A Companion to the Characters
in the Fiction and Drama
of W. Somerset Maugham

A Companion to the Characters in the Fiction and Drama of W. Somerset Maugham

Samuel J. Rogal

Greenwood Press
Westport, Connecticut • London

Library of Congress Cataloging-in-Publication Data

Rogal, Samuel J.
   A companion to the characters in the fiction and drama of W.
Somerset Maugham / Samuel J. Rogal.
      p.   cm.
   Includes bibliographical references and index.
   ISBN 0-313-29917-X (alk. paper)
   1. Maugham, W. Somerset (William Somerset), 1874-1965—Characters—
Dictionaries.   2. Characters and characteristics in literature—
Dictionaries.   I. Title.
PR6025.A86Z855   1996
823'.912—dc20   95-26448

British Library Cataloguing in Publication Data is available.

Copyright © 1996 by Samuel J. Rogal

All rights reserved. No portion of this book may be
reproduced, by any process or technique, without the
express written consent of the publisher.

Library of Congress Catalog Card Number: 95-26448
ISBN: 0-313-29917-X

First published in 1996

Greenwood Press, 88 Post Road West, Westport, CT 06881
An imprint of Greenwood Publishing Group, Inc.

Printed in the United States of America

The paper used in this book complies with the
Permanent Paper Standard issued by the National
Information Standards Organization (Z39.48-1984).

10 9 8 7 6 5 4 3 2 1

Contents

Introduction..vii

The Characters......................................1

Editions and Secondary Sources Consulted............449

Index of Titles.....................................453

Introduction

Critical commentary upon the drama and fiction of William Somerset Maugham (1874-1965) exists clearly as a century-long exercise, beginning with the press and magazine reviews following the publication of <u>Liza of Lambeth</u> (1897) and plodding along (although at times on admittedly weak legs) through to the present moment. Most obviously, within the first eight decades of that exercise, the principal missiles have already been released from the critical cannons, and, barring sudden discoveries of unpublished manuscripts, little ground would appear to remain for some fresh exploration by scholars and commentators of the present and/or future generations. Even a partial and random survey of the topics of extant Maugham scholarship reveals the extent and variety of its substance: the writer's awareness of audience; contrasts to and comparisons with certain contemporaries and near contemporaries (Wilde, Shaw, Wells, Chesterton, Galsworthy, and Coward come quickly to mind); the Victorian, Edwardian, and post-World War I aspects of, and influences upon, his work; his preoccupation with France--with French literature and French art, French cities and towns, French high life low life, French manners, and French thought; his most intense interest in American and and British visitors to France; the East, its people and its religions; British men and women abroad, particularly in the East and at Paris; the so-called clinical attitude toward people and to situations, as prompted by his medical training; the relationship between and among the social classes; England, with the writer's duality of focus on London and Kent; his harsh treatment of Americans in New York, Chicago, and Paris; his variations upon, and recycling of, recurring themes; the necessary masking of his homosexuality and the outward demonstration of his feelings about Jews; the issues of war and peace; various religious commitments and the losses of faith.

The list could flow on and on and occupy several pages. Indeed, the sheer quantity of Maugham's short stories, novels, and plays have produced more than sufficient critical meat upon which academic scholars and critics of more popular media have already chewed loud, long, and fine. Add to the fiction and drama the published biographical facts and gossip associated with Maugham's lengthy and interesting life, scholarly and critical pieces related to his involvements with the London and New York theatres and the cinema studios of England and the United States, and top it all off with Maugham's own sketches of his life and work and his own critical commentaries on others' works, one may have a perfect right to ask, "What next?" "Is there anything left?"

An examination of the full range of critical and biographical study devoted to Maugham's life and work--from The Athenaeum review of Liza of Lambeth on 9 November 1897, to and including Ted Morgan's 1980 biography--might easily lead one to conclude that not much of his fictional, dramatic, or actual worlds remain open for fresh inquiry, discussion, or evaluation. Further, one might be tempted to conclude that, in this final decade of the twentieth century, the majority of Maugham's fiction and drama no longer enjoys the light of what might be termed social or artistic relevance. Nonetheless, to raise such a notion really suggests that his prose fiction and drama, particularly, need no longer be read and then discussed in print from critical, biographical, or social perspectives. However, relevance to the contrary, there exist much in Maugham's novels, short stories, and plays to deserve continued consideration, principally because, no matter how outdated may appear the characters and their situations and conditions, those characters still manage to speak well and their

Introduction

situations still read well.

The art of the writer carries the case against thematic irrelevance. "Because of his readability," wrote John Brophy about Maugham's fiction in the decade immediately preceding Maugham's death, "his knack of securing and retaining the interest of people, all over the world, who normally do not read or at best read trash, he is, especially through his short stories, a valuable popularizer." (1) The word popular, as we know merges from and refers to people; if Maugham is to remain visible to and for literary history (as he certainly will remain visible), he will do so because of his people--literally thousands of them who populate his short stories, novels, and plays. He achieved his popularity at least a full decade before the end of World War I and maintained it for half a century on stage, page, and screen, because his fictional and dramatic characters (his people) appealed and related directly to his real audiences (people). Thus, if for no other reason than their collective wits and personalities, their language and their manners, each of Maugham's characters need to be preserved--to be embalmed (at the risk of morbidity) upon the pages of a reference work that identifies him or her by name and by function, and then captures, for a brief moment, a glimpse of the sketch that Maugham has drawn of him or her.

As the sheer quantity of names that resides within the body of this Companion attests, Maugham literally saturated his fiction and drama with people. In fact, he populated his stories, novels, and plays to the extent that at times their numbers transcend the ability of the normal reading mind and memory to keep track of them. The reader (and/or theatre-goer) comes across active characters with names who speak and act and present themselves to other characters. Some characters stay in a piece but for a brief moment, while others remain throughout, no matter how long the piece (or how much the reader wishes they would go away). There are active characters without names who speak and act, but whose identities remain generic: dressmaker, boy, doctor, waiter, policeman, servant; a number of those generic characters (men, women, children, coolies, sailors) appear as single persons or in clusters of two, three, four, or more. A significant number of characters, both generic and with names, never actually appear, but emerge through direct references by the writer or in off-handed conversations of active characters. Certain characters endure their fictional or dramatic lives with only first names, while the identities of others remain only with their last names, alone (Moreton) or accompanied by a title (Mrs. Nichols). One also finds, with some degrees of frustration and confusion, a character who appears initially with references to the last (or first) name only; then, six chapters or two acts later, that character or other characters announce or reveal the first (or last) name. Certain of Maugham's characters, as the same persons and with the same names, appear in more than a single piece; others appear in more than one piece with the same names, yet are, most obviously and totally, different persons.

Of course, the majority of Maugham's characters live and breathe, but a number no longer hold their credentials for mortality. Maugham even re-created actual persons from history or from his own contemporary world. Some of those do absolutely nothing, while others become fictional or dramatic characters who interact with other characters. Other characters have historical or contemporary names, but they remain purely fictional and function within purely fictional environments. Certain narrators do little more than narrate, while other narrators carry additional responsibilities as partially or fully developed (or even central) characters, with or without names.

Those who have read the several biographies of Maugham realize that he knew a considerable number of persons and that he came into contact with even more whom he did not bother to know well--or, perhaps, whom he did not even want to know. And, as tends to be a habit among biographers and critical commentators, suggestions readily and eagerly come forward as to the intended relationships between characters in fiction or drama and real persons. For example, Ted Morgan tells us that a painter in Paris, Roderic O'Conor, appears in

Introduction

Of Human Bondage as Clutton (first name unknown), an art student at Amitrano's school, Paris; that Henry (Chips) Channon, a wealthy American who spent most of his life cultivating the British aristocracy, and Jerome Zipkin, a friend of Maugham and a member of the mid-1930's international set, combined to serve as models for Elliott Templeton in The Razor's Edge; that Charles Strickland of The Moon and Sixpence mirrored the French painter Paul Gauguin; that Sir Hugh Seymour Walpole, the New Zealand-born novelist, found himself on the pages of Cakes and Ale in the guise of Alroy Kear; that the popular fascination for the Welsh explorer, journalist, and soldier of fortune, Sir Henry Morton Stanley, prompted Maugham (ever attentive to that which attracted the populace), in The Explorer, to paint his portrait of Alexander Mackenzie. (2)

Certainly, Maugham, himself, acknowledged those and numerous other such parallels between fact and his fiction, but he also provided the most reasonable of arguments in that writers needed to go beyond simply photographing real persons and affixing them, "as is," onto the pages of their stories and plays. Rather, he maintained (in 1938) that writers required their own original versions of real life models:

> We know very little even of the persons we know most intimately; we do not know them enough to transfer them to the pages of a book and make human beings of them. People are too elusive, too shadowy, to be copied; and they are also too incoherent and contradictory. The writer does not copy his originals; he takes what he wants from them, a few traits that have caught his attention, a turn of mind that has fired his imagination, and therefrom constructs his character. (3)

Therefore, Maugham paraded across the pages of his fiction and drama a corps of characters drawn only superficially from real life and real experience. Within their new fictional and dramatic environments, those characters marched distinctly but realistically to the drums of their creator's own idiosyncrasies, views, and prejudices.

Sixteen years earlier, in an interview published in Bookman (May 1922), Maugham, then at the height of his popularity, had foreshadowed those sentiments while elaborating on his process for creating fictional and dramatic characters. Although admitting that his actual acquaintances provided him with suggestions for characters, he considered the notion of Person X serving as the "model" for Character Y to be an exaggeration. "I find that by the time I have finished with a character which has engaged my attention, very little is left of the original. It seems to me that very few persons stand so square on their own feet as to make them suitable for fiction." Further, he maintained that "you will know more about a character that you have invented than you possibly can about one who is partially concealed from you by the stubbornness of fact." (4) One must, in the end, accept Maugham at his word, even though there arises the temptation to speculate upon the degree or extent to which he sought to protect his real life originals from biographical scrutiny and himself from the libel courts.

Finally, in that same 1922 interview, Maugham responded to the question about his own favorites among the vast numbers of prose fiction characters whom he had created. "When I look back," he responded, "upon the characters I have invented I find that I am less interested in those that play a leading part in my various novels than in the subsidiary ones. My recollection lingers with most pleasure on a youth called Gerald Vaudrey in Mrs. Craddock [1902] and on Thorpe Athelny in Of Human Bondage [1915]. I think I liked them because they are gay, amusing, and unscrupulous." (5) Of course, between 1922 and 1948 (the last year in which he produced a volume of new fiction or drama), Maugham published nine plays, ten novels, and seven volumes of short stories. Surely, such widely recognized titles as Ashenden (1928), Cakes and Ale (1930), and The Razor's Edge (1944) include more than their share of gay, amusing, and unscrupulous characters, major and minor. The antics of Alroy Kear (with or without the Hugh Walpole connection), the Driffields, Ashenden's coterie of spies and counterspies, and even the decadent sycophants at Paris

Introduction xiii

who slide up and down The Razor's Edge do everything they possibly can to underscore the traditional notion of fiction and drama as mirrors of life. Maugham, perhaps to a lesser degree than any of his more artistic but less popular contemporaries, managed to extract from that mirror as many reflections as a long lifetime of observation and creativity would allow. And, most importantly, he earned a comfortable living while and from doing so.

If Maugham established a discipline and a process for making certain that the thoughts and actions of his characters represented with accuracy the sentiments of his times, one naturally wonders if he applied equal diligence to assigning them their names. Such striking, almost comical, identification tags as Bertram Railing, Valentine and Hermione Lefevre, Gwen Cedar, Tito di San Pietro, George Diogenida, Rev. William Swalecliffe, Isobel Golightly, Rosie Driffield, Alroy Kear, Algernon Peppercorn, Herr Sung, Lady Frederick Barolles, Oliver Haddo, Thorpe Athelny (complete with a phalanx of minor Athelneys, from Edward through Maria de la Concepcion to Maria del Sol), Gerald Vaudry, Canon Theodore Spratte, and Sheppey Miller leap out at the reader from the page as they promenade on the same stage with their more traditionally labeled colleagues: Alec Mackenzie, William Ashenden, Lucy Allerton, Basil Kent, Jenny and James Bush, Bertha Craddock, the Rev. William Carey, Gwendolyn Durant, Robert Colby, Leslie Crosby, James Ford, Catherine Winter, and Isabel Bradley. The selection of names for characters from the East presented Maugham with a totally different problem, but at least in regard to certain classes of persons, he obviously had little to worry about concerning libel suits. No matter what his sources for those names, one cannot help being struck, for example, by the way one group of them bounces across the stage of life as though they represented a measure of notes reverberating from the keyboard of a player piano: Ah-Kay, Ah-Lin, Ah-Ling, Ah-Sing, Ah-Sung, and Ah-Tan.

Although Maugham recycled characters with the same names from story to play to novel and back again, his works still contain sufficient quantities and varieties of names to make the questions of their origins a legitimate one. An apparently reasonable answer, supplied by Maugham himself, yields neither an element of surprise nor any sign of exceptional originality. Following the publication of The Painted Doll (1925)--first in serial form in Nash's Magazine, then in book form--Maugham and his London publisher, William Heinemann, found themselves objects of a libel suit from a Walter and Kitty Lane, a married couple who bore the same first and last names of the principal characters. To compound matters, Heinemann received an official protest from the Assistant Secretary of the government of Hong Kong, objecting to the name of the crown colony being the setting for the work. Maugham quickly changed "Lane" to "Forr" and then "Fane," "Hong Kong" to "Tching-Yen," and then lamented that when writers choose

> . . .the names of their characters at haphazard, from Bradshaw's Guide [Bradshaw's Monthly Railway Guide (1841-1961)], the telephone directory, or, as the practice of the author of his novel [The Painted Veil], from the obituary column of "The [London] Times," it is inevitable that they should sometimes hit upon a name of a living person who may suppose that a reference to him is intended; and for purposes of verisimilitude they give one of their characters a post or office which exists in an actual place, the holder of that post or office is liable to assume a reflection is cast upon him. It is hard to believe that any writer would be such a fool as deliberately to libel a total stranger. (6)

As always, necessity proved the mother of expedience. Whether a comparison of Maugham's characters with various entries in telephone directories and newspaper obituary columns during the the period in which he worked on a novel, play, or short story would prove a worthwhile exercise to determine the the sources for and origins of characters' names depends totally upon the discipline and endurance of the person performing the comparisons.

Introduction

However, one can, with confidence, assume that, despite sporadic examples that combine humor with with a serious regard for developing human personalities, the bestowing of names upon his characters held no extraordinary attraction or fascination for Maugham. Witness the sheer quantities of nameless characters in his fiction and drama, the numbers of names repeated from piece to piece, and the numbers of characters who lack either first or last names. His primary concern lay, instead, with his characters' minds, their hearts, and their voices, not necessarily with their identity cards. Therefore, one must again take Maugham at his word when he declared, as late as 1938, "For the novelist claims to be an artist and the artist does not copy life; he makes an arrangement of it to suit his own purposes. Just as the painter thinks with his brush and paints, the novelist thinks with his story; his view of life, though he may be unconscious of it, his personality, exist as a series of human actions." (7)

In the end, all of Maugham's characters--alive or dead, on or off the page/stage--need to be gathered and housed within a single source, in much the same manner as their creator crowded them onto the pages of his fiction and drama and paraded them across centuries of political and social history and in various parts of the world. As Maugham, himself, accurately noted in an introduction written especially for an abridged edition (1950) of Of Human Bondage, "the author of a piece of fiction is not only subject to the exigencies of the publishers and the public, he is influenced by the climate of opinion prevalent at the time he writes. He is influenced by fashion." (8) Thus we arrive at a principal purpose for this Companion: to provide a vehicle for and to play a role in preserving the "fashion" in which, and for whom, Maugham wrote, thus helping to keep alive his works through his characters and to save them from "the exigencies of the publishers and the public." Further, perhaps as a secondary purpose (but none the less important to the process of Maugham's art), this reference volume allows readers to see the degree and extent to which the playwright and fiction writer recycled his characters and/or their names. In a certain number of instances, there can emerge a composite drawing of a character who appears in two or more pieces; thus emerge the total dimensions of his or her personality.

Be aware, however, that this volume does not intend to serve as a quick and ready substitute for close and careful reading of Maugham's fiction and drama. What follows provides, essentially, physical descriptions of characters and highlights of their principal functions and actions--only enough so that each can be seen as within his or her role as a Maugham person. Entries must not be considered as plot summaries.

As far as possible, complete names appear as headings to entries and within entries, so that readers can easily cross-check one character's connection to another character. The entire arrangement is alphabetical--first by character, then by title of a piece when a name appears more than once--principally so that readers can see the extent to which Maugham did or did not repeat or vary a name. The appendices contain (1) an alphabetical listing (with dates of publication) of stories, novels, and plays; (2) a list of the editions of Maugham's works from which the characters have been extracted; and (3) a brief list of secondary sources helpful to the compilation of this exercise.

Finally, the compiler expresses his gratitude and appreciation to the Carol Bird and Jan Vogelgesang of Jacobs Library, Illinois Valley Community College, for their untiring patience and assistance in locating and obtaining the texts of Maugham's plays, novels, and stories. And, of course, equal gratitude and appreciation must be extended to those unknown librarians across the United States who were kind enough to lend those volumes from their collections.

Notes to the Introduction

1. John Brophy, Somerset Maugham (London: Longmans, Green and Company for the British Book Council and the National Book League, 1958): 36.

2. Ted Morgan, Maugham (New York: Simon and Schus-Schuster, 1980): 207-208, 481, 239, 334, 126.

3. W. Somerset Maugham, "The Summing Up," in Mr. Maugham Himself, selected by John Beecroft (Garden City, New York: Doubleday and Company, Inc., 1954): 633.

4. W. Somerset Maugham, A Traveller in Romance. Uncollected Writings, 1901-1964, ed. John Whitehead (New York: Clarkson N. Potter, Inc., 1984): 126.

5. A Traveller in Romance, 126.

6. From the author's note in the first edition of The Painted Veil (p. 26), quoted in Morgan, 279. See, also, Raymond Toole Stott, A Bibliography of the Works of W. Somerset Maugham (Edmonton: The University of Alberta Press, 1973: 89-91, 312.

7. "Summing Up," 636.

8. W. Somerset Maugham, Of Human Bondage, abridged edition (New York: Pocket Books, Inc., 1950), vi.

The Characters

A

ABAS (Outstation). Native servant whom Warburton procures for Cooper

ABBE #1 (Razor's Edge). At Paris; celebrated for his success in bringing infidels and heretics back into the fold; a great diner out and a noted wit; confined his ministrations to the wealthy and the aristocratic; Elliott Templeton attracted to him

ABBE #2 (Razor's Edge). Young; accompanies the Bishop to Elliott Templeton's house on Antibes; carries the utensils needed to administer the sacrament

ABBE (Theatre). Of St. Malo; dines on Thursday evenings with Madame Carrie Falloux, Mrs. Lambert, and the commandant

ABBESS (Punctiliousness of Don Sebastian). Of a highly respected convent near Xiormonez, Spain; assured Dona Sodina that pickled shrimps were of great efficacy in the begetting of children

ABBOT (East of Suez). Of the Temple of Fidelity and Virtuous Redemption; clears the crown from the room of the Andersons' apartment

ABBOT (Painted Veil). Of the Buddhist monastery, ten miles outside of Meu-fan-fu; beautifully polite; his smile conveyed an irony of resignation

ABBOT (Razor's Edge). At the Benedictine monastery at at Alsace; stood at the refectory door

ABBOTT, Rev. Lewis (Jack Straw). Vicar of Taverner,

Cheshire; husband of Rosie Abbott; young, nice look-looking, and frank

ABBOTT, Rosie (Jack Straw). Wife of Rev. Lewis Abbott; daughter of Jasper Neville; pretty and fragile

ABDUL (Force of Circumstances). Guy's native servant at the station on the Sembulu River, prior to Guy's marriage to Doris

ABDUL-HAMID (Human Element). Exiled the Turkish pasha to Rhodes

ABDUL-SAID (Caesar's Wife). Employed on an estate of the Khedive's mother up the Nile; son of one of the Khedive's mother's maids; has been sentenced to death for the murder of an Armenian merchant

ABRAHAM (Moon and Sixpence). A young Jew whom the Narrator had known as a student, St. Thomas's Hospital, London; blonde, stout, shy, and brilliant; became a house physician and house surgeon, then elected to the staff; eventually ended up as a modest physician in government service at Alexandria, Egypt

ABRAHAMS, Solly (Penelope). Ada Fergusson's friend on the Stock Exchange; offers Ada a splendid tip on a mining stock, the Johannesburg and New Jerusalem

ACABA, Count of (Point of Honour). Father of Soledad; described as an old scamp; heavily in debt; retired to Carmona to escape his creditors, then returned to to Seville after his daughter's marriage

ACHINESE MAN (End of the Flight). Swore to kill the Dutchman for something that the latter had done to him

ACOLYTE (East of Suez). At the Temple of Fidelity and Virtuous Inclination, Peking; tiny; blows out the oil lamps and shuts the temple doors

ACQUAINTANCE (Fact of Life). Has a drink with Nicholas Garnet at Monte Carlo

ACTOR (Painted Veil). At London; married to Waddington's cousin

ACTOR MANAGER (Cakes and Ale). At London; he had given Harry Retford and Rosie Driffield seats for a play; loaned Harry two pounds so that the three of them could go to supper after the performance

ACTORS (Catalina). Employed by the Spanish grandee for his son's wedding; sunk in lethargy and gloom; stare at Diego and Catalina with hostile indifference

ACTORS (Of Human Bondage). From the Comedie Francaise; frequent visitors to the house of the portrait painter at Paris

ACTRESS (Alien Corn). Dinner guest of Ferdy Rabenstein

ACTRESS (Magician). A dinner guest of Arbuthnot at the Savoy, London

ACTRESS (Of Human Bondage). Understudying at a London theatre; Lawson wants her to model for him; attends his luncheon party with Philip Carey and Mrs. Nesbit

ACTRESS (Razor's Edge). Retired from the Odeon; lodges at the same hotel where Larry Darrell lives

ACTRESS #1 (Theatre). An older woman; sound; cast generally for mothers, maiden aunts, or character parts; played Candida opposite Michael Gosselyn in James Langton's repertory company

ACTRESS #2 (Theatre). On stage with Avice Crichton; older and plainer than Avice

ACTRESS #3 (Theatre). Rehearses a part in a revival that Julia Gosselyn had played

ACTRESSES (Magician). At the tavern on the Boulevard des Italiens, Paris

ACTRESSES (Theatre). One or two of them; all leading ladies; they did not like Julia Lambert Gosselyn any better because she called at least two duchesses by their first names

ADAMSON, Dr. (Explorer [novel]). Scottish doctor and surgeon engaged by Alec Mackenzie for three of the latter's expeditions into British East Africa; Alec had known him for years; from Edinburgh; slow drawl and a pawky humor; large--the largest of the white men on the current expedition; deliberate in movement and in conversation; he wishes that the bullet that killed Richardson had, instead, found George Allerton; his quick reaction prevents George from killing Alec; he and Alec attacked by blackwater fever on their way to Nairobi; dies from the disease and is buried at the foot of a great tree

ADAMSON, Dr. (Explorer [play]). Scottish surgeon with Alec Mackenzie's expedition in Africa; large boned and brawny; Scottish accent; has been on three expeditions with Alec

A.D.C. (Man with the Scar). He accompanies General San Ignacio to the execution

A.D.C. (Painted Veil). Accompanied Colonel Yu to Walter Fane's funeral

ADDISHAW, James (Point of Law). Senior partner in the London law firm of Addishaw, Jones, and Braham; the Narrator's solicitor; an old man; his grandfather and father were solicitors; an honest red face; saw Kate Daubernoon twice each year; he offers Ralph Mason an annuity of two thousand pounds per year if he postpones indefinitely his marriage to Kate Daubernoon; refuses to prepare Kate's will; named Kate's executor

ADDISHAW, Mrs. (Point of Law). Wife of James Addishaw; her husband will tell her to ask for the Narrator's new book at Mundie's

ADMIRAL (Painted Veil). Charlie Townsend and the Governor of Hong Kong attended a party on his flag ship

ADMIRERS (Painted Veil). Of Kitty Garstin; two or three of them; proposed more than once to Kitty; penniless

ADOLPHE (Of Human Bondage). Shares a room with Cronshaw on Hyde Street, London; Cronshaw calls him "George"; a waiter; Swiss; brings Cronshaw a bottle of milk before he goes to work

AFRICAN KING (Explorer [novel]). Once gave a dance in Alec Mackenzie's honor, attended by four thousand warriors in war paint

AGATA (Up at the Villa). The cook at the villa in Florence where Mary Panton lives

AGENT (Circle). At Ashton-Adey, Dorset; he holds a conference with Arnold Champion-Cheney

AGENT (Four Dutchmen). Drank beer with the Dutch resident, the captain of the S.S. Utrecht, and the Narrator

AGENT #1 (Gigolo and Gigolette). Wants to book Stella Cotman at Deauville

AGENT #2 (Gigolo and Gigolette). Friend of Syd Cotman; advanced the money for Stella's diving apparatus and booked a Paris engagement for Syd and Stella Cotman

AGENT (Man of Honour). Of Basil Kent; at Chancery Lane, London

AGENT (Narrow Corner). In the British service; supposedly can solve the most complicated code within twenty-four hours

AGENT (Painted Veil). Of the P&O, Hong Kong; Kitty Fane would not be amused by being taken in to dinner by

Characters 5

him
AGENT (Pro Patria). At John Porter-Smith's campaign committee room; not inclined to take events lightly
AGENT (Razor's Edge). The Marseilles agent for a line of freighters from the Near East to New York; a neighbor of Larry Darrell at Sanary; promises Larry a berth on board a ship from Marseilles to New York; Larry presents him with his old Citroen in return for the favor
AGENT #1 (Then and Now). Sent by Caesar Borgia to Milan to collect five hundred Gascon adventurers for his army
AGENT #2 (Then and Now). Sent by Caesar Borgia to hire fifteen hundred Swiss mercenaries for his army
AGENT #3 (Then and Now). Of the Duke of Ferrara; accepted money from Caesar Borgia to induce his master to send troops to Borgia
AGENT #4 (Then and Now). Of Bartolomeo Martelli at Ravenna; writes to Martelli, urging him to come to Ravenna and conclude a business arrangement
AGENT #1 (Winter Cruise). Told Vanetia Reid that from Hamburg to Port au Prince, Haiti, she would have to share her cabin with another woman
AGENT #2 (Winter Cruise). At a small port in Haiti; invited by Captain Erdmann to come aboard the Friedrich Weber for cocktails and supper; the son of a former minister of Haiti to the German court; had lived for many years in Berlin and spoke good German
AGENTS (Good Manners). Had difficulty leasing Graveney Hall, Kent
AGRICULTURAL LABORER (Hour Before the Dawn). A conscientious objector at the exemption tribunal at Lewes; an honest, open face; belonged to a small, obscure sect, the Twelve Apostles
AGURIA, Don Pedro (Point of Honour). Descended from an admiral of Spain under Philip II and of another naval officer who was a close friend of Philip IV; had estates in Cordova, Aguilar, and Seville; married Soledad
AGURIA, Soledad (Point of Honour). Wife of Don Pedro Aguria, although she does not love him; daughter of the Count of Acaba; beautiful; a childhood friend of Pepe Alvarez, and engaged to him before he left for

Cuba
AH KAY (Narrow Corner). Chinese boy; age nineteen; has served Dr. Saunders for six years; slim and comely; large black eyes; skin as smooth as that of a girl; coal black hair cut very short; oval face the color of old ivory; small, white, regular teeth; travels with Saunders from Fu-chou to Takana; acts as his servant and cook at Takana, as well as prepares the doctor's daily intake of opium
AH LIN (Moon and Sixpence). A Chinese boy who waits on tables at the Hotel de la Fleur
AH-LING (Fall of Edward Barnard). A Chinese employee at Cameron's, a trading store at Tahiti
AH-SING (Letter [play]). Chinese boy; a servant at the Crosbies' plantation
AH-SUNG (Mackintosh). The Chinese cook for Walker and Mackintosh
AH TAN (Neil MacAdam). The Chinese boy who washes Neil MacAdam on the day that Neil recovers from his fever
AIR FORCE COMMANDER (Hour Before the Dawn). Of the secret airdrome five miles from Graveney Holt; George Henderson guarantees him of Dora Friedberg's integrity
AIR RAID WARDENS (Hour Before the Dawn). At London; two or three of them; standing outside of the shelter; open the door for Roger Henderson and Jane Foster
AJURIA, Miguel (Of Human Bondage). A Spanish model at Amitrano's art school, Paris; does not consider himself a professional; a writer; a fine figure, with no fat on him; muscular; close cropped and well-shaped head; a short beard; large dark eyes and heavy eyebrows; spoke fluent but broken French; came to Paris to write novels; Philip Carey hangs his charcoal drawing of him in his rooms in Kennington, London
ALAMARI, Georgio (Mask and the Face). The sculptor who flirts with Eliza Zanotti; agrees to cease his flirtation with her
ALBA, Duke of (Point of Honour). The Narrator attempts to tour his house
ALBANESE, Pietro (Making of a Saint). A devoted adherent to the house of Orsi; he will join the conspiracy to assassinate Girolamo Riario; escapes from Forli with Checco d'Orsi, but is captured and returned to

the town prison for execution; hanged from the window of the Palazzo Orsi
ALBANI, Madame (Circle). The stage name of Marie Louise Cecelia Emma Le Jeunesse (1852-1930); an operatic soprano; sang at the London opera
ALBERT (Human Element). Betty Weldon-Burns' chauffeur; speaks fluent Greek; medium height, broad shouldered, squarely built; stocky but not fat; thirty or thirty-one years of age; short thick nose, short fair moustache; formerly the footman for Betty Weldon-Burns' Aunt Louise and a valet for Jimmie Weldon-Burns
ALBERT (Razor's Edge). Wine waiter at the Ritz, Paris; presents the wine card at the Narrator's table; portly, dignified, and an old friend of Elliott Templeton
ALBERT (Sheppey). Barber at Bradley's Hairdressing and Barber's Saloon, Jermyn Street, London
ALBERT, Archduke (Catalina). Commander in chief of the Spanish forces in the Low Countries; on totally unfriendly terms with the Duke of Castel Rodriguez; Don Manuel de Valero stands high in his favor
ALBERT EDWARD, Prince of Wales (Outstation). Had played baccarat with Warburton at Marienbad
ALBERTELLI, Giuliano degli (Then and Now). Florentine; a man of property and now in the flower of his age; childless until he visited San Vitale at Ravena
ALBERTELLI, Signora (Then and Now). Wife of Giuliano degli Albertelli; gave birth to a nine-pound boy nine months after her husband returned from the baths at San Vitale
ALBICINA, Guiseppe (Making of a Saint). Told by Girolamo Riario that Checco d'Orsi may find the hand of the master not so generous as that of a friend
ALDERMAN (Bad Example). Riding the street in his carriage; James Clinton believes him to be a man who has achieved greatness
ALEXANDER VI (Then and Now). Pope; the father of Caesar Borgia
ALEXANDROVNA, Grand Duchess Anna (Road Uphill). At Paris; she telephones Broderick Massen, who tells her that his family has descended from Princess Pocohontas
ALEXEY (Christmas Holiday). A friend of Lydia's mother

and husband of Evgenia; in Paris; provides Lydia Berger with a bed in his house at the Rue du Chateau d' Eau, Paris; lawyer by profession, clever and liberal; a former pupil of Lydia's father; played the violin in an orchestra in a Russian restaurant; father of three children; has not had a job for four years; he drinks

ALFRED (Bishop's Apron). A footman in the employee of Theodore Spratte

ALGERIAN (Christmas Holiday). At the penal colony on French Guiana; always bothering the younger libere; the elder libere "ripped him up the belly"

ALGERIAN CONVICTS (Official Position). Two of them; awaiting execution

ALGERIAN PEDDLARS (Christmas Holiday). At Paris; eyes alert for a possible buyer; cringing but persistent

ALGUAZIL #1 (Catalina). The constable who arrested Domingo Perez on behalf of the Holy Office

ALGUAZIL #2 (Catalina). Accompanied Father Antonio and the civil authorities to see that the sentences of the Inquisition were duly executed

ALGY (Hour Before the Dawn). George Henderson's uncle; he had lived in the Elizabethan cottage barely a mile from Graveney Holt

ALI, Prince (Ashenden/Miss King). An Egyptian; a near relative of the deposed Khedive; small, fat; heavy black moustache; a bitter enemy of the English; dines at the Geneva hotel with his two daughters and Mustapha Pasha

ALICE (Our Betters). Minnie Surennes' aunt and Mary's mother

ALICE (Sacred Flame). The Tabrets' maid

ALI'S DAUGHTERS (Ashenden/Miss King). Two of them; they dine with Prince Ali and Mustapha Pasha at the Geneva hotel; emancipated young women; short and stout; fine black eyes, heavy sallow faces

ALIX (Ashenden/His Excellency). Friend of Yvonne; an acrobat; O'Malley anxious that she pose in the nude for him; broad flat face, wide mouth, upturned nose; china blue eyes; large amount of dyed blonde hair; deep, husky voice

ALLERTON the eldest (Explorer [novel]). Of Hamlyn Purlieu, Hampshire; the founder of his family's fortune;

Characters 9

he and his two wives could be seen, in stone, in the chancel of the parish church
ALLERTON, Fred (Explorer [novel]). Father of George and Lucy Allerton; at age twenty-one the master of Hamlyn Purlieu; the handsomest and most charming of all the family; blue eyes; unscrupulous; became an orphan at age twenty; he lived mostly in Paris and London; an adventurous prodigal; forced to mortgage his lands; married the younger Miss Boulger, and thus managed to pay off his debts; a most persuasive voice; squandered all of his wife's money after she died; accepts Jarrett's offer to purchase Hamlyn Purlieu; owes Dick Lomas two hundred pounds; arrested for operating a fraudulent brokerage house (a "bucket shop") with a man named Saunders, under the assumed names of Vernon and Lawford; taken into custody after being committed for trial; found guilty; sentenced to seven years in Parkhurst Prison; he becomes seriously ill and is set free, a bent and broken man; very thin, constantly trembling hands, sunken cheeks, almost toothless, the light gone from his eyes, and short hair extremely white; Lucy takes him back to Hamlyn Purlieu to die; buried among the ancestors whom he had dishonored
ALLERTON, Fred (Explorer [play]). Father of George and Lucy Allerton; brother-in-law of Lady Alice Kelsey; standing trial for forging a check for three thousand pounds; he has squandered his family's fortune; found guilty and sentenced to seven years in prison; dies
ALLERTON, George (Explorer [novel]). The son of Fred Allerton and brother of Lucy; age twenty; at age ten when his mother dies, after which he went off to school; educated at Winchester College and Oxford; good looking; slender; open, facile smile; frank, blue eyes; radiantly satisfied with the world; dependent upon his sister Lucy; beloved by all of his friends; supposedly he will enter a business in which Lady Alice Kelsey held a large interest, earn sufficient money to pay his father's debts, and perhaps buy back Hamlyn Purlieu; after his father's imprisonment, he accompanies Alec MacKenzie to Africa, where he loses his flabbiness and his good looks; his weak and irresolute nature emerges; he takes to drink; he fires his revolver at Alec when the latter proves

that he (George) had killed the Turkana woman; killed in the last attack against the Arabs and the slavers; lacked courage and died miserably

ALLERTON, George (Explorer [play]). The son of Fred Allerton and brother of Lucy; very young; good looking; a rather weak face; a student at Oxford at the time of his father's arrest; goes to Africa with Alec MacKenzie; turns cowardly and takes to drink; shoots the Turkana woman; fires his revolver at Alec; Alec places him in charge of the Turkanas who plan to turn against him, which leads to his death

ALLERTON, Lucy (Explorer [novel]). The daughter of Fred Allerton and sister of George; twenty-two years of age; fifteen years old when her mother dies; bore a deep love for her father, but then gradually found him weak, unreliable, and shifty; a vehement pride caused her to seek comfort only in her own heart; she loved all ships; transferred her love from her father to George; clear and fresh skin; delicate, sensitive face; bright and fair hair; straight nose; delicately curved lips; tall and strong; slight figure, charmingly lithe; refuses Alec MacKenzie's proposal of marriage, even though she loves him; plans to marry Alec after his return from Africa, despite the accusations of Fergus Macinnery and Alec's refusal to respond to them; eventually believes the accusations that Alec had sacrificed her brother George to save himself, and breaks off her engagement to him; agrees to marry Robert Boulger, then breaks off that engagement; reconciles with Alec and promises to await his return from another expedition to Africa

ALLERTON, Lucy (Explorer [play]). The daughter of Fred Allerton and older sister of George; tall; has lived most of her life in the country, and brings with her a sort of remoteness from the world; beautiful; clear-cut features; rigid moral notions; possessed of marked self control; since age fifteen, has had to care for her father and brother; refuses Alec MacKenzie's proposal of marriage (although she loves him) so that she can be near her father during his prison term and take care of him following his release; becomes engaged to Alec MacKenzie after he returns from Africa; she rejects Robert Boulger's proposal of marriage; breaks off her engagement with Alec MacKenzie when she believes that he did cause George's death; reconciles with Alec and promises to wait for him until he returns from his latest expedition

ALLERTON, Mr. and Mrs. (Explorer [novel]). Parents of Fred Allerton; died when Fred was age twenty

ALLERTON, Mrs. (Explorer [novel]). Younger daughter of Mr. Boulger; deceased wife of Fred Allerton, to whom she had been married for fifteen years; the mother of Lucy and George; younger sister of Lady Alice Kelsey; died suddenly

ALLERTON, Mrs. (Explorer [play]). The deceased wife of Fred Allerton; mother of Lucy and George Allerton; sister of Lady Alice Kelsey; one of three daughters of a Liverpool merchant; died of a broken heart, but still in love with her husband

ALLERTONS (Explorer [novel]). Of Hamlyn Purlieu, Hampshire; for three hundred years they had been men of prudence, courage, and worth; had intermarried with, and had given richly endowed maidens to, the great families of the neighborhood

ALMA-TADEMA, Sir Lawrence (Round Dozen). The Dutch-born British painter (1836-1912) who asked Eleanor Porchester to sit as a model for one of his pictures

ALMOND, Jack (Casual Affair). A former clerk in the Foreign Office, then worked for the shipping firm of Dexter and Farmlow; long brown hair turning grey; short beard; infected with tuberculosis; a confirmed opium smoker; once tall and athletic, with dark brown hair and long lashes; spoke French and German

ALPHONSINE (Jane). French maid in the employ of Jane and Gilbert Napier at the beginning of their Paris honeymoon

ALPHONSO OF SPAIN (Painted Veil). He had hunted at the estate of the Mother Superior's father

ALPHONSO OF SPAIN (Razor's Edge). Had been entertained by Elliott Templeton on the French Riviera

ALVA, Duke of (Catalina). Banished from Court and confined to his castle at Uzeda; he employs Manuel de Valero in his service after having assumed command of Philip II's army in the war against Portugal; defeats King Don Antonio of Portugal and drives him from his kingdom

ALVAREZ, Francisca (Catalina). The daughter of Pedro Alvarez; extremely ugly; offered by her father to Diego Martinez

ALVAREZ, Pedro (Catalina). The wealthy father of Francisca Alvarez

ALVAREZ, Pepe (Point of Honour). A young artillery officer just returned from Cuba; he is brought to the Agurias' box at the opera by the Count of Acaba; a childhood friend of Soledad Aguria, and engaged to her before he left for Cuba

ALVAREZ, Senor (Point of Honour). The father of Pepe Alvarez; a lawyer at Carmona

ALVISI, Count Lodovico (Then and Now). An intimate of Caesar Borgia; a Roman gentleman who employs Piero Giacomini as a page

AMAH (Book Bag). A housemaid in the service of Olive Hardy; a decent, elderly woman

AMAH (East of Suez). Daisy Anderson's elderly Chinese mother; small, thin, and wrinkled; sleek black hair; had been baptized by Catholic, Church of England, Baptist, Presbyterian, and Seventh-Day Adventist missionaries; sold her seventeen-year-old daughter to Lee Tai Cheng for two thousand dollars

AMAH #1 (Painted Veil). At Hong Kong; perhaps has just tried the door to Kitty Fane's bedroom; Walter Fane gives her instructions before Kitty returns from her final meeting with Charlie Townsend

AMAH #2 (Painted Veil). To Kitty Fain at Mei-tan-fu; kneeling on the floor of the bungalow, unpacking Kitty's belongings; accompanies Kitty to the French convent; returns with Kitty to Hong Kong

AMAH #3 (Painted Veil). Of the Mancu woman; brings a pair of shoes to Kitty Fain

AMAHS (Painted Veil). In charge of the orphaned babies at the French convent, Mei-tan-fu

AMBASSADOR (Hour Before the Dawn). Of a foreign power; he and his wife at a dinner with Roger and May Henderson

AMBASSADOR #1 (Our Betters). Sat next to Bessie Saunders at Lady Pearl Grayston's dinner party

AMBASSADOR #2 (Our Betters). Told Flora Della Cercola that Lady Pearl Grayston was the most powerful woman in London

Characters 13

AMBASSADORS (Making of a Saint). Persuade Protonotary Savello to accept the town of Forli for the Pope

AMBASSADORS (Making of a Saint). From Florence and Venice; negotiators in the decision whether to launch an attack upon Forli

AMBASSADORS (Then and Now). From Perugia; surrender their city to Caesar Borgia

AMELIA (Explorer [novel]). A character invented by Julia Crowley and Dick Lomas; no figure; her legs are much too long and she wears corsets; wears quantities of false hair; Dick Lomas's "fiancee"; the granddaughter of a baronet

AMERICAN (Christmas Holiday). Occupies an apartment and studio at Auteuil; employs Madame Berger as a general servant

AMERICAN (Razor's Edge). At the Brasserie Graf, Avenue de Clichy, Paris; he and Maugham went to the same barber at Nice; stout, elderly, grey haired; puffy red face, with heavy pouches under his frightened and unhappy eyes; a Middle Western banker who had left his city after the Crash to avoid investigation

AMERICAN AMBASSADOR (Creative Impulse). Once told Mrs. Forrester that a cup of tea with her was one of the richest intellectual experiences " which it has ever been my lot to enjoy"

AMERICAN COUPLE (Mask and the Face). Eloping; can be heard singing on Lake Como

AMERICAN GIRL (Magician). A dinner guest of Arbuthnot at the Savoy, London

AMERICAN LADY (Razor's Edge). At Paris; wealthy; one of the recent converts of the Abbe #1, whom she introduced to Elliott Templeton

AMERICAN MAN (Of Human Bondage). At the dinner table at Gravier's, Paris; young, handsome, thin ascetic face; dark eyes; ample dark hair

AMERICAN MEN (Of Human Bondage). Two of them; at the Luxembourg Gardens, Paris; young; bearded; wore brown velveteens, enormous trousers, basque caps

AMERICAN PAINTER (Buried Talent). At Paris; Teddie Converse had met Blanche (MacArdle) and Charmian at his party; asked Blanche and Charmian to sing

AMERICAN PUBLISHER (Colonel's Lady). He had sent Evie Peregrine a great spray of orchids; he tells George

Peregrine that Evie's book will be a smash success in America

AMERICAN WOMAN (Alien Corn). A dinner guest of Ferdy Rabenstein; married to an English peer

AMERICAN WOMAN (Cousin Amy). Pretty; taken to dinner by a man, who refuses her request for champagne

AMERICAN WOMAN (Jack Straw). Has a passion for titles; the Pomeranian attache introduced his valet to her as a count; she invited the count/valet to dinner

AMERICAN WOMAN (Moon and Sixpence). Married to Tough Bill; obese and sternly

AMERICAN WOMAN #1 (Razor's Edge). Lived in Paris; at a tea in Louise Bradley's apartment; her hair darkly hennaed; slim figured; excessively made up; sharp features; hungry restless eyes; originally from the Middle West

AMERICAN WOMAN #2 (Razor's Edge). Lived in Paris; at a tea in Louise Bradley's apartment; unnaturally golden hair; slim figured; excessively made up; sharp fea-features; hungry restless eyes; originally from the Middle West

AMERICANS (Christmas Holiday). Six of them (three men and three girls); enter the restaurant at the Avenue du Maine, Paris

AMERICANS (Razor's Edge). A "bunch" of them at the Brasserie Graf, Avenue Clichy, Paris; young, drunk, noisy

AMIEL, Henri Frederic (Of Human Bondage). Born, 1821; professor at Geneva (1849-1881); his brilliancy promised achievement that he never fulfilled; wrote a journal published (1883) two years after his death (1881)

AMY (Cousin Amy). The daughter of the Narrator's grandmother's nephew by marriage; eight years older than the Narrator; lives in the country; growing stout; claims to be a food reformer and a suffragist

AMYNTAS (Choice of Amyntas). The son and first-born of Peter the Schoolmaster and Mrs. Peter; so named because, with that tri-syllable, Peter could finish every stanza of his Horatian ode; age eighteen when his father offers him one guinea (which he never re-receives) and tells him to go forth into the world; sets off for Plymouth and then to Cadiz to become Van

Characters

Tiefel's clerk; loses his money and job prospects at Cadiz; he wanders about Spain and finally enters the accursed cavern; finds the palace and must choose among the four Moorish maidens; selects the Lady of Love (Maiden #4)

ANALYST (Spanish Priest). At London; he wrote to the Englishman at Saville, informing him that the ore received from Vicente Oria y Mazallon was indeed gold

ANASTASIA, Archduchess (Jack Straw). Of Pomerania; has just delivered twins

ANASTASIA, Archduchess (Penelope). Supposedly known to Davenport Barlow; cultivated and pleasant

ANCESTOR (Theatre). Of Michael Gosselyn; he had gambled away his fortune at White's during the Regency

ANDALUSIAN LASSES (Spanish Priest). In the taverns of Gibraltar; dance the balero

ANDALUSIAN WOMAN (Ashenden/Hairless Mexican). A beautiful spy for the President of Mexico, with whom Manuel Carmona falls in love; he cuts her throat

ANDERSON, Daisy (East of Suez). Age twenty-seven (told Henry Anderson she is twenty-two); finacee and then wife of Henry Anderson, whom she met at Shanghai; her mother Chinese; extremely pretty; pale, clear, and slightly sallow skin; beautiful dark eyes; abundant black hair; educated in England at age seven; came to Chung-King at age seventeen; fell in love with George Conway; lived in a Presbyterian mission; her mother sold her to Lee Tain Cheng, a rich Chinese, for two thousand dollars; lived for four years at Singapore with Rathbone; during the war she lived in a Hong Kong Hotel, on familiar terms with "a lot of naval fellows"; still in love with George Conway

ANDERSON, Henry (East of Suez). Age thirty; fair and good looking; pleasant, honest face; on the staff of the British American Tobacco Company, Peking; George Conway his closest friend, brought him to China and saw him through a bout with cholera; engaged to and then marries Daisy, whom he had met at Shanghai; he obtains a transfer from Peking to Chung-King

ANDERSON, Mary (Circle). American actress (1859-1949); her picture appears in an old photograph album owned by Clive Champion-Chaney; her beauty took away one's breath

ANDOVER, Bishop (Bishop's Apron). Of Barchester; at first, dangerously ill; he then dies

ANDREA #1 (Making of a Saint). Master of the guard at Girolamo Riario's palace; waiting for some sign to arrest Checco d'Orsi

ANDREA #2 (Making of a Saint). A nephew of Pietro, the old steward at the Palazzo Orsi; age twenty

ANDREA (Mask and the Face). Count Paolo Grazia's servant; tells Paolo that a fisherman has found Savina Grazia's body in Lake Como

ANDREADI, Constantine (Ashenden/Hairless Mexican). A Greek and an agent of Enver Pasha; on his way from Constantinople with documents

ANDREWS (Mrs. Craddock). The only baker in Leanham who attends church; his bread gives Charles Glover indigestion

ANGELE (Christmas Holiday). One of the girls at the Saraile, Paris; from Tours; well-educated; from an excellent family

ANGELE (Theatre). Annette's niece and assistant at the house of Madame Carrie Falloux; not yet forty years of age; did the rough work

ANGELINA (Happy Couple). Fictional character in a story narrated by Miss Gray; modeled after Mrs. Craig

ANGELIQUE (Lady Frederick). A maid to Lady Frederick Berolles; a jewel of incalculable value

ANGELO (Gigalo and Gigolette). The head waiter at the Casino

ANGELO (Theatre). Head waiter at the Berkeley, London; did not immediately recognize Julia Lambert Gosselyn; takes her to her favorite table

ANGELOTTI, Madame (Our Betters). A guest at Lady Pearl Grayston's dinner party; sang afterward

ANGELS (Judgment Seat). Lead the ghosts to the Presence

ANGRY FATHER (Vessel of Wrath). He sticks a knife into Ginger Ted's back

ANIMALS (Magician). In Margaret Dauncey's vision; creeping; begotten of the slime

ANNE (Camel's Back). The Levefres' maid

ANNE (Moon and Sixpence). A maid to Amy Strickland; she is trim and comely

ANNE OF BRITTANY (Then and Now). Widow of Charles VIII; arranged that she marry Louis XII of France

Characters

ANNETTE (Theatre). Cook, housekeeper, and housemaid for Carrie Falloux and Mrs. Lambert; had been with Madame Falloux for thirty-five years

ANNIE (Before the Party). One of the Skinners' house maids

ANSTEY, Dr. (Cakes and Ale). At Blackstable, Kent; in his dog cart; he passes young Ashenden and the Driffields, the latter three on their bicycles, and reports that fact to Ashenden's aunt and uncle

ANSTEY, Mrs. (Cakes and Ale). Wife of Dr. Anstey; calls upon Ashenden's aunt at Blackstable vicarage

ANTEQUERA, Son of the Duke of (Catalina). At age fifteen, engaged to Beatriz Henriquez y Bragannza; squat and short; mass of coarse black hair; snub nose and a sulky mouth

ANTOINE (Ashenden/Giulia Lazzari). A boatman; refuses a thousand francs to convey Giulia Lazzari from Thonon to Lausanne; turns over to Felix Giulia Lazzari's letter to Chandra Lal

ANTOINETTE (Razor's Esge). The maid engaged by Elliott Templeton to attend to Louisa and Isabel Bradley during their visit to Paris

ANTONIA, Alice (Of Human Bondage). The well-known London serio-comic; large; flaxen hair; boldly painted face; metallic voice; comes to Lynn and Sedley and asks that Mr. Sampson design a new costume for her

ANTONIO (Lotus Eater). The cook at the inn where the Narrator and Wilson dine

ANTONIO (Then and Now). One of Machiavelli's servants; announces that Bartolomeo Martelli wishes to see him; accompanies Machiavelli back to Florence

ANTONIO, Father (Catalina). One of the two secretaries to Blasco de Valero, Bishop of Segovia; formerly a theological pupil of the Bishop at Alcala; secretary to Friar Blasco when the latter served as Inquisitor at Valencia; restrains the other secretary during the Bishop's levitation

AOSTA, Duchess of (Alien Corn). Angry when the King of Italy fell in love with the Princess of Montenegro

A.P.C. (Painted Veil). He and his wife recently came from Mei-tan-fu to Hong Kong

APPLEBY, Fanny (Caesar's Wife). Elderly and homely; the wife of Richard Appleby

APPLEBY, Richard (Caesar's Wife). Member of Parliament; husband of Fanny Appleby (who calls him "George" in Act 3); a north country manufacturer and a self-made man; age sixty; grey beard; short and stout; shrewd, simple, and good-natured

APRIL (Princess September). Fourth daughter born to the King and Queen of Siam; formerly named Summer and Wednesday

ARAB (Man with a Conscience). An old and devout Mohammadan convict; serving a life sentence for murder; looks after the Narrator's bungalow

ARAB #1 (Marriage of Convenience, 1906). At a village on an island off the coast of Tunis; speaks broken French; he asks the Narrator if he wishes to see the Consul; then informs the Narrator that the village has no hotel; carries the Narrator's luggage to the home of a lady

ARAB #2 (Marriage of Convenience, 1906). A gardener who is busy at work at the French consulate on the island village off the coast of Tunis

ARAB BOYS (Spanish Priest). At Gibraltar; little; naked of leg; they trot along the curb whistling "Rule Britannia"

ARAB EMIRS (Explorer [novel]). They ruled a series of independent states in the hinterlands of British East Africa; Alec MacKenzie made treaties with them; filled with jealousy of one another and always eager to fall upon their friends; eventually sign treaties with Great Britain, ending the slave trade

ARAB SLAVERS (Explorer [novel]). Reside in British East Africa; Alec MacKenzie dealt with them diplomatically

ARABS (Explorer [novel]. From across the sea; shouting and jostling on the jetty at Mombassa

ARABS (Explorer [novel/play]). Would have wiped out Alec MacKenzie's men, but they hesitated for ten minutes before attacking

ARABS (Marriage of Convenience). At a village on an island off the coast of Tunis; swarthy; discuss the Narrator and his concerns

ARABS (Narrow Corner). From Baghdad; they owned shops at Takana

ARBOS, Dr. (Ashenden/Miss King). He attends Miss King; Swiss; bearded, grizzled; a member of the Faculty of

Medicine in Geneva

ARBUTHNOT, Dr. (Magician). A London eye specialist; common friend to both Susie Boyd and Arthur Burton; a colleague of Arthur at St. Luke's Hospital, London; a prosperous bachelor; grey hair; red, contented face; well-to-do from a large practice; likes women

ARBUTHNOT, Mr. (Painted Veil). He mentioned the cholera epidemic at Mei-tan-fu

ARCHBISHOP (Romantic Young Lady). Trusted friend of the Duchess de Dos Palos; he tries to dissuade Dina Pilar from marrying Jose Leon

ARCHDEACON (Hero). James Parsons knows him quite well; has a great gift of humor

ARCHITECTS (Punctiliousness of Don Sebastian). Ordered by Don Sebastian to erect an edifice befitting the dignity of Archbishop Pablo de Mantona

ARCHPRIEST (Catalina). Agrees that Don Manuel should attempt to heal Catalina

ARDSLEY, Charlotte (For Services Rendered). The wife of Leonard Ardsley; mother of Sydney, Eva, and Lois Ardsley, and of Ethel Bartlett; sister of Dr. Charles Prentice; over sixty years of age; thin; grey haired; severe face; kind eyes; without an operation, she has only a few months to live

ARDSLEY, Eva (For Services Rendered). Eldest daughter of Leonard and Charlotte Ardsley; sister of Sydney and Lois Ardsley, and of Ethel Bartlett; age thirty-nine; thin and somewhat haggard; gentle and a trifle subdued; restless; her fiance, Ted, killed in the war; looks after Sydney; terribly unhappy; propositions Collie Stratton; she suffers a breakdown after Collie's suicide

ARDSLEY, Leonard (For Services Rendered). The husband of Charlotte Ardsley; father of Sydney, Eva, and Lois Ardsley, and of Ethel Bartlett; age sixty-five; red-faced and hardy; blue eyes and white hair; the only solicitor in Rambleston, Kent; has his office in his house

ARDSLEY, Lois (For Services Rendered). The youngest daughter of Leonard and Charlotte Ardsley; sister of Sydney and Eva Ardsley, and of Ethel Bartlett; age twenty-six, but looks no more than twenty; pretty, gay, and natural; blue eyes and straight nose; an air of immense healthiness; agrees to visit with her Aunt Emily after being propositioned by Howard Bartlett; she suddenly decides to elope to London with Wilfred Cedar

ARDSLEY, Mr. (For Services Rendered). Leonard Ardsley's father; a solicitor; his son followed him in the business

ARDSLEY, Sydney (For Services Rendered). Son of Leonard and Charlotte Ardsley; the brother of Eva and Lois Ardsley, and of Ethel Bartlett

ARGENTINE MAN (String of Beads). Rich; had been "picked up" by Miss Robinson at Deauville, and he went off to Paris with her

ARIADNE (Perfect Gentleman). In the opera, The Island of Naxos; deserted by Theseus; inhabits a lonely cave

ARLES, Bishop of (Then and Now). The Pope's legate in France; tells Caesar Borgia, in a letter, that King Louis has ordered six hundred of his lancers to Parma to be placed in Borgia's service

ARLINGTON, Duchess of (Our Betters). Lost nine pounds by going to Compton Edwardes; she and her husband are scheduled to dine with the Graystons at the country house in Suffolk

ARMENIAN MERCHANT (Caesar's Wife). Had a difference of opinion with Abdul Said, who then shot him to death

ARMSTRONG (Cakes and Ale). The wine steward at Alroy Kear's club, St. James Street, London; he has been employed there for forty-eight years

ARROL, Martin (Love in a Cottage). Nephew of Mrs. Owen Butterfield; a guest at the Hotel Splendide, Varenna, Lake Como; he acts as Owen Butterfield's secretary; believes that Sybil Bruce's money would be useful in furthering his ambition to enter Parliament, and thus proposes marriage to her; conspires with his aunt to have Owen Butterfield confined as a lunatic

ART COLLECTOR (Moon and Sixpence). He had purchased Charles Strickland's painting, "The Woman of Samaria"; he died nine months later, and Christie's again auctioned the piece

ART DEALER (Moon and Sixpence). In Paris; he had once exhibited two or three of Charles Strickland's paintings, but the artist had removed them from his gallery

Characters

ART STUDENT #1 (Of Human Bondage). He had a room on the floor above Miss Wilkinson's apartment on the Rue Breda, Paris; fine eyes; wrote daily love letters to Miss Wilkinson

ART STUDENT #2 (Of Human Bondage). At Paris; young; English; has an affair with Ruth Chalice

ART STUDENTS (Moon and Sixpence). At the London art classes; thought of Strickland's paintings as a joke

ARTHUR, Sister (Of Human Bondage). Nurse at St. Luke's Hospital, London; Griffiths wishes that she could see him washing Philip Carey

ARTILLERY OFFICER (Choice of Amyntas). Marries Maiden #1, who then raises him to dignity and power; is cast down and dies while in exile on a lonely isle

ARTISANS (Mrs. Craddock). Aboard the penny steamboat from London to Greenwich

ARTIST (Catalina). A Greek of Toledo; painted pictures that exalted the devotion of worshipers; his work for the new church at the Escorial rejected by the King

ARTIST #1 (Razor's Edge). He seduced seventeen-year-old Suzanne Rouvier; takes her to live with him in his studio in Montmarte

ARTIST #2 (Razor's Edge). In Montmarte; Suzanne Rouvier goes to live with him after two years, when Artist #1 can no longer afford the luxury of a mistress; a good deal older than Artist #1; he eventually marries an admiring widow with money

ARTIST #3 (Razor's Edge). Young and non-representative; at age twenty, Suzanne Rouvier goes to live with him for a year and a half; a cubist, then a surrealist; marries, and then divorces; Suzanne returns to him after her recovery from typhoid fever

ARTIST #4 (Razor's Edge). A sculptor; Suzanne Rouvier lives with him for six months

ARTIST #5 (Razor's Edge). A young English painter; had money and a car; Suzanne Rouvier's only failure

ASHENDEN (Ashenden/Visit/Giulia Lazzari/Hairless Mexican/His Excellency/Miss King/Mr. Harrington's Washing/Traitor). A writer of fiction and drama; he was recruited into the Intelligence Department by Colonel R.; a self-described humorist; is approaching middle age; balding

ASHENDEN (Sanatorium). A patient at the sanatorium in

the north of Scotland; had contracted tuberculosis of the lungs

ASHENDEN, William (Cakes and Ale). The Narrator; he had known Alroy Kear for twenty years; a novelist; has been writing for thirty-five years; was raised by his aunt and uncle at Blackstable, Kent, where, at age fifteen, he first met Edward and Rosie Driffield; as a boy, dull and not very talkative; for more than a year (between ages twenty and twenty-one) he has an affair with Rosie Driffield

ASHLEY, Algernon (Unattainable). The father of Stephen Ashley; dead

ASHLEY, Caroline (Unattainable). The wife of Stephen Ashley, from whom she has been separated for ten years; has been in love with Robert Oldham during that time, but she does not want to marry him; age thirty-five; attractive; tall and slim; humorous eyes; charming smile

ASHLEY, Stephen (Unattainable). The husband of Caroline Ashley and son of Algernon; had a fine physique; has just died, at age forty-one, at the Edward and Alexandria Hospital, Nairobi, of cirrhosis of the liver

ASKERI (Explorer [novel]). A member of Alec MacKenzie's expedition against the African slave traders; quoted in Fergus Macinnery's second letter to the newspapers

ASSISTANT (East of Suez). To the fat shopkeeper in the crowded Peking street; gives the beggar a few coins

ASSISTANT (For Services Rendered). To Dr. Charles Prentiss; once asked Lois Ardley to marry him; odious and little; a widower with three children and no money

ASSISTANT (Land of Promise). To Dr. Evans; he wants to marry Norah Marsh; nice, but not a gentleman

ASSISTANT (Mrs. Craddock). To Dr. Ramsay, Blackstable, Kent; he accompanies Edward Craddock's body to Court Leys

ASSISTANT #1 (Of Human Bondage). To Dr. South; develops the mumps

ASSISTANT #2 (Of Human Bondage). A substitute when Dr. South's regular assistant went on holiday; a university man; "too damned gentlemanly" for South

ASSISTANT (Penelope). To Dr. Richard O'Farrell; Dickie sends him to see patients whom he ought to have seen himself

Characters 23

ASSISTANT (String of Beads). At Jarrot's Stores; he had mistakenly given Miss Robinson the wrong string of beads

ASSISTANT CHIEF INSPECTOR (Razor's Edge). At Toulon; Larry Darrell and Maugham verify to him the identity of Sophie Macdonald's body after they return from the mortuary

ASSISTANT SECRETARY (Of Human Bondage). At Lynn and Sedley, London; he received from each assistant each month four shillings for washing money, two shillings for the club, and fines

ASSISTANT TAILORS (Perfect Gentlemen). Four of them; to Monsieur Jourdain's tailor

ASSISTANTS (Of Human Bondage). At the drapery department of a London store; draping chintzes and cretonnes; preparing country orders that had come in by mail

ASSISTANTS (Of Human Bondage). Received their pay, once each month, from the secretary of Lynn and Sedley, London

ASSUNTA (Lotus Eater). Wife of the vineyard owner; Thomas Wilson's cook and housekeeper

ASSUNTA (Salvatore). Age twenty-four or twenty-five; extremely ugly; marries Salvatore

ASSUNTA (Up at the Villa). A relative of Agata; rented lodging (with meals) to Karl Richter; both of her sons in military service

ATA (Moon and Sixpence). The Tahitian girl whom Tiare Johnson "married" to Charles Strickland; a relative of Taire; worked and lived at the Hotel de la Fleur; her father and mother were dead; age seventeen; a Protestant; had never been touched but by captains and first mates

ATHELNY, Athelstan (Of Human Bondage). Son of Thorpe and Betty Athelny; rosy, healthy, smiling; at age fifteen, he took to singing, in a cracked voice

ATHELNY, Betty (Of Human Bondage). The common wife of Thorpe Athelny; three inches taller than her husband; fair; blue eyes; a kindly expression; fat and blousy; coarse and red skin; daughter of a farmer from Ferne, Kent, near Blackstable; she claims to have seen Rev. William Carey; formerly a maid in the Athelny house in Kensington

ATHELNY, Edward (Of Human Bondage). Son of Thorpe and Betty Athelny; rosy, healthy, smiling

ATHELNY, Harold (Of Human Bondage). Son of Thorpe and Betty Athelny; rosy, healthy, smiling

ATHELNY, Maria de la Concepcion (Of Human Bondage). Daughter of Thorpe and Betty Athelny; answers to the name of Connie

ATHELNY, Maria de los Mercedes (Of Human Bondage). Daughter of Betty and Thorpe Athelny; answers to the name of Molly

ATHELNY, Maria del Pilar (Of Human Bondage). The third daughter of Betty and Thorpe Athelny; answers to the name of Jane; fair haired; is characterized by her frankness

ATHELNY, Maria del Rosario (Of Human Bondage). Daughter of Betty and Thorpe Athelny; answers to the name of Rosie

ATHELNY, Maria del Sol (Of Human Bondage). Eldest child of Thorpe and Betty Athelny; almost fifteen years of age; answers to the names of Sally and Pudding-Face; tall; even, white teeth; pleasant gray eyes, broad forehead, and red cheeks; apprenticed to a dressmaker in Rogers Street, London; healthy, animal, and feminine

ATHELNY, Mrs. (Of Human Bondage). First wife of Thorpe Athelny; "a lady"; married to her husband for three years; charming; a bore; lived with her husband in a little red brick house in Kensington; she still lives there; refused to divorce her husband

ATHELNY, Thorpe (Of Human Bondage). A journalist; the press representative of Lynn and Sedley, a linendrapery firm in Regent Street, London; age forty-eight; a patient at St. Luke's hospital, suffering from a sharp attack of jaundice; small head and hands; long tapering fingers, with beautiful rosy nails; five feet five inches tall; blue eyes; imposingly bold nose, hooked; small, gray, pointed beard; bald; short-sighted; educated at Winchester; had lived in Spain for eleven years as the secretary of the English water company at Toledo; had been on a tea plantation in Ceylon and was a traveler in America for Italian wines; at one time a police court reporter for an evening paper, sub-editor of a paper on the in the Midlands, and editor of a paper on the Riviera; enjoying a common marriage, with nine illegitimate children alive out of the twelve whom his common wife had delivered; had been (and still is) married to "a lady"

ATHELNY, Thorpe the younger (Of Human Bondage). Eldest son of Betty and Thorpe Athelny; chubby; curly hair; destined for the Navy

ATKIN, Miss (Sanatorium). A patient at the sanitorium during winter; essentially cured; a middle-aged spinster who held the position of honorary librarian

ATKINS, Henry (Liza of Lambeth). Called Harry; young; going to take Sally Cooper to Chingford in the "Red Lion brake [wagon]"; he marries Sally, but beats her when he drinks

ATKINS, Mr. (Cakes and Ale). An hypothetical example of a personality without the reputation to support it; a chartered accountant at a spa in the west of England, taking the waters for his liver

ATKINS, Mr. (Liza of Lambeth). Brother of Harry; he and a friend attend Harry and Sally's wedding

ATKINSON (Narrow Corner). The Australian captain of a pearling schooner from Port Darwin

ATKINSON, Harold (Up at the Villa). Middle-aged American; he and his wife owned a large and sumptuous villa at Florence that had once belonged to the Medici; fine, handsome, and grey haired; plethoric and somewhat corpulent; a terrible flirt

ATKINSON, Mrs. (Up at the Villa). The wife of Harold Atkinson; white haired, kind, and shrewd; seriously thinking of having the singer at the Florentine restaurant trained for the opera

ATTACHE (Theatre). At the Spanish embassy in Paris; aboard the train from Paris to Cannes; black curly hair, beard, and moustache; large eyes; violet and unwrinkled skin; no more than thirty years of age; obtains a sleeping compartment for Julia Lambert Gosselyn

ATTENDANT (Lady Habart). An employee of Captain Smithson; resembled a butler in a family that had come over with the Conqueror

ATTENDANT (Neil Macadam). A Malay; employed at the museum at Kuala Solor

ATTENDANT #1 (Of Human Bondage). At the anatomy theatre at St. Luke's Hospital, London; places a glass of water on the table; carries in a pelvis and two thigh bones

ATTENDANT #2 (Of Human Bondage). At St. Luke's Hospital, London; directs Philip Carey and Dunsford to the dissecting room

ATTENDANT #3 (Of Human Bondage). At the dissecting room of St. Luke's Hospital, London; he assigns a leg to Philip Carey

ATTENDANT (Promise). At Claridge's; tells the Narrator that his wife had telephoned to say that she would not have lunch with him

ATTENDANTS (Mrs. Craddock). Gather Polly Ley's baggage at the railway station at Blackstable, Kent

ATTORNEY (Moon and Sixpence). In France; his failure left Rene Brunot and his wife penniless

ATTORNEY GENERAL (Letter [play]). At Singapore; Leslie Crosby's case in his charge; a very decent person

ATTORNEYS (Closed Shop). They devise a divorce law that proves satisfactory to the new President

AUBURN, Rose (Ashenden/His Excellency). Byring's lover; initially a member of a dance troupe, the Glad Girls, that performed at the Moulin Rouge, Paris; at one time astonishingly beautiful; the best known courtesan in France; graceful and slender; brown hair, large blue eyes; oval face, small nose; lovely white and red skin

AUCTIONEER (Cakes and Ale). At Christie's, London; he followed the customers' gestures with bored eyes and muttered the bids in a drone

AUDLIN, Doctor (Lord Mountdrago). Lord Mountrago's psychoanalyst; tall and thin, with narrow shoulders and a slight stoop; thin grey hair; a long sallow face; large pale blue eyes; large hands and long tapering fingers; conveys the impression of a very sick man; slightly over age fifty; after the war he studied in Vienna and Zurich, and then settled into practice in Wimble Street, London

AUGUST (Princess September). Eighth daughter born to the King and Queen of Siam

AUNT (Christmas Holiday). Of the children of Alexey and Evgenia; lives in Nice; takes one of the daughters of

Alexey and Evgenia to live with her
AUNT (De Amicitia). Of the Narrator; she believes that Ferdinand White and Valentia Stewart should have been married
AUNT (Explorer [play]). Of Dick Lomas; a maiden; left her money to Dick
AUNT (Jack Straw). Of Pierre; widowed; the relic of an egg importer in Soho and a highly respectable person; died
AUNT (Man of Honour). Of John Halliwell; a maiden; sent Basil Kent a woolen comforter when he was at the Cape
AUNT (Of Human Bondage). Of Mildred Rogers; she and Mildred live at Herne Hill, London
AUSTIN (Facts of Life). A tennis player at Monte Carlo; his health uncertain
AUSTRIAN ARCHDUKE (Lord Mountdrago). He talks with the German Ambassador at Lydia Connemara's party
AUSTRIAN NOBLEMAN (Hero). His wine cellar had been purchased by William, Duke of St. Olphert's
AUTHOR #1 (Theatre). Of the play in which Avice Crichton had performed; pale and shattered; made a halting speech at the end of the play
AUTHOR #2 (Theatre). Of Nowadays, a piece that he wrote as a modern version of Sir Arthur Wing Pinero's The Second Mrs Tanqueray (1893)
AUTHORITIES (Explorer [novel]). At Parkhurst Prison; inform Lucy Allerton that because the the grave state of her father's health, they would remit the remainder of his sentence
AVON, Tommy (Bread-Winner). Shot himself last Friday; well known in the city; was one of Charles Battle's clients
AYAHS (Sacred Flame). Employed by the Tabrets in India; Mrs. Tabret wonders what they had taught her children
AZURIA, Juanito (Catalina). The leading man in Alonso Fuentes' acting troupe; young and handsome; runs away with Luisa Fuentes and the troupe's cash

B

B., King (Ashenden/Mr. Harrington's Washing). The ruler of a Balkan state; through his influence, the state was on the verge of declaring war against the Allies

BABIES (Painted Veil). Four of them; at the French convent at Mei-tan-fu; very red; quaint little Chinese faces; queer animals of an unknown species; Walter Fane extremely fond of them

BABY (Merry-Go-Round). Of Fanny Bridger; large blue eyes

BABY (Razor's Edge). Of Girl #2 and Paco; was sent to a nurse in a village near Saville

BACCHUS (Perfect Gentleman). In the opera, The Island of Naxos; young and beautiful; Ariadne throws herself into his arms

BACHELORS (Of Human Bondage). Guests at the boarding house in Brighton; old, funny, with mincing ways

BACHELORS (Razor's Edge). Two or three of them; old; in government offices; lodge at the same Paris hotel where Larry Darrell lives

BACOT, Attihill (Mrs. Craddock). One of the guests at Mrs. Branderton's dinner party; had once contested the Parliamentary seat for the county; looked upon as an authority on the nation's affairs

BADDELEYS (Painted Veil). Mrs. Garstin meets Walter Fane there and asks him to her house

BAGLIONI, Gian Paolo (Then and Now). A mercenary captain in service to Caesar Borgia; lord of Perugia; with Vitellozzo Vitelli, he defeated the Florentines at Arezzo

BAILIFF (Magician). Of Oliver Haddo; died within a year of an altercation with Haddo

BAIN (Pool). Owner of the firm that employs and later dismisses Lawson after his return to Apia

[BAINBRIDGE?], James (Landed Gentry). Mrs. Insoley's cousin; broke his neck in the hunting field; brought to Kenyon Fulton on a stretcher; left Mrs. Insoley all of his debts

BAINBRIDGE, Mr. (Landed Gentry). The deceased father of Mrs. Insoley; would have given Gann the younger only fifteen minutes to reach a decision about Peggy Gann; used to sit on the Times so that no one could read it before he did

BAINBRIDGE, Pamela (Landed Gentry). Great-grandmother of Mrs. Insoley; she supposedly had an affair with the Regent

BAKER (Catalina). Father of Consuelo de Valero; dies

Characters 29

several years after his daughter's marriage
BAKER, Freddy (East of Suez). A manager of the shipping firm of Jardine's, at Fuchow; married a Eurasian
BAKER, Mrs. (East of Suez). A pretty Eurasian; married Freddy Baker at Fuchow
BALLAD SINGER (Making of a Saint). At the market place at Forli
BALLET GIRL (Magician). In Milan; was rumored to have married Oliver Haddo
BAND (Bum). Composed of a guitarist, a blind fiddler, and a harpist; play ragtime in the arcade at Vera Cruz
BANK CLERK (String of Beads). A potential character in Laura's potential story; badly injured in the war; he had lost a leg; half of his face had been shot away; finally marries Miss Robinson
BANK MANAGER (Cakes and Ale). At Blackstable, Kent; the vicar's churchwarden
BANK MANAGER (For Services Rendered). At Rambleston, Kent; preparing to file an arrest warrant against Collie Stratton
BANK MANAGER (Good Manners). At Graveney, Kent; tells Lady Elizabeth of Johann Herz's supposed arrest
BANK MANAGER (Verger). Offers to invest Albert Edward Foreman's money in gilt-edged securities
BANKER (Cakes and Ale). Rich; from London; took a house at Blackstable, Kent, for the summer holidays
BANNOCK (Colonel's Lady). A tenant of George Peregrine; interrupts George's reading of Evie's poems to as for an advance on a pedigree bull that he wants to buy
BANTOCKS (Razor's Edge). Elliott Templeton certain that he and the Bradley women will be invited to one of their large parties
BARBER (Catalina). Is sent for by Maria Perez to bleed Catalina
BARBER (Choice of Amyntas). At Amyntas's village; he wanted an apprentice
BARBER (East of Suez). In a crowded Peking street; he carries the utensils of his trade
BARBER (Razor's Edge). Dressed Elliott Templeton's hair and shaved his face
BARBER (Then and Now). At Imola; shaves Machiavelli and combs his hair; combs Piero Giacomini's hair; directs

Machiavelli and Piero to the house of Bartolomeo Martelli

BARBOY (Footprints in the Jungle). Informs Gaze that a police sergeant wishes to speak to him

BARCHESTER, Lady (Love in a Cottage). The wife of Lord Barchester; a guest at Sybil Bruce's fancy dress ball at Paris; borrows money from Sybil, supposedly to pay her gambling debts

BARCHESTER, Lord (Love in a Cottage). Husband of Lady Barchester; a guest at Sybil Bruce's fancy dress ball at Paris; he and his wife habitually borrow money from their rich friends

BARGEE (Bad Example). He found the girl's body in the River Thames, London; hooked the body into the boat and called the police

BARKER (Hero). A friend of James Parsons and a former adjutant of his regiment; James meets him at his club in London; tells James that Mrs. Pritchard-Wallace is "in a passion" with him

BARKER, Mr. (Of Human Bondage). Of Roxley Farm, near Blackstable Church, Kent; married a cousin, of Betty Athelny

BARKER, Mrs. (Of Human Bondage). The cousin of Betty Athelny and wife of Mr. Barker

BARLOW, Davenport (Penelope). Isobel Golightly's brother; age fifty-two; short and bald; red face; small, neatly curled moustache; fussy and pompous; self-important; attracted to Ada Fergusson

BARLOW, Ruth (Escape). Twice a widow; splendid, dark eyes

BARLOW-BASSETT, Emily (Merry-Go-Round). The mother of Reggie Barlow-Bassett; widow of Frederick Barlow-Bassett; tall; of handsome presence; fine eyes; a confident step; abundant, curling, and grey hair; a widow of means; had devoted her life to the upbringing of of her only son; she enters a private London hospital for an operation; disinherits Reggie after he marries Lauria Galbraith

BARLOW-BASSETT, Frederick (Merry-Go-Round). Deceased husband of Emily Barlow-Bassett and father of Reggie

BARLOW-BASSETT, Reggie (Merry-Go-Round). Son of Emily and Frederick Barlow-Bassett; age twenty-two; tall and strapping; black hair; singularly beautiful fea-

Characters   31

   tures; big-bones, but muscular; very dark; large
   brown eyes; straight nose; olive skin; full, sensual
   mouth; good humored and lazy; unscrupulous and untru-
   thful; has an association with Grace Castillyon; he
   returns every penny that Grace had "lent" him; marries Lauria Galbraith (Annie Higgins) and joins her
   in a career on the stage; fathers an heir; he and his
   wife take up residence at Bournemouth
BARMAID (Cakes and Ale). At the Dolphin pub, Ferne Bay,
   Kent; she wore an engagement ring to give the men a
   chance to tease her
BARMAID (Liza of Lambeth). At the pub near the theatre
   in Westminster; serves Lisa Kemp and Jim Blakeston
BARMAID (Merry-Go-Round). At the Golden Crown, Fleet
   Street, London; a co-worker with Jenny Bush
BARMAIDS (Liza of Lambeth). At the half-way house between Lambeth and Chingford; hand bottles of beer to
   the thirsty passengers from the Red Lion brake
BARMAN (Gigolo and Gigolette). He serves cocktails to
   Sandy Westcott and Cotman; has been instructed to inform Paco Espinel if Cotman returns; serves beer to
   the Cotmans and the Penezzis
BARNABY, Dr. (Wash-Tub). Tall, elderly, and bronzed;
   handsome thin face; thick grey hair cut short; an
   American; Narrator believes him to be a college pro-
   professor, but he is actually a doctor from Pennsyl-
   vania
BARNABY, Mike (Wash-Tub). Known in Arizona as "One-
   Bullet Mike"; a hulking fellow; a miner, but formerly
   a cow puncher and gun runner; also a wealthy oilman;
   the husband of Mrs. Barnaby; actually Barnaby the
   Pennsylvania doctor
BARNABY, Mrs. (Wash-Tub). A wealthy American; came to
   London to "do the season"; the wife of the fictitious
   Mike Barnaby and the real Dr. Barnaby
BARNARD, Edward (Fall of Edward Barnard). Ruddy, tall,
   light brown hair; engaged to Isabel Longstaffe; sent
   to Tahiti in the employ of George Braunschmidt
BARNARD, Mr. (Fall of Edward Barnard). Edward Barnard's
   father; a banker; he shot himself
BARNES, Mr. (Narrow Corner). Premier of Australia; he
   and his wife and the Hudsons invited to dinner at the
   Blakes' house

BARNES, Mrs. (Narrow Corner). Wife of Mr. Barnes; had been to school with Fred Blake's mother

BARRACLOUGH, Lady (Outstation). Officer Hennerley's aunt; wife of Lord Barraclough

BARRACLOUGH, Lord (Outstation). Officer Hennerley's uncle

BARRETT, Eva (Gigolo and Gigolette). Well over fifty years of age; always late; late for her date with Sandy Westcott

BARRETT, Mrs. (Gigolo and Gigolette). The aged widow of Chaloner Barrett; a wealthy American; entertained and gambled extravagantly

BARRISTER (Round Dozen). Nephew of Gertrude St. Clair and once engaged to Eleanor Porchester; had an affair with the daughter of his laundress; eventually married a woman of means and became a high court judge

BARTLE, Charlie (Fortunate Painter). Kept an art studio in the Rue Breda, Paris

BARTLETT, Captain (French Joe). A pilot; completely bald; a resident of the hotel on Thursday Island; he directs the Narrator to French Joe

BARTLETT CHILDREN (For Services Rendered). Of Ethel and Howard Bartlett; away at boarding school

BARTLETT, Ethel (For Services Rendered). Wife of Howard Bartlett; second daughter of Leonard and Charlotte Ardsley; sister of Sydney, Eva, and Lois Ardsley; age thirty-five; married for fifteen years; her children away at boarding school; handsome; regular features; proud; does not wish to admit that she made a mistake in her marriage to Howard

BARTLETT, Howard (For Services Rendered). Husband of Ethel Bartlett; a small tenant farmer who had been an officer in the war; married for fifteen years; age forty; big and somewhat stout; dashing good looks; he drinks; propositions Lois Ardsley

BARTLETT, Mr. the elder (For Services Rendered). Grandfather of Howard Bartlett; died from drink

BARTLETT, Mr. the younger (For Services Rendered). The father of Howard Bartlett; died from drink

BARTON, Mr. (Razor's Edge). Father of Paul Barton; an American; office furniture manufacturer

BARTON, Mrs. (Razor's Edge). The wife of Paul Barton; daughter of a British newspaper magnate who had been

Characters 33

raised to the peerage

BARTON, Paul (Razor's Edge). A young American; at a luncheon party at Carelton House Terrace, London; is interested in seeing the host's art collection; age twenty-three; blonde, good looking, and charming; a beautiful dancer with an ample fortune; he adopted British nationality because he had married the daughter of a British newspaper magnate who had been raised to the peerage; he wants to borrow Elliott Templeton's Count de Lauria costume to attend Edna Novemali's party

BASTIANINI (Hour Before the Dawn). The Italian ambassador; informed everyone that Italy would never fight England

BATTLE, Charles Laurence (Bread-Winner). Age forty-two; father of Judy and Patrick; the husband of Margery Battle; at age twenty-three when he married Margery; distinguished appearance; a stock broker in the firm of Wargrave, Battle, and Company; no sense of humor

BATTLE, Judy (Bread-Winner). Daughter of Charles and Margery Battle; the sister of Patrick; age seventeen; pretty; blonde

BATTLE, Margery (Bread-Winner). Wife of Charles Battle; the mother of Judy and Patrick; arty and highbrow; pretty; slightly faded blonde; less than forty years of age

BATTLE, Patrick (Bread-Winner). The son of Charles and Margery Battle; brother of Judy; age eighteen; nice looking

BAVARIA, King of (Voice of the Turtle). Had an affair with Lola Montez

BAVARIAN PRINCE (Hour Before the Dawn). May Henderson had met him in the Tyrol; he knew that his servants were Nazis

BEADSWORTH, Mr. (Penelope). Husband of Mrs. Beadsworth; the O'Farrells' family solicitor and good friend; middle aged; benign manner

BEADSWORTH, Mrs. (Penelope). Wife of Mr. Beadsworth; attended to her household duties while her husband smoked his pipe

BEARDSLEY, Aubrey Vincent (Alien Corn). The English illustrator; Narrator believes that he should have illustrated Max Beerbohm's book about Ferdy Rabenstein

BEARER (Painted Veil). He wiped his sweaty face with a dirty rag

BEARERS (Explorer [novel]). At Mombassa; had been with Alec MacKenzie during his previous expeditions; Alec engaged them for his expedition against the slave traders of British East Africa

BEARERS (Explorer [play]). Alec MacKenzie believes that when he finally dies in Africa, they will seize his gun and clothes and leave him to the jackals

BEARERS (Painted Veil). Carried Kitty and Walter Fane, in their chairs, to Mei-tan-fu; uttered occasional remarks and uncouth songs

BEARERS (Painted Veil). At Mei-tan-fu; carry Kitty Fane from the compound to the French convent; they give short, sharp cries to urge the coolies to make way

BEARERS (Painted Veil). Carry Kitty Fane, Waddington, and the Chinese officer from the river bank to the center of Mei-tan-fu

BEARERS (Painted Veil). On the journey from Mei-tan-fu to Hong Kong; two carry the amah; four carry Kitty Fane

BECKER, Ellie (Razor's Edge). Widowed daughter-in-law of Herr Becker #1 and Frau Becker #1; she and her three children live on the Becker farm; well under age thirty; thick-set and large black eyes and black hair; a sallow square face and a sullen look; very devout; the daughter of a prosperous farmer; she had attended a girls' gymnasium at Zwingenberg; despises and resents Frau Becker #2

BECKER, Frau #1 (Razor's Edge). The first wife of Herr Becker #1 and mother of Herr Becker #2

BECKER, Frau #2 (Razor's Edge). The second wife of Herr Becker #1; formerly a hired girl from the orphanage who had come to the farm at age fourteen; she married Herr Becker #1 after the death of Frau Becker #1; considerably younger than her husband; full blown, with red cheeks and fair hair; a hungry sensual look; jolly and merry; hates Ellie Becker

BECKER, Herr #1 (Razor's Edge). A German farmer near Zingenberg; husband of Frau Becker #2; hires Larry Darrell and Kosti #2; in his late forties; heavy and grey-haired; wounded in the leg during the war, and

Characters

thus drinks to kill the pain

BECKER, Herr #2 (Razor's Edge). Husband of Ellie Becker and son of Frau Becker #1 and Herr Becker #1; killed at Verdun

BEERBOHM, Sir Henry Maximilian (Alien Corn). English critic, essayist, and caricaturist (1872-1956); he presumably knew Ferdy Rabenstein; Narrator believes that he should have written a book about Rabenstein

BEGGAR (Bum). Vivid red beard and hair; extremely thin; tragic blue eyes; about forty years of age; formerly in the employ of the American Fruit Company in Central America; at one time had wanted to be a waiter

BEGGAR (East of Suez). In a crowded Peking street; gaunt and thin; untidy mop of bristly hair; clad in filthy tatters; stops at a shop and wails

BEGGAR (Making of a Saint). He stops Checco and Matteo d'Orsi and Filippo Brandolini on their way to the Palazzo Orsi; Checco throws him a piece of gold, and he responds with, "God bless you!"

BEGGAR (Painted Veil). At Mei-tan-fu; asks Kitty Fane for alms; hard and rough skin, tanned like the hide of a goat; emaciated bare legs; shock of coarse grey hair; hollow cheeks and wild eyes; possessed the head of a madman

BELGIAN (Buried Talent). Rich; promised, for a price, to get Charmian Pelter into the Brussels opera

BELGIAN COLONEL (Marriage of Convenience). A passenger on the ship out of Bangkok; shy and fat

BELGIAN COUNT (Razor's Edge). He arranges to marry the daughter of Achille Gauvain; authentic title; owns a chateau near Namur

BELGIAN REFUGEE (Hour Before the Dawn). Came to Havre in Roger Henderson's staff car, which he found in a ditch, riddled with machine gun bullets

BELL, Clarence (Of Human Bondage). A cheerful youth, sixteen years of age; non-paid employee in the haberdashery department of Lynn and Sedley, London; he collected stamps

BELL, Dr. (Love in a Cottage). The resident physician at the Hotel Splendide, Varenna, on Lake Como; sees himself as an artist in life; a pipe smoker; wants a private practice in the English countryside; in love with Sybil Bruce; he proposes to Sybil, knowing full well that she will lose her money if they marry

BELLET, Madame (Razor's Edge). She kept a small rooming house and brothel at Toulon, where Sophie Macdonald lodged; an agent of the police; identified Sophie's body

BELLINGHAM, Roger (Lady Frederick). Had an affair with Lady Kate Berolles; dead

BELMONTE, Juan (Mother). A Spanish matador (1892-1962) who fought at Seville during the feast of San Isidro

BENEDICT (Ashenden/Mr. Harrington's Washing). A Jewish interpreter at the British Consulate at Vladivostok; small mop of untidy hair

BENEFACTOR (Painted Veil). Of the French convent at Mei-tan-fu; presented a statue from Paris

BENGALI AGENT (Ashenden/Miss King). In the German secret service; has a black cane trunk with documents of interest to the British government

BENJAMIN (Choice of Amyntas). Son of Peter the Schoolmaster and Mrs. Peter

BENNETT, (Enoch) Arnold (Razor's Edge). Other than the young Narrator, the only serious writer (1867-1931) who would frequent the shabby restaurant in the Rue d'Odess, in the Montparnasse section of Paris

BENNETT, Frederick (Tenth Man). His original name was "Feltman"; secretary of several of George Winter's companies; manages the office; middle aged; small and thin; clean shaven; sharp face; extremely respectable appearance; wears gold spectacles; a former solicitor struck from the rolls; he had spent three years in prison for misappropriating a client's money

BENNETT, Miss (Of Human Bondage). Introduced to Philip Carey by Mrs. Hodges; the belle of Lynn and Sedley, London; buyer in the petticoats department; of massive proportions; large red face, heavily powdered; a bust of imposing dimensions; flaxen hair elaborately arranged; chewed Sens-Sens

BENSON, Sir Frank Robert (Theatre). The Shakespearean actor-manager (1858-1939); had engaged Michael Gosselyn for his Shakespearean tour

BENTIVOGLIO, Ermete (Now and Then). The son of Giovanni Bentivoglio, the Lord of Bologna; attended the meeting of Borgia's captains at La Magione, near Perugia

BENTIVOGLIO, Giovanni (Then and Now). Lord of Bologna;

brother of Protonotary Bentivoglio

BENTIVOGLIO, Protonotary (Then and Now). The brother of Giovanni Bentivoglio; should he come to an agreement with Borgia, he will receive either a Cardinal's hat or the hand of the sister of Cardinal Borgia

BENTLEY (Constant Wife). Butler at the Middleton house, Harley Street, London

BERGER, Colonel (Christmas Holiday). Husband of Leontine Berger and the father of Robert; in the Medical Service; an officer in the Legion of Honor; had lost a leg during the war; dead

BERGER, Leontine (Christmas Holiday). Wife of Colonel Berger and mother of Robert; Robert and Lydia Berger lived with her in Neuilly; widow of a doctor and the daughter of a staff officer, both of whom held the Legion of Honour; tall and thin; dark brown permanently waved hair; sallow skin; fine eyes; delicate straight nose; thin lips; bright, dark, cool, and watchful eyes; in her fifties; following Robert's sentence she becomes a general servant to an American

BERGER, Lydia (Christmas Holiday). Known professionally as Princess Olga; wife of Robert Berger; one of the girls at the Serail, Paris; Russian; perfectly indifferent blue eyes, like windows set flush with a wall; not very tall; heavily made up; not beautiful, but prettyish; high cheekbones; fleshy little nose; neat, trim, slight figure; skin of pale amber hue; broad, white brow; short pale brown hair, curling round the neck; educated in England; had worked at half wages for a Paris dressmaker

BERGER, Robert (Christmas Holiday). Husband of Lydia Berger; at age twenty-two murdered Teddy Jordan; then condemned to fifteen years of penal servitude at St. Laurent, French Guiana; blue-grey eyes; dark brown long wavy hair; strong and wiry; had been almost a first-class tennis player; had worked for a time in a broker's office, but discharged for embezzling funds; a horse player; before his marriage to Lydia he had received a suspended prison sentence for stealing motor cars; had barely escaped another sentence for smuggling heroin from Belgium into France; comes down with malaria while working on the road from St. Laurent to Cayenne, French Guiana

BERNARD (Ashenden/Miss King). A German-Swiss agent in the service of the Intelligence Department; a waiter by calling; stocky, small; bullet-shaped head, close cropped hair; shifty blue eyes, sallow skin

BERNARDO, Messer (Then and Now). A magistrate of Imola; one of the crowd that surges into Borgia's apartment; he recognized the silver as having been stolen from Monna Brigida

BEROLLES, Lady Elizabeth (Lady Frederick). Known as Lady Frederick; age thirty to thirty-five; sister of Sir Gerald O'Mara; Irish; she had married at age seventeen; very nearly ran off with Paradine Fouldes; mother of one child, who died when a boy; handsome and vivacious; dyes her hair; paints; crippled with debts; a friend of Lady Maud Mereston; reportedly had been the mistress of Roger Bellingham

BEROLLES, Lord Frederick (Lady Frederick). Husband of Lady Frederick Berolles for ten years; a confirmed tippler

BEROLLES, Lady Kate (Lady Frederick). The wife of Peter Berolles; small, meek, and mild; had an affair with Roger Bellingham; she told her husband that Roger and Lady Frederick Berolles were lovers; dead

BEROLLES, Lord Peter (Lady Frederick). Brother of Lord Frederick Berolles and husband of Kate Berolles; dead

BERSAGLIERI (Mrs. Craddock). At Rome; with bold cocks' feathers in their hats; the chorus of a comic opera

BESENTZNY, Emil (Magician). He edited a book in German entitled Die Sphinx

BETTY (Back of Beyond). Daughter of Mrs. Moon and Jim; age twenty-two; married for two years and expecting a child

BETTY (Hero). The Parsons' cook; was sent to Howe, the butcher, for some chops

BEVAN, Mr. (Kite). Husband of Mrs. Bevan #1 and then of Mrs. Bevan #2; father of Betty Bevan Sunbury

BEVAN, Mrs. #1 (Kite). Mother of Betty Bevan Sunbury; died

BEVAN, Mrs. #2 (Kite). The step-mother of Betty Bevan Sunbury; she and Mr. Bevan have three children of their own; does not get along with her step-daughter

BIGAMIST (Catalina). He is condemned by the Inquisition

BILL (Liza of Lambeth). One of the several youths on

Vere Street, Lambeth; he calls after Liza as she swaggers down the street; aboard the Red Lion brake for Chingford; he works at the same factory with Jim Blakeston

BIN-MAN (Of Human Bondage). At Ferne, Kent; he supplied each company of hop pickers with strings of hops at their bins

BIRD (Princess September). It sings to September and volunteers to take the place of her parrot

BIRD'S FATHER-IN-LAW (Princess September). He hosts a party, with September's Bird being one of the guests

BISCEGLIE, Alfonso, Duke of (Then and Now). The second husband of Lucrezia Borgia; the handsomest man in Rome; age eighteen when he married her; a year following his marriage, attacked armed men at the Vatican, then later strangled in his bed by Don Michele

BISHOP (Before the Party). Of Hong Kong; guest of Canon Heywood

BISHOP #1 (Bishop's Apron). Asked Lionel Spratte if he were an abstainer; suggested that total abstinence in the clergy served as an example

BISHOP #2 (Bishop's Apron). At the Athenaeum Club, in London; hands a telegram to Lord Stonehenge

BISHOP (Cupid and the Vicar of Swale). Appoints Robert Branscomb as the new vicar of Swale

BISHOP (Lady Frederick). He attends a dinner with Lady Frederick Berolles; told her harrowing details of the distress in the East End of London

BISHOP (Loaves and Fishes). Theodore Spratte meets him at the Athenaeum; tells Spratte that there has been no confirmation that Gray has been appointed Bishop of Colchester

BISHOP (Marriages Are Made in Heaven). As indicated by Jack Rayner, he will dine with you if you give him good dinners

BISHOP #1 (Merry-Go-Round). Of Rochester; a man of no family

BISHOP #2 (Merry-Go-Round). Grandfather of Rev. Collinson Farley

BISHOP (Neil MacAdam). In the civil service at Kuala Solor; receives a punch in the eye from Neil MacAdam after an insulting remark against Darya Munro

BISHOP (Razor's Edge). Of the diocese on the French

Riviera in which Elliott Templeton had his residence; often invited to dine in that house; he had been a cavalry officer before entering the Church; commanded a regiment during the war; rubicand and stout; sturdy and thick set; no more than average height; comes to Antibes to administer the last sacrament to Elliott Templeton

BISHOP, Charlie (Virtue). A friend of the Narrator; a pathologist; both had been medical students together; small but stout; thin, sandy hair, almost bald; blunt features; dark eyes, bespectacled; round, merry, red face; approximately fifty-five years of age

BISHOP, Ivy (Sanatorium). English girl on the sanatorium veranda; age twenty-nine; pretty; red hair and bright blue eyes; red lips, highly colored cheeks; exceptionally white skin; extremely thin face; has been at the sanatorium for two years, but has been in other sanatoria for the past eight years

BISHOP, Margery Hobson (Virtue). The wife of Charlie Bishop; an attractive woman, though not pretty; some ten years younger than her husband; dark hair; leaves her husband for Morton

BISHOP, Mrs. (Sanatorium). Ivy Bishop's mother; led a busy social life

BISHOP, Queenie (Smith). She had an affair with Thomas Freeman at Cambridge

BLACK, Annie (Unknown). She was once engaged to Edward Driffield; expecting a baby; staying at the vicarage with the Pooles; Evelyn Wharton is making the baby's clothes

BLACK, Mrs. (Of Human Bondage). Had a cottage at Ferne, Kent, a half mile from the Athelnys' hut; postmistress and provider

BLACK SLAVES (Choice of Amyntas). Exit from the silver doors of the palace in the secret cavern; assist Amyntas from the boat; lead him into the court of the palace; they bathe, polish, clothe, and perfume him

BLACKBRIDGE, John (Portrait of a Gentleman). An actuary and counsellor-at-law; the author of the Complete Poker Player (1879); middle-aged; clean-shaven and square jawed; thin lips; wary eyes; sallow, somewhat wrinkled face; an American, presumably from the South

BLACKFELLOWS (Narrow Corner). Two of them; row Captain

Characters 41

Nichols from the Takana beach to the lugger; Torres Straits islanders; strong; fine figures

BLACKFELLOWS (Narrow Corner). Two of them; members of the crew of the Australian schooner

BLACKSMITH (Then and Now). At the inn at San Casciana; in a card game in which Machiavelli is a participant

BLAIR DAUGHTERS (Our Betters). Two of them; of Lady Helen Blair; stuffier and dowdier than their mother

BLAIR, Lady Helen (Our Betters). Lived in the country with her two daughters; age fifty-five; stuffy and dowdy; the widowed sister of a duchess

BLAISE, Vesta (Flotsam and Jetsam). Was Vesta Grange's stage name before she married Norman

BLAKE (Sacred Flame). He informed Major Liconda, at the club, that Maurice Tabret had died

BLAKE, Fred (Narrow Corner). [Blake not the real name] Son of Jim Blake; accompanies Captain Nichols into Kim Chin's shop; from Brisbane, Australia; young and tall; broad chest and athletic build; looked no more than twenty years old; slight but wiry; curly dark brown hair; large blue eyes; surly expression; white, small, perfectly shaped teeth; he bites his nails; an accountant; shot Patrick Hudson with the latter's own gun; he has an affair with Louise Frith; according to Captain Nichols, he got drunk at Batavia, threw himself over the side of the Fenton, and drowned

BLAKE, Jim (Narrow Corner). Father of Fred Blake; knows Ryan; the biggest lawyer in Sydney and an important political figure in New South Wales

BLAKE, Mr. (Narrow Corner). The son of Jim Blake and a brother of Fred; married; is involved in one of his father's businesses

BLAKE, Mrs. (Narrow Corner). The wife of Jim Blake and mother of Fred and the other two Blake children; had gone to school with Mrs. Barnes

BLAKELEY, Teddie (Explorer [novel]). Fred Allerton's solicitor; "a man of evil odour"; he specialized in dealing with the most doubtful sort of commercial work; his name was prominent in every scandal for the last fifteen years; surprisingly, he had never followed any of his clients to the jail that he so justly deserved

BLAKESTON, Jim (Liza of Lambeth). He and his family the

the most recent residents of Vere Street, Lambeth; tall and broad; heavy brown beard; large masculine features; pleasant brown eyes; married, with five children, the eldest a girl of fifteen, and then a boy of twelve; age about forty; he has an affair with Liza Kemp

BLAKESTON, Mrs. (Liza of Lambeth). The wife of Jim Blakeston; middle-sized and stout; large fat face; big mouth; between thirty and forty years of age; has given birth to nine children and miscarried a tenth; does her hair funny; a woman of great strength; knows that Jim is having an affair with Liza Kemp

BLAKESTON, Polly (Liza of Lambeth). The eldest of the Blakeston children; looks after her siblings while her parents to to Chingford

BLAND, Sir Adolphus, Bart., M.P. (Alien Corn). Known as Freddy; a resident of Tilby, Sussex; son of Alphonse Bleikogel and Hannah Rabenstein; the nephew of Ferdy Rabenstein; he had been to Eton College and Oxford University; the father of George and Harry Bland

BLAND, George (Alien Corn). The elder son of Freddy and Muriel Bland; age twenty-one; had been dismissed from Oxford University; tall and slim; curly hair, pale brown; blue eyes and straight nose; full and sensual lips; beautiful teeth; skin like ivory; after almost two years in Munich he becomes very fat and untidy in appearance

BLAND, Harry (Alien Corn). Younger son of Freddy and Muriel Bland; student at Eton College; stocky, broad shouldered; black eyes and coarse dark hair, big nose

BLAND, Miriam (Alien Corn). Known as Muriel; wife of Freddy Bland; the mother of George and Harry Bland; fleshy nose; round blue eyes

BLANE, Henry (Colonel's Lady). George Peregrine's solicitor and an old friend; tall and robust; boisterous and jovial

BLANKENSTEIN, Prince (Ashenden/Miss King). He had taken young Higgins to Austria early in the nineteenth century

BLEANE, Lord Harry (Our Betters). Tries to propose to Bessie Saunders every time he sees her; young, pleasant, and clean; penniless

BLEIKOGEL, Alphonse (Alien Corn). He had married Ferdy

Rabenstein's sister, Hannah; later became Sir Alfred Bland; father of Freddy Bland

BLENKINSOP, James (Mrs. Dot). Age forty-five; educated at Eton College; a wealthy bachelor and a cynic; well preserved; a man of fashion

BLISSARD, Colonel (Making of a Millionaire). Father of Janet Blissard; an important person in Shropshire; he refuses to nominate Leslie Rose for membership to Gann's (a London club); then refuses to allow Janet to marry Leslie; he recants after Frederick Rose buys back all of the shares in the New-Lyons Mine

BLISSARD, Janet (Making of a Millionaire). Daughter of Colonel Blissard; engaged to Leslie Rose

BLOOMFIELD, Mrs. (Magician). The invalid friend of Margaret Dauncey, whom Margaret pretends to visit (but actually goes to Oliver Haddo's rooms); has not seen Margaret in three weeks; Susie Boyd and Arthur Burdon go to Chartres with her

BOARDING-MASTER (Moon and Sixpence). At Marseilles; he employed Charles Strickland and Captain Nichols to paint a tramp steamer from Madagascar

BOATMAN (Door of Opportunity). Relates the news of the Chinese coolies' attack upon Prynne's office

BOB (Liza of Lambeth). A boy on Vere Street, Lambeth; asks Liza Kemp to play cricket with his friends and him

BOB (Narrow Corner). The Black crewman on board the Australian schooner; rows Captain Atkinson from the schooner to Captain Nichols' lugger; he and Joe throw the body of the Japanese diver overboard

BOBBIKINS (Hero). Loose-limbed and young; a friend of the Larcher daughters; in the Imperial Yeomanry; came down with a fever in South Africa and was sent home; present at the Larchers' tennis party

BOLLIN, Madame (Winter Cruise). Shares a cabin on the Friedrich Weber with Venetia Reid; a Black

BOLTON, Mr. (Sheppey). Smart looking and middle-aged; claims to be just over forty years of age; grey over the temples; a customer at Bradley's Hairdressing and Barber's Saloon, Jermyn Street, London; wants Sheppey to shave him

BONE SETTER (Unattainable). Maude Fulton's doctor; he does not make love to her more than do other men

BONIFAZIO (Making of a Saint). Has brought an expensive jewel from Milan to Girolamo Riario

BONZO (Bread-Winner). The Battles' dog; sent to the vet to be destroyed

BOOFULS (Voice of the Turtle). She is the third woman in attendance at the sherry party at Bloomsbury; not overly stout or overly tall

BOOKER (Of Human Bondage). At Ferne, Kent; entered the number of hops bushels picked

BOOKSELLER (Merry-Go-Round). At London; advised Bella Langton to purchase (for Herbert Field) [Edward] Dowden's two-volume Life of Shelley (1887)

BOOKSELLER (Portrait of a Gentleman). Owned a secondhand bookshop in Seoul, Korea

BOOKSELLERS (Choice of Amyntas). At Cadiz; none of them willing to employ Amyntas

BORGIA, Angela (Then and Now). Niece of the Pope, who had intended to give her in marriage to the nephew and heir of Guidabaldo da Montefeltro

BORGIA, Caesar (Then and Now). The bastard son of Pope Alexander VI; Louis XII of France created him Duke of Valentinois; also Duke of Romagna, Valencia, and Urbino; Prince of Andria; Gonfaloier; Captain-General of the Church; was married to Charlotte d'Albert; his daughter (and forty thousand ducats) to be given in marriage to the son of the Marquis of Mantuawell; under thirty years of age; a man of striking beauty; average height, broad shoulders, powerful chest, slim waist; vivid coloring; rich auburn hair reaching his shoulders; moustache and beard trimmed to a point; straight and delicate nose; fine and bold eyes under well-marked brows; sensual, well-shaped mouth; clear and glowing skin

BORGIA, Charlotte d'Albert (Then and Now). Married to Caesar Borgia; sister of the King of Navarre

BORGIA, Juan (Then and Now). Cardinal of Monreale; the nephew of Pope Alexander; portly and shrewd

BORGIA, Monna Lucrezia (Then and Now). Sister of Caesar Borgia; she was given an enormous dowry by the Pope to marry the Duke of Ferrara; the first wife of Giovanni Sforza; her second husband Alfonso, Duke of Biscegli

BORGIA, Rodrigo (Then and Now). Pope Alexander VI; past

Characters 45

seventy years of age; of a plethoric condition, but lived a life of a man in his prime

BORSELLI, Count (String of Beads). One of the guests at the Livingstones' dinner party; he knows more about precious stones than anyone else in the world; sits next to Mary Lyngate

BOSS (Narrow Corner). The owner of a Sydney firm for whom Fred Blake worked; called by Jim Blake relative to his son's "illness"

BOULGER, Sir George (Explorer [novel]). The son of Mr. Boulger; the brother of Lady Alice Kelsey and Mrs. Allerton; father of Robert Boulger, to whom he willed the total wealth of Boulger and Kelsey (of which he had been the senior partner); he served in Parliament for a quarter of a century; had been appointed to a baronetcy on the celebration of Victoria's second jubilee; he died of apoplexy at the opening of a park that he had presented to the nation

BOULGER, Mr. (Explorer [novel]). The father of Mrs. Allerton, Lady Alice Kelsey, and George Boulger; a Liverpool manufacturer in partnership with Mr. Kelsey

BOULGER, Robert (Explorer [novel]). The only son of Sir George Boulger; nephew of Lady Alice Kelsey and Fred Allerton; fair hair and clean shaven face; he is not unattractive; educated at Oxford; he inherited the wealth of the firm of Boulger and Kelsey; had succeeded his father as second baronet; in love with his cousin, Lucy Allerton, to whom he has proposed a dozen times; good natured and pleasant, but with no great strength of character; he manages the London branch of Boulger and Kelsey; musical comedy the only form of art that appealed to him; he wins Richard Lomas's seat in Parliament after the latter's retirement; he breaks off his engagement to Lucy Allerton

BOULGER, Robert (Explorer [play]). The nephew of Lady Kelsey; age twenty-two; good looking and spruce; he has been madly in love with Lucy Allerton since he was ten years old; he proposes marriage to Lucy, who rejects him

BOY (Book-Bag). In Featherstone's employ; he tells Featherstone that Sally Hardy wishes to speak with him

BOY (Cakes and Ale). Son of the London banker at Blackstable, Kent; same age as the Narrator

BOY (Casual Affair). The Lows' only servant

BOY (Catalina). A member of Alonso Fuentes' acting company; played second women's parts and served as the troupe's barker

BOY #1 (Christmas Holiday). At St. Eustache, Paris; he sang a canticle; thin, silvery voice

BOY (#2 (Christmas Holiday). Age sixteen; proposes to Patsy Mason during the Christmas holiday

BOY (Consul). Employed by Mr. Pete, who abuses him for not bringing immediately his hat and stick

BOY (Daisy). He is only one of the two employees left in Robert Griffith's carpentry shop

BOY (De Amicitia). Asleep in a moored fishing smack in Holland

BOY #1 (East of Suez). Employed at the Andersons' house in Peking; can exercise the pony

BOY #2 (East of Suez). Son of Coolie #3; age six; he is solemn, shy, and silent; Daisy Anderson gives him presents

BOY (End of the Flight). He serves the District Officer morning tea

BOY (Friend in Need). He gives gin fizzes to Burton and the Narrator at the Grand Hotel, Yokohama

BOY #1 (Explorer [novel]). Chubby; lying in a kraal in British East Africa; has a great spear wound in his body

BOY #2 (Explorer [novel]). Native; a member of Alec Mac Kenzie's expedition against the African slave trade; half dead with exhaustion; Alec told him to sleep until he called him

BOY #1 (Hour Before the Dawn). One of the children evacuated to the Henderson's estate at Graveney Holt; small; remarked that he did not care how long the war lasted

BOY #2 (Hour Before the Dawn). Son of Woman #4; warns his mother of the presence of Germans near the inn

BOY #3 (Hour Before the Dawn). Helped the two old men tend the English garden at Graveney

BOY #1 (Letter [play]). Employed by John Withers; wakes Withers to tell him that the Crosbies' Head Boy wants to see him

BOY #2 (Letter [play]). Sits by Chung Li and idly plays

Characters 47

a Chinese tune on a Chinese flute

BOY (Lion's Skin). Tells Frederick Hardy that fire had broken out in the Forestiers' woods

BOY #1 (Liza of Lambeth). One of the Sunday afternoon cricket players on Vere Street, Lambeth; he maintains that "they always cooks the cats' meat at the shop"; he catches Liza Kemp around the legs and wrestles her to the ground

BOY #2 (Liza of Lambeth). One of the Sunday afternoon cricket players on Vere Street, Lambeth; caught hold of Liza Kemp around the neck and wrestled her to the ground

BOY #3 (Liza of Lambeth). One of the cricket players on Vere Street, Lambeth; accuses Liza Kemp of having been "on the booze yesterday"

BOY #4 (Liza of Lambeth). One of the cricket players on Vere Street, Lambeth; claims that Liza Kemp has "got the needle ter-night"

BOY #5 (Liza of Lambeth). One of the cricket players on Vere Street, Lambeth; advises Liza Kemp not to get into the bad habit of drinking

BOY (Mabel). He brings drinks to the Secretary and the Narrator

BOY (Magician). Small child of the lodgekeeper and the doorman at Skene; played outside the gate; Susie Boyd and Dr. Porheot promise him a shilling to hold their horse

BOY (Marriage of Convenience). Bar waiter on board the ship out of Bangkok

BOY (Masterson). A trim Burmese employed by Masterson; brings drinks to Masterson and the Narrator

BOY (Mirage). At Haiphong; tells the Narrator that an Englishman wants to see him; he speaks very little French

BOY #1 (Moon and Sixpence). A native of Tahiti; asleep on a bench outside of the kitchen of the Narrator's hotel

BOY #2 (Moon and Sixpence). Chinese; waits on tables at the Narrator's hotel

BOY #3 (Moon and Sixpence). Sent by Tiare Johnson to fetch Charles Strickland to have dinner with her

BOY #4 (Moon and Sixpence). Tahitian; climbs a tree to fetch a coconut for Dr. Coutras

BOY #1 (Narrow Corner). At the hotel on Kanda; serves beer
BOY #2 (Narrow Corner). Small; in the hotel dining room on Kanda; draws the punkahs
BOY #3 (Narrow Corner). He comes to Dr. Saunders' hotel room on Kanda; speaks a little English; he announces that someone wants to speak with Fred Blake
BOY #1 (Neil MacAdam). He serves beer at Kuala Solor to MacAdam, Munro, the doctor, the policeman, and Captain Bredon
BOY #2 (Neil MacAdam). Employed by Angus Munro; takes charge of Neil MacAdam's luggage at Kuala Solor
BOY #1 (Of Human Bondage). A pupil at King's School, Tercanbury; asks Rose to walk with him to the football field
BOY #2 (Of Human Bondage). A pupil at King's School, Tercanbury; saw Philip Carey at the station at 4:30
BOY #3 (Of Human Bondage). In the ward at St. Luke's Hospital, London; he has tuberculous ulcers; Philip Carey changes his dressing
BOY #4 (Of Human Bondage). At the dining room of Lynn and Sedley, London; large and fat; in a white coat; brings the knives and forks to the table
BOY (Our Betters). In a business in Portland, Oregon; engaged to Pearl Grayston before she married George Grayston
BOY #1 (Painted Veil). Perhaps has just tried the door to Kitty Fane's bedroom
BOY #2 (Painted Veil). In the employ of Kitty and Walter Fane; brings drinks to Kitty and Charlie Townsend
BOY #3 (Painted Veil). Age twenty; a student at Oxford during the "season" that Doris Garstin became engaged to Geoffrey Dennison; he was the only person to propose to Kitty Garstin
BOY #4 (Painted Veil). Outside of Ku Chow's curio shop, Victoria Road, Hong Kong; on the watch for customers; gave Kitty Fane a broad smile of connivance
BOY #5 (Painted Veil). Chinese; at the Colonial Secretary's office; he asked Kitty Fane to wait; told her that Charlie Townsend would see her in five minutes
BOY #6 (Painted Veil). At the Fanes' bungalow, Mei-tan-fu; served whiskey and soda
BOY #7 (Painted Veil). Employed by Waddington at Mei-

tan-fu; died the week previous to the Fanes' arrival
BOY #8 (Painted Veil). Successor to Boy #7; a fool
BOY #9 (Painted Veil). At Mei-tan-fu; seated on the neck of a water buffalo; drove it slowly home
BOY #10 (Painted Veil). At Waddington's house; brought in bowls of tea, pale and scented with jasmine
BOY #11 (Painted Veil). At the Townsends' house; tells Dorothy Townsend that Kitty Fane has a headache and will not come down to dinner
BOY (Punctiliousness of Don Sebastian). Is sent by the Narrator to fetch the porter at the Chapel of the Duke de Losas
BOY (Salvatore). He tells Salvatore's fiancee and her mother that Salvatore was ill
BOY (Spanish Priest). In the Calle Alfonso Trece, Granada; he leads the English man to the room of Vicente Oria y Mazallon
BOYCE, Colonel (Tenth Man). George Winter's agent; he is spare and tall; bronze skin; grey hair and a grey waxed moustache; dapper
BOYD, Susie (Magician). She shares a flat near the Boulevard du Montparnasse with Margaret Dauncey, her former pupil; age thirty, but she looks older; plain; a large mouth; little round, bright eyes; colorless skin, disfigured by freckles; long, thin nose; pretty hair, sprinkled with white; exceedingly neat figure; white, admirable formed hands; a remarkable talent for dress; had been a mistress in a school for young ladies before receiving a legacy from a distant relative that allowed her to accompany Margaret to Paris and to live in modest independence; studies art at Colarossi's academy merely to amuse herself; her instinct tells her that she was made to be a decent man's wife and the mother of children; in love with Arthur Burdon; she leaves Paris for Italy, then on to Monte Carlo and London (by way of Paris)
BOYLESTON, Clifford (Creative Impulse). A critic and a writer; he remarked that when one looked into a room where Albert Forrester had gone, there was no one there
BOYS (Christmas Holiday). At Paris; coarse-faced; were wearing fezzes and carrying baskets of monkey nuts
BOYS (East of Suez). In a crowded street in Peking;

play around the two gentlemen with the birds and run throughout the crowd

BOYS (East of Suez). Employed at Henry Anderson's residence at Peking; they like Harry's cigars

BOYS (Hour Before the Dawn). Five of them; from the group of children evacuated to Graveney Holt; had gone to the village for church choir practice; return safely

BOYS (Liza of Lambeth). Playing cricket on Vere Street, Lambeth, on Saturday afternoon; wildly excited; Liza Kemp plays with them on a Sunday

BOYS (Liza of Lambeth). Half a dozen of them; on Vere Street, Lambeth, on a Sunday afternoon; surround Liza Kemp and beg her to join in their game of cricket; wrestle with her and throw themselves on top of her

BOYS (Loaves and Fishes). Little; Harry Wroxham would become jealous when Winnie Spratte would talk to them

BOYS (Narrow Corner). They wait on tables at the hotel dining room at Kanda

BOYS (Narrow Corner). On Kanda; they discover Erik Christessen's body

BOYS (Of Human Bondage). Two or three of them; pupils at King's School, Tercanbury; caught scarlet fever toward the end of the term; one of them dies

BOYS (Of Human Bondage). In the dining room of Lynn and Sedley, London; distribute plates of meat and gravy and large dishes of cabbage and potatoes

BOYS (Painted Veil). Had not seen Charlie Townsend come and go from the Fanes' house

BOYS (Painted Veil). One or two of them; younger than Kitty Garstin, but they proposed to her

BOYS (Painted Veil). Employed by Watson at Mei-tan fu; Waddington retained them for the Fanes

BOYS (Painted Veil). At the Townsends' home, Hong Kong; two of them; uniformed; serve savories and cocktails at lunch; later, assist Kitty Fane in the packing of her belongings from her house

BOYS (Taipan). Three of them; waited on the Taipan at his table

BRABAZON, Colonel (Facts of Life). A friend of Henry Garnet; associated with the tennis world; going to Monte Carlo as the non-playing captain of the English tennis team

BRABAZON, Gregory (Razor's Edge). An English decorator, the most successful in London; was a guest at Louisa Bradley's luncheon in Chicago; short and extremely fat; "bald as an egg," but for a ring of curly black hair around his ears and at the back of his neck; a red, naked face; quick grey eyes with bushy eyebrows, sensual lips, and a heavy jowl

BRACKENBRIDGE, Mr. (Theatre). Roger Gosselyn's house master at Eton College; he is always polite to Julia Gosselyn

BRACKLEY, Robert (Man of Honour). Stout and red faced; clean shaven; bald; age forty; always amused at what he says; a poet; would have been given the laureate had it not been abolished at Tennyson's death; he proposes marriage to Hilda Murray, but she initially refuses him

BRADLEY, Chester (Razor's Edge). The father of Myron Bradley; left his family farm to enter a law office in Chicago, where he became wealthy

BRADLEY, Isabel (Razor's Edge). Myron and Louisa Bradley's daughter and youngest child; she and Elliott Templeton want Louisa to have her house redecorated; supposedly engaged to Lawrence Darrell; tall; oval face, straight nose, fine hazel eyes; full mouth, bright brown hair; comely and slightly fat; strong, good, fat hands; fat legs; good skin and high color; sparkling, vivacious, healthy; age nineteen when the Narrator first meets her; conveys to the Narrator the "absurd notion of a pear, golden and luscious, perfectly ripe and simply asking to be eaten"; marries Gray Maturin shortly after the termination of her "engagement" to Larry Darrell; she slims considerably following the births of her two children and the death of her mother; as a mature woman, she appears "chic"

BRADLEY, James (Sheppey). The proprietor of Bradley's Hairdressing and Barber's Salon, in Jermyn Street, London; makes his own hair preparation; married; he offers Sheppey a partnership in his business

BRADLEY, Louisa (Razor's Edge). Myron Bradley's wife, Elliott Templeton's sister, and Isabel Bradley's mother; a widow with three children; lives on Lake Shore Drive, Chicago; perhaps a handsome woman when young; large but good features; fine eyes; sallowish face that sagged; a fine head of white hair; eventually dies from diabetes

BRADLEY, Mr. #1 (Razor's Edge). Myron Bradley's grandfather; left Virginia in 1839 and settled sixty miles from what is now Chicago

BRADLEY, Mr. #2 (Razor's Edge). Myron and Louisa Bradley's elder son; the brother of Templeton and Isabel Bradley; in the diplomatic service at Buenos Aires; eventually charge d'affairs in Tokyo; he could not leave his post at the time of his mother's death

BRADLEY, Mrs. (Razor's Edge). The wife of Templeton Bradley; she accompanies her husband to Chicago when Louisa Bradley's condition is diagnosed as hopeless

BRADLEY, Mrs. (Sheppey). Wife of James Bradley; she will think her husband is up to some "hanky-panky" if he does not get home promptly from the shop

BRADLEY, Myron (Razor's Edge). Louisa Bradley's husband; had been in the diplomatic service, occupying posts in various parts of the world; he became first secretary in Rome; then appointed minister to a South American republic, where he died; he sported a heavy moustache

BRADLEY, Templeton (Razor's Edge). Myron and Louisa Bradley's younger son; brother of Mr. Bradley #2 and Isabel; he served in a government post in the Philippines' married to Mrs. Bradley; occupied a position in the State Department at Washington, D.C., at the time of his mother's death

BRAMANTE, Donato [Bramante, Donato di Pascuccio d'Antonio (1444-1514)] (Then and Now). Italian architect who had built the great dome at Florence, which Machiavelli saw in the distance as he returned to his native city

BRANDERTON, Arthur (Mrs. Craddock). The son of a squire near Court Leys, and of Mrs. Branderton; educated at Eton and Oxford; Lucy Glover had hoped that Bertha Ley would marry him; he asks to be Edward Craddock's best man at his wedding; eventually marries

BRANDERTON, Mrs. the elder (Mrs. Craddock). Mother of Arthur Branderton; Polly Ley does not like her; is small, giggling, and grey-haired; talked stupidly in a high cracked voice

Characters

BRANDERTON, Mrs. the younger (Mrs. Craddock). Wife of Arthur Branderton; pretty and fluffy-haired; nicely bred; properly insignificant

BRANDES, George (Narrow Corner). Danish literary critic (1842-1927); a friend of Erik Christessen's father; he used to read Shakespeare to young Erik

BRANDOLINI (Making of a Saint). The younger brother of Filippo Brandolini; entrusted to a relative, the canon of a cathedral, after Filippo flees Citta del Castello; supposedly to receive all of his brother's lands and palaces

BRANDOLINI, Countess (Making of a Saint). Wife of Giulo Brandolini; originally left her home in the New World to marry Giulo; she desired to publish a biography of Filippo Brandolini; purchased the portraits of several of her husband's ancestors

BRANDOLINI, Filippo (Making of a Saint). A citizen of Castello; a brother of the Order of St. Francis of Assisi, at Campomassa; middle-sized; small black bears and moustache; olive colored oval face; fine dark eyes; after his death, elevated to sainthood as Beato Giuliana; narrates his memoirs; formerly a page at the court of the Bentivogli at Bologna; he served under the Duke of Calabria; he arrived at the town of Forli in 1488; married; suggests to Checco and Matteo d'Orsi the assassination of Girolamo Riario; falls in love with Donna Giulia dall' Aste, then with Claudia Piacentini; is sent by Checco d'Orsi to Florence to transact commercial business with Lorenzo de Medici; he does not escape with the other conspirators from Forli, but remains to take care of the aged Count Orso d'Orsi; disguises himself as a servant (shaves beard and moustache, cuts hair short); he is knocked unconscious defending Orso d'Orsi from the mob, but rescued by Andrea and Pietro and taken to the house of Andrea's mother; he rekindles his love for Giulia dall' Aste; he and Giulia escape from Forli and reach Citta di Castello; he marries Giulia three days after they arrive in Citta di Castello; accompanies Checco d'Orsi to Rome, where he remains for three months before returning (alone) to Citta di Castello; he murders Giorgio dall' Aste, then he leaves Citta di Castello; bests Ercole Piacentini in a sword fight at an inn, but cannot kill him; he becomes the poor monk Giuliano--hair white as snow; eyes dim and sunken; cheeks hollow; skin ashy and wrinkled; he loses his teeth; old, bent, and weak

BRANDOLINI, Giulio (Making of a Saint). The last of the descendants of Filippo Brandolini; narrates, in the late nineteenth century, the "Introduction" to Filippo's memoirs

BRANDOLINI, Leonello (Making of a Saint). The nephew of Filippo Brandolini; after Filippo's death, the family estate devolved to him, as did the manuscript of his uncle's memoirs

BRANDON, Dr. (Happy Couple). Miss Wingford's physician; he signed her death certificate; witnessed her will; arrested in connection with Miss Wingford's poisoning; he eventually assumes the name of George Craig

BRANSCOMBE, George (Cupid and the Vicar of Swale). The uncle of Robert Branscombe; age sixty-five; nephew Robert is his sole heir

BRANSCOMBE, Robert (Cupid and the Vicar of Swale). Is appointed by the bishop as the new vicar of Swale; a gentleman and a second cousin to a peer; a bachelor; forty years of age; tall, good looking, and a fine presence; clean shaven; he gave clear signs of future corpulence; High Church; a passion for Tennyson; has sincere admiration for Edith Strong, but he is disconcerted by the sighs and blushes of Jane Simpson; becomes engaged first to Edith Strong, then to Jane Simpson

BRAUNSCHMIDT, George (Fall of Edward Barnard). A friend of the Barnard family; a South Sea merchant

BREDEN, Captain (Neil MacAdam/Yellow Streak). English captain of the Sultan Ahmed; a small man with a black moustache; good natured

BREDEN, Mrs. (Neil MacAdam). Japanese wife of Captain Breden

BRENTFORD, Mr. the elder (Cakes and Ale). Father of Mr. Brentford the younger; never read a book in his life; drank a bottle of French brandy each day; died at age seventy-eight

BRENTFORD, Mr. the younger (Cakes and Ale). At the Bear and Key, Blackstable; the husband of Mrs. Brentford; Ashenden knew his father (Brentford the elder)

Characters

BRENTFORD, Mrs. (Cakes and Ale). At the Bear and Key, Blackstable; wife of Mr. Brentford; stout; grey hair; tells Katie to show Ashenden "number five"

BRETON, Augustus (Good Manners). A Kentish recluse and an epicure without grossness; age fifty; is scarcely middle sized and slender; small hands and feet; grey beard; well shaped aquiline nose; pale blue eyes

BREVALD (Pool). Ethel Lawson's father; Norwegian; a little old man, knotted and gnarled like an ancient tree; a large hernia in the chest; formerly a mate on a sailing vessel, as well as a blacksmith, trader, planter, and slave trader; ruined financially by the great hurricane of the 1890's; had four native wives

BREVALD, Mrs. #4 (Pool). A very handsome native; middle aged; spoke little English

BRIDET, Monsieur (Ashenden/Miss King). The assistant manager of the Geneva hotel

BRIDGER, Fanny (Merry-Go-Round). A native of Jeyston, Dorsetshire; she went to London in service, got into trouble, and returned with her baby after the father deserted her; white and sunken cheeks; haggard eyes; throws herself in front of the London train so that her father and brothers will not be sent away

BRIDGER, Harry (Merry-Go-Round). An under-gamekeeper on the Castillyon estate; the brother of Jim and Fanny Bridger

BRIDGER, Jim (Merry-Go-Round). An under-gamekeeper on the Castillyon estate; the brother of Harry and Fanny

BRIDGER, Mr. (Merry-Go-Round). Father of Fanny, Harry, and Jim Bridger; he and his two sons under-gamekeepers on the Castillyon estate; he has served the Castillyons for forty years; born in the same cottage in which he and his family now live; middle aged; hard featured and sullen; a tan face; gave an air of savagery; Paul Castillyon told him that he would dismiss him and his two sons if they did not send Fanny and her child away

BRIDGES, Mrs. (Of Human Bondage). At Ferne, Kent; does not know what she would do without the elder Thorpe Athelny

BRIGADIER (Razor's Edge). Of the St. Jean police; an imposing moustache; dirty thumb; asks Maugham to go to Toulon to identify Sophie Macdonald's body

BRIGHELLA (Perfect Gentleman). In the intermezzo; she is a member of a troupe of Italian dancers

BRIGIDA, Monna (Then and Now). Middle-aged; part of the crowd that surges into Borgia's apartment; cousin of Giacomo Fabronio; she claims that the Gascon soldiers stole her silver

BRITISH CONSUL (Ashenden/Mr. Harrington's Washing). At Vladivostok; arranges transportation for Ashenden and Harrington from Vladivistok to Petrograd

BRITISH CONSUL (Mabel). At Cheng-tu, the capital of Szechuan; he examines Chinese curios with George

BRITISH CONSUL (Magician). At Paris; marries Margaret Dauncey to Oliver Haddo

BRITISH CONSUL (Lotus Eater). At Naples; had no funds to assume responsibility for Thomas Wilson

BRITISH OFFICER (Hour Before the Dawn). Roger Henderson responsible for his being arrested and charged with espionage on behalf of Italy; had once dined with May and Roger Henderson at their flat; pleasant

BRITISH WORKMAN (Tenth Man). A hypothetical type, not an actual person; according to Angela Etchingham, he takes his time

BROADSTAIRS, Sir Benjamin (Penelope). A physician; he tried everything, but he could not cure Mrs. Watson

BROKER (Bishop's Apron). Had advised Theodore Spratte to venture on a small flutter in the Stock Exchange, but the shares were not rising with the rapidity that he had promised

BROKER (Gogolo and Gigolette). English husband of the Scottish woman; bluff, military, and hardy

BROKERS (Making of a Millionaire). Three of them; Frederick Rose orders them to buy in, quietly, all of the New-Lyons Mine shares they could find

BROKERS (Razor's Edge). Advised Gray Maturin, following the October 1929 crash, to throw in the sponge

BROMSGROVE, Mrs. (Jack Straw). Of Brixton; used to dine with the Parker-Jennings because her husband was on the L.C.C.

BRONSON, Olive (Footprints in the Jungle). Daughter of Mrs. Cartwright and (supposedly) Reggie Bronson; born four months after Reggie's death; really the daughter of Theo Cartwright and Mrs. Bronson; nice, but not very pretty; age nineteen or twenty; plump; dark but bright and slightly aquiline nose; red cheeks

BRONSON, Reggie (Footprints in the Jungle). Mrs. Cartwright's first husband and Olive Bronson's father; a planter and estate manager; very big and beefy; a loud voice and a bellowing laugh; red face and red hair; handsome; sweated heavily; an athlete; had been a schoolmate of Theo Cartwright

BROOKS, Miss (Of Human Bondage). One of William Carey's neighbors; she resided at the Manor House; shared a subscription to The Times with Carey and Mr. Ellis; since she received the paper late, she would keep it

BROOME, Mrs. (Taipan). Her child is seriously ill

BROTHER (Caesar's Wife). Of Mrs. Appleby; settled in Canada

BROTHER #1 (East of Suez). Of Sen Shi Ming; the two had grown up together; Sen Shi had cheated him out of a house in Hatamen Street

BROTHER #2 (East of Suez). Of Bertha Raymond; one of the clerks in Henry Anderson's office

BROTHER (Explorer [novel]). Of the sultan of the most powerful state in British East Africa; he sought to usurp the sultan's sovereignty

BROTHER-IN-LAW (Mrs. Craddock). Of Arthur Branderton; lives in Yorkshire

BROTHERS (Making of a Saint). Of Giulia dell' Aste; two of them; they hear nothing of nor care anything for their sister

BROTHERS (Narrow Corner). In the Sydney Bulletin; were murdered at a farmstead in the Blue Mountains; they had quarreled with their murderer

BROUGHTON, Rhoda (Cakes and Ale). An English novelist (1840-1920); Mrs. Endcombe knew her; from a very good family

BROUGHTON, Rhoda (Round Dozen). The English novelist (1840-1920) who once informed the Narrator that when she was young, people told her that her books were "fast"

BROWN (Ashenden/His Excellency). Fictitious name of Sir Herbert Witherspoon's supposed friend and fellow junior clerk in the Foreign Office; he came from a family of soldiers and sailors; involved himself with the painters and writers of Paris; madly in love with Alix; presently well known and highly respected; he is actually young Herbert Witherspoon

BROWN (Unattainable). Caroline Ashley tells her friends that he and Stephen Ashley had been connected in a shady deal and that he, not Stephen, had died in the hospital at Nairobi

BROWN, James (Hero). The top boy at Little Primpton School; he recites the poem "Casablanca" (1829) ["The boy stood on the burning deck"], by Felicia Dorothea Browne Hemans (1793-1835), at the welcome home ceremony for James Parsons

BROWNE, Mr. and Mrs. (Mrs. Craddock). They rent Polly Ley's flat in London

BROWNING, George (Daisy). He saw Daisy Griffith and the cavalry officer board the train at Tercanbury, Kent

BRUCE, Arundel (Love in a Cottage). Estranged husband of Sybil Bruce; a wealthy racing man; kills himself

BRUCE,, Sybil (Love in a Cottage). Mrs. Owen Butterfield's nurse; estranged wife of Arundel Bruce; she is considered much too pretty for her job; has been unhappily married and separated from her husband; she longs for money and luxury; inherits the income from her husband's fortune, which she will lose if she remarries; in love with Dr. Bell; she accepts Martin Arrol's proposal of marriage, then tells him what will happen to her money; refuses Dr. Bell's proposal; moves to Paris; determines to marry Dr. Bell and rid herself of her money

BRUNI, Paolo (Making of a Saint). Checco d'Orsi sees him at Girolamo Riario's palace and calls out to him

BRUNOT, Rene (Moon and Sixpence). A middle aged Frenchman; large black beard streaked with grey; sunburned face; large shining eyes; a Breton who had been in the French navy; married, with a son and daughter living in Paris; knew Charles Strickland; one of the guests at the wedding feast of Strickland and Ata; he purchased at least two of Strickland's pictures

BRUNOT, Madame (Moon and Sixpence). The wife of Rene Brunot; taught her children to play the piano and to speak English

BRUTES (Magician). Appear in Margaret Dauncey's vision; noisome; horny scales and round crabs' eyes; uncouth and primeval

BRYANSTON, Sir Mayhew (Theatre). The Chancellor of the

Exchequer; he hosts Charles Tamerley at Henley and accompanies him for a weekend at the Gosselyns' house at Taplow

BRYANT, Mr. (Hero). Is engaged to marry Mrs. Pritchard-Wallace; a landed proprietor

BULFINCH, Corinne (Creative Impulse). Mrs. Forrester's cook; age forty-five; reddish hair and face; buxom; widowed; elopes with Albert Forrester

BULGARIAN AGENT (Ashenden/Miss King). In Ashenden's employ; dines at the hotel in Geneva

BULLEN, Mr. (Footprints in the Jungle). A young man passing through the Club toward the end of the bridge game

BULLOUGH, Mrs. (Unknown). Mother of Sylvia; bed-ridden

BULLOUGH, Sylvia (Unknown). Engaged to John Wharton for seven years; has spent the war tending to her invalid mother; no longer young; pleasant, friendly look; practical, competent, and sensible; decides not to marry John Wharton

BUNCH, Sophie (Hero). A resident of Little Primpton, Kent; she plans to marry a man from Tunbridge Wells

BUONACCORSI, Biagio (Then and Now). A man of methodical habit, hard working and honest; the brother of Monna Francesco Giacomini, Piero's mother; he married the daughter of Marsilio Ficino, who advised him to study Latin and Greek; held a minor government post in the Chancery at Florence under Machiavelli, his friend; thirty-three years of age; mid-sized and plump; round face of high color

BUONAROTTI, Michaelangelo (Then and Now). A Florentine sculptor (1475-1564); to bring the money from Biagio Buonaccorsi to Machiavelli at Imola; hired by Caesar Borgia to draw plans for the fortification of Imola

BURDON, Arthur (Magician). A distinguished surgeon on the staff of St. Luke's Hospital, London; age twenty-six; clean shaven face; very tall and thin; massive bones; high cheekbones; a long, lean face; large nose and mouth; sallow skin; quick dark eyes; son of a Levantine merchant; spent his childhood in Alexandria; as a boy, he had been involved in one of Dr. Porhoet's experiments in seeing things which he could not possibly have known; he worked hard operating, dissecting, and lecturing; had little interest outside of his profession other than golf; admits to no imagination or sense of humor; he can read French and German; a friend of Dr. Porhoet; he comes to Paris to study the methods of the French surgeons and to see Margaret Dauncey, with whom he is deeply in love and to whom he has been engaged for two years; is seven years older than Margaret, whom he has known since he was age seventeen; appointed Margaret's guardian and executor after the death of her father; writes from Paris to his friend, Dr. Frank Hurrell, asking for information about Oliver Haddo; returns to London to private practice and to lecture at St. Luke's; he is appointed visiting surgeon to another London hospital; ages considerably after Margaret's marriage to Oliver Haddo--he loses weight, hair sprinkled with white, face drawn, eyes weary from lack of sleep; is editing a large work on surgery; eases his pain by listening to music; becoming unbalanced and neurotic, believing Margaret Haddo in great danger; spends a week in Chartres and a month in Brittany; pleads with Dr. Porhoet to raise the spirit of Margaret Haddo; he sees Margaret's spirit and realizes that all of his suspicions about her death have been justified; he refuses to leave Venning until Oliver Haddo is dead; sets fire to Haddo's house

BURDON, Mr. (Magician). The deceased father of Arthur Burdon; a Levantine merchant who left Arthur with a modest income; had been Dr. Porhoet's most intimate friend

BURGLAR (Episode). He had been arrested three or four times and sent up for trial, but he had been always able to avoid prison; finally convicted when his wife does not offer an alibi at his trial; requests that Ned Preston visit his wife

BURGLAR'S WIFE (Episode). Visited by Ned Preston; she had always concocted alibis for her husband; at his last trial, she does not offer one

BURKHARDT (Magician). A German who went lion hunting in Africa with Oliver Haddo; he came down with fever and could not stir from his bed; had recently published a book on his adventures in Central Africa; Miss Ley asks Frank Hurrell to meet him; he had met Haddo by chance at Mombassa, East Africa

Characters

BURMESE GIRL (Masterson). Masterson's mistress for five years, with whom he had three children; small and slender, with large solemn eyes; she became an excellent bridge player

BURTON, Edward Hyde (Friend in Need). A rich merchant who had been in business for a number of years in Japan; died at Kobe; five feet four inches tall, and slender; white hair; his face red and wrinkled; blue eyes; sixty years of age when the Narrator met him

BURTON GIRLS (Friend in Need). Two daughters of Edward Hyde Burton and his wife

BURTON, Lenny (Friend in Need). Fairly handsome, with curly hair and pink-and-white cheeks; an excellent bridge player; age thirty-five when he asked Edward Hyde Burton for a job

BURTON, Mrs. (Friend in Need). The wife of Edward Hyde Burton; fat, elderly

BUSH, Annie (Merry-Go-Round). Sister of Jenny and James Bush; she accompanies Jenny Kent to Brighton; plain; graceful figure; she takes up with Mr. Higgins at Brighton; colorless hair; does not have her sister's mellow complexion

BUSH, James (Man of Honour). The brother of Jenny Bush; young; clean shaven face; sharp expression; distinctly vulgar; cockney accent; overly cordial and overly genial; he had been to boarding school at Margate; an auctioneer's clerk involved in a number of schemes

BUSH, James (Merry-Go-Round). Brother of Jenny Bush; had attended a boarding school at Margate; sometimes came to the Golden Crown, Fleet Street; young and weedy; dangling legs; sandy hair; clean shaven, sharp face; pale eyes; small, discolored teeth; pronounced cockney accent; an expression of odious cunning; an auctioneer's clerk; sacked from his job for stealing one hundred and fifteen pounds from his firm; will go to prison unless he repays the money within a week; he comes consistently to Jenny (Bush) Kent for money

BUSH, Jenny (Man of Honour). Is engaged to Basil Kent; formerly a barmaid at the Golden Crown, Fleet Street, London; very pretty; delicate features; beautiful complexion; abundant fair hair; marries Basil; her baby dies; she throws herself into the River Thames

BUSH, Jenny (Merry-Go-Round). For the past three years

a barmaid at the Golden Crown, Fleet Street, London; young; extremely beautiful; bright smile; beautiful eyes; tall; handsomely made; the rounded hips and the full breasts of a passionate woman; short lips; a delicate nose; delicate pink ears; wonderful coloring; rich magnificent hair; perfect, creamy skin; brilliant eyes; engaged to Tom, but breaks away from him after she goes out with Basil Kent; falls in love with Basil; becomes pregnant and marries him; delivers a still-born child and she becomes extremely ill from the process; she throws herself into the Thames, less than eighteen months after her marriage

BUSH, Mr. (Man of Honour). Father of Jenny and James Bush; he had to raise five children on two pounds/ten shillings per week

BUSH, Mr. (Merry-Go-Round). Father of Jenny and James Bush; he and his wife lived at Crouch End, London; according to Jenny, he never earned more than three pounds/ten shillings per week; again, according to Jenny, he had to bring up five children on two pounds and ten shillings per week

BUSH, Mrs. (Man of Honour). Mother of Jenny and James Bush, and of another daughter; following Jenny's death, John Halliwell tells James that Basil Kent plans to give his furniture to her and to her daughter

BUSH, Mrs. (Merry-Go-Round). Mother of James and Jenny Bush; stout; determined manner; Basil Kent surmises in her an alcoholic tendency

BUSINESS PARTNER (Razor's Edge). Of Gray Maturin; in Dallas, Texas; the two had been roommates in college

BUTCHER (Making of a Saint). Gigantic; leads the crowd of mechanics into the square at Forli after the assassination of Girolamo Riario; flourishes a great meat axe

BUTCHER (Of Human Bondage). Mary Ann announces his arrival, thus causing Louisa Carey to forget about Philip's report from school

BUTCHER (Then and Now). At the inn at San Casciano; in a card game in which Machiavelli is a participant

BUTCHER (Unknown). At Stour, Kent; told by Mrs. Wharton (through Kate) to bring two and one-half pounds of the best end of the neck, as well as two kidneys

Characters

BUTCHER, Miss (Cakes and Ale). She maintained a lodging house in Vincent Square, London, near that of Mrs. Hudson; the two feuded

BUTCHERS (Of Human Bondage). At Blackstable, Kent; two of them; they both attended William Carey's church

BUTLER (Ashenden/His Excellency). To Sir Herbert Witherspoon; corpulent

BUTLER (Bishop's Apron). To Mrs. Fitzherbert; asks the brewer, Sir John Durant, if he would drink hock or claret; announces the guests at his mistress's dinner party

BUTLER (Caesar's Wife). English; in service at the Consular Agent's house, Cairo

BUTLER (Cakes and Ale). At Ashenden's apartment, Half Moon Street, London; he answers when Alroy Kear rings the bell

BUTLER (Casual Affair). He announces the Lows at Lady Kastellan's party; he opens the door for Arthur Low

BUTLER #1 (Circle). At Aston-Adey, Dorset; when Lady Catherine Champion-Cheney ran away with Lord Huey Porteus, Clive Champion-Cheney told him (butler) to throw away all of the pictures of her

BUTLER #2 (Circle). At Aston-Adey, Dorset; he announces the guests and calls them to luncheon

BUTLER (Colonel's Lady). Employed by the Peregrines; he brings the morning mail

BUTLER (Cupid and the Vicar of Swale). In the employ of Edith Strong; serves lunch to Robert Branscombe and her

BUTLER #1 (Explorer [novel]). Of Julia Crowley at Court Leys, Kent; he admitted and announced Alec MacKenzie

BUTLER #2 (Explorer [novel]). At Julia Crowley's house, Norfolk Street, London; of imposing dimensions; went well with the house; portentous respectability; his gravity never disturbed by the shadow of a smile; was treated by his mistress as though he were a piece of decoration; looked upon Julia as an outlandish freak, but surrendered entirely his heavy British heart to her; he watched over Julia with a solicitude that amused and touched her

BUTLER (Hour Before the Dawn). He was employed by the Hendersons at Graveney Holt; forced to drive a truck during the war

BUTLER (Human Element). In the employ of Betty Weldon-Burns; an elderly Greek

BUTLER (Jane). Employed by Mrs. Tower

BUTLER (Man of Honour). At Hilda Murray's house in Charles Street, Mayfair, London

BUTLER #1 (Merry-Go-Round). At Elizabeth Dwarris's house, Old Queen Street, London; he is used to his mistress's vagaries

BUTLER #2 (Merry-Go-Round). At Polly Ley's house, Old Queen Street, London; he leads various guests and callers inside

BUTLER #3 (Merry-Go-Round). At Hilda Murray's house, Charles Street, London; he admits and announces Basil Kent; he receives a sovereign from Jenny Kent after telling her that everyone had left Hilda's house

BUTLER #4 (Merry-Go-Round). At the home of Emily Barlow-Bassett; he has no information relative to the marriage of Reggie Barlow-Bassett to Annie Higgins

BUTLER (Mrs. Dot). At Dot Worthley's house on the river; he and the footman bring lunch

BUTLER (Our Betters). At the Graystones' house in Suffolk; tells Thornton Clay that Lady Pearl Grayston is lunching in bed

BUTLER #1 (Razor's Edge). At Elliott Templeton's house on the French Riviera; dressed in white, with gold straps on his shoulders

BUTLER #2 (Razor's Edge). Employed by Elliott Templeton at his Paris apartment during the Maturins' stay there; ushers the Narrator to see Isabel; staid; he serves champagne at dinner, as well as tea at 5:00 p.m.; he arranges the latter with exasperating deliberation; he serves coffee to Sophie Macdonald

BUTLER #3 (Razor's Edge). At Adrienne de Troye's house, off the Avenue Foch, Paris; he projects the image of George Washington

BUTLER (Theatre). At the Gosselyns' home in Stanhope Place, London; phones Charles Tamerley to see if he could lunch with Julia Gosselyn at the Ritz

BUTLER (Three Fat Women of Antibes). Serves Lena Finch a roll of French bread and butter at the Monkey House at Antibes; could prepare at least a half dozen kinds of cocktails

BUTLER (Treasure). He had trained Pritchard

Characters

BUTLER, Captain (Honolulu). A little man; wore round spectacles, blue eyes; plump, with a round face and fat nose; fair short hair; red faced, plump hands and short fat legs; white teeth; age thirty-four or thirty-five; he h d spent all of his life on the Pacific; formerly first officer and then captain of a passenger boat; he had lost a ship and a number of passengers off the coast of California, and with that his certificate; he commanded a small schooner that sailed among the islands of Hawaii

BUTTERFIELD, Mrs. (Love in a Cottage). Invalid wife of Owen Butterfield; Martin Arrol's aunt; a malade imaginaire who gives everyone a terribly difficult time; suggests that Martin Arrol marry Sybil Bruce; trying to have her husband confined as a lunatic

BUTTERFIELD, Owen (Love in a Cottage). A millionaire; he and his wife are guests at the Hotel Splendide, Varenna, Lake Como; tall, thin, and old; a bitter and cynical expression; he likes both Sybil Bruce and Dr. Bell; dying because he has lost all interest in, and feeling for, humanity; he shoots himself

BUYER (Of Human Bondage). In the gentleman's hosiery department of Lynn and Sedley's, London; a well-known reciter of poems; performs at the Monday night social

BWABS (Circle). His picture in Clive Champion-Cheney's old photograph album; Clive had never known a smarter man

BYRING (Ashenden/His Excellency). A successor to Sir Herbert Witherspoon as counsellor in Paris; thirty+ years of age; tall, good looking; in love with Rose Auburn

C

CAB DRIVER (Bishop's Apron). Theodore Spratte promises him a florin if he can get to the Athenaeum Club in three minutes

CAB DRIVER (Explorer [novel]). He takes Dick Lomas and Julia Crowley to Hammersmith

CAB DRIVER (Lotus Eater). Told by the Narrator and his friend to be ready to take them to Anacapri at 5:00

CAB DRIVER #1 (Magician). Takes Margaret Haddo from the Hotel Carlton, London, to Susie Boyd's house

CAB DRIVER #2 (Magician). At Paris; drives Susie Boyd, Arthur Burdon, and Dr. Porhoet to the train station

CAB PROPRIETOR (Smith). At Sydney, Australia; married Smith's sister; owns forty-three cabs

CABINET MINISTER (Our Betters). Bessie Saunders taken in by him at Lady Pearl Grayston's dinner party

CABINET MINISTER (Theatre). Old, fat, bald, and loquacious; sat next to Julia Lambert Gosselyn at Charles Tanerley's luncheon

CABMAN (Flirtation). Bertie Shenton directs him to the Cook's office in Piccadilly, London

CABMAN #1 (Merry-Go-Round). Drives Basil Kent and Jenny Bush to Basil's rooms in the Temple, London

CABMAN #2 (Merry-Go-Round). Takes Mrs. Castillyon and Reggie Barlow-Bassett from Bond Street to Grosvenor Gardens; Reggie tips him five shillings

CABMAN #3 (Merry-Go-Round). Takes Basil and Jenny Kent from Piccadilly Circus to Waterloo station

CABMAN #1 (Mrs. Craddock). Polly Ley tells him to drive furiously from the Trevor-Ropers' to her flat

CABMAN #2 (Mrs. Craddock). He takes Bertha Craddock to Euston station

CACILIE, Fraulein (Of Human Bondage). Age sixteen and fair; a lodger at Helene Erlin's Heidelberg pension; a long pigtail of fair hair down her back; small, square, snub-nosed face; blunt features; her parents in business in South America; she has an uncle who lives in Berlin; falls in love with Herr Sung and runs away with him to Italy

CALABRIA, Duke of (Making of a Saint). Commander of the Neopolitan armies in which Filippo Brandolini served; had always been kind and generous toward Filippo

CALABRIAN PRIEST (Man from Glasgow). He had accompanied Shelley to Naples; of gigantic strength and stature

CALDERON, Pedro (Then and Now). A Spaniard and a chamberlain of the Pope; was killed at Caesar Borgia's command because he had offended the honor of Lucrezia Borgia

CALLIMACO (Then and Now). The name Machiavelli proposes for himself as a character in his play

CAMBRIDGE EXAMINER (Of Human Bondage). Examined Hayward in logic; wore an outrageous collar and elastic-sided boots

Characters 67

CAMERON, Bertie (Letter [play]). He wanted to sell his brand new gun; Robert Crosbie went to Singapore the night of Geoffrey Hammond's murder to purchase it

CAMERON, Mr. (Of Human Bondage). Lecturer in anatomy at St. Luke's Hospital, London; handsome; white hair; clean-cut features; he also lectured at the Royal Academy; he had lived in Japan and had taught at the University of Tokyo

CAMERON, Reverend Septimus (Pro Patria). One of John Porter-Smith's most influential supporters; leader of the Low Church Party in the constituency

CAMP SERVANT (Magician). With Burkhardt's expedition into Asia; he had a desperate quarrel with Oliver Haddo, who shot him

CAMPBELL (Raw Material). A passenger aboard the French liner from Hong Kong to Shanghai; came from New York; his age in the late thirties; small, but well built; large, melancholy eyes; beautiful hands; prematurely bald; supposedly a professional gambler, but actually an eminent banker

CAMPBELL (Sanitorium). He and McLeod have been patients at the sanatorium longer than anyone else; he came there six months after McLeod; long and big-boned; bald; extremely thin; brusque, touchy, bad tempered

CAMPBELL, Miles (Mrs. Craddock). He represented Blackstable, Kent, in Parliament

CAMPERDOWN, Major-General Percy (Cakes and Ale). Father of Emily Kear; grandfather of Alroy Kear; formerly of the Indian Army

CAMPION (Yellow Streak). A mining engineer; sent by the Sultan to Sembulo to find minerals; a little man with a large, bald head; age fifty; strong and wiry; blue eyes; grey moustache; broken and discolored teeth; a continual pipe smoker

CANADIAN AIRMAN (Razor's Edge). A member of Larry Darrell's unit; arrested for passing bad checks; sent to prison for six months

CANADIAN TROOPER (Hour Before the Dawn). At St. James's Park, London; he asks Jim Henderson for directions to Parliament Street

CANDIDATE (Pro Patria). Of the Radicals' party; a Roman Catholic; the opponent of John Porter-Smith

CANON (Making of a Saint). Of the cathedral at Citta di

Castello; a relative of Filippo Brandolini; Filippo entrusts his younger brother to him

CANON (Merry-Go-Round). Of Tercanbury Cathedral, Kent; a widower; he had seven children by his first wife; singularly dull; asked Algernon Langton if he might pay his addresses to Bella Langton

CANONS (Magician). Of St. Sulpice, Paris; followed the seminarians into the church

CANTERBURY, Archbishop of (Mrs. Craddock). While at Mrs. Branderton's dinner party, Mrs. Mayston Ryle related a story about him and the tedious curate

CANTON, Barbara (Promise). She falls in love with Peter Vermont; the youngest daughter of Lord Robert Canton; fair and fluffy

CANTON, Lord Robert (Promise). The father of Barbara Canton; Undersecretary for Foreign Affairs; old and stuffy

CANUTE, Lady (Lord Mountdrago). A patient of Dr. Audlin

CAPELLI, Luca (Then and Now). A merchant at Imola who is attracted to the town by the easy money there; he sells Machiavelli a pair of scented gloves stitched with gold thread, which he sends to Aurelia Martelli; Machiavelli then sends Piero to him to obtain a blue silk scarf with silver embroidery

CAPPELLO Mona Caterina (Then and Now). The mother of Aurelia Martelli; with fine black eyes; black hair; swarthy skin; she had borne her husband six children

CAPPELLO, Signore (Then and Now). Husband of Caterina Cappello and father of Aurelia Martelli; he had owned and captained a sailing vessel that carried merchandise to the Dalmatian cities; he and his son went down with his ship in a storm

CAPTAIN (Four Dutchman). The skipper of a Dutch tramp steamer, the S.S. Utrecht; one of the four Dutchmen; fat and fair; large round bare face

CAPTAIN #1 (Making of a Saint). Of the guard at the Palazzo Orsi, at Forli; spoken to in an undertone by Ercole Piacentini; he orders his men from the chamber after Girolamo Riario storms from the room

CAPTAIN #2 (Making of a Saint). Of the guard; on the street at Forli; he examines the slain attackers of Checco d'Orsi

CAPTAIN #3 (Making of a Saint). He opens the gate at

Characters

Forli, thus allowing Checco d'Orsi and other conspirators to escape from the town

CAPTAIN (Marriage of Convenience). Of the ship out of Bangkok; he addresses the retired French official as "Monsieur le Gouverneur"

CAPTAIN (Narrow Corner). Of the Dutch ship from Merauke to Takana; sat at Kim Ching's and drank beer

CAPTAIN (Taipan). Of the <u>Mary Baxter</u>; perished in the typhoon of 1908 and buried in the English cemetery

CARACCIOLO, Captain (Then and Now). Husband of Dorotea Caracciolo and a captain in the Venetian infantry

CARACCIOLO, Dorotea (Then and Now). Wife of the Captain of the Venetian infantry; kidnapped by Caesar Borgia

CARBERY (Explorer [novel]). A friend of Robert Boulger; at Lady Alice Kelsey's dance

CARBERY, James (Explorer [play]). A young and tall London curate; impressive in appearance; every Wednesday at 4:00 p.m., he reads from <u>Little Lord Fauntleroy</u> to forty charwomen

CARBIS, Lord (Bishop's Apron). A brewer of stout and bitter; is an old fool, according to Sir John Durant, because he refuses to have beer in his house; people only laugh at him

CARDEW, Frederick (Home and Beauty). Son of Victoria and William Cardew; will be two years old next month; named after Major Frederick Lowndes

CARDEW, William (Home and Beauty). Victoria's first husband; believed to have been killed in the battle of Ypres; actually he was seriously wounded and taken prisoner in Germany; lost his memory; holder of the D.S.O.; dark and handsome; jovial; is the father of Frederick Cardew; he suddenly turns up in London

CARDEW-LOWNDES, Victoria (Home and Beauty). A pretty little thing; the daughter of Mrs. Shuttleworth; her first husband, William Cardew, believed to have been killed in France; remarried a year later to Frederick Lowndes; the mother of Frederick Cardew and William Lowndes

CARDINALS (Magician). In Margaret Dauncey's vision; in their scarlet

CAREY, Helen (Of Human Bondage). The mother of Philip Carey; she had been a patient of a St. Luke's surgeon before she married him; an orphan with no relations;

was extremely beautiful and extravagant; straight and dark eye brows; she died shortly after delivering her second child, stillborn, a boy

CAREY, Henry (Of Human Bondage). Philip Carey's father; younger brother of William Carey; a surgeon on the staff of St. Luke's Hospital, London; died suddenly from blood poisoning, six months prior to the death of his wife

CAREY, Louisa (Of Human Bondage). Wife of William Carey and Philip Carey's aunt; had been married to William for thirty years; childless; small and shrivelled; well over fifty years of age; deep wrinkled face; pale blue eyes; grey hair arranged in ringlets; dies while Philip is in Paris

CAREY, Philip (Of Human Bondage). At age nine, brought to his mother's bed after she has just delivered a stillborn baby boy; an only child; has a club foot; after his mother's death, is taken to live with his uncle, Rev. William Carey, at Blackstable, Kent; then educated at King's School, Tercanbury; leaves King's and resides in Heidelberg; at age nineteen, with a very small moustache on his upper lip, he returns to Blackstable; has an affair with Emily Wilkinson, then articled to a London accounting firm; he proceeds to Paris to study art and meets Fanny Price; returns, after two years, to Blackstable, following the death of his aunt; moves to London to study medicine at St. Luke's Hospital; becomes entangled in complex affairs with Mildred Rogers and Norah Nesbit; he loses all of his money; moves in with Thorpe Athelny; becomes a shop floorman at Lynn and Sedley, a London linen drapery firm; returns to St. Luke's Hospital following the death of William Carey; receives his physician's diploma at age thirty, seven years after he had first entered St. Luke's; he spends a pleasant month as a substitute assistant to Dr. South; appointed assistant house physician at St. Luke's; eventually asks Sally Athelny to marry him

CAREY, Rev. William (Of Human Bondage). Philip Carey's uncle; Henry Carey's older brother; well over fifty years of age; of less than average height; inclined to corpulence; hair worn long and arranged to cover his baldness; clean shaven; left in charge of nine-year-old Philip Carey after the death of his mother; had been at Oxford during Edward Manning's secession from the Established Church, and thus had acquired sympathies toward the Roman Catholic Church; in his last years, his face had fallen in strangely, and his skin yellowed; great bags under his eyes; bent and old; he had grown a beard and walked very slowly; his thin hands trembled; he finally dies

CARLISLE, Admiral (Lady Frederick). The father of Rose Carlisle; bluff and downright; against his daughter marrying Gerald O'Mara; pays Gerald's gambling debt to Captain Montgomerie; he proposes marriage to Lady Frederick Berolles

CARLISLE, Rose (Lady Frederick). Daughter of Admiral Carlisle; age nineteen; pretty; she has accepted Sir Gerald O'Mara's proposal of marriage

CARMENCITA (Closed Shop). Spanish owner of a bordello; friend of Madame Coralie; she has two daughters in a convent in New Orleans

CARMICHAEL, Alec (Moon and Sixpence). A physician and friend of the Narrator; recently knighted for his service during the war; on the staffs of a half dozen hospitals

CARMICHAEL, Mr. and Mrs. (East of Suez). George Conway dines with them

CARMICHAEL, Mrs. (Moon and Sixpence). The wife of Alec Carmichael; tall and lovely

CARMONA, Manuel (Ashenden/Hairless Mexican). The hairless Mexican; he claims to have been a general in Victoriano Huerta's army; tall, thin, powerful; brown eyes; bald; yellow skin; without eyebrows and eye-eyelashes; unwrinkled sallow face; wore a pale brown wig; horrifying, repulsive, ridiculous

CARPENTER (Footprints in the Jungle). Hired the Chinese man who found Reggie Bronson's watch

CARPENTER (Loaves and Fishes). Bertram Railing sees him, out of work, in a common lodging house, and he thinks of Jesus Christ

CARPENTER (Unknown). At Stour, Kent; he had employed Edward Driffield as his second man

CARPENTERS (Daisy). Opened shops at Blackstable, Kent, taking business from Robert Griffith

CARR, Bert (Hour Before the Dawn). Son of Mr. and Mrs.

Carr; in the army

CARR, Jack (Flotsam and Jetsam). Manager of the estate across the river from Norman Grange; age thirty-five; a gentleman; had been educated at a public school and then university; tall and slight; crispy curly hair

CARR, Mr. (Hour Before the Dawn). Jim Henderson lodges in his house while working on Jenkins' farm; views Jim's residence in his house as an insult

CARR, Mrs. (Hour Before the Dawn). Wife of Mr. Carr; broad Sussex accent; she tells Jim Henderson that she wants him out of his room

CARREON, Pilar (Romantic Young Lady). See SAN ESTEBAN, Marquesa de

CARRUTHERS, Humphrey (Human Element). Six feet one inch tall, spare, loose-limbed; long face, pale grey eyes; fair, wavy, thinnish hair; clean shaven, pale skin; a clerk in the British Foreign Office; a writer of short stories; sage in the early forties; is in love with Betty Weldon-Burns

CARTER (Cakes and Ale). At Blackstable, Kent; he took young Ashenden's luggage from the vicarage to the train station

CARTER (Creative Impulse). Mrs. Forrester's maid; she "sniggered" when asked by the Narrator, "Is Mrs. Forrester at home? . . .Is there Divine service to-day?"

CARTER (Of Human Bondage). Son of Herbert Carter; had been educated at Rugby School; he is now a student at Cambridge; a thorough sportsman

CARTER, George (Episode). Grace Carter's father; age in the early fifties; not very tall, but sturdy; high color; somewhat heavy; bald; sports a grey, bristled moustache; he had risen from errand boy to draper's assistant, then to the ownership of a draper's shop, with four assistants, on Brixton Road; hard working, honest, intelligent

CARTER, Grace (Episode). Only child of George and Mrs. Carter; pretty, dark haired, dark eyed; tall, slight, good figure; pale skin, white teeth; a student at London University, studying to be a school teacher

CARTER, Herbert (Of Human Bondage). A chartered accountant at London, off Chancery Lane, associated with Albert Nixon; he is willing to take Philip Carey as an articled pupil for five years, at a fee of three

hundred pounds; waxed moustache, grey hair cut short and neat; formerly an officer in the Hertfordshire Yeomanry; is chairman of the Conservative Association
CARTER, Mrs. (Episode). The wife of George Carter and mother of Grace; age in the early fifties; quiet and nice; pleasant face and fairly good looking; had been in domestic service before she married George; she insists that a girl must never lose a man's respect
CARTWRIGHT, Mrs. (Footprints in the Jungle). Wife of Theo Cartwright and mother of Olive Bronson; age in the fifties; untidily arranged white hair; large, pale, tired blue eyes; lined and sallow face; large thin mouth; gaunt and withered neck; she is a heavy cigarette smoker
CARTWRIGHT, Theo (Footprints in the Jungle). A planter near Tanah Merah; Mrs. Cartwright's husband and Olive Bronson's step-father--but, in reality, her natural father; tired and old; of middle height; bald, shiny head and a stubbly grey moustache; wore gold rimmed spectacles; had been a school mate of Reggie Bronson
CASHIER (Ashenden/Miss King). Behind the counter at the Geneva cafe; an imposing brunette with a large bust; reads the local paper
CASHIER (Christmas Holiday). At Charley Mason's Paris hotel; a young woman; excited and curious
CASHIER (Of Human Bondage). The lady at the comptoir, La Closerie des Lilas, Paris; stout, matronly, and middle aged; she laughs over the discussion between Cronshaw and the waiter relative to the contents of the former's whiskey bottle
CASHIER (Verger). Tells Albert Edward Foreman that the bank manager wishes to see him
CASTEL GIOVANNI, Count (Circle). Italian; desperately in love with Lady Catherine Champion-Cheney
CASTEL RODRIGUEZ, Duchess of (Catalina). Wife of the Duke of Castel Rodriguez and the mother of Beatriz Henriquez y Braganza; in poor health; ordered by her doctors to live in a climate less severe than that of Madrid
CASTEL RODRIGUEZ, elder Duke of (Catalina). Father of Beatriz Henriquez y Braganza; a grandee of Spain and a Knight of the Golden Fleece; he occupied important positions in Spain and Italy, where he owned vast

estates; had three sons and a daughter

CASTEL RODGRIGUEZ, younger Duke of (Catalina). Brother of Beatriz Henriquez y Braganza; tells Beatriz of the King's problems with the Greek artist; sends to her as a gift a picture of Lodovico Cardacci, an artist celebrated in Italy

CASTELLAN (Making of a Saint). Of the citadel outside Forli; refused to surrender first to Checco d'Orsi, then to the papal envoy; during the siege of Forli, he turns his cannon on the surrounding houses

CASTER (Pool). He lives with a native wife two or three miles from Apia; an Australian friend of the Narrator

CASTER, Mrs. (Pool). Native wife of Caster and friend of Ethel Lawson

CASTILLYON, Bainbridge (Merry-Go-Round). Son of Mrs. Castillyon and brother of Paul; the agent for the property at Jeyston, Dorsetshire, and the heir to the estate; he attended Eton College and spent a year at Oxford before failing examinations and being sent down; obese; a straggling beard; generally untidy; he speaks slowly in a strong Dorsetshire accent; goes to London once every two years for the agricultural show

CASTILLYON, Grace (Merry-Go-Round). The wife of Paul Castillyon; invited with Paul, to Polly Ley's dinner party; believes it fashionable to arrive late; age thirty-five; a vivacious creature; small and dainty; excitable and restless; loud, shrill voice; thin and small face; high cheekbones; unnaturally fair hair; pretty; vulgar; has the soul of a trollop; treats her husband with impatient contempt; falls in love with Reggie Barlow-Bassett; rediscovers her relationship with her husband

CASTILLYON, Sir John (Merry-Go-Round). Grandfather of Paul and Bainbridge Castillyon; a collector of books

CASTILLYON, Mrs. (Merry-Go-Round). Mother of Paul and Bainbridge Castillyon; small and wizened; wealthy; the only living representative of her family, the Bainbridges of Somersetshire; would give half of her fortune to know that Grace, her daughter-in-law, had gone off to some place with a man; ignorant, narrow, ill-educated, and ill-bred; has an abominable temper

CASTILLYON, Paul (Merry-Go-Round). The husband of Grace Castillyon; son of Mrs. Castillyon and the brother of

Bainbridge; a member of Parliament; dull and pompous; he cannot leave the House until late, and therefore cannot come to Polly Ley's dinner party; is a most important person in Dorsetshire; obese; bald; fleshy, clean-shaven face; commonplace and tedious in his conversation; pompous; rediscovers his relationship with Grace

CASUALTY SISTER (Of Human Bondage). At St. Luke's Hospital, London; told Philip Carey that people commit suicide more for want of money than for want of love

CAYPOR, Grantley (Ashenden/Traitor). An Englishman at Lucerne; a spy for the Germans; born in Birmingham; married for eleven years to a German woman; resident of Lucerne because of his wife's nationality; lives at Ashenden's hotel; had worked in a law office, then became a journalist; had served a short prison term in Shanghai for fraud; he entered into the shipping business; became bankrupt in the London export market and then returned to journalism; once more returned to the shipping business and resided in Southampton; he and his wife moved to Italy in 1915, then went on to Switzerland after Italy entered the war; forty-two years of age, middle height, corpulent; short, dark hair; broad, red, clean-shaven face

CAYPOR, Mrs. (Ashenden/Traitor). Of German birth and parentage; had attended school in Heidelberg for a year; wife of Grantley Caypor; she and her husband resident of Lucerne and of Ashenden's hotel there; "self-effaced and dusty"; a plainish woman, nearly forty years of age; muddy skin, vague features; blue eyes; squarely built, solid, plump; gives Ashenden lessons in conversational German

CEDAR, Gwen (For Services Rendered). The second wife of Wilfred Cedar; age fifty; had been married to Wilfred for twelve years; face painted and hair dyed; hanging on to the remains of her youth

CEDAR, Mrs. (For Services Rendered). The first wife of Wilfred Cedar; her husband forced her to divorce him so that he could marry Gwen

CEDAR, Wilfred (For Services Rendered). Second husband of Gwen Cedar; he has been married to Gwen for twelve years; elderly; stout; red face; grey, crisply curling hair; well preserved; jovial, breezy, sensual; an excellent tennis player; is retired; he and Gwen have rented a house in Rambleston, Kent, for the summer; in love with Lois Ardsley; plans to elope to London with Lois

CEMETERY OVERSEER (Taipan). Denies that a fresh grave had been dug in the English cemetery

CHAIR BEARERS (Taipan). Kept a few paces behind the Taipan as he returned to his office from lunch at the Hong Kong and Shanghai Bank

CHAIRMAN (Hour Before the Dawn). He headed the military exemption tribunal at Lewes; Jim Henderson knew him personally; one of George Henderson's tenants

CHALFORD, Captain Adolphus (Noble Spaniard). Engaged to Lucy; age twenty-seven; adorable whiskers; he appears very gallant and very military

CHALICE, Ruth (Of Human Bondage). One of the students at Amitrano's art school, Paris; English; fine and large brown eyes, languid but passionate; thin face, ascetic but sensual; pale skin like old ivory; long beautiful hands, but with fingers deeply stained from nicotine; large feet; a large corn on the third toe of each foot; she could not do anything that was not deliberately artistic; leaves Lawson for a young English art student

CHAMBERMAID (Razor's Edge). She is employed by Elliott Templeton at Antibes; insists that Templeton receive the last sacraments

CHAMBERS OF COMMERCE (Explorer [novel]). They passed resolutions expressing their appreciation of Alec MacKenzie's services

CHAMBRE ARDENTE (Magician). The tribunal that sat at the Arsenal, Paris, during the reign of Louis XIV (1643-1715); it heard cases of sorcery and magic

CHAMPION-CHENEY, Arnold (Circle). Member of Parliament and holder of Aston-Adey, Dorset; age thirty-five; tall and good looking; fair; a clean cut, sensitive face; the son of Lady Catherine Champion-Cheney and husband of Elizabeth; educated at Oxford; married for three years; Lord Hughie Porteus's godson; initially refuses to allow his wife to divorce him

CHAMPION-CHENEY, Lady Catherine (Circle). She is known familiarly as Kitty; Arnold Champion-Cheney's mother; formerly the wife of Clyde Champion-Cheney and one of the great beauties of her day; thirty years ago, at age twenty-seven, she ran off to Europe (eventually settling in Florence, Italy) with Lord Hughie Porteus (a married man); when young--dark hair, an adorable little nose, dainty, a beautiful little figure; now, thirty years later--dyed red hair and painted cheeks; received into the Catholic Church last winter; at one point she claims her willingness to return to her husband, who rejects the idea

CHAMPION-CHENEY, Clive (Circle). The father of Arnold Champion-Cheney and the husband of Lady Catherine; educated at Eton and Oxford; in his early sixties; tall and spare; a fine head of grey hair; intelligent face; false teeth that fit; handsome; formerly the parliamentary secretary to Lord Hughie Porteus; he resigned his own seat in the House of Commons after his wife left him; now he likes young women; a happy, wicked old man

CHAMPION-CHENEY, Elizabeth (Circle). The wife of Arnold Champion-Cheney; pretty; age twenty-five; married for three years; in love with Edward Luton; she asks her husband to divorce her; runs away with Luton to San Michele in Hughie Porteus's car

CHANDLER (Of Human Bondage). Senior obstetric clerk at St. Luke's Hospital, London; summoned by Philip Carey to attend Woman #19; tall, long nose, and thin face; a man of few words

CHANDRA LAL (Ashenden/Giulia Lazzari). An Indian; fat-faced, swarthy, full lips, fleshy nose; black, thick, straight hair; large, liquid, cow-like eyes; a lawyer by profession; a political agitator

CHAPLIN (Pool). The owner of the Hotel Metropole, Apia, Samoa; mining engineer by profession; small, neither fat nor thin; black hair, turning grey; balding at the crown; small, untidy moustache; red face; a heavy drinker

CHAPLIN, Mrs. (Pool). Manager of the Hotel Metropole; Australian; age forty-five; tall and gaunt

CHAPMAN, Emily (Smith). Age thirty-two; dark and rather haggard; tries to conceal her worn look with heavy applications of rouge and eye shadow; formerly was engaged to Thomas Freeman, a soldier, and a Jew (to the last when she was twenty-seven); is three hundred pounds in debt; eventually refuses Thomas Freeman's offer of marriage; plans to take a job in New South Wales, Australia

CHAP (Man of Honour). Small and scrubby; false teeth; he loitered about the Golden Crown pub, Fleet Street, London, making sheep's eyes at Jenny Bush over innumerable scotch and sodas; supposedly engaged to Jenny

CHAPS (Merry-Go-Round). They and Reggie Barlow-Bassett got "a bit squiffy" at the Empire

CHARING, Roger (Escape). No longer young when he fell in love with Ruth Barlow; strong, hefty, and wealthy

CHARLES (Explorer [novel/play]). The servant of Richard Lomas; according to Dick, he plucks out his master's grey hairs only once each month, at the outside

CHARLES (Mrs. Dot). Gerald Halstane's servant; smokes Gerald's cigars and drinks his whiskey; upset because tradesmen expect gentlemen to pay their bills; has an equal talent for blacking boots and for repartee; has been twice married

CHARLES, Abbe (Razor's Edge). A friend of Elliott Templeton and the bishop's vicar general; he accompanied the bishop when he dined at Elliott Templeton's house on the French Riviera; both austere and cadaverous; Elliott wants him to administer the last sacrament to him

CHARLES, Oscar (Creative Impulse). A young, little, and gnome-like creature; wore gold spectacles; government worker and amateur writer

CHARLIE (Fall of Edward Barnard). A half-caste Tahitian motor car driver

CHARLIE (German Harry). An old friend of German Harry who had recently died; around seventy years of age

CHARLOTTE (Unattainable). Robert Oldham's aunt; she died in the best bedroom of his house

CHARVIN, Jean (Man with a Conscience). Was born at Le Havre; a convict; handsome, tall, erect, lean; flashing dark eyes; clean-cut, strong features; athletic; long brown hair, with natural waves; he works in the accountant's department; murdered his wife; he comes from a respectable family (his father employed by the Customs Service); has had an excellent education; he completed his military service; formerly an accountant at a large exporting house

Characters

CHARWOMAN (Of Human Bondage). Employed by Philip Carey at his rooms in Kennington, London; comes in for an hour in the mornings

CHARWOMAN (Rehearsal). She is the mother (according to the Zampas) of La Ferrari

CHARWOMAN (Tenth Man). Of a bucket shop (an unauthorized office for the sale of stocks); George Winter's mind, she knew more about financial matters than did Francis Etchingham

CHARWOMAN (Virtue). Helps Margery Bishop maintain the flat on Panton Street, London; she tries to awaken Charlie Bishop on the morning of his death

CHAUFFEUR (Bread-Winner). Was directed to drive Charles Battles to the station

CHAUFFEUR (Buried Talent). Drives Teddie Convers from his hotel to Blanche MacArdles's house

CHAUFFEUR (Cakes and Ale). Employed by Amy Driffeld; he meets Alroy Kear and Ashenden at the Blackstable station

CHAUFFEUR #1 (Hour Before the Dawn). Driver of Roger Henderson's staff car in France; killed in an ambush some miles outside of Cassel

CHAUFFEUR #2 (Hour Before the Dawn). Is employed by the Hendersons at Graveney Holt; an elderly man

CHAUFFEUR (Our Betters). Drives Ernest from London to Lady Pearl Grayston's house in Suffolk

CHAUFFEUR #1 (Razor's Edge). Employed by Edna Novemali; he sleeps with her

CHAUFFEUR #2 (Razor's Edge). Is employed by the bishop, and he drives him to Elliott Templeton's residence on Antibes

CHAUFFEUR #1 (Theatre). Employed by Dolly De Vries at Cannes; given orders to fetch Dolly and Julia Lambert Gosselyn from lunch

CHAUFFEUR #2 (Theatre). Is employed by the Gosselyns; Michael Gosselyn proposes to rent him a small flat atop a block of garages near Stanhope Place, London

CHEF (Cakes and Ale). At Alroy Kear's club, St. James Street, London; he is ordered by Kear (by way of the waiter) to choose the asparagus

CHEF (Razor's Edge). For Elliott Templeton; as good as any in Paris; Elliott brings him to his house on the French Riviera

CHEF (Three Fat Women of Antibes). At Antibes; embraced the opportunity to prepare rich, tasty, and succulent dishes for Lena Finch

CHEF DE TRAIN (Theatre). On the train at the station in Paris; told Julia Lambert Gosselyn that every sleeper was engaged

CHEF D'ORCHESTRE (Love in a Cottage). At Sybil Bruce's fancy dress ball in Paris; was in charge of the music

CHERRITON, Guy (Lady Habart). Son of General Cherriton, and Lady Habart's brother; young, tall, good looking, and fair

CHESTER, Henry (Sanatorium). One of the patients at the sanatorium and a London accountant; lunches with Ivy Bishop and Ashenden; stocky, broad shouldered, wiry, and small; his age between thirty and forty; married, with two children; born and bred to live an average life

CHESTER, Mrs. (Sanatorium). The wife of Henry Chester; pleasant, cheerful, and small; not pretty, but neat; persuades her husband to see a doctor; spends a day or two each month at the sanatorium with her husband

CHIEF (Explorer [novel/play]). Of a Turkana tribe; a friend of Alec MacKenzie; told Alec that after George Allerton had shot the Turkana woman, he could not control his young warriors

CHIEF (Hero). Colonel Richmond Parsons' superior officer; he told Parsons after his retreat that "You're only fit to be a damned missionary"

CHIEF (Hour Before the Dawn). Of the War Office; Roger Henderson's superior; congratulated May Henderson on Roger's good work in bringing about the arrest of the British officer

CHIEF (Narrow Corner). Of a large New Guinea village; old; wanted to adopt Jack Swan and provide him with wives

CHIEF AGENT (Painted Veil). At the P.&O. Company, Hong Kong; he arranges a cabin for Kitty Fane on the next ship out of Hong Kong

CHIEF CONSTABLE (Hour Before the Dawn). Of the county in which the Hendersons reside; an old friend of the family; George Henderson strongly guarantees him of Dora Friedberg's personal integrity; he is a grizzled retired colonel; slightly fussy and none too bright

CHIEF CONSTABLE (Tenth Man). James Ford intends to see him concerning George Winter and the missing bonds from the Middlepool Investment Trust

CHIEF ENGINEER (Four Dutchmen). He served on the S.S. Utrecht; one of the four Dutchmen; is fat and fair; large red, round face

CHIEF ENGINEER (Winter Cruise). Of the Friedrich Weber; seated at the same table with Venetia Reed, Captain Erdmann, and the doctor

CHIEF INSPECTOR (Razor's Edge). Of the Toulon police; Corsican; heavy, swarthy, saturnine; with a brusque, insolent manner

CHIEF JUSTICE (Painted Veil). At Hong Kong; is an old friend of Bernard Garstin at the Bar

CHIEF MEDICAL OFFICER (Christmas Holiday). At French Guiana; took a liking to Robert Berger

CHIEF OF BUREAU (Christmas Holiday). Simon Fenimore's supervisor at Paris; has not had an idea in his head for twenty years; shrewd; he had a head cold and sent Simon to deliver a speech in his place

CHIEF OF CONSTABULARY (Causal Affair). A guest at the Lows' dinner party

CHIEF OFFICER (Fortunate Painter). Of the United States Customs, New York; Monsieur Leir writes an anonymous letter to him, alerting him to the Watteau copy with Charlie Bartle's signature

CHIEF OFFICER (Four Dutchmen). He served on the S.S. Utrecht; is one of the four Dutchmen; fat and fair; large red, round face

CHIEF SECRETARY (Before the Party). Harold's superior at Kuala Solor, Borneo; tells Harold he must resign his position unless he stops drinking; suggests that Harold marry

CHIEF SURGEON (Magician). At St. Luke's Hospital, London; his absence requires Arthur Burdon's presence in London, which means that Arthur cannot possibly contact Margaret Haddo

CHIEF WARDER (Episode). At Wormwood Scrubbs; tells Ned Preston that Fred Manson has been asking for him

CHIEF WHIP (Tenth Man). Of the House of Commons; tells Robert Perigal that George Winter proposes to lodge a counter petition for divorce against his wife, thus implicating Robert Colby

CHIEFESS (Moon and Sixpence). Tahitian; old, ill, and a patient of Dr. Coutras
CHIEFS (Explorer [novel]). Of native African tribes; outlandish names; contributed levies of natives, with spears, to accompany Alec MacKenzie on his expedition against the slave traders
CHILD (Bad Example). Age two; it died from starvation
CHILD (Of Human Bondage). At Farnley, Dorsetshire; he has been sent to summon Philip Carey to attend to Mrs. Fletcher
CHILDREN (Bad Example). Gathered around an ice cream stall in a London street; James Clinton eagerly gives a penny's worth of ice cream to each one of them
CHILDREN (Bishop's Apron). In Kensington Gardens; in bright dresses; they shouted merrily as they played
CHILDREN (Explorer [novel]). At a tiny kraal in British East Africa; are little, naked, and playing merrily
CHILDREN (Liza of Lambeth). Playing in Battersea Park, London
CHILDREN (Magician). At the Luxembourg Garden, Paris; brightly dressed; trundled hoops or whipped stubborn tops
CHILDREN (Making of a Saint). At Forli; are hoisted by their parents so that they could see Checco d'Orsi pass; they joined their shrill cries to the general celebration
CHILDREN (Merry-Go-Round). At London slums; they play merrily on the curb
CHILDREN (Moon and Sixpence). Two of them; of Ata and Charles Strickland; the girl dies after Strickland contacts leprosy; the boy becomes a deckhand on a schooner
CHILDREN (Mrs. Craddock). At the railway station at Blackstable, Kent; two or three of them; belong to the pasty-faced clerk and his wife
CHILDREN (Mrs. Craddock). At Rome; they are romping and scampering with merry cries
CHILDREN (Narrow Corner). Naked; playing on the beach at Kanda
CHILDREN (Painted Veil). At the French convent at Mei-tan-fu; ages two and three; black Chinese eyes; black hair; sallow skinned; stunted; flat noses; they play noisily

Characters   83

CHINAMAN #1 (East of Suez). He taught Daisy Anderson to play chess

CHINAMAN #2 (East of Suez). Small, old, and shabby; a coolie; he brings the children of Coolie #3 to Daisy Anderson

CHINAMAN (Moon and and Sixpence). Maintained a wretched inn off of the Rue Bouterie, Marseilles; had only one eye

CHINAMEN (East of Suez). Seated in various shops on a street in Peking; read newspapers through great horn spectacles; smoke waterpipes

CHINAMEN (Moon and Sixpence). Are busy in their shops on the waterfront of Papeete, Tahiti

CHINESE (Painted Veil). Off the Victoria Road, Hong Kong; sat about and stared unpleasantly at Kitty Fane

CHINESE (Painted Veil). Crowding the ferry boat at Mei-tan-fu; had the strange looks of the dead being borne over the water to the land of shadow; stood on shore uncertainly, as though they did not quite know where to go; wandered, desultorily, in twos and threes, up the hill

CHINESE BOY (Book-Bag). Employed by Mark Featherstone at Tenggarah; the Narrator gives him his keys and the ticket for his trunk

CHINESE BOYS (Letter [play]). Several of them at Singapore

CHINESE CHILD (Narrow Corner). Playing outside the shop opposite Kim Ching's store; naked; distended belly; trying to make a sand castle out of the dust of the road

CHINESE CLERK (Taipan). The Taipan sends him off to the English cemetery to ask the coolies about the future occupant of the fresh grave

CHINESE CONTRACTOR (Virtue). He asks for more money to complete a section of the road than Morton can afford to pay; the wounds a coolie in the Chinese gambling house; sentenced by Morton to eighteen months of hard labor on the road

CHINESE CONVERT (Painted Veil). At the French convent at Mei-tan-Fu; supervised the tiny children

CHINESE COOK (Neil MacAdam). A member of the "staff" of Munro's scientific expedition

CHINESE DOCTOR (Vessel of Wrath). Official doctor of

the island group; is a nervous little man from Java; reports the outbreak of cholera

CHINESE GENTLEMAN (East of Suez). Two of them; in a crowded Peking street; stout; airing their pet birds

CHINESE GIRL (Painted Veil). She opens the door of the French convent at Mei-tan-fu for Kitty Fane and Waddington

CHINESE GIRLS (Painted Veil). At the French convent at Mei-tan-fu; a number working at elaborate embroideries; others plain sewing, hemming, and stitching

CHINESE GROCER (Official Position). Sells condiments to Louis Remire

CHINESE LAUNDRYMAN (Moon and Sixpence). Refuses to wash clothes for the man at the Hotel de la Fleur unless he receives payment

CHINESE MAN (End of the Flight). He speaks English and identifies for the Narrator the District Officer's residence

CHINESE MAN (Flotsam and Jetsam). With the Dyak man, he brings the news of the white man to Norman Grange

CHINESE MAN (Footprints in the Jungle). Caught trying to pawn Reggie Bronson's watch

CHINESE MAN (Letter [story]). Fat; is the intermediary between Ong Chi Seng and the Chinese woman

CHINESE MAN #1 (Narrow Corner). On Kanda; fishing from a dugout

CHINESE MAN #2 (Narrow Corner). On Kanda; he directs Saunders, Nichols, and Blake to the hotel

CHINESE MAN #3 (Narrow Corner). At Penang; he buys the Fenton from Captain Nichols

CHINESE MAN (Painted Veil). At Mei-tan-fu; taking down the shutters of his shop

CHINESE MAN (Vessel of Wrath). Was struck over the head with a bottle by Ginger Ted

CHINESE MAN'S FATHER (Footprints in the Jungle). He had confirmed that the suspected Chinese man, his son, had gone from Kabulong to Alor Lipis to get a job with a carpenter

CHINESE MEN (East of Suez). In rickshaws, in a crowded street in Peking; dressed in white ducks

CHINESE OFFICIAL (Painted Veil). Between Mei-tan-fu and Hong Kong; in a sedan; he looks at Kitty Fane with inquisitive eyes

Characters   85

CHINESE SERVANT (Letter [play]). Employed at the Crosbies' house; he assists the Head Boy with Dorothy Joyce's suitcase
CHINESE SERVANTS (Neil MacAdam). Accompany the Munros on the scientific expedition
CHINESE SERVANTS (Painted Veil). At Hong Kong; knew everything, but held their tongues
CHINESE SERVANTS (Painted Veil). At the home of Dorothy and Charlie Townsend; in uniforms; handing out cocktails and olives
CHINESE SOLDIERS (Painted Veil). Three of them; at Mei-tan-fu; accompany Waddington to the Fanes' bungalow
CHINESE WOMAN (Casual Affair). Companion of Jack Almond at the bazaar in Selangor; middle-aged
CHINESE WOMAN (Letter [play]). At Singapore; has been living with Geoffrey Hammond at his bungalow for the past eight months; heavy and middle aged; heavily powdered; bears a certain massive dignity; speaks only Chinese and Malay; she holds a letter in which Leslie Crosbie invites Geoffrey Hammond to her bungalow; she will sell the letter to Robert Crosbie for $10,000 (the total sum of Crosbie's savings)
CHINESE WOMAN (Letter [story]). She lived with Geoffrey Hammond; sends a copy of a letter (supposedly written by Leslie Crosbie to Geoffrey Hammond) to Mr. Joyce; stout; broad, phlegmatic face; black hair; of middle age
CHINESE WOMAN (Vessel of Wrath). She tries to poison herself by swallowing opium because Ginger Ted had deserted her
CHINESE WOMEN (East of Suez). Seated in rickshaws, in a crowded Peking street; wearing long smocks and wide trousers
CHINESE WOMEN (Narrow Corner). At Singapore; wearing trousers; appear as marionettes passing across the stage
CHOIR (Mrs. Craddock). At Leanham church, Kent; sang out of tune
CHOIR MASTER (Hour Before the Dawn). Of the church at Graveney; wanted five of the evacuated boys to sing Christmas carols in the church choir; is known as a sensible fellow
CHORUS GIRLS (Smith). They used to have supper with

Thomas Freeman at the Savoy, London
CHORUS GIRLS (Theatre). Attended the Dexters' luncheon party; young; waved platinum hair
CHRISTESSEN, Erik (Narrow Corner). A Dane; in his twenties; is at least six feet three inches tall; broad shouldered and powerful; clumsily built; broad flat face and flat nose; sallow smooth skin; colorless cheeks; coal black hair cut very short; an ugly face with a good natured expression; raised a Lutheran, became an atheist, then attracted to George Frith's talk about Brahma; was educated at the University of Copenhagen; has represented a Danish company on Kanda for four years; he had actually been in love with Catherine Frith; was unofficially engaged to Louise Frith; shoots himself
CHRISTESSEN, Mr. (Narrow Corner). The father of Erik Christessen; a friend of George Brandes and Holger Drachman
CHRISTESSEN, Mrs. (Narrow Corner). Erik Christessen's mother; a woman of character and courage; those of her sons born prior to Erik had all died
CHRISTIAN HEADMAN (Vessel of Wrath). Of the village on Maputiti; suddenly taken ill
CHRISTOPOULOS, Demetrios (Catalina). Found guilty of holding opinions condemned by the Church; a native of Famagusta, Cyprus, and holder of property; devoted to learning; then went to Italy, where he taught Greek; accompanied the Spanish nobleman to Spain; he taught Greek to Friar Blasco de Valero
CHUAN, Mrs. (East of Suez). A white woman married to a Chinese; she is "outside the pale"
CHUNG HI (Letter [play]). A stout Chinese; a relative of Geoffrey Hammond's mistress, he resides in the same house with her in the Chinese quarter of Singapore; smokes opium
CHURCHWARDENS (Of Human Bondage). They sought William Carey's advice about the drinking habits of Vicar #3
CHURCHWARDENS (Verger). Two of them; at St. Peter's, Neville Square; both elderly; one a lord, the other a general
CIRO (Up at the Villa). Husband of Nina; the Leonards' manservant who went with the house leased from the Leonards by Mary Panton

Characters 87

CITIZENS (Making of a Saint). All prominent; at Forli; present at the meeting between Girolamo Riario and Checco d'Orsi at the Palazzo Orsi; preserved a severe aspect; unsympathetic toward Girolamo's condescension

CITIZENS (Making of a Saint). Of Forli; come to the Palazzo Orsi after they hear about the attack upon Checco d'Orsi

CITY COUNCIL (Magician). At Nuremberg; sent Paracelsus patients who had been pronounced incurable

CLARENCE (East of Suez). The name given to a beggar by George Conway; is excessively thin; a bush of long, bristly hair

CLARENCE (Home and Beauty). From the Ritz Hotel, London; he delivers lunch from Leicester Paton to the Lowndes' house

CLARK DAUGHTER (Hour Before the Dawn). Of Nobby and Mrs. Clark; ten years of age; is puny, but keen faced

CLARK, Ernie (Hour Before the Dawn). The nine-year-old son of Nobby and Mrs. Clark; Nobby had promised to bring him a German helmet; puny, but keen faced

CLARK, Mrs. (Hour Before the Dawn). The wife of Nobby Clark; mother of Ernie and his sister; invites Roger Henderson to tea; small, untidy, and brisk; has thin carroty hair; a missing front tooth; she eventually evacuates, with her two children, to Graveney Holt

CLARK, Nobby (Hour Before the Dawn). A corporal in the British Army; he arrives at Graveney Holt with Roger Henderson; short and sturdy, with bright little eyes; impudent, cheerful grin; ugly, common little face; born and bred in London; a mechanic who had worked in a garage in the Horseferry Road, Westminster; strong cockney accent; he had been taken prisoner by the Germans, but then escaped; he and Roger Henderson escape from France; becomes a messenger for Roger in the War Office

CLARKE, Enid (Back of Beyond). Wife of Knobby Clarke; expecting a baby at the time of her husband's death; blonde and very pretty; a full face, small chin; blue eyes; her profile reminded one of a sheep; at age twenty-six when she married Knobby

CLARKE, Harold (Back of Beyond). Known familiarly as Knobby; close friend of Tom Saffary and his wife; age thirty-eight; planter and estate manager; ugly; high cheek bones and hollow temples; large pale eyes in deep sockets; a large mouth; he died, suddenly and unexpectedly, on his way to England; is buried at sea

CLAUDE, Madame Ada (Lady Frederick). A London dressmaker; Lady Frederick Berolles owes her seven hundred and fifty pounds; stout and genteel; a Cockney accent

CLAUDE, Madame (Penelope). Penelope O'Farrell's London dressmaker

CLAY, Mr. (Our Betters). Father of Thornton Clay; died seven years ago

CLAY, Thornton (Our Betters). An American; was born in Virginia; stout and bald; an effusive manner; speaks with a marked American accent

CLAYSON (Magician). An American sculptor at Paris; a vinous nose; twinkling eyes; red cheeks; with a fair, pointed beard; spoke English with a Parisian accent; he had a tedious habit of saying brilliant things

CLAYTON, Mrs. (Liza of Lambeth). A resident of Vere Street, Lambeth; has just had twins, her tenth and eleventh children

CLAYTON, Mrs. (Woman of Fifty). Laura Greene's mother; a widow

CLEONTE (Perfect Gentleman). He is in love with Lucille Jourdain; a person of no family

CLEOPATRA (Magician). In Margaret Dauncey's vision; she turned away a wan, lewd face

CLERGY (Magician). At Saint Sulpice, Paris; followed the canons into the church to officiate the service

CLERGYMAN (Christmas Holiday). Had kept Simon Fenimore in his family until he was was old enough for school

CLERK (Ashenden/Traitor). Employed at Cook's, Lucerne

CLERK (Bad Example). Articled to a solicitor; on muddy days, he walked on the outside of the street, thus protecting his master from flying mud

CLERK (Consul). An Eurasian; employed by Mr. Pete, who nearly discharges him because he had misspelled two words in a letter

CLERK (End of the Flight). An employee of the District Officer; frightens the Dutchman

CLERK (For Services Rendered). Employed by Leonard Ardsley; Collie Stratton deposits a message with him

CLERK (Happy Couple). To Miss Wingford's lawyer; witnesses her will

Characters   89

CLERK (Making of a Millionaire). Works at the office of
  Frederick Rose; he delivers a telegram to Frederick
CLERK (Making of a Saint). Ushers in Filippo Brandolini
  to see Lorenzo de Medici
CLERK (Marriage of Convenience, 1906). At the Figaro;
  with a malicious grin; he hands Lucien de Pornichet a
  large sack of 748 responses to his advertisement for
  a wife
CLERK (Merry-Go-Round). To Polly Ley's solicitor; he
  witnesses Polly's will
CLERK (Mrs. Craddock). At the station at Blackstable,
  Kent; pasty-faced; with a baby in his arms
CLERK (Mrs. Dot). Aboard a crowded train coming from
  London; pale faced and weary; gave up his seat to a
  strong and bouncing girl
CLERK (Narrow Corner). Sits inside Kim Ching's store at
  Takana; is writing a document in Chinese characters
CLERK #1 (Of Human Bondage). At Messrs. Herbert Carter
  and Company; had to redo Philip Carey's work when Mr.
  Goodworthy was not satisfied with it
CLERK #2 (Of Human Bondage). At Messrs. Herbert Carter
  and Company; accompanied Mr. Goodworthy to Paris to
  do the accounts of a hotel in the Faubourg; took ill
CLERK (Painted Veil). At the P.&O. Company; told Kitty
  Fane that every berth on the next vessel out of Hong
  Kong had been taken
CLERK #1 (Point of Law). In the law firm of Addishaw,
  Jones, and Braham; with an obsequious air, blows the
  Narrator's name up the tube to the family solicitor
CLERK #2 (Point of Law). In the law firm of Addishaw,
  Jones, and Braham; announces that Ralph Mason wishes
  to see Addishaw
CLERK (Spanish Priest). At the copper pyrite mine in
  Seville; told the Englishman that a priest wanted to
  see him
CLERK (Taipan). At the Taipan's office; he had found a
  good jockey to ride the Taipan's horses
CLERK (Unattainable). To Robert Oldham; phones Caroline
  Ashley
CLERK, Nancy (Magician). An old friend of Susie Boyd;
  supposedly the author of a telegram received by Susie
  (actually written and sent by Oliver Haddo), stating
  that she plans to come to Paris, arriving at the Gard

du Nord; she never arrives there

CLERKS (East of Suez). In a crowded Peking street; in black gowns and caps, and black shoes

CLERKS (Making of a Millionaire). In the room adjoining Frederick Rose's office; thought that Frederick had suddenly gone mad

CLERKS (Mrs. Craddock). Aboard the penny steamboat from London to Greenwich

CLERKS (Of Human Bondage). Guests at the boarding house at Brighton; pale faced and middle aged; with their wives; talked about their married daughters and their sons in good positions in the Colonies

CLIBBORN, Clara de Tulleville (Hero). Wife of Colonel Reginald Clibborn and mother of Mary; worldly; once a regimental beauty; at age fifty, she has grown stout; becomes cross if people do not pay her compliments; a flirt; firmly believes that James Parsons has jilted Mary mainly because he loves her (Clara); with equal firmness, she believes that James Parsons killed himself only because he could never claim her (Clara)

CLIBBORN, Mary (Hero). Daughter of Clara and Reginald Clibborn; she resides with her parents at Little Primpton, Kent; has been engaged to James Parsons for five years; gentle, good, and pious; strong hands and solid feet; muscular arms; has guileless blue eyes; pretty hair, arranged simply; skin tanned by wind and weather; a typical country-bred girl; a nurse to the lower classes; considered by those in Little Primpton as a fine pianist; she moves into Primpton house and serves as James Parsons' nurse after he comes down with enteric fever; readily accepts James's marriage proposal; she agrees to marry Thomas Dryland after he his appointment as the vicar of Stone Fairley, Kent

CLIBBORN, Colonel Reginald (Hero). Husband of Clara and the father of Mary; tall; oily black hair, but dyed; aggressively military; worldly; had been in a cavalry regiment (and thus looks down upon infantrymen--such as the Parsons); he considered himself superior and a man of fashion; the perfect dandy

CLIENT (Fortunate Painter). Of Rudolf Kuhn; a California millionaire in New York; he buys the Watteau copy for $60.000

CLINTON, Amy (Bad Example). Wife of James Clinton; the

Characters

second daughter of John Raynor, Esq., of Peckham Rye; mother of two children; a woman of taste; short and stout; black, shiny hair parted in the middle; red and strongly lined face; spirited eyes; aggressive nose; resolute mouth

CLINTON, James (Bad Example). A clerk and the assistant manager in the firm of Haynes, Bryan, and Company; the very essence of respectability; believed in the Church of England and the Conservative Party; earned 156 pounds per year; small and spindly shanked; weak myopic eyes; wore spectacles; scant hair, worn long to conceal the baldness of the crown; has small side whiskers, but otherwise is clean shaven; decayed and yellowed teeth; is married to Amy Clinton; resided in Camberwell, London; father of two children; despised all foreigners; after his experience on the coroner's jury and his recovery from typhoid fever, he reads the Bible and determines to sacrifice everything to help the poor; sacked from his job; gives away all of his money

CLOW, General Sir Charles (Hero). He has recently taken residence in Bath; he has invited Reginald and Clara Clibborn to visit him; is informed by Clara, in a letter, of James Parsons' death; she also tells him of events following the suicide

CLOWN (Making of a Saint). At the piazza in Forli; with bells and bauble; he leads an ass bearing Orso d'Orsi

CLUTTON (Of Human Bondage). One of the art students at Amitrano's school, Paris; thin black hair; enormous nose; a face as long as that of a horse; huge bones seemed to protrude from his body; sharp elbows; he eventually moves away to Gerona, a little town in the north of Spain; returns to Paris and takes a studio at Jardin des Plantes

COACHMAN (Bishop's Apron). Of Lord Stonehenge's small and shabby carriage; in a uniform much the worse for wear; sat on his box in a slovenly, humped-up fashion

COACHMAN (Lady Habart). Ordered by Lady Habart to drive her home

COACHMAN (Liza of Lambeth). He is examining the horses' harness on the Red Lion brake; later announces lunch

COACHMAN (Magician). He takes Margaret Dauncey to the British Consulate at Paris

COACHMAN #1 (Merry-Go-Round). Follows Mrs. Murray and Basil Kent as they walk down the street

COACHMAN #2 (Merry-Go-Round). He drives Polly Ley from Tercanbury to Court Leys, Kent, and then back again

COACHMAN (Mrs. Craddock). At the railway station at Blackstable, Kent; he tips his hat to Bertha Craddock and hands her a note from Edward Craddock

COAL CONTROLLER (Home and Beauty). Acts rudely to Mrs. Shuttleworth

COAL MERCHANT (Man of Honour). He sends Basil Kent a receipt; Jenny Kent believes it to be a letter from Hilda Murray

COAL SHIP OWNERS (Of Human Bondage). Two or three of them; owned houses on the high street of Blackstable

COBBETT (Landed Gentry). Once Mrs. Insoley's milkman

COBBETT, Henry (Landed Gentry). Age twenty-four; very agreeable; a friend of Grace and Claude Insoley; has had an affair with Grace

COBBLER (Ashenden/Traitor). His shop on bottom floor of the building, in Basle, where Gustav Grabow lives

COCO (Razor's Edge). At the cafe on the Rue de Lappe; tall and well built; a great hooked nose; a mat of shining black hair; great sensual lips; looks like an evil Savonarola; tries to force Sophie Macdonald to dance with him

COHEN #1 (Moon and Sixpence). A Jewish trader and seaman; he had acquired one of Charles Strickland's paintings; a little old Frenchman; married to Mrs. Cohen; soft kind eyes and a pleasant smile; owned a cutter and traded in shells and pearls; also owned a Tahiti plantation; hired Strickland as his overseer

COHEN #2 (Moon and Sixpence). The brother of Cohen #1; writes to his brother from Paris concerning Charles Strickland's reputation as a painter

COHEN, Dick (Lady Frederick). A Jewish money lender; he refuses to lend any money to Lady Frederick Berolles; staying at the Hotel de Paris, Monte Carlo

COHEN, Isaac (Smith). A former "employer" of Algernon Peppercorn; generous, but not at all exacting

COHEN, Moses (Rehearsal). Of Grosvenor Square, London; he has implored to marry Genevieve Zampa; formerly associated with a Kaffir Circus, but now he deals in annuities; has agreed to change his name to Courtney

Characters   93

Howard
COHEN, Mrs. (Moon and Sixpence). Wife of Cohen #1; her husband shows her the picture of the plantation that Charles Strickland had painted and then gave to him; she can never throw away anything
COLBY, Robert (Tenth Man). A Member of Parliament; he in love with Catherine Winter; age forty; handsome; spare and active; a refined face and good features; clean shaven; grey hair; has charming manners and old fashioned courtesy; is totally committed to politics; his career will be ruined if George Winter lodges a counter divorce petition against Catherine; is going to lead the War Office in the new Perigal cabinet
COLCHESTER, Bishop of (Loaves and Fishes). He has just died; had been ill for a very long time; a man of no family; an ardent champion of temperance
COLLINS (Of Human Bondage). The name comes up during a conversation at Brighton between Philip Carey and Mildred Rogers; Mildred could not remember the name
COLONEL (Home and Beauty). In the army; is prepared to marry the wife of Gentleman #4; became most offensive toward Rehan when the couple would not divorce
COLONEL (Unknown). Of John Wharton's regiment; wrote to Evelyn Wharton when John was wounded
COLONEL R (Ashenden/ Giulia Lazzari/ Hairless Mexican/ Miss King/Traitor). Is introduced to Ashenden at a party; resident of London; known in the Intelligence Department as "R"; above middle height, lean; yellow, deeply lined face; thin grey hair and a toothbrush moustache; blue eyes--close set, hard, and cruel; a professional soldier who had spent his career in India and the Colonies
COLONIAL GOVERNOR (Marriage of Convenience). Predecessor to the retired French official; a bachelor; had created a scandal by having native girls living with him at the residency
COLORED WOMEN (Razor's Edge). Two of them; following the 1929 stock market crash, the only employees of Isabel and Gray Maturin at their plantation in South Carolina
COMIC MAN (Liza of Lambeth). Performs between the acts at the theatre in Westminster; raised the customary laughter by undressing and thus exposing his nether

garments to the public

COMMANDANT (Christmas Holiday). Of the penal colony on French Guiana; a decent chap; he got the elder Iibere permission to return to France when he still had two years left in his time

COMMANDANT (Man with a Conscience). Of St. Laurent de Maroni Prison; he accompanies the Narrator to Jean Charvin's cell

COMMANDANT (Official Position). Of St. Laurent de Maroni Prison; trusted Louis Remire

COMMANDANT LA GARDE (Theatre). At St. Malo; a retired naval officer; well past seventy years of age; came to dine, on Thursday evenings, with the Abbe, Madame Carrie Falloux, and Mrs. Lambert; small and sturdy; a wrinkled face; white hair cut en brosse; an imposing moustache

COMMANDER (Hour Before the Dawn). Of the R.H.A. battery at a small village near Cassel, France; Roger Henderson brings orders to him

COMMANDING OFFICER (Hero). Of Jamie Parsons' regiment; an old friend of Richmond Parsons

COMMISSIONAIRE (Gigolo and Gigolette). At the casino; directs the Penazzis to the bar to meet the Cotmans

COMMISSIONAIRE (Theatre). At Quag's, London; he calls a taxi for Thomas Fennell and Julia Gosselyn

COMMISSIONER (Explorer [novel]). At Nairobi; he communicates with Alec MacKenzie relative to annexation of the conquered slave trade district to the British Empire

COMMISSIONERS (Explorer [play]). Received from Alec MacKenzie a broad tract of rich, fertile African land

COMMISSIONERS (Then and Now). Two of them; sent by the Florentine Signory to capture Paolo and Vitellozzo Viteli

COMMISSIONERS (Then and Now). Three of them; hanged by Caesar Borgia for providing bad food to his troops

COMMITTEE MEN (Mrs. Craddock). Seven of them; they and Attihill Bacot come to Edward Craddock and ask him to stand for the County Council election

COMPANION (Appearance and Reality). With Lisette Larion when Raymond Le Sueur approached her

COMPOSER (Perfect Gentleman). Of the opera, The Island of Naxos; a pupil of the Music Master; has a charming

Characters   95

gift for composing serenades; he is overcome when he hears that the opera and the harlequinade will be performed together

CONCIERGE #1 (Appearance and Reality). Of the apartment building in the Batignolles district of Paris; spoke well of Lisette Larion

CONCIERGE #2 (Appearance and Reality). Of Lisette Larion's new flat; wanted to place her son in government service; reported to Raymond Le Sueur about Lisette's visitors

CONCIERGE #1 (Christmas Holiday). At Simon Fenimore's building; supposed to come every day to clean; she has varicose veins and hates to climb stairs

CONCIERGE #2 (Christmas Holiday). At Teddie Jordan's building; she cleaned Teddie's flat and brought him coffee; she discovered Jordan's body

CONCIERGE #3 (Christmas Holiday). At Alexey's lodgings in the Rue du Chateau d'Eau, Paris; Lydia Berger leaves her bag with her before accompanying Charley Mason to the Gard du Nord

CONCIERGE #1 (Magician). At Dr. Porhoet's house, Paris; commanded Susie Boyd to ring a tinkling bell at one of the doorways

CONCIERGE #2 (Magician). At Paris; the only person near by when Oliver Haddo put his hand to his heart and fell heavily to the ground; appeals to Margaret Dauncey for help; helps Margaret assist Haddo into Margaret's studio

CONCIERGE #3 (Magician). At the house of Susie Boyd and Margaret Dauncey, Paris; an old woman

CONCIERGE #1 (Moon and Sixpence). At the Narrator's Paris hotel; had never heard of the Hotel des Belges in the Rue de Rivoli

CONCIERGE #2 (Moon and Sixpence). Of the Narrator's apartment building on the Rue des Dames, Paris; she prepares coffee and cleans the apartment

CONCIERGE #3 (Moon and Sixpence). Of the Paris house in which Charles Strickland lives

CONCIERGE #4 (Moon and Sixpence). Of the house in Paris where Dirk and Blanche Stroeve live; Dirk will collect his belongings from her; discovers Blanche on the bed after she has taken the oxalic acid

CONCIERGE #1 (Of Human Bondage). At Philip Carey's art

studio in Paris; calls to Philip that he has received a letter; later, hands him the letter from his Uncle William Carey

CONCIERGE #2 (Of Human Bondage). At the building where Fanny Price lives; she has not seen Fanny in two days

CONCIERGE #1 (Razor's Edge). At Sophie Macdonald's apartment, Paris; she cannot tell Larry Darrell of Sophie's whereabouts; Sophie gives her one hundred francs to tell anyone that she had packed a bag and had gone away in a taxi

CONCIERGE #2 (Razor's Edge). At the Paris apartment of Gray and Isabel Maturin; Maugham concerned that the man had delayed forwarding his letter concerning the failing health of Elliott Templeton to the Maturins

CONDAMINE (Explorer [novel]). A member of Alec MacKenzie's expedition against the African slave traders; took command of the victorious expedition after Alec fell severely ill with blackwater fever; Alec wants him to be appointed sub-commissioner under a chief at Nairobi, and he receives that appointment following Alec's recovery; with shaking voice, reads the burial service for Dr. Anderson from an English prayer book

CONDUCTOR (Bishop's Apron/Loaves and Fishes). Of a bus in London; a nice young man; married; he and Mrs. Railing drink a drop of beer at the end of the ride

CONDUCTOR (Theatre). On the train from Paris to Cannes; he conducts Julia Lambert Gosselyn to her sleeper

CONDUCTORS (Bishop's Apron/Loaves and Fishes). Of the London buses; Mrs. Railing believes them to be good looking gentlemen; earn very good money

CONJURER (Making of a Saint). At the market place at Forli; attracted a gaping crowd

CONNEMARA, Lydia (Lord Mountdrago). Hosts a party in one of Lord Mountdrago's dreams; silly and ill-bred, with bad manners

CONSCIENTIOUS OBJECTORS (Hour Before the Dawn). At the military exemption tribunal at Lewes; are miserable, undersized, and weak

CONSERVATIVE CANDIDATE (Of Human Bondage). Had come to a meeting at Blackstable, which he asked that Josiah Graves (rather than William Carey) chair

CONSERVATIVES (Mrs. Craddock). One hundred of them; all members of the Blackstable Unionist Association; they

Characters 97

   attended Edward Craddock's funeral
CONSTABLE (Hour Before the Dawn). From Graveney; he informs the Hendersons of Tommy Henderson's death; is among the police inspecting the remains of the rick near Jim Henderson's cottage
CONSTABLE (Man of Honour). Informs Basil Kent of Jenny Kent's death
CONSTABLE (Of Human Bondage). Keeps watch over Man #12 at St. Luke's Hospital, London
CONSTANT, Alphonse-Louis (Magician). See LEVI, Eliphas
CONSTANT, Monsieur (Magician). Father of Alphonse-Louis Constant (Eliphas Levi); a bootmaker
CONSTITUENTS (Circle). One or two of them; of Arnold Champion-Cheney; at Aston Adey, Dorset; Arnold has a conference with them
CONSUL (Making of a Saint). Of the Roman Republic; mythical; supposedly founded the family of Brandolini by a somewhat discreditable union with someone else's wife
CONSUL (Taipan). Took care to keep on the right side of the Taipan
CONSULS (Explorer [novel]). Of foreign potentates; two of them at Mombassa; bestow decorations upon Alec MacKenzie
CONTADINI (Up at the Villa). At Florence; have told the violinist about Mary Panton's villa
CONTROLEUR (Narrow Corner). On Kanda; told George Frith that he attributed Erik Christessen's suicide to the heat
CONVERS, Sir Edward (Buried Talent). British Minister Plenipotentiary to the King of Siam; known as Teddie; arrives at Penang, where he must stay until repairs have been made on the rail line to Bangkok; married for nineteen years, with two sons; middle aged; grey hair; keen, intelligent face; at age twenty-two, in Paris, he had been in love with Charmian Pelter and asked her to marry him; he had served in Brazil and Guatemala before coming to the East
CONVERS, Mrs. (Buried Talent). The wife of Sir Edward Convers and mother of their two sons; will join her husband in Siam after the boys return to their school
CONVICT #1 (Man with a Conscience). Is standing idly by the roadside with a pick; has twenty years to scratch

away a blade of grass
CONVICT #2 (Man with a Conscience). Carries a dispatch case under his arm; holds a job in the administration
CONVICT #3 (Man with a Conscience). Carries a basket; a servant in someone's house
CONVICT #4 (Man with a Conscience). Is serving a life sentence for murder; makes the Narrator's bed, tidies his room, and runs errands for him
CONVICT #5 (Man with a Conscience). He spends time at work in a carpenter's shop; had cut his wife's throat
CONVICT #6 (Man with a Conscience). He had come in the ship from France with Jean Charvin; young man; found dead in his hammock with his belly split open
CONWAY, George (East of Suez). Age in the early thirties; tall and dark; handsome and well built; rugged appearance; urbane and self-assured; close friend of Henry Anderson; an Assistant Chinese Secretary; at age twenty-three, had almost married Daisy (now Mrs. Anderson), and still in love with her; attacked and stabbed by Lee Tai Cheng's men, who mistake him for Henry Anderson; plans to leave for Vancouver, Canada; shoots himself
COOK (Bishop's Apron). To Sophia and Theodore Spratte; her ingenuity prolonged Lord Harry Wroxham's torture by the diversity and number of her courses
COOK (Book-Bag). In the employ of the Hardys; taught by Olive to make Italian dishes
COOK (Christmas Holiday). At the restaurant in the Avenue du Maine, Paris; the husband of the patronne
COOK (Constant Wife). At the Middletons' house; makes the best meringues; she has given her notice
COOK (Creative Impulse). Replacement for Mrs. Bulfinch; upset when the porter drops his box
COOK (East of Suez). In a crowded Peking street; serves bowls of rice and condiments to passers-by
COOK (Home and Beauty). At the Lowndes' house; left after one week
COOK (Irish Gentleman). Employed at the Golden Eagle Inn, Wartburg-Hochstein; Robert O'Donnel impresses her with his knowledge of culinary affairs
COOK (Landed Gentry). At Kenyon Fulton, Somersetshire; obese, elderly, and respectable
COOK (Loaves and Fishes). At St. Gregory's Vicarage;

always gets drunk if the guests do not sit down to dinner punctually

COOK (Masterson). In Masterson's employ

COOK #1 (Merry-Go-Round). She has been in Elizabeth Dwarris's employ for twenty-five years; no one other than Polly Ley has ventured to complain about her cooking

COOK #2 (Merry-Go-Round). Of Polly Ley; her mistress is most conceited about her excellence

COOK #1 (Mrs. Craddock). At Court Leys, Barnstable, Kent; she burnt the milk on the day of Bertha Ley's majority

COOK #2 (Mrs. Craddock). Employed by Mrs. Brandenton; sent by her mistress to read the Bible to the poor when they were ill

COOK #1 (Narrow Corner). He works aboard the Australian schooner; cooks breakfast for the Australian captain and Dr. Saunders

COOK #2 (Narrow Corner). Employed by the Blakes; Mrs. Blake tells her not to go near Fred Blake

COOK (Of Human Bondage). Sent by Emma and the maid to look for Mrs. Carey, after the last named had gone to the photographer

COOK (Our Betters). For the Graystons; does not know that Pearl Grayston has asked twelve people to come for dinner

COOK (Painted Veil). For the Fanes at Mei-tan-fu; a Chinese; not bad; held a regard for propriety, des-despite the plague and the difficulty in obtaining provisions

COOK #1 (Smith). Of Mrs. Peppercorn; Algernon Peppercorn claims that she is not as good a cook as the one employed by Rose Dallas-Baker

COOK #2 (Smith). Of Rose Dallas-Baker; single; nearly forty years of age; according to Algernon Peppercorn, a better cook than the one employed by his mother; has sick headaches; advised Smith that, because of Thomas Freeman's proposal, she (Smith) ought to give notice

COOK (Theatre). Is employed at the house of George and Mrs. Gosselyn, at Cheltenham

COOK #1 (Unattainable). At Caroline Ashley's house; she always reads The Times before it goes upstairs

COOK #2 (Unattainable). Formerly in the employ of Dr. Cornish; married the lad who came in to do the boots and knives

COOK (Unknown). At the Whartons' house in Stour, Kent; age forty-five; she is stout and homely; Mrs. Wharton arranged with her that there could be roast beef for lunch

COOK (Verger). In the household of a merchant prince; had tried to teach the twelve-year-old Albert Edward Foreman to read and write

COOKS (Perfect Gentleman). They prepare the banquet at Monsieur Jourdain's house; dance before they bring the dishes to the table

COOLIE #1 (East of Suez). In a crowded Peking street; seated on a stool having his head shaved

COOLIE #2 (East of Suez). Caught by Henry Anderson as one of the attackers upon George Conway

COOLIE #3 (East of Suez). Widowed and the father of two small children; killed

COOLIE #1 (Narrow Corner). Inside Kim Ching's store at Takana; sitting on the floor rolling cigarettes and smoking them; served beer

COOLIE #2 (Narrow Corner). Carries provisions to the Takana beach, then waits for Dr. Saunders

COOLIES (East of Suez). Upon a crowded Peking street; wear blue cotton in various stages of raggedness; half naked; bear great bales on their yokes; utter sharp cries for the people to get out of their way

COOLIES (Mabel). Four of them; carry Mabel in a chair to the door of the British Consulate at Cheng-tu, in Szechuan

COOLIES (Painted Veil). Bore Kitty and Walter Fanes' bedding, stores, and equipment to Mei-tan-fu

COOLIES (Painted Veil). At Mei-tan-fu; fetching water from the river; hurrying to and fro with huge buckets hanging from the yokes on their shoulders, splashing the causeway

COOLIES (Painted Veil). Two of them; at Mei-tan-fu; they help Kitty Fane from the sampan to the shore

COOLIES (Painted Veil). Six of them, at Mei-tan-fu; they carry Walter Fane's coffin to his burial plot

COOLIES (Painted Veil). On the journey from Mei-tan-fu to Hong Kong; straggled disorderly, two or three of

them together
COOLIES (Painted Veil). Between Mei-tan-fu and Hong Kong; they lollop along in a line with their heavy burdens
COOLIES (Taipan). Digging a fresh grave in the English cemetery
COOPER (Of Human Bondage). The partner of Tom Perkins' father in the firm of Perkins and Cooper, St. Catherine Street, Tercanbury; "drank like a fish," thus partially causing the firm's bankruptcy
COOPER (Unattainable). Caroline Ashley's trim parlor maid
COOPER, Allen (Outstation). Warburton's assistant; age about thirty; tall, thin; sallow, colorless face; a large, hooked nose; blue eyes; a large skull covered with short brown hair; weak, small chin; was born and educated at Barbados
COOPER, Jim (Sheppey). A thief; Sheppey saw him stealing the doctor's overcoat out of the latter's car; out of work; he has been in and out of prison a half-dozen times; had not eaten for two days; remanded for a week; Sheppey invites him to lodge and board at his house; ragged looking; tries to steal Sheppey's snuff box
COOPER (Mr. (Bishop's Apron). Husband of Mrs. Cooper; has told Mrs. Railing all about his wife
COOPER, Mrs. (Bishop's Apron). A friend of Mrs. Railing; wife of Mr. Cooper; lives in Shepherd's Bush; tall and gaunt; a nice woman and a thorough lady; she drinks; the mother of seven children; had had trouble with her husband
COOPER, Mrs. (Loaves and Fishes). Mrs. Railing's friend who lives in Shepherd's Bush; takes a little drop too much now and then
COOPER, Mrs. (Liza of Lambeth). Mother of Sally Cooper; she marches arm in arm with Sally's uncle to her daughter's wedding; agrees with Harry Atkins that a woman's place is in the home; has had twelve children and two stillborns, in addition to one miscarriage
COOPER, Sally (Liza of Lambeth). Dances with Liza Kemp on Vere Street, Lambeth, to the tune of the organ grinder; small and thin; sandy hair and blue eyes; very freckled complexion; enormous mouth; terrible

square teeth set wide apart; marries Henry (Harry) Atkins, and then she gives up her factory job; Harry beats her

COPPER (Magician). Margaret Dauncey's terrier; he rubs himself in a friendly fashion against Dr. Porhoet's legs; frightened at the sight of Oliver Haddo; bites Haddo in the hand, and the latter gives him a kick

COPT (Caesar's Wife). Comes every day to teach Arabic to Lady Violet Little

COQUELIN, Benoit Constant (Of Human Bondage). A French actor (1841-1909) who sat next to Miss Wilkinson at a dinner at the Paris home of the portrait painter; he told her that he had never met a foreigner who spoke such perfect French

COQUELIN, Jean (Theatre). The French actor (1864-1944); declared that Julia Lambert Gosselyn had the beaute du diable

CORALIE, Madame (Closed Shop). French proprietor of a bordello

CORELLI, Marie (Mrs. Craddock). English popular novelist (1855-1924); Polly Ley had seen her

CORNISH, Dr. (Unattainable). He is stout, red faced, and jovial; an optimist; he calls on Caroline Ashley; tells her she is suffering from middle age

CORONER (Bad Example). He announces to the jury that it needs to consider only three cases; distraught at the case of the two-year-old child

CORONER (Narrow Corner). In the Sydney Bulletin; commented on the death of the woman who had hanged herself

CORONER (Sacred Flame). Beatrice Wayland will proceed straight to him if Dr. Harvester actually signs Maurice Tabret's death certificate before the autopsy

CORONER'S OFFICER (Bad Example). Allows James Clinton to have another look at the three bodies

CORONER'S OFFICER (Man of Honour). Comes to see Basil Kent on the morning following Jenny Kent's death

CORRESPONDENTS (Explorer [novel]). Of newspapers; come to Alec MacKenzie for a preliminary account of his travels

CORSICAN (French Joe). Helps French Joe to escape from the prison ship at Melbourne

CORSICAN SAILOR (Razor's Edge). At Toulon; a boy friend

of Sophie Macdonald; tall, swarthy, clean shaven; has splendid dark eyes; aquiline nose; raven black wavy hair; muscular; does not look more than twenty years of age

CORYDON (Liza of Lambeth). The faithful swain of the mock idyll that is told at the halfway house between Lambeth and Chingford

COSTANZA, Monna (Then and Now). The widowed sister of Bartolomeo Martelli; she lives at Forli with her two sons, both of whom Bartolomeo has considered adopting

COTMAN, Stella (Gigolo and Gigolette). Australian wife of Syd Cotman; she earned her living by diving into a five-foot tank of flaming water from a ladder sixty feet high; age twenty-six; a small, good figure, but not necessarily pretty; her light wavy brown hair cut short; grey eyes; pale skin; formerly a swimming instructress and diver

COTMAN, Syd (Gigolo and Gigolette). The handsome husband and manager of Stella Cotman; age thirty; short; thick, black, wavy, sleek, and shiny hair; large and flashing eyes; has a Cockney accent; a dancing gigolo since age eighteen

COTTET, Auguste (Razor's Edge). The French painter whom Larry Darrell had known in Paris; he had kept Suzanne Rouvier for a time; went to Saville to paint; lends Larry a cottage at Sanary, on the Riviera, where the latter plans to spend the winter writing

COUNCILLOR (Making of a Saint). At Forli; seconds the sentiment of Antonio Lassi that the town be ceded to Checco d'Orsi

COUNCILLORS (Making of a Saint). Of Girolamo Riario; Girolamo consulted with them before remitting certain of his more oppressive taxes; present at the meeting between Girolamo and Checco d'Orsi at the Palazzo Orsi

COUNCILLORS (Mrs. Craddock). Of the Blackstable Local District Council; attend Edward Craddock's funeral

COUNCILLORS (Punctiliousness of Don Sebastian). Upset when King Philip asked for Don Sebastian's advice on matters of precedence

COUNSEL (Explorer [play]). For Fred Allerton; he told George Allerton that his father's trial was bound to come out all right

COUNTESSES (Circle). Seedy; liked to drive with Lady Catherine Champion-Cheney in the Cascine

COURIER (Magician). He travels about with Oliver and Margaret Haddo

COURIER #1 (Then and Now). Were sent by the Florentine Signory to their agent in Borgia's court, informing him of Machiavelli's arrival at Imola; he awaits Machiavelli at the city gate

COURIER #2 (Then and Now). Brings Biagio Buonaccorsi's letter about the arrival of Machiavelli to Bartolomeo Martelli

COURIER #3 (Then and Now). He arrives at Imola in the morning from Perugia to see Caesar Borgia

COURIER #4 (Then and Now). He arrives at Sforza Palace with letters from the Pope to Caesar Borgia

COURIER #5 (Then and Now). Carries Machiavelli's letter from Castiglione Aretini to the Signory

COURIER #6 (Then and Now). He arrived at Pampalona announcing the death of Caesar Borgia

COURTE, Sir James (Mrs. Craddock). The husband of Lady Courte; father of three daughters

COURTE, Lady (Mrs. Craddock). The sister of Polly Ley; married to Sir James Courte; mother of their three daughters

COURTESANS (Magician). Painted; in Margaret Dauncey's vision

COURTESANS (Magician). At the tavern on the Boulevard des Italiens, Paris; fashionable

COURTIER (Making of a Saint). In the suite of Girolamo Riario; he tells Girolamo and Checco d'Orsi that the bodies of those who had attacked Checco are missing from the Church of San Spirito, Forli

COURTIERS (Making of a Saint). Of Girolamo Riario; in the company of Girolamo at the meeting between Checco d'Orsi and him at the Palazzo Orsi, Forli

COURTIERS (Making of a Saint). Of Caterina Sforza; they snicker as Caterina strips Protonotary Savello of his authority

COUSIN (Bishop's Apron). Of Captain Fitzherbert; on the day Mrs. Fitzherbert marries again, he or she will receive the income from the Captain's estate

COUSIN #1 (Marriage of Convenience). Of the future wife of the retired French official; his political influ-

Characters

ence helps to secure the colonial governorship for his cousin

COUSIN #2 (Marriage of Convenience). Of the future wife of the retired French official; also a friend of the official; he informs the official of his cousin's "availability"

COUSIN #1 (Painted Veil). Of Waddington; had married a celebrated London actor

COUSIN #2 (Painted Veil). Of Odette (Mother Superior); had gone to bid farewell to Madame de Viernot; was much moved

COUSIN (Wash-Tub). Of Mrs. Barnaby; dies and leaves her a large fortune

COUSINS (Painted Veil). Two of them; of Odette (Mother Superior) and staying with her family; they work at tapestries to recover the chairs in the drawing room

COUTRAS, Dr. (Moon and Sixpence). An old Frenchman; he is exceedingly tall and bulky; his body resembled a huge duck egg; sharp blue eyes; a florid complexion; white hair; huge hands; deep resonant voice; he is in possession of one of Charles Strickland's paintings; he diagnosed Strickland's disease as leprosy; he digs Strickland's grave with his one hands

COUTRAS, Madame (Moon and Sixpence). The wife of Dr. Coutras; tall and stout; ample busts; obese; a bold hooked nose and three chins; a copious talker

COWLEY, Mrs. (Cakes and Ale). The owner of the house on Limpus Road, London; rents rooms to Rose and Edward Driffield; she lives in the upper part; formerly a companion to a lady of title

COX, Mr. (Of Human Bondage). Is absent from Blackstable church

CRADDOCK, Bertha (Explorer [novel]). Widow of Edward Craddock and owner of Court Leys, Kent; in Rome; she leases Court Leys to Julia Crowley

CRADDOCK, Bertha (Mrs. Craddock). See under LEY, Bertha

CRADDOCK, Edward (Explorer [novel]). Deceased husband of Bertha Craddock; he broke his neck in the hunting field

CRADDOCK, Edward (Merry-Go-Round). Husband of Bertha Ley; a new tablet in the Leanham church recorded his birth, death, and qualities

CRADDOCK, Edward (Mrs. Craddock). Twenty-seven years of

age tall; is massively set together; big-boned; long arms and legs; a magnificent breadth of chest; large, firm fingers; massive, hard hands; curly hair; grey eyes, clean shaven; is the very picture of health; intense vitality; in love with Bertha Ley; a tenant farmer at Bewlie's Farm, between Leanham and Black-Blackstable, Kent; had spent ten years at St. Regis School, Tercanbury, Kent; marries Bertha Ley; three years later, at age thirty-one; he looks older; gains weight; his features lose their delicacy; stands for and wins election to the County Council; becomes a model farmer, squire, and landlord; thrown from his horse during a hunt and breaks his collarbone; he recovers; thrown a second time by the same horse and dies; his only fault was that his wife once had loved him, and then ceased to do so

CRADDOCK, Mr. (Mrs. Craddock). The father of Edward Craddock; had been Mr. Ley's tenant at Leanham, Kent; educated at St. Regis School, Tercanbury

CRADDOCK, Mrs. (Mrs. Craddock). Mother of Edward Craddock; used to play on the piano such tunes as "The Last Rose of Summer," "Home Sweet Home," and "a lot more like that"

CRAFTSMEN (Explorer [novel]). From Italy; made the lady chapel at Westminster Abbey and, with the Italian sculptor, the effigy of the eldest Allerton and his wife in the chancel of the parish church at Hamlyn's Purlieu, Hampshire

CRAIG, Angelina (Happy Couple, 1908). The wife of Edwin Craig; she and her husband the neighbors of Miss Ley; about forty years of age; tall; masculine in appearance; unattractive fair hair; large nose and mouth; weather-beaten skin; is accused, with her husband, of poisoning Miss Wingfield, but not convicted, faints after she recognizes Frank Hurrell; her real name is Mrs. Brownley; she, along with her husband, infant, and nurse, flee the cottage

CRAIG, Edwin (Happy Couple, 1908). Husband of Angelina Craig; middle aged; handsome; red, honest face; grey moustache and thin grey hair; accused, with his wife, of poisoning Miss Wingfield; his name actually Dr. Brownley; along with his wife and infant, flees the cottage

CRAIG, George (Happy Couple, 1952). A neighbor of Miss Gray; handsome, husband of Mrs. Craig; a red, honest face; grey moustache and thick strong grey hair; is actually Dr. Brandon

CRAIG INFANT (Happy Couple, 1908). Child of Angelina and Edwin Craig; a little more than one year old

CRAIG INFANT (Happy Couple, 1952). Child of George and Mrs. Craig; just learning to walk

CRAIG, Mrs. (Happy Couple, 1952). Wife of George Craig; is tall and masculine in appearance; dull, fair hair; large nose and mouth; with weather beaten skin; forty years of age; actually Miss Starling

CRAMMER (Merry-Go-Round). For Reggie Barlow-Bassett; Reggie lied to his mother, saying that he would be working late with him

CRAMMER #1 (Mrs. Craddock). For the army exams; Gerald Vaudrey "can't stick [him] at any price"

CRAMMER #2 (Mrs. Craddock). He played poker; "skinned" Gerald Vaudrey of every shilling; he said that Gerald was an immoral young dog and was corrupting his house

CRAWFORD, Marion (Lotus Eater). Author of "a sort of" history book containing a story about Sybaria de Crotona; read by Thomas Wilson; actually the American writer of fiction, Francis Marion Crawford (1854-1909)

CREDITORS (Loaves and Fishes). Thomas Spratte is "used to dealing with the beasts"

CREGG, Mother (Liza of Lambert). She had a fight with another woman last year in Vere Street, Lambeth

CREW MEMBER (Red). A Kanaka native; fat and heavy build

CREW, Mr. (Ashenden/Mr. Harrington's Washing). Head of Messrs. Crew and Adams, the Philadelphia firm that J.Q. Harrington represents

CRICHTON, Avice (Theatre). Young actress; pretty; fair; blonde hair; fine blue eyes; a small, straight nose; playing in a Sunday night show; Thomas Fennell told her that he would get her a part in Julia Gosselyn's next play; had been a student with Joan Denver at the Royal Academy of Dramatic Arts; Michael Gosselyn engages her to play the role of Honor in <u>Nowadays</u>

CRICHTON, Colonel (Theatre). Father of Avice Crichton; in the army

CRITIC (Alien Corn). At a dinner hosted by Ferdy Rabenstein

CRITIC (Colonel's Lady). He has dinner with Daphne and tells her of the success of Evie's volume of poetry

CRONSHAW (Ant and the Grasshopper). Is cheated by Tom Ramsay; went off to Monte Carlo with Tom after George Ramsay had settled his law suit

CRONSHAW, J. (Of Human Bondage). A poet; he could be found, between the hours of 9:00 p.m. and 2:00 a.m., at La Closerie de Lilas, a Paris cafe; is large and stout, but not obese; a round face, small moustache, rather small stupid eyes; resembled a pea poised on an egg; a beautiful sonorous voice; a close follower of English cricket; had been dismissed for drunkenness from the staff of an English paper in Paris, but continued to do odd jobs for it; he lived in a dilapidated house on the Quai des Grands Augustins with Woman #4 and their two children; contacts pneumonia and spends seven weeks in the English hospital; moves to London (#43 Hyde Street, Soho); his appearance has become dried-up and yellow; loose and wrinkled skin; his hands trembled continually; very ill with cirrhosis of the liver; dies in his sleep at Philip Carey's residence, Kennington, London

CROSBIE, Leslie (Letter [play]). Has been married for ten years to Robert Crosbie; is Geoffrey Hammond's lover; she shoots Hammond; confined to the prison at Singapore during the length of her trial; acquitted; admits that she still loves Hammond, but will try to make amends with her husband

CROSBIE, Leslie (Letter [story]). The wife of Robert Crosbie; accused of killing Geoffrey Hammond; in the early thirties; fragile, neither short nor tall; with delicate wrists and ankles; white skin; pale lips and light brown hair; she is quiet, pleasant, unassuming

CROSBIE, Robert (Letter [play]). The husband of Leslie Crosbie; a planter at Singapore; age forty; powerful build; a large, sunburned face; a simple and honest man; is unaware both of the contents of the Chinese woman's letter and the price for its purchase--as well as the source for that money; after the trial, he proposes to purchase an estate for sale at $30,000 --$10,000 from his savings and $20,000 on mortgage;

in love with Leslie and cannot continue without her
CROSBIE, Robert (Letter [story[). Over six feet tall; is broad shouldered and muscular; a rubber planter; large hands and feet; the husband of Leslie Crosbie
CROWD (Magician). At the fair at the Lion de Belfort, Paris; surged along the central avenue; bent with a kind of savagery upon amusement; a number of them point out Oliver Haddo to one another; others joke about Haddo's appearance
CROWHURST, Rev. (Mrs. Craddock). The former vicar of Leadham, Kent; a nice old man; he read the ladies' papers to Mrs. Branderton when she was ill
CROWLEY, Julia (Explorer [novel]). An American and recently widowed, who had married an Englishman; owns coal mines in Pennsylvania; young--she admits to age twenty-nine; pretty and rich; quick mind and an alert tongue; diminutive in size; an exquisite figure; the smallest of hands; with good, regular, well-formed features; perfect complexion; agile grace; has leased Court Leys, Kent, from Bertha Craddock; fond of Lucy Allerton; during and after Fred Allerton's trial, she occupies a small house in Norfolk Street, London; in love with Dick Lomas; she refuses Dick's proposal of marriage, although she has every intention of accepting it; then proposes marriage to Dick and weds him; arranges a meeting between Alec MacKenzie and Lucy Allerton
CROWLEY, Mr. (Explorer [novel]). An Englishman and the deceased husband of Julia Crowley
CROWLEY, Nellie (Explorer [play]). A widow; age twenty-eight; small; pretty; vivacious and gesticulative; rejects Dick Lomas's proposal of marriage; she and Dick eventually become engaged
CROWN PRINCE (Voice of the Turtle). Had an affair with La Falterona; he gave her an emerald of immense value
CULVER, Martha (Constant Wife). Daughter of Mrs. Culver and the sister of Constance Middleton; age thirty-two
CULVER, Mrs. (Constant Wife). Mother of Martha Culver and Constance Middleton; elderly; has a pleasant face
CUNNINGHAM, Rex (Unattainable). Young; is nice looking; dark eyes; dark hair brushed back over his head and plastered down; achieves a romantic look; is in love with Caroline Ashley

CURATE (Daisy). Of Blackstable church; rolls his eyes to see who is in church; he "gabbles" the morning prayers

CURATE (Lisa of Lambeth). Young and pale-faced; marries Sally Cooper to Harry Atkins

CURATE (Of Human Bondage). To William Carey at Blackstable village, Kent; he is Emily Wilkinson's tennis partner; recommends to Philip Carey rooms in London at Barnes

CURTIS, Bobbie (Home and Beauty). He sent chocolates to Victoria Cardew-Lowndes

CUSTOMER (Merry-Go-Round). At the Golden Crown, Fleet Street, London; shakes hands with the second barmaid

CUSTOMER (Of Human Bondage). At the tea shop, Parliament Street, London; left the newspaper behind

CUSTOMER #1 (Sheppey). At Bradley's Hairdressing and Barber's Saloon, Jermyn Street, London; has just had his hair cut by Albert and his nails manicured by Miss Grange; his hair getting just a bit thin on top

CUSTOMER #2 (Sheppey). At Bradley's Hairdressing and Barber's Saloon, Jermyn Street, London; being shaved by Sheppey

CUSTOMERS (Sheppey). Of Sheppey, at Bradley's Hairdressing and Barber's Saloon, Jermyn Street, London; they wait for Sheppey, because he always gives them a good laugh

CUSTOMS OFFICER (Fortunate Painter). At New York; he scrapes Charlie Bartle's signature from the copy of Watteau and shows Rudolf Kuhn Watteau's signature

CUSTOMS OFFICIAL (Christmas Holiday). On French Guiana, in the penal colony, French Guiana; used to promise to take liberes over the river for a certain sum; he shot more than thirty of them and took their money

D

DA AMALIA, Agapito (Then and Now). First secretary to Caesar Borgia; related to the great Roman family of the Colonna; Machiavelli had met him at Urbino; he is swarthy, with long black hair and small black beard; pale skin and somber, clever eyes

DA CORELLA, Michele (Then and Now). A Spaniard; one of Caesar Borgia's captains sent to quell an uprising at

Urbino; wounded in a battle with the rebels

DA FERMO, Oliverotto (Then and Now). An ambitious young man; attended the meeting of Caesar Borgia's captains at La Magione, near Perugia; took Camerino by storm

DALLAS-BAKER, Herbert (Smith). Age forty-five; stout; bald; easy going and pompous; a King's Counsel; the husband of Rose Dallas-Baker

DALLAS-BAKER, Rose (Smith). Age thirty; pretty; fair; affected manners; the wife of Herbert Dallas-Baker; sister of Thomas Freeman; dismisses Smith when she learns that Freeman has proposed marriage to her

DALL' ASTE, Giorgio (Making of a Saint). A cousin of Giovanni dall' Aste; returns to Forli; reportedly the only lover that Giulia dall' Aste has kept for more than ten days; young; small, slight, and thin; with abundant golden hair falling over his shoulders; a small golden moustache; pale, fair skin; blue eyes; has an affair with Giulia after she marries Filippo Brandolini and after her new husband has gone off to Rome; Filippo kills him

DALL' ASTE, Giovanni (Making of a Saint). Dead husband of Giulia dall' Aste; driven to his grave, five or six years ago, by his wife

DALL' ASTE, Giulia (Making of a Saint). The widow of Giovanni dall' Aste; the sister of Alessandro and Scipione Moratini; age twenty-three or twenty-four; girlish, merry, and thoughtless; the loveliest woman in Forli; small and graceful; small face, with tiny features; tiny ears; has large brown eyes, soft and caressing; with a mass of dark, reddish brown hair; a fascinating smile; is seduced by Filippo Brandolini; after the fall of Forli, she rekindles her love for Filippo and proposes marriage to him; she and Filippo escape from Forli and reach Citta Di Castello; then marries Filippo three days after their arrival there; renews her love affair with Giorgio dall' Aste during Filippo's three-month absence in Rome; murdered by her father and brother after Filippo kills Giorgio

DA MONCADO, Ugo (Then and Now). A Spaniard and one of Caesar Borgia's captains; he is sent to put down the uprising at Urbino; taken prisoner by the forces of the rebel captains

DA MONTEFELTRO, Duke Guidobaldo (Then and Now). He had

confided in Caesar Borgia's friendship; he lost his estates and barely escaped with his life

DANCING MASTER (Perfect Gentleman). Called in to help M. Jourdain become a gentleman of fashion; Jourdain represents "quite a nice income for him"

DAPHNE (Colonel's Lady). She is George Peregrine's London mistress; age thirty-five; blonde and luscious

DARRELL, Lawrence (Razor's Edge). Supposedly engaged to Isabel Bradley; in 1919, young, just under six feet tall, thin, loose limbed; long, beautifully shaped hands; a tanned face with little color; with regular features; high cheekbones; hollow temples; dark brown hair with slight wave; large deeply set eyes; thick and long lashes; small, white, regular teeth; when the Narrator meets him unexpectedly in Paris some twelve years later, he appears (in his early thirties) tall and thin, with uncut brown hair, extremely white teeth, a heavy brown beard, and deeply tanned neck and forehead; had left St. Paul's School during the war and enlisted as an aviator; at age twenty, he goes to Paris, then he takes a job as a coal miner at Lens, in northern France; at age twenty-three, goes with Kosti #2 into Belgium and Germany; he leaves the Becker farm and proceeds to Bonn, and from there to Father Ensheim's Benedictine monastery in Alsace; to Paris, then to Spain, Italy, the East, India (for two years), and back to Paris; inform Isabel Maturin that he plans to marry Sophie Macdonald, but he never does

DARRELL, Mr. #1 (Razor's Edge). Lawrence Darrell's grandfather; had neither brother nor sister

DARRELL, Mr. #2 (Razor's Edge). Lawrence Darrell's father; an only son; from Baltimore; taught Romance languages at Yale ("or something like that"); he died twelve years before the Narrator first met his son

DARRELL, Mrs. (Razor's Edge). The mother of Lawrence Darrell; from Philadelphia and old Quaker stock; an only daughter; she died after giving birth to her son

DASHWOOD, Henry (Colonel's Lady). He writes a raving review of Evie Peregrine's book; tall and thin; high forehead; beard; long nose; walks with a stoop; he is introduced to George Peregrine by George's friend at the St. James's Street club

DAUBERNOON, Kate (Point of Law). Only daughter of Roger

and Mrs. Daubernoon; at age twenty-two, after the death of her mother, is left to care for her invalid father; a skillful nurse; not pretty; the years spent caring for her father only robbed her of her country freshness; grew prim and old maidish before her time; contracts consumption; at age forty: she is thin and haggard; hair streaked with grey; coughed constantly; tells Addishaw that she plans to marry Ralph Mason, which she does; does at Rome, intestate

DAUBERNOON, Mrs. (Point of Law). The wife of Roger Daubernoon and mother of Kate; died shortly after her husband's accident

DAUBERNOON, Robert (Point of Law). Cousin to Roger Daubernoon; an officer on half pay, with a large family; Kate Daubernoon's only relative and natural heir; he inherits all of Roger's and Kate's real property

DAUBERNOON, Roger (Point of Law). His family one of the oldest clients of the law firm of Addishaw, Jones, and Braham; a North Country squire with large estates in Westmorland; he injured his spine in a hunting accident and thus lingered a cripple for twenty years

DAUDET, Alphonse Marie Leon (Of Human Bondage). French writer (1867-1942); a guest at the Paris home of the portrait painter; gave Miss Wilkinson a copy of Sapho

DAUGHTER (Bad Example). Of the seventy-year-old man; had not been heard of for thirty years

DAUGHTER (Hero). Of John; according to Mary Clibborn, she had arranged her father's pillows badly

DAUGHTER (Magician). Of Herodias; subtle; in Margaret Dauncey's vision

DAUGHTER (Making of a Saint). Of a tradesman at Citta de Castello; unmarried mother of Ercole Piacentini

DAUGHTER (Marriages Are Made in Heaven). Of a doctor; engaged to marry Herbert Paton; fair hair and blue eyes

DAUGHTER (Of Human Bondage). Of Dr. and Mrs. South; she marries a farmer in Rhodesia; had taken her husband's part in a quarrel with her father; had not been in England in ten years; has one child

DAUGHTER (Of Human Bondage). Of the Jewish tailor shop owner on Harrington Street, London; age twenty; went around the house and extinguished the lights when the work day ended; allowed herself to be made love to by one of the tailors

DAUGHTER (Penelope). Of Mrs. Watson; accompanying her mother to the Riviera; married

DAUGHTER (Razor's Edge). Of a millionaire in South America; Prince Colombey had left the Marquese de Clinchant to marry her

DAUGHTER (Round Dozen). Of the laundress; she has an affair with the nephew of Gertrude St. Clair; married into her own class and became proprietor of a public house in Canterbury; Eleanor Porchester is godmother to her eldest child

DAUGHTER (Sheppey). Of Gentleman #2; her father told her, on the day before he died, that if he appeared before God looking as a gentleman, he would owe that to Sheppey

DAUGHTER (Theatre). Of the Spanish attache in Paris; is with her father and mother at Cannes

DAUNCEY, Margaret (Magician). Possesses beauty, grace, and sympathy; age nineteen; a delightful enthusiasm for every form of art; adores Arthur Burdon, to whom she has been engaged for two years; is seven years younger than Arthur, whom she has known since she was age ten; has been studying art at Colarossi's Paris academy for the past two years; shares a flat off the Boulevard du Montparnasse with Susie Boyd, her former schoolmistress; she comes under the hypnotic spell of Oliver Haddo, who gets her to admit that she loves him; marries Haddo; Arthur Burdon hustles her away from her husband; she then stays with Susie Boyd in a cottage in Hampshire, opposite the Isle of Wight; she suddenly leaves the cottage and returns to Haddo; dies, and is buried at Skene

DAUNCEY, Mr. (Magician). Father of Margaret Dauncey; a country barrister; died penniless, many years after the death of his wife

DAUNCEY, Mrs. (Magician). Mother of Margaret Dauncey; she died many years before her husband passed away

DAUNCEYS (Explorer [novel]). Of Malden Hall, Hampshire; they had given daughters to the Allertons of Hamlyn's Purlieu

DA VENAFRO, Antonio (Then and Now). Attended the meeting of Borgia's captains at La Magione, near Perugia; trusted adviser and confident of Pandolfo Petrucci,

Lord of Siena, and the mastermind of the conspiracy against Caesar Borgia; serves as an emissary from the Orsini to Caesar Borgia; arrives at Sforza Palace in the evening, and he departs the next day, supposedly carrying a peace offer from the rebel captains

DAVIDSON, Rev. Alfred (Rain). Missionary; silent, sullen, reserved; is tall and thin, long limbed, hollow cheeked, and with high cheek bones; has full, sensual lips; long fingers; long hair, dark eyes

DAVIDSON, Mrs. (rain). Missionary; the wife of Alfred Davidson; small; brown, dull hair; blue eyes; long, sheep-like face; high, metallic voice

DAVIES (Landed Gentry). The coroner, local doctor, and advanced Radical; in charge of the inquest into Peggy Gann's death

DA VINCI, Leonardo (Then and Now). The noted Florentine sculptor, painter, and engineer (1452-1519); produced a number of drawings of Caesar Borgia; sent by Borgia to Piombino to drain the marshes, then to Cesena and Cesenatico to cut a canal and form a harbor

DAVIS (Before the Party). The Skinners' gardener and acting chauffeur

DAWSON (String of Pearls). Butler at the Livingstones' dinner party; whispers to Miss Robinson that two men in the hall wish to speak with her

DAWSON, Constance (Love in a Cottage). The sister of Eleanor Dawson; an eccentric old maid; a guest at the Hotel Splendide, Varenna, on Lake Como; embroiders; she and her sister beg money from Sybil Bruce, who refuses them

DAWSON, Eleanor (Love in a Cottage). The sister of Contance Dawson; an eccentric old maid; a guest at the Hotel Splendide, Varenna, on Lake Como; paints watercolors

DAYTON, Margaret (Road Uphill). Pretty; girlish manner; she marries Ford Sheridan and bears him a daughter

DEACON (Explorer [novel]). A member of Alec MacKenzie's expedition against the African slave traders; Alec sends him to bring in the Latukas to reinforce his men for the attack from the slavers and the natives

DEACON, Dr. (Of Human Bondage). Elderly and bland; he diagnoses Philip Carey's illness as influenza

DEALER (Facts of Life). At the baccara game at Monte

Carlo; member of the Greek Syndicate; impassive face; watchful eyes

DEAN (Cakes and Ale). Of Westminster Abbey; denies the request of Edward Driffield's admirers to have the writer buried in the Abbey

DEAN (Magician). Late of Christ Church, Oxford; Oliver Haddo would preach blasphemous sermons, while imitating his voice

DEAN (Mirage). Of the medical college at St. Thomas's Hospital, London; threatens Grosely with penalties if he continues to neglect his studies

DEAN (Mrs. Craddock). Of Tercanbury Cathedral; a guest at Mr. Branderton's dinner party

DEAN (Of Human Bondage). Of Tercanbury Cathedral; he supported with zeal the candidacy of Thomas Perkins as headmaster of King's School

DE BATHE, Lady (Gigolo and Gigolette). Flora Penezzi introduced herself to her

DE BECEDAS, Don Miguel (Catalina). The steward of Dona Beatriz's estates; he administered her charities; ordered to determine who had possession of Catalina's crutch; sent to the archpriest to demand the crutch from him; instructed by Dona Beatriz to inquire into the backgrounds of Manuel de Valero, Diego Martinez, and Diego's father

DE BELMONTE, Hernando (Catalina). Duke of Terranova; he prevented officials of the Holy Office from arresting some wealthy vassals in Moorish dress; sentenced by Blasco De Valero to perpetual seclusion in a convent

DE BRIDES, Madame (Ashenden/Giulia Lazzari). Ugly, but a lovely figure; mistress of Grand Duke Theodore; one of the most influential and clever women in Europe

DE CAPIT, Lord (Merry-Go-Round). Young; tall and fair; wealthy; one of Marguerite Vizard's lovers

DE CARANERA, Marquesa (Catalina). The widowed niece of Prioress Dona Beatriz; age twenty-four; left ill-provided by her husband who, with their only son, had died of a distemper; resided at the Carmelite convent at Castel Rodriguez; eventually becomes sub-prioress of the Carmelite convent at Castel Rodriguez

DE CARMONA, Baltasar (Catalina). The junior Inquisitor; a doctor of laws and a rigid moralist; a dried-up little man; long sharp nose; tight lips and restless eyes; suffered from an intestinal disorder

DE CEPEDA, Teresa (Catalina). A nun at the Convent of the Incarnation at Avila; claimed she had seen Jesus Christ, the Blessed Virgin, and various saints; known as Mother Teresa of Jesus; hated by Dona Beatriz; a woman of energy, determination, and courage; founded the Discalced Order of Carmelites

DE CHAUEAU-GAILLARD, Gracie (Razor's Edge). A member of the Franco-American set at Paris; Elliott Templeton tries, unsuccessfully, to convince Larry Darrell to meet her

DE CHAUMONT, Monsieur (Then and Now). Ordered by King Louis of France to send three hundred of his lancers from Milan to Caesar Borgia

DE CLINCHANT, Marquese (Razor's Edge). Pretty; small; she had tried to poison herself because her lover, the Prince de Colombey, had left her to marry the daughter of a South American millionaire

DE COLOMBEY, Prince (Razor's Edge). The lover of the Marquese de Clinchant; left her to marry the daughter of a South American millionaire

DE FLORIMOND, Marie Louise (Razor's Edge). Age forty; delicately beautiful; an insatiable sexual voracity; expected to dine with Elliott Templeton; she combined irreproachable connections with notorious immorality

DE HIGGINS, Baroness (Ashenden/Miss King/Giulia Lazzari). An Austrian who had settled in Geneva during the war; spoke perfect English with no more than a trace of a German accent; found it convenient to make her name look as French as possible; a granddaughter of a Yorkshire stable boy; obviously a spy for the Austrians; over forty years of age; still extremely beautiful; a high-colored blonde with golden hair of a metallic luster; fine features; blue eyes, straight nose, pink and white skin; the skin stretched over the bones a trifle tightly; white and ample bosom; Ashenden considered the possibility of a flirtation with her

DE LA RAMEE, Marie Louise (Cakes and Ale). The English writer (1839-1908); her pseudonym "Ouida"; Mrs. Endcombe met her at Florence, Italy

DE LANCRES, Monsieur (Then and Now). Will command the six hundred lancers from Milan to be sent to Caesar

Borgia for his attack upon Parma

DELILAH (Ashenden/Mr. Harrington's Washing). The name by which J.Q. Harrington addressed Anastasia Alexandrovna Leondidov

DELLA CERCOLA, Princess Flora (Our Betters). Formerly Miss van Hoog; married at age twenty; separated from her husband, an Italian, when their only child died; a friend of Pearl Grayston; age thirty-five; tall and thin; pale, haggard face; large dark eyes; gentle and kind; has wealth and distinction

DELLA CERCOLA, Prince Marino (Our Betters). The Italian husband of Flora Della Cercola; small and ordinary; his family had been ruined by speculation

DELLA MIRANDOLA, Lodovico (Then and Now). He headed the advanced guard of fifteen hundred of Caesar Borgia's troops upon Sinigaglia

DELLA MIRANDOLA, Pico (Making of a Saint). Young; long oval face; bones of the face and chin very strongly marked; skin like brown ivory; black hair that fell over his forehead and ears; large and melancholy brown eyes

DELLA ROVERE, Giuliano (Then and Now). A bitter enemy of the Borgias; succeeds Pius II (1405-1464) to the papal throne as Pope Julius II (1443-1513); vindictive, crafty, unscrupulous, ruthless

DELLA ROVERE, Leonardo (Making of a Saint). Father of Pope Sixtus IV (1414-1484); founder of the family; a common sailor at Rovese

DELLA TRECCIA, Amtrogio (Making of a Saint). Was one of Giulia dall' Aste's lovers; on one occasion almost caught by old Bartolomeo Moratini; he had had to slip out of Donna Giulia's window to escape unnoticed

DE LORQUA, Ramiro (Then and Now). The most trusted of Caesar Borgia's commanders; good soldier and an able administrator; governor of Romagna, where his cruelty and dishonesty made him hated by the people; he conducted the retreat of the routed forces after the battle of Fossombrone, thus saving them to fight for another day; reported to have been a lover of Lucrezia Borgia; arrested and beheaded by Caesar Borgia

DE LOSAS, Duchess of (Punctiliousness of Don Sebastian) Second wife of the first Don Sebastian; the richest heiress in Spain

Characters

DE LOSAS, Seventh Duke of (Punctiliousness of Don Sebastian). His only son had not been born of any duchess

DE MANTONA, Pablo (Punctiliousness of Don Sebastian). Brother of the first Duque de Losas; archbishop of the See; great favorite of the King and of the Pope; a connoisseur; as a young priest, he assisted in the marriage ceremony of Don Sebastian and Dona Sodina; Don Sebastian's only living relative; poisoned by Don Sebastian

DE MERODE, Mlle. Cleo (Of Human Bondage). She had made popular the fashion of wearing the hair over the ears

DE MEYER, Baron and Baroness (Narrow Corner). Seated in the omnibus box at a Covent Garden theatre, London; she caught Dr. Saunders' eye and bowed

DE MEDICI, Lorenzo (Making of a Saint). The Florentine statesman and ruler ((1449-1492); Checco d'Orsi has commercial transactions with him at Florence that need to be concluded; bent, wrinkled, and mean; ugly features; a large coarse nose; heavy sensual mouth; small, sharp and glittering eyes; thin, short hair; muddy, yellowed, and wrinkled skin; refuses to assist Checco d'Orsi against the invading forces of Lodovico Sforza

DE MONTADOUR, Emily (Razor's Edge). A member of the Franco-American set at Paris; Elliott Templeton tries unsuccessfully to convince Larry Darrell to meet her

DE MORET, Count (Noble Spaniard). The French husband of Kate De Moret

DE MORET, Countess Kate (Noble Spaniard). English wife of Count De Moret

DENBY, Dr. (Honolulu). A Honolulu physician who attends to Captain Butler

DENISIEV, Alexander (Ashenden/Mr. Harrington's Washing) The father of Anastasia Alexandrova Leonidov; he is a revolutionary who had escaped from Siberia after being sentenced to penal servitude for life; then had settled in England; a writer

DENNIS, Miss (Home and Beauty). Manicurist of Victoria Cardew-Lowndes; age twenty-five; neat and trim; with slight cockney accent; engaged

DENNISON, Dr. (Painted Veil). A prosperous surgeon; Geoffrey Dennison's father; had received a baronetcy during the war; said that he had never seen a child finer than his grandson

DENNISON, Geoffrey (Painted Veil). Becomes engaged to Doris Garstin and eventually marries her; the only son of a prosperous surgeon; he will inherit both his father's title and comfortable fortune

DENNORANT, Lady Cecily (Theatre). Formerly Lady Cecily Laweston; wife of Lord George Dennorant; pretty; at the London restaurant where Thomas Fennell and Julia Gosselyn dine

DENNORANT, Lord George (Theatre). The husband of Lady Cecily Dennorant; is at the London restaurant where Thomas Fennell and Julia Gosselyn dine

DENNORANT, Marquess of (Theatre). The father of Charles Tamerley; had married an heiress

DENTIST (Bishop's Mantle). Always administered gas to Theodore Spratte when extracting a tooth

DENTIST (Circle). Fitted Lord Hughie Porteus with new teeth; told Lady Catherine Champion-Cheney that her teeth would last until she is fifty; as he scrapes his patients' teeth, he tells them about the Dowager Empress of China

DENTIST (Razor's Edge). At Paris; he is very busy; Joan Maturin a patient of his

DENTIST (Treasure). He will see Richard Harenger on Tuesday, the sixth of the month

DENVER, Joan (Theatre). One of the two girls whom Tom Fennell and Roger Gosselyn picked up after they had been to the theatre; age between nineteen and twenty-two; pretty little face; snub nose; close cropped curls; had been a student with Avice Crichton at the Royal Academy of Dramatic Arts; Tom knew her; Jill's roommate; an actress; asked Roger if he could get her an understudy in Julia Gosselyn's next play; puts an end to Roger's virginity

DE PAOLI, Joseph (French Joe). Age ninety-three; known as French Joe; had lived in the hospital on Thursday Island; is small and shriveled; a Corsican; vivacious eyes, short white beard, bushy black eyebrows; he had entered the French army in 1851

DE PORNICHET, Lucien (Marriage of Convenience, 1906). A French consul at a village on an island off the coast of Tunis; small; grey hair cut very short; large grey moustache, excessively fierce and bristling; alert eyes; trim and neat figure; age fifty-seven; husband of Sophie de Pornichet; formerly a major in the colonial army at Algeria, Senegal, and Tonquin; forced to retire at age forty-five because of ill health

DE PORNICHET, Sophie (Marriage of Convenience, 1906). Wife of Lucien de Pornichet; Swiss; from Geneva; she is devoted to English novels; a polished linguist; amiable and stately; her cousin reportedly a professor at the Sorbonne; she married Lucien at age thirty

DEPUTY BARMAN (Gigolo and Gigolette). At the Casino

DEPUTY PUBLIC PROSECUTOR (Letter [story]). Prosecutes the case of the Crown vs. Crosbie; he is a kindly man

DE RAIS, Gilles (Magician). Practiced human sacrifice at his castle

DE RETHEL, Marquise (Razor's Edge). Appointed to the embassy at Madrid; he is willing to sublet his rez-de chaussee to Larry Darrell

DE ROUEN, Cardinal (Then and Now). First minister to the King of France

DE SAINT ORME, Marquise (Love in a Cottage). A guest at Sybil Bruce's fancy dress ball at Paris

DE SAN JOSE, Dona Ana (Catalina). The mistress of the novitiates at the Convent of the Incarnation; she is discreet, intelligent, reliable; totally devoted to Prioress Dona Beatriz

DETECTIVE (Appearance and Reality). Private investigator hired by Raymond Le Sueur; inquires about Lisette

DETECTIVE (Christmas Holiday). Interviewed the tailor who made Robert Berger's grey suit

DETECTIVE (Happy Couple). Sent from Scotland Yard to investigate Miss Wingford's murder

DETECTIVE (Home and Beauty). Called in by Miss Montmorency to protect her from Gentleman #6

DETECTIVES (Ashenden/Giulia Lazzari). Two of them; they escort Giulia Lazzari on the train from Boulogne to Paris; then they accompany her and Ashenden to Thonon

DETECTIVES (Christmas Holiday). Two of them; come to take Robert Berger to the Commissariat

DETECTIVES (Tenth Man). From Scotland Yard; George Winter believes that they are on their way to arrest him

DE TROYE, Adrienne (Razor's Edge). Isabel Maturin met her at a dress show in Paris; the smartest kept woman in the city; age forty-five; not pretty

DE VALERO, Blasco Suarez (Catalina). Bishop of Segovia and canon of Malaga; the eldest son of Juan Suarez and Violante de Valero; brother of Manuel and Martin De Valero; had been a student with Domingo Perez at the seminary of Alcala de Henares; when as a young seminarian home on leave to recoup his health, he had caught the attention of Beatriz Henriquez y Braganza; he held the degrees of Master of Arts and Doctor of Theology; entered the monastic order of the Dominicans; appointed professor of theology at the university of the Alcala de Henares; became, at age thirty-seven, Inquisitor of the Holy Office at Valencia; head shaven, except for a ring of black hair touched with grey; hollow temples; sunken cheeks; a deeply lined face; large, dark, luminous eyes

DE VALERO, Consuelo (Catalina). Daughter and only child of a baker and the wife of Martin de Valero; she bore her husband four children

DE VALERO, Juan Suarez (Catalina). Father of Blasco, Martin, and Manuel de Valero; husband of Violante; an old and a very pure Christian, but a very poor one

DE VALERO, Manuel (Catalina). A captain in the King's armies and Count of San Costanzo, Kingdom of Naples; the second son of Juan Suarez and Violante de Valero; brother of Blasco and Martin de Valero; handsome and strong; bold black eyes and handsome moustache; he is conceited; he served the Duke of Alva and helped King Philip II regain the northern provinces; received the Order of Calatrava; unscrupulous, ruthless, intrepid, able; age forty-five

DE VALERO, Martin (Catalina). Third son and last child of Juan Suarez and Violante de Valero; the brother of Blasco and Manuel de Valero; good natured; content to farm his father's property; is married to Consuelo de Valero, the daughter of a baker; proposes, after the death of his father-in-law, to operate the bakery, and he does so with considerable success; age thirty-four; jolly, red-faced, corpulent

DE VALERO, Violante (Catalina). The daughter of a gentleman of Castel Rodriguez; wife of Don Juan Suarez de Valero; mother of Blasco, Manuel, and Martin--the three of her ten children who survived adolescence

Characters

DE VENDOME, Duchess (Razor's Edge). Supposedly told the Abbe of the high level of Elliott Templeton's intelligence

DEVERILL, Charley (Theatre). An old Paris friend of Julia Lambert Gosselyn; made her clothes for her; he takes Julia to dinner at the Bois

DE VIERNOT, Madame (Painted Veil). A widowed friend of the Mother Superior's family; she left for the Carmel without telling any of her relatives

DE VRIES, Dolly (Theatre). Age sixty; widow; short and very fat; a fine Jewish nose and fine Jewish eyes; heavy red lips; short hair dyed a rich copper; a loud and deep voice; Roger Gosselyn's godmother; she had advanced the money for Michael and Julia Gosselyn to begin their own theatre company, and thus she owned shares in it

DEXTER, Archie (Theatre). The husband of Grace Hardwell Dexter; Julia Lambert Gosselyn's leading man in The Powder Puff; a quick wit

DEXTER, Grace Hardwell (Theatre). An actress and the wife of Archie Dexter; pretty

DIAGHILEV, Sergei Pavlovich (Ashenden/Mr. Harrington's Washing). Russian ballet producer and art critic; he frequented the Regent Park section of London

DICK (Bad Example). The office boy at Hanes, Bryan, and Company, London; he usually arrived at the office two minutes before James Clinton

DICKENSON, Dr. (Camel's Back). Summoned to the Lefevre house by Hermione Lefevre; he finds everyone in good health; then administers a psychiatric examination to Valentine Lefevre

DIMITRI, Grand Duke (Razor's Edge). Elliott Templeton, although in bed following an attack of uremia, plans to lunch with him on Saturday

DINAH (Mrs. Craddock). An Irish terrier once owned by Edward Craddock; had litters as regular as clockwork

DINNER GUEST (Jane). Balding; white hair; sharp, intelligent face

DIOGENIDIA, George (Ashenden/Hairless Mexican). Fictitious "friend" of Manuel Carmona

DIPLOMATIST (Caesar's Wife). Stuffy and old; asks Lady Violet Arthur to dance

DIPLOMATIST (Lady Frederick). He told risque stories to

Lady Frederick Berolles all through dinner

DIRECTOR #1 (Christmas Holiday). Of the hotel in the Rue St. Honore, Paris; spoke fluent English

DIRECTOR #2 (Christmas Holiday). Of the hotel near the Gare Montparnasse off the Rue de Rennes, Paris; takes Charley Mason to his room; affable; he spoke perfect English and wore a morning coat

DIRECTOR (Explorer [novel]). Of the North East Africa Trading Company; a friend of Walker's family; offered Walker a position after the latter had squandered his inheritance

DIRECTOR (Man with a Conscience). He is Jean Charvin's employer at Le Havre; he has business connections at Lille, Lyons, and Marseilles; he asks Charvin if Utel would hire Henri Renard

DIRECTORS (Explorer [novel]). Of the North East Africa Trading Company; gladly accepted Alec MacKenzie's offer to join their forces with his in exploiting the commercial possibilities of the area; grow anxious when they hear nothing from Alec; proposed to have a question raised in Parliament or begin an outcry in the newspapers which would oblige the government to relieve or avenge Alec; they communicate with Alec relative to annexing the former slave trade district to the British Empire

DIRK, Lord Philip (Mrs. Craddock). Confided to Arthur Branderton that he had not often seen one ride as well as did Edward Craddock; he invites Edward to a tennis tournament and a ball

DI SAN GIORGIO, Cardinal (Then and Now). Purchased the pseudo antique cupid in marble by Michaelangelo Buonarotti from a dealer; returned it to the dealer when he discovered that is was a fraud

DI SAN PIETRO, Count Carlo (Woman of Fifty). Age fifty; is tall, thin, and handsome; dark liquid eyes; thick snow-white hair; a bronzed face; the widowed and poor father of Tito di San Pietro; lives in a fifteenth-century villa thirty miles from Florence; formerly in the Italian diplomatic service, an attache in London

DI SAN PIETRO, Tito (Woman of Fifty). Age twenty-six; the son of Count Carlo di San Pietro; an admirer of Laura Clayton, whom he eventually marries; a bold and reckless poker player; good looking; medium height;

Characters

black eyes, thick brown hair, olive skin

DISRAELI, Benjamin (Mrs. Craddock). British statesman (1804-1881); at Mrs. Branderton's dinner party, Atthill Bacot tells the story about Disraeli and the agricultural laborer

DISSENTING MINISTERS (Of Human Bondage). Three of them, at Blackstable, Kent; Louisa Carey would cross on the other side of the street so as to avoid meeting them

DISTRICT OFFICER (End of the Flight). A friend of the Narrator; sturdy, ruddy, and jovial; age thirty-five; the Narrator relates a "funny" story to him

DISTRICT OFFICER (Flotsam and Jetsam). Investigated the murder of Jack Carr

DISTRICT VISITOR (Of Human Bondage). A nurse to the poor mothers of newborn infants; opened windows without asking and poked her nose into corners

DIVORCEE (Explorer [novel]). An American; swooned when Richard Lomax poured into her shell-like ear facts about the McKinley tariff (1890)

DIXON, Howard (Camel's Back). Engaged to Enid Lefevre; tells Hermione Lefevre that Enid has broken off the engagement

DOCTOR (Ashenden/Giulia Lazzari). He pronounces Chandra Lal dead from Prussic acid

DOCTOR #1 (Bad Example). Said that the seventy-year-old man was terribly emaciated and that he had died from starvation; shrugged his shoulders when he announced that the two-year-old child had died from starvation; he announced that there were signs on the body of the twenty-two-year-old girl of extremely great privation

DOCTOR #2 (Bad Example). A slow, cautious Scotsman; he claimed that James Clinton had caught cold and he had something wrong with his lungs; then determined that Clinton had typhoid

DOCTOR (Bishop's Apron). According to Theodore Spratte, he has advised Canon Spratte to take horse exercise

DOCTOR (Book-Bag). He attempts to prevent Featherstone from seeing Olive Hardy

DOCTOR (Cakes and Ale). Advises Rosie Iggulden to keep down her weight

DOCTOR (Casual Affair). A guest at the Lows' dinner party

DOCTOR (Catalina). He attends Bishop Blasco de Valero

after the latter has received penance from Antonio and another friar; orders the Bishop to remain in bed

DOCTOR #1 (Christmas Holiday). Informs the girl at the Serail, Paris, that she must be operated on at once

DOCTOR #2 (Christmas Holiday). Escaped from the penal colony, French Guiana; practicing somewhere in South America and doing well

DOCTOR (East of Suez). He has treated George Conway's knife wound; says that George is perfectly all right

DOCTOR #1 (Explorer [novel]). Of Richard Lomas; he has ordered Dick to go abroad for the rest of the winter; Dick wrote the prescription and gave him two guineas

DOCTOR #2 (Explorer [novel]). On the Isle of Wight; an old man, touched by Lucy Allerton's grief; examines Fred Allerton after his release from prison; he tells Lucy that he can only alleviate her father's pain

DOCTOR (Home and Beauty). After William Cardew's death, he told Victoria Cardew that she would need considerable attention for the next ten years

DOCTOR (Hour Before the Dawn). At the French village near Michel's farm; Jeannette brings him to care for Roger Henderson; rough, uncouth; nervous; competent

DOCTOR (Land of Promise). He attended Emma Sharp at the birth of only one of her children

DOCTOR #1 (Liza of Lambeth). Said that Mrs. Kemp was to be rubbed with liniment that he prescribed for her

DOCTOR #2 (Liza of Lambeth). Delivered Liza Kemp; he thought (according to Mrs. Kemp) that Mrs. Kemp would not survive the ordeal of childbirth

DOCTOR #3 (Liza of Lambeth). Treats Kitie Stanley for her cut head at the hospital

DOCTOR #4 (Liza of Lambeth). Treats Liza Kemp after her miscarriage

DOCTOR #1 (Man of Honour). Tells Jenny Bush that she is going to have a child

DOCTOR #2 (Man of Honour). He tends to Jenny Bush after the birth of her baby; sends a bill for fifty pounds

DOCTOR #1 (Merry-Go-Round). Tells Jenny Bush that she is going to have a child

DOCTOR #2 (Merry-Go-Round). At Tercanbury, Kent; he attends to Herbert Field during the latter's illness

DOCTOR #3 (Merry-Go-Round). At Rome; explained to Bella and Herbert Field the condition of Herbert's lungs;

Characters 127

agreed that Herbert ought to go to Naples
DOCTOR #4 (Merry-Go-Round). He warned Bella Field that Herbert could die at any moment
DOCTOR #5 (Merry-Go-Round). He has tended Jenny Kent during her illness; he sends a bill for fifty pounds
DOCTOR #6 (Merry-Go-Round). At Tercanbury, Kent; tends to Herbert Field during his last hemorrhage; brings Herbert back to consciousness
DOCTOR #7 (Merry-Go-Round). At London; by Jenny Kent's body; had stopped all efforts to restore life; offers to walk home with Basil Kent
DOCTOR #1 (Moon and Sixpence). At Paris; he prescribes medicines for Charles Strickland
DOCTOR #2 (Moon and Sixpence). Attends Blanche Stroeve after she takes the oxalic acid; a small, bearded man
DOCTOR (Mother). He arrives immediately following the death of Rosalia
DOCTOR (Mr. Know-All). Ship's physician; the Narrator, Max Kelada, and Ramsay are seated at his table; lazy
DOCTOR #1 (Mrs. Craddock). At Naples, Italy; he thought it strange that Bertha Ley should remain alone there after the death of her father
DOCTOR #2 (Mrs. Craddock). At London; Bertha Craddock sees him periodically for an imaginary illness
DOCTOR #1 (Narrow Corner). English; treated the foreign residents of Fu-chou
DOCTOR #2 (Narrow Corner). At Singapore; told Captain Nichols that his dyspepsia came from domestic unpleasantness
DOCTOR #3 (Narrow Corner). On Kanda; a half-caste; Catherine Frith beyond his help by the time he had reached her bungalow
DOCTOR #4 (Narrow Corner). He declared that Mrs. Hudson needed a complete change
DOCTOR #5 (Narrow Corner). Fred Blake's uncle and his mother's brother; would not send Fred to the hospital until the scarlet fever symptoms declared themselves
DOCTOR Neil MacAdam). Was introduced to Neil MacAdam at Kuala Solor by Captain Bredon; he is small and brisk
DOCTOR (Noblest Act). At Singapore; he told Mrs. Farley that there was nothing seriously the matter with her
DOCTOR #1 (Of Human Bondage). At Mrs. Carey's bedside; removes the child, Philip, from his mother's bed and

hands him to the nurse

DOCTOR #2 (Of Human Bondage). He suggested that Philip Carey's convalescence from scarlet fever be spent by the seaside

DOCTOR #3 (Of Human Bondage). Tends to Mildred Rogers' pregnancy; he informs her that she should expect no trouble; charges fifteen guineas

DOCTOR #4 (Of Human Bondage). Operated a dispensary at Fulham Road, London; would not hire Philip Carey as an unqualified assistant

DOCTOR #5 (Of Human Bondage). The new man at Blackstable, Kent; had been there for ten years; clever; not much of a practice among the better people

DOCTOR #6 (Of Human Bondage). At Farnley, Dorsetshire; on the cliff; attends to the wealthy

DOCTOR (P.&O.). Is extremely attentive to Mrs. Linsell

DOCTOR (Penelope). A mere nobody who had rudely treated Mrs. Watson; he told her that she had nothing wrong with her

DOCTOR #1 (Razor's Edge). A specialist in diabetes; at London

DOCTOR #2 (Razor's Edge). The Narrator, as a young man, knew him; rather than practice, he spent time in the British Museum; he wrote and published, at his own expense four or five pseudoscientific, pseudophilosophic books that no one read; married, with a wife and two children

DOCTOR #3 (Razor's Edge). Tends to Elliott Templeton on the French Riviera; sees his patient twice a week and injects into an alternate buttock a hypodermic needle with the fashionable serum of the moment; recommends the cure at Montecatini, a spa in the north of Italy; he refuses to allow Elliott to drink alcohol; takes a grave view of Templeton's condition after the attack of uremia; Elliott tells him that he must cure him by Saturday, in time for luncheon

DOCTOR #4 (Razor's Edge). At Paris; retained by Larry Darrell to look after Sophie Macdonald

DOCTOR (Sanatorium). A specialist; tells Henry Chester that he might be able to return to work in two years

DOCTOR (Sheppey). Has his coat stolen from his car by Jim Cooper

DOCTOR (Taipan). He reads The Times in the club reading

room
DOCTOR #1 (Three Fat Women of Antibes). At Carlsbad; he treated Miss Hickson, Mrs. Richman, Mrs. Sutcliffe with the same ruthlessness; he cooked vegetable soup that tasted like hot water into which a cabbage had been well rinsed
DOCTOR #2 (Three Fat Women of Antibes). He tells Lena Finch that she must eat; recommended that she drink burgundy at lunch and champagne at dinner
DOCTOR #1 (Unconquered). Of the village near the Perier farm; had been called into the army
DOCTOR #2 (Unconquered). At Soissons; an old man and a devout Catholic
DOCTOR #3 (Unconquered). At Soissons; an old man; was arrested by the German and held hostage
DOCTOR (Virtue). He administers a sedative to Margery Bishop
DOCTOR (Winter Cruise). Is seated at the same table as Venetia Reid, Captain Erdmann, the chief engineer, and the first mate; age sixty; thin grey hair, grey moustache; small, bright blue eyes; silent and bitter
DOCTOR'S DAUGHTER (Razor's Edge). Of Doctor #2; is very pretty; a second-rate actress who played small parts with second-rate companies in the provinces; returned home to nurse her ill mother
DOCTOR'S SON (Cakes and Ale). At Blackstable, Kent; had gone to school with Ashenden; succeeded his father in the practice; a fine head; has three grandchildren
DOCTOR'S SON (Razor's Edge). Of Doctor #2; he wanted a career in the army; no money available to send him to Sandhurst; enlisted; killed in the war
DOCTOR'S WIFE (Footprints in the Jungle). She asks Mrs. Bronson (later Mrs, Cartwright) if she were not tired of having a stranger (Theo Cartwright) in the house
DOCTOR'S WIFE (Razor's Edge). Of Doctor #2; became ill after years of drudgery
DOCTORS (Catalina). Examine Catalina after she has been trampled by the bull; pricked her leg with needles; bled and purged her
DOCTORS (Catalina). Cannot discover why Beatriz loses her appetite and her high spirits
DOCTORS (Razor's Edge). Inform Louisa Bradley that she has developed diabetes

DOCTORS (Sanatorium). Dr. Lennox's assistants; care for the patients when Lennox goes fishing

DOCTORS (Then and Now). Are consulted by Giuliano degla Albertelli and his wife in their attempt to conceive a child

DOG (Landed Gentry). Of Mrs. Insoley; male; he sits on various laps and chairs

DOMINICAN FRIAR (Then and Now). He is Monna Costanza's confessor at Forli

DOMINICAN FRIARS (Catalina). Three of them; hoods drawn over their shaven heads; they follow the Bishop and his secretaries to the Carmelite church

DON AGOSTO (Closed Shop). Proprietor of the Grand Hotel

DON MANUEL (Closed Shop). Current president; had once been employed by Madame Coralie as errand boy; tall, stout, and handsome

DON PEDRO the Cruel (Point of Honour). A character in Pedro Calderon's El Medico de su Honora (c.1629)

DON SEBASTIAN Emanuel de Mantona (Punctiliousness of Don Sebastian). The first Duque de Losas; small black moustache; a stern heavy face; prominent cheek bones; sensual lips; a massive chin; husband of Dona Sidona, to whom he had been engaged since age ten and married when he had reached age twenty-two; he poisons his brother, Pablo de Mantona; after the death of Dona Sidona, goes to Madrid, where he becomes an advisor to the King and receives the appointment as Admiral of the Fleet; created Duke de Losas and marries the richest heiress in Spain

DON SEBASTIAN Emanuel de Mantona (Punctiliousness of Don Sebastian). Present Duque de Losas; at Xiormonez, Spain; is small and dark; the crown of his hair less than thin; charged one franc per person to view the bones of his ancestors; he sold to the Narrator, for thirty-one shillings and threepence, the manuscript account of how Dona Sodina had raised her husband to the highest dignities in Spain; is a bachelor and the last of his line; he has not yet reached age forty

DONA SODINA DE BERRUGUETE (Punctiliousness of Don Sebastian). First wife of the first Don Sebastian; fat and broad face; short graceful nose; little, nobbly chin; thick neck; married Don Sebastian at age sixteen; she died fifteen years later from having eaten

Characters 131

excessively of pickled shrimps; had an affair with Pablo de Mantona

DONALDSON (Straight Flush). A Scot; is short and stout; red, clean-shaven face; no hair; gentle eyes; now age seventy-nine; had gone to California as a boy and had made considerable money from mining; formerly a heavy drinker and a desperate gambler; is on board the ship from Hong Kong

DONALDSON, Mr. (Of Human Bondage). A young electrical engineer; he proposes to Sally Athelny; good looking, fair, and clean shaven; pleasant regular features; an honest face; tall

DONIANI, Prince (Lady Frederick). He will be asked to lunch by Lady Frederick Berolles; a handsome fellow

DONNA LUCIA (Lotus Eater). The wife of the host at Morgano's, a cafe at Capri; middle aged and portly; she has large, liquid eyes; once a recognized beauty

DONS (Explorer [novel]). At Oxford; according to Dick Lomas, only they wanted to read Alec MacKenzie's verses, which he composed in the classical languages

DOORMAN (Mabel). At the British Consulate in Cheng-tu, the capital of Szechuan

DOORMAN (Magician). At Oliver Haddo's estate, Skene, in Staffordshire; husband of the lodgekeeper and father of the boy; he tries to prevent Arthur Burdon from entering the house

DORANTE (Perfect Gentleman). A friend of Monsieur Jourdain; he owes Jourdain sixteen hundred louis; he is elegant, condescending, and aristocratic; is in love with Dorimene

DORIA, Andrea (Then and Now). A Genoese commander and statesman (1466?-1560); left to defend the citadel of Sinigaglia after the widow of the Duke of Urbino and her son fled the city; bribed by both the Orsini and Caesar Borgia to refuse to surrender the citadel to no one but Borgia

DORIMENE, Countess (Perfect Gentleman). An attractive widow

DORIS (Force of Circumstance). Married to Guy; before marriage secretary to a member of Parliament; brown eyes, short dark hair; only child of a widowed mother

DORMER, Clementine (Razor's Edge). A friend or acquaintance of Isabel Bradley; her house had been decorated by Gregory Brabazon

D'ORSAY, Count (Irish Gentleman). He had given a ring to Robert O'Donnel

DORSET, Eleo (Our Betters). Took lessons from Woman #2 and with in three months she lost her American accent

D'ORSI, Checco (Making of a Saint). Husband of Clarice d'Orsi; son of Orso d'Orsi; cousin of Matteo d'Orsi; age forty; has sons; tall, thin, and dark; full beard and moustache; dark hair and brown eyes; eight years ago he did all he could to bring the town of Forli to the allegiance of Count Girolamo Riario; his life threatened by Girolamo; under pressure to engage in an assassination attempt on Girolamo; kills Girolamo on 14 April 1488; he escapes with other conspirators from Forli to Citta di Castello; after a year there journeys to Rome (with Filippo Brandolini) to seek papal assistance in an attack upon Forli; after six years, he dies in exile, suffering of a broken heart

D'ORSI CHILDREN (Making of a Saint). Of Checco and Clarice d'Orsi; they play at hide and seek and bind man's bluff with Filippo Brandolini; are embraced by Checco during his day of triumph; leave Forli with their mother in light of the impending siege

D'ORSI, Clarice (Making of a Saint). The wife of Checco d'Orsi and mother of their children; refuses to leave Forli at the time of the planned assassination upon Girolamo Riario; is embraced by her husband during his day of triumph; leaves Forli with her children prior to the siege of the city

D'ORSI, Matteo (Making of a Saint). A cousin of Checco d'Orsi; brings Filippo Brandolini to Checco's house at Forli; dark hair and eyes; a broad face; prominent bones; the rough skin of a soldier; he escapes from Forli with Checco and arrives at Citta di Castello; returns to the life of a soldier of fortune; dies in a battle against a foreign invader

D'ORSI, Count Orso (Making of a Saint). The father of Checco d'Orsi; age eighty-five; deaf and blind; weak and decrepit; dead eyes; sunken and wrinkled cheeks; long, shriveled hands that tremble incessantly; thin, weak, and trembling voice; he remains quietly in his room; originally opposed to the appointment of Count Girolamo Riario as Lord of Forli; excellent in war and in all of the arts of peace; noted for his skill in commerce; was the first politician of his city; a great and generous patron of the arts; he refuses to leave Forli at the time of the planned assassination of Girolamo Riario; refuses again to leave Forli at the time of the impending siege; would rather die in his own town and palace; than rush about the country in search of safety; he refuses a third time to leave Forli and escape with Checco from the wrath of Lodovico Sforza; is carried off to prison after the mob ransacks the palace; is placed on an ass and led into the piazza; forced to witness the destruction of the Orsi Palace, stone by stone; is put to death by being dragged around the piazza by the hangman, tied at the end of his horse; is buried in the cloisters of the church at Forli

DOS PALOS, Duchess de (Romantic Young Lady). Mother of Pilar Carreon; was married at age fifteen; a widow of high birth and social connection; on bad terms with the Countess de Marbella

DOS PALOS, Duke of (Romantic Young Lady). Son of the Duchess de Dos Palos; cannot, of course, fight a duel with the Countess de Marbella's coachman

DOUGLAS (Back of Beyond). Plays billiards against Tom Saffary at the club at Timbang Belud

DOWAGER (Explorer [novel]). Asked Richard Lomas of his intentions; Dick flung at her astonished head an article from the Encyclopaedia Britannica

DOWAGER (Mrs. Dot). She once asked James Blenkinsop his intentions; he flung at her head an entire article from the Encyclopaedia Britannica

DOWAGER MARCHIONESS (Loaves and Fishes). According to Lady Sophia Spratte, Theodore Spratte discusses the simple life with her at tea-table

DOWAGERS (Circle). Used to jump on chairs to get a good look at Mrs. Langtry whenever she came into a drawing room

DRACHMANN, Holger (Narrow Corner). Noted Danish poet, dramatist, and novelist (1846-1908); a friend of Erik Christessen's father; came often to the Christessen house

DRAGOMAN (In a Strange Land). Hands the Narrator a hot water bottle from Signora Niccolini

DRAPER (Narrow Corner). From Liverpool; father of Mrs. Nichols

DRAPER (Sheppey). A Baptist, and one of Bessie Legros' regulars at her flat in Kensington; came on Tuesdays and Fridays; talked religion after he had his bit of fun

DRAYTON (Point of Law). A clerk in the law firm of Ad-Addishaw, Jones, and Braham; pale and young; he witnesses the signature of the Narrator's will

DRESSMAKER (Christmas Holiday). At Paris; "a little woman 'round the corner'" who made Venetia Mason's dresses

DRESSMAKER (Explorer [novel]). To Julia Crowley; charming

DRESSMAKER (Explorer [play]). To Nellie Crowley; charming

DRESSMAKER (Flirtation). To Mrs. Parnaby; charming

DRESSMAKER (Kite). A little woman; she lives around the corner from Beatrice Sunbury; made black dresses for her

DRESSMAKER (Magician). Of Margaret Dauncey at Paris; Margaret sent her newly purchased clothes to her

DRESSMAKER (Mrs. Craddock). Bertha Ley's, at Naples, Italy; she is "not bad"

DRESSMAKER #1 (Of Human Bondage). At Blackstable; down the street from the vicarage; had made Louisa Carey's tight black dress

DRESSMAKER #2 (Of Human Bondage). She makes a dress for Mildred Rogers; Philip Carey refuses to pay for it

DRESSMAKER (Razor's Edge). At a village in Anjou; Suzanne Rouvier apprenticed to her at age fifteen, for two years

DRESSMAKER (Smith). Of Emily Chapman; willing to lend Emily the money to pay her debt until she (Emily) gets married

DREW, John (Theatre). American theatre manager; offers Michael Gosselyn a part in his company

DRIFFIELD, Amy (Cakes and Ale). Widow and second wife of Edward Driffield; almost forty years younger than her husband; formerly a hospital nurse; she married Edward Driffield after she had nursed him through an attack of pneumonia; Alroy Kear had just recently stayed with her; Ashenden had lunched with Driffield

Characters

and her six years ago; wrote to the press in support of having her husband buried near Blackstable, Kent; at age forty-five when Ashenden first met her; small sallow face; with neat sharp features; slight figure, neither tall nor short; trim, competent, alert; is a great talker; gay and sprightly

DRIFFIELD DAUGHTER (Cakes and Ale). Of Rose and Edward Driffield; the reason for their marriage; she died of meningitis when she was six years old

DRIFFIELD, Edward (Cakes and Ale). On his last visit to London, he lunched with Alroy Kear at the latter's club in St. James's Street; died at age eighty-four; one of the greatest novelists of the day; the last of the Victorians; his collected works run to thirty-seven volumes; Ashenden first met him at Blackstable, Kent; he used to sing in the church choir; short; bearded; pale blue eyes; good humored expression; was born in Blackstable parish; was educated at Haversham School; ran away to sea; drove a cab at Maidstone; he had been a clerk in a booking office at Birmingham; taught young Ashenden how to ride a bicycle; he and Rosie Driffield lived at Lime Cottage, Blackstable, next to the Congregational church; leaves Blackstable for London, and becomes literary editor of a weekly paper; divorces Rosie Driffield; six years before his death, he appears very thin; head barely covered with fine silvery hair; clean shaven; skin almost transparent; very pale blue eyes; rims of his eyelids red; white false teeth; thin and pallid lips; a wrinkled scraggy neck

DRIFFIELD, Rosie (Cakes and Ale). Formerly Rosie Gann, the daughter of Josiah Gann; she and Mary Ann went to Sunday School together; was the first wife of Edward Driffield; formerly a barmaid for three years at the Railway Arms, Blackstable, Kent, then at the Prince of Wales's Feathers, Haversham; extremely unfaithful to her husband (the twenty--year-old Ashenden among one of her activities); ample golden hair; was over thirty years of age when young Ashenden first met her; unexpectedly meets Ashenden in London during his term as a medical student at St. Luke's Hospital; her skin as smooth as a child's; short, thick nose; small eyes, a large mouth; blue eyes; red, sensual lips; no color in her face; pale golden hair; a reader of historical biography; eventually runs off with George Kemp and ends in the Albermarle Hotel, Yonkers, New York, under the name of Rosie Iggulden; now at least seventy years of age when Ashenden last sees her: her nails blood colored, eyebrows plucked; is stout and double chinned; a red bosom and face; white hair; her teeth the best that money could buy

DRISCOLL, Professor (Road Uphill). Professor of Psychology at the university; he is impressed by Joseph Sheridan's book

DRIVER (Cakes and Ale). Of a four-wheeler; in the fried fish shop in Horseferry Row, London

DRIVER (Magician). Of a Paris cab; Susie Boyd tells him where she, Arthur Burden, and Margaret Dauncey want to go; held his horse's neck after Oliver Haddo had touched it

DRIVER (Moon and Sixpence). Of the carriage that returns Dirk Stroeve and the Narrator from Blanche's funeral; asks his passengers where they wished to be let off

DRIVER (Razor's Edge). At Lens; of the tractor that hauled the trucks carrying the coal from the mine to the elevators; a poor mechanic; is succeeded by Larry Darrell

DRIVER #1 (Traveller in Romance). Of the post chaise from St. Moritz into Italy; Germany; he gets off at Vicosoprano

DRIVER #2 (Traveller in Romance). Of the post chaise from St. Moritz into Italy; Italian; he gets on at Vicosoprano; he called upon San Antonio whenever the four horses stumbled

DRUMMERS (Making of a Saint). A part of the escort for the execution of Pietro Albanese and Marco Scorsacana at the piazza in Forli; beat their drums incessantly and maddeningly

DRUNKEN REVELER (Up at the Villa). In a car on a secluded road about five miles from Mary Panton's villa in Florence; sings "La Donna e mobile"

DRUNKS (Razor's Edge). In a large sedan in Chicago; driving eighty miles per hour; crashed head on into Bob Macdonald's car, thus killing him and his child

DRYADE (Perfect Gentleman). In the opera. The Island of

Naxos; companion of Ariadne

DRYLAND, Rev. (Hero). The father of Thomas Dryland; for over a quarter of a century, the vicar of Easterham

DRYLAND, Thomas (Hero). The curate of Little Primpton, Kent; large and stout; reddish hair; his complexion like squashed strawberries and cream; a large, heavy, and hairless face; scanty red eyebrows; blue eyes; a small mouth; possessed a fine sense of order; a fat, full, and modulated voice; age thirty-three; directed the welcoming home ceremony for James Parsons; wants to marry Mary Clibborn; he proposes to Mary again a month following James Parsons' death; appointed vicar of Stone Fairly, Kent, after which Mary Clibborn finally accepts his offer of marriage

DRYSDEN, Lord Justice (Point of Law). Mr. Addishaw had to deal with his will

DUBOIS, Adele (Hour Before the Dawn). The wife of Andre Dubois; old; resides at a small villa on the coast of France, facing the sea; working in the garden; pleasant homely face; admittedly a coward

DUBOIS, Andre (Hour Before the Dawn). Resides, with his wife Adele, at a small villa on the coast of France; old; respectable in appearance; small and thin; thick grey hair; an untidy grey beard; a professor at the University of Rouen; owns a cutter that he willingly gives to Roger Henderson and Nobby Clark

DUCHESS (Caesar's Wife). Hosted a weekend party where Violet first met Sir Arthur Little

DUCHESS (Cakes and Ale). Big, young, and fat; intense admiration for Edward Driffield

DUCHESS (Catalina). Wife of the Spanish grandee; gives Catalina a gold chain

DUCHESS (Jack Straw). Arrives at the Parker-Jennings home in Cheshire

DUCHESSES (Explorer [novel]). At London; with strawberry leaves around their snowy brows; ask Dick Lomas to tea so that he will tell them of Alec MacKenzie's childhood; Dick promises to bring Alec to lunch with them

DUCLERC #1 (Razor's Edge). Older son of Madame Duclerc; a coalminer; age nineteen; tall and good looking; he will soon enter military service

DUCLERC #2 (Razor's Edge). Age eighteen; younger son of

Madame Duclerc; a coal miner; tall and good looking

DUCLERC, Madame (Razor's Edge). A widow at a mining village near Lens, in northern France; her husband had been killed, and her two sons worked in the coal mine; rents Larry Darrell a bed in her house; tall and gaunt; greying hair; large, dark eyes; two front teeth missing; good features; might have been nice looking at one time

DUCROZ, Monsieur (Of Human Bondage). At Heidelberg; he comes every day to Frau Professor Erlin's pension to teach French to Philip Carey; a citizen of Geneva; is tall and old; sallow skin and hollow cheeks; thin, long grey hair; he had fought in Italy with Garibaldi against the Pope; expelled from Geneva for political offenses; extremely poor

DUDLEY, Lady (Circle). Her picture in an old photograph album owned by Clive Champion-Cheney

DUENA (Catalina). To Beatriz Henriquez y Braganza; a widow and distantly related to the Duke of Castel Rodriguez; had lived at Castel Rodriguez all of her life; devout, censorious, and penniless; complacent regarding her mistress's reading habits; accompanied Beatriz to Mass every morning; entered a convent at Castel Rodriguez at the same time that Beatriz went to Avila

DUENAS (Spanish Priest). At Gibraltar; accompany the girls on their walks

DUKE (Catalina). A Spanish grandee; the husband of the Duchess; celebrates the marriage of his son and heir; employs the troupe of actors; gives Diego a gold ring

DUNSFORD (Of Human Bondage). A medical student at St. Luke's Hospital, London; age eighteen; fresh-complexioned; heavy; pleasant blue eyes; curly dark hair; large limbed; is slow of speech and movement; a sweet smile; from Clifton; had no friends in London; stupid but good humored

DURAND-RUEL (Of Human Bondage). Art dealer on the Rue Lafitte, Paris; always pleased to show the shabbiest student what he wanted to see

DURANT, Gwendolyn (Bishop's Apron). The only daughter of Sir John Durant; is making up her mind to marry Lionel Spratte; pretty; a complexion of robust coloring that suggested the best of health; abundant wavy

Characters 139

brown hair handsome figure; she eventually accepts Theodore Spratte's proposal of marriage

DURANT, Gwendolyn (Loaves and Fishes). She is linked romantically with Lionel Spratte; age twenty-two or twenty-three; fairly tall; languid; the daughter of a wealthy brewer; she accepts Canon Theodore Spratte's proposal of marriage

DURANT, Sir John (Bishop's Apron). A brewer; one of ten children; the father of Gwendolyn Durant and her six brothers (three of whom are still alive); told Lionel Spratte that since he had received his Jubilee baronetcy, people have been sending him, weekly, a family tree; proposes to give his daughter one hundred and fifty thousand pounds as her marriage portion; age fifty; stout; a capacious paunch; his few remaining hairs arranged judiciously over a shining pate; broad and merry face; his little eyes bright with hilarity; disproportionately short legs; is rubicand and good humored; he and the British people knew that Durant's Half-Crown Family Ale was the best beer in England; began his working life as a van boy; shrewd, blunt, outspoken

DURANT, Mr. (Loaves and Fishes). Father of Gwendolyn Durant; a brewer

DURHAM, Marie-Louise (Constant Wife). Wife of Mortimer Durham; is pretty and small; large eyes; a friend of Constance Middleton; is having an affair with John Middleton; at dinner, she told Bernard Kersal that Constance and John Middleton were the most devoted couple she had ever known

DURHAM, Mortimer (Constant Wife). The husband of Marie-Louise Durham; stout and big; age forty; red face and an irascible manner; his only ambition in life is to make a million; believes that a woman loves him just because he loves her

DUSE, Eleanora (Merry-Go-Round). Italian actress (1859-1924); according to Frank Hurrell, Londoners who rave over her do so in the name of culture

DUTCH CAPTAIN (Moon and Sixpence). Of a fishing smack; married to Dirk Stroeve's sister

DUTCH MERCHANT (Catalina). A Lutheran; caught smuggling into the country a Spanish translation of the New Testament; admitted under torture that he had given a copy to Demetrios Christopoulos

DUTCH OFFICIAL (Narrow Corner). On Kanda; in a white uniform with brass buttons; an incomprehensible name; he tells Dr. Saunders and Fred Blake that Erik Christessen had shot himself; is in charge of the inquiry

DUTCH OFFICIALS (Narrow Corner). On Kanda; present at Erik Christessen's funeral

DUTCH REGISSEUR (Narrow Corner). Visited Takana only at rare intervals

DUTCH RESIDENT (Four Dutchmen). He drank beer with the Agent, the Captain of the S.S. Utrecht, and the Narrator; invited the Narrator and the four Dutchmen to dinner

DUTCH TRAVELER (Catalina). Went to Spain in the latter part of the reign of Philip IV (c. 1660); he recorded the appearance of Catalina in her later years

DUTCHMAN (Ashenden/Hairless Mexican). Shot in Mexico by Manuel Carmona when he stepped between the bar and the Mexican

DUTCHMAN (End of the Flight). He slept at the District Officer's residence on the night before the Narrator arrived; blue eyes

DUTCHMAN #1 (Narrow Corner). In the hotel dining room on Kanda; eating; sunburned

DUTCHMAN #2 (Narrow Corner). In the hotel dining room on Kanda; dark enough skin to suggest that he had native blood in him

D'UZES, Duchesse (Razor's Edge). Told Elliott Templeton that the most recalcitrant male becomes amenable to suggestions during a picnic lunch eaten in perfect comfort

DWARRIS, Elizabeth Ann (Merry-Go-Round). An old, unmarried spinster of means who loved to feel her power; massive, with commanding presence; is known as Aunt Eliza to her relations; she died at last in a passion over a trifling misdemeanor of her maid

DYAK BOY (Flotsam and Jetsam). He paddled Vesta Grange across the river following the murder of Jack Carr

DYAK GIRL (Yellow Streak). Very small and shy; graceful; immobile face; feeds drinks to white men

DYAK HUNTERS (Neil MacAdam). Four of them; accompany the Munros and MacAdam on the scientific expedition

DYAK MAN (Flotsam and Jetsam). With the Chinese man, he

carries the news of the white man to Norman Grange

DZERJINSKY [Dzerzhinsky, Felix Edmundovich (1877-1926)] (Christmas Holiday). Russian revolutionary; Alexey defended him at one of his trials; he later arrested Alexey as a counter-revolutionary and sent him, for three years, to Alexandrovsk; the head of the Cheka (secret police) and the real master of Russia; he is extremely thin from the tuberculosis that he contacted in prison; tall; not bad looking; terrifying eyes

E

EARL (Rehearsal). Belted; asked for permission to marry and to pay his addresses to Genevieve Zampa; Monsieur Zampa refused him

EASTNEY, Lady (Bishop's Apron). Attended the Hollingtons' dinner party

EBOLI, Princess of (Catalina). Sent a copy of Mother Teresa de Jesus's autobiography to Prioress Dona Beatriz

ECHO (Perfect Gentleman). In the opera, The Island of Naxos; companion of Ariadne

EDITOR (Mrs. Craddock). Of the Blackstable Times; told Edward Craddock that he could have a thousand copies of the report of his speech

EDITOR (Of Human Bondage). Of a paper; he suggests that Hayward write some criticism for him

EDWARDES, Compton (Our Betters). The great reducer of London; he has cut off Minnie Surennes from her tea

EDWIN (Happy Couple). A fictional character in a story narrated by Miss Gray; is modeled after George Craig

EGBERT (Marriage of Convenience). One of the Wilkins' monkeys; drinks lemonade from a straw

EGYPTIAN (Magician). A friend of Dr. Porhoet at Alexandria; an interpreter at the French Consulate; he had often begged Porhoet to see the sheik who could show, through a mirror, persons absent or dead; brought the sheik to Porhoet

ELDERS (Making of a Saint). Of the Council at Forli; Girolamo Riario asks their advice about the state of his affairs

ELDRIDGE (Of Human Bondage). A pupil at King;s School, Tercanbury; is the cleverest boy in Mr. Turner's form

ELECTRICAL ENGINEER (Of Human Bondage). According to Thorpe Athelny, the man has taken to drink because his daughter, Sally Athelny, refused to share her hymnal with him

ELIZABETH (Lady Frederick). An aunt to Lady Frederick Berolles; died of an apoplectic fit

ELIZABETH, Lady (Good Manners). A friend of Augustus Breton; she pleads with Breton to visit the Baron von Bernheim

ELLINGHAM, Sir Peter (Love in a Cottage). Age forty; lean and good looking; guest at the Hotel Splendide, Varenna, Lake Como; is separated from his wife, upon whom he is financially dependent; in love with Sybil Bruce, and he suggests to her that they become lovers

ELLINGHAMS (Razor's Edge). Elliott Templeton is certain that he and the Bradley women will be invited aboard their yacht at Cowes

ELLIS, Mortimer (Round Dozen). Shabby little man; long thin nose, pale blue eyes; sallow skin; he could have been anywhere in age from thirty-five to sixty; a bigamist; had married one of his eleven wives at St. Martin's Church, Elsom; supposedly, he achieves his ambition of a twelfth marriage by eloping with Eleanor Porchester

ELLIS, Mr. (Of Human Bondage). A neighbor of William Carey; he resided at the Limes; was one of the shared subscribers to The Times

ELMER (Marriage of Convenience). One of the Wilkins' monkeys

ELNA, Bishop of (Then and Now). A cousin to Caesar Borgia; he meets with Caesar Borgia and Agapito da Amalia to consider letters from the Pope--thus delaying Machiavelli's appointment with Aurelia Martelli

EMBALMER (Razor's Edge). He rouges Elliott Templeton's cheeks and reddens his lips

EMIL (Of Human Bondage). A stupid lout; untidy, clumsy; phlegmatic face; he waits at tables and does most of the housework at Helen Erlin's pension at Heidelberg

EMILY (Cakes and Ale). Servant at Blackstable vicarage, Kent; young, flighty

EMILY (For Services Rendered). The Ardsley children's aunt; Lois Ardsley's godmother; Charlotte Ardsley's sister-in-law; lives near Canterbury; says that she is going to leave Lois something in her will; Lois loathes the idea of having to spend time with her

EMILY (Of Human Bondage). Sister of Louisa Carey; the widow of a naval officer

EMMA (Of Human Bondage). Nine-year-old Philip Carey's nurse in London; tall and big-boned; fair hair and large features; from Devonshire

EMPEROR (Jack Straw). Of Pomerania; growing old; being broken down by domestic problems; he consents to the marriage of the Archduke Sebastian and Ethel Parker-Jennings

ENCOMBE, Mrs. (Cakes and Ale). A cousin of Mrs. Greencourt and the wife of an Oxford don; small; eager, wrinkled face; grey short hair; the first example of the New Woman ever to have been seen in Blackstable

ENGINEER (Red). Long and lean; scraggy neck; thin arms tattooed from elbow to wrist

ENGLISH AMBASSADOR (Irish Gentleman). Robert O'Donnel states firmly that he will appeal his arrest by John-Adolphus to him

ENGLISH LADIES (Spanish Priest). At Gibraltar; mature in age; ride by, with callow subalterns in attendance

ENGLISH LADY (Gigolo and Gigolette). Disappointed that Stella Cotman's dive is over so quickly

ENGLISH LORD (Gigolo and Gigolette). He and his wife members of the Casino dinner party; both are long and lean; prepared to dine with anyone who would provide a free meal

ENGLISH MAN (Lotus Eater). Thomas Wilson meets him at the feast of the Assumption, at Punta di Timberio

ENGLISH MAN #1 (Of Human Bondage). An India-rubber merchant at Slough; the father of English Man #2; he did not approve of his son's marriage to Thekla Erlin

ENGLISH MAN #2 (Of Human Bondage). Is engaged to Thekla Erlin; the son of an India-rubber merchant at Slough (English Man #1)

ENGLISH MAN #1 (Razor's Edge). At the Brasserie Graf, Avenue de Clichy, Paris; tall, long, washed-out face; thinning wavy hair

ENGLISH MAN #2 (Razor's Edge). In a vision while Larry Darrell meditates; belongs to the sixteenth century; young; cheerful, ruddy countenance; a bold, reckless, wanton look

ENGLISHMAN (Spanish Priest). Meets the Narrator at a tavern on Gibraltar; wiry; sunburned; age fifty; a hard drinker; his restless face revealed strength and character; blue eyes, sharp and alert; strong, large, and obstinate nose; a mining engineer who has lived in Spain for thirty years; formerly the manager of a copper pyrite mining company in Saville; resigned his post and went to Granada in search of Vicente Orias y Mazallon and/or information on the old Roman mine; he spends three years of work searching for the mine

ENGLISHMEN (Land of Promise). Two bachelors in British Columbia; they would not have anything to do with the Indians because the latter were so dirty

ENGLISH NOBLEMAN (Making of a Saint). In possession of a portrait of Filippo Brandolini painted in 1488; he refuses to part with it

ENGLISH PARSON (Mrs. Craddock). At the villa in Naples, Italy; thought that Bertha Ley ought not to be alone after the death of her father

ENGLISH PUBLISHER (Colonel's Lady). He informs George Peregrine about the success of Evie Peregrine's book and the quality of the reviews

ENGLISH SEA CAPTAIN (Moon and Sixpence). The father of Tiare Johnson; he had settled in Tahiti and married a native woman; he forced his daughter to marry Captain Johnson after her affair with the mate

ENGLISH SHIPMASTER (Catalina). Arrested and confessed to being a member of the Reformed faith; tortured by the Inquisition until he consented to become a Roman Catholic; condemned by Blasco de Valero to ten years labor in the galleys, then to perpetual imprisonment

ENGLISH STOKER (Moon and Sixpence). When he died, Tough Bill then provided Charles Strickland with his papers

ENNISMORE, Dr. (Sheppey). A friend of Dr. Jervis at St. Mary's of Bethlehem Hospital for the insane; one of the greatest authorities in England on the diseases of the mind; he ascribes philanthropy to repressed homosexuality; examines Sheppey and believes that he suffers from acute mania, visual hallucinations, and religious paranoia

ENSHEIM, Father (Razor's Edge). A lodger, with Larry Darrell, at the boarding house of the professor's widow at Bonn; a Benedictine monk; Alsatian; is very learned; tall and stout; sandy hair; prominent blue eyes and a round red face; shy and reserved; had once taught philosophy

ENVER PASHA (Ashenden/Hairless Mexican). He employs Constantine Andreadi as his agent

ENVOY (Then and Now). Of the Pope, at Perugia; the Orsini had come to assure him of their loyalty to the Pope

ENVOYS (Then and Now). Sent by the Venetians to Caesar Borgia to demand the return of Dorotea Caracciolo

ENVOYS (Then and Now). Three of them; from Siena; they ask Caesar Borgia why he plans to attack their city

EQUERRY (Irish Gentleman). Informs Robert O'Donnel that Prince John-Adolphus will dine with him at the Golden Eagle that afternoon

ERDMANN, Captain (Winter Cruise). Captain of the Friedrich Weber; short and thick set; a clean-shaven head; red, clean-shaven face; hairy chest; a jovial fellow; asthmatic; married, with grown children

ERLIN, Adolf (Of Human Bondage). The husband of Helene Erlin and the father of Anna and Thekla; tall; middle aged; large fair head; his hair turning to grey; mild blue eyes; he speaks correct but archaic English; a professor at the local high school; teaches German to Philip Carey

ERLIN, Anna (Of Human Bondage). The younger of Adolf and Helene Erlin's daughters; tall, plain; a pleasant smile; high cheekbones, large misshapen nose; always made herself useful

ERLIN, Helene (Of Human Bondage). Wife of Adolf Erlin and mother of Anna and Thekla; operates a pension in Heidelberg, where Philip Carey lodges and studies German; short and very stout; tightly dressed hair; red face; small sparkling eyes; speaks broken English

ERLIN, Thekla (Of Human Bondage). The elder daughter of Adolf and Helene Erlin; is no more than age twenty-five; short; a pretty face and abundant dark hair; engaged to English Man #2, who had spent a year at the pension studying German; painted little pictures

ERNEST (Bread-Winners). Hairdresser; said he could dye Margery Battle's hair so that no one would know it was not natural

ERNEST (Our Betters). A London dancer and dancing-master; he charges twenty guineas for lessons; small and dark; large eyes; his long black hair is neatly plastered down

ERNESTINE, Mademoiselle (Christmas Holiday). The sous-maitresse at the Serail, Paris; her age in the late thirties; is good looking in a cold, hard way; strait nose; thin painted lips; firm chin

ERNIE (Liza of Lambeth). The captain of one of the Vere Street cricket teams; put himself in first; unwillingly gave his bat to Liza Kemp

ESPINEL, Paco (Gigolo and Gigolette). A young Argentinian who had exhausted all of his money; arranged the events with which the Casino attracted its visitors

ESTATE AGENT (Hour Before the Dawn). Of General George Henderson; old and none too competent; he had allowed the estate to fall into poor condition; his death led to the appointment of Richard Murray as estate agent

ESTATE AGENT (Razor's Edge). He tells the Narrator that after the outbreak of the Depression, 48,000 properties from Toulon to the Italian border had to be sold

ESTATE MANAGER (Up at the Villa). For Rowley Flint's property in Kenya; Rowley plans to dismiss him because he is no good

ETCHINGHAM, Lady Angela (Tenth Man). The wife of Lord Francis Etchingham; mother of Catherine Winter and Anne Etchingham; age fifty; is handsome and well preserved; dyed red hair; massive and imposing presence

ETCHINGHAM, Anne (Tenth Man). Daughter of Lady Angela and Lord Francis Etchingham; the sister of Catherine Winter; small and slight; bright and vivacious; she is engaged to Edward O'Donnell

ETCHINGHAM, Lord Francis (Tenth Man). Husband of Lady Angela Etchingham; the father of Anne Etchingham and Catherine Winter; at age fifty; middle height; bald; amiable, weak face; good natured; suffers from gout; chairman (but in name only) of a half-dozen of George Winter's companies; unwittingly in debt to George and a mere pawn in his son-in-law's business schemes

ETERNAL (Judgment Seat). In bad humor; he has just been told by the Philosopher of his total disbelief in Him

ETHEL'S GRANNY (Pool). Nothing but a wrinkled old woman

ETHERIDGE, Anne (Caesar's wife). Age forty; is handsome and pleasant; sympathetic; a woman of the world; the sister of Ronald Parry; one of Sir Arthur Little's oldest friends

EUGENE (Razor's Edge). A butler in the employ of Louisa Bradley; he is a tall and stout Negro with white hair

EURASIAN GIRL (East of Suez). She almost married the twenty-three-year-old George Conway

EVANS, Dr. (Land of Promise). He advised Norah Marsh to remain home and not to attend Miss Louisa Wickham's funeral; Clement Wynne's brother-in-law

EVANS, Rev. (Bad Example). The curate of the parish in which the Clintons live; young; thin and short; red faced; long nose; weak eyes; his shoulders screwed up into a perpetual shiver; comes to see what he can do with James Clinton; Clinton chases him from the room

EVIE (Theatre). The maid and dresser to Julia Lambert Gosselyn; she had been with her mistress since the latter's engagement at Middlepool; a cockney; thin, raddled, and angular; untidy red hair; two of her front teeth missing

EVGENIA (Christmas Holiday). Wife of Alexey; friend of Lydia's mother; mother of three children; managed the ladies' cloak room at the Russian restaurant in Paris

EX-INDIAN GOVERNOR (Christmas Holiday). The party wants to find a safe seat in Parliament for him, so Wilfred Terry-Mason will then exchange his seat for a peerage

EXECUTIONER (Catalina). He had to be bribed to give the sufferer the quick release of death, thus allowing him or her to escape the agony of death by fire

EXECUTIONER (Official Position). He was Louis Remire's predecessor; had held the position for only two years before his nerves gave way; burly and sanguine; was ardently passionate

EXECUTIONER'S ASSISTANT #1 (Official Position). Nerves had given way; had developed scruples about capital punishment; suffering from neurasthma; had been sent to the Ile St. Joseph

EXECUTIONER'S ASSISTANT #2 (Official Position). Lived with Louis Remire; tall, gawky, ungainly; deeply set staring eyes; cavernous jaws; formerly a cook; rapist and murderer

EXPLORER (Explorer [novel]). Dick Lomas labels him a lunatic; wanted to find out about an African district to which no one had ever been; he returned to England crippled with fever and having failed in his attempt; Alec MacKenzie pursued his mission

F

FABIO (Making of a Saint). The steward of Filippo Brandolini; Filippo has entrusted his palace at Citta di Castello to him during his absence, both at Forli and at Rome; held to the memory of Filippo's father with more than human love; he tells Filippo that his wife Giulia (dall' Aste) has betrayed him

FABRIZIO (Making of a Saint). The servant placed in the particular charge of old Orso d'Orsi; Orso would take food only from him and insisted that he be near him every moment of the day; had been among the first of the palace servants to fill his pockets and leave

FABRONIO, Giacomo (Then and Now). One of the crowd that surges into the apartment of Caesar Borgia; a silversmith of Imola; cousin to Monna Brigida; bought the silver pieces from the Gascon soldiers

FAFNER (Ashenden/Miss King). Geneva detective #1, so named by Ashenden for one of the giants in the Rhinegold; he is powerfully built; stout; black moustache

FALLOUX, Carrie (Theatre). The sister of Julia Lambert Gosselyn's mother; was married very young to a French coal merchant at St. Malo; she became a Catholic; her only son killed in the war; now widowed

FALLOUX, Monsieur (Theatre). Husband of Madame Carrie Falloux and uncle of Julia Lambert Gosselyn; a French coal merchant at St. Malo; dead

FAMILIARS OF THE HOLY ORDER (Catalina). Eight of them in Castel Rodriguez; have the power to determine if Catalina should be delivered to the Tribunal of the Inquisition; two of them bring Catalina before Bishop Blasco de Valero

FANE, Kitty (Painted Veil). Wife of Walter Fane, whom she hates; daughter of Bernard and Mrs. Garstin and sister of Doris; she is having an affair with Charlie Townsend; a beauty from the time she was a child; large, liquid, and vivacious dark eyes, with long lashes; her lovely skin her greatest beauty; brown curling hair with a reddish tint; exquisite teeth; overly square chin; nose too big; her beauty depended upon her youth; married Walter, at age twenty-five, in a panic; then accompanies Walter to Mei-tan-fu; volunteers to work at the French convent and placed in charge of the babies and younger children; she discovers that she is with child; Walter's death a relief to her; returns to Hong Kong and stays with the Townsends; renews her relationship with Charlie; returns to England; will, in the end, accompany her father to the Bahamas, to live with him and have her baby there

FANE, Dr. Walter (Painted Veil). Husband of and in love with Kitty Fane; M.D. and government bacteriologist, Hong Kong; grave face, a trifle stern; sweet smile; short, but not thick-set; slight, rather than thin; dark and clean shaven; regular, clean-cut features; eyes almost black, but not large; straight, delicate nose; fine brow; well-shapen mouth; not good looking; had no gaity; his shyness was a disease; offers to go to Mei-tan-fu and take charge during the cholera epidemic there; he will file a petition for divorce if Kitty does not accompany him; dies of cholera; his last words a line from Oliver Goldsmith:

[But soon a wonder came to light,
   That shew'd the rogues they lied,
  The man recover'd of the bite,]
   The dog it was that died.
(Vicar of Wakefield, Chapter 17, "An Elegy of the Death of a Mad Dog," line 4, stanza 8)

FANNING (Daisy). The postman at Blackstable, Kent

FANNY (Man of Honour). The housemaid of Jenny and Basil Kent at Putney

FANNY (Merry-Go-Round). Servant of Jenny and Basil Kent at their house in Bares, London

FARINELLI, Giacomo (Then and Now). A Florentine exiled with the Medici; a clever accountant in the employ of Caesar Borgia

FARLEY CHILDREN (Noblest Act). Of Dr. James and Kate Farley; had been left in England when the oldest was only nine years of age; grown up and almost strangers to their mother

FARLEY, Rev. Collinson (Merry-Go-Round). Vicar of All Souls, Grosvenor Square, London; the most fashionable cleric in London; Dr. Frank Hurrell detested him; of middle size; iron grey hair; fine head; well manicured hands, soft and handsome; an inclination toward obesity; a suave manner coupled with intelligent conversation; once a country rector; his grandfather a bishop; proposes marriage to Hilda Murray; presides over the marriage of Hilda and Basil Kent; he tells Miss Ley that he will marry Florence, Lady Newhaven

FARLEY, Dr. James (Noblest Act). The husband of Kate Farley; he and his wife have been in the Malay States for thirty years; big, bluff, handsome; clear blue eyes; a thatch of curling grey hair; immense vitality

FARLEY, Kate (Noblest Act). Wife of Dr. James Farley; a native of Yorkshire; thin, wan, and frail; worn face; terribly homesick for England; worn out from all the years in the tropics; one more year there will no doubt kill her

FARMER (Painted Veil). Father of Sister St. Joseph; a good old man; used to whip his daughter because she was a naughty girl who played pranks

FARMER (Razor's Edge). In Germany; said he would hire Kosti #2, but not Larry Darrell

FARMERS (Bishop's Apron). At Barchester; on market day, they would lead their cattle and sheep to the town

FARMERS (Good Manners). Near Graveney, Kent; dreamed pleasant dreams of new prosperity, believing that Baron von Bernheim would stand for Parliament

FARMERS (Magician). Near Skene, Staffordshire; if they aroused Oliver Haddo's anger, Haddo exercised an evil influence over their crops and cattle

FARMERS (Making of a Saint). In certain districts near Forli; because of the taxes, they did not have grain to sow in their fields

FARNESE, Alexander (Catalina). Commander of the Spanish forces in the northern provinces

FARRAR, Frederick William (Mrs. Craddock). The Dean of Canterbury (1831-1903); Polly Ley had once met him

FASOLT (Ashenden/Miss King). Geneva detective # 2, so named by Ashenden after one of the giants from the Rhinegold; powerfully built, stout; a black moustache

FAT MAN (Ashenden/His Excellency). Acrobat; large black moustache; is dressed in ill-fitting pink tights with green satin trunks; he performs at the Metropolitan, Edgware Road, London

Characters

FAT MAN (Fall of Edward Barnard). Warehouse manager at Braunschmidt and Company, Tahiti; stout, spectacled, bald headed

FATHER (Casual Affair). Of Lady Kastellan; permanent Under-Secretary for Foreign Affairs; insisted that his daughter and Jack Almond not meet

FATHER (Christmas Holiday). Of Lydia Berger; he had studied at Berlin; a professor of economics at the University of Leningrad; a socialist who, with his family; had to flee from the Bolsheviks; was murdered upon his return to Russia

FATHER #1 (East of Suez). Of Daisy (Anderson); an English merchant; sent Daisy to school in England; when he died, he left all of his money to his relatives in England, but nothing to Daisy

FATHER #2 (East of Suez). Of Amah; very poor; sent Amah to become a Christian

FATHER (Fortunate Painter). Of Rosie; he will not let Rosie marry Charlie Bartle unless the latter produces five thousand pounds or proves that he is earning two hundred and fifty pounds per year

FATHER (Hour Before the Dawn). Of May Henderson; was a naval officer who had lost his life in the last war

FATHER (Noble Spaniard). Of Matilda Proudfoot; he gave Sebastian Proudfoot his first brief

FATHER #1 (Painted Veil). Of Dorothy Townsend; a retired colonial governor; he lives in a small house in Earl's Court, London

FATHER #2 (Painted Veil). Of Mrs. Garstin and her four sisters; a Liverpool solicitor; he told his daughter that Bernard Garstin would go far

FATHER #3 (Painted Veil). Of Odette; her decision to join the Church was very hard on him

FAUSTINE (Magician). In Margaret Dauncey's vision; was haggard; with eternal fires of lust

FAWCETT, Barbara (Constant Wife). A widow; age forty; trim and business-like; in the decorating business

FEATHERSTONE, Mark (Book-Bag). The acting resident at Tenggarah, Malaya; thirty-five years of age; tall and handsome; fine eyes, strong face; a wiry black moustache, bushy eyebrows; had been to Oxford and belonged to a good London club; is in love with Olive Hardy

FEAVERHAM, Lord (Marriages Are Made in Heaven). When he

married, he settled twelve hundred pounds per year on Lottie Vivyan

FEBRUARY (Princess September). Second daughter born to the King and Queen of Siam; was formerly named Day, Autumn, and Monday

FELIX (Ashenden/Giulia Lazzari). A French agent of the Surete; comes from the Tonon police station to see Ashenden at his hotel; with small, dark; sharp eyes

FELLAH WOMAN (Magician). At the fair at the Lion de Belfort, Paris; wife of Mohammed; inside the tent; sat motionless, in ample robes of dingy black; face hidden by a long veil; a queer brass ornament in the middle of her forehead; large somber eyes; her lashes darkened with kohl; her fingers brightly stained with henna

FELLOWS, Miss (Cakes and Ale). The Narrator's landlady in Half Moon Street, London; had been a cook in some very good places; spare and upright; with determined features; middle aged; wore eyeglasses; businesslike, quiet, coolly cynical, very expensive

FELTMAN (Tenth Man). See Frederick BENNETT

FEMALE CORPSE (Mask and the Face). Unrecognizable; was found in Lake Como by a fisherman and taken inside Villa Grazie

FEMALE CYCLIST (Liza of Lambeth). At Battersea Park, London; she rode by Liza Kemp and Jim Blakeston

FEMALE PARISHIONER (Bad Example). Wealthy; Rev. Evans calls upon her after leaving James Clinton's house; she gives him two cups of tea to help him recover his equilibrium

FEMALE SLAVE (Magician). Black; a virgin; the sheik saw her in his mirror

FEMALE SLAVES (The Choice of Amyntas). Enter the palace room with salvers laden with choice food

FENCING MASTER (Perfect Gentleman). Called in to help M. Jourdain become a gentleman of fashion; blustering and authoritative; a loud voice and an abrupt manner

FENIMORE, Mr. (Christmas Holiday). Father of Simon; in the Indian Forest Department; divorced; thin, slight build; sallow lined face; tight lipped mouth; died of cirrhosis of the liver when Simon was age twelve

FENIMORE, Mrs. (Christmas Holiday). Mother of Simon; her husband divorced her because of her promiscuous adultery; had left India and vanished into obscurity

FENIMORE, Simon (Christmas Holiday). Oldest friend of Charley Mason; as a boy--thin and weedy; pale face and enormous black eyes; with abundant straight, dark hair; large sensual mouth; at age seventeen he declared his mother a whore and his father a drunk; he had left Cambridge at the end of his second year; while at school an ardent socialist, and at Cambridge was a communist; Leslie Mason had gotten for him a job as a Paris correspondent for a London newspaper; is harsh, cynical, unscrupulous; he lives in the Rue Campagne Premiere, Paris; at age twenty-three--lanky, of average height; a long, thin, pale face; hard, shining, inquisitive, suspicious, dark, opaque eyes; large, ironical mouth; small irregular teeth; pointed chin; prominent cheek bones; a face of tortured beauty; high pitched voice

FENNELL, Mr. (Theatre). Father of Thomas Fennell; a north London solicitor; buys his son a share in the firm of Lawrence and Humphreys

FENNELL, Thomas (Theatre). A young accountant; age twenty-two; extremely shy; frank, open face; curly, light brown hair; pale blue eyes; fresh color; white skin; well shaped teeth; an articled clerk employed by the firm of Lawrence and Humphreys, where he eventually becomes a junior partner; he examines Michael Gosselyn's books; he has an affair with Julia Lambert Gosselyn; is in love with Avice Crichton; hard times force a cut in his salary

FENWICK, Arthur (Our Betters). An intimate friend of Lady Pearl Grayston, whom he loves, keeps, and calls "girlie"; provides bad food to the working classes of the United States at an exorbitant price; elderly; tall; red face and grey hair

FERDINAND (Punctiliousness of Don Sebastian). King of Spain; in exchange for money, he continued the titles and honors of the house of Losas on to the illigitimate son of the seventh Duke

FERDINAND (Then and Now). King of Naples; he ordered Caesar Borgia to prison

FERGUSSON, Ada (Penelope). At age thirty, handsome and showy; close friend of Penelope O'Farrell; having an affair with Dickie O'Farrell; her husband is in the navy and stationed at Malta

FERGUSSON, Mr. (Penelope). Husband of Ada Fergusson; in the naval service; on a man-of-war stationed at Malta

FERGUSSON, Mr. and Mrs. (East of Suez). Out riding with Sylvia Knox

FERNANDEZ (Man from Glasgow). A chemist at San Lorenzo; played tresillo (the card game of ombre) with Robert Morrison

FERNE, Henry (Daisy). Recognizes Daisy Griffith as the principal's boy in a pantomime at Tercanbury, Kent

FERRARA, Cardinal (Then and Now). A brother of the Duke of Ferrara; Caesar Borgia and the Pope have conferred benefits upon him

FERRARA, Duke of (Then and Now). He has married Caesar Borgia's sister, Lucrezia

FERRYMAN (Razor's Edge). In India; he refused to convey the Yogi across the river because he had no money

FICINO, Marsilio (Then and Now). An Italian philosopher and Latin and Greek scholar (1433-1499); father-in-law of Biagio Buonaccorsi; directed Biagio's studies; a celebrated scholar who was patronized by the Medici

FIDDLER (Christmas Holiday). At the Serail, Paris; part of a three-piece orchestra

FIDDLER (Razor's Edge). At a cafe on the Rue de Lappe, Paris; an old and tired man

FIELD, Bella (Merry-Go-Round). See under Bella LANGTON

FIELD, Herbert (Merry-Go-Round). Age twenty; a bank clerk at Tercanbury, Kent; attended St. Regis School, Tercanbury; writes mediocre poetry; with fair hair; transparent, delicate skin; a thin, oval face; blue eyes; thin figure; shapely, long, exquisite hands; he becomes consumptive; marries Bella Langton, and she takes him to Italy; dies at the deanery in Tercanbury

FIELD, Mr. (Merry-Go-Round). Father of Herbert Field; a linen draper at Blackstable, Kent; he died from consumption less than a year after he first contacted it and before his son could continue on to Cambridge

FINCH, Lena (Three Fat Women of Antibes). A widow; she had been married to a cousin of Francis Hickson, who had recently died; is just recovering from a nervous breakdown; same age as Miss Hickson (approximately forty-eight); pale and ordinary looking

FIREMAN (Theatre). At Sarah Siddons Theatre, London; he

Characters 155

had been told to let Julia Lambert Gosselyn out at the front

FIRST MATE (Taipan). Of the Mary Baxter; he perished in the typhoon of 1908; buried in the English cemetery

FISCHER, [Ernst] Kuno [Berthold] (Of Human Bondage). A German philosopher (1824-1907); lectures on Schopenhauer at the University of Heidelberg; Philip Carey attends his course

FISHERMAN (Mask and the Face). Finds an unrecognizable female body in Lake Como

FISHERMAN (Of Human Bondage). At Blackstable, Kent; he is sitting on his doorstep and mending his nets

FISHERMEN (Razor's Edge). Two of them; brought the body of Sophie Macdonald to shore from the Toulon harbor

FISHMONGER (Bishop's Apron/Loaves and Fishes). Lionel Spratte to officiate at his funeral

FITZGERALD, Colonel (Ashenden/Traitor). Old, tall, and bent; Irish; had served in the Egyptian war; he and his wife residents of Vevey, Switzerland; spend their summers in Lucerne; guests at Ashenden's hotel' share the bathroom with the Caypors

FITZGERALD, Mary (Loaves and Fishes). A widow and guest at St. Gregory's vicarage, South Kensington, London; she is having her house redecorated; age thirty-five; tall and handsome; self-confident and keenly alive to her own advantages; is possessed of humor; she has an income of five thousand pounds per annum, and she tells potential suitors that it will cease if she remarries; she accepts Theodore Spratte's proposal, but releases him from it

FITZGERALD, Mr. (Loaves and Fishes). Deceased husband of Mary Fitzgerald; left his wife everything he had; lived longer than anyone had expected

FITZGERALD, Mrs. (Ashenden/Traitor). Wife of Colonel Fitzgerald; old; she and her husband are residents of Vevey and guests at Ashenden's Lucerne hotel; she had never opened a door for herself; received mountain flowers from Grantley Caypor

FITZHERBERT, Sir Augustus (Lord Mountdrago). Physician of Lord Mountdrago the younger

FITZHERBERT, Captain (Bishop's Apron). Husband of Mrs. Fitzherbert, whom he had met at the wedding of Theodore Spratte and Dorothy Frampstone; was stationed at various parts of the world, and rarely returned to England; fell ill and eventually died

FITZHERBERT, Mrs. (Bishop's Apron). An old friend of Theodore Spratte, with whom she had, at age eighteen, been deeply in love; accepted Dorothy Frampstone's invitation to be bridesmaid at her wedding to Theodore Spratte; there she met Captain Fitzherbert, whom she later married; spent several years nursing her husband on the Riviera and Italy; a handsome widow, age forty-five; singularly fine teeth and a charming smile; the years had only increased her attractiveness; she sees Theodore Spratte as the most desperate humbug whom she has ever known; her income of five thousand per year will cease on the day she remarries

FITZHERBERT, Mrs. (Round Dozen). Drove with the Prince Regent to the coffee-room of the Dolphin Inn, Elsom

FLAMENCO SINGER (Razor's Edge). At Etrenia, in Seville; Auguste Cottet, Larry Darrell, and two girls go to hear her sing

FLANAGAN (Of Human Bondage). Student at Amitrano's art school, Paris; a regular at Gravier's restaurant; an American from Seattle, Washington; son of a businessman; young; short; snub-nosed, jolly face, and laughing mouth; broad Western accent; eventually returns to the United States and enters his father's business

FLEMING (Explorer [novel]). A character invented by Julia Crowley and Dick Lomas; a most objectionable little beast and a prig; has been used to the saddle since he was three years old; he was the best swimmer at Harvard and a wonderful shot

FLEMING, Dr. (Of Human Bondage). Headmaster of King's School, Tercanbury, for a quarter of a century; had retired a year prior to Philip Carey's entry; he had become too deaf to continue

FLETCHER (Smith). Porter of the flats; he is Algernon Peppercorn's favorite candidate as the father of a future little Smith; steady; has proposed marriage to Smith

FLETCHER, Mrs. #1 (Of Human Bondage). She sold sandwiches that the employees of Lynn and Sedley ate for supper; funny, old, and very fat; a broad red face; black hair; dirty, greasy hands; wore a black bonnet and a white apron; everyone called her "Ma"

FLETCHER, Mrs. #2 (Of Human Bondage). Resides at Ivy Lane, Farnley, Dorchester; Philip Carey treats her
FLETCHERS (Explorer [novel]). A family Of Horton Park, Hampshire; had given daughters to the Allertons of Hamlyn's Purlieu
FLINT, Mrs. #1 (Up at the Villa). First wife of Rowley Flint; engaged to another man when she married the twenty-three-year-old Rowley; she divorced him after three years
FLINT, Mrs. #2 (Up at the Villa). Second wife of Rowley Flint; he left her two or three years after their marriage
FLINT, Rowley (Up at the Villa). English; is just over thirty years of age; at Florence; he had been paying attention to Mary Panton; not much to look at; has a tolerable figure; of average height; has uneven white teeth; fresh color, but unclear skin; abundant hair, vague brown, between dark and fair; with fairly large pallid blue eyes; an air of dissipation and a shifty look; his principal quality was his sex appeal; had been married at least twice; inherited an income; a cousin of Lady Grace Trail; proposes to Mary Panton
FLORENTINE MERCHANT (Then and Now). In partnership with Bartolomeo Martelli's father
FLORENTINE MERCHANT'S DAUGHTER (Then and Now). Wife of the elder Martelli and mother of Bartolomeo Martelli
FLORRIE (Liza of Lambeth). Dances with another girl to the music of an organ grinder on Vere Street, Lambeth
FLOWER GIRL (Bad Example). She passes James Clinton on a London street and offers him a yellow rose; small and grimy; unkempt brown hair
FLOWER-WOMEN (Merry-Go-Round). Along Fleet Street and the Strand; they offered gay vernal blossoms for sale
FOGLIATI, Giovanni (Then and Now). Uncle of Oliverotto da Fermo (his mother's brother); he raised the child of his sister
FOINET (Of Human Bondage). A master at Amitrano's art studio, Paris; small and shrivelled; bad teeth and a bilious air; an untidy grey beard; savage eyes; high voice, with a sarcastic tone; he came on Fridays; a difficult person; a landscape painter who had been repeating the same art work for the past twenty years
FOLLOWERS (Magician). Of Paracelsus, in Asia; their

minds still influenced by him; Paracelsus appears to them in visible and tangible substance

FOOTLEY, Mr. (Liza of Lambeth). The finest among the undertakers in Lambeth

FOOTMAN (Casual Affair). For Lady Kastellan; he takes Arthur Low's hat and coat and leads him to Lady Kastellan's drawing-room

FOOTMAN #1 (Jack Straw). At the Parker-Jennings' home, Cheshire; he carries Maria Parker-Jennings' letter to Count Adrian von Bremer

FOOTMAN #2 (Jack Straw). At the Parker-Jennings' home, Cheshire; is present at Jack Straw's breakfast table

FOOTMAN (Landed Gentry). At prayers in the dining room at Kenyon Fulton

FOOTMAN (Love in a Cottage). At Sybil Bruce's house in Paris; announces the arrival of the ex-King of Pomerania

FOOTMAN (Magician). At Westminster Abbey, London; opens the carriage door for Eliphas Levi

FOOTMAN #1 (Merry-Go-Round). At Lady Edward Stringer's house in Kensington, London; powdered; he took Basil Kent's hat

FOOTMAN #2 (Merry-Go-Round). At Lady Edward Stringer's house, Kensington, London; seized Basil Kent's coat

FOOTMAN (Mrs. Dot). At Frances Worthley's house on the river; he and the butler serve lunch

FOOTMAN (Razor's Edge). At Elliott Templeton's house on the French Riviera; he is dressed in white, with gold straps on his shoulders

FOOTMAN (Smith). Recently employed by the Rosenbergs; six feet four inches tall; Cynthia Rosenberg is proud of him

FOOTMEN (Ashenden/His Excellency). Three of them; for Sir Herbert Witherspoon; are all very tall Englishmen

FOOTMEN (Catalina). Two of them; in livery; carry the church pillows of the Duchess of Castel Rodriguez and Beatriz

FOOTMEN (Explorer [novel]). A little crowd of them clustered at the steps of the house opposite that of Lady Alice Kelsey in London

FOOTMEN (Hour Before the Dawn). Two of them; employed by the Hendersons at Graveney Holt; called into the army

FOOTMEN (Human Element). Two of them; in the employ of Betty Welldon-Burns; they are smart and picturesque

FOOTMEN (Our Betters). Two of them; at Lady Pearl Grayston's house

FOOTMEN (Perfect Gentleman). Four of them; immense; one of them announces a change in the program: the opera and the harlequinade will be performed together

FOOTMEN (Up at the Villa). Two of them; employed at the Atkinsons' luncheon; they serve cocktails and food

FORD, James (Tenth Man). The richest man in Middlepool and a director of the Middlepool Investment Trust; is married, with sons; friendly with George Winter for twenty years; he is large, stout, and oldish; a north country accent; he is one of the controllers of the Dissenting interest in Middlepool; built a Congregational church out of his own pocket; twice mayor of Middlepool; is extremely honest, and thus cannot be bought (the "tenth man")

FORDE, Quentin (Cakes and Ale). He is a regular among the Driffields' Saturday visitors; small and stocky; straight nose and handsome eyes; neatly cropped gray hair; black moustache; affluent; his only occupation to cultivate the arts; attracted to Rosie Driffield

FOREIGN SECRETARY (Explorer [novel]). He had asked Alec MacKenzie to submit reports to the Foreign Office on matters relating to the countries that he (Alec) knew

FOREMAN (Bad Example). Of the coroner's jury; he turned around and whispered to the jury for a minute

FOREMAN (Outstation). He had been Warburton's valet in "the old days" at Ascot, Goodwood, and Cowes

FOREMAN (Razor's Edge). Of the coal mine near Lens, in northern France; arranges to have Larry Darrell work with Kosti #2

FOREMAN, Albert Edward (Verger). Verger at St. Peter's, Neville Square, for the past sixteen years; clean cut and distinguished features; tall, slim, grave, and dignified; had been in service in very good houses-- page boy, footman, single-handed butler, butler with two men under him; he could neither read nor write

FOREMAN, Mrs. (Of Human Bondage). A Kennington neighbor of Philip Carey and Mildred Rogers; visits Mildred and stares hard at Philip's nude drawings on the wall

FOREMAN, Mrs. (Verger). Wife of Albert Edward Foreman;

she writes letters for her husband

FORRESTIER, Eleanor (Lion's Skin). The American wife of Captain Robert Forestier; born in Portland, Oregon; she stayed with the Hardys after her husband's death; absurd, homely, foolish; as tall as the average man; large mouth and a great hooked nose; pale blue eyes; shortsighted; big ugly hands; skin lined and weather beaten; long hair dyed gold; age fifty

FORESTIER, Mr. the elder (Lion's Skin). Robert Forestier's great-grandfather; was one of the bucks of the Regency period; had brought financial ruin upon the family

FORESTIER, Mr. the younger (Lion's Skin). The father of Robert Forestier; a friend of Thompson; a wine waiter at one of the clubs

FORESTIER, Robert (Lion's Skin). English; the second husband of Eleanor Forestier; was two or three years younger than his wife; handsome; wavy, abundant gray hair; a handsome moustache; weather beaten, healthy, tanned skin; tall, lean, and broad shouldered; a good golfer and bridge player; a connoisseur of wines; had once worked as a car washer at Bruton Street, where he first came in contact with Frederick Hardy; also had been a page boy, trooper, and a valet; he met his death in a forest fire trying to save his wife's dog

FORESTRY OFFICER (Razor's Edge). Indian; lived on the outskirts of a village near Ashrama; was a devotee of Shri Ganesha; offers Larry Darrell a bungalow in the mountains where he can meditate

FORLIVESI, Count (Making of a Saint). He has deigned to accept Checco d'Orsi's invitation to the great gathering at Palazzo Orsi

FORMS (Magician). Shadowy; appear in Margaret Dauncey's vision; they are swept along like waves of the sea

FORRESTER, Albert (Creative Impulse). Shared the London flat with Mrs. Forrester and paid the rent; a London currant merchant; an expert on the choice of cigars; the proud bright eyes of a pedigree hen; of average height; spare and frail; short, white hair and stubby white moustache; pale and tired blue eyes; he is well mannered; a bore; has been married to Mrs. Forrester for thirty-five years; he elopes with Mrs. Bulfinch

FORRESTER, Mrs. Albert (Creative Impulse). A writer of

prose and verse; author of the novel, The Achilles Statue; age fifty-seven; lived in a London flat, not far from Marble Arch; she is a woman of authoritative presence; large boned, tall, and strong; dark skin; large, bright, black eyes; fleshy nose, square chin, big mouth; thick, solid grey hair piled atop her head

FORSTER, Fraulein (Of Human Bondage). Is an old Dutch spinster; masculine appearance; a permanent lodger at Helen Erlin's pension at Heidelberg; is troublesome

FORSYTH, Major William (Hero). The brother of Frances Parsons; a bachelor living in London; he considered himself a typical man of the world and in society; a haunter of military clubs; wanted to be thought of as a rake; he blamed the War Office rather than his own incompetence for having been retired on half pay; Frances Parsons needs him to attempt to salvage the relationship between Mary Clibborn and James Parsons; age fifty-three; red faced; scanty hair parted in the middle; wore a moustache that bristled with a martial ardor; a fine set of artificial teeth; wrinkled skin; old eyes; he had managed to gain a complete dominance over Richmond and Frances Parsons

FORTESQUE, Captain (Sheppey). He calls Bradley's Hairdressing and Barber's Saloon to book an 11:30 a.m. appointment with Sheppey; cursed and swore earlier in the day when he came to the shop and found Sheppey not there

FOSTER, Ian (Hour Before the Dawn). The husband of Jane Foster; age forty; large and heavy; he weighed two hundred pounds; red face; great booming voice; obese; he had been in the Grenadiers before his marriage; is entirely dependent upon Jane; made a security officer and sent to France; survives Dunkirk; he loses all of his front teeth when his ship is torpedoed; treated at a hospital in York; sent to Egypt (with a new set of teeth)

FOSTER, Jane (Hour Before the Dawn). Eldest child of General George and Mrs. Henderson; is married to Ian Foster; sister of Roger, Jim, and Tommy; age thirty-four; she is tall, gaunt, rather masculine; horsey; naturally dark hair, hennaed; heavy make up; wears a rimless monocle in her left eye; she played the piano better than one could have expected; is bombed out of her London house, and so she returns to Graveney Holt

FOSTER, Mrs. (Of Human Bondage). Housekeeper at Blackstable vicarage; had been with William Carey since the death of Louisa Carey

FOTHERINGHAM (Razor's Edge). A young attache with the British embassy at Paris; he was invited to Elliott Templeton's dinner party; affluent; is interested in Isabel Bradley

FOULDES, Paradine (Lady Frederick). Lady Maud Mereston's brother; around forty years of age; a bachelor; self-possessed, worldly, and urbane; has run through two fortunes; he had very nearly run off with Lady Frederick Berolles; he pays Lady Frederick's debt to Captain Montgomerie; later, proposes marriage to Lady Frederick Berolles

FOWLER, Jane (Jane). Mrs. Tower's sister-in-law (Mr. Tower's sister); she married a manufacturer from the north of England; a well-to-do widow; age fifty-five; a large woman; grey hair; weather-beaten face; short sighted, thus wore spectacles; marries Gilbert Napier

FOYOT, Madame (Of Human Bondage). The wife of Monsieur Foyot; mother of two daughters; Jewish; affluent; has no figure; Miss Wilkinson had been a governess in her house

FOYOT, Mademoiselles (Of Human Bondage). Two of them; the daughters of the Paris portrait painter and his Jewish wife; tall; Miss Wilkinson was their governess until they eventually married

FOYOT, Monsieur (Of Human Bondage). A fashionable portrait painter at Paris; he married a Jewish wife of means; father of two daughters; Miss Wilkinson had been a governess in his house; she claimed that he attempted, violently, to make love to her

FRAMONTI, Andrea (Making of a Saint). A captain of the guard at the Palazzo Orsi; came every day to receive the password from Girolamo Riario; was killed by the conspirators

FRAMPSTONE, Lord (Bishop's Apron). His youngest daughter, Dorothy, married Theodore Spratte

FRANCIS, Mr. (Before the Party). The successor to Mr. Simpson as the assistant resident at Kualo Solor

FRANCISCAN FRIAR (Catalina). Was engaged in healing the sick by supernatural means; then arrested by the Holy

Characters 163

Office and never hard from again
FRANCISCAN FRIAR (Making of a Saint). Was situated at an inn a half-day's ride from Citta di Castello; he collected alms for the sick and needy
FRANÇOIS (Road Uphill). Broderick Madden's valet; Madden provokes him into giving notice, but the two then reconcile
FREDERICK (Home and Beauty). He is Victoria's present husband; the holder of the D.S.O.; dark and handsome
FREEHOLDER (Magician). In the neighborhood of Skene, Staffordshire; he refused to sell some of his land to Oliver Haddo; ruined by disease that attacked every animal on his farm
FREEMAN, Mr. (Smith). Father of Thomas Freeman and Rose Dallas-Baker; had to pay money to get Thomas out of a scrape with Queenie Bishop
FREEMAN, Thomas (Smith). Age thirty-five; strong and muscular; hearty and enthusiastic; a boyish laugh; Rose Dallas-Baker's brother; was formerly engaged to Emily Chapman; ruined in the Stock Exchange; took a job as a luggage porter in a Johannesburg hotel, then bought a two-thousand-acre farm in Rhodesia; he has been away from England for eight years; in search of a wife; he proposes marriage first to Emily Chapman, then to Smith
FREEMASONS (Mrs. Craddock). Of Lodge No. 31,899, Blacktable, Kent; attended Edward Craddock's funeral; they lined the road, attired in white gloves and aprons
FRENCH CALVINIST (Catalina). Stated that he had heard Demetrios Christopoulos uttering Protestant opinions
FRENCH CAPTAINS (Then and Now). At Cesena; angry over their abrupt dismissal from service by Caesar Borgia
FRENCH CONVICTS (Official Position). Awaiting execution
FRENCH GOVERNESS (Razor's Edge). Was employed by Louisa Bradley to take charge of Isabel
FRENCH MINISTER (Ashenden/Miss King). Travels to Nice to recover from a cold; is drugged by a yellow-haired lady who relieves him of his dispatch case containing important documents
FRENCH MINISTER (Marriage of Convenience). At Bangkok; he had escorted the retired French official on board the ship
FRENCH OFFICIAL (Marriage of Convenience). Is retired;

former governor of one of the French colonies; holder of the Legion of Honor; retired from the navy at age forty-nine; a little man, below average height; ugly little face; bushy grey hair and bushy grey eyebrows; a passenger on the ship out of Bangkok; he and his wife on a tour of the world

FRENCH PAINTER (Moon and Sixpence). At the cafe in the Avenue de Clichy, Paris; he occasionally plays chess with Charles Strickland; the Narrator forms a casual acquaintance with him

FRENCH PEASANT (Unconquered). He gives Hans and Willi misleading directions

FRENCH PRISONER OF WAR (Unconquered). Escaped through Switzerland; he wrote to Annette and informed her of Pierre Gavin's death

FRENCH TRADERS (Marriage of Convenience). Two of them; they were passengers on board the ship out of Bangkok

FRENCH TRAVELER (Magician). He supposedly saw Solomon Trismosinus alive at the end of the seventeenth century

FRENCH WOMAN #1 (Of Human Bondage). At the hotel at the edge of the forest of Fontainbleau; fat, middle aged; broad obscene laugh; triple chin and large belly; a former prostitute; she spent the day fishing for fish that she never caught; spoke a little broken English

FRENCH WOMAN #2 (Of Human Bondage). Elderly; she opens the door of the house on Hyde Street, London, where Cronshaw lives

FRENCHMAN (Louise). Tall, handsome, and young; lunches at the Ritz, in Paris, with Louise

FRENCHMAN (Magician). Gallant; had called Susie Boyd a belle laide to her face, which almost flattered her

FRENCHMAN (Mirage). An old resident of Haiphong; speaks English; formerly in the Customs Service; a friend of Grosely

FRENCHMAN #1 (Moon and Sixpence). At the Paris cafe; plays chess with Charles Strickland; fat and bearded

FRENCHMAN #2 (Moon and Sixpence). Friend of Rene Brunot who lends the latter money to purchase an island in the Paumotus

FRENCHMAN (Of Human Bondage). He played dominoes with Cronshaw at La Closerie de Lilas, Paris

FRENCHMAN (Razor's Edge). Grouchy and elderly; he is

making a retreat at the Benedictine monastery, Alsace

FRENCHMEN (De Amicitia). The acquaintances of Ferdinand White, who spoke to them about Valentia Stewart; they shrug despairingly when White states to them that he had never once kissed Valentia on her classic mouth

FRENCHMEN (Magician). A few of them; painters; in a small room with three tables, always reserved for them and their wives (or nearly wives), at the Chein Noire, Paris

FRENCHMEN (Magician). Two of them; at the gaming tables at Monte Carlo; talking laughingly and grossly about Margaret and Oliver Haddo; they claim that Haddo uses Margaret simply as a mascot

FRENCHMEN (Merry-Go-Round). Bearded; at shabby little restaurants in Soho; are languishing away from their native land

FRIAR #1 (Catalina). He brings a message to the Bishop from the Prior, requesting an audience

FRIAR #2 (Catalina). One of the two friars spending the final night with Demetrios Christopoulos; tells Friar Blasco de Valero that the Greek has refused to listen to his exhortations

FRIAR (Then and Now). Lodging at the inn at Castiglione Aretino; is on his way from one monastery to another; Machiavelli plays cards with him

FRIARS (Catalina). Are sent by Friar Blasco de Valero to convince Demetrios Christopoulos of his errors

FRIARS (Making of a Saint). At Forli; placed the naked body of Girolamo Riario on a stretcher, covered it, and bore it to their church

FRIEDA (Razor's Edge). A retired actress; she builds a sumptuous residence on the Riviera, close to Elliott Templeton's estate; she always kept an open house

FRIEDBERG, Dora (Hour Before the Dawn). Pretty and intelligent; is without a home and a country; Austrian; age twenty; fair hair; large, blue, intelligent eyes; honey colored skin; slender; elegant little head set on a lovely neck; a blond and healthy radiance; firm chin; the Hendersons had met her at Kitzbuhl, in the Austrian Tyrol, during the winter that had preceded Anschluss; a beautiful skier; a pleasant voice, with only a trace of an accent; she comes to live with the Hendersons at Graveney Holt while she looks for work;

secretly marries Jim Henderson; refuses to consider the possibility of having children; she eventually reveals herself as a spy for the Germans; Jim Henderson chokes her to death

FRIEDBERG, Frau (Hour Before the Dawn). Mother of Dora Friedberg; a distinguished appearance; a German who betrayed her husband to the Nazis

FRIEDBERG, Herr (Hour Before the Dawn). Father of Dora Friedberg; an Austrian lawyer; ardent socialist and an anti-Nazi; murdered in a Nazi concentration camp

FRIELINGHAUSEN, Sir Jacob (Alien Corn). Husband of Lady Frielinghausen and father of Violet

FRIELINGHAUSEN, Lady (Alien Corn). The mother of Violet Frielinghausen; a friend of the dowager Lady Bland; disliked by Muriel Bland

FRIELINGHAUSEN, Violet (Alien Corn). Daughter of Lady and Sir Jacob Frielinghausen; proposed as a "match" for George Bland

FRIEND (Bishop's Apron). Of Mrs. Fitzherbert; his or her illness obliged Mrs. Fitzherbert to go immediately into the country

FRIEND (Christmas Holiday). Of Robert Berger; he stated that he had met Berger, on the night of the murder, walking in the direction of Teddie Jordan's apartment

FRIEND (Constant Wife). Of Mrs. Culver; her husband was neglecting her; did not want her mother to know that she had made a mistake

FRIEND (Letter [play]). Of Ong Chi Seng; he supposedly would lend money to Robert Crosbie on the security of the latter's properties

FRIEND #1 (Liza of Lambeth). Of Liza Kemp and Sally Atkins; proclaims to Sally that Liza is "barmy [mad, eccentric]"

FRIEND #2 (Liza of Lambeth). Of Harry Atkins' brother; attends the wedding of Harry and Sally

FRIEND #1 (Magician). Of Oliver Haddo; he took Haddo to see the snake charmer at Madras

FRIEND #2 (Magician). Of Dr. Porhoet, at Alexandria; Porhoet asks him to send his (friend's) son to him

FRIEND #3 (Magician). Of the mature-aged lady; was to assist at the complete evocation, but had to withdraw

FRIEND #4 (Magician). Of the French physician Lesebren; he prepared and ingested the remedy to prolong life;

he lost his nails, but experienced no pain in the process
FRIEND #5 (Magician). Of Susie Boyd; invites Susie to Italy for the winter
FRIEND #6 (Magician). Of Susie Boyd at Rome; a gossip; tells Susie about the eccentricities and extravagances of Oliver and Margaret Haddo
FRIEND (Making of a Saint). Of Giulio Brandolini; he lately wrote a story of the London poor; attacked by the critics because of his characters' bad language and behavior
FRIEND #1 (Merry-Go-Round). Of Bella Langton; she asked Bella to spend a month in Brittany
FRIEND #2 (Merry-Go-Round). Of Rev. Algernon Langton; Algernon asked him if his wife had heard news of his daughter Bella
FRIEND #1 (Mrs. Craddock). Of Edward Craddock; Edward tells him that women are like chickens
FRIEND #2 (Mrs. Craddock). Of Polly Ley; young; Polly writes to her from Paris, detailing and explaining Bertha Craddock's condition and situation
FRIEND (Razor's Edge). Of both Suzanne Rouviere and Achille Gauvin; introduces them to each other
FRIEND, Mr. (Daisy). The Baptist minister at Blackstable, Kent; asks Mrs. Griffith to attend his chapel
FRIENDS (Bishop's Apron). Of Theodore Spratte; one or two of them; Theodore nods to them as he walks along Saville Row
FRIENDS (Explorer [play]). Of George Allerton; George cannot face them after his father's trial
FRIENDS (Magician). Of the snake charmer at Madras; accompanied him home from the marriage feast; would have killed the cobra that had bitten the charmer, but the latter prevented them
FRIENDS (Making of a Saint). Of Vitelli the elder; were strung up from the windows of the Palace by Vitelli the younger
FRIENDS (Mrs. Craddock). Of Polly Ley; rent Polly's flat in Chelsea while she and Bertha Craddock go to Paris
FRIENDS (Sacred Flame). Of Beatrice Wayland; live on the South Coast
FRITH, Catherine (Narrow Corner). Wife of George Frith;

mother of Louise; was a widow when she married George Frith; had died the previous year from heart disease, her age close to fifty

FRITH, George P. (Narrow Corner). Englishman on Kanda; the father of Louise Frith; he receives copies of the Sydney Bulletin with every mail; he resides with his daughter on a nutmeg plantation; a widower; at age thirty-six when he married Catherine Swan; big and fat; grey hair, small grey moustache; growing bald; imposing forehead; red face, unlined and round; long yellow tooth in the middle of his mouth; walks with a pronounced limp; has rheumatism; educated at one of the smaller public schools, then went to Cambridge; formerly a schoolmaster; he operated a book shop in Singapore and a hotel at Bali; he has spent the last four years working on a translation of The Lusiads (1572), by the Portuguese poet Luis de Camoens (1524-1580)

FRITH, Louise (Narrow Corner). George Frith's daughter; fair, thick, long, and ashy pale hair; slim and long legged; the narrow hips of a boy; her skin burned by the sun to rich honey color; an attitude of indolent beauty; long, slender, brown hands; blue eyes; fine, regular features; an extremely pretty young woman; age eighteen; sent to school at Aukland, but returned to Kanda after her mother's death; is unofficially engaged to Erik Christessen; has an affair with Fred Blake

FRITZ (Hour Before the Dawn). One of the German motor-cyclists who drinks champagne with Roger Henderson at the French village inn

FRITZI (Ashenden/Traitor). Grantley Caypor's pet bull terrier; acquired in 1914

FROBISHER, Sir Reginald (Jane). English admiral; age fifty-three; a dinner guest; a regular guest at Jane Napier's Tuesday parties; plans to marry Jane Fowler after she obtains her divorce from Gilbert Napier

FUENTES, Alonso (Catalina). Owner of the theatre troupe engaged by the Spanish grandee and living at the inn; a playwright; husband of Luisa Fuentes; small, bald, and fat

FUENTES, Luisa (Catalina). The wife of Alonso Fuentes; leading lady in her husband's acting troupe; ran away

Characters

with the leading man and all of the troupe's money

FULTON, Maude (Unattainable). A spinster; approximately forty years of age; bright eyes; a vivacious manner; a sharp tongue; has known Caroline Ashley for twenty years

FUORUSEIETI (Making of a Saint). In pursuit of Filippo Brandolini to arrest him in the name of Vitelli the elder; called back by Vitelli the younger

FYODOR, Grand Duke (Outstation). He and Warburton broke the bank at Monte Carlo

G

GALBRAITH, Lauria (Merry-Go-Round). Professional name of Miss Higgins; an actress; marries Reggie Barlow-Bassett

GALLAGHER (P.&O.). Native of Galway, Ireland; well over six feet tall; broad, stout; red, bloated skin; dark eyes; thick black hair; age forty-five; strong Irish brogue; a full, loud, and hearty voice; a planter and estate manager

GALLOWAY (Cakes and Ale). Curate to the vicar of Blackstable, Kent; tall, thin, and ungainly; untidy black hair; small, sallow, dark face; young; spoke quickly and gesticulated; energetic; is walking with Edward Driffield when the fifteen-year-old Narrator first sees the writer

GAMBLERS (Magician). Noble; often in the company of the Haddos at Monte Carlo

GAME, Polly (Hero). The top girl of Little Primpton Parish School, Kent; she presents Mary Clibborn with a bouquet at the welcome home ceremony for James Parsons

GANDIA, Duke of (Then and Now). Fished out of the River Tiber with nine wounds in his body; he supposedly had loved Lucrezia Borgia

GANDY, Mrs. (Hero). One of Mary Clibborn's patients at Little Primpton, Kent; attended to by Dr. Higgins; is ill, weak, and in need of strengthening

GANGSTER (Sheppey). In the film seen by Ernie Turner and Florrie Miller; good looking

GANN the elder (Landed Gentry). The father of Gann the younger; he had come to work at Kenyon-Fulton fifty-four years ago

GANN the younger (Landed Gentry). Employed as Claude Insoley's gamekeeper; son of Gann the elder; father of Peggy; short, sturdy, and grizzled; wild, stubborn hair; a fringe of beard around his chin; he has been employed at Kenyon-Fulton for all of his life (forty years); he faces dismissal because Peggy has gotten into trouble and he will not send her away

GANN, Josiah (Cakes and Ale). The father of Rosie Gann Driffield; he joined the army and came home with a wooden leg; a painter who worked seldom; he and his family lived in Rye Lane, Blackstable, next door to Mary Ann

GANN, Margaret (Landed Gentry). Daughter of Gann the younger; known as Peggy; has gotten into trouble in London; young and pretty; pale; black rings around her eyes; she kills herself

GANN, Mr. (Of Human Bondage). Farmer near Ferne, Kent; married Betty Athelny's sister; father of Peter Gann

GANN, Mrs. (Cakes and Ale). Mother of Rosie Gann and wife of Josiah Gann; used to send young Rosie to Mary Ann's house for tea; after the Driffields settle in London, she meets with Rosie on occasion at the hotel in Haversham

GANN, Mrs. (Unknown). Shopkeeper, living at Stour, Kent

GANN, Peter (Of Human Bondage). He is the son of Betty Athelny's sister; his father is a farmer near Ferne, Kent; he is interested in Sally Athelny; tall, spare, straight; sunburned face; long, easy stride

GANN, Rosie (Cakes and Ale). See under Rosie DRIFFIELD

GARAGE OWNER (Masterson). Provides Narrator with a dilapidated Ford to take him and his luggage to Taunggi

GARCIA, Father (Catalina). A Dominican who hears the confessions of Beatriz Henriquez y Braganza; agrees that she should enter religion

GARDENER (Caesar's Wife). Works at the Consular Agent's establishment in Cairo; exchanges greetings with the Servant

GARDENER (Cakes and Ale). At the Blackstable vicarage, Kent; he initially tries to help young Ashenden mount his bicycle

GARDENER (Hero). At Little Primpton, Kent; he gossiped with Colonel Richmond Parsons

GARDENER (Mrs. Craddock). At the Craddocks' home, Court Leys, near Blackstable, Kent; Edward Craddock gives him orders
GARDENER #1 (Of Human Bondage). Works at the vicarage, Blackstable, Kent; an old sailor; makes a hammock in which Philip Carey lies and reads
GARDENER #2 (Of Human Bondage). He works at Blackstable vicarage; sent by Mrs. Foster to bring the curate to the vicarage
GARDENER (Sacred Flame). At Millie Tabret's house; will help Alice with Beatrice Wayland's trunk
GARDENER (Unknown). At the Whartons' house in Stour, Kent; just as old as Colonel Wharton, but not nearly as active
GARMAN, Mrs. (Daisy). She resides at Blackstable, Kent; her daughter has, in some manner, dishonored her
GARNET GIRL #1 (Facts of Life). Twelve-year-old daughter of Henry Garnet and his wife
GARNET GIRL #2 (Facts of Life). Sixteen-year-old daughter of Henry Garnet and his wife
GARNET, Henry (Facts of Life). A broker; hearty and in good health; affluent; an excellent bridge and tennis player
GARNET, Mrs. (Facts of Life). Wife of Henry Garnet and the mother of Nicholas and the two Garnet girls; not opposed to Nicholas playing tennis at Monte Carlo
GARNET, Nicholas (Facts of Life). The only son of Henry Garnet and his wife; age eighteen; he is six feet two inches tall; lithe, muscular, broad shouldered, slim waisted; pale brown hair; has blue eyes and long dark lashes; red mouth; tanned and clear skin; regular and extremely white teeth; an excellent tennis player; a student at Cambridge University
GARRODS (Explorer [novel]). Of Penda, Hampshire; had given their daughters to the Allertons of Hamlyn's Purlieu
GARSTIN, Bernard (Painted Veil). The husband of Mrs. Garstin and father of Kitty Fane and Doris Dennison; lived in South Kensington; no reason why he should not soon become a judge; is small and wizened; tired eyes; long upper lip; thin mouth; painstaking, industrious, and capable; once an unsuccessful candidate for Parliament; appointed Recorder of a Welsh town;

had not the will to advance himself; looked upon by his daughters only as a source of income; age sixty when his wife dies; is offered the position of Chief Justice of the Bahamas

GARSTIN, Doris (Painted Veil). Daughter of Bernard and Mrs. Garstin; younger sister of Kitty Fane; gave no sign of good looks; an overly long nose and a lumpy figure; at age eighteen became engaged to Geoffrey Dennison; married him and produced a child; expecting another

GARSTIN, Kitty (Painted Veil). See under Kitty FANE

GARSTIN, Mrs. (Painted Veil). Wife of Bernard Garstin, K.C., and mother of Kitty Fane and Doris Dennison; age fifty; thin and flat chested; has abundant smooth black hair; fine black eyes; one of five daughters of a Liverpool solicitor; she is hard, cruel, managing, ambitious, parsimonious, and stupid; she despised her husband; enters a nursing home for an operation; dies before Kitty can return to England

GASCON SOLDIER #1 (Then and Now). Is dragged and pushed into Caesar Borgia's apartment; shabby; nondescript garments; scowling; age forty; a powerful physique; thick black beard; livid scar on his forehead; states that the silver objects belonged to the soldiers as rightful loot of war; Borgia orders him to be hanged in the city square

GASCON SOLDIER #2 (Then and Now). Is dragged and pushed into Caesar Borgia's apartment; shabby; nondescript clothes; a smooth-faced boy; sallow skin; shifty but frightened eyes; he confesses to stealing the silver pieces; Borgia orders him to be hanged in the square

GASKELL AND BIRCH (Unattainable). A London real estate firm; Caroline Ashley engages them to let her house

GATE KEEPER (Painted Veil). At the water gate at Mei-tan-fu; stands with a torch

GAUVAIN, Achille (Razor's Edge). A manufacturer from Lille; he takes a fancy to Suzanne Rouvier; married, with two children; establishes Suzanne in an apartment in Montparnasse and with two thousand francs per month in exchange for her company one night every two weeks; small--half a head shorter than Suzanne; iron grey hair and neat grey moustache; plump, with a pot belly; he brings M. Meyerheim to view Suzanne's art

Characters   173

GAUVAIN, Madame (Razor's Edge). The wife of Achille Gauvain; the only child of a businessman in the same line as Gauvain; good woman and a good Catholic; her marriage was a union of business interests; her death leaves her husband free to marry Suzanne Rouvier.

GAUVAIN, Monsieur (Razor's Edge). Son of Achille and Madame Gauvain; engaged to a wealthy girl; sensible enough to realize the soundest basis for a happy marriage is the community of financial interests; he becomes suitably married and does well in the firm

GAVIN, Pierre (Unconquered). Engaged to Annette; taught at a boys' school; small and frail; a prisoner of war in Germany; is shot during an uprising in the prison

GAZE, Major (Footprints in the Jungle). The head of the police at Tanah Merah; is the Narrator's host; due to retire in two or three years; ugly face

GELONI, Abbe (Magician). An Italian mystic and Rosicrucian; he and the Count Johann-Ferdinand von Kuffstein made humunculi in five weeks

GENERAL (Cakes and Ale). At Alroy Kear's club in St. James Street, London; old; he and another member sit in a corner, talk in undertones, and glance hostilely at Kear and Ashenden

GENERAL (Man with the Scar). His broad red scar ran in a crescent, from his temple to his chin; round, fat, good-humored face; is powerful; of more than average height; he offers lottery tickets for sale; an exile from Nicaragua; he was once a revolutionary general

GENERAL (Sanatorium). An old patient at the sanatorium; he lunched, because of his rank, at the table with McLeod, Campbell, and Miss Atkin

GENERAL'S WIFE (Man with the Scar). A dead white face; young; slim; regular features; enormous eyes; she is beautiful

GENEVAN CITIZENS (Ashenden/Miss King). The two of them; fat; black beards; they play dominoes in the cafe

GENTLEMAN (Creative Impulse). Middle-aged; wears side whiskers; a benign expression; corpulent; powerfully built; a fellow passenger with Mrs. Forrester on the tram

GENTLEMAN #1 (Home and Beauty). Engaged to marry Miss Dennis; originally attracted to her by her polished nails

GENTLEMAN #2 (Home and Beauty). Of the house where Mrs. Pogson last worked; he lit the fire every morning and brought Mrs. Pogson a cup of tea and a slice of thin bread and butter every day before she arose

GENTLEMAN #3 (Home and Beauty). Had arranged to marry Rehan's client after her divorce; fled to the Continent upon discovering that the woman had false teeth

GENTLEMAN #4 (Home and Beauty). Mr. Rehan recommended that he hit his wife a few strokes with a stick; he became overly excited and administered her a severe beating to her, which aroused his wife's adoration

GENTLEMAN #5 (Home and Beauty). Actually wanted to go to bed with Miss Montmorency, but she told him that would never do

GENTLEMAN #6 (Home and Beauty). Had been sent to Miss Montmorency by a firm of solicitors in a cathedral city; he refused to drink anything but ginger beer; he wanted to kiss Miss Montmorency and to combine business with pleasure

GENTLEMAN (Hour Before the Dawn). At St. James's Park, London; old; sitting on a bench, reading a newspaper

GENTLEMAN (Irish Gentleman). A companion of Princess Mary of Wartburg-Hochstein

GENTLEMAN (Making of a Saint). Present at the gathering at Palazzo Orsi; comments upon the happy condition of present times, wherein there are ten different wars in as many parts of the country

GENTLEMAN (Moon and Sixpence). At Paris; pays Cohen #2 thirty thousand francs in return for Charles Strickland's picture of the Tahiti plantation

GENTLEMAN (Mrs. Dot). He lives upstairs from Gerald Halstane; Gerald has lent the man his telephone book

GENTLEMAN #1 (Of Human Bondage). From London; he rents, for six weeks during the summer, the house opposite the vicarage at Blackstable, Kent; he has two boys

GENTLEMAN #2 (Of Human Bondage). Guest at the boarding house at Brighton; single; he generally went to the Metropole for his holiday

GENTLEMAN #3 (Of Human Bondage). At the Monday evening social of Lynn and Sedley, London; he sang two songs: "Bid Me Good-bye" and "Sing Me to Sleep"

GENTLEMAN (Razor's Edge). Comes, every Thursday, to see his mistress who lodges at the same Paris hotel where

Larry Darrell resides

GENTLEMAN #1 (Sheppey). One of Sheppey's customers at Bradley's Hairdressing and Barber's Saloon, in Jermyn Street, London; told Sheppey that if things did not improve, he would have to give away either his yacht or his racing stable

GENTLEMAN #2 (Sheppey). A steady customer of Sheppey at Bradley's Saloon; very nice; left Sheppey a snuff box in his will; Sheppey shaved him after he had died

GENTLEMAN (Treasure). Had sent Pritchard to a tailor's shop to learn how to press clothes

GENTLEMEN (Magician). In Margaret Dauncey's odd vision; gay, attired in their periwigs

GENTLEMEN (Making of a Saint). Several of them; at the gathering at the Palazzo Orsi; advance to the farther end of the hall with Checco d'Orsi and Ercole Piacentini

GENTLEMEN (Making of a Saint). Of the Court of Girolamo Riario at Forli; are present at the meeting between Girolamo and Checco d'Orsi at the Palazzo Orsi

GENTLEMEN (Merry-Go-Round). Strangers who visited Lady Vizard; slipped sovereigns into young Basil Kent's hands

GENTLEMEN (Razor's Edge). At the Brasserie Graf, Avenue Clichy, Paris; old; early risers; wear thick-lensed spectacles

GENTLEMEN (Round Dozen). The two of them; guests at the Dolphin; elderly golfers; red faces and baldish heads

GENTLEMEN (Sheppey). Three or four of them; respectable tradesmen with wives and families; they used to visit Bessie Legros regularly at her flat in Kensington

GENTRY (Magician). Live at Skene, Staffordshire; Oliver Haddo had quarrelled with all of them

GEORGE (Circle). The footman to Arnold Champion-Cheney; he serves tea to Arnold and Lady Catherine Champion-Cheney; delivers Edward Luton's letter from the Champion Arms hotel and pub to Elizabeth Champion-Cheney

GEORGE (Mabel). Tall, thin, bronzed; large moustache; has been married to Mabel for eight years

GEORGE (Mrs. Dot). He is James Blankinsop's servant

GEORGE (Narrow Corner). The owner of the bar in Sydney, Australia; gave Captain Nichols a dirty look and told him to wait outside until he decided to buy a drink

GEORGE (Theatre). The doorkeeper to Julia Lambert Gosselyn's dressing room; he guarded Julia's privacy between performances

GEORGE V (Hour Before the Dawn). King of England (1936-1952); he addresses the nation on the radio on the evening following the Nazi German invasion of Poland

GERMAN AMBASSADOR (Lord Mountdrago). He talks with an Austrian archduke at Lydia Connemara's party

GERMAN DOCTOR (Penelope). Mrs. Watson read that he had discovered a new medicine for nerve cases

GERMAN GOVERNESS (Human Element). A fictional character in Humphrey Carruthers' "Week-End"; all action seen through her eyes

GERMAN HARRY (German Harry). A Dane; the only resident at Trebucket; once an able seaman on a sailing ship that had wrecked off Trebucket; refused to be taken from the island; is over seventy years of age; bald gray beard, hatchet face; blue eyes

GERMAN MOTORCYCLISTS (Hour Before the Dawn). The two of them come to Michel's farmhouse; want directions to Andrecy

GERMAN MOTORCYCLISTS (Hour Before the Dawn). There are six of them; they enter the inn at the small French village; Roger Henderson, disguised as the barkeeper, drinks champagne with them

GERMAN OFFICER (Home and Beauty). Had a difference of opinion with William Cardew, who quickly laid him out

GERMAN OFFICER (Unconquered). Commander at Soissons; elderly and easy-going

GERMAN PAINTER (Punctiliousness of Don Sebastian). The Narrator met him at Xiormonez, Spain; a cautious man; tried to solve the mystery of the whereabouts of the railway officials at Xiormonez

GERMAN PROSTITUTE (Ashenden/Miss King). Small; China blue eyes, doll-like face; dines at the Geneva hotel

GERTRUDE (For Services Rendered). The parlormaid at the Ardsley house; brings in meals and announces visitors

GIACOMINI, Monna Francesca (Then and Now). The widowed mother of Piero Giacomini; sister of Biagio Buonaccorsi

GIACOMINI, Piero (Then and Now). Biagio Buonaccorsi's nephew; age eighteen; he accompanies Machiavelli to Imola; tall and handsome; had been taught history by

Machiavelli; eventually enlists in the army of Caesar Borgia, becomes a page to Count Lodovico Alvisi, and, finally, marries Aurelia Martelli

GIACOMO (Mask and the Face). He is listed, but not described in the summary

GIBBONS (Jasper (Cakes and Ale). One of the most celebrated poets of his day; born at Walsall; after only one volume of verse, fourteen critics claimed to have discovered him; the first poet to have his name engraved at the bottom of an "At Home" card; recited his work at the home of Mrs. Barton Trafford; he was inclined to drink; once arrested for being drunk and disorderly in Piccadilly

GIBBONS, Mr. (Of Human Bondage). The buyer of the furnishing drapery department of a London store; he is middle aged, short, and corpulent; black beard and dark greasy hair; brisk movements and a clever face

GIGOLO (Gigolo and Gigolette). A friend of Syd Cotman; had married a woman old enough to be his mother; she gave him a car and money

GIGOLO (Lion's Skin). At the Casino; he asks Eleanor Forestier to dance; is nearly knocked down by Robert Forestier

GILLIAN, Mr. and Mrs. (Theatre). Thomas Fennell saved them hundreds of pounds on their income tax

GILLIATT, Mrs. (Unattainable). Calls to remind Caroline Ashley that she is to have tea with her at Rumplemeyer's; Caroline has no intention of going

GINGER TED (Vessel of Wrath). He is the only white man, besides Rev. Owen Jones, who lived on Baru; and Englishman; a drunkard; age thirty-one; middle height; fat; a bloated red face; curly, red hair; white skin

GIOVANNI (Then and Now). The hired man employed by the Machiavellis; he ate with his masters in the kitchen; caught the dozen larks for their dinner

GIOVANNI (Up at the Villa). The head waiter at the Florentine restaurant on one of the banks of the Arno; could speak half a dozen languages fluently, but he understood none; he tells the Princess San Ferdinando that the singer is sick

GIPSY (Sheppey). On the pier; said that Florie Miller had a gift for languages

GIRL (Bad Example). Age twenty; found dead in the River

Thames, a confused black mass; pregnant; had written a letter to the coroner, apologizing for the trouble she would cause

GIRL #1 (Bishop's Apron). Maid to Mrs. Railing; frowzy; dishevelled head

GIRL #2 (Bishop's Apron). Happy eyed; dancing around the ballroom in an ecstasy of delight

GIRL (Buried Talent). A fellow voice student of Blanche (MacArdle) in Paris; she believed that Blanche was jealous of Charmian Pelletier success; claimed that Charmian owed her success to her looks, rather than to her voice

GIRL #1 (Christmas Holiday). At Paris; is walking by herself; a seamstress or a typist; going home after a day's work; Charley Mason sees her from his taxi

GIRL #2 (Christmas Holiday). At Paris; with a fur round her neck; walking arm-in-arm under an umbrella with a young man; Charley Mason sees her from his taxi

GIRL #3 (Christmas Holiday). At Paris; English; wanted to come with Simon Fenimore and share his squalor; works with the International Communist Bureau; the daughter of a dean; held a degree in economics from Oxford; she looked upon promiscuous fornication as a sacred duty

GIRL #4 (Christmas Holiday). At Paris; Norwegian; she wanted to come with Simon Fenimore and to share his squalor; works as the Sorbonne

GIRL #5 (Christmas Holiday). At Paris; French; out of work dressmaker; wanted to come with Simon Fenimore and share his squalor; she is gentle and affectionate

GIRL #6 (Christmas Holiday). The daughter of Alexey and Evgenia; she goes to live with her aunt at Nice

GIRL #7 (Christmas Holiday). The daughter of Alexey and Evgenia; has gone into service

GIRL #8 (Christmas Holiday). At the Serail, Paris; she is suddenly taken ill; Simon Fenimore took her to a nursing home, paid for the operation, and paid her expenses to a convalescent home

GIRL #9 (Christmas Holiday). With Man #5 at the cellar bar, Paris; twenty years younger than her companion; sleek black hair; face powdered dead white; scarlet lips; eyes heavy with mascara; dances with Charley Mason

Characters   179

GIRL (East of Suez). The daughter of Coolie #3; shy, solemn, and silent; Daisy Anderson gives her presents

GIRL (Hero). A slender Amazon; in a London park; smiles at a man who raises his hat to her

GIRL #1 (Honolulu). Tall, graceful, alert; brown skin; thick black hair coiled around her head; small, even, white teeth

GIRL #2 (Honolulu). Captain Butler's first girl who ran away with the first Chinese cook

GIRL #1 (Liza of Lambeth). On Vere Street, Lambeth; she dances with Florie to the tune of the organ grinder

GIRL #2 (Liza of Lambeth). On Vere Street, Lambeth; she asks Liza Kemp if she is wearing her new dress

GIRL #3 (Liza of Lambeth). On Vere Street, Lambeth; she asks Liza Kemp where she got her new dress

GIRL #4 (Liza of Lambeth). One of Liza Kemp's fellow factory workers; she asks Liza why she is shivering

GIRL (Merry-Go-Round). A typist; "a real love touch"; Reggie Barlow-Bassett wants to dine with her without his mother knowing about it

GIRL (Moon and Sixpence). Age fifteen; granddaughter of the old Tahitian woman who had helped Ata through her pregnancy; she comes to stay with Ata and Charles Strickland; sent by Ata with a hundred franc note to bring Dr. Coutras to tend to Strickland

GIRL (Mrs. Dot). On a crowded train from the city; she is strong and bouncing; never thanks the clerk for giving his seat to her; she does not, in turn, offer to give her seat to an old woman

GIRL (Neil MacAdam). Serves pale tea at the Japanese brothel, Singapore

GIRL #1 (Of Human Bondage). She played with a touring company; had an affair with Watson, the brewer's son

GIRL #2 (Of Human Bondage). The baby born to Mildred Rogers; Emil Miller the father; Mildred is undecided whether to name her Madeleine or Ceclia; dies before she is three years old

GIRL #3 (Of Human Bondage). Attends the Monday evening social of Lynn and Sedley, London; a great deal of hair; played the piano

GIRL #1 (Painted Veil). At the French convent, Mei-tan-fu; age six; an idiot, with huge hydrocephalic head; small, squat body; large vacant eyes; drooling mouth;

spoke hoarsely a few mumbled words; became attached to Kitty Fane and followed her about
GIRL #2 (Painted Veil). At the French convent at Meitan-fu; little; confident in the Mother Superior's interest; showed her a fantastic toy
GIRL #1 (Razor's Edge). Lives with Auguste Cottet at Seville, where he had initially met her
GIRL #2 (Razor's Edge). At Seville; is a friend of the flamenco singer; age eighteen; pretty; she had gotten into trouble with Paco, a boy from her village, and expected a baby; went to work in a tobacco factory; goes to live with Larry Darrell; leaves him to return to Paco and their baby
GIRL (Round Dozen). Plain; she wears a Tam o'Shanter
GIRL (Salvatore). Eyes like forest pools; pretty; lives on the Grande Marina; becomes engaged to Salvatore
GIRL (Smith). She works in the flat upstairs from the Dallas-Bakers; Fletcher goes out with her after Smith refuses him
GIRL #1 (Theatre). At the Globe Restaurant, London; she was "picked up" by Michael Gosselyn when he was playing with Benson's Company
GIRL #2 (Theatre). An acquaintance of Evie; a total stranger bought her a hat in a Bond Street shop; she walked out of the shop while he waited for the change
GIRL (Unattainable). Engaged for seven years to Man #2 in South Africa; when she came to Durban, his courage failed him, and he ran; she chased him up and down Africa, caught him, and married him
GIRL (Vessel of Wrath). Fancied by Evert Gruyter at the same time that she had been according her favors to Ginger Ted
GIRL'S FATHER (Salvatore). He would not give permission for his daughter to marry Salvatore
GIRL'S MOTHER (Salvatore). Sits on the doorstep of her house with her daughter
GIRLS (Bad Example). Young; half a dozen of them; they dance to the music of a barrel organ; James Clinton gives them money
GIRLS (Bishop's Apron). Dowdy; have spent their lives in Bayswater or in small, dull terraces at South Kensington; after their fathers have become peers, they bear their twopenny titles self-consciously and marry

obscure young men from the City

GIRLS (Bishop's Apron). Some acquaintances of Winnie Spratte; they have married beneath their class and struggle to keep up appearances and to make ends meet

GIRLS (Christmas Holiday). At the Dome, Paris; bare headed; in raincoats

GIRLS (Christmas Holiday). Two of them; they dance together at the Serail, Paris; dance with the woman in black

GIRLS (Hero). In a London park; they hurry past James Parsons on ponies or bicycles; convey an impression of light-heartedness; their cheeks glow with healthiness; a happy tenderness is revealed in their eyes

GIRLS (Hour Before the Dawn). Employed by Jenkins as farm laborers

GIRLS (Liza of Lambeth). On Vere Street, Lambeth; they are chiefly employed in skipping rope; they dance to the music of the Italian organ grinder

GIRLS (Liza of Lambeth). Three of them; little; seen in front of the theatre in Westminster; sang sentimental songs and collected money

GIRLS (Liza of Lambeth). Noticed Liza Kemp's black and blue eye

GIRLS (Moon and Sixpence). Four of them; employed by Amy Strickland in her typing office in Chancery Lane, London

GIRLS (Mrs. Craddock). Aboard the penny steamboat from London to Greenwich; noisy

GIRLS (Painted Veil). Chinese; two of them; live at the French convent at Mei-tan-fu; attacked by cholera; nothing can save them

GIRLS (Painted Veil). At the French convent at Mei-tan-fu; in Kitty Fane's charge; little; stiff black hair; round yellow faces; staring, sloe-black eyes; in ugly uniforms

GIRLS (Penelope). Two of them; from Francoise, at The Modeste; they bring hats for Penelope O'Farrell

GIRLS (Spanish Priest). At Gibraltar; in mantillas and accompanied by duenas; they walk quickly, with modest bearing

GIUSEPPE (Wash-Tub). A waiter at the hotel at Positano; also functioned as porter, chambermaid, and cook; an old friend of the Narrator

GLADSTONE, William (Mrs. Craddock). The British liberal statesman (1809-1898); had appointed Andover Bishop of Barchester

GLADSTONE, William (Mrs. Craddock). The British liberal statesman (1809-1898); at Mrs. Branderton's dinner party, Atthill Bacot tells a story about him and the table at the House of Commons

GLASER, Miss (Voice of the Turtle). La Falterona's secretary; English; age fifty; haggard; grey hair and a sallowed, wrinkled face; plays the piano

GLOSTER, Eleo (Our Betters). An American woman married to an Englishman; she is unfaithful to him

GLOVER, Charles (Merry-Go-Round). The vicar of Leanham, Kent; brother of Fanny Glover

GLOVER, Charles (Mrs. Craddock). The vicar of Leanham, Kent; brother of Fanny Glover; over forty years of age; is tall, angular, fair, and thin; red-cheeked; a somewhat feminine edition of his sister; smelled of antiseptics

GLOVER, Fanny (Merry-Go-Round). The sister of the Rev. Charles Glover

GLOVER, Fanny (Mrs. Craddock). Sister of Rev. Charles Glover; worthy, but tedious; good natured and charitable; bashful and self-conscious; age twenty-eight; colorless hair; no figure; dry and hard skin drawn tightly over her bones; a red flush covered her prominent cheekbones; a determined nose and mouth; pale blue eyes; according to Mrs. Branderton, her "great ankles are positively pornographic"; keeps house for her brother

GNOCCHI, Cesare (Making of a Saint). Son of Bartolomeo Moratini; related to the d'Orsi on his mother's side

GO-BETWEEN (Bishop's Apron). Sent unofficially by the Government to Josiah Spratte to learn of his views on the Lord Chancellor appointment

GODMOTHER (For Services Rendered). Of Eva Ardsley; left Eva a thousand pounds

GOLDING, Mr. (Daisy). A fisherman at Blackstable, Kent

GOLDSMITH (Making of a Saint). The best one in Rome; he made a gold chain for Girolamo Riario

GOLIGHTLY, Charles (Penelope). The husband of Isabel Golightly; the father of Penelope O'Farrell; tall and spare; grey hair; clean shaven; he is a professor of mathematics who maintains that 2+2=5

GOLIGHTLY, Isabel (Penelope). Davenport Barlow's sister and wife of Charles Golightly; the mother of Penelope O'Farrell; middle aged; extremely stout; good natured

GOMEZ (Ashenden/Traitor). A young Spaniard whom Grantley Caypor had met in Zurich; a member of the British Secret Service; was tried, convicted, and shot by the Germans

GOOD FOLK (Explorer [novel]). Aboard panting ferries that carried them across the water to buy goods in Southampton or to sell the produce of their farms

GOODHART, Colonel (Gigolo and Gigolette). A gentleman from the City; no one knew how he came by his rank; at the Casino dinner party

GOODWORTHY, Mr. (Of Human Bondage). Managing clerk at Messrs. Herbert Carter and Company, London; small and thin; a large head; prominent pale eyes; thin sandy hair; uneven whiskers; pasty and yellow skin; badly decayed teeth

GORDON, Rev. B.B. (Of Human Bondage). The master of the middle-third form at King's School, Tercanbury; known as "Squirts"; ill-suited to be a schoolmaster; he is impatient and choleric; of middle height; corpulent figure; short, sandy hair turning grey; small bristly moustache; a large, naturally red face that grew dark and purple when he became angry; small blue eyes; a nail biter; eventually dies of apoplexy

GORDON, Mr. (Of Human Bondage). An actor; he and his wife touring the provinces; Norah Nesbit invites them to lunch on a Sunday

GORDON, Mrs. (Of Human Bondage). The wife of Gordon the actor

GORING (Yellow Streak). A police officer at Kuala Solor and a resident of the rest house there

GOSSELYN, George (Theatre). Father of Michael Gosselyn; a retired army colonel; he had little more than his pension on which to live; had retired with honorary rank after an entirely undistinguished career; he had served for some time in India; thin and rather small; a lined face; close-cropped white hair; civil, but reserved; he dies during the influenza epidemic after the war

GOSSELYN, Julia Lambert (Theatre). A noted actress; age

forty-six; the wife of Michael Gosselyn and mother of Roger; a native of Jersey and daughter of a veterinarian there; learned French from her aunt, Madame Carrie Falloux, and acting from Jane Taitbout; at age sixteen a student at the Royal Academy of Dramatic Art, Gower Street, London; following two years on the stage, James Langston engaged her (at age twenty) for his company at Middlepool; one year later, she met Michael Gosselyn; a lovely figure; fairly tall; long legs; low, rich voice; she falls in love with Thomas Fennell

GOSSELYN, Michael (Theatre). Husband of Julia Lambert Gosselyn and father of Roger; age fifty-two; short chestnut hair turning very grey; a good figure; handsome; six feet tall; educated at Cambridge; had been five years in the war; at age twenty-five, engaged by James Langton's company at Middlepool; spent a single season in America; served in France during World War I, emerging at age thirty-six with the rank of major, the Military Cross, and the Legion of Honour; becomes manager of the Sarah Siddons Theatre; he is a tidy businessman; as a young actor (the best looking one on the English stage): a great mass of curling chestnut hair; wonderful skin; large dark-blue eyes; a straight nose; small ears

GOSSELYN, Mrs. (Theatre). The wife of Colonel George Gosselyn and mother of Michael; invited Michael and Julia Lambert to visit for a week at Cheltenham; tall and stout; elderly; much taller than her husband; her hair parted in the middle, with a bun on the nape of her neck; possessed the remains of good looks; shy; dies during the influenza epidemic following the war

GOSSELYN, Roger (Theatre). The son of Julia and Michael Gosselyn; age seventeen; curly red hair; blue eyes; his only good features were his teeth and his hair; educated at Eton (where he had been entered a week after birth); one year away from entering Cambridge; leaves Eton and goes to Vienna; searches for reality

GOVERNESS (Explorer [novel]). She is in charge of Lucy Allerton following the death of her mother

GOVERNESS (Pro Patria). Engaged by Fanny Porter-Smith's sister; John Porter-Smith had behaved badly with her

GOVERNESS (Razor's Edge). Employed by the Maturins; she

Characters 185

is afraid to take Joan Maturin to see the dentist
GOVERNMENT OFFICIAL (Moon and Sixpence). A guest at the Stricklands' dinner party
GOVERNMENT SURVEYOR (Casual Affair). He is a guest at the Lows' dinner party
GOVERNOR of French Guiana (Man with a Conscience). He lives at Cayenne; the Narrator lives in his bungalow at St. Laurent de Maroni
GOVERNOR of Hong Kong (Painted Veil). After Kitty and Walter Fane first arrived in Hong Kong, he took in Kitty as a bride; Charlie Townsend will have to tell him about his affair with Kitty Fane; according to Charlie, he will curse like hell; a good fellow who will fix Charlie's problems somehow and avoid scandal by bringing pressure to bear upon Walter Fane
GOVERNOR of Pago Pago (Rain). He is large and handsome; a sailor; grey, toothbrush moustache
GOVERNOR of Rhodes (Human Element). A guest at Betty Weldon-Burns' dinner party
GOVERNOR of the Prison Island (Official Position). Pays no attention to the fears and the appeals of Louis Ramire's predecessor
GRABAU DAUGHTERS (Razor's Edge). Two of them; of Frau and Professor Grabau; at Bonn; middle aged; did the cooking and the housekeeping work at their mother's boarding house
GRABOW, Frau (Ashenden/Traitor). Wife of Gustav Grabow
GRABOW, Gustav (Ashenden/Traitor). Secret service agent and a resident of Basle; represents a Swiss firm with branches in Germany; is possessed of a keen instinct; dapper little man with close shaven round head; wears spectacles
GRAND DUKES (Magician). Russians; with their mistresses and often in company with the Haddos at Monte Carlo
GRAHAM, Mr. (Cakes and Ale). Occupies the same rooms as Ashenden had, thirty-five years earlier, at the house of Mrs. Hudson, Vincent Square, London
GRANDFATHER (Man of Honour). Of Jenny Kent; he is her mother's father; supposedly a gentleman
GRANDFATHER (Merry-Go-Round). Of Mrs. Castillyon; Emily Barlow-Bassett discovered that he was actually a lord
GRANDFATHER (Mrs. Dot). Of Gerald Halstane; on Gerald's mother's side; he lived to the age of ninety-seven

GRANDFATHER (Razor's Edge). The Quaker father of Larry Darrell's mother; he was lost at sea when a young man

GRANDFATHER (Sheppey). Of Gentleman #2; he received the snuff box from King George V

GRANGE, Miss (Sheppey). A manicurist at Bradley's Hairdressing and Barber's Saloon, Jermyn Street, London; very refined

GRANGE, Norman (Flotsam and Jetsam). A rubber planter at Borneo; close cropped gray hair; a gray moustache; red, broad fleshy face; a large mouth; short, pugnacious nose; small, mean eyes; he was born at Sarawak, Borneo; his father was a government worker

GRANGE, Vesta (Flotsam and Jetsam). The wife of Norman Grange; is small and elderly looking;; age forty-six; short hair, dyed yellow; dry skin; a tic causes her head and hand to jerk; an actress, known as Vesta Blaise before she married Norman, sixteen years ago

GRANGER, Alfred (Bread-Winner). Husband of Dorothy and father of Diana and Timothy; a solicitor; tall, well set, and middle aged; red faced; hearty, blustering, jovial manner; he laughs at everything that he says

GRANGER, Diana (Bread-Winner). Daughter of Alfred and Dorothy Granger; the sister of Timothy; age eighteen; she is dark and pretty; with fine eyes; a fresh color

GRANGER, Dorothy (Bread-Winner). Wife of Alfred Granger and the mother of Diana and Timothy; less than forty years of age

GRANGER, Timothy (Bread-Winner). The son of Alfred and Dorothy Granger; brother of Diana; age seventeen; is slim, tall, and dark

GRAVE DIGGERS (Painted Veil). At Mei-tan-fu; they cover Walter Fane's coffin with dirt

GRAVENEYS (Good Manners). The owners of Graveney Hall, Kent, the largest house in the neighborhood; forced to lease their lands and move to a villa in Regent's Park

GRAVES, Josiah (Of Human Bondage). The manager of the Blackstable bank; choir master (of the best choir in Kent), church treasurer, and church warden; is tall; thin sallow face; long nose; extremely white hair; is referred to (in private) by Rev. William Carey as "Bismarck"; takes charge of William Carey's funeral arrangements and of his will

GRAVES, Miss (Of Human Bondage). The sister of Josiah Graves; kept house for her brother; secretary of the Maternity Club, dedicated to easing the problems of the pregnant poor; along with Louisa Carey, attempted to reconcile the differences between Josiah Graves and William Carey

GRAVINA, Duke of (Then and Now). The nephew of Pagolo Orsini; he accompanied his uncle to the meeting of Caesar Borgia's captains at La Magione, near Perugia

GRAY (Red). A store owner

GRAY, Dr. (Bishop's Apron). The headmaster of Harbin School; formerly a tutor to one of Lord Stonehenge's children; the newspapers announce, prematurely, his appointment as Bishop of Barchester; Lord Stonehenge eventually appoints him to that post; has an apoplectic stroke and dies

GRAY, Dr. (Loaves and Fishes). The headmaster of Harbin School; Lionel Spratte reports that he has been announced as Bishop of Colchester

GRAY, Miss (Happy Couple). A neighbor and old friend of the Narrator; of mature age

GRAY, Miss (Hero). Daughter of Mrs. Gray; wears bright colors to church, to which Mary Clibborn objects

GRAY, Mrs. (Hero). The mother of Miss Gray; she is one of Mary Clibborn's patients at Little Primpton, Kent

GRAYSTON, Lord George (Our Betters). Husband of Lady Pearl Grayston; an Englishman; he wants to live nine months of the year in the country and have a baby every five minutes; he resides in Abbots Kenton, Suffolk, when Pearl lives in London; moves to London whenever Pearl entertains in Suffolk

GRAYSTON, Lady (Our Betters). The mother of Lord George Grayston; according to Lady Pearl, a peculiarly plain woman

GRAYSTON, Lady Pearl (Our Betters). Wife of Lord George Grayston; Bessie Saunders' sister; an American from New York; she occupies a house in Grosvenor Street, Mayfair, London; age thirty-four; handsome and dashing; red hair; outrageously painted face; was once engaged to a boy in business in Portland, Oregon

GRAZIA, Count Paola (Mask and the Face). The husband of Savina Grazia; extremely jealous; claims that a man who pardons infidelity must resort to suicide; he further claims that he would kill his wife if she were to be unfaithful to him; lacks the determination to kill himself or to strangle Savina; goes on trial and is acquitted for the murder of his wife--who is not dead at all; then reconciles with Savina upon her return from abroad

GRAZIA, Savina (Mask and the Face). Wife of Count Paola Grazia; attractive; is ordered by her husband to go abroad and to change her name; believed to have been murdered by Paolo; returns and reconciles with him

GREEK GIRL (In a Strange Land). She worked at the Niccolinis' hotel; the mother of the two Niccolini boys

GREEK MAN (String of Beads). Becomes intimate with Miss Robinson in Paris, after she disposes of the rich Argentinian

GREEK WOMAN (Moon and Sixpence). Lives in Alexandria with Abraham; supposedly ugly and old

GREEN, Howard (Road Uphill). A mutual friend of Joseph Sheridan and Ruth Latimer; he promises to become a millionaire in two years; has intentions toward Ruth Latimer, whom he marries; ruined financially when his speculations fail; faces prison; kills himself in an airplane crash

GREEN, Lady (Hero). Formerly, Miss Lake; supposedly a friend of Major William Forsyth; she supposedly tells William he has found the secret of perpetual youth

GREEN, Ruth (Road Uphill). See below under Ruth LATIMER

GREENCOURT, Major (Cakes and Ale). Had taken the Three Gables, Blackstable, Kent; has an attack of the gout

GREENCOURT, Mrs. (Cakes and Ale). Wife of Major Greencourt; her father made china and her grandfather had been a factory hand

GREENE, Emery (Woman of Fifty). The brother of Jasper Greene; husband of Fanny Greene; composer and teacher at a New York music school; twenty-seven or twenty-eight years of age

GREENE, Fanny (Woman of Fifty). Wife of Emery Greene; small and pretty; an unemployed actress

GREENE, Jasper (Woman of Fifty). Instructor at a small Midwest university; is Laura Greene's second husband; large and plump; a moon face; black, coarse, unkempt hair; wears spectacles; slightly over thirty years of age

GREENE, Laura Clayton (Woman of Fifty). Wife of Jasper Greene; is originally from San Francisco; she teaches Renaissance and Italian literature; once married to Tito de San Pietro; age fifty; grey hair; stout; with large pale blue eyes; poor complexion

GREENGROCER (Rehearsal). The father (according to the Zampas) of La Ferrari

GREENGROCERS (Fortunate Painter). Located in the Rue Breda, Paris; they argue with the ladies

GREGSON (East of Suez). His death causes Henry Anderson to leave Peking for Tientsin and Kalgan, as well as delays for one year Harry's transfer to Chung-King

GREY, Rev. Charles (Daisy). The vicar of Blackstable church, Kent; husband of Mrs. Grey

GREY, James (Daisy). A nephew of Rev. Charles and Mrs. Grey

GREY, Mr. (Before the Party). The Resident of the State of Sembulu, Borneo

GREY, Mrs. (Before the Party). Wife of the Resident of the State of Sembulu, Borneo; middle aged and kindly

GREY, Mrs. (Daisy). The wife of the Rev. Charles Grey

GRIFFITH, Daisy (Daisy). Daughter of Robert and Mary Ann Griffith; sister of George; she was educated at Tercanbury; studied singing and dancing; eloped with Captain Hogan, who abandons her in London; takes a situation in London; begs to return to Blackstable; pale; blue eyes, dim and lifeless; eyelids heavy and red; beautiful hair, dishevelled; becomes (according to her brother, George) a London streetwalker; then she turns up at Tarcanbury in a pantomime (as Dick Whittington); marries Lord Herbert Ously-Farrowham; returns to Blackstable to visit her parents; tall and dignified, with grave blue eyes

GRIFFITH, George (Daisy). Son of Herbert and Mary Ann Griffith; brother of Daisy, of whom he is jealous; educated at the church school, Blackstable; engaged to Edith Pollett, whom he eventually marries; he is employed as a clerk to a coal merchant at a salary of one pound per week; is sent by Mary Ann Griffith to London to tell Daisy that she and Robert will have nothing to do with her

GRIFFITH, Mary Ann (Daisy). The wife of Robert Griffith and mother of George and Daisy; small hard grey eyes;

hard features; firm clear complexion; looks down upon Daisy with utter contempt; she intercepts Daisy's letters to Robert Griffith

GRIFFITH, Robert (Daisy). Husband of Mary Ann Griffith and father of George and Daisy; a carpenter; churchwarden at Blackstable church; is not more than fifty years of age; bearded; he lacks the courage to oppose his wife

GRIFFITHS, Dr. (Of Human Bondage). The father of Harry Griffiths; practiced medicine in a small village in Cumberland; he had not the heart to be angry with his extravagant son

GRIFFITHS, Harry (Of Human Bondage). He is a fifth-year medical student at St. Luke's Hospital, London; lived on the floor above Philip Carey; had been to Oxford; tall, with a quantity of curly, red hair; blue eyes; white skin; red mouth; everyone liked him; he nurses Philip Carey during the latter's bout with influenza; appointed house surgeon at a hospital in the north of London; later, he falls in love with Mildred Rogers

GRIFFITHS, Mr. (Lord Mountdrago). A Welsh miner; father of Owen Griffiths; he witnessed Lord Mountdrago's humiliation of his son in the House of Commons

GRIFFITHS, Mrs. (Lord Mountdrago). The mother of Owen Griffiths; witnessed Lord Mountdrago's humiliation of her son in the House of Commons

GRIFFITHS, Mrs. (Of Human Bondage). The mother of Harry Griffiths and wife of Dr. Griffiths; an old-fashioned person for whom a telegram proved an event to excite tremor

GRIFFITHS, Owen (Lord Mountdrago). A Welsh Labour Party member of Parliament; he appears in Lord Mountdrago's dreams; a former miner and the son of a miner; once a schoolmaster and journalist; scrawny and grey-faced; filthy hands

GRIGGS, Mrs. (Man of Honour). Is Basil Kent's landlady

GROOM (Bishop's Apron). He only bores Gwendolyn Durant

GROOM (Then and Now). Of Bartolomeo Martelli; he accompanies his master

GRUYTER, Mynheer Evart (Vessel of Wrath). Is the Dutch controleur of the Alas Islands; resides at Baru; age thirty; five feet, four inches tall; extremely fat; round and red; a round, protruding belly; a florid

complexion; his head and face always shaved; eyebrows barely visible; little twinkling blue eyes; fluent in English, Dutch, and Malay
GUARD (Magician). At the Luxembourg Gardens, Paris; in the romantic cloak of a brigand in comic opera; wears a peaked cap
GUARD #1 (Making of a Saint). At the town gate, Forli; he tells Filippo Brandolini and Matteo d'Orsi to stop
GUARD #2 (Making of a Saint). Tries to explain why all of the so-called robbers who attacked Checco d'Orsi have been slain
GUARD #3 (Making of a Saint). At the Palazzo Orsi, in Forli; salutes Checco d'Orsi and other conspirators as they pass to enter Girolamo Riario's apartment
GUARD (Punctiliousness of Don Sebastian). On duty at the railway station at Xiormonez, Spain; he told the Narrator where he was
GUARDS (Making of a Saint). Escort Caterina Sforza and her three children from the Palazzo Orsi to Checco d'Orsi's house
GUARDS (Then and Now). Two of them; escort Machiavelli from the Sforza Palace back to Serafina's house
GUARDSMAN #1 (Bishop's Apron). Young; he is comfortably asleep in the smoking room of his club; then, rudely awakened by Lord Josiah Spratte to make a fourth for whist; told Lord Spratte to stop "ragging him like a fish-wife" and to mind his manner
GUARDSMAN #2 (Bishop's Apron). He claims a dance with Gwendolyn Durant
GUBBINS, Miss (Outstation). The maiden name of Mr. Warburton's mother
GUEST #1 (Treasure). Of Richard Harenger; is served immediately by Pritchard
GUEST #2 (Treasure). Converses with Richard Harenger about the value and appearance of Pritchard
GUESTS (Explorer [novel]). Attended Lady Alice Kelsey's dance; they huddle around the door, waiting for their carriages and cabs
GUESTS (Magician). Of Oliver Haddo, at a Monte Carlo restaurant; furious with Haddo for having given the waiter a counterfeit coin
GUESTS (Magician). Two of them; at the last moment cannot attend Dr. Arbuthnot's dinner party at the Savoy

GUY (Force of Circumstances). He is married to Doris; age twenty-nine; born in Sembulu, Malaya; small and round; a red face; with pimply complexion; blue eyes

GWEN (Theatre). A young lady engaged to the young man who confronts Julia Lambert Gosselyn in the Edgware Road, London; she collects autographs; pert-looking

GWENNIE (Of Human Bondage). The middle aged daughter of Lady #6; she and her mother guests at the boarding house in Brighton

H

HABART, Lady Dollie (Lady Habart). A widowed gentlewoman, under thirty years of age; she is the sister of Guy Cherriton; naturally cold brown hair altered to a delicate reddish gold; great blue eyes; a rose-like mouth; pencilled eyebrows and long black lashes; perfect teeth; beautiful; she owes Captain Smithson three thousand pounds

HABART, Lord (Lady Habart). He had broken his neck five years earlier in a hunting field; unable to will away a penny of his property; deceased husband of Dollie

HABERDASHER (Catalina). The father of La Clara; at odds with Diego Martinez

HADDO, Margaret (Magician). See under Margaret DAUNCEY

HADDO, Mr. (Magician). Father of Oliver Haddo; always unlucky in speculation; he lost his power of speech shortly before he died; his son called him from the grave a year later, and the father conveyed his dying words--advice to purchase a stock that, in the end, did poorly

HADDO, Mrs. (Magician). The mother of Oliver Haddo; has been in an asylum for the past twenty-five years; of great stature; revolting, excessive corpulence; huge, impassive face, smooth and unwrinkled; grey, disheveled, and scanty hair; bears an appalling likeness to Oliver

HADDO, Oliver (Magician). An Englishman; large; six feet two or three inches tall; was extremely handsome when young, with a magnificent figure; now, is vastly obese, with a paunch of imposing dimensions; a large and fleshy face; not old, but his corpulence adds to his apparent age; good features, with small ears and delicately shaped nose; pale blue eyes; large teeth, white and even; a large mouth; heavy moist lips; the neck of a bullock; dark, curling hair retreating from his temples; a bald crown; clean shaven; had the look of a wicked, sensual priest; pompous; was educated at Eton and Oxford (which he left in 1896), where he had a reputation for athletics and eccentricity; claims to have been one of Dr. Frank Hurrell's most intimate friends; is rumored to have been married to a ballet-girl in Milan, Italy; Dr. Porhoet meets him at the Arsenal Library, Paris, where both studied the old alchemists; read Hebrew and Arabic, and had studied the Kabbalah (or Cabala) in the original; claims to be a magician, but wishes to be known as a Brother of the Shadow; possesses extraordinary courage, but is, at the same time, wantonly cruel; terribly vain; he claims to have shot more lions than any man alive; still possesses Skene, the family estate in Staffordshire; proposes marriage to Margaret Dauncey, whom he marries; he engages in the practice of creating human forms; his corpulence becomes a positive disease; all of his features sink into a hideous obesity; he dies from suffocation

HALL, Louisa (Landed Gentry). The companion to Mrs. Insoley; self-effacing and silent; of uncertain age; she is always anxious to make herself useful

HALLIWELL (Man of Honour). Employed in the meat trade; he is an acquaintance of James Bush

HALLIWELL, John (Man of Honour). The husband of Mabel Halliwell; age twenty-six; good-humored; is neither handsome nor plain; blunt and open

HALLIWELL, Mabel (Man of Honour). The younger sister of Hilda Murray; wife of John Halliwell; small; pretty, rather than beautiful; she is vivacious and talkative

HALSTANE, GERALD (Mrs. Dot). Related to the long line of the Dowager Duchess of Hollington; Dot Worthley is in love with him

HAMLYN, Mr. (P.&O.). The husband of Mrs. Hamlyn; age fifty-two; bald, stout; employed as a silk merchant in Yokohama; he had fallen in love with Dorothy Lacom

HAMLYN, Mrs. (P.&O.). Mr. Hamlyn's wife; large; forty years of age

HAMMOND, Geoffrey (Letter [play]). His age in the late

thirties; supposedly an acquaintance of the Crosbies, but he is actually Leslie Crosbie's lover; tall; good looking, and breezy; generous with his money, and a favorite with the ladies; was the best dancer between Penang and Singapore; wounded in the knee during the war; left Leslie for the Chinese woman at Singapore; shot by Leslie, who claimed that he tried to rape her

HAMMOND, Geoffrey (Letter [story]). Is Killed by Leslie Crosbie; his age in the late thirties; wounded and decorated in World War I; tall, handsome; blue eyes; has black, curling hair; played tennis and billiards

HANCOCK DAUGHTERS (Mrs. Craddock). Of General Hancock; two of them; they accompanied their father to Mrs. Branderton's dinner party; their combined ages came to sixty-five years

HANCOCK, General (Mrs. Craddock). One of the guests at Mrs. Branderton's dinner party

HANGMAN (Making of a Saint). Enters the piazza at Forli on a huge black stallion; large; dressed in flaming red, with a red hood over his head; rides the horse around the piazza, dragging Orso d'Orsi at the end of a rope

HANLEY, Mrs. (Our Betters). Supposedly washed miners; clothes in California

HANNAH (Unknown). Maid at the Whartons' house, Stour, Kent

HANNAWAY, Ellen (Creative Impulse). She is one of Mrs. Forrester's most devoted admirers

HANNAY, Mrs. (Door of Opportunity). The wife of the governor of Singapore

HANNAY, Percy (Door of Opportunity). The Governor of Singapore; grey hair, eyes, and face; looks tired and depressed

HANS (Unconquered). A German soldier; tall, slim, broad shouldered; fair, curly hair; blue eyes; the son of a farmer; had been to school in Munich and then to an agricultural college; called "Jean" by Madame Perier

HANS' BROTHER (Unconquered). Lives with his parents on the family farm in Bavaria

HANS' PARENTS (Unconquered). They live and work on the family farm in Bavaria

HARDING, Bessie (Woman of Fifty). The wife of Colonel

Harding
HARDING, Colonel Charley (Woman of Fifty). Had occupied an important position in the Red Cross; had a villa in the Via Bolognese, Florence
HARDING, Mrs. (Of Human Bondage). At Hove, in Brighton; she is willing to keep Mildred Rogers' baby for seven shillings per week; elderly and stout; gray hair; red fleshy face; she lived in a small but clean and tidy house in a back street; she is the wife of a curate
HARDING, Rev. (Of Human Bondage). The husband of Mrs. Harding; a curate; old; he substituted for vicars on holidays or during their illness; he received a small pension from a charitable institution
HARDY BOYS (Lion's Skin). Two of them; small children of Sir Frederick and Lady Hardy
HARDY, Sir Frederick (Lion's Skin). The neighbor and an acquaintance of the Forestiers; Robert Forestier, who had known him formerly as Captain Fred Hardy, did not like him; women and horses had forced him into bankruptcy at age twenty-five; formerly a car salesman, outside broker, commission agent, and actor; finally married when well over forty years of age; now well past age fifty and the recipient of a baronetcy; his hair close cropped; slightly built
HARDY, Lady (Lion's Skin). Wife of Sir Frederick Hardy; small in stature; a former actress
HARDY, Mr. (Book-Bag). Father of Tim and Olive Hardy; former husband of Mrs. Hardy; is a retired naval man; he raised Tim after his divorce; a hard liver and a heavy drinker
HARDY, Mrs. (Book-Bag). The deceased mother of Tim and Olive Hardy; after her divorce, she raised Olive in Italy
HARDY, Olive (Book-Bag). Tim Hardy's sister; educated in Florence, Italy; spoke fluent Italian and French; her soft brown eyes liquid and appealing; especially attractive
HARDY, Sally (Book-Bag). Married to Tim Hardy; pretty; fair; enormous, blue eyes; a small, straight nose; exquisite "milk and roses" skin; at age nineteen when she married Tim; resides in England
HARDY, Tim (Book-Bag). Excellent bridge player; plays with the Narrator and Featherstone at the club; owns an estate; large, fine hands with long fingers; clean

shaven; an oval face; rounded chin; thick brown hair turning grey; his brown eyes are gentle, but very sad

HARENGER, Richard (Treasure). He is of considerate and generous disposition; is employed in the Home Office; tall, slim, erect; small feet; thin hair; brown eyes; approaching age fifty; had been married in his early twenties, but then both he and his wife agreed to an amicable separation

HARENGER, Mrs. (Treasurer). Wife of Richard Harenger; separated from him

HARLEKIN (Perfect Gentleman). In the intermezzo; he is a member of a troupe of Italian dancers

HARLOT (Moon and Sixpence). At a Paris tavern; laughing eyes and charming mouth; young; she has a drink with Charles Strickland and the Narrator; wants to go home with Strickland

HARLOT (Of Human Bondage). She stops Philip Carey on Piccadilly, London; puts her hand on his arm; goes to dinner with him

HARLOT (Razor's Edge). At the Brasserie Graf, Avenue de Clichy, Paris; in the company of the American banker

HARNESSMAKER (Moon and Sixpence). He lived next door to the Stroeve family in Holland; as a boy, Dirk Stroeve said that he would marry his daughter

HARNESSMAKER'S DAUGHTER (Moon and Sixpence). Lived next door to young Dirk Stroeve in Holland; a little girl with blue eyes and a flaxon pigtail

HAROLD (Before the Party). Millicent's husband, who, supposedly, had committed suicide eight months prior to the opening of the story; an alcoholic; murdered by Millicent

HARRINGTON, John Quincy (Ashenden/ Mr. Harrington's Washing). An American; he travels with Ashenden from Vladivostok to Petrograd; he represents a firm in Philadelphia; thin, less than middle height; yellow, bony face; large pale blue eyes; large, bald head; he spoke with a New England accent; his family had come from Devonshire in the early eighteenth century; is a compulsive talker and a bore

HARRINGTON, Mrs. (Ashenden/Mr. Harrington's Washing). John Quincy Harrington's wife; a cultivated woman in delicate health

HARRIS (Cakes and Ale). The butcher at Blackstable; the

Driffields in debt to him for more than thirty pounds

HARRIS (Of Human Bondage). Employee of Lynn and Sedley, London; tall, thin, and young; a hooked nose; pasty face; unevenly shaped long head; large, red, inflamed acne spots on his forehead and neck

HARRIS, Jack (Our Betters). Is one of Minnie Surennes' former lovers

HARRISON, Robbie (Unknown). Clever, nice looking, and amusing; killed in the war

HARRISONS (East of Suez). Formerly occupied residence in the Temple of Fidelity and Virtuous Inclination, Peking

HARROW, Dr. (Back of Beyond). Informs Enid Clarke that she is pregnant

HARRY (Footprints in the Jungle). The doctor; he prescribes brandy, instead of water, for Mrs. Bronson

HARVEYS (Circle). Reside near Ashton-Adey, Dorset; they have furnished their most perfect Georgian house with dreadful Victorian furniture

HASSAN (Letter [play]). The Crosbies' chauffeur; drives the Head Boy to fetch John Withers

HASSAN (Vessel of Wrath). An attendant at Owen Jones's dispensary

HASSAN (Yellow Streak). He is Izzart's native servant

HAYWARD, Dr. (Painted Veil). Told Kitty Fane to get out of the heat of Hong Kong if she did not want to go all to pieces

HEAD BOY #1 (Book Bag). The servant of Featherstone

HEAD BOY #2 (Book-Bag). Servant of Tim Hardy; informed Featherstone of Olive Hardy's attempted suicide; he drove Sally Hardy from the Hardys' house to Featherstone's residence

HEAD BOY (Hero). Of Little Primpton School; he led the shout of "three cheers" for James Parsons at the welcome home ceremony

HEAD BOY #1 (Letter [play]). At the Crosbies' bungalow; age forty; a small, fat Chinaman; Leslie Crosbie tells him that there has been an accident; he is sent to tell John Withers that Geoffrey Hammond is dead

HEAD BOY #2 (Letter [play]). Of Geoffrey Hammond; old and fat

HEAD BOY (Outstation). Servant to Warburton and liaison with Cooper's servants; Abas's uncle

HEAD BOY (Painted Veil). At the Fanes' house in Hong
   Kong; he had been left in charge of the place during
   Kitty and Walter Fanes' stay in Mei-tan-fu
HEAD BOY (Vessel of Wrath). Employed by Evert Gruyter;
   he announces the presence of Owen Jones; he brings an
   assortment of women to satisfy Gruyter's young man's
   fancy
HEAD CLERK (Vessel of Wrath). He is employed by Evert
   Gruyter; a Dutch half-caste
HEAD MAN (Explorer [novel]). Of Alec MacKenzie's latest
   African expedition; ordered to take up the loads; at
   sunset, he blew his whistle, asked if all men were
   present, reported to Alec, and received orders for
   the next day
HEAD MAN (Flotsam and Jetsam). Steering the prahu when
   Skelton discovered that he had malaria; brings Kong
   to Skelton
HEAD MAN (Hero). Of the unruly Madda Khel hill tribes
   in India; agrees to give up their rifles to Colonel
   Richmond Parsons, then he tricks him into a serious
   defeat
HEAD OF CUSTOMS (Making of a Saint). At Forli; almost
   torn to pieces by the people as he walked toward the
   palace
HEAD WAITER (Jack Straw). At the Grand Babylon Hotel;
   promised to overlook Pierre's absence if the latter
   could find a substitute
HEATHER, Lord William (Merry-Go-Round). Is the biggest
   scoundrel whom Polly Ley ever knew; is a cheat and a
   blackmailer; kept out of prison only by a miracle and
   his family's influence; nonetheless he is a gentleman
HEIRESS #1 (Bishop's Apron). Of important connections;
   Josiah Spratte wants his son, Viscount Rallington, to
   marry her; she proved willing, but Rallington refused
HEIRESS #2 (Bishop's Apron). French; according to Rev.
   Theodore Spratte, in the seventeenth century, she
   married a prominent member of the English branch of
   the Montmorency family, thus forming the antecedents
   of the Sprattes
HEIRESS (Punctiliousness of Don Sebastian). An acquaintance of the Narrator at Hampstead; he provides the
   present Duque de Losas with an introduction to her
HEN (Magician). Of Lesbebren's friend; aged; given the

remedy for prolonging life; lost all of its feathers, but then grew new ones and soon began to lay eggs

HENDERSON DAUGHTERS (Hour Before the Dawn). Two of them born to George and Mrs. Henderson, between Roger and Jim; both died in childhood

HENDERSON, George (Hour Before the Dawn). Husband of Mrs. Henderson; father of Roger, Jim, and Tommy, and of Jane Foster; squire of Graveney Holt; a retired military man

HENDERSON, Jim (Hour Before the Dawn). Son of George and Mrs. Henderson; brother of Roger and Tommy, and of Jane Foster; age twenty-one; at Oxford, studying for the law; a pacifist; tall, broad shouldered, well built; a handsome, sensitive face; in love with Dora Friedberg; declares himself a conscientious objector; announces suddenly that Dora and he have been married since last August; murders Dora, then shoots himself

HENDERSON, May (Hour Before the Dawn). At age twenty-eight; pale brown hair; dark brown eyes; is slim and tall; a straight nose, with delicate nostrils; candid brow; a well-shaped mouth; clear, white skin; very pretty; daughter of a naval officer, killed in the last war; married to Roger Henderson for eight years; in love with Dick Murray; she wants to divorce Roger, then changes her mind after he returns from France; finally feels that she needs to be with the invalid Dick Murray

HENDERSON, Mr. and Mrs. (Penelope). Penelope O'Farrell plans to motor to Cornwall with them

HENDERSON, Mrs. (Hour Before the Dawn). Wife of George Henderson; the mother of Jim, Roger, Tommy, and Jane Foster; daughter of a soldier; age fifty-three; tall, handsome, and grey haired; fine features; with mildly friendly eyes; was age nineteen when Jane was born

HENDERSON, Roger (Hour Before the Dawn). George and Mrs. Henderson's oldest son; brother of Jim and Tommy and of Jane Foster; age thirty-three; May's husband; was educated at Sandhurst; an officer in the military intelligence; had been stationed in Japan, the United States, Spain, France, Poland, and the Balkans; tall, broad shouldered, and well knit; strong face; moves from the War Office to the Imperial General Staff of the Commander-in-Chief (Viscount John Standish Gort,

1886-1946); thought to have been killed in an ambush near Cassel, France; he suddenly turns up in Graveney Holt, a bullet lodged in his shoulder and a bullet wound in his leg

HENDERSON, Tommy (Hour Before the Dawn). Is George and Mrs. Henderson's youngest son; age thirteen; brother of Roger and Jim, and of Jane Foster; away at school; skinny legs and arms; slender body; he returns to and remains at Graveney Holt after transference of his preparatory school to Canada; killed in an air raid

HENNERLEY (Outstation). Police officer at Kuala Solor; he was educated at Eton College and Oxford University

HENRY (Fall of Edward Barnard). A warehouse employee of Braunschmidt and Company, Tahiti

HENRY (Moon and Sixpence). The Narrator's uncle; for twenty-seven years the vicar of Whitestable, Kent; he solicited subscriptions for the Additional Curates Society (founded 1837)

HERBARTUS (Ashenden/ His Excellency/Mr. Harrington's Washing). A Galician Pole; he is an indefatigable and determined agent in Ashenden's employ; he had been engaged in the arrangement of a scheme to blow up munitions factories in Austria; a heavy, clean shaven face; large hairy hands; big, dark, powerfully built; fierce black eyes; massive strength; disinterested, ruthless, and completely unhampered by any scruples

HERBERT, Barbara (Tenth Man). Close friend of Catherine Winter; accompanied Catherine on a tour to northern Italy, and will accompany her again after Catherine leaves George Winter

HERDSMAN (Merry-Go-Round). In Italy; with a rifle slung across his back; he is wild, handsome, and debonair

HERDSMEN (Choice of Amyntas). In the Spanish countryside; point to the mountains and direct Amyntas to the brigands

HEREFORD, Duchess of (Alien Corn). The loveliest, most gallant, and dashing of the beauties at the end of Victoria's reign; involved in a twenty-year affair with Ferdy Rabenstein

HEREFORD, Duke of (Outstation). Present at Warburton's club on the night before the latter sails for Borneo

HERMANOS, Ferdinand Francisco Maria de Lomas y Oria, Duke of (Noble Spaniard). A Spaniard; "as regular as

Characters 201

the tides and more persistent than a nun"; is in love with Marion Nairne; rich and distinguished; dark; has charming blue eyes
HEWITT (Tenth Man). A broker
HEYWOOD, Canon (Before the Party). The father of Gladys Heywood; host of the garden party
HEYWOOD, Gladys (Before the Party). The only unmarried daughter of Canon Heywood
HIGGINS, Annie (Merry-Go-Round). The second daughter of Jonathan Higgins; marries Reggie Barlow-Bassett; an actress who goes under the stage name of Miss Lauria Galbraith; small; older than her husband (age near or beyond twenty-eight); is by no means pretty; handsome eyes; fine black hair; a shrewish mouth; is an eager smoker; she expects an heir for the Barlow-Bassetts
HIGGINS, Baron (Ashenden/Giulia Lazzari/Miss King). The grandfather of Baroness de Higgins; was a Yorkshire stable boy who went to Austria with Prince Blankenstein; good looking; he had a charming and romantic career; he attracted the attention of an archduchess; he ended life as a baron and the minister plenipotentiary to an Italian court
HIGGINS, Baroness von (Ashenden/Giulia Lazzari/Miss King). An Austrian resident of the hotel in Geneva; granddaughter of Yorkshire stable boy who eventually became the Austrian plenipotentiary to an Italian court; spoke fluent English and French; is over forty years of age; extremely beautiful; has golden blonde hair; blue eyes; straight nose; pink and white skin; white and ample bosom; an agent in the service of the Austrian government
HIGGINS, Dr. (Hero). At Little Primpton; is burly and broad shouldered; Mary Clibborn sees him as a horrid, vulgar man; he and Mary clash over treating patients
HIGGINS, Jonathan (Merry-Go-Round). Of Wimbledon; the father of Annie Higgins (Lauria Galbraith)
HIGGINS, Mr. (Merry-Go-Round). Young; very smart; takes up with Annie Bush at Brighton
HIGHBURY, Mr. (Bishop's Apron). Is a colleague of Lord Stonehenge; officious
HIRED MAN (Razor's Edge). Employed by Herr Becker; is gored by a bull and confined to hospital until after the harvest

HODGES, Mr. (Of Human Bondage). Husband of Mrs. Hodges; a barrister; he treated his wife "simply shocking"

HODGES, Mrs. (Liza of Lambeth). Wife of Mr. Hodges; a midwife; she tends to Liza Kemp after Liza has had a miscarriage

HODGES, Mrs. (Of Human Bondage). Is an employee of Lynn and Sedley, London; small; age forty-five; badly dyed hair; a yellow face, with a network of of small veins all over it; pale blue eyes with yellow whites; had left her husband; she accompanies Philip Carey to the Monday evening social

HODGKINS (Mrs. Craddock). He is the foreman of a group of laborers cutting down trees at Court Leys, Kent

HODGSON, Mr. (Of Human Bondage). He, his wife, and the three children occupy rooms on the first floor of the house in the little street between Chancery Lane and Holborn, London; Thorpe Athelny introduces Philip Carey to them

HODGSON, Spencer (Our Betters). The father of Minnie Surrenes

HODMARSH, Lady (Cakes and Ale). A clever and handsome American; she lived in Tercanbury, Kent; entertained persons connected with the arts; a neighbor of Edward Driffield

HODMARSH, Lord (Cakes and Ale). The husband of Lady Hodmarsh; a sporting baronet with no intelligence; charming manners

HOGAN, Captain (Daisy). Cavalry officer from the depot at Tercanbury; married; elopes to London with Daisy Griffith, then leaves her

HOLDEN, Rev. (Of Human Bondage). He is the Dissenting minister at Blackstable; William Carey would never speak to him; yet, he sent a wreath to Louisa Carey's funeral

HOLLAND, Ambrose (Jack Straw). Is age thirty-five and elegant; at one time an actor in a traveling company

HOLLINGTON, Lord Charles (Outstation). Of Castle Reagh; friend of Warburton; had given the latter a bottle of forty-year-old port wine

HOLLINGTON, Clara (Our Betters). She told Lady Pearl Grayston that she had lost over a stone (c. fourteen pounds+) by going to Compton Edwards

HOLLINGTON, Dowager Lady of (Mrs. Dot). Grandmother of

Lord Hollington; a relative of Gerald Halstane

HOLLINGTON, Lord George (Mrs. Dot). Gerald Halstane's distant cousin; last winter he broke his neck in the hunting field

HOLLINGTON, Lady (Bishop's Apron). Had the fashionable craze for asking literary and artistic persons to her parties

HOLLINGTON, Lady (Penelope). Davenport Barlow has promised to look in on her after dinner

HOLLINGTON, Lord (Mrs. Dot). A grandson of the Dowager Lady Hollington; a soldier; young; is engaged to be married; is killed in the northwest frontier of India while leading a military expedition; fifteenth cousin of Gerald Halstane

HOLLINGTON, Lord and Lady (Bishop's Apron). Invite Rev. Theodore Spratte to dine with them

HOLLINGTON, Lord and Lady (Jack Straw). Guests at the Parker-Jennings' garden party in Cheshire

HOLLINGTONS (Magician). Had been proud to give their daughters to the house of Haddo

HOLT, Wyman (Woman of Fifty). A professor of English literature at a small Midwest university

HOLZMINDEN, Count von (Ashenden/Miss King). A German agent; dines at the hotel in Geneva; related to the Hohenzollerns; tall and thin; close-cropped Prussian head; charming manners; interested in the fine arts

HOME GUARDS (Hour Before the Dawn). Two of them; carry Tommy Henderson's body to the house at Graveney Holt

HOME OFFICE OFFICIAL (Episode). Interviewed Ned Preston for the unpaid position of prison visitor at Wormwood Scrubbs; dour and shrewd

HOMUNCULI (Magician). Supposedly created by the old alchemists; forms in which life became manifest; male and female; ten made by Count Johann-Ferdinand von Kuffstein and the Abbe Geloni

HORE-BELISHA, Leslie (Hour Before the Dawn). Secretary of State for war and lawyer (1893-1937); George Henderson tries to see him to volunteer for the war; he is too busy to see George

HORN, Jo (Rain). A trader, with rooms to rent; a half-caste

HORN, Mrs. (Rain). A native of Pago-Pago and wife of Jo Horn

HORNBY, Colonel (Land of Promise). The husband of Mrs. Hornby and father of Reginald; he paid off his son's gambling debts and then told him to go off to Canada

HORNBY, Mrs. (Land of Promise). Wife of Colonel Hornby and mother of Reginald; had been a close friend of Louise Wickham

HORNBY, Reginald (Land of Promise). Son of Colonel and Mrs. Hornby; educated at Harrow and Oxford; young and good looking; dark and sleek hair; a small, trim, and curled moustache; "a nut"; he had been in the motor car business in London; goes to Canada; eventually, he is able to return to England

HORTENSE (Love in a Cottage). Sybil Bruce's Paris maid

HOSPITAL ORDERLY (Book-Bag). He attempts to prevent Featherstone from seeing Olive Hardy

HOST (Lotus Eater). Friend of the Narrator; the latter stays at his villa in Capri; identifies Wilson to the Narrator

HOSTESS (Episode). Of the dinner party attended by the Narrator and Ned Preston; she never invited the wives with their husbands

HOTEL KEEPER (Merry-Go-Round). At Naples; Herbert Fields announces to him his intention to leave for Brindisi

HOTEL MANAGER (Four Dutchmen). Of the Van Dorth Hotel, Singapore; a genial Dutchman

HOTEL MANAGER (French Joe). A woman in a red flannel dressing gown; long black hair; stoutish; keen eyes; red nose

HOTEL MANAGER (Gigolo and Gigolette). Made remarks if the gigolos did not dress well

HOTEL MANAGER (Narrow Corner). On Kanda; he is away at Batavia when Dr. Saunders, Captain Nichols, and Fred Blake arrive; later asks Saunders to sign for a cable that has just arrived for him

HOTEL MANAGER (Of Human Bondage). Of the Hotel St. Georges, Paris; a good friend of Mr. Goodworthy; he spoke English; stout and pleasant

HOUSE BOY (Back of Beyond). He is in the employ of the Saffrays; he brings brandy to revive Violet Saffray; later, takes dinner to her

HOUSE BOY (Door of Opportunity). He serves drinks to Captain Stratton and Alban Torel

Characters 205

HOUSE BOY (Flotsam and Jetsam). Accompanies the Chinese and the Dyak up the stairs and into the Grange house

HOUSE BOY (Force of Circumstance). Is employed by Doris and Guy; he has a scuffle with women from the kampong

HOUSE BOY (Painted Veil). Is at the Fanes' bungalow at Mei-tan-fu; he holds a hurricane lamp for Waddington

HOUSE BOYS (Vessel of Wrath). Three of them; they serve meals to Evert Gruyter

HOUSE MAID (Cakes and Ale). At Blackstable; was nearly engaged by Amy Driffield before the latter discovered that she was Edward Driffield's great-niece

HOUSE MAID (Mrs. Craddock). At Court Leys, Blackstable, Kent; was surprised when Bertha Craddock removed the antimacassars (chair and sofa covers) and threw them into the fireplace

HOUSE MAIDS (Landed Gentry). Two of them; at prayers in the dining room at Kenyon Fulton

HOUSE PHYSICIAN (Of Human Bondage). Present at the out-patients' room at St. Luke's Hospital, London; dapper little man; excessively conscious of his importance

HOUSE SURGEON (Of Human Bondage). He is on duty at the accident station, St. Luke's Hospital, London; faced with a dilemma when patients are brought in by police

HOUSEKEEPER (Hour Before the Dawn). Of Dick Murray at Graveney; receives a letter from Mrs. Murray stating that Dick has been wounded in Egypt

HOWARD, Courtenay (Rehearsal). See above, Moses COHEN

HOWE (Hero). He is the local butcher at Little Primpton

HOWLETT, Mrs. (Daisy). Widow at Blackstable, Kent; she learns from Miss Reed that Daisy Griffith has eloped

HUBBARD, Miss (Round Dozen). She was once engaged to Mortimore, which would have made her his twelfth wife

HUBBARD, Mrs. (Land of Promise). Resides at Tunbridge Wells; wealthy and old; employs Agnes Pringle as her companion

HUDSON, Florie (Narrow Corner). In the <u>Sydney Bulletin</u>; the wife of Patrick Hudson #1; she is extremely thin; scraggy neck; tallish; a long thin face, with hollow cheeks; her skin brown, rather leathery; untidy black hair; enormous black eyes; nothing attractive about her; engaged in an affair with Fred Blake; she hanged herself while, according to a coroner's jury report, temporarily insane; she has been suspected but never accused, of the of the murder of her husband; at age forty-two

HUDSON, Patrick #1 (Narrow Corner). Name in the Sydney Bulletin; the suicide of his wife, Florie, leaves his murder unsolved; he is a resident of Sydney; railroad worker; he is a member of the Labour Party; a Roman Catholic; considerable influence among the Irish and Italian workers; big, powerful, and strong; shot by Fred Blake with his own gun

HUDSON, Patrick #2 (Narrow Corner). Identified as the former resident magistrate in New Guinea; he had been dead for a number of years

HUNTER, Bateman (Fall of Edward Barnard). An American; native of Chicago; handsome, tall, and slender; thin lips; dark, but pale of face; close friend of Edward Barnard

HUNTER, Mr. (Fall of Edward Barnard). Father of Bateman Hunter; tall and slender; thin lips; a motor vehicle manufacturer (Hunter Motor Traction and Automobile Company)

HURET, Maurice (Moon and Sixpence). He wrote an article regarding Charles Strickland in the Mercure de France and thus rescued the unknown painter from oblivion

HURRELL, Dr. (Merry-Go-Round). Of Ferne, Kent; old; the father of Dr. Frank Hurrell; he has a large general practice; has not gone on holiday for thirty years; he and his wife looked upon every sovereign that he earned as held in trust for their only son; wants to retire and be near Frank

HURRELL, Dr. Frank (Happy Couple). A physician; one of the medical experts called by the prosecution at the Wingfield trial; recognizes the Craigs, and they him

HURRELL, Dr. Frank (Magician). Assistant physician at St. Luke's Hospital, London; always interested in odd personalities; Oliver Haddo claims to be an old friend of his; he writes to Arthur Burdon on what he knows about Haddo, whom he cordially dislikes and has not seen for years; could not bear Haddo's company, but could never resist seeing the man whenever the opportunity arose; recommends that Arthur avoid Haddo like the plague

HURRELL, Dr. Frank (Merry-Go-Round). At age thirty, an assistant physician at St. Luke's Hospital, London, with a practice at Harley Street; broad shoulders and a solid build too great for his height; heavy brows; square jaw; mocking, expressive eyes; a deep romantic voice; small black moustache; a well shaped mouth; regular and excellent teeth; extremely reserved; he and Basil Kent close friends at Oxford; is a regular visitor to the home of Polly Ley; he examines Herbert Field and diagnoses his illness as consumption; then contracts a septic inflammation of the throat from post-mortem examinations; upon his recovery, plans to holiday at Ferne, Kent (with his father), and then at Jeyston, Dorsetshire (with the Castillyons); wants to leave the medical profession; is mentioned in Polly Ley's will to receive one-third of her estate; calls regularly upon the dying Herbert Field at Tercanbury

HURRELL, Mrs. (Merry-Go-Round). Wife of Dr. Hurrell and mother of Frank; both she and her husband looked upon every sovereign earned by the doctor as held in trust for their only son; wants to retire and be near Frank

HUSBAND (Home and Beauty). On Mr. Raham's instructions, hits his wife (Rahan's client) in the jaw, knocking out her false teeth

HUSBAND (Lisa of Lambeth). The first husband of Kitty Stanley; he was a gentleman and a Christian; a man of education and a teetotaler

HUSBAND (Mask and the Face). Of the eloping American woman; complaisant

HUSBAND #1 (Of Human Bondage). Of expectant mother; if there had been a number of babies prior to the expected arrival, he proved indifferent

HUSBAND #2 (Of Human Bondage). Of newly married woman; nervous and often drunk

HUSBAND #3 (Of Human Bondage). Of the twins; he proves ferociously sullen; he resented his newborn children; has murder in his soul

HUTCHINSON (Yellow Streak). The Resident; educated at Winchester School; he is tall, stout, and red-faced

I

IBSEN, Henrik (Ashenden/Mr. Harrington's Washing). The Norwegian playwright and poet (1828-1906); Ashenden had once observed him drink a glass of Munich beer

IBSEN, Henrik (Of Human Bondage). His A Doll's House (Et Dukkehjem 1879) had appeared at Heidelberg the winter previous to Philip Carey's arrival there; it shocked the "decent" people, especially Adolf Erlin

IDLERS (Making of a Saint). At Forli; wandering to and fro and joining themselves into groups

IGGULDEN, Rosie (Cakes and Ale). See Rosie DRIFFIELD

IL MORO, Lodovico (Then and Now). The son of Francisco Sforza; had commissioned Leonardo's equestrian statue of his father; held prisoner in the castle of Loches

INDIAN #1 (Razor's Edge). Friend of Larry Darrell; went to the Himalayas with him; sprained his ankle; Larry relieves him of his pain

INDIAN #2 (Razor's Edge). At Benares; he bathed and prayed in the Ganges; tall and gaunt; mass of tangled hair and a ragged beard; long arms

INDIAN #3 (Razor's Edge). Larry Darrell meets him first at Benares, then, two years later, at Madura; long black hair; had become a holy man

INDIAN AGENT (Ashenden/Miss King). Comes to Ashenden's Geneva hotel with instructions

INDIAN CIVILIAN (Ashenden/Miss King). Retired; he and his wife guests at the Geneva hotel

INDIAN CIVILIAN (Painted Veil). Retired; a K.C.I.E.; age fifty-three; proposed marriage to Kitty Garstin

INDIAN CIVILIAN (Sanatorium). Is an old patient at the sanatorium; he had been there longer than anyone but McLeod and Campbell; he had once ruled a province

INDIANS (Christmas Holiday). Three of them; young; ate in moody silence at the restaurant in the Avenue du Maine, Paris

INDIANS (Land of Promise). In British Columbia; would have nothing to do with the two Englishmen who lived among them

INFANTA (Poet). A proud descendant of the Bourbons; was loved by the King and Santa Ana; was rejected by the latter and sent to a convent by the former

INFANTRYMEN (Mrs. Craddock). Two of them; seen at the railway station at Blackstable, Kent; trim; saunter down the platform

INHABITANTS (Making of a Saint). Of the houses at Forli bombarded from the citadel; hurried for their lives to safer parts of the town

Characters	209

INNKEEPER (De Amicitia). At Monnickendam; he brings Ferdinand White and Valentia Stewart their lunch

INNKEEPER (Irish Gentleman). Of the Golden Eagle, in the capital, the Principality of Wartburg-Hockstein; he conveys the visitors' book to Robert O'Donnel

INNKEEPER (Making of a Saint). Of the inn at Forli; fat

INNKEEPER #1 (Then and Now). At Castiglione Aretino, where Machiavelli lodges on his way back to Florence; he proposes that his guest sleep in the same bed with his wife and him, but Machiavelli declines the offer

INNKEEPER #2 (Then and Now). At an inn at San Casciano; in a card game in which Machiavelli is a participant

INQUISITOR GENERAL (Catalina). Saw no reason to reverse the tribunal's decision about the death of Demetrios Christopoulos

INQUISITORS (Catalina). They exile Domingo Perez from Salamanca, as well as from the immediate neighborhood

INSOLEY, Archibald (Landed Gentry). Brother of Claude; is vicar of Kenyon-Fulton, Somersetshire; age thirty-four; good looking; a humorous manner and a kindly expression; initially curate of Wakefield; he admits that his class means more to him than his calling, and that he really knows very little of the world

INSOLEY, Claude (Landed Gentry). Owns Kenyon-Fulton, in Somersetshire; husband of Grace Insoley; brother of Archibald; age thirty-five; is dried up and precise; neither good looking nor plain; a slightly diplomatic and authoritative manner

INSOLEY, Grace (Landed Gentry). She has been married to Claude Insoley for ten years; middle class; formerly Grace Robinson of London; now age thirty; beautiful; eager, earnest face; fine eyes; restless; dislikes the country and her husband; has had an affair with Henry Cobbett; eventually determines that she loves Claude

INSOLEY, Mr. (Landed Gentry). Deceased father of Claude and Archibald Insoley; had declared Gann the younger to be the best gamekeeper he had known; when he made up his mind to do anything, it was done

INSOLEY, Mrs. (Landed Gentry). Widowed mother of Claude and Archibald Insoley; formerly Miss Bainbridge; she is small and old; corpulent; has the appearance of a charwoman in her Sunday best; she had wanted Claude to marry Helen Vernon; dislikes Grace; controls the family money

INSOLEY, Robert (Landed Gentry). Uncle of Claude and Archibald Insoley; Archibald's predecessor as vicar of Kenyon Fulton

INSPECTOR (Land of Promise). At the Taylor farm located in Prentice, Manitoba; condemns Frank Taylor's crop because it is infected with mustard weed

INSPECTOR (Mrs. Craddock). At the Euston rail station, London; comes along to look at tickets

INTERMEDIARY (Then and Now). He is sent by Bartolomeo Martelli to Monna Caterina Cappello to propose that Aurelia become his mistress and, perhaps later, even his wife

INTERPRETERS (Mrs. Craddock). Employees of Cook's; are everywhere in Paris

INTERVIEWERS (Explorer [novel/play]). From the London evening newspapers; ask Alec MacKenzie about Fergus Macinnery's charges; Alec refuses to speak to them

IRONMONGER (Bishop's Apron). Retired; had built, in the first years of Queen Victoria's reign, the house at Beachcombe, which Josiah Spratte the younger had purchased, sixty years ago, to gain the standing of a country gentleman

IRVING, Sir Henry (Round Dozen). British Shakespearean actor (original name John Henry Brodribb, 1838-1905) whom Edwin St. Clair had met at the Garrick Club

ISMAIL, Khedive (Magician). He had summoned Dr. Porhoet unexpectedly to Cairo, thus causing the latter to miss Arthur Burdon's birth

ITALIAN (Razor's Edge). Picked up by Sophie Macdonald in a Chicago speakeasy; he was wanted by the police

ITALIAN COUNTESS (Gigolo and Gigolette). A guest at the Casino dinner party; neither Italian nor a countess; an excellent bridge player

ITALIAN OFFICER (Voice of the Turtle). He pays considerable attention to La Falterona on the voyage from New York to Europe

ITALIAN PEASANT (Love in a Cottage). Close by the Hotel Splendide, Varenna, Lake Como; when the guests at the hotel hear a shot, they conclude that he has been playing with firearms

ITALIAN PRINCE (Merry-Go-Round). Offered Polly Ley his

hand and his heart; she refused him because he was so virtuous
ITALIAN PRINCES (Circle). Vague; glad to borrow a few francs from Lord Hughie Porteus
ITALIAN SCULPTOR (Explorer [novel]). Had been lured to England to do the recumbent effigy, in stone, of the eldest Allerton and his two wives in the chancel of the parish church at Hamlyn's Purlieu, Hampshire
ITALIAN SERENADERS (Love in a Cottage). On Lake Como; entertain the guests at the Hotel Splendide, Varenna
ITALIAN TENOR (Marriage of Convenience). A passenger on the ship out of Bangkok; a Neopolitan on his way to Hong Kong to rejoin his company; enormously fat; podgy and beringed fingers; considerable long, curly, greasy hair
ITALIAN WOMAN (Woman of Fifty). She is engaged by Laura Clayton to teach her Italian
IZZART (Yellow Streak). He had been in Borneo since the war; spoke both Malay and Dyak; educated at Harrow; legs like broomsticks; over six feet tall, powerfully built; neat black moustache and neat black hair; dark eyes; handsome
IZZART, Mrs. (Yellow Streak). Izzart's mother; a half-caste; she lives in London; fat, old, with grey hair; smokes cigarettes

J

J (Princess September). Youngest son and last of the nineteen children born to the King and Queen of Siam
JACK (Pool). The native bartender at the English Club, Apia
JACKSON, Rev. Archibald (Hero). The vicar of Little Primpton, Kent; husband of Maria Jackson; small and dried up; earnest and without humor; appointed to the living while James Parsons was serving in India
JACKSON, Arnold (Fall of Edward Barnard). Mrs. Longstaffe's brother; a resident of Tahiti; former banker and philanthropist; he served seven years in jail for fraud; tall, thin, curly white hair; thin face, large hooked nose, expressive mouth
JACKSON, Eva (Fall of Edward Barnard). Arnold Jackson's daughter; dark eyes, red mouth, brown skin, black and

straight, black hair; she is "like a goddess of the Polynesian spring"

JACKSON, Lavina (Fall of Edward Barnard). Tall, handsome Tahitian woman, "wife" of Arnold Jackson; mother of Eva Jackson

JACKSON, Maria (Hero). Wife of Archibald Jackson; small and dried up; earnest and without humor; a busybody; attempts to convince James Parsons that he has a duty to marry Mary Clibborn

JACOBS, Mr. (Of Human Bondage). An assistant surgeon on the out-patients' department at St. Luke's Hospital, London; short, fat, and exuberantly jolly; bald head and loud voice; cockney accent; Philip Carey assigned to him as a dresser

JAGSON (Magician). A lanky youth, very tall, thin, and fair; with very long hair; held himself as though an exhausted lily; he reminds Susie Boyd of an Aubrey Beardsley caricature that has been dreadfully smudged; a painter without talent

JAMES (Jack Straw). One of the footmen at the Parker-Jennings' home in Cheshire; fetches a brandy and soda for Jack Straw

JAMES, Miss (Sheppey). The cashier at Bradley's Hairdressing and Barber's Saloon, Jermyn Street, London

JANE #1 (Choice of Amyntas). The daughter of Peter the Schoolmaster and Mrs. Peter

JANE #2 (Choice of Amyntas). The servant of the Parson; she brings her master a second bottle of port wine

JANE (Mrs. Craddock). Polly Ley's maid; packs Bertha Craddock's boxes

JANUARY (Princess September). The eldest daughter and first-born child of the King and Queen of Siam; she formerly named Night, Spring, and Sunday

JAPANESE DIVER (Narrow Corner). On board the pearling schooner out of Port Darwin; ill from a severe attack of dysentery; is treated by Dr. Saunders; coal black eyes; he dies

JAPANESE GENTLEMEN (P.& O.). Trim and neat; they look European and speak English; play deck quoits

JAPANESE PROSTITUTES (Neil MacAdam). Four of them; with shining black hair; staff the Japanese brothel at Singapore

JAPANESE WOMAN (Neil MacAdam). Stout, middle aged; she

oversees the staff of the Japanese brothel, Singapore
JARRETT (Explorer [novel]). Fred Allerton's broker and principal creditor; he submitted to Fred an offer for the purchase of Hamlyn's Purlieu, which Fred accepted
JASPER, Brother (Faith). A young Franciscan monk at San Lucido, the poorest monastery in Spain; great black eyes; shaven chin; resembles a living corpse; he does not believe; after he has been whipped he momentarily believes that Jesus Christ has appeared to him; he freezes to death
JAVANESE (Narrow Corner). A half-caste; he represented the Dutch government at Takana; he spoke no English
JAY, Lottie (Daisy). Daughter of Mrs. Jay; everyone in the village of Blackstable knows about her goings on
JAY, Mrs. (Daisy). Mother of Lottie Jay; is ashamed and ignored
JAY, Mrs. (Moon and Sixpence). A writer; a guest at Amy Strickland's luncheon
JEANNETTE (Hour Before the Dawn). The French woman who finds Roger Henderson after he had escaped from the German ambush; stocky; young; flat face and apple red cheeks; small, black, shrewd eyes, like buttons; she is Michel's daughter-in-law
JEDDY, Mrs. (Treasure). The cook employed by Richard Harenger during the past twelve years, first at his house in St. John's Woods, and later at his flat near Whitehall
JENKINS (Hour Before the Dawn). A farmer near Cornford, Essex, six miles from Graveney Holt, who cultivated his own land; hires Jim Henderson as a laborer; small and wiry; gray thinning hair; a lined, bony face; red rimmed eyes; constantly berates Jim with obscenities
JENKINSON, Mr. (Rehearsal). The manager of the Olympia Theatre of Varieties; dark and stout; hair redolent of cosmetic; his accent betrayed his Teutonic nationality and his Jewish origin
JEPHSON, Mr. (P.&O.). A consul going home to England on leave
JERROLD, Douglas (Round Dozen). As ugly as he was witty
JERVIS (Mackintosh). Half-caste trader at Talua; small, dark, black beard burning gray; has handsome eyes and flashing teeth; servile
JERVIS, Dr. (Sheppey). He tends to Sheppey after he had

fainted at home; believed that Sheppey had a stroke, and he tells him that he should stay in bed and not return to work; is middle aged and red faced; hearty; Sheppey believes that he will be bald in six months; he examines Sheppey's state of mind; wants to commit Sheppey to a home

JERVIS, Harry (Vessel of Wrath). He found "a pretty big pearl" during Ginger Ted's six months' jail sentence

JERVIS, Mrs. (Mackintosh). A trader's wife; daughter of a chief and a chief in her own right; she owned much land; huge, old, and obese

JERVIS, Mrs. (Sheppey). Wife of Dr. Jervis; always says that her husband has nice hair

JERVIS, Mrs. Onslow (Home and Beauty). A friend and a colleague of Miss Montmorency; the widow of the vicar of Clacton; she has two sons in the army; assigned to Frederick Lowndes; a perfect lady; has charm, manner, and ease

JERVIS, Teresa (Mackintosh). A trader's daughter; she is swarthy and broad featured

JESSIE (Cakes and Ale). The maid at Rosie Driffield's rooms, the Albermarle Hotel, Yonkers, New York; black

JEVONS (Theatre). The cook employed by the Gosselyns; Margery warned her that a guest would be coming to the Gosselyns' for lunch

JEW (Moon and Sixpence). At Paris; bought all of Dirk Stroeve's possessions, with the exception of a box of clothes and a few books

JEW (Razor's Edge). In a vision while Larry Darrell meditates; tall and gaunt; thick dark hair; studious look of the scholar

JEW (Smith). Once engaged to Emily Chapman; rich; gave Emily lovely things; made co-respondent in a divorce case

JEWELL, Miss (Of Human Bondage). An employee of Lynn and Sedley, London; she referred to Philip Carey as "Phil"; apparently, she is going to marry a doctor

JEWELLER (Irish Gentleman). At Wartburg-Hochstein; buys Robert O'Donnel's ring for only half of its value

JEWISH TAILOR SHOP OWNER (Of Human Bondage). Has a shop on Harrington Street, London; married, with two small boys and a girl twenty years old

JEWISH VENDORS (Merry-Go-Round). In London; had removed

to new shops since Algernon Langton had last visited
JEWS (Marriage of Convenience, 1906). Are on the island village off of the coast of Tunis; as picturesque as they are dirty
JEZEBEL (Magician). In Margaret Dauncey's vision; she looks out upon Margaret from beneath painted brows
JILL (Theatre). One of the two young girls whom Thomas Fennell and Roger Gosselyn picked up after they left the theatre; is Joan Denver's roommate; Tom knew her
JIM (Back of Beyond). Husband of George Moon's ex-wife; retired
JIM (Of Human Bondage). A London builder; came home one afternoon, three days after his wife's confinement, to tell her that he had been dismissed; small, rough, uncouth; weather beaten face and long white scar on his forehead; large, stubbly hands
JOAN (Before the Party). Millicent's daughter; pale and grave for her age, preferring to play quiet games of her own invention
JOE (Narrow Corner). A Black member of the crew of the Australian schooner; sitting on his haunches on the floor by the Japanese diver; he helps Bob throw the diver overboard after he dies
JOHN (Choice of Amyntas). Son of Peter the Schoolmaster and Mrs. Peter
JOHN (Hero). He is old and poor; a resident of Little Primpton, Kent; lying in bed and writhing with pain; one of Mary Clibborn's patients
JOHN (Honolulu). Captain Butler's second Chinese cook; short, thick set, totally ugly; limped badly; bristly gray hair; a broad, flat, square face; deeply pitted complexion; a pronounced hairlip; a huge, yellow fang
JOHN (Judgment Seat). Husband of Mary; ten years older than Ruth, with whom he had fallen in love; he was a passenger on a ship that had been torpedoed by a submarine; might have saved himself had he not tried to save his wife, whom he hated
JOHN (Liza of Lambeth). A resident of the same house as the Blakestons, on Vere Street, Lambeth; hesitant to disrupt the fight between Jim Blakeston and his wife
JOHN-ADOLPHUS, Prince (Irish Gentleman). Despotic ruler of Wartburg-Hochstein; he is huge; gray hair and gray moustache; bushy eyebrows and scowling eyes; he dines

with Robert O'Donnel at the Golden Eagle inn
JOHNSON (Neil MacAdam). Police officer at Kuala Solar; he shared a house with Waring
JOHNSON, Captain (Moon and Sixpence). First husband of Tiare Johnson; older than his wife, but good looking; six feet three inches tall; died
JOHNSON, Tiare (Moon and Sixpence). Proprietress of the Hotel de la Fleur, Tahiti, where the Narrator lodges; the daughter of a Tahitian native and an English sea captain; is age fifty, but she looked older; tall and extremely stout; arms like legs of mutton and breasts like giant cabbages; broad and fleshy face; a set of vast chins; with long, dark, curly hair; young and vivacious eyes; known as the best cook on the island
JOHNSTON (Bread-Winner). The Battles' female servant; she packs Charles Battle's clothes
JOHNSTON, Miss (Merry-Go-Round). The companion to Mrs. Castillyon; age forty; demure; "ate with admirable complacency the bread of servitude"
JOHNSTON BLAKE, Mr. and Mrs. (Home and Beauty). They are planning to divorce
JOJO (Christmas Holiday). Proprietor of Jojo's Bar, behind the Boulevard de la Madeleine, Paris; he speaks with the reporter about Teddie Jordan's murder; he is a police informer
JONES, Martha (Vessel of Wrath). Owen Jones' sister; taught in the mission school and helped her brother with his medical work; age, over forty; flat chested, tall, thin; long, thin, red nose
JONES, Mr. (Mrs. Craddock). Edward Craddock's tenant at Bewlie's Farms; husband of Mrs. Jones; he had known Edward in the days of his poverty
JONES, Mrs. (Mrs. Craddock). Wife of Edward Craddock's tenant at Bewlie's Farms, Kent
JONES, Rev. Owen (Vessel of Wrath). Is in charge of the Baptist mission on the Alas Islands, headquartered on Baru; the only qualified medical doctor in the area; of Australian Welsh descent; age forty; tall, thin, melancholy; long face, sallow and drawn; brown hair turned white; is extremely narrow minded and dogmatic
JORDAN, Teddie (Christmas Holiday). He is an English bookmaker at Paris; small; a former jockey; he had served a nine-month term at Wormwood Scrubs for false

pretenses; lived in Paris for ten years; a suspected drug trafficker; age thirty-six; he lived alone in a ground floor flat; he was murdered by Robert Berger

JOSE (Man from Glasgow). Is a resident on the company estate at San Lorenzo

JOSEPH (Razor's Edge). Elliott Templeton's manservant; tends to the luggage of Isabel and Louisa Bradley at Paris; delivers messages; he is forbidden by Elliott Templeton to address him as "Monsieur le Comte"; he informs the Narrator of Elliott Templeton's attack of uremia; at that point, he had been in the employ of Elliott for forty years; he is devoted to him; a free thinker who believes all religion is nothing but a conspiracy of the priests to gain control of people

JOURDAIN, Lucille (Perfect Gentleman). The daughter of Madame and Monsieur Jourdain; is old enough to marry

JOURDAIN, Madame (Perfect Gentleman). Wife of Monsieur Jourdain; a clear and practical person; unsympathetic toward her husband's ambitions; is middle aged, dour, and highly opinionated

JOURDAIN, Monsieur (Perfect Gentleman). He is a wealthy tradesman who has determined to storm the barricades of exclusive society; possesses absolutely no taste; he arranges an elaborate musical entertainment, but sleeps through it all

JOURNALIST (Of Human Bondage). He meets Hayward at Lawson's studio in London; he is charmed by the former's conversation

JOURNALIST (Virtue). He occupies a flat upon the same landing as the Bishops; upon seeing Charlie's body, he instructs the charwoman to go summon a policeman

JOYCE, Dorothy (Letter [play]). Wife of Howard Joyce; age forty; buxom, florid, and handsome; prepares the Crosbies' bungalow to welcome Leslie Crosbie home after her trial; celebrated throughout the Federated Malay States for her cocktails

JOYCE, Dorothy (Letter [story]). Mr. Joyce's wife; she is talkative and vivacious; known for her cocktails

JOYCE, Howard (Letter [play]). Leslie Crosbie's lawyer and the senior partner in the law firm of Joyce and Simpson; age forty-five; he is thin, spare, and clean shaven; he has been Robert Crosbie's oldest and best friend; suspicious of Leslie; he purchases Leslie's letter to Geoffrey Hammond from the Chinese woman for $10,000--advancing the money from his own account

JOYCE, Mr. (Letter [story]). Partner in the law firm of Ripley, Joyce, and Naylor, at Singapore; by nature a silent man; is Leslie Crosbie's lawyer at her trial

JUDGE (Explorer [novel/play]). At Fred Allerton's trial at the Old Bailey, London; Richard Lomas and Bobbie Boulger left as he was summing up; sentences Fred to seven years in prison

JUDGE (For Services Rendered). Leonard Ardsley believes that he will be lenient in sentencing Collie Stratton

JUDGE (Land of Promise). Old; from India; used to come to Louisa Wickham's house two or three times a week for tea; he would talk to Norah Marsh about the East

JUDGES (Bishop's Apron). Presided over cases argued by Josiah Spratte; the really weak ones were like wax in Josiah's hands

JUDGES (Christmas Holiday). At Robert Berger's murder trial; two of them; middle aged; never opened their mouths

JUDGES (Painted Veil). Mrs. Garstin proved herself most obsequious to them

JUDY (Lion's Skin). Eleanor Forestier's Sealyham dog

JUGE D'INSTRUCTION (Christmas Holiday). Is in charge of Robert Berger's case; puzzled because the money that Berger supposedly had stolen from Teddie Jordan's flat could not be found

JULY (Princess September). Seventh daughter born to the King and Queen of Siam

JUNE (Princess September). Sixth daughter born to the King and Queen of Siam; she was formerly named Friday

JURIES (Bishop's Apron). Trembled at Josiah Spratte's ferocious glance

JURY (Explorer [play]). At the Old Bailey, London; they required no more than ten minutes to find Fred Allerton guilty

JURY (Landed Gentry). They passed a vote of censure on Claude Insoley following the suicide of Margaret Gann

JURY (Letter [play]). At Leslie Crosbie's trial; Howard Joyce declares, to Robert Crosbie, that not a single member will get into the box without already having made up his mind to bring a verdict of "Not Guilty"

JURY (Merry-Go-Round). At the Vizard divorce trial; its

members found the charges against Lady Vizard to be not proven

JURYMEN (Bad Example). At the coroner's inquest; laugh at James Clinton's witticisms

JUSTICE OF THE PEACE (Sheppey). He Used to visit Bessie Legros regularly at her flat in Kensington

JUSTICES (For Services Rendered).They will refer Collie Stratton's case to quarter sessions if he decides to be tried by jury

K

KAMMERER, James (Magician). Butler and famulus (private secretary) to Count Johann-Ferdinand von Kuffstein; maintained a diary; refers to <u>homunculi</u> as prophesying spirits

KASTELLAN, Lady (Casual Affair). A resident of Carlton House Terrace, London; described as beautiful; hosted a party attended by the Narrator and the Lows; tall; massive figure; lovely skin; large blue eyes; a broad face; has pale brown hair; the wife of Lord Kastellan

KASTELLAN, Lord (Casual Affair). The husband of Lady Kastellan; Under-Secretary at the Home Office; large person; middle aged; red faced; has sleek black hair; little, shrewd eyes; he knew of his wife's infidelity

KATE (Land of Promise). Parlormaid at Louisa Wickham's house in Tunbridge Wells; of decent age and respectable appearance

KATE (Road Uphill). She is a maid to Cornelia Sheridan

KATE (Unknown). The Whartons' servant; is middle aged

KATIE (Cakes and Ale). At the Bear and Key inn, Blackstable; ancient and haggard; untidy mop of gray hair; ushers William Ashenden into a small, grubby room

KEAR, Alroy (Cakes and Ale). A novelist; the author of thirty books; had achieved a considerable position on little talent; educated (Winchester and New College, Oxford); appointed the tutor to the delicate son of a very noble lord; he resigned that position to devote himself totally to literature; had once lectured at the University of Virginia; six feet tall, athletic build, broad shoulders; confident; not handsome, but manly; wide blue eyes; curly light brown hair; short broad nose and square chin; a bachelor; at age forty-nine or fifty when William Ashenden meets him again

KEAR, Emily (Cakes and Ale). Wife of Sir Raymond Kear and mother of Alroy

KEAR, Sir Raymond (Cakes and Ale). Father of Alroy Kear and husband of Emily; a civil servant; the colonial secretary, Hong Kong; then governor of Jamaica; after retirement, he lived near Stroud, in Gloucestershire

KEARON, Hugh (Merry-Go-Round). Had affairs throughout Europe, including one with a Princess

KEITH, Miss (Razor's Edge). Edna Novemali's secretary; a middle aged Scottish woman; sandy hair and freckled face; she wore a pince-nez on her prominent nose; the daughter of a minister who bore the air of determined virginity; had been a secretary for twenty-one years

KELADA, Max (Mr. Know-All). Short, sturdily built, and clean shaven; dark skin; a fleshy hooked nose; large eyes; long black hair, sleek and curly; supposedly a British subject, but a native of the Levant; a trader in pearls

KELLER, Dr. (Unknown). Specialist at Canterbury; he is clever; Dr. Macfarlane refers George Wharton to him

KELSEY, Lord Alfred (Explorer [novel]). Deceased husband of Lady Alice Kelsey and son of Mr. Kelsey; was a merchant and a partner in the firm of Boulger and Kelsey; he surrendered his seat in Parliament to a defeated cabinet minister in exchange for knighthood

KELSEY, Lady Alice (Explorer [novel]). She is the elder daughter of Mr. Boulger and sister of Mrs. Allerton; widow of Lord Alfred Kelsey; she has a house on the Thames and another in Charles Street, London; would have married Fred Allerton had her sister not done so; she offers to pay George Allerton's expenses to Oxford; childless; in love with Fred Allerton for the past twenty-five years; repays Mrs. Sabidon the eight thousand pounds that Fred Allerton and Saunders had swindled from her

KELSEY, Lady Alice (Explorer [play]). Age fifty; kind and emotional; sister-in-law of Fred Allerton; one of three daughters of a Liverpool merchant; the aunt of Robert Boulger and Lucy and George Allerton

KELSEY, Mr. (Explorer [novel]). Father of Lord Alfred Kelsey; a Liverpool merchant in partnership with Mr. Boulger

KEMP, George (Cakes and Ale). A coal merchant at Blackstable, Kent; he is known familiarly as Lord George; married and the father of three children; carried on with Rosie Gann; stout; a pointed beard; florid; high color, bold blue eyes; his building venture at Blackstable fails and he becomes ruined financially; runs off with Rosie Driffield; he then changes his name to Iggulden after he and Rosie flee to America; dies at age seventy+

KEMP, Harold (Cakes and Ale). One of Lord George Kemp's sons; is in business at Maidstone; supposedly, he has informed Amy Driffield of Rosie Driffield's death

KEMP, Liza (Liza of Lambeth). Age eighteen; dark eyes; lives with her mother on Vere Street, Lambeth; she is a factory worker; has an affair with Jim Blakeston; becomes pregnant; her death the result of miscarriage

KEMP, Mr. (Liza of Lambeth). Liza Kemp's father; dead; a soldier and a radical

KEMP, Mrs. (Liza of Lambeth). Liza Kemp's mother; age sixty-five; short, rather stout; red face; gray hair brushed tight back over her forehead; widowed for a number of years; she claims to have given birth to thirteen children; lives with Liza on Vere Street, Lambeth; she exists on her husband's pension and by charring; she drinks

KEMP, Robert (Of Human Bondage). He and his mother are residents of Ferne, Kent; a member of the Athelneys' hop garden

KENNING (Casual Affair). Is a member of the club in the north of Borneo; knew Jack Almond

KENSINGTON, Duchess of (Rehearsal). Is the principal character in Lucien Smith's ballet; dances in skirts and high heels

KENT, Basil (Man of Honour). Age twenty-six; bachelor, barrister, and writer; is good looking; clean shaven; delicate face and clean-cut features; was educated at Harrow; he had served in the Boer War, earning the D.S.M.; is engaged, out of necessity, to marry Jenny Bush, which he does; really in love with Hilda Murray

KENT, Basil (Merry-Go-Round). A barrister and a writer; lives modestly on an income of three hundred pounds per year; son of Mr. Kent #1 and Marguerite Vizard; has the face of a knight in an early Italian picture;

slender limbs, well made; has white and comely hands; somewhat long, brown curly hair; fine color in his face; dark brown eyes; thin cheeks; has full sensual mouth; went to Harrow, then to Oxford, where he and Frank Hurrell became close friends; following his mother's divorce trial, he enlisted in the Imperial Yeomanry and sailed for South Africa, where he spent three years; he returned to England and read for the Bar; he has an affair with young Jenny Bush; in love with Hilda Murray, but is forced to marry Jennie Bush and settle in Barnes; then publishes his novel, which receives generally poor reviews; following Jenny's suicide, he thinks about jumping into the river or shooting himself, but can do neither; then spends the winter in Seville; after his return to England, he becomes engaged to, and then marries, Hilda Murray

KENT, Jenny (Man of Honour/Merry-Go-Round). See Jenny BUSH

KENT, Mr. #1 (Merry-Go-Round). Father of Basil Kent and first husband of Lady Marguerite Vizard; cousin of Mr. Kent #2; died four years after his marriage, when Basil was a child

KENT, Mr. #2 (Merry-Go-Round). Of Ouseley; a cousin of Mr. Kent #1

KENT, Mrs. (Merry-Go-Round). Maternal grandmother of Basil Kent; she raised Basil after her son's death and his mother's marriage to Lord Vizard

KENYON, Montie (Smith). He had lunch at the Ritz with Cynthia Rosenberg

KERSAL, Bernard (Constant Wife). Tall; brown hair and brown eyes; age forty-five; tanned; good looking; a bachelor; a merchant in Kobe, Japan; he has not seen Constance Middleton in the last fifteen years; he once proposed marriage to her

KHEDIVE (Ashenden/Miss King). Deposed; had spent three weeks at the hotel in Geneva in closed meetings with Prince Ali

KHEDIVE, (Caesar's Wife). He has quarrelled with his secretary; asks Sir Arthur Little to recommend to him an English secretary

KIM CHING (Narrow Corner). A rich Chinese merchant at Takana; age seventy; formerly a coolie; is tall and stout; he has expensive gold teeth; sight is failing;

Characters   223

Dr. Saunders successfully removes his cataract; he had dismissed Captain Nichols eight or ten years ago

KINDERSELY, Colonel (Noble Spaniard). Cousin of Matilda Proudfoot; Matilda could have married him

KING of Cambodia (Princess September). Marries Princess September

KING of Denmark (Razor's Edge). Entertained by Elliott Templeton on the French Riviera

KING of England (Narrow Corner). Dr. Saunders clearly remembers seeing him in the old days, in the omnibus box at a Covent Garden theatre; obese; great paunches under his eyes

KING of Siam (Princess September). The father of nine daughters and ten sons

KING of Sweden (Razor's Edge). Entertained by Elliott Templeton on the French Riviera

KING of Uganda (Explorer [play]). Gave a dance in Alec MacKenzie's honor; ten thousand warriors in war paint participated

KING, Lady Eleanor (Jack Straw). Maria Parker-Jennings does not believe that she is the type of person who would be willing to have luncheon with Rosie Abbott

KING, Lady Eleanor (Penelope). According to the Morning Post notice, she leaves for Paris in the morning

KING, Miss (Ashenden/Miss King). Serves as Chaperone and governess to Prince Ali's daughters; a little old English woman, well over eighty years of age; black eyes; deeply furrowed face

KING'S COUNCIL #1 (Moon and Sixpence). A guest at the Stricklands' dinner party

KING'S COUNCIL #2 (Moon and Sixpence). Lives in South Kensington, London; plans to dine with Amy Strickland

KING'S PROCTOR (Merry-Go-Round). An "absurd gentleman" who presides over respectable divorce proceedings

KINGS (Rehearsal). Of Europe; Genevieve Zampa claims to have danced before all of them, and without heels

KINGSFORD, Mr. (Of Human Bondage). Forty years of age; clean shaven; long, fair hair; reddish skin; pale and tired eyes; large nose and large mouth; has prominent facial bones; is of more than average height; broad shouldered; a journalist and the editor of one of Alfred Harmsworth's (Viscount Northcliffe, 1865-1922) magazines; is engaged to marry Norah Nesbit after her divorce becomes final

KITCHEN MAID (Landed Gentry). At prayers in the dining room at Kenyon Fulton

KNIGHT (Catalina). Long, cadaverous face, short ragged beard, immense moustache; wears rusty, old fashioned armor; confronts Diego and Catalina on their way from the fort to the inn

KNIGHT OF THE BATH (Painted Veil). A widower with three children; Kitty Garstin had refused his proposal of marriage

KNOX, Harold (East of Suez). Young; brother of Sylvia Knox; pleasing appearance; serves on the staff of the British American Tobacco Company, at Peking; he is a Presbyterian; drinks; been in China for seven years

KNOX, Mr. (East of Suez). Father of Harold and Sylvia Knox; he thought that Sylvia ought to go to China

KNOX, Sylvia (East of Suez). Sister of Harold Knox; age twenty-two; Presbyterian; pretty; a simple, healthy, and attractive girl; is spring-like and fresh; her fiance killed in the war

KONG (Flotsam and Jetsam). Is Skelton's Chinese servant

KOSTI #1 (Razor's Edge). Father of Kosti #2; supposedly a general under the Czar

KOSTI #2 (Razor's Edge). A Polish coal miner who shared a room with Larry Darrell at the mining village near Lens, in northern France; tall (two or three inches taller than Larry) and is heavily built; pale fleshy face, broad short nose, and a big mouth; blue eyes, hard and shrewd; big lashes; ugly and uncouth; he had gone to school in Warsaw; he spoke very good French, with hardly a trace of a Polish accent; he is highly educated; a devout Catholic; had entered the nobleman's cadet school as a child; a cavalry officer in the late war; hated the Polish marshal, statesman and first president, Jozef Klemens Pilsudski (1867-1935); claimed to have been involved in an abortive plot to kill Pilsudski, and then escaped across the frontier after his associates had been captured; yet, others claimed that he had been cashiered from the army because he had been caught cheating at cards at the officers' club in Warsaw

KRAUSE, Hans (Winter Cruise). First mate on the Friedrich Weber; is seated at the same table with Venetia

Reed, Captain Erdman, the chief engineer, and the doctor; is young, handsome, and strong; married less than a year

KRAUSE, Mrs. (Winter Cruise). Married to Hans Krause for less than a year; she is in Hamburg, waiting and yearning for her husband

KREISLER, Fritz (Our Betters). The Austrian violinist (1875-1962); Arthur Fenwick boldly assures Lady Pearl Grayston that he can engage him to play at one of her parties

KU CHOW (Painted Veil). The owner of the filthy little curio shop off of the Victoria Road, Hong Kong, where Kitty Fane and Charlie Townsend generally met; small and fat-faced

KU FAUNG MIN (East of Suez). An old merchant at Peking; wants to place an order to Henry Anderson

KUHN, Rachel (Fortunate Painter). The only daughter of Monsieur Leir; married to Rudolf Kuhn

KUHN, Rudolf (Fortunate Painter). He is a New York art dealer; married to Rachel Kuhn, Monsieur Leir's only daughter

KUYPER, Jack (Cakes and Ale). Joins the regular guests at the Driffields' Saturday afternoon tea parties in Limpus Road, London; a Dutch Jew; a diamond merchant from Amsterdam spending a few weeks in London; tall, stout, and dark; bald; a big hooked nose; fifty years of age; powerful, determined, sensual, and jovial; he is attracted to Rosie Driffield

L

LA BARBERINA (Then and Now). A procuress at Imola with a well established and a respectable business; lets rooms in her house to Nina; she acquaints Machiavelli with sundry and not too expensive young women who on occasion assuage his passions

LA BRETONNE, Mimi (Lady Frederick). Is a singer at the Folies Bergeres; pretty; four or five years ago she had rooms at the Hotel de Paris, in Monte Carlo; she had an affair with Lord George Mereston; fell desperately ill and nursed by Lady Frederick Berolles

LA CACHIRRA (Mother). Real name Antonia Sanchez; mother of Currito Sanchez; moves from Triana to the tenement house in La Macarena, Seville; age forty; haggard and thin; bony hands, claw-like fingers; sunken cheeks; yellow and wrinkled skin; pale heavy lips; pointed teeth; hair black and coarse; large, black, deeply set eyes; her face bore a fierce expression; she had spent seven years in prison for committing a murder

LA CAROLINA (Then and Now). A grand woman of Florence who had been kept by a Cardinal; is extremely clever

LA CLARA (Catalina). The daughter of a haberdasher; her father and the Martinezes intend that she marry Diego Martinez; described by Diego as having a hump on her back, a squint in her eye, and hair like that of a mangy dog; Catalina sees her as having been marked by the smallpox, with yellow teeth (one of them missing)

LA FALTERONA, Maria (Voice of the Turtle). Is a prima donna; she no longer sang opera, but still toured; a neighbor of the Narrator on the Riviera; claimed to be Hungarian, but spoke excellent English; her accent suggested that she came from Kansas City; her father was supposedly a political exile who had escaped to America; raven black hair and black eyes; large mouth and nose; fleshy face

LA FERRARI (Rehearsal). Ballet dancer; the deadly rival of Genevieve Zampa; according to the Zampas--is age forty; weighs seventeen stone (238 pounds); she has thirteen children; her father a greengrocer and her mother a charwoman; "she cannot dance for nuts"

LA GORDA (Closed Shop). Is the Spanish proprietor of a bordello; a woman of ample proportions, with a highly visible moustache; her son attends Harvard University

LA MALAGUENA (Ashenden/Giulia Lazzari). Stage name of Giulia LAZZARI

LA MARISHKA (Christmas Holiday). Singer at the cellar bar in Paris; age forty; haggard and somber; gaunt, masculine features; brown skin; has enormous blazing eyes; black, heavy, and arching brows; raucous voice

LA MARQUEZA (Ashenden/Hairless Mexican). An old woman who kept a house in Mexico City

LABOURER #1 (Mrs. Craddock). At Bewlie's Farm, Kent; he tends to Edward Craddock's sick cow

LABOURER #2 (Mrs. Craddock). At the railway station at Blackstable, Kent; he saunters down the main platform

LABOURER (Of Human Bondage). Old; sits next to Philip

Carey at the Jolly Sailor, Ferne, Kent

LACOM, Dorothy (P.&O.). Wife of Mr. Lacom; age forty-eight; a handsome woman; bold black eyes, red mouth, lovely hair; is the object of Mr. Hamlyn's affections

LACOM, Mr. (P.&O.). Dorothy Lacom's husband; is a silk merchant in Yokohama

LAD (Hour Before the Dawn). Pasty faced; comes to the London air raid shelter and tells Mrs. Clark that the woman who lives in her house has been asking for her

LAD (Of Human Bondage). At the Jolly Sailor, in Ferne, Kent; a shiny face; a love lock plastered on his red forehead; age seventeen; he sits next to Philip Carey

LAD (Unattainable). He formerly served in the employ of Dr. Cornish; came in to do the boots and knives; then married the cook

LADIES (Bishop's Apron). Old; placed Theodore Spratte's biography of his father beside their devotional works and had it read to them during hours of mental stress

LADIES (Cakes and Ale). Two of them; elderly; walked along the beach at Blackstable, Kent

LADIES (Catalina). Sent for Catalina, made her parade before them, and gave her presents; cautioned her not to become conceited

LADIES (Cupid and the Vicar of Swale). Called upon Mr. Simpson to protest against the destruction of the old cottages on his estates

LADIES (Fortunate Painter). Gay; seen in the Rue Breda, in Paris; Charlie Bartle watched them make their purchases for luncheon; several had sat for Charlie

LADIES (Fortunate Painter). Old; English; owned the signed Watteau painting that Charlie Bartle copied

LADIES (Hero). Wives of officers of a native Indian regiment; advised Pritchard-Wallace not to marry the daughter of the riding master and his Portuguese wife

LADIES (Magician). In Margaret Dauncey's vision; in powder and patch

LADIES (Magician). Great and of doubtful fame; often in company of Oliver and Margaret Haddo at Monte Carlo

LADIES (Making of a Saint). A score of them; at the gathering at the Palazzo Orsi; they beckon to Matteo d'Orsi from different parts of the room

LADIES (Making of a Saint). Several of them; they have accompanied Caterina Sforza to the piazza at Forli

LADIES (Making of a Saint). At Forli; after his return from Florence, Filippo Brandolini attentive to all of them

LADIES (Merry-Go-Round). At shabby little restaurants in Soho; their positions in society had been scarcely acknowledged; exchanged confidences with one another

LADIES (Of Human Bondage). Two of them; visiting with Henrietta Watkin and her sister shortly after Mrs. Carey's death

LADIES (Of Human Bondage). Two of them; widows; old; are permanent lodgers at Helene Erlin's Heidelberg pension; troublesome

LADIES (Of Human Bondage). A few of them; at the cheap but respectable restaurant in Soho; of easy virtue

LADIES (Of Human Bondage). Guests at the boarding house in Brighton; old, with their elderly maiden daughters

LADIES (Sanitorium). One or two; patients at the sanitorium; middle aged; try unsuccessfully to learn from Ivy Bishop her relationship with George Templeton

LADIES (Theatre). At St. Malo; invited to tea by Carrie Falloux and Mrs. Lambert

LADY #1 (Bishop's Apron). She is of great position and suffering under some brutal affront; she tells Josiah Spratte that people are wondering "who this sprat is that we are asked to follow"

LADY #2 (Bishop's Apron). Cleans St. Gregory's Church; supposedly told Theodore Spratte that she wanted her little drop of beer, but that she favored spirits

LADY #3 (Bishop's Apron). From the Gaiety chorus; Lord Thomas Spratte loved her dearly, but she jilted him

LADY #1 (Cakes and Ale). Of title; when she died, she left all of her furniture to Miss Cowley, her former companion

LADY #2 (Cakes and Ale). A barmaid at the Bear and Key, Blackstable, Kent; young; shingled hair; in the bar reading a book by Mr. Compton Mackenzie (1883-1972)

LADY #1 (Catalina). A boarder at the convent; went to see friends in the city and told them of the Bishop's levitation

LADY #2 (Catalina). A boarder at the convent; pasty faced, lethargic, and corpulent; her husband away at the wars; she tells Catalina that she only wished she were free to become a religious

Characters   229

LADY #3 (Catalina). From the city; pinches Catalina's cheek and tells her that surely a saint will be in the convent in the near future

LADY (Christmas Holiday). At the restaurant at Jouy; forgets her handbag

LADY (Episode). Employed Grace Carter's mother before she married George Carter; told the former that she would leave her something in her will if she stayed with her until she died

LADY (Hero). At Little Primpton, Kent; married; one of Mary Clibborn's patients; she is about to be confined

LADY (Irish Gentleman). She is an older companion of the Princess Mary of Wartburg-Hochstein; she thanks Robert O'Donnel for his rescuing of the Princess Mary

LADY (Jack Straw). Could kick higher than anyone else in the world; Sebastian asked her to marry him, but his grandfather refused his consent; taken away over the frontier; she could claim three lawful husbands

LADY (Liza of Lambeth). One of the passengers from the Red Lion brake at Chingford; she is of quite mature appearance; announces to the coachmen that "we're not hanimals [sic]; we don't drink water"

LADY (Making of a Saint). In waiting to Caterina Sforza at the Palazzo Orsi; when she sees the conspirators, she shrieks and runs back

LADY #1 (Magician). Sitting in a carriage in front of Westminster Abbey, London; she is of mature age; gray eyebrows; bright, black eyes of preternatural fixity; speaks French with a marked English accent; she shows Eliphas Levi her collection of vestments and magical instruments, and she lends him books

LADY #2 (Magician). At Skene, Staffordshire; old, the mother of a landowner near Oliver Haddo's estate; she called upon Margaret Haddo when the latter first came there, but she had not been admitted

LADY (Merry-Go-Round). A small woman; Reggie Barlow-Bassett had taken her to dinner on a Saturday night

LADY #1 (Mrs. Craddock). Complained that Lucy Glover treated expectant mothers among the lower classes as though they were not married

LADY #2 (Mrs. Craddock). An expectant mother who had already delivered sixteen children; prepared to offer Lucy Glover actual proof of her marriage

LADY #1 (Of Human Bondage). Seen dining with Mr. Turner at the Cafe Royal; perhaps she was a near relative

LADY #2 (Of Human Bondage). She resided in Kensington Square, London; formed a platonic relationship with Hayward; is married to an official in India, soon to come home on leave

LADY #3 (Of Human Bondage). Lives on the drawing room floor of the house on Vauxhall Bridge Road, London; she provided Mildred Rogers with an account of her confinement

LADY #4 (Of Human Bondage). Is in confinement at Mrs. Owen's nursing home; her husband in the Indian civil service

LADY #5 (Of Human Bondage). At the boarding house in Brighton; Mildred Rogers becomes friends with her; she had taken a fancy to Mildred's baby

LADY #6 (Of Human Bondage). Is a guest at the boarding house at Brighton; old; with a middle-aged daughter; she is having her beautiful house in London redone

LADY #1 (Razor's Edge). Former employer of Miss Keith; found herself three months' pregnant when her husband had been shooting lions in Africa for six months; she took an expensive trip to Paris, and all proved well

LADY #2 (Razor's Edge). Appears to Larry Darrell in a vision while he meditates; elderly; lace cap and gray ringlets hanging over her ears; a lined face; kindly, sweet, mild; is dressed in the clothing of the 1870's

LADY (Round Dozen). Guest at the Dolphin; middle aged; by herself

LADY (Tenth Man). Young and married; in a thirty-year-old photograph that Angela Etchingham shows to Robert Perigal; Perigal had been in love with her and he had asked her to run away with him

LAG (Christmas Holiday). An old cat burglar whom Robert Berger met while awaiting trial; he specialized in jewelry; he told Berger stories about his exploits

LAKE, Lord Edward (Daisy). Is married to Lady Lake, Sir Herbert Ousley-Farrowham's sister

LAKE, Lady (Daisy). Is Lord Herbert Ousley Farrowham's sister; married to Lord Edward Lake

LAKE, Miss (Hero). See above, identified as Lady GREEN

LAMBERT, Julia (Theatre). See Julia Lambert GOSSELYN

LAMBERT, Miss (Counsel). See below, listed as Mrs. YU

Characters   231

LAMBERT, Mr. (Consul). Father of Mrs. Yu; in a "very
   good position" when he died
LAMBERT, Mr. (Theatre). The father of Julia Lambert
   Gosselyn; was a native of Jersey, where he practiced
   veterinary medicine; he died shortly after the war
LAMBERT, Mrs. (Counsel). Mrs. Yu's mother; takes in a
   lodger, Mr. Yu, after her husband's death; is against
   her daughter's marriage to Yu
LAMBERT, Mrs. (Theatre). The mother of Julia Lambert
   Gosselyn; after the death of her husband went to live
   with her widowed sister, Madame Carrie Falloux, at
   St. Malo; became Catholic; her age well over seventy
LAMBERVILLE, Mr. and Mrs. (Jack Straw). They are guests
   at the Parker-Jennings' garden party held in Cheshire
LAND AGENT (Point of Law). In Westmorland; had employed
   Ralph Mason as a clerk
LANDLADY (Ashenden/Traitor). Of Ashenden's second-class
   hotel at Lucerne; curious as to why Ashenden had come
   to Lucerne during the "dead season"; is a blonde and
   blowsy Swiss, outwardly good-humored and talkative
LANDLADY (Cakes and Ale). Of the house in the Vauxhall
   Bridge Road, London, where the Driffields had rooms;
   a former tart; she refused to allow Ted and Rosie
   Driffield to nurse their sick child in her house
LANDLADY #1 (Of Human Bondage). In the building where
   Philip Carey lodged at Barnes, in southwest London;
   funny looking, little, and old; a shriveled body and
   a deeply wrinkled face; she and her husband had a
   married daughter
LANDLADY #2 (Of Human Bondage). Of the house on the
   Vauxhall Bridge Road, where Philip Carey finds rooms
   for Mildred Rogers; small; a middle-aged cockney; she
   has an amusing sense of humor and a quick tongue
LANDLADY #3 (Of Human Bondage). At Kennington, London;
   an austere and silent woman; Philip Carey rents four
   unfurnished rooms from her for nine shillings a week;
   wants nothing more to do with Philip than receive her
   rent; she and her husband the only other residents of
   the house
LANDLADY #4 (Of Human Bondage). At the London rooms of
   Harry Griffiths; had orders to tell Mildred Rogers,
   whenever she called, that Griffiths was not at home;
   told Griffiths that on one occasion, Mildred had sat

on the doorstep for hours, crying
LANDLORD #1 (Cakes and Ale). Of the Dolphin, Ferne Bay, Kent
LANDLORD #2 (Cakes and Ale). In or about Blackstable, Kent; Edward Driffield converses with him about crops and the price of coal
LANDLORD (Catalina). Of an inn; tells Diego that he has no vacancies
LANDLORD (Making of a Saint). At an inn one half-day's ride from the Citta di Castello; he offers food to Filippo Brandolini and brings him wine
LANDLORD (Man from Glasgow). Of a shabby inn at Algeciras; he played cards
LANDLORD (Moon and Sixpence). Of the bar off of the Rue Bouterie; he stood for no nonsense from his customers
LANDLORD (Mother). At Triana; evicts La Cachirra from his house
LANDLORD (Mrs. Craddock). Of the villa in Naples; Miss Bertha Ley gives him notice after her father's death
LANDLORD (Noble Spaniard). Of the villa at Boulogne; he might not like it if the Duke of Hermanos chooses to kill himself on his property
LANDLORD (Razor's Edge). Owner of Elliott Templeton's apartment; he charged Templeton dearly to rent it
LANDLORD (Spanish Priest). Of the house in the Callo Alfonso Trece, Granada, where Vicente Oria y Mazallon lived; he feared difficulty with the police if someone tampered with with Vicente's belongings; agrees to rent Vicente's room to the English man
LANDLORD (Then and Now). At Machiavelli's inn at Sinigaglia; provides a mattress for Machiavelli and Piero at the foot of the bed of his wife and children
LANDON, Sir Edward (Happy Couple). A member of the same club to which the Narrator belonged; a judge at the Old Bailey; he had presided over the Wingford murder trial; a long white face, thin lips, pale blue eyes; age in middle to late sixties
LANGTON, Algernon (Merry-Go-Round). Dean of Tercanbury, Kent; Polly Ley's old friend and a distant cousin; father of Bella Langton, for whose fortieth birthday he composed a set of Latin verses; is a widower; old, tall, spare, and bent; has very white hair; pallid, almost transparent skin; cold, blue eyes; very gentle

Characters 233

  expression; a dignity and grace of bearing; his first
  curacy was at Portsmouth; refused ever to see Bertha
  Ley because she had married a farmer; now denies his
  consent to Bella's marriage to Herbert Field; then he
  reconciles with Bella and Herbert Field; administers
  the Holy Sacrament to Herbert
LANGTON, Bella (Merry-Go-Round). Daughter of Algernon
  Langton; age forty; not pretty; squarely built; with
  pleasant brown hair; overly broad features; an oddly
  weather-beaten complexion; kindly, gray eyes; short,
  thick-set, ungraceful hands; good-humored expression;
  falls in love with Herbert Field; proposes marriage
  to Herbert after she learns that he has consumption,
  then marries him; takes Herbert to Italy; her hair
  begins to turn gray; she reconciles with her father;
  after Herbert's death, collects his verses and wishes
  to publish them, accompanied by a prefatory biography
  that she has written
LANGTON, James (Theatre). The manager of a repertory
  theatre at Middlepool; age forty-five when he engaged
  the twenty-five-year old Michael Gosselyn; is fat and
  bald; rubicund; eccentric, arrogant, vain, charming;
  a bad actor
LANGTON, Mrs. (Merry-Go-Round). The wife of Algernon
  Langton and mother of Bella; brown eyes; she has been
  dead for thirty-five years
LANGTRY, Emily Charlotte Le Breton (Alien Corn/Gigolo
  and Gigolette/Circle). A famous beauty (1852-1929),
  known as "the Jersey Lily"; a guest in the country
  house where Ferdy Rabenstein had one resided; has an
  exquisitely shaped head; blue eyes; remembered Flora
  Penezzi perfectly; her picture in an old photograph
  album owned by Clive Champion-Cheney; a lovely nose;
  she and Clive went riding once
LANTERN BEARERS (Painted Veil). At Mei-tan-fu; they led
  Kitty Fane, Waddinton, and the Chinese officer across
  the courtyard to Walter Fane's room
LARCHER (Hero). A sapper whom Reggie and Clara Clibborn
  met at Simla, India; he sported a large red moustache
LARCHER DAUGHTERS (Hero). Of Mr. and Mrs. Larcher; two
  of them; buxom and healthy looking; they shook hands
  vigorously; James Parsons converses with one of them
  about the cricket week at Canterbury

LARCHER, Mr. (Hero). Father of Reginald Larcher and the two Larcher daughters; the husband of Mrs. Larcher; rosy-cheeked and bewhiskered; he is dapper and suave; owns the largest flower conservatory around Ashford

LARCHER, Mrs. (Hero). Mother of Reginald Larcher and the two Larcher daughters; wife of Mr. Larcher; wrote twice to James Parsons, inviting him to come to see her; hosting a tennis party when James finally visits

LARCHER, Reginald (Hero). A subaltern; age eighteen; an only son; fair hair and blue eyes; is from Ashford, Kent, near Little Primpton; he had been in Jamie Parson's regiment in South Africa for three or four weeks; shot in the leg; Jamie bandages the wound and carries him; shot in the neck; dies in Jamie's arms

LARION (Appearance and Reality). He is Lisette Larion's father; a wounded hero of World War I; he operated a tobacco shop in a small country town in the southwest of France

LARION, Lisette (Appearance and Reality). French; age nineteen; modeled clothes at an expensive and highly fashionable Paris establishment; tall, with slim hips and a slim waist; long legs; large brown eyes; a red mouth; clear but slightly freckled skin

LASCELLES, Emily (Tenth Man). Rumored to be in line for the Secretary of the Home Office; she does not know a single word of French, and thus she cannot entertain

LASSI, Antonio (Making of a Saint). Is a member of the Council at Forli; Girolamo Riario had raised him from a humble position; supports his master's determination to raise taxes; after the assassination of Girolamo Riario, he suggests that Forli be handed over to Checco d'Orsi

LATIMER, Mrs. (Road Uphill). Invalid and then deceased mother of Ruth Latimer

LATIMER, Ruth (Road Uphill). She is engaged to Joseph Sheridan; refuses to marry Joseph and accompany him to Paris; marries Howard Green and bears him a son

LATUKAS (Explorer [novel]). Friendly tribe in northeast Africa; Alec MacKenzie orders Deacon and Rogers to bring them in as reinforcements against an attack by the slavers and the natives

LAURA (String of Beads). She dines with the Narrator

LAVENDER MAN (Our Betters). On Grosvenor Street Mayfair

Characters 235

LAWESTON, Lady Cecily (Theatre). See Cecily DENNORANT

LAWSON, Andrew (Pool). Son of Bertie and Ethel Lawson

LAWSON, Bertie (Pool). Is small and thin; a long sallow face; a narrow weak chin; large and bony nose; large shaggy eyebrows; large and dark eyes; heavy drinker; had come from England to manage the local branch of an English bank; husband of Ethel, father of Andrew

LAWSON, Ethel (Pool). The wife of Bertie and mother of Andrew; a half-caste; daughter of Old Brevald; she is extremely young (age twenty-two or so); is adorably pretty; no darker than a Spaniard; small; beautiful, with tiny hands and feet; in all, delicate and dainty

LAWSON, Frederick (Of Human Bondage). Is a student at Amitrano's art school, Paris; a regular at Gravier's restaurant; young; thin; has freckled face; red hair; bright green eyes; he is very sensitive to criticism; he eventually moves to London, then returns to Paris, and finally back to London

LAWYER (Happy Couple, 1908). Successfully defends Dr. Brownley and Miss Wingfield's companion; that trial made his name

LAWYER (Happy Couple, 1952). Draws Miss Wingford's will

LAWYER (Merry-Go-Round). Engaged by Lord Vizard for his divorce; is the cleverest criminal lawyer of the time

LAWYER (Treasure). He arranged the separation between Richard Harenger and his wife

LAWYER (Up at the Villa). An old, shrewd man and an old friend of Mary Panton; advised her that, next time, she should marry not for love, but for position and companionship

LAWYERS (Catalina). Engaged by Don Manuel de Valero to determine Blasco de Valero's eligibility for canonization; they report to Manuel that the chances seem far better for one's beatification than for sainthood

LAWYERS (Up at the Villa). Gathering what was left of Mr. Panton's squandered fortune

LAY BROTHER (Catalina). Tells Blasco de Valero that his brother, Don Manuel, desired to see him; later, he ushers Domingo Perez directly to the bishop's oratory

LAY SISTERS (Catalina). Performed menial work at the convent of Castel Rodriguez to allow the nuns there more time for their devotion and occupations of honor

LAZZARI, Giulia (Ashenden/Giulia Lazzari). The woman

with whom Chandra Lal believes he has fallen in love; she is approximately thirty-five years of age; is an Italian prostitute; is almost swarthy; skin lined and sallow; coal black eyes; she is a "rotten" performer of Spanish dances; she calls herself "La Malaguena"; married to a Spaniard; a spy

LECTURER (Mirage). In anatomy at the medical college, St. Thomas's Hospital, London; discovers one of his students is reading a newspaper during his lecture

LECTURER (Unconquered). To the German troops at Soissons; he tells them that a third of the French farms remain uncultivated because of a lack of male workers

LEE TAI CHENG (East of Suez). A rich Chinese; big and stout, with a smooth yellow face; black eyes; is a graduate of the University of Edinburgh; spent a year each at Harvard and Oxford; bought seventeen-year-old Daisy (Anderson) from her mother for two thousand dollars; he gives Daisy a necklace after she has been married to Henry Anderson for a year; Daisy's hatred for him is a sharp and bitter sauce that tickles his appetite; is married; Robert Burns his favorite poet

LEFEVRE, Enid (Camel's Back). Is the niece and ward of Valentine Lefevre; worth ten thousand pounds a year; is in love with Denis Armstrong, although she is to marry Howard Dixon within six weeks; breaks off her engagement to Dixon and becomes engaged to Armstrong

LEFEVRE, Hermione (Camel's Back). The wife of Valentine Lefevre for sixteen years; Enid's aunt; she dyes her hair; tells her family that Valentine is out of his mind; eventually, she reconciles with her husband

LEFEVRE, Mrs. (Camel's Back). Is the widowed mother of Valentine Lefevre; daughter of a clergyman; married to her husband for forty years; a resident of a hotel in Oxford Street, London; fully supported by her son; she desperately wants to continue her independence

LEFEVRE, Valentine (Camel's Back). Husband of Hermione Lefevre and Enid's uncle; is a humorless and rumbling barrister; a prospective candidate for Parliament; he believes that his wife dresses too young; trustee of Enid's money until she reaches age thirty-five; he disapproves of Denis Armstrong; he insists that Enid must marry Howard Dixon; he threatens to cut off his mother's income unless she comes to live with him;

announces that he will divorce Hermione because he believes that she has had an affair with Denis Armstrong; then reconciles with his mother and Hermione

LEGGATT, Edward (Moon and Sixpence). Is a friend of the Narrator; an able writer and admirable painter; wrote (1917) a critical book on Charles Strickland's work

LEGRAND, Colonel (Christmas Holiday). An old friend of the Berger family; an army doctor who had served with Robert Berger's father; is present at the marriage of Robert and Lydia Berger

LEGROS, Bessie (Sheppey). She is pretty, painted, and is no longer young; one of Sheppey Miller's drinking companions at the Bunch of Keys pub, London; a tart; her initial situation when she came to London was at Gloucester Place; went by the name of Mrs. Gloucester when she had her flat in Kensington; after recovering from double pneumonia, she found that her gentleman clients could no longer afford luxuries; Sheppey then openly invites her to lodge and board at his house

LEIR, Monsieur (Fortunate Painter). An art dealer; the father of Rachel Kuhn; small and old; a lonely man; he had known many painters; liked artists and found satisfaction in their society; occupied an apartment in the same house as Charlie Bartle

LEMBERG, Count Max (Magician). He had seen homunculi

LEMOINE, Maitre (Christmas Holiday). He defended Robert Berger at his murder trial; one of the best criminal lawyers at the French bar; very tall and thin; a long sallow face; immense, black eyes; black, thick hair; eloquent hands; deep, powerful voice; an actor and an orator; kind toward Lydia Berger, but he is impatient because she would not divorce her husband after his sentence

LENNOX, Dr. (Sanatorium). A small, brisk, and genial Scotsman; an avid fisherman; visits Ashenden morning and evening; Ivy Bishop's physician; he advises Major Templeton to stop smoking

LEON, Jose (Romantic Young Lady). The coachman to the Countess de Marbella; Pilar wishes to marry him; he is extremely handsome;he belonged to an ancient and distinguished Adalusian family

LEONARDS (Up at the Villa). English people; bought the Florentine villa from the impoverished descendants of a noble Florentine; they then lent it to Mary Panton

LEONIDOV, Anastasia Alexandrovna (Ashenden/Mr. Harrington's Washing). Daughter of Alexander Denisiev; lived with her husband in London; fine eyes; a voluptuous figure; high cheekbones; snub nose; wide mouth; large square teeth; pale skin; has an affair with Ashenden

LEONIDOV, Vladimir Semenovich (Ashenden/Mr. Harrington's Washing). Husband of Anastasia Alexandrovna Leonidov; an exile from Russia; small; a large, long head, with a great shock of unruly hair; he taught Russian and wrote for the Moscow papers

LEPARD, Lady (Theatre). At the London restaurant where Thomas Fennell and Julia Gosselyn dine; she hosted a large party in Cheshire

LERIN, Count of (Then and Now). He is the most powerful of the rebel captains' barons; Caesar Borgia planned to attack his castle

LERMA, Duke of (Catalina). The favorite of King Philip III of Spain; engages the services of Don Manuel de Valero

LEROUX, Andre (East of Suez). Is having an affair with Mrs. Stopfort; George Conway not sure that Andre will marry Mrs. Stopfort after her divorce

LESEBREN (Magician). A physician to Louis XIV; recounts experiments that he witnessed relative to a remedy to prolong life

LESTER, Sir Henry (Unattainable). Is Caroline Ashley's principal solicitor

LE SUEUR #1 (Appearance and Reality). Son of Raymond and Madame Le Sueur; he played tennis nearly like a professional, and danced and played bridge expertly

LE SUEUR #2 ((Appearance and Reality). The Daughter of Raymond and Madame Le Sueur; married a very nearly authentic prince

LE SUEUR, Madame (Appearance and Reality). The wife of Raymond Le Sueur; age fifty; tall, angular; heiress to a flourishing steel works

LE SUEUR, Raymond (Appearance and Reality). Locomotive manufacturer, with controlling interests in a sugar refinery, a film company, a motor car company, and a newspaper; a member of the French Senate; large and fat; gray beard

LETTER, Arthur (Bread-Winner). Chairman of a great bank

in London; agrees to lend Charles Battle enough money to meet his obligations

LEVANTINE #1 (Of Human Bondage). An itinerant vendor of cheap rugs; a partner of Levantine #2; he enters the Closeries de Lilas, Paris; clad in shabby European clothes; gray, cold face; middle aged; black beard; a cringing smile like a mongrel; he shows Cronshaw a pornographic picture

LEVANTINE #2 (Of Human Bondage). Partner of Levantine #1; clad in shabby European clothes; a gray and cold face; age eighteen; a deep face scarred by smallpox; one eye

LEVANTINES (Christmas Holiday). At the Dome, in Paris; they are all swarthy, gesticulating, and loquacious

LEVI, Eliphas (Magician). His real name Alphonse-Louis Constant; the son of a bootmaker; destined for the priesthood; he fell in love with a fair damsel and married her; they parted when she took a lover; the most celebrated occultist of recent years; supposedly he knew more of the mysteries than any adept since Paracelsus (see below); did not look like a magician; a good natured face; a long, gray beard that covered nearly his entire breast; was short and corpulent; in London in the spring of 1856

LEVITSKI, Aaron (Lady Frederick). A money lender and father of Captain Montgomerie; a Polish Jew who came to England with three shillings in his pocket; then married an English woman; at his death, he left his son the name and the arms of the Montgomerie family and over one million pounds

LEWIS, Edith (Landed Gentry). Age twenty and pretty; a resident of London

LEWISHAM, Mannie (Tenth Man). The head of a group of business rivals of George Winter in Central America; George has been fighting him for ten years; in the end, he offers to join with Winter in the Camp del Oro mining venture

LEY, Bertha (Merry-Go--Round). Widow of Edward Craddock and a niece of Polly Ley; when she married a farmer, Rev. Algernon Langton, her relative, refused to see her again; in Italy; Polly Ley would like to see her marry Dr. Frank Hurrell; is mentioned in Polly Ley's will to receive one-third of her Aunt Polly's estate

LEY, Bertha (Mrs. Craddock). Age twenty-one; a niece of Polly Ley; an orphan; tall and handsome; dark eyes; small and pink ears; full, red lips; even, glistening teeth; dark hair; olive skin; small and exquisitely modelled hands, tapered fingers, and soft pink nails; statuesque neck; finely formed arms; shapely body; has lived with her Aunt Polly Ley for three years at Court Leys, between Leanham and Blackstable, Kent; in love with Edward Craddock and, a month after reaching her majority, marries him; her first child, a boy, still born; is told that she can never have another child; she leaves Court Leys (gone six weeks) to stay with her Aunt Polly in London, then accompanies her to Paris; returns to Court Leys and realizes that she no longer loves Edward Craddock; leaves her husband a second time and accompanies Polly Ley to Rome, and then to London; falls in love with Gerald Vaudrey; is somewhat over thirty years of age when her husband dies in a riding accident; pale, but still beautiful

LEY, Mary (Merry-Go-Round). Known familiarly as Polly; the most distant of Elizabeth Dwarris's cousins; she is slender and of middle size; plain hair beginning to turn gray; a wrinkled face; thin, expressive, and mobile lips; is neither handsome nor pretty, but not without grace or fascination; very bright eyes; has beautiful hands; shapely feet; plain spoken; a keen wit; at age fifty-seven she is appointed executrix of Elizabeth Dwarris's will, and receives her real and personal property--and three thousand pounds per year

LEY, Mary (Mrs. Craddock). Known familiarly as Polly; aunt of Bertha Ley; a sister of Betty Vaudrey; has lived with her niece, Bertha Ley, for three years at Court Leys, near Blackstable, Kent; is a forty-seven-year-old spinster, passionately devoted to her own liberty; neither short nor tall; very slight; a thin and wrinkled face; mouth not large; lips a trifle too thin; cold eyes; thin, gray hair; she leaves Court Leys following the marriage of Bertha to Edward Craddock; her story will be continued in Merry-Go-Round

LEY, Miss (Happy Couple, 1908). The most delightful of old maids; took a house on the river for a fortnight

LEY, Miss (Magician). Friend of both Frank Hurrell and Arthur Burdon; she asked Frank to meet the German explorer, Burkhardt

LEY, Mr. (Merry-Go-Round). Father of Polly Ley; when he stormed into a passion, he called it righteous anger

LEY, Mr. (Mrs. Craddock). Father of Bertha Ley and the brother of Polly Ley and Betty Vaudrey; irascible; he and Polly not on speaking terms for years; also not on speaking terms with his brother-in-law, General Vaudrey; went abroad with Bertha following the death of his wife; he had died in Italy three years ago

LEY, Mrs. (Mrs. Craddock). Bertha Ley's mother; sister-in-law of General and Betty Vaudrey; she had left her daughter a small income

LEY, Polly (Merry-Go-Round/Mrs. Craddock). See Mary LEY

LIBRARIAN (Magician). At the Arsenal library, in Paris; could not help Dr. Porhoet find seemingly impossible authorities

LICENCEE (Of Human Bondage). At Ferne, Kent; knew all his customer by name

LICONDA, Major (Sacred Flame). Is a retired official of the Indian Police; tall and middle aged; gray hair; sunburned face; spare of build; active and alert; has taken over the furnished house on the golf links; he has known Mrs. Tabret (to whom he is still deeply attached) for thirty years; he first met Mrs. Tabret in India; a good golfer

LIEUTENANT (Good Manners). In the navy; a guest at one of Augustus Breton's little dinners; breezy ways and an adventurous air

LIFAR, Serge (Casual Affair). The Russian-born dancer and choreographer (1905-1986), in attendance at Lady Kastellan's party

LIFTMAN (Ashenden/Miss King). At the hotel in Geneva

LIFTMAN (Human Element). At the Plaza Hotel, Rome; an old acquaintance of the Narrator; tells the Narrator that the hotel is almost empty

LIGURIO (Then and Now). The name of the character that Machiavelli ascribed to Piero Giacomini in his play

LINSELL (P.&O.). Naval officer attached to the British Embassy in Tokyo; Mrs. Linsell's submissive husband

LINSELL, Mrs. (P.&O.). Wife of Mr. Linsell; had become engaged to Linsell while she was still at school; is a small woman; the object of the surgeon's affections

LINTON, Julia (Constant Wife). An acquaintance of Mrs.

Culver; she married an Egyptian pasha

LITTLE, Sir Arthur (Caesar's Wife). Consular Agent at Cairo; the husband of Lady Violet Little; brother of Christina Pritchard; then only recently married; age forty-two; alert; young in manner; intelligent; is an experienced dipolmatist; almost nothing escapes him

LITTLE, Lady Violet (Caesar's Wife). Wife of Sir Arthur Little; age twenty; is very pretty; fresh and English looking; met Sir Arthur at a weekend party; in love with Ronald Parry

LITTLEWOOD, Archie (Unknown). Elder son of Charlotte Littlewood and brother of Ned; badly wounded on the Somme; eventually killed

LITTLEWOOD, Charlotte (Unknown). The mother of Ned and Archie Littlewood; she has lost both of her sons and refuses to mourn for them; small and elderly; wants to leave Stour and move to London; has known Evelyn Wharton for thirty years

LITTLEWOOD, Ned (Unknown). The younger son of Charlotte Littlewood; brother of Archie; age nineteen; died at Boulogne

LIVERPOOL MANUFACTURER (Outstation). Relative on George Warburton's mother's side, from whom the mother inherits, and then squanders, a hundred thousand pounds

LIVINGSTONE, Mr. (String of Beads). Husband of Sophie Livingstone; hosts a dinner party for fourteen people

LIVINGSTONE, Sophie (String of Beads). The wife of Mr. Livingstone; hosts a dinner party for fourteen people

LIZZIE (Home). When she carries a cup of tea to Uncle George Meadows, she discovers that he is dead

LOCKSMITH (Of Human Bondage). Opens the door to Fannie Price's lodgings

LOCKSMITH (Spanish Priest). He gained the English man admission to Vicente Oria y Mazallon's room

LODGEKEEPER (Magician). At Oliver Haddo's estate in Staffordshire; tries unsuccessfully to keep Arthur Burdon, Dr. Porhoet, and Susie Boyd from entering Skene; wife of the doorman; mother of the little boy

LODGER (Dream). Found the body of the Russian's wife at the bottom of the stairs

LOMAS, Mr. (Explorer [novel]). Father of Richard Lomas; spent seven years in China; he sent Dick to America before his son proceeded to Oxford

LOMAS, Richard (Explorer [novel]). An old friend of the Allertons; he is a bachelor, barrister, and member of Parliament; educated at Oxford; age thirty-seven to thirty-nine; is wiry and small; a sharp, good-humored face; sparkling eyes; thinning hair; is whimsical and gay; an excellent bridge player; tells Lucy Allerton that her father has lost everything and that Hamlyn's Purlieu must be sold; proposes to retire from active life and devote himself to the graces of life; Fred Allerton owes him two hundred pounds; he begins his retirement with holiday in Naples; proposes marriage to Julia Crowley, who refuses; accepts Julia's proposal (demand, actually) of marriage and marries her

LOMAS, Richard (Explorer [play]). Is a witness at Fred Allerton's trial; clean shaven and dapper; sharp face and good natured smile; age between thirty-five and forty; slim and youthful; a barrister; is the trustee for the remains of Mrs. Allerton's fortune; a member of Parliament; preparing to retire; accompanies Alec MacKenzie on his expedition to Africa; he suffers a slight wound in the arm; proposes marriage to Nellie Crowley, but she refuses; he then spends the summer touring Scotland, Germany, and Italy; he and Nellie Crowley finally become engaged

LOMBARDOS (Ashenden/Hairless Mexican). Fictitious name under which the agent Constantine Andreadi travels

LONDON COUNTY COUNCILLOR (Jack Straw). The most exalted person Ethel Parker-Jennings had ever met until she reached the age of sixteen

LONDON THRONG (Merry-Go-Round). Well-dressed; in gay June weather; sat about on chairs or lounged up and down, looking at their neighbors; they talked light heartedly of the topics of the hour

LONG, Major (Pro Patria). Jovial and red-faced; he is a most influential supporter of John Porter-Smith

LONGSTAFFE, Isabel (Fall of Edward Barnard). American (native of Chicago); cool, gray eyes; slim, straight; delicate features; an aristocratic, short upper lip; wealth of fair hair; she is engaged to Edward Barnard

LONGSTAFFE, Mary (Fall of Edward Barnard). Mother of Isabel Longstaffe and the sister of Arnold Jackson

LONGSTAFFE, Mr. (Fall of Edward Barnard). The father of Isabel Longstaffe; husband of Mary

LONSDALE, Lady (Circle). Her picture is an old photograph album owned by Clive Champion-Cheney

LOUIS XII (Then and Now). King of France (1462-1515; 1498-1515) and the paramount power;he had received a dispensation from the Pope to eliminate his barren and scrofulous wife (daughter of Louis XI) so that he might marry Anne of Brittany

LOUISE (Human Element). Betty Weldon-Burns' aunt, with whom she had lived before her marriage; she was the former employer of Albert

LOULOU (Christmas Holiday). At the cellar bar in Paris; she is a little bit drunk; sits next to Charley Mason

LOUNGERS (Bishop's Apron). At the Corn Exchange, Barchester

LOVER (Magician). Of the wife of Eliphas Levi; he ran away with her

LOVER (Theatre). Of Jane Taitbout; had settled a small pension on Jane when, after many years of faithful concubinage, he and she parted

LOW, Arthur (Casual Affair). District Officer; lives on an island on the north coast of Borneo; he hosts the Narrator; his age in the late thirties; quiet; small; married, with two young children; once a fairly close with Jack Almond; the principal narrator of the story

LOW, Bee (Casual Affair). Wife of Arthur Low; small and plump; dark eyes, fine eyebrows; she is attractive, although not pretty

LOWNDES, Major Frederick (Home and Beauty). Is Victoria Cardew-Lowndes' second husband; the father of William Lowndes; he had been William Cardew's best man at his wedding to Victoria; employed at the War Office; tall and soldierly

LOWNDES, Victoria (Home and Beauty). See under Victoria CARDEW-LOWNDES

LOWNDES, William (Home and Beauty). Son of Victoria and Frederick Lowndes; he has been named after Victoria's first husband, William Cardew

LUARD (Of Human Bondage). One of the pupils at King's School, Tercanbury, Kent; a friend of Philip Carey

LUCIA (Making of a Saint). Servant-maid of Donna Guilia dall' Aste; carries a message from her mistress to Filippo Brandolini, at the house of Andrea's mother

LUCREZIA (Then and Now). The name of a character in the

play by Machiavelli; will represent Aurelia Martelli

LUCY (Noble Spaniard). Age eighteen; a sister of Marion Nairne; she is engaged to Captain Adolphus Chalford

LUIGI (Then and Now). A son of Monna Serafina; destined for the priesthood; shares a room in his house with Piero Giacomini

LUKAS, Monsieur (Christmas Holiday). The Commissaire de Police; investigates the murder of Teddie Jordan; he searches the Berger house; big, fat, and hearty; red cheeks; heavy moustache; large, shining, black eyes

LUNCHEON GUEST (Up at the Villa). Is at the Atkinsons' villa, in Florence; he sits next to Mary Panton; he has the reputation as an expert on all Italian art

LUTCHKOV, Princess (Neil MacAdam). The mother of Darya Munro; after the death of her first husband and exile to Yokohama, she married a fellow exile; divorced him after two years; died penniless

LUTHERAN MINISTER (Narrow Corner). Officiates at Erik Christessen's funeral

LUTON, Edward (Circle). Is known familiarly as "Teddy"; young and attractive; the manager of a rubber estate in Malaya; in love with Elizabeth Champion-Cheney; he runs away with Elizabeth in Lord Hughie Porteus's car to San Michele

LYCETT, James (Mrs. Craddock). A guest at Mrs. Branderton's dinner party; husband of Mrs. Lycett; a red-faced squire who possesses highly dogmatic opinions

LYCETT, Mrs. (Mrs. Craddock). Accompanies her husband, James, to Mrs. Branderton's dinner party; is thin, quiet, and staid

LYNGATE, Mary (String of Beads). A guest at the Livingstones' dinner party; she sits next to Count Borselli

M

MABEL (Mabel). The wife of George, for eight years

MACADAM, Neil (Neil MacAdam). Assistant Curator of the museum at Kualo Solor, Borneo; Scottish; age twenty-two; six feet, two inches tall; long, loose limbs and broad shoulders; narrow hips; brown curly hair; large blue eyes; short, blunt nose; a big mouth; determined chin; broad face; smooth, white skin; patch of red on each cheek; son of a country doctor; the nephew of a

Glasgow merchant; B.Sc., with honors, the University of Edinburgh; he is a highly trained taxidermist

MACALISTER (Of Human Bondage). A Scot; had studied at Cambridge with Hayward; a London stockbroker, as well as a philosopher; a student of Kant; he introduced Hayward to the tavern in Beak Street; big boned; too short for his width; a large, fleshy face; soft voice

MACANDREW, Fred (Moon and Sixpence). Brother-in-law of Amy Strickland and the husband of Dorothy Macandrew; formerly a colonel in the Guards; was a guest at the Stricklands' dinner party; tall and lean; age fifty; drooping moustache and gray hair; pale, blue eyes and weak mouth; a foolish face; died two years before his wife

MACANDREW, Dorothy (Moon and Sixpence). Older sister of Amy Strickland, wife of Colonel Fred Macandrew, and a guest at the Stricklands' dinner party; outlived her husband by two years, and left money to her sister

MACARDLE, Dr. Andrew (Buried Talent). A Scot; tall and big-boned; abundant curly white hair and white beard; red cheeks; husband of Blanche MacArdle; his youthful solemnity had become pleasant cheer and encouragement

MACARDLE, Blanche (Buried Talent). Middle aged; big and stout; gray hair; handsome, dark eyes, but with bags under them; a heavy jowl; coarse, sallow skin; ample bosom; Scottish; married to Dr. Andrew MacArdle (at age twenty-four) for twenty-six years; was a handsome creature when young--fine eyes and a good profile; a magnificent contralto, who gave away her career to marry and then accompany her husband to the Federated Malay States; had shared a room with Charmian Pelter near the Boulevard Raspail, Paris; Charmian referred to her as "a constipated virgin"; takes her own life

MACDONALD (Tenth Man). He is George Winter's expert on mining; is the soundest man in the profession; George sends him to Campo del Oro; he determines that the Lewishams' mine is worthless

MACDONALD, Bob (Razor's Edge). The husband of Sophie; a lawyer; he and their child killed in an automobile crash in Chicago

MACDONALD CHILD (Razor's Edge). Of Sophie and Bob Macdonald; killed with her father in an automobile crash in Chicago

Characters 247

MACDONALD, Mr. (Social Sense). The host of the dinner party; husband of Mrs. Macdonald

MACDONALD, Mrs. and Mrs. (Razor's Edge). Paternal grandparents of Bob Macdonald; Sophie Macdonald had lived with them after her parents' divorce; they would not allow Sophie to return

MACDONALD, Mr. and Mrs. (Razor's Edge). Bob Macdonald's parents; nice, quiet people; are upset by Sophie's conduct following the death of Bob and their grandchild; provided Sophie with an allowance, but forced her to live abroad

MACDONALD, Mrs. (Social Sense). The host of the dinner party; wife of Mr. Macdonald

MACDONALD, Sophie (Razor's Edge). At age fourteen, had long hair brushed back from her forehead, and a thick black bow at the back; freckled serious face; modest, high-minded, idealistic; talked with Larry Darrell, whom she loved, about books; wrote poetry; in 1919, before her marriage, she found herself seated next to Maugham (the Narrator) at Louisa Bradley's dinner; her grandparents lived at Marvin, Illinois; is shy, drab, and seemingly very young; at age seventeen--not pretty, but with an amusing face; small, tilted nose, wide mouth, greenish blue eyes; sandy brown hair; is thin and flat chested; is eventually married to Bob Macdonald; spent four months in a sanitorium after the death of her husband and child; took to drink and sleeping with men; twelve years later--appeared tall and thin; dyed red hair cut short and loosely curled; outrageously made up; green eyes; confronts Maugham, Larry Darrell and Isabel and Gray Maturin at the cafe on the Rue de Lappe, Paris; she is terribly drunk and deeply affected by opium; after running out on Larry Darrell, who had planned to marry her (the marriage actually prevented by Isabel Maturin), she goes to Toulon, where Maugham meets her; takes up residence at the Commerce et la Marine hotel; she is found in Toulon harbor, in her underwear, with her throat cut

MACDOUGAL (Of Human Bondage). An office boy at Messrs. Herbert Carter Company, London; long nose; and pimply face; Scottish accent; age about nineteen or twenty

MACDOUGAL, Henry Beard (Cakes and Ale). Is an assistant professor of English literature at the University of

Virginia; he wishes to look at the Driffield house and garden; tall, young, broad shouldered, and clean shaven; a swarthy face; spectacles; thick black hair; is on a literary tour of England

MACDOUGAL, Mr. (Unattainable). He is persuaded by Mr. Petersen and Mrs. Macdougal to allow for the divorce

MACFARLANE, Dr. (Unknown). Is an old fashioned country doctor at Stour, in Kent, where he had practiced for fifty years; has no interest in attending church; he brought both Sylvia Bullough and John Wharton into the world; he tends to Colonel George Wharton, and he encourages George to see a specialist; he is old and eccentric; small; with long, white hair; rosy cheeks

MACFARLANE, Mrs. (Unknown). Wife of Dr. Macfarlane; had seen John Wharton in church

MACFARREN, Mr. and Mrs. (Letter [story]). Host a tennis party, where Leslie Crosbie last met Geoffrey Hammond

MACGREGOR, Eliza (Mrs. Dot). Dot Worthley's aunt; age fifty-five; quiet; thin; angular; good humor; amiable

MACHIAVELLI, Bernardo the elder (Then and Now). Father of Niccolo Machiavelli; he inhabited the white house near the company estate at San Lorenzo; had been dead for twenty years

MACHIAVELLI, Marietta (Then and Now). Wife of Niccolo Machiavelli; was a young woman of no great beauty; of reputable family; she had brought her husband a good dowry; married to Machiavelli for less than a year

MACHIAVELLI, Niccolo (Then and Now). Age thirty-three; husband of Marietta Machiavelli, to whom he had been married for less than a year; is of middle height; so thin that he looked taller than he was; a small head; very black hair, cut short; small and restless dark eyes; a long nose; thin lips, tightly closed when he was not speaking; a sallow face; a wary, thoughtful, severe, cold expression; was not a man with whom you could play pranks; had cherished the conviction that men are always the same and have the same passions; when circumstances are similar, the same cause leads to the same effects; sent to the city of Imola by the Florentine Signory on a mission to Duke Caesar Borgia

MACINNERY, Fergus (Explorer [novel]). A member of Alec MacKenzie's latest expedition into Africa; Alec had found him, half starving, at Mambassa; he had made a nuisance of himself; he and George Allerton got into a scrape with some native women; Alec sends him back to the coast; publishes a letter in the Daily Mail, accusing Alec of sending George Allerton to his death to save himself (Alec); challenges Alec to bring an action for criminal libel against him; then writes a second letter to the newspapers, once again accusing Alec MacKenzie of causing George Allerton's death

MACINNERY, Fergus (Explorer [play]). A member of Alec MacKenzie's expedition to Africa; Alec dismissed him after he and George Allerton got blind drunk at the station at Muneas; writes letters to the London Times and blames Alec Mackenzie for George Allerton's death

MACK, Mrs. (Penelope). Name invented by Ada Fergusson and Dickie O'Farrell; Dickie's fictional patient; she is a pretense for Ada and Dickie meeting each other

MACK, Walker (Penelope). Is the fictional Mrs. Mack's fictional husband; he has been dead for forty years

MACKENZIE, Alexander (Explorer [novel]). Dick Lomas's friend for twenty years; belonged to an old family of the Scottish Highlands; educated at Eton and Oxford; just under six feet tall; spare and well made; well-knit limbs, without superfluous flesh; dark hair, cut very close; a short red beard and a moustache; square chin; a determined mouth; eyes fixed, but not large; skin tanned by continued exposure to tropical suns; jumped into the Atlantic Ocean to rescue Dick Lomas when the latter fell overboard; after leaving Oxford, embarked upon a brief expedition to Algeria to shoot; then followed fifteen years of traversing throughout Africa; he is a man of considerable means, his income depending chiefly upon a colliery in Lancashire, as well as family inheritance; sold his estate in Texas and then borrowed on his interests in Lancashire to conduct a private expedition of three hundred men against the slave traders of British East Africa; was badly wounded in battle against the native forces of Mohammed the Lame; has read papers before the Royal Geographical Society; he acquired, within a year, a working knowledge of botany and geology, the elements of surveying, the treatment of maladies associated with tropical climates, and the elements of surgery; he had explored those countries that afterward became

British East Africa; he plays bridge extraordinarily well; had arrived in England two months earlier from Mombassa; in less than one month, he would return to Africa, and with an expedition of four hundred armed men, renew his struggle against the slave traders; endowed with an extreme gift of concentration; falls in love with Lucy Allerton and proposes marriage to her; after four years, he succeeds in driving all the slavers out of British East Africa; both he and Dr. Adamson attacked by blackwater fever on their way to Nairobi; near death, but recovers; falsely accused by Fergus Macinnery of causing George Allerton's death; leads the rescue of the thirty entombed miners from the pit in Lancashire; after Lucy Allerton breaks her engagement with him, he proposes to return to Africa to work in the Congo Free State on behalf of the King of Belgium; he and Lucy Allerton eventually reconcile

MACKENZIE, Alexander (Explorer [play]). He is the the great traveler; he met Dick Lomas on board a ship and rescued him when he fell overboard; is preparing to return to Africa; is tall, wiry, and well knit; dark hair, small, red moustache; a beard cut close to the face; age thirty-five; he proposes marriage to Lucy Allerton, who refuses him; he becomes engaged to Lucy after returning from Africa; then plans to go back to Africa after Lucy angrily breaks off their engagement

MACKENZIE, Mr. and Mrs. (Explorer [novel]). Parents of Alec Mackenzie; had died during their son's childhood

MACLAREN (Tenth Man). A broker

MADAM (Sheppey). She kept the house in Gloucester Place where Bessie Legros practiced her profession when she first came to London; Bessie thought her a nice lady

MADDEN (Explorer [novel]). Of Brise, Hampshire; because of his rank and opulence, was the most distinguished person in the county

MADDEN, Broderick (Road Uphill). A brother of Cornelia Sheridan; he is a gentleman dandy who lives in Paris

MADDENS (Explorer [novel]). Of Brise, Hampshire; gave their daughters to the Allertons of Hamlyn's Purlieu

MADGE (Merry-Go-Round). One of Reggie Barlow-Bassett's lady friends

MAFALDA, Princess (Razor's Edge). Expected at Frieda's residence; a comely young woman

Characters   251

MAGGIE (Ashenden/Giulia Lazzari). Raymond's fictitious aunt
MAGISTRATE (Explorer [novel]). At the Bow Street Police Court, London; agreed to set bail for Fred Allerton at five thousand pounds; later, he committed Fred to trial and declined to renew his bail
MAGISTRATE (Mirage). At a London police court; remands Grosely for a week and refuses bail
MAGISTRATE (Painted Veil). At Mei-tan-fu; ill with the cholera; has lost his head
MAGISTRATE (Sheppey). At the Lambeth Police Court, London; heard the case of the man who stole the doctor's coat out of his car
MAGNUS, Albertus (Magician). The German philosopher, bishop, and doctor of the Church (1200?-1280); knew about the Tinctura Physicorum, one of the greatest of the alchemical mysteries
MAHENDRA (Razor's Edge). A teacher at the university at Benares; the same age as Larry Darrell; nice, kindly, and intelligent
MAHON, Mrs. (Pro Patria). Is Fanny Porter-Smith mother; resides in South Kensington; is tall and buxom; fair hair; has a comfortable smile; is fifty years of age
MAID (Appearance and Reality). Called upon by Lisette Larion to bring in a hot coffee for Raymond Le Sueur
MAID (Ashenden/Miss King). At the Geneva hotel; Swiss; she conveys a message from Miss King to Ashenden
MAID #1 (Cakes and Ale). Works at the Driffield house, in Blackstable, Kent; is little; the Driffields leave without paying her three months' wages, but then she receives her money at a later time, through the mail
MAID #2 (Cakes and Ale). At the Driffield house on the Limpus Road, London; has Ashenden wait in the parlor
MAID #1 (Christmas Holiday). At Charley Mason's Paris hotel; she is stout and middle aged; serves coffee to Charley and Lydia Berger
MAID #2 (Christmas Holiday). Employed by Madame Berger at her house in Neuilly; is young and stolid looking; serves tea
MAID (Closed Shop). Told by Comencita to call La Gorda
MAID (Episode). Employed by the Carters; she conveys a message to Ned Preston
MAID #1 (Explorer [novel]). To Lady Alice Kelsey; told

by her mistress to phone Dick Lomas and to tell him to come at once

MAID #2 (Explorer [novel]). Is Julia Crowley's treasure

MAID (Explorer [play]). To Nelly Crowley; Nellie tells her, after she does her hair so badly, that she will never speak to her

MAID #1 (Hour Before the Dawn). Employed by Roger and May Henderson; May sends her to by a sole and some cutlets for her dinner with Dick Murray

MAID #2 (Hour Before the Dawn). She is employed by Mrs. Henderson to clean Dick Murray's house at Graveney

MAID #3 (Hour Before the Dawn). At the Henderson estate at Graveney Holt; calls May Henderson to the phone

MAID #1 (Landed Gentry). At the Insoley house at Kenyon Fulton; told Edith Lewis that Grace Insoley had not yet come to her room; is absent from morning prayers

MAID #2 (Landed Gentry). To Mrs. Insoley; at prayers in the dining room at Kenyon Fulton

MAID #3 (Landed Gentry). To Helen Vernon; a Catholic; highly respectable and well over forty years of age

MAID (Lion's Skin). Employed by Eleanor Forestier; she informs Eleanor that Judy, the dog, remains in the burning house

MAID (Man from Glasgow). At a shabby inn at Algeciras; slatternly

MAID #1 (Merry-Go-Round). Was in service to Elizabeth Dwarris; she committed a trifling misdemeanor leading first to her mistress's anger, and then to her death

MAID #2 (Merry-Go-Round). Of Lady Marguerite Vizard; was named as a co-respondent in the divorce counter-petition of her Lady Marguerite against Lord Vizard

MAID #3 (Merry-Go-Round). Of Marguerite Vizard; she is dismissed every time she does her mistress's hair badly; she has been with Lady Vizard for five years

MAID #4 (Merry-Go-Round). Of Polly Ley; she is sent on to London while her mistress remains in Rochester

MAID #5 (Merry-Go-Round). Of the Castillyons at Jeyston, Dorsetshire; when she came to draw the blinds, Grace Castillyon told her to call the trap for the station

MAID (Moon and Sixpence). At Amy Strickland's house on Camden Hill, London; trim

MAID (Mrs. Craddock). Of Mrs. Vaudrey; has been carrying on with Gerald Vaudrey; age forty; her complexion like parchment and very much the worse for wear; has been sent away in hysterics

MAID (Narrow Corner). She is employed by the Blakes; Mrs. Blake tells her directly not to go near Fred

MAID #1 (Of Human Bondage). She helps Emma assist Mrs. Carey after the latter returns from the photographer

MAID #2 (Of Human Bondage). At Hayward's lodgings in London; she tells Philip Carey that Hayward had gone to Brighton for the weekend

MAID #3 (Of Human Bondage). At Mildred Rogers' lodging, London; she tells Philip Carey that Mildred has not returned from Oxford; later tells Philip that Mildred has moved away

MAID #4 (Of Human Bondage). At Norah Nesbit's house

MAID #5 (Of Human Bondage). At the first boarding house in Brighton; untidy; fetches her mistress at Philip Carey's request

MAID #6 (Of Human Bondage). Is employed by Dr. South

MAID (Penelope). At the O'Farrells' house; tells Ada Fergusson that Dickie O'Farrell is in his dispensary

MAID #1 (Sanatorium). She brings Ashenden his meals

MAID #2 (Sanatorium). Carries messages back and forth between McLeod and Campbell relative to the latter's violin playing

MAID (Tenth Man). Scottish; with religious principles; accompanied Catherine Winter and Barbara Herbert on their tour of northern Italy

MAID (Theatre). At the Gosselyns' house at Taplow; she tended to Thomas Fennell's needs

MAID (Then and Now). In service to Niccolo and Marietta Machiavelli; she ate in the kitchen with her masters; she brought Machiavelli a half dozen larks roasted on a skewer; washed the dishes

MAID (Virtue). Of the Marshes; summons Janet Marsh to see Margery Bishop

MAID (Wash-Tub). At the Marina restaurant, in Positano

MAIDEN #1 (Choice of Amyntas). The eldest of the four palace maidens; a queenly aspect; beautiful and clear features; proud and fiery eyes; masses of raven hair; has the power to make a great warrior of the man who chooses her; after rejection by Amyntas, she marries an artillery officer; leaves him for a youth with a withered hand

MAIDEN #2 (Choice of Amyntas). The second of the four palace maidens; clad most gorgeously of all; has the gift of wealth and riches; after being rejected by Amyntas, she gives her favors to the first comer, everyone welcome; lives in the palace in the capital of an island in the north, dominating the inhabitants

MAIDEN #3 (Choice of Amyntas). The third of the four palace maidens; beautiful, pale, and thoughtful; hair yellow as corn; she speaks mournfully; all that is beautiful and good and wise is in her province; after Amyntas rejects her, wanders lonely through the world

MAIDEN #4 (Choice of Amyntas). The fourth of the palace maidens; ravishingly beautiful; long eyelashes; lips like a perfect rose; skin like a peach; auburn hair, curled, that falls to her waist; is the Lady of Love

MAIDEN LADY (Of Human Bondage). Mistress of the second boarding house, Brighton; bustling; with shrewd eyes and voluble speech; can rent Philip Carey two rooms; at meals, she sat at the head of the table and carved

MAIDENS (Hero). At Little Primpton, Kent; Mary Clibborn taught them sewing; Mary cannot understand why, in their poverty, they remain happy

MAIDS (Cakes and Ale). Two of them; at the Driffields' luncheon at Ferne Court, Blackstable, Kent; in brown uniforms; buxom Kentish girls; healthy color and high cheekbones

MAIDS (Christmas Holiday). Are employees of the Leslie Masons; appear well trained and wear neat uniforms

MAIDS (Happy Couple). Italian; two of them; employed by the Craigs; live in the village

MAIDS (Hour Before the Dawn). Employed by Jane Foster in London; she sends them to the shelter before the air raid actually begins

MAIDS (Moon and Sixpence). Two of them; employed by Amy Strickland; trim and comely

MAIDS (Razor's Edge). Three of them; are employed at Elliott Templeton's residence on Antibes; they cry as the Bishop leaves the house; each kisses the Bishop's ring

MAIDS (Unattainable). Dr. Cornish tries new medicines on them, but they evidence no interest in science

MAIDS OF HONOUR (Princess September). Could not comfort September when her parrot died

Characters 255

MAITLAND, Iris (Louise). The daughter of Louise and Tom Maitland; after finishing school, she comes to London to live with her mother; eventually marries a young friend of the Narrator

MAITLAND, Louise (Louise). Wife of Tom Maitland, then of George Hobhouse; the mother of Iris; had known the Narrator intimately for twenty-five years; before her first marriage, seemed frail and delicate, with large melancholy eyes; at age forty, still thin and frail, with large pale eyes and pale cheeks; scarlet fever left her with a weak heart

MAITLAND, Tom (Louise). The husband of Louise Maitland; father of Iris; wealthy; big, husky, good looking, and a fine athlete; died of a cold

MAITRE D'HOTEL (Promise). At Claridge's; has a set and hostile face; tells the Narrator that every table was occupied

MAKART, Lea (Alien Corn). Acknowledged as the greatest woman pianist in Europe; friend of Ferdy Rabenstein; in her youth, she was slight and pale; enormous eyes; magnificent black hair; age, early forties; now grown stout, with a broad face

MALACCA CHINAMAN (Letter [play]). He is in financial difficulty; willing to sell his estate in Sumatra to Robert Crosbie

MALAY (Back of Beyond). Overseer of the billiards game between Tom Saffary and Douglas, held at the club at Timbang Belud

MALAY (Narrow Corner). Servant of George Firth; brings in a bottle of whiskey and a siphon; he serves dinner

MALAY DRIVER (Narrow Corner). On Kanda; drove Saunders, Blake, Christessen, and Nichols in the old Ford to Frith's plantation

MALAY GIRL (Four Dutchman). Accompanied the Captain of the S.S. Utrecht on one of his voyages

MALAY GIRL (P.&O.). Lived with Gallagher; fat; she put a curse on him when he left

MALAY GIRL (Yellow Streak). Lives with Hutchinson; she bore him two children; she is young; fine, dark eyes

MALAY SERVANTS (Letter [play]). Several of them; at the Crosbie bungalow; they rush into the drawing room from the kampong after they hear the sound of shots

MALAY WOMEN (Letter [play]). One or two of them; they

walk softly up the steps of the Crosbies' bungalow to view Geoffrey Hammond's corpse

MALAYS (Narrow Corner). Three of them; dark skinned; at Takana; they are seen working on a prahu on the beach

MALAYS (Neil MacAdam). They man the four prahus for Angus Munro's scientific expedition

MALLINS (Explorer [novel/play]). Is a friend of Robert Boulger; in attendance at Lady Alice Kelsey's dance

MAN (Ashenden/Giulia Lazzari). He gives the letter from Chandra Lal to Giulia Lazzari to Felix; afterward, he informs Ashenden of Chandra Lal's arrival at Thonon

MAN (Ashenden/Mr. Harrington's Washing). He addresses a small crowd in Petrograd

MAN (Back of Beyond). At the club at Timbang; discovers the newspaper notice concerning Knobby Clark's death

MAN #1 (Bad Example). Age seventy; respectable and hard working; suffered a paralytic stroke, which left one side of him completely powerless; lost his job; wife was dead; had not heard from his daughter for thirty years; he spent his savings, then sold or pawned all of his possessions; eventually died from starvation

MAN #2 (Bad Example). Husband of the mother of the two-year-old child and of one other child; he left them

MAN #3 (Bad Example). Dirty and ragged; half-starved; smelt distinctly alcoholic; James Clinton brings him home and proposes (to his wife) to provide him food and shelter; Amy Clinton chases him out of the house

MAN #1 (Bishop's Apron). At Westminster; he is selling a terrier that Lord Thomas Spratte wanted to examine

MAN #2 (Bishop's Apron). Is handsome; Mrs. Fitzherbert nodded with complete satisfaction when he passed her

MAN (Book-Bag). Married; he plays bridge with Featherstone, Hardy, and the Narrator

MAN (Catalina). Hired by Martin de Valero to manage and to work on his father's farm

MAN (Choice of Amyntas). Rich; in a mountain village in Spain; looking for a swineherd

MAN #1 (Christmas Holiday). At the Serail, Paris; is a sightseer; speaks with the two girls dancing together

MAN #2 (Christmas Holiday). From the window of his Paris hotel room, Charley Mason observes him lying on his bed, clad in his shirtsleeves, reading

MAN #3 (Christmas Holiday). At the restaurant at Jouy;

companion of the lady who had forgotten her handbag; he manages to retrieve the purse from Robert Berger

MAN #4 (Christmas Holiday). At the cellar bar in Paris; is sinister looking; the scar of a razor wound on his face; offers Charley Mason and Lydia Berger a glass of wine

MAN #5 (Christmas Holiday). At the cellar bar in Paris; short and thick set; red face; magnificent moustache; hairy chest; profusely tattooed arms

MAN #6 (Christmas Holiday). At the cellar bar in Paris; he and Man #7 have completed their sentences at the penal colony in French Guiana; he knew Robert Berger there; Lydia Berger meets with him and Man #7; she and Charley Mason lunch with the two of them at the Palatte, Paris; age thirty; was a cook who had killed another man in the kitchen of the restaurant where they had worked; two or three inches taller than his companion; thin; a sallow and colorless face; skin drawn tightly over the bones; he appeared ill; large eyes; an electrician

MAN #7 (Christmas Holiday). See, also Man #6; age about forty; thin and short, but sturdy; well knit figure; a sallow, colorless, and much lined face; large eyes; an electrician; his mother dead; wife and children have left him; saw Robert Berger when he went to the hospital to have his appendix removed

MAN (Colonel's Lady). At the St. James Street club; a friend of George Peregrine; he relates to George the success of Evie Peregrine's book and introduces him to Henry Dashwood

MAN (Cousin Amy). Took a pretty American out to dinner; he refused her request for champagne

MAN (Cupid and the Vicar of Swale). He is Unsympathetic toward Rev. Robert Branscombe; suggested the vicar's conceit to be phenomenal

MAN (Daisy). Only one of two employees left in Robert Griffith's carpenter's chop

MAN (De Amicitia). Is seen in a moored fishing smack in Holland; sitting in the prow, fishing

MAN (Episode). He is one of the three men present at the dinner party, the Narrator and Ned Preston being the other two

MAN #1 (Explorer [novel]). Seen at some tiny kraal in

British East Africa; in the agony of death, streaming with blood

MAN #2 (Explorer [novel]). Older employee in charge of the northern station of North East Africa Company; he had returned home on leave, to be replaced by Walker

MAN #3 (Explorer [novel]). A member of Alec MacKenzie's expedition against the East African slave traders; George Allerton had him flogged because he did not cook George's food to his satisfaction

MAN (Explorer [play]). Is a member of Alec MacKenzie's African expedition; Alec hanged him from a tree for having outraged a native woman

MAN #1 (Facts of Life). A Knight of the Cross; he plays bridge with Henry Garnet and Man #2 and Man #3; asks Garnet about the state of the market

MAN #2 (Facts of Life). A Home Office official; plays bridge with Henry Garnet and Man #1 and Man #3; asks Garnet about his son

MAN #3 (Facts of Life). Is an eminent surgeon; he plays bridge with Henry Garnet and Man #1 and Man #2

MAN #4 (Facts of Life). Stands next to Nicholas Garnet at the roulette table at Monte Carlo

MAN #1 (Hero). Is a member of Major William Forsyth's London club; his first cousin had served under Lord Frederick Sleigh Roberts (1832-1914) in India

MAN #2 (Hero). In a London park; he raises his hat to a slender Amazon

MAN #3 (Hero). A friend of James Parsons whom he had known in India; meets James in Piccadilly; bound for Scotland; gives James Mrs. Pritchard-Wallace's London address

MAN #4 (Hero). The husband of Woman #3; was cured of his swearing when his wife responded in kind to his vulgarisms

MAN (Hour Before the Dawn). At London; badly wounded in the air raid

MAN #1 (Liza of Lambeth). On Vere Street, Lambeth; he teases Liza that her new dress came from a pawnbroker

MAN #2 (Liza of Lambeth). Comes out of the public house with a horn in his hand

MAN #3 (Liza of Lambeth). Sees Liza Kemp and Jim Blakeston turning into upper end of Vere Street, Lambeth

MAN #4 (Liza of Lambeth). One of Jim Blakeston's fellow

workers; gave his wife a week's wages in return for an illegal end to their marriage

MAN #5 (Liza of Lambeth). He referees the fight between Liza Kemp and Mrs. Blakeston

MAN #6 (Liza of Lambeth). Resident of the same house as the Blakestons, on Vere Street, Lambeth; discourages John from interfering in the fight between Jim Blakeston and Mrs. Blakeston

MAN #1 (Loaves and Fishes). At Westminster; he wanted to sell Thomas Spratte a terrier

MAN #2 (Loaves and Fishes). Told Theodore Spratte that the moment of his greatest dismay came when he saw his engagement announcement in The Morning Post

MAN #1 (Lord Mountdrago). Buried under the earth by a bursting shell and struck dumb; his speech restored by Dr. Audlin

MAN #2 (Lord Mountdrago). Paralyzed after an airplane crash; the use of his limbs restored by Dr. Audlin

MAN #3 (Lord Mountdrago). Is in a dream, in a Limehouse pub; calls Mountdrago "Bill" and offers him a drink

MAN #1 (Magician). Dull; plays at Monte Carlo and puts his money on the colors

MAN #2 (Magician). At the fair at the Lion de Belfort, Paris; is cutting silhouettes in black paper; Oliver Haddo poses for him

MAN #3 (Magician). At Alexandria; learned; Dr. Porhoet operated on him for a cataract; he gave the doctor an ancient Koran

MAN #4 (Magician). Met Frank Hurrell at dinner at Queen Anne's Gate, London, and told him about Oliver Haddo

MAN #1 (Making of a Saint). At the gathering, Palazzo Orsi; he asks Matteo d'Orsi if he has been travelling

MAN #2 (Making of a Saint). Recognizes one of the slain attackers of Checco d'Orsi as a Girolamo Riario guard

MAN #3 (Making of a Saint). In the square at Forli; he tears the gold chain from the neck of the body of Girolamo Riario and runs away with it

MAN #4 (Making of a Saint). In the square at Forli; he snatches Girolamo Riario's gold chain from Man #3

MAN #5 (Making of a Saint). At Forli; he pushed through the guards protecting Caterina Sforza and placed his hand on her bosom; receives a sharp slap on the face from her for his efforts

MAN #6 (Making of a Saint). Old; member of the Council at Forli; he expressed the thanks of the citizens for the freedom that Checco d'Orsi had bestowed upon them

MAN #7 (Making of a Saint). At Forli; he ascended the ramparts and reported that Protonotary Savello had a letter from the Pope promising relief of the siege

MAN (Man from Glasgow). Pursues a youth from a shop in Naples and stabs him with a knife

MAN Man of Honour). Had seen Jenny Kent walk along the Thames tow path and then throw herself into the river

MAN (Marriages Are Made in Heaven). Sends a letter to Jack Rayner and awaits an answer

MAN (Masterson). On board the ship from Columbo; tall, dark, and aloof; had spent five years at Keng Tung; convinces the Narrator that he should visit there

MAN (Mayhew). A friend of Mayhew and a member of his club; having only recently returned from Italy, he tells Mayhew and the others about the house at Capri

MAN #1 (Merry-Go-Round). Old; resides at Carbis Water, Cornwall; he rented rooms in a fisherman's cottage to Basil and Jenny Kent on their honeymoon; amiable and simple; he told them delightful and simple stories

MAN #2 (Merry-Go-Round). At London; got Fanny Bridger in trouble; deserted after the birth of their child

MAN #3 (Merry-Go-Round). At Jeyston, Dorsetshire; tells Paul Castillyon Fanny Bridger has just killed herself

MAN #4 (Merry-Go-Round). A member of Paul Castillyon's club; is in the process of divorcing his wife; he sought, in the club smoking room, to excite sympathy toward himself by narrating his wife's infidelities

MAN #5 (Marry-Go-Round). Came toward Jenny Kent as she walked along the the river bank; did not notice her

MAN #6 (Merry-Go Round). Saw Jenny Kent throw herself into the river and drown before he could summon help

MAN #1 (Moon and Sixpence). A resident of the Hotel de la Fleur, Tahiti; had fallen on adversity, and thus did not pay for board and lodging

MAN #2 (Moon and Sixpence). He drove the mail cart from Taravao to Papeete; told by Ata to inform Dr. Coutras that Charles Strickland was fast approaching death

MAN #1 (Mrs. Craddock). Is at Barnstable, Kent; Edward Craddock claimed he drove a good bargain with him

MAN #2 (Mrs. Craddock). At the station at Barnstable,

Kent; from the city; is swearing volubly because his luggage had gone off to Margate

MAN #3 (Mrs. Craddock). In the United States; he tells Gerald Vaudrey that he need not plan to begin his new position until the end of this month or the next one

MAN (Mrs. Dot). Requests help from Dot Worthley; he has lost one leg in a railway accident and the other in a colliery explosion

MAN #1 (Narrow Corner). Is outside the bar at Sydney, Australia; on the other side of the street; standing in the shadow of buildings, watching Captain Nichols

MAN #2 (Narrow Corner). In the Sydney Bulletin; he had received sentence at Newcastle for an insurance fraud

MAN #3 (Narrow Corner). A Kanda acquaintance of Captain Nichols; lends Nichols his black suit for Erik Chrisstessen's funeral; is taller and stouter than Nichols

MAN #4 (Narrow Corner). He and his wife neighbors of the Hudsons; is awakened by Florrie Hudson after she returns from the picture palace; he calls the police

MAN #1 (Of Human Bondage). Is at the gallery door of a London theatre; tries to converse with Philip Carey

MAN #2 (Of Human Bondage). At a party at the West End, London; observed by Philip Carey, who remarked that he would never be able to stand in that man's place

MAN #3 (Of Human Bondage). Is standing at the door of Amitrano's art studio, Paris; held a dish to collect a half-franc from each one of the persons who entered

MAN #4 (Of Human Bondage). On the Boulevard St. Michel; in a blouse; Philip Carey thinks of him as "ripping"

MAN #5 (Of Human Bondage). Dead; on the slab in the dissecting room at St. Luke's Hospital, London; thin; tense skin; forty-five years of age; thin gray beard; scanty, colorless hair; eyes closed; lower jaw sunken

MAN #6 (Of Human Bondage). At the cheap but respectable restaurant in Soho; tall; a mane of gray hair; ragged and thin beard; he looks like a dangerous anarchist

MAN #7 (Of Human Bondage). Takes Mildred Rogers to the Tivoli; young and smoothed-face; sleek hair; the look of a commercial traveler

MAN #8 (Of Human Bondage). An out-patient at St. Luke's Hospital, London; is rough and illiterate; exercised self-control when he was told his case was hopeless

MAN #9 (Of Human Bondage). An out-patient at St. Luke's

Hospital, London; strong; is bothered by a persistent ache; told he must have rest or he will die; he has a wife and children

MAN #10 (Of Human Bondage). The Father of Ernie, the boy with the club foot; tells Philip Carey that his son's deformity hinders his ability to earn a living

MAN #11 (Of Human Bondage). At London; short; wears a bowler hat; Mildred Rogers attempts to attract his attention by Swan and Edgar's; he stares at her for a moment, then passes on

MAN #12 (Of Human Bondage). An accident patient at St. Luke's Hospital, London; a great gash from ear to ear from an attempted suicide; sullen, silent, and angry

MAN #13 (Of Human Bondage). Attempted suicide victim; threw himself into the Thames; fished out and brought to St. Luke's Hospital, London; ten days later, he developed typhoid from swallowing Thames water; died

MAN #14 (Of Human Bondage). Attempted suicide; he could not get work, then lost his wife; pawned his clothes to buy a revolver, with which he shot out an eye and a piece of his face; he recovered and lived happily

MAN #15 (Of Human Bondage). An applicant for a sales position at a drapery department in a London store; he looks forward to getting his refusal soon enough to be able to look elsewhere

MAN #16 (Of Human Bondage). An applicant for a sales position at the drapery department of a London store; he asks Philip Carey if he has had any experience

MAN #17 (Of Human Bondage). Former employee of Lynn and Sedley, London; had done well for himself at Bradford and owned five shops; after fifteen years, returned to London, visited with Mrs. Fletcher, and gave her a gold watch

MAN #18 (Of Human Bondage). The husband of Woman #18; at London; huge, burly, drunk; rousts Philip Carey to attend to his wife; he had been a soldier in India

MAN #1 (Painted Veil). At the curio dealer's house off Victoria Road, Hong Kong; old; led Kitty Fane to the back of the shop and then up a dark flight of stairs

MAN #2 (Painted Veil). Seen at the foot of the compound wall, Mei-tan-fu; on his back with his legs stretched out and arms thrown over his head; is dead of cholera

MAN #3 (Painted Veil). At Mei-tan-fu; with a lantern;

Characters

runs in front to the chair
MAN (Poet). Old, tall, exceedingly thin; skin the color of old ivory; has abundant white hair and dark bushy eyebrows; an aquiline nose and a closely set mouth; occupies house next to the poet Calisto de Santa Ana
MAN (Point of Honour). Denies the Narrator admission to the Duke of Alba's house
MAN #1 (Razor's Edge). He tends to the desk at Larry Darrell's Paris hotel; in shirtsleeves and waistcoat in thin black and yellow stripes; attired in an apron
MAN #2 (Razor's Edge). Is with Sophie Macdonald in the cafe on the Rue de Lappe, Paris; he tries to stop her from staggering across the floor
MAN #3 (Razor's Edge). At the cafe on the Rue de Lappe, Paris; big and fat; great head of greasy hair; in his shirtsleeves; he offers a chair to Sophie Macdonald
MAN #4 (Razor's Edge). Is an acquaintance of Maugham in Spain; married to a whore
MAN #5 (Razor's Edge). At the Brasserie Graf, Avenue de Clichy, Paris; little; is quietly dressed; neat black beard; wore a pince-nez
MAN #6 (Razor's Edge). At the Brasserie Graf, Avenue de Clichy, Paris; in evening dress; orders a substantial breakfast; tired but satisfied mien
MAN (Salvatore). Had been engaged to Assunta; killed in Africa during his military service
MAN (Sanatorium). Patient at the sanatorium; is evicted by Dr. Lennox for "carrying on" with the Woman
MAN (Smith). A big, hulking brute; drunk; on board the ship bound for the Cape; he attempts to force Thomas Freeman to drink with him; Tom hits him over the head with a whiskey bottle; he is in bed for a fortnight
MAN (Spanish Priest). Some day he will stumble upon the biggest fortune in the world, somewhere in Andalusia; millionaires will be mere paupers by the side of him
MAN #1 (Taipan). A former member of the Taipan's firm, senior to the latter; had he lived, he would have been the taipan
MAN #2 (Taipan). Hums incessantly while playing bridge
MAN #3 (Taipan). Insists on drinking beer with a straw
MAN #4 (Taipan). Partner in bridge game with the Taipan
MAN #1 (Theatre). Bought a girl whom he had never seen before a hat in a Bond Street shop; she walked out of

the shop while he waited for his change
MAN #2 (Theatre). Walking along Edgware Road, London; does not return Julia Lambert Gosselyn's bold stare
MAN #1 (Then and Now). On horseback in the streets of Imola
MAN #2 (Then and Now). In the streets of Imola; leading a string of donkeys bearing a large load of firewood
MAN #3 (Then and Now). In the street of Imola; he sauntered by with female asses, whose milk was good for pregnant women; he announced his presence with a loud melodious call
MAN #4 (Then and Now). In the saddler's shop at Imola
MAN #5 (Then and Now). At Imola; in the barber shop, having his hair cut
MAN (Traveller in Romance). On the post chaise from St. Moritz into Italy; gets on at Kampfer; immense size; massive bones and large hands; a huge nose; a strong, square chin; a commercial traveler; a Pole; he worked for his firm in an office, in Liverpool, before the opportunity came for him to travel
MAN #1 (Unattainable). In Regent's Park, London; Maude Fulton believes that he is following her as she makes her way to see Caroline Ashley
MAN #2 (Unattainable). Robert Oldham knew him in South Africa; engaged to a girl in England; could not send for her until they had been engaged for seven years; when she arrived, his courage failed him, and he ran; she finally caught up with him, and they were married
MANAGER (Cakes and Ale). At New York; in the employ of William Ashenden
MANAGER (Explorer [novel]). Of the mine in Lancashire; his house turned into a hospital after the explosion
MANAGER (Letter [play]). Of the estate of the Malacca Chinaman on Sumatra; a European
MANAGER (Making of a Millionaire). Of the mine in New-Lyons; he sends a cable, in cipher, to Frederick Rose
MANAGER (Narrow Corner). Of a plantation on Kanda; his wife has just delivered a son, and he has a feast for the occasion
MANAGER (Of Human Bondage). At the linen drapery firm of Lynn and Sedley, London; florid; sandy hair and a large sandy moustache; has large and protruding upper teeth that appeared loose

MANAGER #1 (Razor's Edge). Of the coal mine at Lens, in northern France; is married to the sister of Larry Darrell's Greek teacher; is small and fat; red cheeks

MANAGER #2 (Razor's Edge). Of a bank in Chicago, where Larry Darrell has an account; tells Isabel Maturin of Larry's bank drafts from China, Burma, and India

MANAGER #3 (Razor's Edge). Of the Brasserie Graf, in the Avenue de Clichy, Paris; he intercedes in the argument between a man and a heavily painted woman

MANAGER (Tenth Man). Of the Campo del Oro mine; he has misled Macdonald by not showing him the new shaft

MANAGER (Traveller in Romance). Of a first-class Swiss hotel; according to the commercial traveler on the post chaise, he possesses the soul of a reptile

MANAGER (Virtue). Of the kutch factory; a member of the club in Morton's district at Borneo; not on speaking terms with his assistants

MANAGERESS (Of Human Bondage). Of the tea shop in Parliament Street, London; impressed by Philip Carey's drawing of Mildred Rogers; has, on occasion, gone to Eastbourne for the weekend with a man; marries a man in the glove trade; moves to Tulse Hill, South London

MANAGERESS (Round Dozen). Of the Dolphin Inn, at Elsom; she identifies the St. Clairs for the Narrator

MANCHU LADIES (East of Suez). Seated in rickshaws, in a crowded Peking street; with faces like masks; wearing embroidered silk

MANCHU WOMAN (Painted Veil). Is from a distinguished Hankow family; she lives with Waddington and loves him to distraction; slim and tall; large black eyes; hands preternaturally long, slender, and the color of ivory, suggesting breeding of uncounted centuries; exquisite nails, painted; she appeared more like an idol than a woman; high voice, like the twittering of birds in an orchard; sits, paints, writes poetry, and smokes opium in moderation

MANICURIST (Sheppey). In the country; did a bad job on Mr. Bolton's nails

MANNERS, Henry (Circle). His picture appears in an old photograph album owned by Clive Champion-Cheney; seen wearing his eyeglass

MAN-O'WAR'S MAN (Spanish Priest). He drinks his grog in the taverns of Gibraltar

MANSON, Fred (Episode). Good looking, tall, well built; blue eyes, good features, friendly smile; thick head of red wavy hair; thick eyebrows are lighter than his hair; smooth olive skin; bold eyes; age twenty-two; a postman at Brixton, London; is extremely sociable; he becomes engaged to Grace Carter

MANSON, Gerrard (Social Sense). Had died, at age sixty, on the afternoon of the Macdonalds' dinner party; was passionately attached to Mary Warton for twenty-five years; small and shrivelled; faded blue eyes; he wore spectacles; a high and shiny bald head; a critic and essayist; married, and the father of grown daughters

MANSON, Mr. (Episode). Father of Fred Manson; has, for the past twenty-four years, driven a postal van

MANSON, Mrs. (Social Sense). Wife of Gerrard Manson; fat, frowsy, and boring; mother of grown daughters

MANTUA, Cardinal (Then and Now). Brother of the Marquis of Mantua; elevated to his position by Caesar Borgia and the Pope after depositing with Borgia the sum of forty thousand ducats

MANTUA, Marchioness of (Then and Now). Thought that a pair of scented gloves stitched with gold would be a gift worthy of the acceptance of the Queen of France

MANTUA, Marquis of (Then and Now). The brother of the Cardinal of Mantua; pays part of the forty thousand ducats to the Pope and to Caesar Borgia for his brother's elevation to Cardinal; Borgia supposedly sent him the marble cupid of Michaelangelo Buonarotti

MANUEL (Mother). A policeman; refuses to inquire into the activities of La Cachirra

MANUFACTURER (Moon and Sixpence). At Lille; wealthy; he fled the city on the approach of the Germans; he had owned Strickland's portrait of the retired plumber

MANUMA (Mackintosh). Son of Chief Tangatu; tall, handsome, copper colored; fuzzy hair dyed red with lime

MAPUTITI NATIVES (Vessel of Wrath). Two of them; Miss Jones gives them the small medical kit

MARBELLA, Countess de (Romantic Young Lady). Pilar Carreon and the Narrator had danced together at her parties; a French woman who had married a Spaniard; hair of brilliant gold

MARCEL (Christmas Holiday). Landlord of the cellar bar in Paris; Lydia Berger knows him; large; he has the naked look of a fat priest

MARCEL (Razor's Edge). A Swede; immensely tall; great broad shoulders and a magnificent chest; slim waist, fat stomach, and muscles like a professional athlete; gold wavy hair; a skin of honey; Suzanne Rouvier fell in love with him; she lived with him for three years and bore him a girl, Odette; he knew Larry Darrell

MARCH (Princess September). Third daughter born to the King and Queen of Siam; also named Winter and Tuesday

MARGARITA (Alien Corn). Mother of the King of Italy; she was a "great friend" of the dowager Lady Bland

MARGHERITA (Razor's Edge). Of Italy; she had extended kindness to Louisa Bradley and her husband when Mr. Bradley had served in Rome as the first secretary

MARGERY (Theatre). She is secretary to Michael Gosselyn

MARIA (Catalina). The daughter of the shepherd Joachim; she meets Catalina outside the church attached to the convent of the Carmelite nuns; she wears a long cloak that reaches her feet; is fairly tall for a Spanish woman; young; an unlined face; dark eyes; smooth and soft skin; hair parted in the middle; small, delicate features; Catalina believes her to be the Blessed Virgin; serves as the second witness to the marriage of Catalina and Diego Martinez

MARIE (Hour Before the Dawn). The Dubois' maid; sturdy and middle aged; broad face

MARIE (Magician). Is the maid at the Chien Noir, Paris; little; hard visaged; mature; a large mouth; looked busily after the various wants of the customers; she has recently broken away from her lover

MARIE (Razor's Edge). The cook at the Maturins' Paris apartment; she provides the dainties for tea, as well as the soup, chicken, and the souffle for dinner

MARQUESS (Razor's Edge). He hosts a luncheon party at Carlton House Terrace; Paul Burton interested in his art collection; Elliott Templeton had purchased a Titian from that collection

MARQUIS (Home and Beauty). A client of Rahan and Miss Montmorency; suffered from dyspepsia; gave Mrs. Montmorency pepsin tablets when she suffered indigestion

MARSDEN, Mr. (Bishop's Apron). He is Theodore Spratte's tailor on Saville Row, London; Theodore had given him an order for two pairs of trousers

MARSDEN, Peter (Penelope). A London surgeon; schedules an important operation on the same day as a horse race so that he cannot attend the race and lose money

MARSH, Bill (Virtue). Is a A member of Charlie Bishop's London club; also is an acquaintance of the Narrator

MARSH, Edward (Land of Promise). The brother of Norah Marsh; husband of Gertrude; is good natured and easy going; a small moustache and untidy hair; he farms in Dyer, Manitoba, Canada

MARSH, Gertrude (Land of Promise). The wife of Edward Marsh; is dark and small; dried skin; hard look; thin and nervous; sharp tongue; has earned her own living since the age of thirteen; formerly a waitress in a scrubby little hotel in Winnipeg; eventually pregnant

MARSH, Mrs. (Land of Promise). The mother of Norah and Edward Marsh; she would refer to her son as "Eddie"

MARSH, Norah (Land of Promise). Age twenty-eight; with a pleasant and honest face; a happy smile; gentle and quiet manners; quick tempered; a passionate nature; sister of Edward Marsh; companion to Louisa Wickham for ten years; left out of Miss Wickham's will; goes to live with her brother, Edward, in Canada; out of desperation marries Frank Taylor and returns with him to his farm in Prentice, Manitoba; eventually falls in love with Frank; she receives five hundred pounds ($2500 Canadian) from James Wickham, which she turns over to Frank Taylor when his crop has been condemned

MARTELLI, Aurelia (Then and Now). Is he third wife of Bartolomeo Martelli and twenty years younger than he; a native of Sinigaglia, a port on the Adriatic; made shirts for her husband; had been taught embroidery by the nuns, and (according to her husband) no other woman in Imola can rival her skill in art; naturally dark hair dyed fair; handsome black eyes and eyebrows plucked thin; a small straight nose and lovely mouth; small, even, white teeth; slim figure; virginal, ripe quality in her beauty

MARTELLI, Bartolomeo (Then and Now). Is an alderman at Imola and a man of property there; husband of Aurelia Martelli; he had spent some years of his youth in Smyrna; had inherited from his mother two houses in Florence; cousin to both Biagio Buonaccorsi and Piero Giacomini; brought about the capitulation of Imola to

Caesar Borgia without a struggle; is forty years of age; corpulent; a red face and double chin,; imposing paunch; long hair receding from his forehead; a full black beard

MARTELLI, Signora #1 (Then and Now). The first wife of Bartolomeo Martelli; the marriage had been arranged by Martelli's parents; died, eight years later, from cholera; she bore her husband no children

MARTELLI, Signora #2 (Then and Now). The second wife of Bartolomeo Martelli; she died some eleven years after their marriage; she bore her husband no children

MARTELLI, Signore (Then and Now). Father of Bartolomeo Martelli; made money by trade in the Levant; had been in partnership with a Florentine merchant of good family and eventually married his daughter; distantly related to Biagio Buonaccorsi

MARTHA (Merry-Go-Round). Is Elizabeth Dwarris's maid; she has been ordered to pack Polly Ley's boxes

MARTHA (Razor's Edge). Dr. Robert Nelson's hired help; a rigid Baptist; she frightened young Larry Darrell by describing the hell, fire, and brimstone to which all sinners of the world would be committed eternally

MARTINEZ (Catalina). The father of Diego Martinez; is a successful tailor; made clothes for the most notable persons in the city; small, dried up; sharp nose and querulous expression

MARTINEZ, Diego (Catalina). The son of a tailor and he, himself, a tailor; age eighteen; was engaged to marry Catalina, but that was before her accident; tall and strapping, fine legs; slim waist and broad shoulders; handsome head of oily hair; olive skin and bold black eyes; sensual mouth and straight nose; Prioress Dona Beatriz proposes to endow him with an estate and to confer upon him the title Don Diego de Quintamilla, so that he can then join the army of Archduke Albert

MARTINS (Man of Honour). John Halliwell was seen by Hilda Murray at their house

MARY (Choice of Amyntas). The daughter of Peter the Schoolmaster and Mrs. Peter

MARY (Judgment Seat). The wife of John; a passenger on a ship that has been torpedoed by a submarine

MARY (Liza of Lambeth). Liza Kemp's aunt; the only one of Liza's mother's sisters who had never "gone in ter double figures [she had only three children]. . .but she wasn't married"

MARY, Princess (Irish Gentleman). Of Wartburg-Hochstein; when Robert O'Donnel stops her runaway horse, she slips from the saddle and faints in his arms

MARY ANN (Cakes and Ale). Servant and cook at Blackstable vicarage, in Kent; had come to the vicarage at age eighteen; a Blackstable girl who had never been to London; age thirty-five when young Ashenden first met the Driffields; small; snub nose; decayed teeth; fresh colored

MARY ANN (Of Human Bondage). She is the maid employed by William and Louisa Carey for eighteen years; age thirty-five; is chubby and small; the daughter of a fisherman and his wife, who lived in a little house off Harbour Street; had come to the vicarage at age eighteen; was dismissed after Louisa Carey's death

MARY JANE (Noble Spaniard). She is the Proudfoots' maid

MASON #1 (Christmas Holiday). Son of Sibert Mason and brother of Sir Wilfred Terry-Mason; killed in the war

MASON #2 (Christmas Holiday). Daughter of Sibert Mason and a sister of Sir Wilfred Terry-Mason; killed by a fall in the hunting field

MASON (Explorer [novel]). A member of Alec MacKenzie's expedition against the East African slave traders

MASON (Loaves and Fishes). Is carrying his rod; Bertram Railing believes that Christ looks at him through the Mason's eyes

MASON (Mother). He brings news to tenement residents of a friend in Triana who knew all about La Cachirra

MASON (Of Human Bondage). Is a pupil at King's School, Tercanbury; one of Philip Carey's early tormentors

MASON, Bertha (Bishop's Apron). The wife of Sir Peter Mason; she thinks it bad form that her husband should drive around in a dog cart to see patients, at five shillings per visit

MASON, Charley (Christmas Holiday). Son of Leslie and Mrs. Mason; brother of Patsy; age twenty-three; he he been born during the war; he has been educated at Rugby and Cambridge; he studied bookkeeping for four months with the firm of accountants employed by the Mason Estate; he joined his father at Lincoln's Inn Fields; spends an eventful Christmas holiday in Paris

Characters   271

MASON, Dr. (Bishop's Apron). Father of Sir Peter Mason; president of a medical body at the Jubilee; scraped together the thirty thousand pounds necessary for him to accept at baronetcy

MASON, Kate (Point of Law). See above, Kate DAUBERNOON

MASON, Leslie (Christmas Holiday). Father of Charley Mason; the youngest of Sibert Mason's grandchildren; educated at Rugby School and Cambridge; in his early fifties; tall, good figure; blue eyes; fine gray hair worn long; a high color; a sportsman, but also keenly interested in the arts; secretary of the Mason Estate

MASON, Martha (Christmas Holiday). Was Charley Mason's great aunt; his great grandfather's eldest child; a grim featured spinster; sallow, wrinkled face; small and thin, tight lips; terrified Charley when he was young; lived in Sibert Mason's house; died several years ago, and she left Charley five hundred pounds

MASON, Mrs. (Christmas Holiday). Wife of Sibert Mason; a cook at a grand palace in Sussex; near age to forty when she married; she bore her husband eight children

MASON, Patsy (Christmas Holiday). Daughter of Leslie and Mrs. Mason; the sister of Charley; age eighteen; studying at the Royal Academy of Music; pretty; blue eyes and fair hair; slim figure and attractive smile

MASON, Sir Peter (Bishop's Apron). As a medical student his only ambition was to buy a little practice in the country and marry his cousin, Bertha; inherited his father's baronetcy; he lives in Essex because it is cheap; tries to maintain dignity on a thousand pounds per year; he is desperately bored

MASON, Ralph (Point of Law). Marries Kate Daubernoon; tall, and perhaps fifteen years younger than Kate; handsome; a beautiful moustache; is the land agent's clerk; an ordinary, common, and provincial tradesman; hard drinker, with a violent temper; unscrupulous; a provincial Lothario; his scheme gains him forty-three pounds, seven shillings, and threepence a halfpenny

MASON, Sibert (Christmas Holiday). Head gardener at a grand palace in Sussex; he married the cook at age forty; he combined their savings, bought a few acres north of London, and established himself as a market gardener; then engaged as a real estate developer and became affluent; he died at age eighty-four

MASON, Venetia (Christmas Holiday). The wife of Leslie Mason and mother of Charley and Patsy; daughter of John Peron, painter; middle aged and comely; nearly as tall as her husband; blue eyes; soft brown hair slightly streaked with gray; is inclined to be stout; a broad brow, open countenance, and a diffident smile

MASSEUR (Our Betters). Recommended to Minnie Surennes by Compton Edwardes

MASSEUR (Razor's Edge). He called on Elliott Templeton every morning to keep his elegant body in perfect condition

MASTER (Cakes and Ale). At Westminster School; lodged on the drawing room floor of Mrs. Hudson's house, in Vincent Square, London

MASTER (Moon and Sixpence). Of the Paris art studio; when he saw Charles Strickland's work, he raised his eyebrows and walked on

MASTER #1 (Of Human Bondage). At King's School, Tercanbury; he held the degree of doctor of philosophy from the University of Heidelberg; had spent three years in a French lycee; he taught French and German to the upper forms; not ordained

MASTER #2 (Of Human Bondage). Of King's School, Tercanbury; taught systematic mathematics; was no ordained

MASTER #3 (Of Human Bondage). Of Trinity Hall, Cambridge; expressed his satisfaction that Hayward would be attending his college

MASTER OF PHILOSOPHY (Perfect Gentleman). Is engaged by Monsieur Jordain

MASTERS (Tenth Man). Is a campaign worker at Middlepool for George Winter

MASTERSON (Masterson). Met the Narrator at the club in Mandalay; originally from Cheltenham; lived in Thazi; age in the early thirties; a pleasant, friendly face; curling, dark hair speckled with gray; handsome dark eyes; spoke with a musical voice; he spent most of the year traveling up and down Burma on business

MATADOR (Point of Honour). At Seville, Spain; he fell and, miraculously, escaped from the horns of the bull

MATE (Narrow Corner). He and Jack Swan had their own cutter; a New Zealander and a former bank manager who had involved himself in some form of trouble; he was decapitated by New Guinea natives

MATE (Red). A Kanaka; handsome, swarthy, and with "the look of a later Roman emperor"; is inclined to stoutness; fine and clean cut face

MATEO (Catalina). Actor; skinny; long nose and a large loose mouth; with horse-like face and a shrill voice

MATHILDE (Home and Beauty). Made Victoria's mourning dress following the death of her first husband

MATHILDE (Magician). The ancient bonne (house maid) at Dr. Porhoet's house in Paris

MATRON (Home). Of the sailors' home at Portsmouth; she wrote to George and Emily Meadows about their Uncle George's condition

MATRON (Letter [story]). Stout, middle aged, English; at the prison at Singapore; attends to Leslie Crosbie

MATRON (Sanatorium). On friendly terms with Miss Atkin

MATRON (Smith). At a London hospital; she told Emily Chapman that she was not what they wanted as a nurse

MATURIN, Gray (Razor's Edge). Henry Maturin's only son; he is six feet three or four inches tall; great broad shoulders; large heavy eyebrows; a rugged, unfinished look; short blunt nose; a sensual mouth; florid Irish complexion; thick, sleek, and raven black hair; clear blue eyes; powerful; is in love with Isabel Bradley; is Lawrence Darrell's best friend; he marries Isabel shortly after the termination of her engagement to Darrell; is ruined after the October 1929 crash, from which he suffers a nervous breakdown; he and Isabel and their two children move to a plantation in South Carolina, then they occupy Elliott Templeton's Paris apartment; by his early thirties his hair has receded on the temples, with a small bald patch on the crown; puffy red face; a double chin; heavy and gross; after recovering from his breakdown (with Larry Darrell's help) and after Elliott Templeton's death, he finds an opportunity (with Isabel's share of Elliott's money) with an oil corporation in Dallas, Texas

MATURIN, Henry (Razor's Edge). Gray Maturin's father; he is slightly past fifty years of age; resides in an enormous house on the river in Marvin, Illinois; one of the richest men in Chicago; the head of a Chicago brokerage house; he built a new church in Marvin and gave a million dollars to the University of Chicago; had offered Larry Darrell a job; a large; fleshy face with a great jowl; blunt and aggressive nose; small, blue, shrewd eyes; rapidly thinning, snow-white hair; dies, in his sixties, from a heart attack following the October 1929 crash

MATURIN, Isabel (Razor's Edge). See Isabel BRADLEY

MATURIN, Joan (Razor's Edge). Older daughter of Isabel and Gray Maturin; sister of Priscilla; age eight when the Narrator first sees her; tall; frail; black hair and hazel eyes

MATURIN, Mr. (Razor's Edge). The grandfather of Gray Maturin; shanty Irish

MATURIN, Mrs.#1 (Razor's Edge). The grandmother of Gray Maturin; once a Swedish waitress in an eating house

MATURIN, Mrs. #2 (Razor's Edge). Wife of Henry Maturin and Mother of Gray; is thin, raddled, and frail; her death interrupts the whirl of gaiety that surrounds Isabel and Gray Maturin

MATURIN, Priscilla (Razor's Edge). Younger daughter of Isabel and Gray Maturin; sister of Joan; age six when the Narrator first sees her; tall; frail; black hair and hazel eyes

MAUGHAM, Mr. (Razor's Edge). The Narrator; novelist and playwright; in Chicago in 1919, on his way to the Far East; had known Elliott Templeton for fifteen years

MAUNDYS (Door of Opportunity). Had arranged to meet the Strouds at the popular Tracadero Grill Room, London

MAUPASSANT, Guy de (Of Human Bondage). French writer of fiction (1850-1893); Miss Wilkinson hints that he had made love to her

MAY (Princess September). Fifth daughter born to the King and Queen of Siam; her former name Thursday

MAYHEW (Mayhew). A Detroit lawyer; had achieved a large and successful practice at age thirty-five; totally insensible to beauty; big, brawny, with a powerful physique; he has thick black hair and beard; he loses considerable weight during his stay on Capri, with his skin becoming pale and waxy

MAYNE, Lydia (Theatre). An actress with notorious sex appeal; played the vamp; indecent glance, serpentine gestures, lazy drawl

MAYOR (Appearance and Reality). Delivers a long speech at the wedding of Lisette Larion and the young traveling silk salesman

MAYOR (Mask and the Face). Of the town near the Villa Grazie; wants to provide Count Paolo Grazia with an official welcome and to hold a banquet in his honor; presides over what he believes to be the funeral of Savina Grazia

McCORMACK, Charlie (Vessel of Wrath). He married during the six months of Ginger Ted's sentence

McDERMOTT, Eddie (Straight Flush). The brother of Jamie McDermott; he had staked out a claim with Donaldson; over six feet tall; handsome

McDERMOTT, Jamie (Straight Flush). The brother of Eddie McDermott; he staked out a claim with Donaldson; over six feet tall; handsome; killed Eddie in a poker game

McEVOY, Ambrose (Theatre). The English portrait painter (1878-1927); his portrait of Julia Lambert Gosselyn in the National Portrait Gallery

McFARRENS (Letter [play]). They hosted a tennis party; Leslie and Robert Crosbie and Geoff Hammond attended

McLEOD (Sanatorium). Both he and Campbell have been patients at the sanatorium longer than anyone there; he has been there for seventeen years; tall; skin stretched tight over his bones; has hollow cheeks and temples; emaciated face; large bony nose; brother and two sisters have families, and they do not want him

McLEOD, Mrs. (Liza of Lambeth). Lived in the house next to Sally and Harry Atkins, in Vere Street, Lambeth; Sally had gone to speak with her

McPHAIL, Dr. Alec (Rain). He has red hair, bald patch, freckled; age forty; a thin, pinched face; pale blue eyes; Scots accent; timid

McPHAIL, Mrs. (Rain). The wife of Dr. Alec McPhail; shy

MEADOWS (Noblest Act). Colonial Secretary at Singapore; he asks James Farley to remain in the Malay States

MEADOWS, Albert (Home). Great-nephew of George Meadows #2; had gone to Portsmouth to bring George #2 back to his ancestral home

MEADOWS, Billie (Yellow Streak). He is an acquaintance of Campion in Sinaloa

MEADOWS, Lord Billie (Yellow Streak). A horse owner and acquaintance of Izzart

MEADOWS, Charlie (Letter [play]). He is willing to lend Robert Crosbie $20,000 on mortgage

MEADOWS, Charlie (Letter [story]). The person from whom

Robert Crosbie intends to borrow $10,00 with which to purchase his wife's letter from the Chinese woman

MEADOWS CHILDREN (Home). Of George Meadows #1 and his wife; the five of them--two sons and three daughters

MEADOWS, Emily (Home). The wife of Tom Meadows; seventy years of age; tall, upright, dignified; gray hair and wrinkled face; has bright and shrewd eyes; originally Emily Green

MEADOWS, George #1 (Home). Age fifty; husband of Mrs. Meadows; son of Tom and Emily Meadows

MEADOWS, George #2 (Home). The older brother of Tom Meadows; uncle of George Meadows #1; gone away to sea after Tom had married Emily Green; for the last ten years, crippled with rheumatism; thin; skin hung on his bones; yellow, wrinkled face; had lost nearly all of his teeth

MEADOWS, Mrs. (Home). Wife of George Meadows #1; age forty-eight or forty-nine; is known as Mrs. George

MEADOWS, Tom (Home). Husband of Emily Meadows; father of George #1 and the younger brother of George #2

MEASURER (Of Human Bondage). At Ferne, Kent; in company with the booker, he went on his rounds to determine the number of hops that the pickers had gathered

MECHANICS (Making of a Saint). Rush into the Forli town square following the assassination of Girolamo Riario

MECHANICS (Vessel of Wrath). Two of them; one middle aged, the other a youth; form the crew of the launch from Maputito to Baru

MEDICAL MISSIONARY (Explorer novel]). Condamine brings Alec MacKenzie to his station; for weeks, he and his wife attend to Alec and deliver him from danger

MEDICAL MISSIONARY (Painted Veil). At Mei-tan-fu; died of cholera

MEDICAL STUDENT #1 (Of Human Bondage). Is at St. Luke's Hospital, London; tall; fierce, red moustache; might have been thirty years of age

MEDICAL STUDENT #2 (Of Human Bondage). Is at St. Luke's Hospital, London; perhaps twenty-eight or twenty-nine years of age; black hair

MEDICAL STUDENT #3 (Of Human Bondage). Is at St. Luke's Hospital, London; bespectacled; his beard quite gray

MEDICAL STUDENT #4 (Of Human Bondage). Is at St. Luke's Hospital, London; at the dissecting table with Philip

Carey, working on the opposite leg

MEDICAL STUDENT #5 (Of Human Bondage). Was enrolled the year prior to Philip Carey's entrance to St. Luke's Hospital, London; had cut himself at the dissecting table, failed to wash to wound with antiseptic, and died from speticaemia

MEDICAL STUDENT #6 (Of Human Bondage). Is at St. Luke's Hospital, London; he had been in the Royal Navy, but dismissed for drunkenness; age thirty; red face and brusque manner; loud voice

MEDICAL STUDENT #7 (Of Human Bondage). Is at St. Luke's Hospital, London; married, with two children; he had lost money through a defaulting solicitor; serious difficulty committing facts to memory

MEDICAL STUDENT #8 (Of Human Bondage). Is at St. Luke's Hospital, London; he had heard that Philip Carey had studied in Paris, and tried to discuss art with him

MEDICAL STUDENT #9 (Of Human Bondage). Is at St. Luke's Hospital, London; to make money, he bought items at sales on credit and then pawned them; his father made good on the young man's debts, then sent him overseas

MEDICAL STUDENT #10 (Of Human Bondage). At St. Luke's Hospital, London; he fell to the glamor of the music halls and bar parlors; became a clerk to a bootmaker

MEDICAL STUDENT #11 (Of Human Bondage). At St. Luke's Hospital, London; has a gift for singing and mimicry; left the hospital for the chorus of a musical comedy

MEDICAL STUDENT #12 (Of Human Bondage). At St. Luke's Hospital, London; uncouth manner and interjectional speech; he left the medical world to work on a farm

MEDICAL STUDENTS (Merry-Go-Round). Colleagues of Frank Hurrell; they spent their nights in revelry while he worked; became sober, tedious general practitioners

MEDICAL STUDENTS (Of Human Bondage). At the surgery in the outpatients' department at St. Luke's Hospital, London; they giggle when Jacobs orders Philip Carey to remove his sock and shoe

MEDICAL STUDENTS (Of Human Bondage). At St. Luke's Hospital, London; they look in on Philip Carey after the operation on his foot

MELITA, Antonio (Circle). Said that he would shoot himself if he could not have an affair with Catherine Champion-Cheney

MELLOR (Of Human Bondage). Is a pupil at King's School, Tercanbury; Sharp reported that he had told Rose to kick Philip Carey

MELROSE, Peter (Voice of the Turtle). Novelist; twenty-two or twenty-three years of age; of middle height; appeared squat; reddish skin that fit tightly over the bones; with large Semitic nose; alert green eyes; bushy eyebrows; short brown hair; generally uncouth

MEMBER OF PARLIAMENT (Loaves and Fishes). Of the House of Lords; a "funny old thing who was mumblin' away in his beard"

MEMBER OF PARLIAMENT (Moon and Sixpence). He could not leave the House and, therefore, could not attend the Stricklands' dinner party

MEMBERS OF PARLIAMENT (Bishop's Apron). Associates and opponents of Josiah Spratte; Josiah trampled on them with impartiality

MEMBERS OF PARLIAMENT (Loaves and Fishes). In House of Lords; twenty old buffers lying about on red benches

MEN (Back of Beyond). Several of them; at the club at Timbang; read and comment upon the newspaper notice of Knobby Clarke's death

MEN (Bad Example). Two or three of them; rough; drinking in a pub in a London slum; James Clinton talks with them

MEN (Buried Talent). They exploited and robbed Charmian Pelletier

MEN (Buried Talent). Are coarse and vulgar; Charmian Pelletier sold herself to them for a hundred francs

MEN (Buried Talent). At Paris; now and then tried to be familiar with Blanche (MacArdle)

MEN (Cakes and Ale). Attend at Christie's auction sale, London; dark and small; passed pieces of Victorian silver among one another

MEN (Cakes and Ale). Two of them; they row a dinghy in the Thames, near Vauxhall Bridge

MEN (Choice of Amyntas). In the mountains of Spain; two of them; crouching behind a rock; run away when they see Amyntas

MEN (Choice of Amyntas). Venturous; they had gone to discover the terrible secret of the accursed cavern, but have never returned

MEN (Christmas Holiday). At the Serail, Paris; two of

them; with dispatch cases; are extracting papers and talking business
MEN (Christmas Holiday). Two of them; are sentenced to prison for smuggling heroin from Belgium into France; associated with Robert Berger, who escapes sentence
MEN (Closed Shop). Young; two of them; are seen in the president's audience chamber; heavily armed; they are lying on sofas, reading papers, smoking cigarettes
MEN (De Amicitia). At Volendam, Holland; are sitting at their doors mending their nets; big, sturdy; rough, weather-beaten faces; they are wearing huge earrings
MEN (East of Suez). In a crowded Peking street; wild looking; they are accompanying a string of camels
MEN (East of Suez). Three of them; they carry George Conway from the street into the Andersons' apartment
MEN (Explorer [novel]). At some tiny kraal in British East Africa; worked in the fields or lounged idly by
MEN (Explorer [novel]). With Alec MacKenzie's latest expedition to Africa; at the halt in mid-day, some are sick, while others stop to adjust a load; still others, weak or lazy, lag behind
MEN (Hour Before the Dawn). At a dinner party; having finished their port, they would gather about Jane Foster and shout with coarse laughter while she aired her views
MEN (Hour Before the Dawn). Two or three of them; old; they dutifully tended the English garden at Graveney
MEN (Hour Before the Dawn). Four of them; seated upon the floor, the London air raid shelter, playing cards
MEN (Hour Before the Dawn). Two or three of them; trying to douse the rick fire near Jim Henderson's farm
MEN (Landed Gentry). A few of them; old; touched their hats as Mrs. Insoley passed
MEN (Liza of Lambeth). On Vere Street, Lambeth; some leaning against the walls; others smoking or sitting on the sills of the ground floor windows
MEN (Liza of Lambeth). Two of them; on Vere Street, in Lambeth; they waltz around the circle, to the tune of the organ grinder, and with the gravity of judges
MEN (Liza of Lambeth). At the Westminster theatre; told the women to keep close and hold tight
MEN (Liza of Lambeth). Four of them; all residents of Vere Street, Lambeth; come across to Liza Kemp and

Jim Blakeston on the Albert Embankment; they do not believe Liza's story about her visiting a sick friend

MEN (Liza of Lambeth). Loafing about the public house, in Vere Street, Lambeth; they are viewing the altercation between Liza Kemp and Jim Blakeston's wife

MEN (Liza of Lambeth). Two of them; young; constituted themselves as seconds for Liza Kemp during her fight with Mrs. Blakeston

MEN (Magician). Their imaginations raise them above the humdrum of mankind; willing to lose their all if they have the chance at a great prize

MEN (Magician). At the fair at the Lion de Belfort, Paris; stand at the doors of booths and vociferously importune people to enter

MEN (Magician). In Son #2's vision; enter Jean-Marie Porhoet's room with a long box; kneel before the bed

MEN (Magician). In Margaret Dauncey's vision; are at the point of death; Margaret clearly heard their shrill cries, peels of laughter, terrifying rattle

MEN (Magician). Are at the tavern on the Boulevard des Italiens, Paris; laughed boisterously

MEN (Magician). Strange, over-dressed, and scented; in company with Oliver and Margaret Haddo at Monte Carlo

MEN (Magician). During the reign of Louis XIV; some are hanged, some sent to the stake on evidence contained in the old books housed in the Arsenal library, Paris

MEN (Making of a Saint). Group of them at the gathering at the Palazzo Orsi; talking with Giulia dall' Aste

MEN (Making of a Saint). Two of them; they, along with Filippo Brandolini and Checco and Matteo d'Orsi, the only persons remaining at the gathering at Palazzo Orsi after the departure of Girolamo Riario's party

MEN (Making of a Saint). Four of them; they attack Checco d' Orsi and Filippo Brandolini on their way back from the Palazzo Orsi; all four of them die

MEN (Making of a Saint). Seen at the piazza at Forli, following the assassination of Girolamo Riario; they stand about as sheep, in dismayed and confused states

MEN (Making of a Saint). At the piazza at Forli, after the assassination of Girolamo Riario; they are seen mounted on barrows and loudly haranguing the people

MEN (Making of a Saint). At Forli; waved their caps and threw them in the air upon learning that Checco d'

Characters

Orsi planned to place the town under Papal protection

MEN (Making of a Saint). A few of them; rapacious; they wandered about the ransacked Palazzo Orsi as though they were scavengers, to see if anything remained

MEN (Making of Saint). At Forli; lamented about what they, as inexperienced townsmen, could do against the trained army of Lodovico Sforza

MEN (Making of a Saint). Two of them; at the piazza in Forli; they hold on to the bridle of the hangman's huge black stallion

MEN (Merry-Go-Round). Polly Ley met them at Venice and Capri; they confessed to her how they abandoned the greatness of the world; spoke of their past zeal with indulgent irony

MEN (Merry-Go-Round). Of science; they are dining at Frank Hurrell's London club; have the diverting air of middle-aged schoolboys

MEN (Merry-Go-Round). Had cared passionately for Jenny Bush and had been willing humbly to do her bidding; devoured Jenny with their eyes and trembled when they touched her hand; turned pale with desire when Jenny smiled on them

MEN (Moon and Sixpence). Authors; at a London tea party attended by the young Narrator; are not eccentric in appearance; tired looking

MEN (Mrs. Craddock). Cutting down beech trees at Court Leys, Kent; Bertha Craddock quickly stops their work

MEN (Narrow Corner). Stand outside the bar in Sydney, Australia; Captain Nichols tries to engage them in conversation, but they want nothing to do with him

MEN (Of Human Bondage). A few of them; queer; at the cheap but respectable restaurant in Soho; came in for hurried, scanty meals

MEN (of Human Bondage). Young; are patrons of the Jolly Sailor, Ferne, in Kent; they throw rings on a stick

MEN (Painted Veil). Over forty years of age; they began to be attracted to Kitty Garstin

MEN (Painted Veil). A group of them; in a corner tea house at Mei-tan-fu; they are eating an early meal

MEN (Perfect Gentleman). Twenty of them; the tailor put them to work on Monsieur Jourdain's clothes

MEN (Razor's Edge). Young and strapping; members of the Household Brigade; they call on Isabel Bradley at

Claridge's, London

MEN (Razor's Edge). Young and elegant; from the Foreign Office; call on Isabel Bradley at Claridge's, London

MEN (Razor's Edge). Two acquaintances of Maugham from the East; they married whores

MEN (String of Beads). Two of them; come from Jarrot's Stores; they attended the Livingstones' dinner party and exchanged necklaces with Miss Robinson

MEN (Taipan). Three of them--ages twenty-five, twenty-six, and twenty-seven; died from drink and buried in the English cemetery

MEN (Tenth Man). At Parker and Gibbons, in Middlepool; George Winter scheduled to speak to them

MEN (Tenth (Man). A dozen of them at Middlepool; they are sent by Colonel Boyce to Parker and Gibbons to fetch George Winter

MEN (Theatre). Two or three of them; walking along the Edgware Road, London; they thought that Julia Lambert Gosselyn smiled at them

MEN (Then and Now). With torches; convey Machiavelli to the Sforza Palace for a meeting with Caesar Borgia

MEN (Then and Now). Eight of them; ordered by Caesar Borgia to escort the rebel captains to the palace at Sinigaglia

MEN (Traveller in Romance). Two of them; on the post chaise from St. Moritz to Italy; stout; middle aged; they appeared to have a business connection; blended bad German and worse Italian; they got off at Kampfer

MENAGE (Of Human Bondage). One or two; at the cheap but respectable restaurant in Soho; had their own napkins reserved for them

MEN-AT-ARMS (Making of a Saint). Present at the meeting between Girolamo Riario and Checco d'Orsi, held at the Palazzo Orsi, Forli

MERCHANT (Catalina). Harbored a fugitive from the Holy Office

MERCHANT (Explorer [play]). At Liverpool; the father of Alice Kelsey, Mrs. Allerton, and of another daughter

MERCHANT (Of Human Bondage). At Berlin; the father of Fraulein Hedwig

MERCHANT (Sheppey). At Baghdad; he sent his servant to market to buy provisions; he then lends his servant a horse to ride to Samarra to escape Death; later, he

confronts Death in the market place
MERCHANT (Then and Now). He has recently come to Imola from the Levant; sold Machiavelli a flask of attar of roses, which he sent as a gift to Aurelia Martelli
MERCHANTMEN (Explorer [novel]). Are honest, laborious, trustworthy, and of good courage; took foul weather and peril in a day's journey, and they made no outcry
MERCHANTS (Choice of Amyntas). At Cadiz; none of them willing to employ Amyntas
MERCHANTS (East of Suez). In a crowded Peking street; clad in black gowns and caps, and wearing black shoes
MERCHANTS (Making of a Saint). Seen at Forli; after the assassination of Girolamo Riario, they keep calm and appear unafraid
MERCIA (Punctiliousness of Don Sebastian). Eighteen-year-old cousin and ward of Don Sebastian; is being educated in a convent near Xiormonez, Spain; she is beautiful; becomes maid of honor to the Queen, then mistress to the King
MERESTON, Lord Charles (Lady Frederick). Is age twenty-two; the son of Lady Maud and Sir George Mereston; wealthy; in love with Lady Frederick Berolles; asks her to marry him
MERESTON DAUGHTER (Sheppey). Of Lord and Lady Mereston; for her coming out, her father must give a ball for seven hundred people and buy champagne at eighteen shillings per bottle
MERESTON, Sir George (Lady Frederick). Deceased husband of Lady Maud Mereston and the father of Lord Charles; wore side whiskers; a religious man who believed the worst about his neighbors; the president of the Broad Church Union; he had an affair with Mimi La Bretonne
MERESTON, Lady (Flirtation). Is hosting a party; Bertie Shenton one of the guests
MERESTON, Lady (Sheppey). Wife of Lord Mereston; her husband had paid two thousand pounds for a diamond bracelet for her for their silver wedding anniversary
MERESTON, Lord (Sheppey). Shaved by Sheppey Miller at Bradley's Hairdressing and Barber's Saloon, in Jermyn Street, London; married to Lady Mereston; a son and a daughter; he told Sheppey about the expenses of life
MERESTON, Lady Maud (Lady Frederick). Age forty; sister of Paradine Fouldes; a handsome woman; mother of Lord

Charles and the widow of Sir George; a friend of Lady Frederick Berolles

MERESTON, Marchioness of (Penelope). According to the Morning Post, she has arrived at 89 Grosvenor Square, London

MERESTON, Marchioness and Marquess of (Jack Straw). Are Guests at the Parker-Jennings' garden party, Cheshire

MERESTON SON, M.P. (Sheppey). Of Lord and Lady Mereston; nursing a constituency that costs his father fifteen hundred pounds per year

MERESTONS (Magician). They had been proud to give their daughters to the house of Haddo

MESSALINA (Magician). In Margaret Dauncey's vision; has and insatiable mouth and wanton eyes

MESSENGER (Catalina). He carries Beatriz's letter to Blasco de Valero, in which she reveals her knowledge of the Bishop's levitation

MESSENGER (Escape). Carries Roger Charing's response to Ruth Barlow

MESSENGER (Explorer [novel]). Native; sent from Mondabi to Alec Mackenzie

MESSENGER #1 (Making of a Saint). Sent by Checco d'Orsi to Protonotary Savello recounting the events at Forli

MESSENGER #2 (Making of a Saint). Sent by the Pope to Protonotary Savello, stating that the former was preparing an army to come to the assistance of Forli

MESSENGER (Narrow Corner). From Kim Ching; he asks Dr. Saunders to visit Kim Ching

MESSENGER (Of Human Bondage). Generally a little girl; informs the porter at St. Luke's Hospital, London, that a woman is in labor; is sent across the road to where Philip Carey lodges

MESSENGER (Painted Veil). Is sent by the nuns of the French convent at Mei-tan-fu with a cross of dahlias to Walter Fane's funeral

MESSENGER (Then and Now). Brings news to Sforza Palace that Caesar Borgia's rebel captains have actually signed articles of agreement

MESSENGER BOY (Of Human Bondage). Philip Carey sends him to Mildred Rogers' house with a letter; returns, telling Philip Mildred has not come back from Oxford

MESSENGER BOY (Smith). Brings Algy Peppercorn's dinner clothes from his mother to the Dallas-Bakers' house

Characters

MESSENGER BOY (Tenth Man). Sent by George Winter to the Etchinghams' house with a toothbrush for Catherine Winter

MESSENGERS (Explorer [novel]). Carried to Rofa Alec Mac Kenzie's intent that the latter would come to the royal kraal before mid-day

MESSENGERS (Making of a Saint). Sent from Forli to Rome and to Florence, requesting help against the armies of Lodovico Sforza

MESSENGERS (Making of a Saint). Sent from Forli to Rome urging the Pope to negotiate with Lodovico Sforza

MESSENGERS (Making of a Saint). Sent from the Council at Forli to open negotiations with Lodovico Sforza

MEURICE, Madame (Man with a Conscience). She is Marie-Louise Meurice's mother; an invalid

MEURICE, Marie-Louise (Man with a Conscience). Daughter of a captain in the colonial army who had, following her father's death, she accompanied her mother to Le Havre; was born at Tonkin; age eighteen when she met Henri Renaud and Jean Charvin; small, pretty figure; large, gray eyes; pale soft skin; mouse colored hair; beautiful, not pretty; eventually weds Jean Charvin

MEYER (Magician). A landscape painter; lives in Paris with Madame Meyer; clean shaven; a large quantity of gray curling hair; handsome face

MEYER, Madame (Magician). The wife of Meyer, the Paris landscape painter; formerly a governess in Poland, but too pretty to remain as such; is small and gay

MEYERHEIM (Razor's Edge). Art dealer and gallery owner located on the moneyed side of the Seine, Paris; an international reputation; Suzanne Rouvier to have an exhibition of her paintings there

MICHEL (Hour Before the Dawn). A French farmer; Roger Henderson is taken to his farm, where he spends ten days; thin and wizened; mean face; fears the Germans will burn the farm if they discover Roger to be there

MICHELE, Don (Then and Now). He is a Spaniard known as Michelotto; sent by Caesar Borgia to bring Oliverotto da Fermo at Sinigaglia; big, hairy, and of powerful build; bushy eyebrows, hard eyes; short, blunt nose; an expressive, cold ferocity; strangled Pagolo Orsini

MIDDLETON, Constance (Constant Wife). Daughter of Mrs. Culver, sister of Martha Culver, and the wife of John

Middleton; age thirty-six; handsome; has been married to John for fifteen years; knows that her husband is involved in a love affair with Marie-Louise Durham

MIDDLETON, Helen (Constant Wife). Daughter of John and Constance Middleton; age fourteen; at boarding school

MIDDLETON, John (Constant Wife). Husband of Constance Middleton; is a surgeon; age forty; tall and spare; involved in a love affair with Marie-Louise Durham

MIDWIFE (Choice of Amyntas). Was present at the birth of each of Peter the Schoolmaster's children; placed the child in its father's arms

MIDWIFE #1 (Of Human Bondage), Of the woman in labor; talked naturally with Philip Carey

MIDWIFE #2 (Of Human Bondage). For the mother of the twins; speculates that "Maybe the Lord 'll see fit to take 'em to 'imself"

MIDWIFE #3 (Of Human Bondage). At London; attends Woman #19; sobbed noisily after she dies

MIDWIFE (Unconquered). At Soissons; gives Annette some medicine that only makes her ill

MILIOTTI, Mario (Mask and the Face). He is the local magistrate; marries Wanda Serini

MILITARY MAN (Cakes and Ale). Retired; walked along the beach at Blackstable, Kent

MILITARY OFFICIAL (Hour Before the Dawn). A "big shot," with ribbons all over his chest; he told Jane Foster that the French army was on its toes and thus would surprise the Germans

MILITARY TAILOR (Making of a Millionaire). He made Mr. Rose's clothes

MILKMAIDS (De Amicitia). At Monnickendam, Holland; with huge-limbs; milking the cows and pouring the pails of milk into huge barrels

MILKMAN (Mrs. Craddock). Employed on Edward Craddock's farm; more useful than a milkmaid

MILLAIS, Sir John Everard [Everett] (Round Dozen). The Pre-Raphaelite painter (1829-1896); he took the St. Clairs to the Garrick Club; met Henry Irving there

MILLER (Explorer [novel/play]). Is the butler at Lady Alice Kelsey's house, Charles Street, Mayfair, London

MILLER (Merry-Go-Round). Lady Vizard's butler at her husband's house in Charles Street, London; had given evidence at the divorce trial of Lady and Lord Vizard

Characters

MILLER (Pool). Is one of the men in the lounge shaking dice for drinks; a German-American, formerly named "Muller"; big, fat, and bald; round face; wore large gold-rimmed spectacles; a heavy drinker; represented a San Francisco jobbing firm; hires Lawson after his dismissal by Bain

MILLER (Then and Now). In a card game at the inn of San Casciano in which Niccolo Machiavelli participates

MILLER, Ada (Sheppey). Married to Sheppey Miller for twenty-three years; the mother of Florence; stout and middle aged; good natured and homely face; kind eyes and a pleasant smile; an excellent cook; a cook in service from the time she was age fifteen until she married Sheppey

MILLER, Emil (Of Human Bondage). A naturalized German; is a regular customer at the tea shop in Parliament Square, London; sandy hair and a bristly moustache; admired Mildred Rogers; of middle height; round head; sallow face; in business at Birmingham, where he has a wife and four children; he leaves Mildred Rogers shortly after she becomes pregnant with his child

MILLER, Florence (Sheppey). Daughter of Sheppey and Ada Miller; permanently waved, short hair; pretty, alert, and self-assured; has been a typist in the city, but gave her notice after Sheppey won the prize in the Sweepstakes; studies French in expectation of her Paris honeymoon; engaged to Ernest Turner for two years

MILLER, Joseph ["Sheppey"] (Sheppey). Husband of Ada Miller and father of Florence; known as Sheppey; a hairdresser at Bradley's Hairdressing and Barber's Saloon, Jermyn Street, London, for the past fourteen years; middle aged; stoutish; red face and twinkling eyes; bald, but sports a fine head of black wavy hair during working hours; a jovial and well fed look; was born on the Isle of Sheppey, in Kent (and thus the origin of his name); married for twenty-three years; a Conservative; is the best salesman that Bradley has ever had; has high blood pressure; wins a residuary prize in the Irish Sweepstakes; faints in the shop, then later at home; tenders his notice to Bradley and refuses the latter's offer of a partnership in the shop; plans to give his money to the needy; he dies

MILLER, Mr. (Sheppey). Sheppey Miller's father; he had

Sheppey scrub his back during his bath

MILLER, Mrs. (Of Human Bondage). Wife of Emil Miller; she discovers her husband's relationship with Mildred Rogers; threatens to divorce him

MILLICENT (Before the Party). Mrs. Skinner's daughter; Harold's widow; Joan's mother; age thirty-six; sallow and muddy skin; blue eyes; stocky; she murders Harold

MILLIONAIRE (Merry-Go-Round). Frank Hurrell knows him; makes his only son work ten hours a day in a bank; he believes that work provides the boy useful training

MILLIONAIRE (Razor's Edge). From South America; Prince de Colombey had left the Marquese de Clinchant to marry his daughter

MILTON, Mrs. (Lord Mountdrago). A patient of Dr. Audlin

MIMI (Christmas Holiday). Simon Fenimore's hypothetical example of a poor brute who no longer has the money to lead the Latin Quarter life; hard working; a trade unionist; she loses her virtue but she keeps her head

MINDABI (Explorer [play]). Sent a native messenger to Alec MacKenzie

MINER #1 (Explorer [novel]). He is age fourteen; son of Miner #2 and brother of Miner #3; entombed in the pit at Lancashire with his brother; blue eyes, a laughing mouth, and cheeky brightness

MINER #2 (Explorer [novel]). The father of Miner #1 and Miner #3; killed in the explosion at Lancashire; his charred and disfigured body lay in a nearby mortuary

MINER #3 (Explorer [novel]). Older brother of Miner #1 and son of Miner #2; he is married and the father of children; entombed in the pit at Lancashire with his brother; he dies

MINERS (Explorer [novel]). At Alec MacKenzie's mine in Lancashire; a number of them killed or buried in an explosion; about thirty of them entombed in a pit

MINISTER (East of Suez). He wired to George Conway from Peking, stating that George would have to resign if he married Daisy (now Mrs. Anderson); he then transferred George from Chung-King to Canton

MINISTER (Hour Before the Dawn). Told Jane Foster over the telephone that the B.E.F. had become trapped and that it would be a true miracle if more than thirty or forty thousand escaped

MINISTER (Marriage of Convenience, 1906). Had offered

Characters 289

    Lucien de Pornichet the governorship of the island off the coast of Tunis, but only if he married; gave Lucien six weeks to find a wife

MINISTER (Razor's Edge). At Chicago; he recommends to a rich old woman that she invest in a wildcat scheme

MINISTER OF FINANCE (Razor's Edge). Stationed at of one of the smaller states in northern India; a European education, including Oxford; wore European clothes; nice looking; stout; age forty-nine; a close cropped and neat moustache; has a wife and children; when he reaches age fifty, he plans to dispose of everything and become a wandering mendicant

MINISTER OF FINE ARTS (Razor's Edge). At Paris; under obligation to Achille Gauvain; he will open Suzanne Rouvier's art exhibition at Meyerheim's gallery, in Paris, with a speech on Suzanne's virtues as a woman

MINISTER TO THE COLONIES (Marriage of Convenience). He appointed the retired French official as a colonial governor after he had completed his naval service

MINISTERS OF THE CROWN (Hour Before the Dawn). Three of them; invited to Jane Foster's for dinner; possessed an intimate acquaintance with all of the modern poets

MINOR CANONS (Merry-Go-Round). Of Tercanbury, in Kent; they talked with gusto concerning the Royal Academy

MINSTRELS (Merry-Go-Round). At Brighton; they sang and played sentimental ditties

MISSION BOY (Vessel of Wrath). Helps nurse Owen Jones

MISSIONARIES (Taipan). Two men, with their wives and children; massacred during the Boxer Rebellion (1900-1901); they are all buried in the English cemetery

MISSIONARY (P.&O.). To China; reads the burial service at Gallagher's funeral

MISSIONARY LADIES (East of Suez). At Fuchow; they turn up their noses at Freddy Baker's half-caste wife

MISTRESS (Of Human Bondage). Of the first boarding house in Brighton; middle aged, stout, and business-like; tells Philip Carey that she has nothing but a single room

MOB (Making of a Saint). Storms and plunders Palazzo Orsi after the assassination of Girolamo Riario; then does the same to the treasury at the Gabella; storms the palace once again after the surrender of the city

MODEL #1 (Of Human Bondage). At Amitrano's art school,

Paris; sulky; the first naked woman Philip Carey has seen; is not young; shriveled breasts; colorless fair hair; face covered with large freckles

MODEL #2 (Of Human Bondage). At Amitrano's art school, at Paris; he is an old man, with a vast gray beard

MODELS (Merry-Go-Round). At Rome; in the dress of the Campagna; lounged about Bernini's easy steps of the Piazza di Spagna

MOHAMMED (Magician). He is at the fair at the Lion de Belfort, Paris; an Egyptian snake charmer from Assiut and the husband of the fallah woman; he sat at the entrance to a canvas booth, cross legged and listlessly beating a drum; bright teeth; claimed to have shown serpents to Lord Kitchener

MOHAMMED THE LAME (Explorer [novel]). A new leader who arose among the Arabs; had been a camel driver; his leg had been badly set after a fracture; he is shrewd and far-seeking, ruthless and ambitious; attacked the capital of a small state in the north of British East Africa and proclaimed himself its king; seized with a serious illness during the three months that Alec MacKenzie had spent in England; he took the field against his rebellious son, thus weakening his forces

MOLLY (Lord Mountdrago). In a dream; at a pub in Limehouse; a prostitute; blowsy, old, and drunk; decayed teeth; sits on Lord Mountdrago's lap

MOLSON, Mr. (Mrs. Craddock). Husband of Mrs. Molson; a guest at Mrs. Branderton's dinner party; a red-faced squire with dogmatic opinions

MOLSON, Mrs. (Mrs. Craddock). Accompanies her husband to Mrs. Branderton's dinner party; is insignificant

MONA LISA (Magician). Is in Margaret Dauncey's vision

MONGOLS (East of Suez). Two of them in a crowded Peking street; astride shaggy ponies; wear high boots and Astrakhan caps

MONK (Making of a Saint). At the church in Forli; he is dark-robed; admits Andrea and Filippo Brandolini, bearing the body of Orso d'Orsi, into the cloisters

MONK #1 (Moon and Sixpence). At the Asile de Nuit, in Marseilles; read Charles Strickland's papers and then addressed him in English

MONK #2 (Moon and Sixpence). At the Asile de Nuit, in Marseilles; entered the common room with a huge Bible and he began the service to which all of the lodgers were subject

MONK #3 (Moon and Sixpence). Stalwart; responsible for dislodging the lodgers at Aisle de Nuit, Marseilles, from their beds at 5:00 a.m.

MONK (Mrs. Craddock). At Rome; Franciscan; a figure of a romantic play

MONKS (East of Suez). Members of the Temple of Fidelity and Virtuous Inclination, Peking; clad in gray gowns; shaven heads

MONKS (Faith). At the monastery of San Lucido; recited service in heavy drones; harsh voices; drag Brother Jasper to the cloisters, strip him of his cowl, bind him by the hands to a pillar; witness his whipping

MONKS (Making of a Saint). Four of them; barefooted and bearing crucifixes; they accompany Marco Scorsacana and Pietro Albanese

MONKS (Painted Veil). At the Buddhist monastery, ten miles outside of Mei-tan-fu; smiling; seemed to stay there on sufferance, waiting notice to quit the place

MONKS (Razor's Edge). There are two of them; at the refectory door of the Benedictine monastery at Alsace

MONSIGNORE (Circle). Lady Catherine Champion-Cheney met him at Monte Carlo; he acted wonderfully toward her

MONSORE, Begum of (Noble Spaniard). She could find no fault with Captain Adolphus Chalford's appearance

MONTAGUE, Oliver (Circle). His picture appears in an old photograph album owned by Clive Champion Cheney

MONTANEZ, Duke of (Poet). Killed in a duel by Santa Ana because of Pepa Montanez

MONTANEZ, Pepa (Poet). A dancer; because of her, Santa Ana had fought a duel with the Duke of Montanez

MONTEZ, Lola (Voice of the Turtle). Told the Narrator about her love affair with the King of Bavaria

MONTGOMERIE, Captain (Lady Frederick). Age thirty-five; polished and well groomed; son of Aaron Levitski, the Jewish money lender; rich; is thinking of going into Parliament at the next election; proposes marriage to Lady Frederick Berolles; he holds the papers for the debts of both Lady Frederick and Sir Gerald O'Mara

MONTGOMERIE, Florence (Voice of the Turtle). Told the Narrator about her affair with Crown Prince Rudolf

MONTGOMERY, Ludovic (Cakes and Ale). He is one of the

fictitious names that young Ashenden had invented to replace his own

MONTMORENCY (Bishop's Apron). Father of Josiah Spratte the elder and great-grandfather of Thomas, Sophia, and Theodore Spratte; Theodore believed him to have been a gentleman, but Thomas maintains that he was a greengrocer; he waited at dinners in Bedford Square and had a sly drink of sherry when no one was looking

MONTMORENCY (Loaves and Fishes). Great-grandfather of Sophia, Thomas, and Theodore Spratte; Theodore holds the belief that he was a gentleman, but Sophia claims he was merely a greengrocer; Thomas asserts that he waited on tables at dinner parties at Bedford Square, drinking sherry on the sly when no one was looking

MONTMORENCY, Aubrey de (Bishop's Apron). Was an early (c.1631) antecedent of the Spratte family; he had, according to Rev. Theodore Spratte, assumed the name "des Prats" upon his marriage to a French heiress; he was killed in about 1642 while (again, according to Theodore) fighting for the freedom of the people

MONTMORENCY, Aubrey de (Loaves and Fishes). The ancestor to the Sprattes; married in 1631 and killed in 1642, while fighting for the freedom of his people

MONTMORENCY, Esmeralda (Home and Beauty). An employee of A.B. Rahan; an intervener in adultery cases; comes from one of the best families in Shropshire; a spinster, approximately fifty-five years old; resembles a hard boiled egg; speaks with a slight drawl; a very good card player; she does facial massages for ladies personally recommended; is assigned to William Cardew

MONTMORENCY, Roger de (Loaves and Fishes). Second son of Aubrey de Montmorency; beheaded by King James II; the current Sprattes are directly descended from him

MOON, George (Back of Beyond). Resident at Timbag Belud in Malaya; ready to retire and return to England; age fifty-five; tall; narrow shoulders; thin, yellow face wrinkled and tight-lipped; thin gray hair; gray eyes

MOON, Mr. (Back of Beyond). Married son of George Moon and his ex-wife; age twenty-seven; New Zealand farmer

MOON, Mrs. (Back of Beyond). Ex-wife of George Moon; large, fat, and dark; remarried

MOOR (Catalina). Was convicted of killing a chicken by cutting off its head

Characters 293

MOOR (Choice of Amyntas). Father of the palace maidens; one of the wealthiest of his people; lived in Spain; built the palace after the Spanish authorities drove his people from the country; very learned; one day he lost himself in metaphysical speculation, and he has never been found

MOORE (Landed Gentry). Claude Insoley's butler; he is elderly and impressive

MOORISH SLAVE (Catalina). Impregnated by Domingo Perez before he turned twenty years of age

MORATINI, Allesandro (Making of a Saint). A brother of Giulia dall' Aste and Scipione Moratini; the son of Bartolomeo Moratini; delicate features; in a room at the Palazzo Orsi; Checco d'Orsi signals him to close the door; he escapes with Checco prior to the fall of Forli; settles with his family at Citta di Castello

MORATINI, Bartolomeo (Making of a Saint). The father of Giulia dall' Aste, Allesandro and Scipione Moratini, Fabio Oliva, and Cesare Gnocchi; age sixty; rugged and upright; grave and dignified; a charming smile; blind love for his daughter, Giulia; he flattered her folly and believed totally in her virtue; he almost caught Amtrogio della Treccia with Giulia; he and his family will enter into the conspiracy to assassinate Girolamo Riario; he escapes from Forli with Checco d'Orsi; he eventually settles in Citta di Castello

MORATINI, Scipione (Making of a Saint). Is a brother of Giulia dall' Aste and Allesandro Moratini; a son of Bartolomeo Moratini; has delicate features; attended Checco d'Orsi; a pleasant person; escapes from Forli and then settles with his family in Citta di Castello

MORATINI, Signora (Making of a Saint). Wife of Bartolomeo Moratini; mother of Giulia dall' Aste and Allesandro and Scipione Moratini; once a very beautiful woman; somewhat gay

MORET, Count de (Our Betters). Married Minnie Surennes' cousin, Mary

MORET, Mary (Our Betters). Is Minnie Surennes' cousin; married the Count de Moret

MORETON (Narrow Corner). He walked across New Guinea, unarmed, with a walking stick and with his police

MORGAN, Pierpont (Constant Wife). When he died, he was found to own seven million dollars of worthless stock

MORISCO WOMEN (Catalina). Four of them; consigned as heretics to the Inquisition; their beauty excites the admiration of all

MORO, Lodovico (Making of a Saint). He and his armies at Milan; enters Forli in triumph after the flight of Checco d'Orsi and the conspirators

MORRISON (Tenth Man). Is the Tory candidate for George Winter's seat in Parliament to represent Middlepool

MORRISON, Robert (Man from Glasgow). Scottish; broadly built; sunburned face; short hair; large mouth, ears, and nose; wrinkled skin pale blue eyes; ragged gray moustache; employed by the Glasgow and South of Spain Oil Company Limited

MORTON, Gerald (Virtue). Is known as Gerry; a district officer in Borneo; unmarried; hosts the Narrator for a week; twenty-eight years of age; obsessed with the building of a road; he takes up with Margery Bishop

MOTHER (Bad Example). Of the two-year-old child and one other; pale and small; thin, hollow cheeks; eyes red and dim with weeping; her husband had left her; out of work; she had suckled her child as long as she could before it died

MOTHER #1 (Caesar's Wife). Of the Khedive; has asked Lady Violet Little to see her at 3:30 p.m.; attempts to intercede in the murder case against Abdul Said, to whose mother she gave a dowry when she married

MOTHER #2 (Caesar's Wife). Of Abdul Said; a maid to the Khedive's mother, from whom she received a dowry when she married

MOTHER #1 (Cakes and Ale). Of Mary Ann; did the washing for the Blackstable vicarage

MOTHER #2 (Cakes and Ale). Of the young lady at the vicarage tea party; announced that she had brought her daughter's music

MOTHER (Christmas Holiday). Of Lydia Berger; she was the daughter of a customs official; granddaughter of a serf; worked in Paris addressing letters; died from malnutrition

MOTHER (Circle). Of Elizabeth Champion-Cheney; she died when Elizabeth was a baby

MOTHER (Hour Before the Dawn). Of May Henderson; her husband's death left her with little more than a pension; school friend of Mrs. Henderson; she and May occupied one of the cottages at Graveney, a mile from Graveney Holt; died before May wed Roger Henderson

MOTHER (Liza of Lambeth). Of Mrs Kemp; Mrs. Kemp claims that, when a girl, she (Mrs. Kemp) gave her money to her; she never had to ask her daughter for anything

MOTHER (Magician). Of Madame Rouge; is old and stout; possessed the remains of beauty; she refers to her husband's lover as her son-in-law

MOTHER (Making of a Saint). Of Andrea; Filippo Brandolini stays at her house in Forli after escaping from the mob

MOTHER (Narrow Corner). Of Japanese diver; Dr. Saunders imagines her in Japanese dress and elaborately done hair, taking her son, as a little boy, to the cherry blossoms and the temple

MOTHER #1 (Of Human Bondage), Of Mrs. Otter; introduced to Philip Carey by her daughter

MOTHER #2 (Of Human Bondage). Of the expectant mother; she talked naturally with Philip Carey

MOTHER #3 (Of Human Bondage). Of twins; when told of the event, she let forth a long shrill wail of misery

MOTHER #4 (Of Human Bondage). Of Mother #3; she does not know how the babies will be fed

MOTHER (Our Betters). Of Minnie Surennes; she could not bear her sister Alice; determined that Minnie should marry a duke

MOTHER #1 (Painted Veil). Of Sister St. Joseph; she is old; fond of her daughter-in-law, son, and grandson

MOTHER #2 (Painted Veil). Of Odette (Mother Superior); maintained that a well-bred woman will do nothing that will make people talk about her

MOTHER (Razor's Edge). Of Sophie Macdonald). Divorced from her husband; married a Standard Oil man in China

MOTHER (Sanatorium). Of Mrs. Chester; an old woman; she did not mind at all that she was dying

MOTHER (Unknown). Of Charlotte Littlewood; both she and Charlotte were the first people in Stour to call upon young Evelyn and George Wharton when they came there

MOTHER (Up at the Villa). Of Mary Panton; had told her nineteen-year-old daughter that the forty-three-year-old Sir Edgar Swift was in love with Mary; she died

MOUNTDRAGO, Lady (Lord Mountdrago). Is the wife of Lord Mountdrago the younger; the daughter of a duke and an

American heiress; age eighteen when she married Lord Mountdrago; mother of two sons

MOUNTDRAGO, Lord the elder (Lord Mountdrago). Father of Lord Mountdrago the younger; in the House of Lords

MOUNTDRAGO, Lord the younger (Lord Mountdrago). At age forty-two; he prides himself on his punctuality; able and distinguished; appointed Secretary for Foreign Affairs before he had reached the age of forty; the ablest politician in the Conservative Party; speaks several languages; is married and the father of two sons; a fearful snob, arrogant and selfish; large and heavy; graying hair receding on the forehead; puffy face with bold regular features

MULLER (Pool). See above; same person as MILLER (Pool)

MULOCK, Edward (Taipan). He is buried in the English cemetery; drank himself to death at age twenty-five

MUNRO, Angus (Neil MacAdam). Curator of the museum at Kualo Solor, Borneo; a graduate of the University of Edinburgh; age forty; tall and thin; hollow cheeks; gray eyes; thin, aquiline nose and pale lips; close-cropped brown hair turning gray

MUNRO, Darya (Neil MacAdam). The Russian wife of Angus Munro; age thirty-five; of medium height; pale brown face; pale blue eyes; pale brown hair, parted in the middle and wound into a knot on the nape of her neck; broad face, high cheekbones; a fleshy nose; has large hands; not pretty, but graceful; she speaks English perfectly; father killed in the war; her mother was Princess Lutchkov

MURDERER (Narrow Corner). In the Sydney Bulletin; of two brothers on a farmstead in the Blue Mountains; he surrendered to the police, but pleading self-defense

MURPHY, Mr. (Mrs. Dot). Husband of Mrs. Murphy; a bedridden lunatic

MURPHY, Mrs. (Mrs. Dot). The wife of Mr. Murphy; Dot Worthley had sent her fifteen pounds six months ago because she had nine children; she now has eleven; she and her husband produce twins twice each year

MURRAY, Captain (Man of Honour). Late husband of Hilda Murray; a cavalryman; he left his wife five thousand pounds per year

MURRAY, Captain (Merry-Go-Round). Late husband of Mrs. Murray; a cavalryman; stupid; did two wise things in his life: he made his will, leaving his wife a large fortune, and (2) he promptly departed this world

MURRAY, Dr. (For Services Rendered). Is a physician at Stanbury, with whom Charles Prentice has consulted concerning Charlotte Ardsley's health; he examines her and recommends she undergo an immediate operation

MURRAY, Hilda (Man of Honour). Older sister of Mabel Halliwell; tall and handsome; self-possessed; widow of Captain Murray; in love with Basil Kent; initially refuses Robert Brackley's marriage proposal

MURRAY, Hilda (Merry-Go-Round). A tall, handsome widow with five thousand pounds per year; hair neither dark nor fair; gray and tender eyes; a sweet smile; long white arms; beautiful hands; self-possessed; in love with Basil Kent, and eventually marries him; she and Basil Kent lay roses on the grave of Jenny Kent

MURRAY, Mrs. (Hour Before the Dawn). Widowed mother of Richard Murray; her financial reverse caused her son to abandon the notion of entering the army; writes to Dick's housekeeper that her son has been wounded

MURRAY, Richard (Hour Before the Dawn). He is George Henderson's estate agent; a bachelor; his age between twenty-nine and thirty; thick and wavy hair, prematurely gray; has tanned, unlined skin; fine blue eyes; thick lashes; blunt features; white regular teeth; heavily built; broad shoulders; average height; is a member of the Territorials; an old friend and school fellow at Sandhurst) of Roger Henderson; in love with May Henderson; joins his regiment at Norfolk, then goes off to France; survives Dunkirk and returns to England; sent to Egypt, rises to the rank of captain, and is blinded; returned to England and to a hospital

MUSETTE (Christmas Holiday). Serves as Simon Fenimore's hypothetical example of a poor brute who no longer has the money to lead the Latin Quarter life; hard working; a trade unionist; loses her virtue but keeps her head

MUSIC MASTER (Perfect Gentleman). Is called in to help Monsieur Jordain become a gentleman of fashion; blunt and downright; M. Jourdain represents "quite a nice little income" for him

MUSICIAN (East of Suez). Is in a crowded Peking street; stands on the curb and plays a tuneless melody on a

one-stringed fiddle
MUSICIANS (Catalina). Hired to play for Beatriz Henriquez y Braganza during her illness
MUSICIANS (Magicians). Seen in a Hungarian band at the tavern on the Boulevard des Italiens, Paris; played in a distant corner
MUSTAPHA PASHA (Ashenden/Miss King). Serves as Prince Ali's secretary; dines with Prince Ali and Ali's two daughters at the Geneva hotel; age forty-five; huge and fat; has large eyes; sports a big black moustache

N

NAIRNE, Jack (Noble Spaniard). The deceased husband of Marion Nairne; broke his neck within two years of his marriage; liked gin and water more than he did Marion
NAIRNE, Marion (Noble Spaniard). Young widow of Jack Nairne; fascinating; handsome; Lucy's sister; wealthy
NAJADE (Perfect Gentleman). In the opera, The Island of Naxos; companion of Ariadne
NAPIER, Gilbert (Jane). A young architect; age twenty-four; slight, not tall; fair hair; clean shaven and blue eyed; pleasant amiable face; marries Jane Fowler
NAPIER, Jane (Jane). See below; listed as Jane FOWLER
NAPLES, King of (Making of a Saint). He negotiates with the Pope and Checco d'Orsi about an attack upon Forli
NAPOLEON (Rehearsal). He offered his Imperial crown to Celestine Zampa, but she simply refused to accept it
NARRATOR (Alien Corn). Is a novelist and playwright; a friend of both the Blands and of Ferdy Rabenstein
NARRATOR (Ant and the Grasshopper). Apologizes for telling something that everyone is supposed to know; expresses disapproval of prudence and common sense
NARRATOR (Appearance and Reality). Relates the story as told to him by a professor of French literature at an English university
NARRATOR (Book-Bag). He is a writer; also a reader from force of habit; books constitute a necessity for him
NARRATOR (Bum). A professional writer who sees himself as doing nothing at all; had come from Vera Cruz to Mexico City to board a ship for Yucatan
NARRATOR (Casual Affair). A novelist; he does relate the story, but is in no way part of it; guest of the

District Officer on an island off the north coast of Borneo; had known Jack Almond
NARRATOR (Closed Shop). Is identified only as a writer
NARRATOR (Cousin Amy). Is a cousin of Amy, although he cannot imagine that they are related; at age thirty-five, he is eight years younger than Amy
NARRATOR (Creative Impulse). Explains how Mrs. Albert Forrester came to write The Achilles Statute
NARRATOR (Cupid and the Vicar of Swale). Sees Swale as strikingly picturesque and most eminently respectable
NARRATOR (De Amicitia). Relates the story of Valentia Stewart and Ferdinand White to his aunt
NARRATOR (Dream). Traveling from New York to Petrograd, by way of Vladivostok, on the Trans-Siberian Railway; supposedly a journalist, but who also writes fiction
NARRATOR (End of the Flight). Lands in a remote town in Borneo; then narrates the District Officer's story
NARRATOR (Episode). A guest at the dinner party and a friend of Ned Preston
NARRATOR (Escape). He knew only one man who managed to extricate himself from the grasp of a woman who had determined to marry him
NARRATOR (Footprints in the Jungle). A traveler and an observer of those who comprise the European quarter of Tanah Merah, Malaya
NARRATOR (Four Dutchman). He stayed at the Van Dorth Hotel, Singapore; passenger aboard the S.S. Utrecht, a steamer from Merauke, in New Guinea, to Macassar
NARRATOR (French Joe). Came from Sydney, on a Japanese tramp steamer, to Thursday Island
NARRATOR (Friend in Need). Has been studying his fellow men for the past thirty years
NARRATOR (German Harry). Travels on a pearling lugger from Thursday Island to Merauke, New Guinea
NARRATOR (Good Manners). Is a guest at one of Augustus Breton's little dinners
NARRATOR (Happy Couple). Did not really like Sir Edward Landon, but regards him as sufficiently good company
NARRATOR (Happy Man). Unwillingly forced to point the finger of fate; as a young man, he lived in a modest London apartment located near Victoria Station; is a non-practicing physician; a writer
NARRATOR (Hero). Wishes that someone would write an

invective against the blanc-mange (milk pudding), surely the most detestable of all the national dishes
NARRATOR (Home). Had never seen a more united household than that of the Meadows family
NARRATOR (Honolulu). Obviously as experienced traveler
NARRATOR (Human Element). A novelist who spends his time "revisiting places or pictures that are endeared to me by old associations"
NARRATOR (In a Strange Land). Of a "roving disposition" and one who travels to see people
NARRATOR (Jane). Lately returned to London from China
NARRATOR (Kite). Is writing an odd story told to him by Ned Preston; he has read a great deal of Freud's work
NARRATOR (Lady Habart). Observes Lady Habart to have been made up uncommonly well
NARRATOR (Lion's Skin). He suddenly enters the story in the midst of the fourth paragraph; an element of the story, rather than a particular character
NARRATOR (Lotus Eater). Curious to meet Thomas Wilson
NARRATOR (Louise). He had known Louise intimately for twenty-five years
NARRATOR (Luncheon). A writer; he catches sight of the woman at the play; has not seen her in twenty years
NARRATOR (Mabel). On a steamer from Pagan, Burma, to Mandalay
NARRATOR (Man from Glasgow). Is a visitor to Algeciras
NARRATOR (Man with a Conscience). English; is a visitor to St. Laurent de Maroni, the center of the French penal settlements in Guiana; a writer; his objective is to tell a story
NARRATOR (Man with a Scar). He frequents the bar of the Palace Hotel, Guatamala City
NARRATOR (Marriage of Convenience, 1906). A writer; in his youth sailed on a Spanish cargo boat from Cadiz to Valencia, Tarragona, and Tunis
NARRATOR (Marriage of Convenience, 1952). He sails from Bankok on a shabby, dirty little ship
NARRATOR (Masterson). Convinced to journey to Keng Tung because it offered "contentment"
NARRATOR (Mayhew). Fascinated by men "who take life in their own hands and. . .mould it to their own liking"
NARRATOR (Mirage). Had been wandering about the East for months before reaching Haiphong; he had been, in

1892, a student at the medical college, St. Thomas's Hospital, London

NARRATOR (Moon and Sixpence). A writer; as a young man in London had lived near Victoria Station; first met Charles Strickland's wife at an afternoon tea party at Rose Waterford's house; age twenty-three when he first met Charles Strickland; for a time a resident of Paris; was taken to Tahiti by the hazards of war

NARRATOR (Mr. Know-All). Shared a cabin with Max Kelada from San Francisco to Yokohama

NARRATOR (Outstation). Comments upon the financial ruin of Mr. Warburton

NARRATOR (Poet). Not really interested in celebrities

NARRATOR (Point of Honour). Writing a book about Spain in the Golden Age; he had read <u>El Medico de su Honora (The Physician of His Honour</u> [c.1629]), by Pedro Calderon de la Barca (1600-1681); as a young man, he had gone (after the Spanish-American War), to Seville to see the celebration of the Feast of Corpus Christi

NARRATOR (Point of Law). A writer; he makes his will whenever he feels more than usually poor

NARRATOR (Pool). Pipe smoker; "the link with the world" that Bertie Lawson "regretted"

NARRATOR (Portrait of a Gentleman). He had arrived at Seoul by rail from Peking; describes himself as "an ignorant person"

NARRATOR (Promise). Married to a very punctual woman; lunches with Elizabeth Vermont at Claridge's, London

NARRATOR (Punctiliousness of Don Sebastian). He is on an express train to Madrid; he gets off at Xiormonez

NARRATOR (Raw Material). Novelist; he is traveling from Haiphong to Peking on a French liner

NARRATOR (Razor's Edge). Discussed above under MAUGHAM

NARRATOR (Romantic Young Lady). He admits that old age sometimes provides an "opportunity of seeing. . . the outcome of certain events you had witnessed long ago"

NARRATOR (Round Dozen). Is a frequent visitor to Elsom; goes there two or three years after World War I to recuperate from an attack of influenza; is a novelist

NARRATOR (Salvatore). He had first known Salvatore as a boy of fifteen years of age

NARRATOR (Social Sense). He is a resident of Half Moon Street; invited to the Macdonalds' dinner party and

sits next to Mary Warton
NARRATOR (Spanish Priest). A frequenter of a tavern on Gibraltar; sits for hours, watching people's faces
NARRATOR (Straight Flush). Is traveling on board a ship from Hong-Kong; a writer
NARRATOR (String of Beads). A writer; dines with Laura and listens to her story
NARRATOR (Traveller in Romance). He is a passenger on the post chaise traveling from San Moritz into Italy
NARRATOR (Vessel of Wrath). He recommends the "Sailing Directions" published by the Hydrographic Department
NARRATOR (Virtue). Is obviously a person of leisure who enjoys food and a good cigar after meals; at one time a medical student; now a novelist
NARRATOR (Voice of the Turtle). A writer who accepts an invitation to a sherry party in Bloomsbury, London
NARRATOR (Wash-Tub). Will spend a few days at Positano
NARRATOR (Woman of Fifty). Over sixty-five years of age and friend of Wyman Hold; he had known Laura Greene twenty-five years ago
NARRATOR'S ACQUAINTANCE (Man with a Conscience). Accompanies the Narrator on a walk in St. Laurent de Maroni
NARRATORS' ACQUAINTANCE (Man with the Scar). He drinks martinis with the Narrator at the bar of the Palace Hotel, Guatamala City; Guatamaltecan; speaks Spanish
NARRATOR'S WIFE (Promise). She is very punctual; late for lunch at Claridge's, London
NATIVE (Explorer [novel]). From the interior of British East Africa; is shouting and jostling on the jetty at Mombassa
NATIVE (Narrow Corner). Of Tanaka; walks past the store of Kim Chang, carrying sugar cane
NATIVE DOCTOR (Honolulu). A little old man; he is thin, wrinkled, and totally bald; bright eyes; is bowed and gnarled like an old tree
NATIVE MESSENGER (Explorer [play]). Is sent to Alec Mac Kenzie by Mindabi
NATIVE WOMAN (Door of Opportunity). Lived with Prynne and bore him two children; is shy, pretty, and small
NATIVE WOMAN (Narrow Corner). At the hotel on Kanda; is on the veranda
NATIVES (Explorer [novel]). Are with Alec MacKenzie's latest African expedition; struck up a strange and

Characters

musical chant as they left the camp

NATIVES (Explorer [novel]). Men and women; at the camp of Alec MacKenzie's expedition; they streamed in with baskets of grain, flour, and potatoes, as well as with chickens, and pots of honey

NATIVES (Explorer [novel/play]). On Alec MacKenzie's expedition against the slave traders; refer to Alec as "Thunder and Lightning"

NATIVES (Explorer [play]). Are with Alec MacKenzie's African expedition; twenty of them are badly wounded after the last Arab attack

NATIVES (Magician). In Asia; treated overbearingly by Oliver Haddo

NATIVES (Narrow Corner). Three or four of Dr. Saunders' patients at Takana; wanted to consult with Saunders

NAVARRE, King of (Then and Now). The brother-in-law of Caesar Borgia; in a war with his barons, he placed Borgia in command of his army

NEAPOLITAN PRINCE (Voice of the Turtle). Is one of the former husbands of La Folterona

NEGRO (Christmas Holiday). At the Serail, Paris; is in Turkish dress; opens the door for Charley Mason and Simon Fenimore

NEGROES (Christmas Holiday). Two of them seen at Paris; dark faces, pinched with cold; nothing in the world for them to do but wait

NEIGHBOR (Bad Example). A friend of Amy Clayton; visits with Amy during James Clayton's illness

NEIGHBORS (Man of Honour). Of Basil and Jenny Kent; know that the Kents have bills with the tradesmen

NEIGHBORS (Merry-Go-Round). Of Basil and Jenny Kent, in Barnes; Basil loathed them, believing that they and Jenny discussed him; led narrow lives; they know that Basil has accumulated bills with the local tradesmen

NEIGHBORS (Spanish Priest). Of Vicente Oria y Mazallon; they could not tell the English man anything about Don Vicente except hid name

NEILSON (Red). Swedish; a small gray beard; thin face; speaks English with a slight accent; middle aged; is sick, weak, ugly; falls in love with Sally, and she eventually becomes his wife

NELSON (Pool). He is the supercargo of the ship Manoa

NELSON, Robert (Razor's Edge). A physician and an old

village friend of Lawrence Darrell's father; resides in Marvin; is a bachelor who raised Larry after the death of his father; remains his guardian; tall and stout; red face; middle aged; he invents gadgets for planes; drinks; is an agnostic who attended church to satisfy his patients; also sent young Larry to Sunday school for the very same reason; he died fairly soon after the marriage of Gray Maturin and Isabel Bradley

NEPHEW (Happy Couple). Of Miss Wingford; he had been told by the maid that his aunt had been poisoned

NEPHEW (Noble Spaniard). Of Sebastian Proudfoot; is in strained circumstances

NEPHEW (Painted Veil). Of Sister St. Joseph; son of her brother; only a child when his aunt left France for China; promised to have a fist that could fell an ox

NEPHEWS (Theatre). Dolly De Vries' only relatives; live in South Africa

NESBIT, Norah (Of Human Bondage). Has rooms at Vincent Square, London; age twenty-five; small; pleasant and ugly face; bright eyes; high cheekbones; large mouth; white skin; red cheeks; has thick black hair and eyebrows is separated from her husband; one child; wrote penny novelettes under the name of "Courtenay Paget"; also engaged in part-time acting

NEVILLE, Jasper (Jack Straw). Father of Rosie Abbott

NEWCOMER (Pool). Drinks Scotch with Lawson at the bar

NEWHAVEN, Lady Florence ((Merry-Go-Round). Will marry Collinson Farley, the rector of All Soul's, London, at the end of the season

NEWS AGENT (Explorer [novel]). He sends papers to Lady Alice Kelsey

NEWSBOYS (Mrs. Dot). On Grafton Street, London; calling out the news of the catastrophe in India and the death of Lord Hollington

NEWSMITH, General (Hero). He showed Frances Parsons his stamp collection (she thought it inferior to her husband's); he had lived for several years on Mauritius

NEWSON (Of Human Bondage). Is a medical student at St. Luke's Hospital, London; Philip Carey's partner at the dissecting table; much at home with his subject

NEWSPAPER BOY (Mrs. Craddock). At the railway station, Blackstable, in Kent; Edward Craddock buys Punch and Sketch from him

NEWSPAPER MAGNATE (Razor's Edge). Is the father of Paul Barton's wife; British; was elevated to the peerage

NEWSPAPER PROPRIETOR (Christmas Holiday). Very rich; is prepared to give a brilliant young man a chance; he is impressed by Simon Fenimore

NEWTON, Allgood (Cakes and Ale). Is The best critic in England; large, fat, and blond; a fleshy, white face; pale blue eyes; graying fair hair

NICCOLINI, Masters (In a Strange Land). The two sons of Signor Niccolini and a Greek who worked at the hotel

NICCOLINI, Signor (In a Strange Land). A former chef to Lord Ormskirk; was very handsome; Signora Niccolini's husband; he has been dead for the past fifteen years

NICCOLINI, Signora (In a Strange Land). Is an English woman, with a trace of a cockney accent; maiden name Parker; was formerly in the service of the late Lord Ormskirk; Signor Niccolini's widow; proprietor of the hotel in a little town in Asia Minor; elderly; small and stout; spoke fluent Turkish

NICHOLE (Perfect Gentleman). Monsieur Jordain's servant girl; from the country; possessed of a sharp tongue

NICHOLS, Captain (Moon and Sixpence). He approaches the Narrator at his hotel on Tahiti to talk about Charles Strickland, whom he said he had met at the Aisle de Nuit, Marseilles; an outrageous liar; English; lean, of average height; gray hair cut short and a stubbly gray moustache; his deeply lined face burned brown; small, blue, shifty eyes; with broken and discolored teeth; suffered from dyspepsia; the Narrator does not believe a word of his story

NICHOLS, Miss (Moon and Sixpence). She is Captain and Mrs. Nichols' daughter; age seven; pale faced; sullen

NICHOLS, Mrs. (Moon and Sixpence). The wife of Captain Nichols; daughter of a policeman; age twenty-eight; been married to Nichols for eight years; plain face; narrow lips; tight skin, tight hair, and tight smile

NICHOLS, Mrs. (Narrow Corner). The wife of Captain Tom Nichols; daughter of a Liverpool draper; had to go into service at Sydney because her husband could not find work; short and stout; a flat, pasty face; somewhat protruding eyes, round and shining like buttons; eventually catches up with her husband at Singapore

NICHOLS, Tom (Narrow Corner). English captain; husband

of Mrs. Nichols; is middle aged; sallow, lined face; white hair and the scrub of a white moustache; middle height; spare; hideously decayed teeth; cunning and restless eyes, small and pale; he claims to have been raised a Baptist; he has been sailing the Archipelago for thirty years; a highly competent sailor; claims that he has known Kim Ching for twenty years; he had been a heavy drinker, but now suffers from dyspepsia; he captained a shabby little pearling lugger, the Fenton; had been fired by Kim Ching, then he lost his certificate over trouble with an insurance company; has been married for twenty-five years; one daughter

NICI, Messer (Then and Now). Name of the character in Machiavelli's play; he represents Bartolomeo Martelli

NICOLO (Making of a Saint). A young man at the gathering at Palazzo Orsi; believes swords of Matteo d'Orsi and Filippo Brandolini may not prove useful at Forli

NIECE (Merry-Go-Round). Of Elizabeth Dwarris; her illness forced Elizabeth to solitude in March and April

NIECES (Explorer [play]). Two of them; of Dick Lomas; desperately plain; with red noses; Dick's only living relatives

NIECES (Happy Couple). Two of them; of Miss Wingford; told by the maid that their aunt had been poisoned

NIGGERS (Liza of Lambeth). Two of then; in front of the Westminster theatre; sang, danced, and made faces; then moved to the pit doors

NIGHT PORTER (Ashenden/Miss King). At the Geneva hotel; discovers Miss King in her room following her stroke

NIGHT PORTER (Of Human Bondage). At St. Luke's Hospital in London; he awoke Philip Carey to inform him of a woman in labor

NIGHT PORTER (Treasure). Is on duty at the flats where Richard Harenger lives; receives an icy glance from Harenger on the elevator

NIGHT PORTER (Up at the Villa). At Rowley Flint's hotel in the town; he takes Mary Panton's call and puts it through to Rowley's room

NIGHT WATCHMAN (Christmas Holiday). At Charley Mason's hotel off the Rue de Rennes, Paris; sleepy; he opens the door for Charley and Lydia Berger and takes them upstairs in the lift

NINA (Then and Now). A maid in the house of Bartolomeo

Martelli; serves wine and a dish of sweetmeats to the assembled guests

NINA (Up in the Villa). Is Mary Panton's Italian maid; married to Ciro; a young woman who liked to gossip

NIXON, Albert (Of Human Bondage). He is William Carey's family lawyer; resident of London; he and William co-executors for the late Henry Carey's estate; discourages Philip Carey from entering law; is a sportsman; Philip recommends Mildred Rogers to him after she separates from Emil Miller; he disapproves of Philip

NON-COMMISSIONED OFFICER (Ashenden). Is at Colonel R's headquarters in London; opens the door for Ashenden

NORTON (Of Human Bondage). Is a pupil at King's School, Tercanbury; could not attend Oxford unless he won a scholarship

NOVELIST (Bishop's Apron). At Lady Hollington's dinner party; he entertained Lady Patricia Stonehenge with his theories upon art and literature

NOVELLI, Ermeto (Circle). The great Italian tragedian; told Lady Catherine Champion-Cheney that he had never seen such a Lady Teazle (School for Scandal) as she

NOVEMALI, Edna (Razor's Edge). An American of immense wealth; the widow of Prince Novemali; age sixty; the fascists drove her out of Italy, and thus she built a Florentine villa behind Cannes; a malicious tongue; stupid; entertained extravagantly; has not invited aged and dying Elliott Templeton to her fancy dress party intended for the night of the August full moon

NOVEMALI, Prince (Razor's Edge). The deceased husband of Edna Novemali; the head of a great family that is descended from a condottiere (mercenary)

NOVICE (Catalina). At the Dominican convent; informs Father Vergara that the Bishop is ready to see him

NOVICE (Faith). He is at the monastery of San Luciso; a youth; hurried away from Brother Jasper without even responding to the latter's question

NOVICE (Razor's Edge). At the Benedictine monastery at Alsace; he stood near the refectory door, and in a monotone read from an edifying work

NUN #1 (Catalina). Of the Carmelite Convent; asserted that Elias, the founder of the order, appeared to her in her cell; she receives a whipping by the prioress

NUN #2 (Catalina). A member of the Carmelite Convent of

the Incarnation; intimate friend of Maria Perez Orta;
Maria tells her Catalina's experience with the Woman
NUN #3 (Catalina). A native of Toledo; informed Beatriz
of a Greek in Toledo who painted pictures exalting
the devotion of worshipers
NUN #4 *Catalina). Is told by Beatriz to bring Catalina
NUN #5 (Catalina). She waits with Catalina in the Lady
Chapel preparatory to seeing the Bishop of Segovia
NUN #6 (Catalina). Excitedly tells Catalina that the
Bishop of Segovia will attempt to cure her affliction
NUN #7 (Catalina). Tells Catalina how much all of the
nuns at the convent love her and hope that she will
remain with them
NUNS (Catalina). Two of them; are sent by Dona Beatriz
to Maria Perez's house to learn of the specifics of
Catalina's healing
NUNS (Painted Veil). Initially, seven of them; French;
at the French convent at Mei-tan-fu; doing what they
can for those stricken by cholera; four died, to be
replaced by others from Canton; six of them alive
when the Fanes arrive; have an unbounded admiration
for Walter Fane
NUNS (Painted Veil). From Canton; two of them; they are
expected to come to the French convent at Mei-tan-fu
NURSE (Circle). Of young Arnold Champion-Cheney; Lady
Catherine Champion-Cheney thought that she drank
NURSE (French Joe). She sat at the end of French Joe's
hospital bed as he told his story to the Narrator
NURSE (Happy Couple, 1908, 1952). Tends to the Craigs'
infant
NURSE (Home and Beauty). The Nannie to William Lowndes
and Frederick Cardew; she wears a neat gray uniform
NURSE (Hour Before the Dawn). At London; is too busy to
attend the pregnant woman living in the Clarks' house
NURSE (Loaves and Fishes). To young Theodore and Sophia
Spratte; an excellent judge of character; a woman of
no education
NURSE (Love in a Cottage). She succeeds Sybil Bruce in
tending to Mrs. Owen Butterfield at Hotel Splendide
NURSE (Mrs. Craddock). Arrives at Court Leys to tend to
Bertha Craddock prior to her delivery; old; had been
tending to the neighborhood gentry for twenty years
NURSE (Moon and Sixpence). At the Paris hospital; tells

Characters

the Narrator and Dirk Stroeve that Blanche Stroeve's condition has improved

NURSE #1 (Of Human Bondage). Is at the Bedside of Mrs. Carey (Philip's mother)

NURSE #2 (Of Human Bondage). Tends to Mildred Rogers after the birth of her daughter

NURSE #3 (Of Human Bondage). Is at St. Luke's Hospital, London; she expresses her approval of Philip Carey's skill in bandaging

NURSE #4 (Of Human Bondage). On night duty with Philip Carey at St. Luke's Hospital, London; gray haired; is masculine in appearance; had been night nurse in the casualty department for twenty years; she referred to every dresser as "Mr. Brown"

NURSE (Painted Veil). A type imagined by Kitty Garstin; in a hospital at Hong Kong; she is the daughter of a clergyman; she appears dull, plain, flat-footed, and strenuous; such a wife would suit Walter Fane nicely

NURSE #1 (Razor's Edge). Is sent by Elliott Templeton's doctor from the English hospital between Nice and Beaulieu to attend the unconscious Elliott on Antibes

NURSE #2 (Razor's Edge). At a village near Saville; she takes care of the baby of Girl #2 and Paco

NURSE (Sanatorium). Helps Ashenden dress; takes him to the sanatorium veranda; then introduces him to McLeod

NURSE (Smith). For Cynthia and Otto Rosenberg's baby

NURSES (Bishop's Apron). In Kensington Gardens, London; they gossiped idly

NURSES (Hour Before the Dawn). At the hospital in York; fuss over Ian Foster as though he were a hero; ask him about his bowels

NURSES (Magician). At the Luxembourg Gardens in Paris; some wear the white caps of their native province; others with satin streamers of the nounou; marched by sedately in pairs, wheeling perambulators and talking

NURSES (Sacred Flame). Three or four of them; tended to Maurice Tabret before the arrival of Nurse Wayland; all more or less odious

NURSES (Sanitorium). Tend to Ashenden at the sanatorium

O

OAKLAND, Harry (Creative Impulse). A versatile critic;

one of Mrs. Forrester's staunchest admirers; refined and beautiful features; not yet thirty years of age
OAKLEY (Door of Opportunity). He is Prynne's assistant manager; attacked by the Chinese coolies; small, dark skinned native; flattened features; thick coarse hair
OAKLEY, Mr. (Treasure). He telephones Richard Harenger, inviting him to a cocktail party at the Savoy, London
O'BRIEN, Mr. (Magician). Irish painter at Paris; tall, dark; strongly marked features; untidy hair; a ragged black moustache; a failure as an artist; can forgive no one who is unsuccessful; speaks French perfectly
OBU, Tom (Narrow Corner). A Black crew member aboard Captain Nichols' lugger; tall; solid build; very gray and crisp curly hair; a Torres Straits islander; he served as cook and steward
O'CONNOR, Miss #1 (Of Human Bondage). Sister of Miss O'Connor #2; guest at a tennis party at the vicarage at Blackstable, Kent; the daughter of a retired major in an Indian regiment; pretty; age nineteen or twenty
O'CONNOR, Miss #2 (Of Human Bondage). Sister of Miss O'Connor #1; guest at a tennis party at the vicarage at Blackstable, Kent; daughter of a retired major in an Indian regiment; pretty; age seventeen or eighteen
ODETTE (Painted Veil). Mother Superior of the French Convent at Mei-tan-fu; is her parents' only daughter; age between forty and fifty; very few wrinkles on her smooth, pale face; a dignified bearing; strong and beautiful hands; long face; large mouth; large, even teeth; delicate and sensitive nose; thin black brows; large, black, compelling eyes; her face intense and tragic; a deep, low, and controlled voice; an air of authority tempered by Christian charity; a remarkable woman; she belongs to one of the greatest families in France; impossible to ask her an indiscrete question
ODETTE (Razor's Edge). Daughter of Suzanne Rouvier and Marcel; rosy, fair-haired, blue-eyed; is left in the care of Suzanne's mother at Anjou; Achille Gauvain to see that she is sent to a convent for good education and then trained to earn a living as a typist and stenographer; at age sixteen, has neither the talent to be an actress nor the temperament to be a whore
O'DONNEL, Robert (Irish Gentleman). Age twenty-eight; handsome; florid complexion; white teeth; bold eyes;

hair disordered; abundant whiskers; travels through Germany in pursuit of artistic emotion; maintains a journal; he had taught Latin, acted, written for booksellers, and gambled; stops Princess Mary's runaway horse; revives her after she faints in his arms

O'DONNELL, Edward (Tenth Man). He is age twenty-three; insignificant, amiable, and good looking; engaged to Anne Etchingham; educated at Harrow; failed entrance into the army; he becomes a lackey for George Winter

O'FARRELL, Dr. (Tenth Man). He attends to Lord Francis Etchingham during his attack of gout

O'FARRELL, Penelope (Penelope). Wife of five years of Dr. Richard O'Farrell; the only child of Isabel and Charles Golightly; she wants a divorce from Dickie

O'FARRELL, Dr. Richard (Penelope). Is more familiarly known as Dickie; husband, of five years, of Penelope O'Farrell; age thirty-five; is a physician of modest income; he is having an affair with Ada Fergusson

OFFICER (Human Element). Young and smart; in the lounge of the Hotel Plaza, Rome, at tea time, with a woman

OFFICER (Irish Gentleman). At the frontier; he examines Robert O'Donnel's passport and looks at him with suspicion; refuses to let him leave Wartburg-Hochstein

OFFICER (Man with the Scar). In charge of the execution of the General and four others

OFFICER #1 (Painted Veil). At Mei-tan-fu; Colonel Yu shot him because he refused to enter the house of a person dead from the cholera

OFFICER #2 (Painted Veil). He is sent by Colonel Yu to Waddington, to inform him of Walter Fane's illness

OFFICER #3 (Painted Veil). At Mei-tan-fu; he stood by motionless at the foot of Walter Fane's draped pallet

OFFICER #1 (Then and Now). Of Caesar Borgia's forces; he escorts Niccolo Machiavelli to see Caesar Borgia

OFFICER #2 (Then and Now). Ushered Niccolo Machiavelli into the room, at the Sinigaglia palace, for an audience with Caesar Borgia

OFFICER #3 (Then and Now). He informs Agapito da Amalia and Caesar Borgia that two Gascon soldiers have been caught looting

OFFICERS (Hero). Under the command of Colonel Richmond Parsons in India; looked at their colonel with bitter contempt and anger, because he had forced them to

retire before the enemy
OFFICERS (Human Element). Several of them; accompany the Governor of Rhodes to Betty Weldon-Burns' dinner party; smart in their uniforms, attentive to Betty; the young ones callow; the older ones fat and bald
OFFICERS (Making of a Saint). Command the soldiers in the piazza at Forli
OFFICERS (Narrow Corner). Off of the Dutch ship from Merauke to Takana; drank beer at Kim Ching's store
OFFICIAL (Closed Shop). He conducts the three bordello owners to the audience chamber of the President
OHLSON, Fred (Rain). A Danish trader and a drunkard
OLD CRONE (Razor's Edge). At the Brasserie Graf, Avenue de Clichy, in Paris; she offered newspapers for sale
OLD FAT WOMAN (Ashenden/Mr. Harrington's Washing). Lies on top of J.Q. Harrington when snipers fire at the Petrograd tram
OLD LADY (P.&O.). Rheumatic; joins with Mrs. Hamlyn in casting her vote against the Christmas Eve ball
OLD MAID (Mirage). Known by the Narrator in his youth; she was "a relic of the Victorian age"; wore black silk mittens; she had suffered terribly in her youth
OLD MAN (Man from Glasgow). He and his wife cared for the company estate at San Lorenzo and looked after Robert Morrison
OLD WOMAN #1 (Ashenden/Mr. Harrington's Washing). She was attacked by two soldiers on a Petrograd sidewalk
OLD WOMAN #2 (Ashenden/Mr. Harrington's Washing). The Petrograd laundress who reluctantly allowed J.Q. Harrington to take his washing
OLD WOMAN (Mirage). Mother of Grosely's wife; carries tray, opium, and opium pipe to Grosely and his wife
OLDHAM, Robert (Unattainable). A lawyer; he has been in love with Caroline Ashley for the past ten years, but does not want to marry her; age forty-five; tall and handsome; inclined to stoutness
OLIPHANT, Mary (Razor's Edge). Owner of Raney Castle; one of Louisa Bradley's most intimate friends; her residence had been decorated by Gregory Brabizon
OLIVA, Fabio (Making of a Saint). The son of Bartolomeo Moratini; is related to the Orsi on his mother's side
O'MALLEY (Ashenden/His Excellency). A talented Irish portrait painter and a member of the Royal Academy; a

Characters

friend of Brown, when both were young and in Paris
O'MARA, Sir Gerald (Lady Frederick). Brother of Lady Frederick Berolles; was educated at Trinity College, Dublin; age twenty-six; handsome and penniless; is a gambler; he owes Captain Montgomerie nine hundred pounds; he has proposed marriage to Rose Carlisle
O'MARA, Mrs. (Lady Frederick). Mother of Lady Frederick Berolles and Sir Gerald O'Mara; she thought that her daughter's marriage to Lord Frederick Berolles had been a good match
ONG CHI SENG (Letter [play]). Serves as Howard Joyce's confidential clerk; a Cantonese; is small and trimly built; holds a degree in law from the University of Hong Kong; has learned English as a foreign language, and he speaks it perfectly; he serves as the contact between Joyce and the Chinese woman; is a disciple of the late Herbert Spencer (1820-1903); influenced by Friedrich Wilhelm Nietzsche (1844-1900), George Bernard Shaw (1856-1950), and H.G. Wells (1866-1946)
ONG CHI SENG (Letter [story]). A Cantonese; studied law at Gray's Inn, London; is spending a year or two with Ripley, Joyce, and Nailor, Singapore, in preparation for his private law practice; speaks precise English; is industrious, obliging, and of exemplary character
OPERATOR (Magician). Is a French surgeon at the Hotel Dieu, Paris; sought to dazzle Arthur Burdon by feats that savored almost of legerdemain; his methods contained a hint of charlatanry; he demonstrated an audacious sureness of hand
OPPRESSED THRONGS (Magician). In Margaret Dauncey's vision; innumerable as the sands of the sea; faces are thin, earthy, and cavernous from disease; their eyes terribly dull with despair; English and French
ORCHARDSON, Sir William Quiller (Bishop's Apron). The Scottish portrait painter (1831-1910); had painted a portrait of Canon Theodore Spratte, which the latter gave to his wife on their tenth wedding anniversary
ORDELAFFI, Count (Making of a Saint). Formerly Lord of Forli; was ousted by Checco d'Orsi and succeeded by Girolamo Riario
ORDERLIES (Painted Veil). Three or four of them; they stand by Walter Fane's pallet
ORDERLY (Ashenden/Giulia Lazzari). Escorts Ashenden to

Colonel R's room in the Hotel Lotti, at Paris; he is a sub-lieutenant and a civilian with a temporary commission; his age in the early thirties

ORDERLY (Back of Beyond). In the employ of George Moon; informs Moon of a visitor

ORDERLY (Door of Opportunity). He is in service to the Governor of Singapore

ORGAN GRINDER (Liza of Lambeth). Plays on Vere Street, in Lambeth; an Italian; a shock of black hair and a ferocious moustache

ORGANIST (Mrs. Craddock). At Leanham church, Kent; made horrid sounds

ORGANIST (Verger). At St. Peter's, Neville Square; had gotten into trouble

ORIA Y MAZALLON, Vicente (Spanish Priest). The Spanish priest; unattached to any diocese; age sixty; tall; with grizzled hair and a three days' growth of white beard; a long, lean face; yellow skin, as though he suffered from chronic jaundice; is exceedingly thin; great, sharp bones; sallow cheeks; lives in Granada; discovers an old Roman mine near Granada and brings a sample of the ore to the English man at the mine in Seville; he wants half of everything that the English man can get from the mine; three years later, the English man finds him dead in a cave; is shriveled like a mummy, merely a skeleton of skin and bones

ORMONDE, Lady (Casual Affair). Wife of the Governor of the Federated Malayan States; she is a terrible snob

ORMONDE, Lord (Casual Affair). He is Governor of the Federated Malayan States

ORMSKIRK, Lady (In a Strange Land). The wife of Lord Ormskirk; Signora Niccolini served as her lady's-maid

ORMSKIRK, Lady (Outstation). The birth announcement of her son noticed by Warburton on pages of the Times

ORMSKIRK, Lord (In a Strange Land). Former employer of Signor and Signora Niccolini; always traveled with a hot water bottle

ORPHANS (Painted Veil). Living at the French convent at Mei-tan-fu; they scrub the floors of the convent

ORSINI, Cardinal (Then and Now). The brother of Pagolo Orsini; he accompanied his brother to the meeting of Caesar Borgia's captains at La Magione, near Perugia; was imprisoned and died at the Castle of San Angelo

Characters

ORSINI, Chevalier (Then and Now). He is a bastard in the family in the service of Caesar Borgia; reported from Siena that the leaders of the conspiracy wished to re-enter Borgia's service

ORSINI, Pagolo (Then and Now). A mercenary captain in the service of Caesar Borgia; head of the Roman house of Orsini; he is vain, loquacious, effeminate, and silly; middle aged, plump, and baldish; round, smooth face; strangled by Michelotto

ORTA, Maria Perez (Catalina). Catalina's mother; two of her children had died before the birth of Catalina; pious; she lives with her daughter and her brother, Domingo Perez; supports herself and her daughter by doing difficult needle work for Church ceremonies; once pretty, but now, at middle age, has grown stout

ORTA, Pedro (Catalina). Catalina's father; had sailed for the Americas to make his fortune soon after the birth of Catalina; he has not been heard from since

ORTA Y PEREZ, Maria de los Dolores Catalina (Catalina). Is crippled with paralysis; she cannot walk without a crutch; age sixteen; very beautiful; is tall for her age; small hands and feet; large, dark, shining eyes; black, naturally curly hair that reached well below her waist; brown, soft skin; rosy cheeks and a red moist mouth; taught to read and write by her uncle, Domingo Perez; a quick memory; eventually becomes a famous actress; in her later years described (by the Dutch traveler) as corpulent and several times a grandmother, but yet could still portray on the stage a girl of sixteen

ORTH, Dr. Egon (Ashenden/Mr/ Harrington's Washing). The chief among the three Czechs sent to Russia to assist Ashenden in his mission; minister of a church in the Midwestern Untied States; a doctor of divinity; tall; small gray beard; merry twinkle in his eye and a dry humor; speaks fluent Russian

OSBORNE, Bernal (Circle). His picture appears in an old photograph album owned by Clive Champion-Cheney; the wittiest man Clive had ever known

OSMAN PASHA (Caesar's Wife). He is a swarthy, bearded Oriental; obese, elderly, and dignified; an official in the Khedival service; speaks only French; although he speaks and understands English, he will not utter a word unless Lady Violet Little, whom he respectfully admires, speaks it; a Muslim of the old school, with a bitter hatred of the English; once tried to poison Sir Arthur Little, and has never forgiven him for recovering; had one of his wives beaten to death and thrown into the Nile; he wants to establish a technical college in Cairo; Sir Arthur Little had recommended that he be appointed minister of education; confined to his country estate for his part in a plot to kill Sir Arthur Little

OSTLER (Making of a Saint). He takes care of Filippo Brandolini's horse at an inn a half-day's ride from Citta di Castello

OTTER, Lucy (Of Human Bondage). She is the massiere of Amitrano art school, Paris, where she is in charge of the common fund; was recommended to Philip Carey by Hayward; an insignificant woman, thirty years of age; separated from her husband; had been studying art for three years; is meek, mediocre, and self-satisfied

OUSLEY-FARROWHAM, Daisy (Daisy). See Daisy GRIFFITH

OUSLEY-FARROWHAM, Sir Herbert (Daisy). Staying at the George in Tercanbury, Kent; age twenty-nine; he has a house in Cavendish Square, London; he marries Daisy Griffith; bestows an allowance of five pounds a week upon the Griffiths

OUTRIDERS (Pro Patria). Clad in scarlet; are employed by John Porter-Smith to help in his election campaign

OUVREUSES (Razor's Edge). Sour-faced and unwashed women at the Theatre Francaise; they show patrons to their seats and, with domineering looks, await their tips

OVERSEER'S DAUGHTER (Narrow Corner). On Kanda; a friend of Louise Frith since childhood; is the same age as Louise; married for four years; she has three babies

OWEN, Mrs. (Of Human Bondage). Owner of the house where Mildred Rogers plans to undergo her confinement; she recommended a doctor to Mildred

P

PACO (Razor's Edge). Lover of Girl #2 and the father of their baby; completes his military service in Spanish Morocco; then returns to Cadiz to live with Girl #2

PADRE (Door of Opportunity). Sees the Torels off from

Characters

Singapore
PADRE (Unknown). Of John Wharton's regiment; told John that the Almighty meant not one so much able to do all things, but one being powerful over all things
PADRE'S WIFE (Door of Opportunity). Invites the Torels to stay with her at Port Wallace while they await the steamer; she and her husband see the Torels off from Singapore
PAGE (Cakes and Ale). At Alroy Kear's club, St. James Street, London
PAGE (Making of a Saint). At Filippo Brandolini's house in Citta di Castello; he whispers timidly to Filippo that Fabio is in the chapel
PAGE (Punctiliousness of Don Sebastian). Asleep outside Don Sebastian's door; awakened by his master and told to bring a light
PAGE (Then and Now). Accidentally spilled some wine as he carried it to Ramiro de Lorqua; the latter had him thrown into the fire and burnt alive
PAGE-BOY (Ashenden/Miss King). Is at Ashenden's Geneva hotel; brings a note from a lady staying at the hotel
PAGE-BOY (Making of a Saint). At the gathering at the Piazza Orsi; he tells Claudia Piacentini that her husband wants her to come to him
PAGE-BOY (Treasure). He is at Richard Herenger's club; informs Herenger of a call from his flat indicating that he had left without his keys
PAGET, Courtenay (Of Human Bondage). The pen name under which Nora Nesbit wrote penny novelettes
PAGLIANINO (Making of a Saint). A devoted adherent to the house of Orsi; he will gladly join the conspiracy to assassinate Girolamo Riario
PAINTER (Alien Corn). Friend of George Bland at Munich
PAINTER (Magician). At the Luxembourg Gardens, Paris; sketching with half-frozen fingers
PAINTER (Moon and Sixpence). He is at the Villa Medici; referred to Dirk Stroeve as "Le Maitre de la Boite a Chocolats"
PAINTER (Mrs. Craddock). He had said that Bertha Ley's skin had in it "all the colours of the setting sun, of the setting sun at its borders, where the splendour mingles with the sky"
PAINTER (Of Human Bondage). From Brittany; formerly a

stock broker, with a wife, family, and large income; seen as a queer fellow; no one but Clutton, who had been greatly influenced by his work, had ever heard of him; goes to Tahiti

PAINTERS (Magician). English or American; a small party of them; a room with three tables at the Chien Noir, Paris, always reserved for them

PAINTERS (Moon and Sixpence). Are colleagues of Dirk Stroeve at Italy and Paris; they demonstrate outward contempt for his work, but borrow (or take) his money

PALACE, Mrs. (Flotsam and Jetsam). The wife of Victor Palace; played the lead roles in his acting company

PALACE, Victor (Flotsam and Jetsam). The manager of a London acting company traveling to Egypt, India, the Malay States, China, and Australia; he employs Vesta Blaise (eventually to be Mrs. Grange) for minor roles

PALMER, Rev, Archibald (Love in a Cottage). An English clergyman; he and his wife are guests at the Hotel Splendide at Varenna, on Lake Como; he attempts to borrow money from Sybil Bruce, but she refuses him

PALMER, Mrs. (Bad Example). A resident of No. 17 Adonis Road, Camberwell; is, supposedly, a terrible drinker

PALMER, Mrs. (Love in a Cottage). The wife of Archibald Palmer

PALMERS (Virtue). Mr. and Mrs.; friends of Morton whom the Narrator had met at Sarawak; Mrs. Palmer's mother taken ill in Scotland

PAN (Magician). In Margaret Dauncey's vision; playing on his pipe; has a horrible face and lecherous eyes; then changes to a lovely youth, titanic but sublime

PANSECCHI, Lodovico (Making of a Saint). A soldier in the service of Girolamo Riario; had not been paid for four years; formerly in pay of the Duke of Calabria; joins the conspiracy to assassinate Girolamo Riario

PANTON, Mary (Up at the Villa). Leased the Florentine villa from the impoverished descendants of the noble Florentine; age thirty; with dark, rich, golden hair; large, deep brown eyes; pale golden skin; initially, after the death of her husband, she had no intention of ever hazarding again the risks of wedlock; her father had been in the Indian civil service; she had been, before marriage, to Matthew Panton, an actress

PANTON, Matthew (Up at the Villa). The husband of Mary

Characters   319

   Panton; killed a year ago in an automobile accident;
   a gambler and a drunkard; had squandered his fortune
PAPER BOYS (Liza of Lambeth). They are in front of the
   Westminster theatre; offer Tit-Bits (1881-1984) and
   extra specials
PAPERLEIGH, Lady (Merry-Go-Round). Has a box for The
   Bells of Petersburg, and has asked Grace Castillyon
   to bring Reggie Barlow-Bassett
PARACELSUS, Philippus Aureolus (Magician). A Swiss-born
   alchemist and physician (1493-1541); Dr. Porhoet be-
   ieves him to have been the most interesting of all of
   the alchemists; belonged to the celebrated family of
   Bombast, called Hohenheim after their ancient residence near Stuttgart; he traveled in Germany, France,
   Italy, the Netherlands, Denmark, Sweden, Russia, and
   India; taken prisoner by the Tartars and brought to
   the Great Khan; served as a surgeon in the imperial
   Italian army; vain, ostentatious, intemperate, and
   boastful; wrote in German instead of Latin; died as
   the result of a tavern brawl and buried in Salzburg
PARENTS (Fortunate Painter). Of Rosie; want her to end
   her relationship with Charlie Bartle; they say there
   is not a chance of Charlie ever earning any money
PARENTS (Painted Veil). Of Sister Francis Xavier; they
   are fisher folk, in Brittany
PARISHIONER (Merry-Go-Round). Of Rev. Algernon Langton
   at Portsmouth; Algernon advised him to marry a woman
   whom he had gotten pregnant; he cut his wife's throat
   six months after their marriage; he was duly hanged
PARKER (In a Strange Land). See under Signora NICCOLINI
PARKER (Mrs. Craddock). The Craddocks' footman at Court
   Leys, Blackstable, Kent
PARKER, George (Yellow Streak). Educated at Winchester;
   a member of Izzart's regiment
PARKER, Mrs. (Letter [play]). Matron of the prison at
   Singapore; stout, middle aged; English; overly chatty
PARKER-JENNINGS, Ethel (Jack Straw). Daughter of Maria
   and Robert Parker-Jennings and sister of Vincent; she
   is charming and pretty
PARKER-JENNINGS, Maria (Jack Straw). The wife of Robert
   Parker-Jennings; mother of Ethel and Vincent; claims
   her name to be Marion; is originally from Brixton;
   is growing exclusive; a determined appearance; vulgar

PARKER-JENNINGS, Robert (Jack Straw). Husband of Maria Parker-Jennings; father of Ethel and Vincent; small and stout; common and self-assertive; originally from Brixton; as shrewd a man as one would meet between Park Lane and Jerusalem; the head of Jennings' Patent Hardware; worth eighty thousand pounds per year; has provided books for Andrew Carnegie's free libraries

PARKER-JENNINGS, Vincent (Jack Straw). Son of Maria and Robert Parker-Jennings, and brother of Ethel; he is showy and aggressive; he has been educated at Oxford

PARKLEIGH, Sir Robert (Bishop's Apron). Was an eminent lawyer; had claim upon the office of Lord Chancellor; had held office in a previous government, where he waived his right to promotion to achieve greater end; was a person of vigorous understanding; learned and urbane; from a great family

PARLIAMENTARIAN (Bishop's Apron). In the House of Lords and mumbling away in his beard

PARLIAMENTARIAN (Lord Mountdrago). Labour Member; observes that Owen Griffiths looks "pretty dicky today"

PARLIAMENTARIANS (Bishop's Apron). Seen in the House of Lords; twenty old buffers lying about on red benches; half of them asleep

PARLIAMENTARY SECRETARY (Human Element). A character in Humphrey Carruthers' "Week End"; worked for a cabinet minister; a young man

PARLOUR MAID (Cakes and Ale). At Amy Driffield's house, Ferne Court, Blackstable, Kent; trim; brings in two cards on a small salver

PARLOUR MAID (Mrs. Craddock). At Court Ley, Kent; pink cheeks and golden hair

PARNABY, Lord (Lady Frederick). His urbanity gained him the premiership, but his brilliancy overthrew him

PARNABY, Mrs. (Flirtation). A guest at Lady Mereston's party; pretty widow of twenty-nine; dainty shoulders

PARNABY, Viscount (Jack Straw). She is a guest at the Parker-Jennings' garden party in Cheshire

PARNABYS (Magician). They had been proud to give their daughters to the house of Haddo

PARRY, Ronald (Caesar's Wife). He is a brother of Anne Etheridge; one of Sir Arthur Little's secretaries; an Arabic scholar; he is young and good looking; fresh, pleasant, charming; has been appointed to a position in the Foreign Office at Paris; is in love with Lady Violet Little; Sir Arthur Little recommends him to the Khedive to be his secretary; uncovers the plot to kill Sir Arthur Little

PARSON (Choice of Amyntas). Peter the Schoolmaster had confessed to him that the writing of twelve odes on paternity poses a severe tax one's imagination; he arranged that Peter should name the first child and Mrs. Peter the remainder; huge body; red face; he is completely satisfied with the world; readily gives Amyntas a glass of port, a Bible, and ten guineas

PARSON (Mrs. Craddock). He is one of Gerald Vaudrey's crammers; told Gerald that he was making his place into a gambling hall

PARSONS, Frances (Hero). The wife of Colonel Richmond Parsons and mother of James; sister of Major William Forsyth; age fifty-five; is taller than her husband; a placid, smooth brow; calm eyes; hair parted in the middle and drawn back; a firm mouth and square chin; gentle, kind-hearted; does not like Clara Clibborn

PARSONS, James (Hero). Known as Jamie; son of Richmond and Frances Parsons; been engaged to Mary Clibborn for five years; he had gone from Sandhurst to India, where he distinguished himself; he fell in love with Mrs. Pritchard-Wallace; at the outbreak of the Boer War, sent directly to Capetown; severely wounded in the arm attempting to save the life of Larcher #1; recommended for the Victoria Cross; he has been away from England for the past five years; breaks off his engagement to Mary Clibborn and then he leaves Little Primpton for London; he returns to Little Primpton, where he comes down with enteric fever; after his recovery, he asks Mary Clibborn to marry him; meets Mrs. Pritchard-Wallace in London; then shoots himself

PARSONS, Colonel Richmond (Hero). Husband of Frances Parsons and father of James; he and his wife of more than thirty years reside at Primpton House, Little Primpton, Kent, some four miles from Tunbridge Wells; thin, bent, and frail; long wisps of silvery hair brushed over the crown to conceal baldness; hollow and wrinkled cheeks; a white moustache; a weak, good-natured mouth; blue eyes; old and worn; pious, mild, and even-tempered; in India, he tried to act like a

Christian and a gentleman, but then tricked by rebels of the Madda Khel tribes and routed; forced from the service in ruin, disgrace, and dishonor; left India a broken man; eventually finds peace; collects stamps

PARTISANS (Making of a Saint). Of Checco d'Orsi; at the piazza, Forli; rush into the crowd; proclaim liberty

PARTNER (Explorer [novel]). Was taken into the firm of Boulger and Kelsey at the death of Sir Alfred Kelsey; managed the main part of the business in Manchester

PARTNER (Straight Flush). With Donaldson, in a mining claim; present when Jamie McDermott shot his brother

PASSENGER (Liza of Lambeth). Aboard the rake bound for Chingford; admonishes Man #2 when the latter blows a discordant sound on his horn

PASSENGERS (Explorer [novel]). They are aboard the ship from Gibraltar to England; they never recognize Alec MacKenzie as the famous explorer

PASSENGERS (Liza of Lambeth). At the Waterloo Station, London; in wraps and overcoats; walking to and fro, awaiting the last train

PASSENGERS (Narrow Corner). Of the Dutch ship from Merauke to Takana; drink beer at Kim Ching's store

PASSERS-BY (Painted Veil). In the streets, Mei-tan-fu; seemed intent only on their affairs; cowed, listless

PAT (Of Human Bondage). Is a master at King's School, Tercanbury, Kent; present at dinner when Dr. Fleming announced that Thomas Perkins would succeed him

PATIENT (Narrow Corner). Of Dr. Saunders at Takana; he carries the luggage to the beach

PATIENT (Penelope). Of Dr. Richard O'Farrell; a timid little man; a bald head; gold spectacles; nervous and apologetic; he drinks nothing at luncheon, and only claret and water at dinner

PATIENT (Sanatorium). He has a fit of coughing and then looks anxiously at his handkerchief

PATIENTS (Painted Veil). The two of them; dead; on the floor of the French convent at Mei-tan-fu; lay side by side, and are covered with a piece of blue cotton

PATON, Herbert (Marriages Are Made in Heaven). A friend of Jack Raynor; he had been to school with Jack and served with him in South Africa; is young and grave; slightly heavy; devoid of humor; Jack has asked him to be his best man; attempts to prevent the marriage

Characters

between Jack and Lottie Vivyan

PATON, Leicester (Home and Beauty). Is small and fat; exceedingly prosperous and well pleased with himself; Mrs. Shuttleworth wishes that Victoria had married him instead of Frederick Lowndes; he wears spats; a ship builder; can wangle almost anything one wants; is in steadfastly love with Victoria Cardew Lowndes

PATRON (Magician). Of the Chien Noir, Paris; a retired horse dealer; he is a cheery soul, with a loud voice

PATRON #1 (Razor's Edge). Of the country inn in France where Larry Darrell took Suzanne Rouvier and Odette; he kindly lent them his Citroen to drive into town

PATRON #2 (Razor's Edge). Of a cafe in the Rue de Lappe in Paris; he cleared a table for the Narrator and Isabel Maturin

PATRONNE (Christmas Holiday). At the restaurant on the Avenue du Maine, Paris; wife of the cook; foresees a lucrative order from the six Americans

PATSY (Razor's Edge). The young airman who died saving Larry Darrell's life; small; red hair; funny face and funny grin; absolutely without fear; age twenty-two; slightly older than Larry; six inches shorter than he; planned to marry a girl in Ireland after the war

PATTI, Adelina (Circle). Spanish-born Italian operatic soprano (1843-1919); she had sang at the London opera

PAUL (Christmas Holiday). Son of Alexey and Evgenia; becomes a gigolo; does the night clubs at Montmarte

PAVLOVA, Anna (Ashenden/Mr. Harrington's Washing). The Russian ballerina (1881-1931); she had been a frequent visitor to the Regent's Park section of London

PAWNBROKER (Footprints in the Jungle). He recognizes Reggie Bronson's watch and detains the Chinese man who tries to pawn it

PAXTON, Anthony (Our Betters). The present companion of Minnie Surennes; age twenty-five; handsome; engaging manners; charming smile; in love with Pearl Grayston

PEARLING LUGGER OWNER (German Harry). Asks the Narrator to stop at the island of Trebucket and deliver the supplies to German Harry

PEARS, Lady Patricia (Loaves and Fishes). Rev. Theodore Spratte plans to meet her at dinner; is the aunt, by marriage, of the second wife of the Prime Minister's youngest son; holds all the ecclesiastical patronage

PEASANT (Faith). White and startled face; discovers the frozen body of Brother Jasper and informs the porter at the monastery of San Lucido

PEASANT GIRL (Magician). Seen at Saint Sulpice, Paris; little; with a Breton coiffe; is fresh, healthy, and innocent; she had little to confess

PEASANT WOMAN (Ashenden/Miss King). Old; fat, red face; from French Savoy; sold butter and eggs at the Geneva market; carried instructions to Ashenden; corpulent

PEASANTS (Making of a Saint). Are in the country around Forli; their houses were falling into decay because of the taxes; begin to flock into Forli with their families and cattle, fearful of the approach of the army of Lodovico Sforza

PEASANTS (Painted Veil). Four of them; at the wall of Mei-tan-fu; pass, quick and silent, with a new coffin

PEASANTS (Painted Veil). At Mei-tan-fu; three of them; lolloped, with sidelong gait, under their heavy loads

PEASANTS (Painted Veil). At Mei-tan-fu; seen working industriously in their rice fields

PEASANTS (Painted Veil). Between Mei-tan-fu and Hong Kong; on their way to market

PEDERSON (Pool). Is a half-caste who offers Lawson more salary than does Miller, but Lawson refuses to work under the orders of a half-caste; however, he does accept Lawson after the latter leaves Miller's employ

PEDDLER (Then and Now). At Imola; sells pins, needles, threads, and ribbands

PEDDLERS (Choice of Amyntas). In the Spanish countryside; point to the mountains and direct Amyntas to the brigands

PELLETIER, Charmian (Buried Talent). See Charmian PELTER

PELTER, Charmian (Buried Talent). She is now deceased; a singer who had formerly shared a room with Blanche (MacArdle) off the Boulevard Raspail, Paris; soprano voice of exquisite purity, not powerful, but sweet; a lovely creature, with very white skin; straight nose; large shining eyes; exuberant in her youth; careless and extravagant; refused Teddie Convers' proposal of marriage; changed her name to Pelletier prior to her debut in Brussels; her Paris debut launched her to fame; began to squander her life; periodically hissed off the stage; the curtain of the Opera-Comique had to be lowered because she was too drunk to finish the scene; her voice lost its tone and she gained weight; her career dragged down by drink and drugs; at age forty-three, fished out of the harbor at Toulon, with a knife in her back

PENDER, Miss (Caesar's Wife). A young American, age nineteen or twenty, staying at the same Cairo hotel (Ghezireh Palace) as the Applebys; wonderful hair; pretty; a beautiful dancer; plays tennis; monopolized Ronald Parry at the hotel dance; is in love with him

PENEZZI, Carlo (Gigolo and Gigolette). An Italian; age seventy-eight; is big and stout; mass of white hair, white eyebrows, and an enormous white moustache; once a circus ringmaster; married to Flora Penezzi; now owner of a pension

PENEZZI, Flora (Gigolo and Gigolette). Wife of Carlo Penezzi; well past seventy years of age; small; she wore an ill-fitting, raven black wig; deeply wrinkled skin hanging loosely on her face; large bold eyes; at one time she was an an acrobat (a human cannonball)

PENITENT #1 (Catalina). Died after two hundred lashes

PENITENT #2 (Catalina). Broken by torture; he died from shock during the reading of his sentence

PEOPLE (Bishop's Apron). On the Peckham High Street; Winnie Spratte saw stupid mediocrity in their faces

PEOPLE (Explorer [novel]). In Alec MacKenzie's expedition; they were too frightened to stand up to Rofa

PEOPLE (Landed Gentry). Stood outside the Insoley Arms; hissed at Claude Insoley as he passed; gave Claude no credit for good intentions

PEOPLE (Loaves and Fishes). Two or three of them; they mentioned to Herbert Railing that Theodore Spratte would succeed the Bishop of Colchester

PEOPLE (Magician). At Oxford; disliked Oliver Haddo, but showed a curious pleasure in his company; abused Haddo behind his back, but they could not resist his fascination

PEOPLE (Magician). In the south of Bavaria; in 1698, witnessed the phenomenon of the Tinctura Physicorum penetrating the soil; believed that to be a miracle

PEOPLE (Magician). At Saint Sulpice, Paris; Margaret Dauncey watched them go to and fro

PEOPLE (Magician). At the tavern on the Boulevard des

Italiens, Paris; admire Margaret Dauncey's beauty

PEOPLE (Magician). Along the Madeleine, Paris; Margaret Dauncey watched them

PEOPLE (Magician). At Monte Carlo; babbled of satanism and necromancy; amused and outraged at Oliver Haddo's bulk and vanity

PEOPLE (Magician). At a London restaurant; appear gay

PEOPLE (Magician). Lounging about the Chien Noir, Paris

PEOPLE (Making of a Saint). At Forli; sent by Caterina Sforza to Protonotary Savello, assuring him of her good will and asking him to join her at the cathedral

PEOPLE (Mrs. Craddock). Six of them; are present at the Barnstable railway station when Polly Ley arrives

PEOPLE (Punctiliousness of Don Sebastian). A few of them at Xiormonez, Spain; returning from their riots, they see Don Sebastian wandering about, in silence

PEPE (Catalina). Sacristan of the priest who marries Catalina and Don Diego; also witnesses the marriage

PEPPERCORN, Algernon (Smith). He is age twenty-seven or twenty-eight; clean shaven and carefully groomed; was formerly in the motor car business; a social parasite

PEPPERCORN, Mrs. (Smith). Algernon Peppercorn's mother; Algy telephones her to send his dinner clothes over to the Dallas-Bakers' house; can afford to give her son board and lodging, but not money with which to buy clothes and tobacco

PEPPINO (Up at the Villa). Owner of the restaurant at Florence where the Princess San Ferdinando hosts a dinner party

PERCY (Marriage of Convenience). One of the Wilkens' monkeys

PERCY (Sheppey). The brother of Ada Miller; he died of meningitis at age seven

PEREGRINE Eva Katherine Hamilton (Colonel's Lady). Wife of George Peregrine; a published poet; when married, was pretty and petite, with creamy skin, light brown hair, and a trim figure; presently nearing age forty-five; drab skin and hair; extremely thin; no makeup

PEREGRINE, Colonel George (Colonel's Lady). Husband of Evie Peregrine; slightly over fifty years old; tall; curly, gray hair, only slightly beginning to thin; blue eyes; high color; had been in the Welsh Guards before his marriage; received the M.C. and the D.S.O.

in the last war; he had settled down to the life of a country gentleman and the justice of the peace on the Sheffield family estate; friendly, affable, popular

PEREGRINE, Mrs. (Colonel's Lady). Is George Peregrine's sister-in-law; mother of Peregrine the younger and widow of Peregrine the elder; considered by George a fool for sending her son to a coeducational school

PEREGRINE the elder (Colonel's Lady). Brother of George Peregrine; killed in a motor car accident; left a son

PEREGRINE the younger (Colonel's Lady). The nephew and heir of Col. George Peregrine; his father, George's brother, had been killed in a motor car accident; he is attending a coeducational school

PEREZ (Catalina). The father of Maria Perez Orta and Domingo Perez; he had sent his son to the seminary of Alcala de Henares, then supported him for eight years at Salamanca

PEREZ, Domingo (Catalina). Catalina's uncle and Maria Perez Orta's brother; age forty-seven; lives with his sister and his niece; he had been destined for the priesthood; became a fellow student of Bishop Blasco Suarez de Valero at the seminary, Alcala de Henares; spent eight years at Salamanca, supposedly studying law; became a strolling player, as well as a writer of plays and verse; afterward soldiered and gambled in Italy; at age forty by the time he returned to his birthplace, following a turbulent, headstrong, and dissipated existence; earns money by writing letters for the illiterate and sermons for lazy priests; is skinny and loose-limbed; gray hair; lined yellow face

PERIER the elder (Unconquered). French farmer; father of Annette and Perier the younger; husband of Madame Perier; he attempts to rescue his daughter from Hans

PERIER the younger (Unconquered). Is Annette's brother; mobilized into the French army; died at a hospital in Nancy from pneumonia

PERIER, Annette (Unconquered). Daughter of the farmer and Madame Perier; a teacher; formerly a governess to two little girls Stuttgart; opens the door for Hans and Willi; fine dark eyes, straight nose; pale face; raped by Hans

PERIER CHILD (Unconquered). The boy born to Annette Perier and Hans; he has fair hair and blue eyes

PERIER DOG (Unconquered). Old; obviously dislikes Hans
PERIGAL, Robert (Tenth Man). Prime Minister of England; stout; of middle height; clean shaven; abundant gray hair, worn long; a sensual, shrewd, and bland face; a first cousin to Angela Etchingham
PERKINS (Explorer [novel/play]). He is a member of Alec MacKenzie's current expedition against the African slave traders; is delirious, with a bad dose of fever
PERKINS, Freddie (Mrs. Dot). Age twenty-two; vivacious; the son of Rev. Perkins; a friend of Gerald Halstane; the nephew and secretary of Dot Worthley; educated at Eton and Oxford; falls in love with Nellie Sellenger and runs off with her
PERKINS, Mr. (Of Human Bondage). The father of Thomas Perkins; is a linendraper in the firm of Cooper, St. Catherine's Street, Tercanbury; filed for bankruptcy just before Tom took his degree
PERKINS, Rev. (Mrs. Dot). Father of Freddie Perkins
PERKINS, Thomas (Of Human Bondage). Appointed, at age thirty-two, headmaster of King's School, Tercanbury; tall and lean; dark, untidy hair; large eyes; black moustache and a beard that came almost to his cheek bones; he had entered King's School as a day boy on scholarship; went on to Magdalen College, Oxford; he took Holy Orders; assistant master first at Wellington, then at Rugby; son of a Tercanbury linendraper
PERON, John (Christmas Holiday). The father of Venetia Mason, Leslie Mason's wife; is a member of the Royal Academy; he painted pictures of women in eighteenth-century costume
PERRUQUIER (Lady Frederick). Taught Angelique the art of hairdressing; stated that a good hairdresser could express every mood and passion of the human heart
PERSIAN CATS (Magician). Of Dr. Porhoet; two of them; sit in front of the fire and meditate on the problems of metaphysics; run about in terror whenever Oliver Haddo appears
PERSIAN SCHOLAR (Caesar's Wife). Is the best one in the Foreign Office; he has spent the last six years in Washington, D.C.
PERSON (Spanish Priest). In the Calle Alfonso Trece, at Granada; tells the Englishman that he has not seen Vicente Oria y Mazillon for the past several days

PERSON OF RANK (Catalina). He Lends a carriage to Juan Suarez and Violante de Valero and to Martin de Valero and his family

PERSONS (Magician). Of distinction at London; concerned with the supernatural; Eliphas Levi bore letters of introduction to them; were trivial and indifferent

PERSONS (Magician). One or two of them; are outside the Carlton Hotel, London; they stared at Margaret Haddo coming from the hotel in a tea gown and without a hat

PERSONS (razor's Edge). Two of them; at a cafe on the Rue de Lappe, Paris; they were unhappy because the patron had cleared them away from their seats to make room for the Narrator and Isabel Maturin

PERUGINO (Then and Now). Painter and teacher at Urbino

PERUZZI, Carlo (Then and Now). The father of the grandmothers of Bartolomeo Martelli and Biagio Buonaccorsi

PETE, Mr. (Consul). He had been in the consular service for more than twenty years; bachelor; absent minded; an ardent collector; small and frail; large head, but exceedingly bald; pale blue eyes; he wore spectacles; drooping moustache

PETER (Choice of Amyntas). A son of Peter the Schoolmaster and Mrs. Peter

PETER, Mrs. ((Choice of Amyntas). A farmer's daughter; married Peter the Schoolmaster and bore him twelve children; buxom; she is a careless but charming soul

PETER THE SCHOOLMASTER (Choice of Amyntas). A scholar and a man of of letters; lived in the West Country of England; is poor; he fell in love with and married a farmer's daughter (Mrs. Peter); the father of twelve children; composed a Latin ode upon the birth of each child; tall and lean; thin, white hair; blue eyes; he has rosy, wrinkled cheeks; incessant snuff-taking had given a special character to his nose; he wore spectacles; father of Amyntas

PETERS (Taipan). He is immediately junior to the Taipan

PETERSEN, Mr. (Unattainable). Robert Oldham had known him for twenty years; had been devoted to Mrs. Macdougal for years before she divorced and they were married; divorcing her after eighteen months of marriage; is dull when he is sober and brutal when drunk

PETERSEN, Mrs. (Unattainable). Formerly Mrs. Macdougal; married Mr. Petersen; is now, after eighteen months of marriage, divorcing him; Robert Oldham her lawyer

PETERSON (Raw Material). Is a passenger on the French liner bound from Hong Kong to Shanghai; had come from New York; big and burly; red face; crisp, black hair; powerful and pugnacious; supposedly a professional gambler, but actually a distinguished mining engineer

PETRUCCI, Pandolfo (Then and Now). Lord of Siena; the mastermind behind the rebellion of the captains against Caesar Borgia

PEYTON (Penelope). Parlormaid at the O'Farrell house on John Street, London

PHILADELPHIA SURGEON (Ashenden/Mr. Harrington's Washing). Is a friend of J.Q. Harrington; he offers to operate on the sons of Harrington at the same time

PHILIP (Punctiliousness of Don Sebastian). The King of Spain; he asks Don Sebastian's advice, first on petty matters, then he turns to him on affairs of state

PHILIP, Prince (Catalina). Son of the King of Spain; he sent Blasco de Valero two hundred ducats and a letter of congratulations for t he pious zeal with which he conducted the business of the Inquisition; as King, he appoints Blasco to the bishopric of Segovia

PHILLIPS, Miss (Of Human Bondage). Of Blackstable; she thought to have been engaged

PHILLIPS, Miss (Theatre). Masseuse; gave Julia Lambert Gosselyn a light massage prior to her performance

PHILOSOPHER (Judgment Seat). He told the Eternal to His face that he did not believe in Him

PHILOSOPHY STUDENT (Alien Corn). Friend of George Bland at Munich

PHOTOGRAPHER (Cakes and Ale). Is one of the fashionable artists of the period; photographed Rosie Driffield

PHOTOGRAPHER (Of Human Bondage). Takes a dozen photographs of Mrs. Carey shortly before she delivers her second child

PHOTOGRAPHER'S ASSISTANT (Of Human Bondage). Recognized Mrs. Carey's condition and suggested that she come another day

PHYLLIS (Liza of Lambeth). The amorous shepherdess in the mock idyll related at the half-way house between Lambeth and Chingford

PHYSICIAN #1 (Merry-Go-Round). At St. Luke's Hospital, London; his death allowed Frank Hurrell to move into

Characters   331

   the position of resident
PHYSICIAN #2 (Merry-Go-Round). At St. Luke's Hospital,
   London; he tends to the wards; Dr. Frank Hurrell will
   perform his duties throughout August and September
PHYSICIAN (Of Human Bondage). Philip Carey had clerked
   for him at St. Luke's Hospital, London; he invites
   Philip to a "solemn dinner"
PHYSICIANS (Magician). At Nuremburg; they all denounced
   Paracelsus as being a quack, charlatan, and imposter
PIACENTINI, Claudia (Making of a Saint). Wife of Ercole
   Piacentini; handsome, voluptuous, and massive; full-
   breasted and high colored; a massive white neck, the
   veins showing clear and blue; with deep, red, heavy,
   sensual, and moist lips; returned with her husband to
   Citta di Castello after the death of Girolamo Riario;
   tells Filippo Brandolini, after his return from Rome,
   that Giulia dall' Aste had been carrying on with
   Giorgio dall' Aste
PIACENTINI, Ercole (Making of a Saint). The husband of
   Claudia Piacentini; is the bastard son of a Castello
   nobleman and the daughter of a tradesman; a principal
   favorite of Girolamo Riario; a citizen of Citta di
   Castello; big, heavy looking; ugly and sallow-faced;
   Filippo Brandolini hates him immediately; needlessly
   disagreeable; declares that Matteo d'Orsi and Filippo
   have good steeds and imaginations; Girolamo Riario
   and he try to kill Checco d'Orsi; returned to Citta
   di Castello after the death of Girolamo; Filippo is
   influential in banishing him from Citta di Castello;
   he loses a sword fight to Filippo at a country inn
PIACENTINI, Lord (Making of a Saint). Unmarried father
   of Ercole Piacentini; a nobleman of Citta di Castello
PIANIST (Christmas Holiday). At the Serail, Paris; part
   of the three-piece orchestra
PIANO PLAYER (Razor's Edge). At a cafe on the Rue de
   Lappe, Paris; young man; pale, dissipated; wipes his
   face with a dirty handkerchief after the music stops
PICADOR (Point of Honour). At the celebration of the
   Feast of Corpus Christi at Seville; consciously proud
   of his picturesque uniform
PICKLE, Sir Courteny (Camel's Back). Supposed "friend"
   of Dr. Dickinson; actually the head of various homes
   for idiots and imbeciles; calls on Valentine Lefevre

PIERRE (Jack Straw). Is a waiter at the Grand Babylon Hotel, and is of somewhat striking physique; attends the funeral of an elderly aunt in Soho

PIETRO (Making of a Saint). Is a steward at the Palazzo Orsi, Forli; old; white hair; stood by, wringing his hands, as the servants looted the palace and ran off

PILAR (Mother). One of the residents of the tenement in La Macarena, Seville

PILOT (Narrow Corner). A friend of Captain Nichols at Brisbane; crippled by rheumatism; walked on crutches

PILSUDSKI, Jozef (Razor's Edge). A Polish revolutionary leader (1867-1935); first president of independent Poland (1918-1922); supposedly shot those associates of Kosti #2 who had planned to kill him and whom he had captured

PIUS III [IV] (Then and Now). Elected Pope after the death of Alexander VI (1431-1503); he is old and sick

PIUS XI [1857-1939] (Razor's Edge). Elliott Templeton shows him a photograph of the Romanesque church of St. Martin, which Elliott had built for him; he then compliments Templeton for having impeccable taste

PLANTATION OWNERS (Mrs. Craddock). On an orange plantation in Florida; acquaintances of Polly Ley; Gerald Vaudrey stayed with them during his visit to Florida

PLANTER (Narrow Corner). At Singapore; is young; deeply sunburned; is seen striding past the Van Dyke Hotel

PLANTER (P.&.O.). He suggests inviting the second-class passengers aboard the ship to the Christmas Eve ball

PLATTER, Mrs. (Merry-Go-Round). She inhabited a flat in Shaftesbury Street, London; named as a co-respondent in a divorce counter-petition filed by Lady Vizard against Lord Vizard

PLUMBER (Moon and Sixpence). Retired; Charles Strickland had painted his portrait for two hundred francs; a great, red face like a leg of mutton; on his right cheek was an enormous mole with hair growing from it

POGSON, Mrs. (Home and Beauty). Sent by the Alexandra Employment Agency to inquire into the position of cook at the Lowndes' house; she is large, heavy, and authoritative; dressed like an undertaker's widow; drives a Ford automobile

POKER PLAYER (Straight Flush). He sat next to Rosenbaum during a game in San Francisco

Characters 333

POLE (Alien Corn). A friend of George Bland at Munich; studies Oriental languages

POLE (Our Betters). The butler at Lady Pearl Grayston's house; he conveys Fleming Harvey's flowers to Bessie Saunders; also announces various guests and arrivals

POLICE (Mother). They break into La Cachirra's room and handcuff her

POLICE CHIEF (Official Position). Of Lyons; he is well disposed toward Louis Remire

POLICE DOCTOR (Narrow Corner). Determined that Patrick Hudson #1 had been dead about for two or three hours

POLICE INSPECTOR #1 (Hour Before the Dawn). At Lewes; admits to no negative evidence against Dora Freidberg

POLICE INSPECTOR #2 (Hour Before the Dawn). Graveney; inspects the charred rick near Jim Henderson's farm

POLICE INSPECTOR (Merry-Go-Round). He tells Basil Kent that Jenny Kent has thrown herself into the river

POLICE SERGEANT (Cakes and Ale). He escorts the Driffields' maid to the house, where both discover that the Driffields have left

POLICE SERGEANT (Door of Opportunity). Is in charge of eight policemen at the time the Chinese coolies raid Prynne's estate

POLICE SERGEANT (Footprints in the Jungle). Tells Gaze of the dead white man (Reggie Bronson) lying in the jungle path

POLICE SERGEANT (Vessel of Wrath). Is knocked flat by Ginger Ted when he tries to arrest him

POLICE SERGEANT (Letter [play]). He is a Sikh; at the Singapore jail; tall, bearded, and dark; he conducts Robert Crosbie to the cells, see his wife, Leslie

POLICE WOMAN (Christmas Holiday). Grim-faced; she conducts the body searches of Lydia and Leontine Berger

POLICEMAN (Bad Example). Finds James Clinton after the latter had fainted; shakes him and asks him his name

POLICEMAN (Bishop's Apron). Standing on Saville Row; he watched with gaping mouth as Rev. Theodore Spratte and Gwendolyn Durant raced their horses at full speed

POLICEMAN (Bum). Tries to protect public from beggars

POLICEMAN (Cakes and Ale). Is on point duty in London; gave Ashenden and Rosie Driffield a stare of suspicion and twinkle of comprehension as they passed him

POLICEMAN (Hour Before the Dawn). One of those inspect-

ing the remains of the rick near Jim Henderson's cottage; discovers charred pieces of the <u>New Statesman</u>
POLICEMAN (Liza of Lambeth). He passes Liza Kemp as she goes to meet Jim Blakeston; he wonders whether she is contemplating some illegal act
POLICEMAN (Loaves and Fishes). In the words of Bertram Railing, throughout the winter, he walks up and down the Thames embankment to prevent poor and homeless wretches from sleeping in case they freeze to death
POLICEMAN (Mackintosh). A picturesque figure in white jacket and Samoan loin cloth; he beats the red-haired beggar with his thong
POLICEMAN (Magician). He was brought to a Monte Carlo restaurant to force Oliver Haddo to exchange the counterfeit coin that he had given to the waiter
POLICEMAN (Merry-Go-Round). Rings a bell at the Kents' house; he tells Basil that Jenny has had an accident
POLICEMAN (Neil MacAdam). Introduced by Captain Bredon to Neil MacAdam at Kuala Solor; heavy and swaggering
POLICEMAN (Of Human Bondage). He says a good morning to Philip Carey as the latter returns from his last case
POLICEMAN (Razor's Edge). At Toulon; accompanies Larry Darrell and Maugham to the mortuary to view Sophie Macdonald's body
POLICEMAN (Smith). Algernon Peppercorn believes him to be a candidate to father a future little Smith; Rose Dallas-Baker says she will place a wager on him, also
POLICEMAN (Vessel of Wrath). Accompanies Ginger Ted to the launch for Baru
POLICEMAN (Virtue). He calls the police station for an ambulance to take Charlie Bishop's body to Charing Cross Hospital
POLICEMEN (Ashenden/Miss King). Two of them; are at the quay at Geneva to observe the passengers disembark
POLICEMEN (Casual Affair). Two of them; they accompany Arthur Low to the Chinese woman's house in the bazaar
POLICEMEN (Unattainable). Caroline Ashley has noticed how young they are
POLISH CONVICT (Official Position). Awaiting execution
POLISH PRINCE (Magician). Supposedly, the blasphemous ceremonies of the Black Mass had been celebrated in his house at Monte Carlo

POLISH PRINCES (Razor's Edge). In the words of Elliott Templeton, they would drink zubrovka by the tumbler "without turning a hair"
POLITICIAN (Bishop's Apron). Famous; Theodore Spratte passes the time of day with him as they walk along Saville Row
POLITICIANS (Painted Veil). Are promising; Mrs. Garstin made much of them
POLITICIANS (Tenth Man). Enthusiastic; are turned out of the public houses at Middlepool; sing and cheer for George Winter
POLLETT, Edith (Daisy). Engaged and eventually married to George Griffith; ready to break the engagement if Daisy Griffith comes to Blackstable; steel-gray eyes; dictates a letter toRobert Griffith to send to Daisy
POLLY (Liza of Lambeth). A resident of Vere Street, in Lambeth; her next child is due in one or two months
POLLY (Of Human Bondage). A patient of Philip Carey; he saw her at the dinner hour; she is the wife of Herb
POLSON, Mr. and Mrs. (Hero). Mary Clibborn plays golf with them at Tunbridge Wells
POMERANIA, Ex-King of (Love in a Cottage). Is invited to attend Sybil Burton's fancy dress ball at Paris
POMERANIAN ATTACHE (Jack Straw). Adrian von Bremer has had to send him packing back to Pomerania; he played a practical (unmentioned) joke on an American woman
PONSONBY (Bishop's Apron). A gentleman's butler and an imposing personage; in the employ of Theodore Spratte; large, flabby, and corpulent; rotund calves; loose, smooth skin; puffy, lower eyelids; fish-like eyes; a fleshy, immobile face; earnest and obsequious voice
PONSONBY (Loaves and Fishes). He is the butler at St. Gregory's vicarage; of a most impressive appearance; he combines the self-confidence of a Parliamentarian and the dignity of a mute at a very expensive funeral
POOLE, Dorothy (Unknown). Wife of Rev. Norman Poole; middle aged; dour; is brisk, competent, and firm; she resembles her husband
POOLE, Rev. Norman (Unknown). Is vicar of Stour, Kent; husband of Dorothy Poole; tall, thin, and bald; he is energetic, breezy, and cheerful; resembles his wife; he has problems with his lungs; formerly in charge of the parish of St. Jude, in Stoke Newington, London

POPE (Making of a Saint). Is against Girolamo Riario, although he pretends to support him; Checco d'Orsi decides, after the assassination of Girolamo Riario, to offer Forli to him

PORCHESTER, Eleanor (Round Dozen); Niece of Dr. and Mr. St. Clair; between fifty-one and fifty-four years of age; a slim and youthful figure; she is tall; long legs; abundance of brown hair; straight and delicate nose of a Greek goddess; beautiful mouth; large blue eyes; she has wrinkles on her forehead and about her eyes; is a spinster; she runs off with Mortimer Ellis

PORHOET, Dr. (Magician). Son of Jeanne-Marie Porhoet; a small, fragile body; stooped shoulders; thin face, sallow from long exposure to tropical suns; hollow cheeks; a thin, gray beard; an habitual weariness of expression; sunken eyes; a native of Brittany; spent the best part of his life in Egypt in the practice of medicine; had conducted studies in Mala fever; speaks English fluently; a friend of Arthur Burdon, whom he has known since birth; has recently published a book on old alchemists; interested in the oddities of mankind; a necromancer; recalls Margaret Haddo's spirit

PORHOET, Jeanne-Marie (Magician). Widowed mother of Dr. Porhoet; old; her son, living in Alexandria, had not received news of her for several weeks; she has died

PORTER (Ashenden/Miss King). Of Ashenden's hotel at Geneva; he receives generous tips from Ashenden for trifling services

PORTER (Bishop's Apron). At the Athenaeum Club, London; servants will ask him if Lord Wroxham is in the club

PORTER #1 (Cakes and Ale). Is employed at Alroy Kear's club, St. James Street, London; aged

PORTER #2 (Cakes and Ale). Is at the Albermarle Hotel, Yonkers, New York; black; in uniform; he telephoned Ashenden's name up to Rosie Driffield's apartment

PORTER #3 (Cakes and Ale). At the Albermarle Hotel, in Yonkers, New York; conveys Ashenden on the elevator

PORTER #1 (Catalina). Is at the Dominican convent; will not immediately admit Domingo Perez

PORTER #2 (Catalina). At the episcopal palace, Segovia; ushers Domingo Perez to see Bishop Blasco de Valero

PORTER #1 (Christmas Holiday). Is at the Paris railway station; takes Charley Mason's bag

Characters 337

PORTER #2 (Christmas Holiday). At the hotel in the Rue St. Honore, Paris; spoke fluent English

PORTER #3 (Christmas Holiday). At Charley Mason's Paris hotel; smilingly benevolent

PORTER (Creative Impulse). Drops Mrs. Forrester's new cook's box

PORTER #1 (Explorer [novel]). At Fred Allerton's house in Shaftesbury Avenue, London; had no key to Fred's flat and did not know exactly when Fred would return

PORTER #2 (Explorer [novel]). Was with Alec Mackenzie's expedition against the African slave traders; seized his load and carrying it off to lash on his mat and cooking pot; ate a few grains of roasted maize or the remains of last night's game

PORTER Faith). He is at the monastery at San Lucido; he administers thirty-eight strokes to Brother Jasper with a heavy knotted scourge, and he sweats heavily

PORTER (Happy Man). At the hotel in Seville; he directs the Narrator over to the English doctor in the city

PORTER (Hero). At James Parson's London club; he hands James a letter sent over from Mrs. Pritchard-Wallace

PORTER (Magician). He is at the Carlton Hotel, London; informed Arthur Burdon that Oliver Haddo had gone out

PORTER #1 (Merry-Go-Round). At Brighton; he carries the traps of Jenny Kent and Annie Bush from the station to their lodgings

PORTER #2 (Merry-Go-Round). Waterloo Station, London; he thinks the distraught Jenny Kent had been drinking

PORTER (Mirage). At the Haiphong hotel; helps the Narrator direct the rickshaw boy to the Grosleys' house

PORTER (Mother). He carries the rest of La Cachirra's belongings to the tenement house in the La Macarena, Seville; argues with her over payment

PORTER #1 (Mrs. Craddock). Is at the railway station at Blackstable, Kent; Edward Craddock calls out to him

PORTER #2 (Mrs. Craddock). The railway station, Blackstable; takes Bertha Craddock's luggage to the coach

PORTER #1 (Of Human Bondage). Is at Blackstable, Kent, sixty miles from London; takes charge of the luggage of William and Philip Carey±

PORTER #2 (Of Human Bondage). Tercanbury train station; Philip Carey asks him when the next train will arrive

PORTER #3 (of Human Bondage). Heidelberg; Philip Carey

follows him from the station to Frau Erlin's pension
PORTER #4 (Of Human Bondage). Is at the building where Fanny Price lives; sullen; accompanies Philip Carey to the police
PORTER #5 (Of Human Bondage). Out-patients' room, St. Luke's Hospital, London; sends in the old patients
PORTER #6 ()f Human Bondage). St. Luke's Hospital, London; gets Philip Carey when he is about to go to bed
PORTER (Penelope). At Davenport Barlow's club; believes the gout to be a mark of a good family
PORTER #1 (Punctiliousness of Don Sebastian). Is at the railway station, Xiormonez, Spain; told the Narrator that everyone was asleep; carries the Narrator's bag from the station
PORTER #2 (Punctiliousness of Don Sebastian). For the Chapel of the Duke de Losas, Xiormonez, Spain; he and his wife both have gone into the country for the day
PORTER (Romantic Young Lady). Is at the new hotel in Seville; tells the Narrator that the Marquessa de San Esteban had been asking for him
PORTER (Round Dozen). Of the Dolphin Inn, at Elsom; he carries the St. Clairs' rugs and cushions from the landau to the hotel; conveys Mr. St. Clair's request for a copy of <u>Whitaker's Almanack</u> to the Narrator
PORTER (Smith). At the Waterloo Station, London; asks Thomas Freeman if he wants him to call for a taxi
PORTER (Treasure). At the flats where Richard Harenger lives; knows of someone who might fit Harenger's need for a house maid or parlor maid
PORTER, Mr. (Yellow Streak). Is a resident of the rest house at Kuala Solor
PORTERS (Choice of Amyntas). Of the great men of Cadiz; none willing to employ Amyntas
PORTERS (Door of Opportunity). Several; at the London train station and hotel off St. Jermyn Street, London
PORTERS (Explorer [novel]). Are with Alec MacKenzie's expedition against the African slave traders; quoted in Fergus Macinnery's second letter to the newspapers
PORTERS (Hero). At Victoria Station, London; lift heavy packages onto the bellied roofs of the hansom cabs
PORTERS (Liza of Lambeth). One or two of them; seen at Waterloo Station, London; standing about and yawning
PORTERS (Marry-Go-Round). The port in Brindisi, Italy;

they are swarthy; with red sashes
PORTERS (Mrs. Craddock). Are on the train from London to Blackstable, Kent; with noticeable Kentish drawls
PORTERS (Mrs. Craddock). Two of them; at the station at Blackstable; waddle toward the van to remove the bags
PORTER-SMITH, Fanny (Pro Patria). Wife of John Porter-Smith; daughter of Mrs. Mahon; is ravishing, slender, and delicate; she is separated from her husband
PORTER-SMITH, John (Pro Patria). Is a carpet-bagger (a candidate without a connection to the place he wishes to represent); the candidate of the Unionists; he is moustached; an Imperial Yeoman who had fought in the war in South Africa, where he suffered a scratch on the hand; before the war, committed an indiscretion with the governess of his wife's sister; he has not communicated with his wife, Fanny, for over a year
PORTEUS, Lord Hughie (Circle). Married to Lady Porteus; educated at Eton and Oxford; he had formerly served in Parliament; everyone thought that he would become the Prime Minister; he ran away to Europe (eventually settling in Florence, Italy) with Catherine Champion-Cheney; is Arnold Champion-Cheney's godfather; as a young man--handsome; yellow hair and blue eyes; good figure; thirty years later--is very bald and elderly; ill-fitting false teeth; rheumatic; snappy and gruff
PORTEUS, Lady (Circle). Wife of Lord Hughie Porteus; not a very attractive woman; she refused to divorce her husband after he ran away with Lady Catherine Champion-Cheney (whom she hated)
PORTRESS (Catalina). Unlocks the door of the Carmelite church for the Bishop
PORTUGUESE WOMAN (Hero). She is from Goa; the mother of Mrs. Pritchard-Wallace and wife of a riding master
POSTILIONS (Pro Patria). In handsome red coats; in the employ of John Porter-Smith for his election campaign
POSTMAN (De Amicitia). At Volendam, Holland; is walking down the street; he has no letter for Ferdinand White
POSTMAN (Smith). Herbert Dallas-Baker's candidate to father a future little Smith
POSTMAN (Traveller in Romance). Sat beside the driver on the post chaise coming from St. Moritz into Italy
POTENTATES (Explorer [novel]). Foreign; two of them; through their consuls at Mambassa, bestow decorations

upon Alec Mackenzie

POTMAN (Liza of Lambeth). At the half-way house between Lambeth and Chingford; they draw beer for the thirsty passengers from the Red Lion brake

POTTER (Of Human Bondage). He is an American student at Amitrano's art school, Paris; attends the party given by Philip Carey and Lawson; he offers his studio to Philip Carey for two months when he goes off to Italy

POTTS (Mrs. Craddock). An old sheep raiser at Herne, in Kent; Edward Craddock will see him about some sheep

PREFECT (Of Human Bondage). Of the lodging house on Harrington Street, London, for the employees of Lynn and Sedley; he would turn out the gas at 11:15 p.m.

PRENTICE, Dr. Charles (For Services Rendered). Brother of Charlotte Ardsley; is elderly and thin; iron-gray hair; he has a severe, stern face and searching eyes

PRESIDENT (Closed Shop). Of free and independent state on the American continent; had an eye to pretty women

PRESIDENT (Point of Honour). Of the bullfight, Seville; his appearance signals the beginning of the event

PRESIDING JUDGE (Christmas Holiday). At Robert Berger's murder trial; small and old; the wrinkled face of a monkey; tired, flat voice

PRESS REPRESENTATIVE (Cakes and Ale). At New York; an employee of William Ashenden's manager; he advertises Ashenden's arrival

PRESS REPRESENTATIVE (Gigolo and Gigolette). Is a small haggard woman; untidy head; Sandy Westcott tells her the names of the guests attending the dinner party

PRESS REPRESENTATIVE (Theatre). Of the Sarah Siddons Theatre; had only informed a few newspapers of Julia Lambert Gosselyn's departure for St. Malo, France

PRESTON, Ned (Episode/Kite). A Scot; bachelor friend of the Narrator; good humored and merry; has a gift for telling a story; suffered from chronic tuberculosis; became an unpaid prison visitor at Wormwood Scrubbs; died at age fifty-five of a hemorrhage

PRICE, Albert (Of Human Bondage). The brother of Fanny Price; lives in Surbiton, Surrey; refuses to lend his sister five pounds; is common looking; small; stubbly moustache; a cockney accent; easily upset; a rubber merchant; father of three children

PRICE, Fanny (Of Human Bondage). Student at Amitrano's

art school, Paris; introduced to Philip Carey by Mrs. Otter; age twenty-six; abundant dull gold hair; large face; has broad, flat features; small eyes; pasty and unhealthy skin; colorless cheeks; serious and silent; formerly a governess at London; hangs herself because she was starving; buried in a Montparnasse cemetery

PRICE, Mrs. (Of Human Bondage). Wife of Albert Price; mother of three children

PRIEST #1 (Catalina). He has heard the confessions of Beatriz Henriquez y Braganza, and he reports to her mother concerning the girl's desire for domination

PRIEST #2 (Catalina). Short, fat, red-faced; witnessed Catalina and Diego Martinez being thrown from their horse; Catalina bribes him to marry Diego and her

PRIEST (Christmas Holiday). At St. Eustache, in Paris; administers communion

PRIEST (Human Element). Leads tired, eager, and pious pilgrims to Rome

PRIEST #1 (Magician). In the vision of Son #2; of the Breton village where Jeanne-Marie Porhoet lives; in a white surplice with a cross in his hands; outside of the vision, writes a letter to Dr. Porhoet at Alexandria, announcing the burial of his mother (the very day upon which Son #2 had seen the image in his hand)

PRIEST #2 (Magician). Is in the confessional at Saint Sulpice, Paris

PRIESTS (Magician). At Saint Sulpice, Paris; chanting; words and movements meaningless for Margaret Dauncey

PRIESTS (Mrs. Craddock). At Rome; old and fat; taking the sun and smoking cigarettes; they appear at peace with themselves and with the rest of the world

PRIESTS (Mrs. Craddock). At Rome; young and restless; the flesh unsubdued shining out of their dark eyes

PRIESTS (Razor's Edge). Two of them; they are guests at the Benedictine monastery at Alsace; passing by and had stopped off for dinner

PRIME MINISTER (Bishop's Apron). Offered Josiah Spratte the position of Lord Chancellor of England

PRIME MINISTER (Caesar's Wife). Told Lady Violet Little that her husband was the most competent man who he had ever met

PRIME MINISTER (Cakes and Ale). Presented Edward Driffield the Order of Merit on his eightieth birthday

PRIME MINISTER (Loaves and Fishes). Theodore Spratte states, ironically, that he will inform him that an eighteen-hole golf course is a sine qua non of his elevation to the episcopacy

PRINCE (Catalina). He sat in the balcony during the Inquisition proceedings; swore to obey the Catholic faith and the Holy Office

PRINCE (Marriage of Convenience). Had accompanied the retired French official to the ship lying at Bangkok

PRINCE, Miss (Winter Cruise). Friend of Miss Reid; the daughter of the late vicar of Camden; saw Miss Reid off at Plymouth

PRINCE OF WALES (Gigolo and Gigolette). Came to the Old Aquarium, in London, to see Flora Penezzi, the human cannonball

PRINCE OF WALES (Theatre). Attended Lady Lepard's large party in Cheshire

PRINCE, Rev. (Winter Cruise). The late vicar of Camden; father of Miss Prince

PRINCE REGENT (Round Dozen). Rode with Mrs. Fitzherbert to drink tea in the coffee-room, Dolphin Inn, Elsom

PRINCESS (Lion's Skin). Guest at Forestiers' luncheon; according to Robert Forestier, "a malignant old cat"

PRINCESS (Merry-Go-Round). She had an affair with Hugh Kearon; she bored him to death

PRINCESS (Razor's Edge). A minor one, of the House of Windsor; she hosts Elliott Templeton and Louisa and Isabel Bradley in her Royal box at the London opera

PRINGLE, Agnes (Land of Promise). A companion to Mrs. Hubbard, a wealthy old lady at Tunbridge Wells; she is middle aged; has narrow shoulders; weatherbeaten, tired face; gray hair; eventually leaves Mrs. Hubbard to live with her brother

PRINGLE, Mr. (Land of Promise). The widowed brother of Agnes Pringle; she can always stay with him if she is without a situation

PRINGLE, Mrs. (Land of Promise). Wife of Mr. Pringle; Agnes Pringle's sister-in-law; she dies

PRINTERS (Tenth Man). At Bishop and Jones, Middlepool; Boyce telephones them with instructions for posters

PRIOR #1 (Catalina). Of the same order as Bishop Blasco de Valero; keeps the Bishop informed of his family's condition; he wants Catalina's healing to be a large

ceremony; the Bishop of Segovia refuses his request
PRIOR #2 (Catalina). Carries the standard of the Holy Office in the Inquisition procession
PRIOR #3 (Catalina). Of the remote convent to which Bishop Blasco de Valero retires; pleads with the aged friar to forego the more severe of his austerities
PRIOR #1 (Faith). Lives at the monastery of San Lucido; Brother Jasper goes to him for help; old and wasted; had lived at the monastery for for fifty years; older than anyone else there; white haired and wrinkled; clear, rosy skin; soft blue eyes; his sight weakened by cataract; always happy and kind; contracts cancer; suffers greatly and dies
PRIOR #2 (Faith). Succeeds Prior #1 at the monastery at San Lucido; tall and gaunt; a great hooked nose and heavy lips; keen dark eyes and shaggy brows; young; hated Jews and heretics
PRIOR (Of Human Bondage). Employee in the silks department, Lynn and Sedley, London; once in the army; tall
PRIORESS #1 (Catalina). Of the Carmelite Order; whips the nun and forces her to confess that she invented the story about Elias
PRIORESS #2 (Catalina). Of the Carmelite Convent of the Incarnation at Avila; is sister of the Duke of Castel Rodriguez
PRIORESS #3 (Catalina). She is appointed the head of the Duke's convent at Castel Rodriguez until Beatriz becomes of a suitable age to assume her position
PRISONERS (Noble Spaniard). They consider it a pleasure to have been sentenced by Judge Sebastian Proudfoot
PRITCHARD (Treasure). Hired by Richard Harenger as his house parlor maid and valet; age thirty-five; tall; good features and high color; pale brown hair; she is neither fat nor thin; a widow
PRITCHARD, Christina (Caesar's Wife). Mother of Henry Pritchard and sister of Sir Arthur Little; tall and spare; turning gray; comely and upright; is honest, direct, and truthful; not without humor; kept house for her brother for ten years; she has a true genius for household organization and order
PRITCHARD, Henry (Caesar's Wife). The son of Christina Pritchard and nephew of Sir Arthur Little; he holds a badly paid position in the Ministry of Education; can

speak Arabic; he has the mind of an official; he is pleasant and clean, but lacks imagination and charm

PRITCHARD, Mr. (Treasure). The late husband of Pritchard; was shorter than his wife; he had never worked a single day during the period of their marriage

PRITCHARD-WALLACE, Mrs. (Hero). Is Richard Pritchard-Wallace's wife; the daughter of a riding master and a Portuguese woman; is small; dark haired; olive skin; large brown eyes; common, but excessively pretty; she flirts with James Parsons, but she is not seriously in love with him; meets James in London and tells him that she is engaged to marry Mr. Bryant

PRITCHARD-WALLACE, Richard (Hero). Was an officer in a native regiment in India; husband of Mrs. Pritchard-Wallace; a good friend of James Parsons; gentle and good humored; large; heavy moustache; kind eyes; died of fever in Durban at the beginning of the Boer War

PROFESSOR (Appearance and Reality). He teaches French literature at an English university; is a man of high character; he relates the story to the Narrator

PROFESSOR (Marriage of Convenience, 1906). Teaches at the Sorbonne; Genevan; friend of Lucien de Pornichet; advises Lucien to advertise for a wife in the Figaro

PROPRIETOR (Of Human Bondage). Owns the restaurant in Soho; a good man from Rouen

PROPRIETOR (Razor's Edge). Of a bar in the cellar near Notre Dame, Paris, frequented by gangsters and their molls; knew Maugham

PROPRIETORS (Liza of Lambeth). Of the coconut-shy at Chingford; look with concern upon Jim Blakeston for his steady ability to hit the coconuts with the balls

PROPRIETORS (Making of a Saint). In the country around Forli; dismiss their laborers because of heavy taxes

PROUDFOOT DAUGHTERS (Cupid and the Vicar of Swale). Of Sir George and Lady Proudfoot; they play tennis

PROUDFOOT, Sir George (Cupid and the Vicar of Swale). Dead husband of Lady Proudfoot; received his K..G.B. after he bungled an important affair in the Colonies

PROUDFOOT, Lady (Cupid and the Vicar of Swale). She is a resident of Swale; widow of Sir George Proudfoot; more than anyone else in Swale, she is concerned with the matrimonial affairs of the Rev. Robert Branscombe

PROUDFOOT, Matilda (Noble Spaniard). Wife of Sebastian

Proudfoot; age forty-five; stout; she brought thirty thousand pounds to her marriage
PROUDFOOT, Sebastian (Noble Spaniard). The husband of Matilda Proudfoot; age fifty-five; a judge; pompous; fond of a joke
PROVOST (Facts of Life). Of Nicholas Garnet's Cambridge college; knows Colonel Brabazon; has no objection to Nicholas leaving college for tennis at Monte Carlo
PRYCE, Mr. (P.&O.). Looks after machines on Gallagher's estate; small, sturdy, self-assured; a London cockney
PRYNNE (Door of Opportunity). Manages rubber estate up river; age thirty-five; red face; black hair; uneducated; lived with native woman and their two children
PRYNNE CHILDREN (Door of Opportunity). Of Prynne and a native woman; a boy and girl; they fancy Anne Torel
PUBLIC PROSECUTOR (Christmas Holiday). At the trial of Robert Berger; age between thirty-five and forty; he is stout and rubicund; subjected Leontine Berger to a merciless examination; oozing with self-satisfaction
PUBLISHER (Moon and Sixpence). At Berlin, Germany; had reproduced several of Charles Strickland's paintings and sent copies to Amy Strickland
PUBLISHERS (Explorer [novel]). Telegraphed offers to Alec MacKenzie for a book they assumed he would write
PUCCI, Piero (Mask and the Face). In love and engaged to Wanda Sereni; he releases her from that engagement
PURCHASERS (Making of a Saint). At the market place at Forli; they walk along and carefully examine goods
PURSER (Ashenden/Mr. Harrington's Washing). The only man aboard the ship from Yokohama to Vladivostok who spoke English
PURSER (Moon and Sixpence). Of the Oahu; he told Tiare Johnson that he had never met a nicer girl on all the islands than Ata

Q

QUACK (Making of a Saint). Is at the market place at Forli; extracting teeth
QUEEN OF SIAM (Princess September). She is the mother of nine daughters and ten sons
QUERN, Sir Giles (Human Element). The Englishman from whom Betty Weldon-Burns purchased her house in the

city; he is from Cornwall

QUERN, Mary (Human Element). Cousin of Sir Giles Quern; she had married one of Betty Weldon-Burns' relatives

R

R (Ashenden). See above, discussed under COLONEL R

RABENSTEIN, Ferdy (Alien Corn). Age fifty when he meets the Narrator; is nearly seventy years of age when the story occurs; born in South Africa; came to England at age twenty; on Stock Exchange until he inherited a considerable fortune from his father; has abundant, coarse, curly white hair; has a fine Semetic profile; shiny black eyes; tall, a lean; oval face; clear skin

RABENSTEIN, Hannah (Alien Corn). Dowager Lady Bland; Ferdy Rabenstein's sister; married Alphonse Bleikogel (Sir Alfred Bland); at the time of the story, is age eighty and a resident of Portland Place, London; she is tall and stout, and she wears a metallic brown wig

RADIO OPERATOR (Winter Cruise). On board the Friedrich Weber; above middle height; square shouldered, with narrow hips; erect and slender; tanned smooth skin; large blue eyes; curly blonde hair; age twenty-one; neither married nor engaged

RADLEY (For Services Rendered). Collie Stratton owes him 187 pounds; he wants his money by the first of the month

RADLEY, Dr. (Hero). Physician at Little Primpton, Kent; he announces that James Parsons has enteric fever

RADZIWELLS (Razor's Edge). Elliott Templeton used to drink zubrovka at their house whenever he lodged with them for the shooting

R.A.F. OFFICER (Hour Before the Dawn). At Lewes, with the chief constable and the police inspector; is from the secret airdrome near Graveney; convinced that the Germans know the airdrome exists; obstinate, insular, and narrow-minded

RAGGLES (Magician). A still-life painter at Paris; he is young; bow legged; neat, smooth hair; at the Chien Noir, he represented the artist of rank and fashion

RAHAM, A.B. (Home and Beauty). Victoria Cardew-Lowndes' solicitor; has arranged more divorce cases than any man in England

RAILING, Bertram (Bishop's Apron). Son of James Samuel and Mrs. Railing; the brother of Louise and Florrie; interested in model dwellings for the London poor; age twenty-eight; as beautiful as a Greek god; dark; skin smoother than polished ivory, with the glowing color of Titian's young Adonis; long curling hair; dark, fine, sincere eyes; broad forehead; a straight nose; well-shaped sensual mouth; square jaw; powerful and statuesque neck; a somber expression; clever; a Christian socialist who writes for the radical papers and devotes his entire life to "a passionate striving for reform"; his income is approximately 150 pounds per year; in love with and engaged to Winnie Spratte

RAILING, Bertram/Herbert (Loaves and Fishes [see 1st ed., London: William Heinemann Ltd., 1924: ii,iv, 21, 43]]). Brother of Louise and Florri Railing; a Christian Socialist and author of The Future of Socialism; flaunting good looks that attract women; dark; fine eyes; age twenty-five; of a romantic appearance; fine hair that he wears long; is engaged to Winnie Spratte

RAILING, Florrie (Bishop's Apron/Loaves and Fishes). Is the elder daughter of James Samuel and Mrs. Railing; sister of Bertram and Louise; is not quite right in her head, the result of a fall down the stairs when she was a only a child; she resides in an asylum

RAILING, Mr. James Samuel (Bishop's Apron/Loaves and Fishes). Father of Florrie, Louise, and Bertram Railing; first mate on a collier trading from Newcastle; died before he had reached age thirty-five; fine legs

RAILING, Louise (Bishop's Apron). Younger daughter of James Samuel and Mrs. Railing; sister of Bertram and Florrie; lives with her mother in Peckham; teaches at a Board school; careful to speak the King's English correctly; with a pinz-nez; radical "from top to toe"

RAILING, Louise (Loaves and Fishes). Sister of Bertram and Florrie Railing; an advanced radical and social worker; she was once engaged to a solicitor's clerk; is determined and very aggressive; wears a pinz-nez

RAILING, Mrs. (Bishop's Apron). Widow of James Samuel Railing; the mother of Florrie, Louise, and Bertram; lives with Louise in Peckham; is not highly educated; short, stout; red face; excessively black hair; fat, good-natured voice; aggressive cockney tongue; drinks

RAILING, Mrs. (Loaves and Fishes). Mother of Florrie, Louise, and Bertram Railing; she is short and stout; red face; gray hair tightly drawn

RAILING, Thomas (Bishop's Apron). The father of James Samuel Railing; had sailed on the brig Mary Ann; wore side whiskers that were of considerable luxuriance

RAILWAY DIRECTORS (Good Manners). Baron von Bernheim petitioned them for a rail station at Graveney, Kent

RAILWAY OFFICIALS (Punctiliousness of Don Sebastian). At Xiormonez, Spain; the German painter believed that they spent time eating garlic and smoking cigarettes

RAINEY, George (Moon and Sixpence). Second husband of Tiare Johnson; was nearly six feet three inches tall; Tiare divorced him because he treated her so decently

RAMSAY, Anne (Bishop's Apron). Nurse to young Theodore and Sophia Spratte; lived in the country on a small pension; she had been attacked by a fatal illness

RAMSAY, Dr. (Mrs. Craddock). A general practitioner at Blackstable, Kent; is Bertha Ley's guardian; big and broad shouldered; a mane of fair hair turning white; mutton-chop whiskers and shaven chin; red-cheeked; florid complexion; jovial; married; he is opposed to the intended marriage of Bertha and Edward Craddock; bandages Edward Craddock when the latter breaks his collarbone after having been thrown from his horse

RAMSAY, Elmer (Mr. Know-All). He and his wife sit at the doctor's table, with the Narrator and Max Kelada; described as dogmatic; is a member of the American Consular Service, stationed at Kobe, Japan; from the Midwest; he is heavy, with loose fat under tight skin

RAMSAY, George (Ant and the Grasshopper). The brother of Tom Ramsay; respectable; age forty-seven; married, and the father of four daughters

RAMSAY, Mr. (Mrs. Craddock). Father of Dr. Ramsay; a farmer; he has been dead for thirty years; he made no pretense of being a gentleman

RAMSAY, Mrs. (Mr. Know-All). The wife of Elmer Ramsay; small and pretty; modest

RAMSAY, Mrs. (Mrs. Craddock). The wife of Dr. Ramsay; meekly submitted to her husband

RAMSAY, Tom (Ant and the Grasshopper). The brother of George Ramsay; age forty-six; had gone into business, married, and had two children; left his wife and his

business, and then lived off of his brother's money
RAMSDEN (Of Human Bondage). Is a medical student at St. Luke's Hospital, London; is a close friend of Harry Griffiths; very tall; small head; attempts to affect a reconciliation between Griffiths and Philip Carey
RAMSDEN, Freddy (Lady Habart). Had been engaged to Lady Habart when she was known as Dolly Cherriton; is the younger son of a country squire; his eldest brother died and left him the estate; Dolly jilted him for Lord Habart, after which he went off to Africa for five Africa; he is big and broad shouldered; grayish hair, heavy moustache; is deeply bronzed from the sun
RANDOLPH, Lady (Circle). Her picture appears in Clive Champion-Cheney's old photograph album
RATHBONE, Mr. (East of Suez). American; lived in Singapore for four years with Daisy (now Mrs. Anderson), but never married her; he died
RAVENSWORTH, Roderic (Cakes and Ale). A fictitious name young Willie Ashenden invented to replace his own
RAWLINGSON, Mrs. (Of Human Bondage). Wife of the vicar of Ferne; thirty-two wreaths were sent to her funeral
RAWLINGSON, Rev. (Of Human Bondage). Vicar of Ferne and husband of Mrs. Rawlingson
RAYMOND (Ashenden/Giulia Lazzari). Code name for Col. R
RAYMOND, Bertha (East of Suez). A Eurasian; very nice
RAYMOND, Jane (Love in a Cottage). Sybil Bruce's friend and companion at Paris
RAYNER, Jack (Marriages Are Made in Heaven). He is age thirty-two; sunburnt, lined, and worn face; an aura of weariness suggests that he had lived very hard and found life difficult; poor; preparing to marry Lottie Vivyan; educated at Oxford; he served in South Africa in the war; worked as a farmer, miner, and bartender
RAYNOR, Adolphus (Bad Example). Son of John and Mrs. Raynor; brother of Amy Clinton; died at age two years
RAYNOR, John, Esq. (Bad Example). Father of Amy Clinton and Adolphus Raynor; he is a resident of Peckham Rye
RAYNOR, Mrs. (Bad Example). Wife of John Raynor and the mother of Adolphus Raynor and Amy Clinton; assisted her daughter and James Clinton, prior to their marriage, in the selection of a place to live; agreed with James's choice of the left side the road (as opposed to the right)

REAR GUARD (Explorer [novel]). With Alec Mackenzie's latest expedition against the African slavers; they would not allow a single man to remain behind them

REBELS (Making of a Saint). Some fifty of them; thrown into the prison at Forli by Caterina Sforza; executed

REBELS (Man with the Scar). Are four of them; spend the night in jail playing poker with the General; they are executed the next day

RECEPTION CLERK (Human Element). At the Hotel Plaza, at Rome; tells Narrator that the hotel is full

RECTOR (Catalina). Of the University of Salamanca; vain and irascible; he turned over Domingo Perez's name to the inquisitors of the Holy Office

RECTOR (Explorer [novel]). A bachelor and a former don; given living of Hamlyn's Purlieu by Fred Allerton; spare, gray-haired, and gentle; lived as a recluse, spending most of his time with his books; a man of varied learning and remote information; eccentric; he responds to Lucy Allerton's request to bring her father home to die, offering her rooms in the rectory

RECTOR (Good Manners). Guest at one of Augusta Breton's dinners; youngish; iron-gray hair; an ascetic manner

RECTOR (Merry-Go-Round). Of Jeyston, Dorsetshire; he is vulgarly independent

RED (Red). An American sailor; flaming hair, with a natural wave; extremely handsome; one or two inches over six feet; broad shoulders, thin flanks; suave, feminine grace; white, milky skin; dark blue eyes; dark eyebrows; long dark lashes; eventually becomes a schooner captain--taciturn; tall, more than six feet; very stout; red face; blotchy, bloodshot eyes; bald, except for the fringe of long, curly hair, nearly white, at the back of his head; immense forehead; fat chest covered by reddish hair; large belly, fat legs

REED, George (Letter [story]). Announced as having an appointment with Mr. Joyce at twelve o'clock; he rescheduled for 3:00 p.m.

REED, Miss (Daisy). A resident of Blackstable, Kent; a gossip and a meddler; tells Mrs. Howlett that Daisy Griffith has eloped

REED, Mr. (Letter [play]). Of Reed and Pollack; Howard Joyce has an appointment with him at 12:30 p.m., but he must wait

Characters   351

REEVES, Mrs. (Cakes and Ale). The owner of the Railway Arms, Blackstable, Kent

REGIMENTAL SURGEON (Painted Veil). At Mei-tan-fu; was trained by Walter Fane and, in turn, he treats Walter during his illness

REGISTRAR (Jane). Marries Jane Fowler to Gilbert Napier

REID (Winter Cruise). Venetia Reid's grandfather; had been a naval officer

REID, Venetia (Winter Cruise). Her legal Christian name is Alice; a passenger on the Friedrich Weber; owner of a tea room at a celebrated beauty spot in the west of England; an avid reader, but an excruciating bore; long, stupid face; large brown eyes and thick lashes; brown hair cut short; neither fat nor thin; generally drab appearance; is approximately forty years of age

REITUNG, Hans (Alien Corn). A friend of George Bland at Munich; a young poet

RELATIVE (Sanatorium). Comes to the sanatorium from Glasgow to attend McLeod's funeral

REMIRE, Adele (Official Position). Murdered by her husband, Louis Remire; an intolerable woman; dressmaker

REMIRE, Louis (Official Position). A widower; serving a twelve-years sentence at St. Laurent de Maroni, in French Guiana, for killing his wife; former policeman from Lyons; the public executioner; sturdy and broad shouldered; of middle height; ruddy complexion; blue eyes; thick brown hair, gray at the temples; handsome moustache; age fifty; he is quick tempered, but good natured; a great fisherman

RENARD, Henri (Man with a Conscience). Known as Riri; inseparable companion, at Le Havre, of Jean Charvin; his father an official in the Customs Service; light hearted and athletic; thoroughly enjoyed his leisure

RENARD, Monsieur and Madame (Man with a Conscience). Henri Renaud's parents; host a party to celebrate the engagement of their daughter

REPORTER (Bishop's Apron). Of the London Daily Mail; he comes to the vicarage of St. Gregory's to interview Theodore Spratte following his appointment as Bishop of Sheffield

REPORTER (Christmas Holiday). He had conducted his own investigation concerning the murder of Teddie Jordan

REPORTER (Sheppey). For the Daily Echo; young and pasty

faced; he interviews Sheppey Miller after the latter wins a prize in the Irish Sweepstakes

REPORTERS (Landed Gentry). Seen at the inquest on the suicide of Margaret Gann; made Claude Insoley appear a perfect brute

REPORTERS (Razor's Edge). Of the Herald and the Mail; Miss Keith sees that they receive a good supper and a bottle of Edna Novemali's second best champagne

RESIDENT (Buried Talent). At Penang; tells Sir Edward Convers to stay with him, but the former declines

RESIDENT (Masterson). At Taunggyi; he arranges for the Narrator to secure mules and ponies for the journey from Taunggyi to Keng Tung

RESIDENTS (Explorer [novel]). At Mombassa; they held a dinner in Alec MacKenzie's honor

RETFORD, Harry (Cakes and Ale). Is a regular visitor to the Driffields' house on Saturdays; he is an often unemployed actor; took Rosie Driffield to be photographed; age thirty; has a pleasantly ugly face; gay, charming, vain, boastful, and unscrupulous; killed at Ladysmith in the Boer War

REVIEWER (Cakes and Ale). Of a lady's paper; excitedly claimed one of Alroy Kear's books as a work of genius

RHODESIAN FARMER (Of Human Bondage). Wed the daughter of Dr. and Mrs. South; had a quarrel with the doctor

RIARIO, Girolamo (Making of a Saint). Is the husband of Caterina Sforza; nephew (illegitimate son?) of Pope Sixtus; the common people of Forli once struggled to lick the ground upon which he trod; the people begin to murmur about his extravagance; claimed that to be popular, he had to be magnificent; is tall, muscular, strong; a big, heavy face; prominent jawbones; long, hooked nose; small, keen, mobile eyes; unpleasant red and coarse skin; he and his father prime movers in the conspiracy that murdered the brother of Lorenzo de Medici, nearly killing Lorenzo himself; eventually assassinated in the conspiracy led by Checco d'Orsi

RIARIO, Ottaviano (Making of a Saint). The small son of Girolamo Riario and Caterina Sforza; innocently sang a popular song of scorn against his father; Girolamo nearly killed him in a passion of rage

RICE, Mr. (Of Human Bondage). The young master of the lower second form at King's School, Tercanbury; red face; a pleasant voice; jolly; he had only taken his degree the previous year

RICHARDSON (Explorer [novel/play]). Is a member of Alec MacKenzie's expedition against the East African slave traders; he is killed in fierce battle with the Arabs

RICHARDSON, Dr. (Magician). Attended Margaret Haddo at Skene, Staffordshire; told Mrs. Smithers that Margaret died from heart disease (endocarditis); small; at age fifty-five; a fair beard, nearly white; prominent blue eyes; broad Staffordshire accent; obstinate and foolish; he has practiced medicine thirty-five years; also chairman of the board of magistrates at Venning

RICHARDSON, Mrs. (Magician). Wife of Dr. Richardson; hosting a few lady-friends to tea

RICHMAN, Beatrice (Three Fat Women of Antibes). She is a widow; age in the early to mid-forties; enormously fat; fine eyes

RICHTER, Hans (Narrow Corner). Celebrated German conductor (1843-1916); led the music at Covent Garden Theatre, London, with passion and melodious splendor

RICHTER, Herr (Up at the Villa). Is the father of Karl Richter; he had been head of the police in a small Austrian town during the Dollfuss regime (1932-1934); favored the restoration of the Archduke Otto; he shot himself when the Germans marched into Austria (1934)

RICHTER, Karl (Up at the Villa). The violinist at the Florentine restaurant on one of the banks of the River Arno; is Austrian; a strange head, with close-cropped, black hair; high cheekbones, hollow cheeks; pallid skin; a strained look; self-proclaimed student of art; actually studied art history at a university, planning to become a schoolmaster; he also admits to being a terrible violinist; is a substitute for the singer; age twenty-three, and poor; dark and slender; enormous, hungry eyes; has a melancholy look; smooth, pinched, and thin face; spoke English well, but with a foreign accent; spent three months in concentration camp, then escaped into the Italian Tyrol; he has an affair with Mary Panton; after that he shoots himself

RICKABY, Duke and Duchess of (Theatre). To have supper at the Savoy with Julia Lambert Gosselyn and Thomas Fennell; they will go anywhere for a free meal

RICKSHAW BOY #1 (Mirage). He conveys the Narrator to

Grosely's house

RICKSHAW BOY #2 (Mirage). He carries Grosely to find a woman

RICKSHAW BOYS (East of Suez). They are In a crowded Peking street; they shout for the crowd to make way

RIDING MASTER (Hero). Is the father of Mrs. Pritchard-Wallace; husband of a Portuguese woman

RISENBAUM, Benjy (Voice of the Turtle). Of considerable wealth; a lover of La Folterona

RIXON, Mrs. (Mrs. Dot). Is Gerald Halstane's solicitor; short and rubicund; white whiskers; a hearty manner

ROAD, George (Moon and Sixpence). A writer and guest at Amy Strickland's luncheon

ROBERTSON (Penelope). He is Richard O'Farrell's broker; Dickie asks his advice about the Johannesburg and New Jerusalem mine

ROBEY, Sir George (Unknown). A London comedian (1869-1954) and "the Prime Minister of Mirth"; Charlotte Littlewood and her woman companion see him in London

ROBINSON, Grace (Landed Gentry). Under Grace INSOLEY

ROBINSON, Miss (String of Beads). Is the Livingstones' governess; asked by the Livingstones to dinner when one of the guests fails to arrive; twenty or twenty-one years of age; rather pretty; clergyman's daughter

ROBINSON, Mr. (Sheppey). Husband of Mrs. Robinson; out of work for the past eight months

ROBINSON, Mrs. (Sheppey). Has delivered twins to add to her four other children; Ada Miller makes calves-foot jelly for her; is the wife of unemployed Mr. Robinson

ROBINSON, Peter (Casual Affair). Bee Low bought a frock for Lady Kastellan's party at his London dress shop

ROBINSONS (Ashenden/Miss King). A Swiss family at the Geneva cafe; so named by Ashenden; a father, mother, four children; sit around a table and drink two small cups of coffee

ROCCAMARE, Prince (Three Fat Women of Antibes). Accompanies Arrow Sutcliffe on a brisk walk; is young and good looking; he has a palace in Rome and a castle in the Apennines

RODOLPHE (Christmas Holiday). Simon Fenimore's hypothetical example of a poor brute who no longer has the money to lead the exciting life in the Latin Quarter

RODRIGO (Catalina). Is a wine seller in Segovia, Spain

Characters 355

ROFA (Explorer [novel]). The barbaric native king of an African region; became friends with Alec MacKenzie; he wanted to marry his sister--except that Alec did not have one

ROGERS (Explorer [novel]). A member of Alec MacKenzie's expedition against the African slave traders; Alec sends him to bring in the Latuka tribe to reinforce his men against an attack by the natives and slavers

ROGERS (Love in a Cottage). [Listed, but not described in the summary]

ROGERS (Mrs. Craddock). Is a huntsman near Blackstable, Kent; he cautioned Edward Craddock about the horse he had bought from Arthur Branderton

ROGERS (Tenth Man). Is one of George Winter's campaign workers at Middlepool

ROGERS, A.W. (Mrs. Craddock). Landlord of the Pig and Whistle, Blackstable, Kent; he leads the cheering for Edward Craddock after his political speech at the Blackstable town hall; he is in attendance at Edward Craddock's funeral; he maintains that had Edward been there, the funeral would have ended a half-hour ago

ROGERS, Dr. (Penelope). Is a physician in John Street, London; he is located just opposite Dickie O' Farrell

ROGERS, Mildred (Of Human Bondage). Is a waitress at a London tea shop, Parliament street; age twenty-four; Dunsford admired her; tall, thin; narrow hips; the chest of a boy; small, regular features; blue eyes; a broad, low brow; considerable hair, done over the forehead in an Alexandra fringe; is anemic; pale lips and delicate skin, with greenish pallor; good teeth; small, thin, white hands; she generally suffered from dyspepsia after a meal; her parents are dead; lives with her aunt, at Herne Hill; goes to live with Emil Miller; expects a baby; Miller leaves her; falls in love with Harry Griffiths; eventually "vanished [but temporarily] into the anonymous mass of the population of London"; resurfaces as a London streetwalker; in one room in Highbury with her baby; moves in with Philip Carey; they part and she returns to the street

ROGERS, Mr. (Of Human Bondage). Mildred Rogers' father; supposedly, he kept a dog cart and three servants

ROLLIN, Michel (Of Human Bondage). Is an art master at Amitrano's art studio in Paris; elderly; white beard;

florid complexion; impervious to the progress of art, but he was an excellent teacher; he came on Tuesdays

ROLLO, Monsieur (De Amicitia). An old French painter at Paris; the American girls call him Popper; Valentia Stewart writes to him from Holland, declaring that she does not think of Ferdinand White as a man, but as a companion; he writes and calls her a philosopher

ROMAN EMPERORS (Magician). A part of Margaret Dauncey's hypnotic vision; clad in purple

ROMANO (Cakes and Ale). Owner of a London restaurant; Harry Retford knew him; spoke in funny broken English

RONALDSON, Major (Moon and Sixpence). Husband of the Stricklands' daughter; is an officer in the Gunners

RONALDSON, Mrs. (Moon and Sixpence). Daughter of Amy and Charles Strickland; dark, thick, shoulder-length hair; a kindly expression; sedate, untroubled eyes; married to Major Ronaldson

RONCHI, Jacopo (Making of a Saint). The commander of a troop; stationed himself by the Church of San Stefano to await Girolamo Riario; he has not received his pay for months; will join a plot to assassinate Girolamo

ROOME, Colonel (Merry-Go-Round). A co-respondent in the divorce petition of Lord Vizard against Lady Vizard

ROONEY (Landed Gentry). The chauffeur at Kenyon Fulton; he is afraid that Henry Cobbett will miss the train

ROSALIA (Mother). Daughter of Pilar; pretty; high color and fine, bold eyes; glossy black hair; full figured

ROSE (Of Human Bondage). A pupil at the King's School, Tercanbury; large hands and big bones; charming eyes; laughed constantly; became a friend of Philip Carey

ROSE, Betty (Making of a Millionaire). Frederick Rose's wife and mother of Leslie; threatens to leave if her husband does not buy back shares of New-Lyons Mine

ROSE, Frederick (Making of a Millionaire). Betty Rose's husband and father of Leslie; is tall and stout; gray hair and heavy moustache; his eye had a good-humored twinkle; frank expression; a retired soldier; he has made a fortune on the Stock Exchange; twenty years earlier, he had undergone prosecution for a swindling charge; narrowly escaped a prison term; currently engaged in a gigantic fraud that turns out legitimate

ROSE, Leslie (Making of a Millionaire). Son of Betty and Frederick Rose; is handsome; educated at Oxford;

athletic; engaged to Janet Blissard; he threatens to leave for America if his father does not buy back all of the shares in the New-Lyons Mine

ROSEBERY, Archibald Primrose, Earl of (Mrs. Craddock). British statesman (1847-1929); whenever he makes a speech, the news journals of his own party promptly report him in the first person and at full length

ROSENBAUM (Straight Flush). Small, hunched, fairly, old (age seventy-six), and rich; emaciated; on board the ship for Hong Kong

ROSENBERG (Christmas Holiday). He is an art dealer, Rue de Seine, Paris

ROSENBERG BABY (Smith). Six-week-old child of Cynthia and Otto Rosenberg; sickly; dies

ROSENBERG, Cynthia (Smith). The wife of Otto Rosenberg; formerly Cynthia Russell; she is young, pretty, and rosy cheeked; elaborately arranged golden hair; the mother of a six-week-old infant who is always ill

ROSENBERG, Lydia (Smith). Sister of Otto, Rachel, and Pom-Pom Rosenberg; she has thirty thousand pounds

ROSENBERG, Otto (Smith). Husband of Cynthia Rosenberg; brother of Lydia, Rachel and Pom-Pom; is considerably older than Cynthia; a German-Jew, but a naturalized British citizen for ten years; on the Stock Exchange

ROSENBERG, Pom-Pom (Smith). The sister of Otto, Rachel, and Lydia Rosenberg; she has thirty thousand pounds

ROSENBERG, Rachel (Smith). The sister of Otto, Lydia, and Pom-Pom Rosenberg; she has thirty thousand pounds

ROSIE (Fortunate Painter). Engaged to Charlie Bartle; her parents pressuring her to end the relationship

ROTHCHILDS (Razor's Edge). They are hosting a ball at Paris, to which Elliott Templeton has adeptly managed to obtain entry cards for Isabel and Louisa Bradley

ROUGE (Magician). Does all of the illustrations for La Semaine; more a prosperous tradesman than an artist

ROUVIER, Madame (Razor's Edge). The mother of Suzanne Rouvier; a widow; native of Anjou, where she retired after the death of her husband

ROUVIER, Monsieur (Razor's Edge). The husband of Madame Rouvier and father of Suzanne; was a minor government official; he died when his daughter was only a child

ROUVIER, Suzanne (Razor's Edge). Known both to Maugham and Larry Darrell, whom she had met through Marcel;

Larry told her about the young airman who died saving his life; she tells the story, in French, to Maugham; had been a mistress to at least six artists in Paris before she contacted typhoid fever; mother of Odette; has a brief affair with Larry Darrell; becomes the mistress of Achille Gauvain, manufacturer from Lille; takes up painting; close to forty years of age when Maugham sees her again; is rather ugly; tall (a short body, long legs and arms); hair often reddish brown; small square face; prominent cheekbones; large mouth; good skin; strong white teeth; large vivid blue eyes

ROYAL PERSONS (Magician). Dr. Frank Hurrell believes that one day Arthur Burdon will relieve them of their veriform appendixes

RUDOLF, Crown Prince (Voice of the Turtle). He had an affair with Florence Montgomerie

RUMANIAN PRINCE (Razor's Edge). Is at a tea hosted by Louisa Bradley at her Paris apartment; small, dark; little darting black eyes; clean shaven swarthy face

RUSSELL (Lady Habart). A butler employed by Lady Habart

RUSSELL, Cynthia (Smith). See under Cynthia ROSENBERG

RUSSIAN (Dream). He shares a table with the Narrator at the station restaurant at Vladivistok; he is tall and stout, with a vast paunch; small hands; long, dark, thin hair; becoming bald; huge sallow face; double chin; clean shaven; small, button nose; small, black, shining eyes; large red mouth; an ugly man; of noble birth; a lawyer and a widower; he is a heavy smoker

RUSSIAN CHILDREN (Ashenden/Mr. Harrington's Washing). Two of them; belong to a bearded Russian and his wife

RUSSIAN DANCERS (Casual Affair). Two of them; the provided the entertainment for Lady Kastellan's party

RUSSIAN MAN (Ashenden/Mr. Harrington's Washing). Father of two children; bearded; suffers from deep emotion

RUSSIAN PRINCE (Gigolo and Gigolette). A guest at the Casino dinner party; has designs upon the aged Mrs. Chaloner Barrett; he sells motor cars, champagne, and Old Masters on commission

RUSSIAN WOMAN (Ashenden/Mr. Harrington's Washing). Wife of the bearded Russian man and mother of their two children; she tells the station master her life story

RUSSIAN'S WIFE (Dream). Native of Geneva, Switzerland; cultivated woman who spoke English, German, Italian,

French, and Russian; she taught languages to nobles' daughters at Petrograd; small, thin; bad complexion; extremely jealous

RUTH (Judgment Seat). Broken in health from hard work and devotion; died, after she had heard of the death of John, whom she loved; ten years younger than John; charming, graceful, lovely; became fiercely religious

RYAN (Narrow Corner). At the bar in Sydney, Australia; is a big bully; had something to do with politics; he always had plenty of money; married, with children; offers Captain Nichols a job to run a pearling lugger

RYLE, Mrs. Mayston (Mrs. Craddock). Is a guest at Mrs. Branderton's dinner party; wore a wonderful black wig

S

SABIDON, Mrs. (Explorer [novel]). She brought an action against Fred Allerton and Saunders; she had entrusted more than eight thousand pounds to them for investment, which they, in turn put to their personal uses

SACRISTAN #1 (Then and Now). He is a lay brother at Fra Timoteo's church

SACRISTAN #2 (Then and Now). San Vitale, Ravenna; for a gratuity allows one to remain all night in the church

SAFFARY, Tom (Back of Beyond). A planter; one of George Moon's Tamil overseers; husband of Violet Saffary; manager of one of the largest rubber estates in the district; thirty-eight years of age; is large, burly, and stout; a red face; double chin; with curly, black hair; blue eyes; strong; a heavy eater and drinker

SAFFARY, Violet (Back of Beyond). Wife of Tom Saffary; age thirty-four or thirty-five; small; is not pretty, but pleasant to look at; is the daughter of a doctor killed in the war

SAILES, Corrie (De Amicitia). One of Valentia Stewart's leaving Paris and going home

SAILOR (Christmas Holiday). He had accompanied Teddie Jordan to Jojo's Bar; is a suspect in Teddie's murder

SAILOR (French Joe). He carried the Narrator's luggage from the steamer and then directed him to the hotel on Thursday Island

SAILOR (Moon and Sixpence). On board a sailing vessel from Aukland to San Francisco; points out Tahiti to

Charles Strickland

SAILORS (Ashenden/Miss King). Two of them; on board the steamer from Thonon to Geneva; inform Ashenden that the boast has crossed Lake Leman

SAILORS (Cakes and Ale). Two or three; sit outside the warehouse in Blackstable, Kent, and stare at Ashenden

SAILORS (Merry-Go-Round). At Brindisi; lounge about the port

SAILORS (Moon and Sixpence). Residents of Tough Bill's boarding house; told Charles Strickland that Tough Bill had sworn to kill him

SAILORS (Mrs. Craddock). Three or four of them; at the station, Blackstable, Kent; saunter down the platform

SAILORS (Razor's Edge). Bring opium from the East into Toulon

SAILORS (Spanish Priest). Of all nations, at Gibraltar; lounge idly

SAISE #1 (Caesar's Wife). The Consular Agent's house, Cairo, Egypt; he brings in a salver with coffee cups

SAISE #2 (Caesar's Wife). The Consular Agent's house, Cairo; bears a small tray on which is a silver vessel containing Turkish coffee

SAISE #3 (Caesar's Wife). The Consular Agent's house, Cairo; turns out the lights after the dancers leave

SALADIN, Madame (Appearance and Reality). Widowed aunt of Lisette Larion; lived with Lisette in a two-room apartment within the Batignolles district of Paris

SALESMAN (Sheppey). He had persuaded Bradley to give the German hair preparation a trial in his shop

SALLY (Red). A Samoan native girl who fell in love with Red at age sixteen (he then being nineteen); tall and slim; large eyes; black hair; small hands; eventually marries Neilson; she ages into a fat old native woman

SALVATORE (Salvatore). A pleasant, ugly face; laughing mouth and carefree eyes; contacts form of rheumatism while on naval service; a fisherman and worker in his father's vineyard; marries Assunta

SALVATORE'S CHILDREN (Salvatore). Two boys, one three years old and the other almost two

SALVATORE'S FATHER (Salvatore). A fisherman and owner of a small vineyard; two sons younger than Salvatore

SALVATORE'S MOTHER (Salvatore). Tells her son that she did not know the whereabouts of his fiancee

Characters 361

SALVIATI, Giacomo (Then and Now). Sent to succeed Machiavelli as the Florentine ambassador to Caesar Borgia

SAMPSON (Of Human Bondage). Buyer at Lynn and Sedley, London; he is small, pleasant, and fussy; age thirty; he considers himself and Philip Carey both gentlemen

SAMSON (Ashenden/ Mr. Harrington's Washing). Name given to J.Q. Harrington by Anastasia Alexandrovna Leonidov

SAN ESTEBAN, Marques (Romantic Young Lady). Pursues and finally marries Pilar Carreon

SAN ESTEBAN, Marquesa de (Romantic Young Lady). Stout; more than middle aged; dark, red, and dyed hair; a fine figure of a woman; a widow; former name, Pilar Carreon, a daughter of the Duchess de Dos Palos; age twenty when she initially met the Narrator; when a young woman, magnificent eyes and peach-like skin; slim, tall, red mouth, white teeth; shiny black hair

SAN FERDINANDO, Prince (Up at the Villa). A Roman; the husband of Princess San Ferdinando; had been dead for a quarter of a century

SAN FERDINANDO, Princess (Up at the Villa). Hosting a dinner party at Florence to which Mary Panton and Sir Edgar Swift had been invited; an old tyrant; she is an American; iron-gray, tightly-waved hair; manner is authoritative; upright carriage; determined features; fine eyes; had lived in Italy for forty years without ever having returned to America; has little money; a caustic tongue but a good nature; reportedly had been unfaithful to the Prince; her two sons in the Italian army; had discovered a singer in a restaurant on the banks of the River Arno

SAN IGNACIO, General (Man with a Scar). The commander of the government troops; he attends the execution of the General and his four companions

SANCHEZ, Antonia (Mother). See above under LA CACHIRRA

SANCHEZ, Currito (Mother). The son of La Cachirra; age twenty; a lean face, and white, even teeth; hair cut close and shaved at the temples; bearded; brown skin

SANTA ANA, Calisto de (Poet). A Spanish poet; he lived in seclusion in his native Andalusian town of Ecija

SANTAGUADOR, Duchess Conchita de (Point of Honour). The cousin to Don Pedro Aguira; converses with him at the Seville opera house; weeks later, she dances with him at a party

SANTI, Pepe (Mother). He is murdered by La Cachirra for beating Currito Sanchez

SARAH (Camel's Back). The Lefevres' buxom young cook; insists on spoon-feeding a bowl of gruel to Valentine Lefevre; Valentine flirts with her and gets her to believe that he will take her off to Paris; dismissed by Hermione Lefevre

SARAH (Choice of Amyntas). The daughter of Peter the Schoolmaster and Mrs. Peter

SARAH (Noble Spaniard). Matilda Proudfoot's aunt; went down on her bended knees and begged Matilda not to marry a common lawyer

SATTERWHAITE, Mr. and Mrs. (Razor's Edge). They occupy a great stone house on Lake Shore Drive, Chicago; host a large party

SAUNDERS (Explorer [novel]). In partnership with Fred Allerton in a fraudulent brokerage operation (bucket shop) under the name of Vernon and Lawford; the sort of man who only uses his own name on the charge sheet of a police court

SAUNDERS, Dr. (Narrow Corner). English; had practiced medicine for fifteen years at Fu-chou; is short, just over five feet six inches tall; slim; slight paunch; soft, small, and podgy hands, with tapering fingers; ugly; snub nose and large mouth; big, yellow, uneven teeth; bushy gray eyebrows; green eyes; blotchy skin; a high color; purple flush over cheekbones; somewhat inclined to corpulence; hair nearly white and thin on the crown; had studied medicine in England; removed from the Register; is skilled in treating ills that affect the eye; he spoke fluently the dialect of Fu-chou; smoked opium regularly, but with moderation; not a great reader; occupied a shabby little Chinese house over the Min River; he was persuaded by money to go to Takana, where he would operate on Kim Ching

SAUNDERS, Elizabeth (Our Betters). Known as Bessie; a very pretty American girl; age twenty-two; Lady Pearl Grayston's sister; fair hair and blue eyes; at age sixteen had been asked by Fleming Harvey to marry him

SAUNDERS, Mr. (Our Betters). Father of Bessie Saunders and Pearl Grayston; American; owns a hardware store

SAUNDERS, Mrs. (Our Betters). Mother of Bessie Saunders and Pearl Grayston; has a fancy for Seventy-Second

Characters 363

    Street, New York
SAUNDERS, Mr. Sergeant (Round Dozen). He is the father of Gertrude St. Clair
SAVELLO, Protonotary (Making of a Saint). He is Papal governor of Cesena; through him, Checco d'Orsi offers Forli to the Pope; he accepts; middle sized; stout; great round belly and fat red face; double chin; bull neck; huge ears; tiny piggish eyes, sharp and shrewd; pale and thin eye brows; shaven cheeks; scanty hair, the crown being quite bald and shiny; he takes refuge in a Dominican monastery after the fall of Forli; he goes to the cathedral to worship with Caterina Sforza
SAXOPHONIST #1 (Christmas Holiday). Is a part of the three-piece dance orchestra at the Serail, in Paris
SAXOPHONIST #2 (Christmas Holiday). At the cellar bar in Paris; accompanies Las Marishka
SAXOPHONIST (Razor's Edge). A cafe on the Rue de Lappe, Paris; he made a discordant noise on his instrument
SCALLION, Lord (Cakes and Ale). Young; is possessed of violent literary inclinations; wrote detective novels
SCARABS (Magician). In Margaret Dauncey's vision; huge, limping, and shelled
SCARAMUCCIO (Perfect Gentleman). In the intermezzo; a member of a troupe of Italian dancers
SCAVENGER (Loaves and Fishes). Sweeps the city streets; Bertram Railing believes that Jesus Christ speaks to him through the scavenger's humility
SCHAFER, Wilbur (Ashenden/His Excellency). American ambassador to X; from Kansas City; big, stout; no longer young; white hair; square red face; clean shaven; a little snub nose and determined chin; rubbery face
SCIENTIFIC BODIES (Explorer [novel]). Of all countries; conferred on Alec MacKenzie those distinctions which were in their power to give
SCHOOL CHILDREN (Hero). Of Little Primpton, Kent; come to the Parsons' house to welcome James Parsons home
SCORSACANA, Marco (Making of a Saint). He is a devoted adherent to the house of Orsi; he will eagerly join the conspiracy to assassinate Girolamo Riario; he escapes from Forli with Checco d'Orsi, but then he is captured; returned to the town prison for execution; in the end, hanged from a window of the Palazzo Orsi
SCOT (Spanish Priest). Drinks whiskey in the taverns of

Gibraltar

SCOTCH WOMAN (Gigolo and Gigolette). Is a member of the Casino dinner party; gaunt; her "face like a Peruvian mask that had been battered by the storms of ten centuries"

SCRAGGY GIRL (Creative Impulse). Age fifteen; long legs and tousled head; in same building as Mrs. Bulfinch

SCULPTOR (Explorer [play]). Second-rate; Alec MacKenzie believes that after his death, the man will make a fancy statue of him that will be placed in front of the London Stock Exchange

SCULPTORS (Punctiliousness of Don Sebastian). Directed by Don Sebastian to make one image of him and another of Dona Sodina, so that his new chapel might also function as a burial site

SEAFARE, Lord (Up at the Villa). Secretary of State for India; Edgar Swift's superior; offers Sir Edgar the governorship of Bengal

SEAMSTRESS (Vessel of Wrath). At the mission at Baru; one of the many native women ill-used by Ginger Ted

SEBASTIAN, Archduke (Jack Straw). Of Pomerania; disappeared four years ago; he writes to the Emperor of Pomerania every Christmas from a different part of the world; he passes himself off as Jack Straw

SECOND MATE (Marriage of Convenience, 1906). Aboard the Spanish cargo boat sailing from Cadiz; he told the Narrator that the vessel sometimes carried passengers

SECOND MATE (Taipan). Of the Mary Baxter; perished in the typhoon of 1908; buried in the English cemetery

SECOND OFFICER (Four Dutchmen). In charge of the S.S. Utrecht whenever the four officers and the Narrator dined with the Dutch Resident

SECRETARIES (Catalina). Two of them; to Bishop Blasco de Valero; they hold membership in his own order

SECRETARIES (Closed Shop). Seated at little tables in the president's audience chamber; only in their shirt sleeves, and with revolvers on hips; are busy typing

SECRETARIES (Explorer [novel]). At the Foreign Office; timorous; they did not know into what difficulties a determined Alec MacKenzie might eventually lead them

SECRETARIES (Making of a Saint). To Lorenzo de Medici; they can arrange the commercial transaction between Lorenzo and Checco d'Orsi

Characters

SECRETARIES (Marriage of Convenience). With the French ministry at Bangkok; they had accompanied the retired French official to the ship at Bangkok

SECRETARIES (Then and Now). To Caesar Borgia; convey Niccolo Machiavelli to Sforza Palace to meet Borgia

SECRETARY (Appearance and Reality). Handled confidential arrangements for Raymond Le Sueur; calls Madame Saladin to schedule a dinner meeting among Lisette, her aunt, and Raymond Le Sueur

SECRETARY (Caesar's Wife). Of the Khedive; quarrelled with the Khedive

SECRETARY #1 (Cakes and Ale). To Alroy Kear; connects the Narrator's (William Ashenden) phone call to Kear

SECRETARY #2 (Cakes and Ale). Medical school, St.Luke's Hospital, in London; refers Ashenden to Mrs. Hudson

SECRETARY (Catalina). Read in a loud voice the oath by which all present at the Inquisition proceedings did swear obedience to the Holy Office and pledge themselves to persecute all heretics

SECRETARY (Closed Shop). To President Don Manuel; he presents the letter from the three bordello owners to the president

SECRETARY (Door of Opportunity). To the Governor of Singapore

SECRETARY #1 (Hour Before the Dawn).To Roger Henderson; phones from the War Office, London, to say that Roger has just left for his parents' house at Graveney Holt

SECRETARY #2 (Hour Before the Dawn). To Leslie Hore-Belisha; tells George Henderson that this will be a young man's war

SECRETARY (Lord Mountdrago). To Lord Mountdrago the younger; contacted Dr. Audlin on Mountdrago's behalf

SECRETARY (Mabel). Of the club at the village; relates to the Narrator the story concerning George and Mabel

SECRETARY #1 (Of Human Bondage). St. Luke's Hospital, London; provides Philip Carey with list of potential lodgings; also suggests that he begin dissection with a leg; held out no hope of Philip finding students to tutor; is a pleasant little man; black beard; affable

SECRETARY #2 (Of Human Bondage). At Lynn and Sedley's, London; paid employees their wages once each month

SECRETARY (Punctiliousness of Don Sebastian). To the Archbishop Pablo de Mantona; prepares to read to his master, but the latter sends him away

SECRETARY (Razor's Edge). From the American embassy; at a tea hosted by Louisa Bradley at her apartment in Paris; suave and silent

SECRETARY #1 (Then and Now). To Caesar Borgia; comes to escort Machiavelli to the Sforza Palace on the night of his arranged appointment with Aurelia Martelli

SECRETARY #2 (Then and Now). To Caesar Borgia; brought a portfolio to Borgia, which he handed Machiavelli, of Leonardo's drawings of Borgia

SECRETARY #3 (Then and Now). To Caesar Borgia; sent to tell the captains that Borgia will come to Sinigaglia

SECRETARY (Wash-Tub). To Mrs. Barnaby; she supposedly writes all the invitations to her employer's parties

SEIS #1 (Book-Bag). In the employ of Mark Featherstone; drives Featherstone from Hardys' house to hospital

SEIS #2 (Book-Bag). In the employ of the Hardys; takes message from Olive Hardy's amah to Mark Featherstone

SEIS (Footprints in the Jungle). Sent by Major Gaze to the police station with instructions to send two men to the site of Reggie Bronson's body

SELIM (Explorer [novel/play]). A servant on Alec MacKenzie's expedition against the African slave trade; tells George Allerton Alec wishes to speak with him

SELLINGER, Eleanor (Mrs. Dot). She is known as Nellie; daughter of Lady and General Sir Robert Sellenger; age twenty-one; has been engaged to Gerald Halstane for the past three years; pretty and graceful; falls is in love with Freddie Perkins and runs off with him

SELLENGER, Lady (Mrs. Dot). Widow of General Sir Robert Sellenger and mother of Nellie; age fifty; refused, three years ago, to allow Nellie to marry Gerald Halstane; stout; pompous, alert, and extremely clever

SELLENGER, General Sir Robert (Mrs. Dot). Late husband of Lady Sellenger and father of Nellie

SELLERS (Making of a Saint). Are at the market place at Forli; a joyful crew; all gaily attired; they are bargaining, joking, quarreling, laughing, shouting

SEMANARISTS (Magicians). At St. Sulpice, Paris; a long procession of them; from the college by the church; some young; one or two possess a wan, ascetic look

SEMINARISTS (Mrs. Craddock). Are at the garden of the Mattei, Rome; sauntered along the grass-grown avenues

Characters 367

SENATORS (Making of a Saint). Of the Council at Forli; all of them prejudiced against Girolamo Riario, but voted to reimpose taxes

SENIOR PARTNER (Of Human Bondage). Of Macalister's investment firm; bought five hundred shares of South African gold mine stock for both of his sisters

SEN SHI MING (East of Suez). He cheated his brother out of a house in Hataman Street; he heard someone in the street crying for help and ran out; was found an hour later with a dagger in his heart

SEPOYS (Hero). In Colonel Richmond Parson's command; the most ignorant among them thought their colonel incapable and mad

SEPTEMBER (Princess September). Ninth daughter of the King and Queen of Siam; marries the King of Cambodia

SERAFINA, Monna (Then and Now). A poor widow of one of Bartolomeo Martelli's former business associates in the Levant; the mother of three children, two of whom live with her; lodges Machiavelli, Piero Giacomini, and their servants in her house; thin and tall; with a lined and worn face; has sullen eyes and gray hair

SERGEANT (Marriage of Convenience, 1906). French; at a village on an island off the coast of Tunis; regards Narrator with considerable suspicion; he arrests him

SERGEANT (Painted Veil). At Mei-tan-fu; told Waddington that Walter Fane was still alive

SERGEANT OF THE COURT (Vessel of Wrath). Announces the entrance into Court of Evert Gruyter

SERGISON, Mr. (Book-Bag). A policeman at Sibuku, Malaya

SERGISON, Mrs. (Book-Bag). Wife of Mr. Sergison; thinks that Mark Featherstone and Olive Hardy will marry

SERINI, Wanda (Mask and the Face). The young niece of Cirillo Zanotti; she is engaged to Piero Pucci, but he releases her so that she can marry Marco Milotti

SERLO, Lady (Jack Straw). Widow of Lord Serlo the elder and mother of Lord Ned Serlo; Maria Parker-Jennings believes that she is not the sort of person who would lunch with Rosie Abbot

SERLO, Lord the elder (Jack Straw). The late husband of Lady Serlo and the father of Lord Ned Serlo; formerly ambassador to Pomerania

SERLO, Marchioness of (Penelope). According to a notice

in the Morning Post, she goes to Paris in the morning

SERLO, Lord Ned (Jack Straw). Maria and Robert Parker-Jennings try to arrange a marriage between him and their daughter Ethel; an insignificant person; has no other means of a livelihood aside from his title

SERPENTS (Magician). Are in Margaret Dauncey's hypnotic vision; winged

SERVANT (Alien Corn). In the Employe of the Blands; is instructed by Muriel Bland to tell George Bland to stop playing the piano

SERVANT #1 (Bishop's Apron). Of Josiah Spratte; handed his master a dish of potatoes baked in their skins; stood petrified as Josiah hurled each one at the pictures on the wall

SERVANT #2 (Bishop's Apron). Is at the Athenaeum Club, London; Theodore Spratte asks him to ask the porter if Lord Wroxham is in the club

SERVANT (Caesar's Wife). Native Egyptian; of the Consular Agent's establishment at Cairo; exchanges greetings with the gardener

SERVANT #1 (Catalina). Sent by Friar Blasco de Valero with coins to induce executioner to kill Demetrios Christopoulos, and thus preventing his death by fire

SERVANT #2 (Catalina). He is sent by the archpriest to retrieve Catalina's crutch from the church

SERVANT (East of Suez). At the Andersons' residence; he opens the door of Harold and Sylvia Knox

SERVANT #1 (Explorer [novel]). At Lady Alice Kelsey's dance; told by Robert Boulger to fetch Lucy Allerton

SERVANT #2 (Explorer [novel]). Of Alec MacKenzie; he is ordered to follow to Lancashire with Alec's clothes

SERVANT #1 (Explorer [play]). Is at Dick Lomas's London club (and in Dick's imagination); obsequious; brings Dick grilled rump steak and a plate of fried potatoes

SERVANT #2 (Explorer [play]). At Dick Lomas's London club (and in Dick's imagination); obsequious; brings Dick a pewter tankard and a large bottle of ale

SERVANT (Good Manners). Of Augustus Breton, who tells him that he will not wait luncheon for Baron von Bernheim later than 2:10 p.m.

SERVANT #1 (Hero). Of the Parsons; brings the telegram from James Parsons to his parents

SERVANT #2 (Hero). Of the Clibborns; he informs James

Parsons that Mary Clibborn is in the drawing room; he smiles eagerly at James with obtrusive friendliness

SERVANT (Jack Straw). Of the Parker-Jennings at their country home in Cheshire; announces various guests

SERVANT #1 (Lady Frederick). At the Hotel de Paris, in Monte Carlo; employed by Lady Mereston

SERVANT #2 (Lady Frederick). To Lady Frederick Berolles at Monte Carlo; fetches his mistress's dispatch box

SERVANT #3 (Lady Frederick). Informs Lady Frederick Berolles that Madame Claude wishes to speak with her

SERVANT (Lady Habart). Of Lady Habart; brings in coffee

SERVANT #1 (Magician). Of Dr. Porhoet in Alexandria; dispatched by the doctor to an intimate friend of his

SERVANT #2 (Magician). Of Lesebren's friend; an old woman who partook of the remedy to prolong life; she regained at least one of the characteristics of youth

SERVANT #3 (Magician). Is in Arthur Burdon's consulting room, London; shows Oliver Haddo outside

SERVANT (Making of a Millionaire). At the Roses' house, London

SERVANT #1 (Making of a Saint). Of Checco d'Orsi; he announces the presence of Lord Girolamo Riario at the gathering at Palazzo Orsi

SERVANT #2 (Making of a Saint). Of Lorenzo de Medici; he announces that Pico della Mirandola had gone away

SERVANT #3 (Making of a Saint). He informs the crowd of citizens at the house of Checco d'Orsi, at Forli, that Checco is dressing and will be with them at once

SERVANT #4 (Making of a Saint). At the house of Checco d'Orsi; drops dinner plates, causing Checco to swear

SERVANT #5 (Making of a Saint). He admits Checco d'Orsi and the other conspirators into Girolamo Riario's private apartment; stabbed to death by Matteo d'Orsi

SERVANT #6 (Making of a Saint). Meets Checco d'Orsi at the Palazzo Orsi and tells him a messenger awaits him with important news

SERVANT #7 (Making of a Saint). Of Giorgio dall' Aste; remained in the chapel at Citta di Castello all night by the body of his master; thanks Filippo Brandolini for burying Giorgio; offers to serve Filippo, but the latter declines

SERVANT (Marriages Are Made in Heaven). Lives in Lottie Vivyan's house in London

SERVANT (Masterson). At Madrassi; he is employed by the Narrator to secure his luggage in and onto the Ford
SERVANT #1 (Merry-Go-Round). Of Polly Ley; he takes Polly's dinner invitation to Frank Hurrell to Harley Street
SERVANT #2 (Merry-Go-Round). Is at Frank Hurrell's consulting room; fetches Bella Langston
SERVANT #3 (Merry-Go-Round). Is at the lodging house in Brighton; announces visitors
SERVANT #4 (Merry-Go-Round). At the Castillyon's house, Jeyston, in Dorsetshire; announced that Mr. Bridger wanted to speak with Paul Castillyon
SERVANT #5 (Merry-Go-Round). To Emily Barlow-Bassett; instructed wire to Reggie Barlow-Bassett at Brighton
SERVANT #1 (Mrs. Craddock). At Court Leys, the Leys' home near Blackstable, Kent; opens doors for visitors
SERVANT #2 (Mrs. Craddock). At the vicarage in Leanham, Kent; brought a basket of eggs, sat through the evening lesson, and lit the candles
SERVANT #3 (Mrs. Craddock). At Court Leys, Blackstable, Kent; told by Mrs Branderton that she could find her own way to Bertha Craddock's room
SERVANT #4 (Mrs. Craddock). At Polly Ley's London flat; tells Gerald Vaudrey that Polly is not in, but that Bertha Craddock is there
SERVANT #1 (Of Human Bondage). A woman; enters the room where the nine-year-old Philip Carey sleeps; tells him his mother wants him, and carries him downstairs
SERVANT #2 (Of Human Bondage). At the boarding house in Brighton; is treated by Mildred Rogers with insolence
SERVANT (Point of Honour). Employed by the Spaniard and tends the gate of the house
SERVANT (Punctiliousness of Don Sebastian). Sent by Don Sebastian from Madrid to Xiormonez to fetch Mercia
SERVANT (Razor's Edge). At Maugham's house at Cape Ferrat; tells Maugham that the police wish to see him
SERVANT (Sheppey). Of the merchant of Baghdad; sent to the market to buy provisions; jostled by Death; rides to Samarra on his master's horse to escape Death
SERVANT #1 (Then and Now). Of Bartolomeo Martelli; he carries a letter from his master to Niccolo Machiavelli inviting Piro Giacomini and Niccolo to dinner; on another occasion, rides with his master to Ravenna

Characters 371

SERVANT #2 (Then and Now). Told by Machiavelli to bring a jug of wine to the parlor for Fra Timoteo and him

SERVANT #3 (Then and Now). Told by Machiavelli to bring a pail of hot water to his bedroom; later told by Machiavelli to take a copy of Caesar Borgia's treaty with the rebel captains to the Signory at Florence

SERVANT GIRL (Bad Example). Employed by the Clintons; opens the door for Rev. Evans

SERVANTS (Bishop's Apron). Of Josiah Spratte; trembled before their master

SERVANTS (Caesar's Wife). Are at the Consular Agent's house, Cairo; bring tea

SERVANTS (Catalina). Of Don Manuel de Valero; frequent the same tavern as Domingo Perez

SERVANTS (Circle). At Clive Champion-Cheney's cottage, Aston-Adey, Dorset; too busy with their own affairs to serve their employer lunch

SERVANTS (Daisy). Are at the Ousley-Farrowhams' London house; tell Daisy that her husband is in his study

SERVANTS (Hour Before the Dawn). Of a Bavarian prince; Nazi spies who reported on the prince and his family

SERVANTS (Magician). A suite of them; travel about with Oliver and Margaret Haddo

SERVANTS (Magician). At Oliver Haddo's house, in Skene, Staffordshire; not permitted to sleep there; after dinner, they are sent to various cottages in the park

SERVANTS (Making of a Millionaire). Are at the Roses' house, London; Mrs. Rose tries to show them that she was not suffering from an indescribable torment

SERVANTS (Making of a Saint). Of Girolamo Riario; they dine after Girolamo has eaten his mid-day meal and he has retired to a private room

SERVANTS (Making of a Saint). Of Checco d'Orsi; twenty of them; armed; are waiting at the piazza at Forli to come to guard Palazzo Orsi and assist conspirators; they accompany Checco into the piazza following the assassination of Girolamo Riario

SERVANTS (Making of a Saint). At the Palazzo Orsi; tell one another that Checco d'Orsi has left Forli; fear for their lives; take no notice of Filippo Brandolini (disguised as a servant); loot the palace and leave

SERVANTS (Making of Saint). Of Filippo Brandolini at Citta di Castello; they accompany their master to the house of Bartolomeo Moratini after Filippo had killed Giorgio dall'Aste; after Filippo returns from Bartolomeo's house, they shrink back, with averted faces, as if afraid to look at him

SERVANTS (Merry-Go-Round). Of Elizabeth Dwarris; two of them; witnessed their mistress's will

SERVANTS (Merry-Go-Round). Brought by Lord Vizard to the divorce proceedings to testify to Lady Vizard's most private habits

SERVANTS (Merry-Go-Round). At the Castillyons' house in Jeyston, Dorsetshire; Paul and Grace Castillyon mean to convince them that nothing unusual has happened

SERVANTS (Merry-Go-Round). They tell their mistress, Emily Barlow-Bassett, how Reggie Barlow-Bassett had lived during the past two years; are told by Emily to throw Reggie into the street if he should show his face at her house

SERVANTS (Mrs. Craddock). At a villa at Naples; Bertha Craddock gives them notice after her father's death

SERVANTS (Point of Law). Two; at Daubernoon Manor, in Westmorland; witness Kate Daubernoon's invalid will

SERVANTS (Punctiliousness of Don Sebastian). Of Don Sebastian; go to Toledo, Burgos, Salamanca, Cordova, Paris, and Rome to purchase books for their master

SERVANTS (Smith). Eight of them; employed by Cynthia and Otto Rosenberg

SERVANTS (Then and Now). Two of them; taken by Niccolo Machiavelli on his lengthy journey to Caesar Borgia

SERVINGMAN (Then and Now). In the employ of Bartolomeo Martelli; he opens the door for Machiavelli and Piero Giacomini; suspicious eyes; beetle-browed and sullen; great bony nose and cruel mouth; he is Nina's lover

SETTA, Marta (Mask and the Face). Is engaged to Luciano Spina; reproaches Luciano for delaying their wedding; she suspects the intrigue between Luciano and Savina Grazia; eventually marries Luciano

SEXTON (Of Human Bondage). Of the Blackstable church, in Kent; he waited at the door to take the communion plate from William Carey

SFORZA, Caterina (Making of a Saint). Wife of Girolamo Riario; the bastard of old Francisco Sforza of Milan; the common people of Forli once struggled to lick the ground upon which she walked; wonderfully beautiful;

is tall and well made; clear, strong features; strong piercing eyes; her complexion is of rare delicacy and softness; chestnut hair; a full, low masculine voice; courageous; born to be a queen; apparently willing to sacrifice the lives of her children rather than give away the citadel at Forli; faints when Checco d'Orsi prevents Protonotary Savello from carrying out the execution of her children; she received Lodovico Moro after his triumphant entry into Forli and accompanies him to the cathedral for mass

SFORZA Caterina (Then and Now). Is a thrifty woman; had built the Palace at Imola; held prisoner at Rome by Caesar Borgia

SFORZA (Cesare (Making of a Saint). The son of Caterina Sforza and Girolamo Riario; the younger brother of Ottaviano; age seven; ordered hanged by Protonotary Savello, but saved by Checco d'Orsi

SFORZA, Count Francisco (Making of a Saint). Of Milan; King of Codottieri; father of Caterina Sforza; he had raised himself from a mere soldier of fortune to the proudest duchy in the world; clear, strong features; strong, piercing eyes; pock-marked skin; courageous

SFORZA, Giovanni (Then and Now). The first husband of Lucretia Borgia; escaped death by fleeing to Pesaro

SFORZA, Lodovico (Making of a Saint). Half-brother of Caterina Sforza; cannot assist Caterina and Girolamo Riario because he is occupied with the Venetians; after the assassination of Girolamo, people in Forli believe that he will bring vengeance upon them from Milan; he marches on Forli with five thousand men and lays siege to the town

SFORZA, Ottaviano (Making of a Saint). Son of Caterina Sforza and Girolamo Riario; age nine; elder brother of Cesare; ordered hanged by Protonotary Savello, but saved by Checco d'Orsi

SHAREHOLDERS (Making of a Millionaire). Frederick Rose had considerable practice in dealing with them; he could make them gracefully accept the inevitable

SHARP (Of Human Bondage). Is a pupil at King's School, Tercanbury; from London; heavy; loutish hair; he is beginning to form a moustache; connected and bushy eyebrows; soft hands; suspicion of a cockney accent; disliked school; he leaves King's and goes to Germany

SHARP, Clary (Liza of Lambeth). Is aboard the brake for Chingford; with Bill

SHARP, Emma (Land of Promise). Wife of Sidney Sharp; middle aged; stout; red in the face; mother of five children

SHARP, Sidney (Land of Promise). Is a neighbor of Frank Taylor; age forty; the husband of Emma Sharp; rough looking; he had been a noncommissioned officer in an English regiment; retains the look of a soldier; the father of five children

SHAW, Lady Justitia (Mrs. Craddock). Polly Ley knew her in Italy; she married her footman; drank heavily; she died, after the death of her husband some forty years later, from a violent attack of the delirium tremons

SHAW, Lord (Mrs. Craddock). Husband of Lady Justitia Shaw; her former footman; his wife made him take her name; drank heavily; married forty years, then died

SHEFFIELD, Bishop of (Bishop's Apron). He dies in his sleep after a long illness

SHEFFIELD, Bishop of (Jack Straw). He is a guest at the Parker-Jennings' garden party in Cheshire; tells Jack Straw harrowing stories about the immorality of the very best people

SHEIKH (Magician). Able, by means of a magic mirror, to show persons who were absent or dead; tall and stout; fair complexion; dark brown beard

SHELLEY, Percy Bysshe (Man from Glasgow). English poet (1792-1822); he witnessed murder of a youth in Naples

SHENSTONE, Mrs. Anna (Circle). Age forty; a friend of Elizabeth and Arnold Champion-Cheney; very pleasant; elegant appearance

SHENSTONE, Mr. (Circle). Father of Anna Shenstone; once referred to Lord Hughie Porteus as the ablest man in the House of Commons and the future Prime Minister

SHENTON, Bertie (Flirtation). Age forty; clean shaven; slight of build; with quick eye and a laughing mouth

SHEPHERD (Faith). Of the arid plain of San Lucido; sat on a rock; moody; payed no heed to his sheep; dully looking at the desert around him

SHEPHERD, Mrs. (Cakes and Ale). An old woman; the vicar of Blackstable announces that she died last night

SHEPHERDS (Choice of Amyntas). Are in the mountains of Spain; clothed in skin

Characters

SHEPPEY (Sheppey). Discussed above under Joseph MILLER
SHERIDAN, Cornelia (Road Uphill). Mother of Ford and Joseph Sheridan; sister of Broderick Madden; resident of Chicago
SHERIDAN, Ford (Road Uphill). Younger son of Cornelia Sheridan; brother of Joseph; is attracted to Margaret Dayton; writing a play; he decides to give up writing to enter the bond business; marries Margaret Dayton
SHERIDAN, Joseph (Road Uphill). Older son of Cornelia Sheridan; brother of Ford; engaged to Ruth Latimer; he achieved a distinguished record as a flier during World War I; does not want to work at a regular job; goes to Paris to study painting; writes a book on art and art criticism
SHERIDAN, Margaret (Road Uphill). See Margaret DAYTON
SHERIFF (Making of a Saint). Sent by Girolamo Riario to Checco d'Orsi because the latter had not paid certain dues owed to the Treasury
SHERWIN, Duke of (Jack Straw). Vincent Parker-Jennings claims that he is a thorough sportsman; Lord Serlo does not know of him
SHIP'S CHANDLER (Honolulu). Lends Captain Butler $250 to purchase Girl #2 from her father
SHOP ASSISTANT (Razor's Edge). At Charvat's, Paris; he asks Elliott Templeton if he would like to see the silk drawers that he had made especially for him
SHOPKEEPER (East of Suez). In a crowded Peking street; fat; he tells his assistant to give some coins to the wailing beggar
SHOP MASTER (Casual Affair). Chinese; leads Arthur Low to the Chinese woman's living quarters
SHUTTLEWORTH, Mrs. (Home and Beauty). She is the mother of Victoria Cardew-Lowndes; elderly and gray haired
SIGHS (Of Human Bondage). Is a master at King's School, Tercanbury; age fifty-seven; present when Dr. Fleming announces the appointment of Thomas Perkins as the new headmaster; he had conducted the fifth form for twenty-five years with an unparalleled incompetence
SIKHS (Door of Opportunity). Twenty of them; under the command of Captain Stratton; set out to attack the Chinese rioters
SIMMONDS, Mr. (Of Human Bondage). He is William Carey's curate at Blackstable; administers the last communion

to William Carey

SIMMONS (Creative Impulse). Mrs. Forrester's literary agent; round face; wore strong glasses

SIMMONS (Painted Veil). The Colonial Secretary at Hong Kong; supposedly will retire soon, to be succeeded by Charlie Townsend

SIMPSON DAUGHTERS (Cupid and the Vicar of Swale). Of Simpson the landlord; they are totally innocuous

SIMPSON, Jane (Cupid and the Vicar of Swale). She is the eldest daughter of Simpson the landlord; is age twenty-nine; homely; has matrimonial designs toward Rev. Robert Branscombe; she is worth at least one hundred thousand pounds, total, in solid securities

SIMPSON, Mr. (Before the Party). Assistant Resident at Kuala Solor, Borneo; is age twenty-four; thin, weedy, wavy hair

SIMPSON, Mr. (Cupid and the Vicar of Swale). Father of Jane Simpson and other daughters); landlord at Swale; decided to remove the old cottages on his estate and erect new ones, with sanitary conveniences and modern improvements; died before he could begin the project

SINCLAIR, Lady Evelyn (Caesar's Wife). Fat and old; is invited to Sir Arthur and Lady Violet Little's party

SINGER (Of Human Bondage). Pupil at the King's School, Tercanbury; age eleven; is the biggest boy in Philip Carey's dormitory; one of Philip's early tormentors

SINGER (Up at the Villa). At a restaurant on one of the banks of the Arno River; discovered by the Princess San Ferdinando

SINGERS (Merry-Go-Round). At a London music hall; they leave Jenny Bush restless

SINGERS (Perfect Gentleman). Men and women; perform at various occasions in the house of Monsieur Jourdain

SINNERY, Dr. (Christmas Holiday). Is the Masons' family doctor; he delivered Charley Mason; in the treatment of certain social diseases, "He's discretion itself"

SISTER (Caesar's Wife). Of Violet Little; she cannot imagine why Sir Arthur Little would propose to Violet

SISTER #1 (Explorer [novel]). Of Julia Crowley; takes ill, forcing Julia to cancel her trip to Egypt and return to America

SISTER #2 (Explorer [novel]). Of Woman #4; she lives in Jonesville, Ohio

Characters   377

SISTER (Merry-Go-Round). Of Herbert Field; she died from consumption after an illness of only four months
SISTER (Narrow Corner). Of Fred Blake; she is married
SISTER #1 (Of Human Bondage). One of the waitresses at the tea shop, Parliament Street, London; she and her husband occasionally go to Eastbourne for the weekend; sees the manageress there, at a boarding house
SISTER #2 (Of Human Bondage). In the ward at St. Luke's Hospital, London; greets Philip Carey when he is late
SISTER (Pro Patria). Of Fanny Porter-Smith; engaged the governess with whom John Porter-Smith had misbehaved
SISTER (Perfect Gentleman). Of Monsieur Jourdain; Jourdain has arranged for his wife to dine with her
SISTER (Razor's Edge). Of the person who taught Larry Darrell Greek; her husband the manager of a coal mine at Lens, in northern France
SISTER (Sheppey). Of Albert; she had champagne at her wedding
SISTER (Smith). Of Smith; married; lives in New South Wales, Australia; formerly a cook; says that Smith can come and stay with her
SISTER (Tenth Man). Of James Ford; a shareholder in the Middlepool Investment Trust
SIXTUS IV (Making of a Saint). Pope (1414-1484) and the uncle or father of Girolamo Riario; he squandered the riches of the Church to satisfy the whims and fancies of Caterina Sforza; obtained possession of Forli for his nephew, Girolamo; is dead
SKELTON (Flotsam and Jetsam). Ill with malaria; brought to the Grangers' house; he is an anthropologist
SKINNER, Alfred (Before the Party). The husband of Mrs. Skinner; a lawyer, who has offices at Lincoln's Inn Fields,London; he is clean shaven and extremely bald
SKINNER, Kathleen (Before the Party). The daughter of Alfred and Mrs. Skinner; she enjoys making lists; age thirty-five; the honorary secretary of a ladies' golf club; she is thin, with red cheeks from playing golf
SKINNER, Mrs. (Before the Party). Is Kathleen Skinner's mother, Harold's mother-in-law, Joan's grandmother
SKIPPER #1 (End of the Flight). Captain of the vessel that conveys the Narrator to the remote Borneo town
SKIPPER #2 (End of the Flight). The captain of the boat that runs between Singapore and Kuching; lives at the

Van Wyck Hotel between trips

SKIPPER (German Harry). Captain of a purling lugger on Thursday Island; hired by the Narrator to transport him to New Guinea; he then tells German Harry of Old Charlie's death

SKIPPER (Mabel). The captain of the steamer from Pagan, Burma, to Mandalay; directs the Narrator to a club at a village where the ship stops for the night

SKIPPER (Marriage of Convenience, 1906). Of the Spanish cargo ship from Cadiz; plays cards with the Narrator

SKIPPER #1 (Narrow Corner). Of one of Butterfield's boats on the Yang-tze River; he ruined himself by becoming addicted to opium; ended up as a tout for a fantan house in Shanghai

SKIPPER #2 (Narrow Corner). Of a Dutch ship; told the young George Frith about Kanda

SKIPPER #3 (Narrow Corner). Of a schooner; the first husband of Catherine Frith; a New Zealander; in the island trade; he drowned at sea in a great hurricane

SKIPPERS (Explorer [novel]). Of the ferry boats that carried people across the water to Southampton; they were sturdy, but assumed the airs of self-importance

SLAVE MERCHANT (Explorer [novel]). The surviving inhabitants of a raid upon a small kraal in British East Africa would eventually be delivered into his hands

SMITH (Cakes and Ale). The hypothetical friend of Alroy Kear; is an example of how one could "use a man very shabbily without afterward bearing him the slightest ill-will"

SMITH (Narrow Corner). A man given this fictitious name by Fred Blake; rushed to the Fever Hospital outside Sydney under Fred Blake's name (itself fictitious); he dies there of scarlet fever

SMITH, Lucien (Rehearsal). Composer of the new ballet that would set the Thames on fire; is long and lean; auburn hair; he is engaged to marry Genevieve Zampa

SMITH, Mary (Smith). The Dallas-Bakers' parlormaid; age twenty; tall and handsome; fair; walks with grace and dignity; she has perfect health of mind and body; a farmer's daughter; she had been in service at several country houses before being brought to London by the Dallas Bakers; is a very good needlewoman; eventually rejects Fisher's marriage proposal; finally accepts

Thomas Freeman's offer to marry him
SMITH, Mr. (Smith). Father of Mary Smith and ten other children (including the married daughter in New South Wales, Australia); he has a farm near the site where the Dallas-Bakers once vacationed
SMITH, Mrs. (Smith). Mary Smith's mother; has asked the Dallas-Baker's cook to keep her eye on daughter Mary
SMITH, Sidney (Bishop's Apron). The English journalist, clergyman, and wit (1771-1845); the most brilliant parson of his day; Canon Theodore Spratte wanted his own name to go down to posterity with that of Smith
SMITHERS, Mr. (Bishop's Apron/Loaves and Fishes). Is a builder in Peckham; he complains to Mrs. Railing that people no longer look at houses without bathrooms
SMITHERS, Mrs. (Magician). The landlady at the hotel at Venning, Staffordshire, some three miles from Skene; Arthur Burdon tells her he wants to see a farm advertised to let; she calls Oliver Haddo insane; informs Arthur, Susie Boyd, and Dr. Porhoet of the death of Margaret Haddo
SMITHSON (Cakes and Ale). A Blackstable draper; sang a comical song at the annual concert at the Assembly Rooms; gentry reminded him of the presence of ladies
SMITHSON (Lady Habart). A Christian money lender and a captain in the militia; educated in a public school and at Oxford; a classicist; he is a gentleman and a sportsman; he occupied chambers near Piccadilly; age thirty; handsome; a fine, carefully waxed moustache; wore an eyeglass; tells Guy Cherriton and then Lady Habart that the latter must pay her debt in one week
SNAKE CHARMER (Magician). The most noted one in Madras; Oliver Haddo claims to have seen him die two hours after he had been bitten by a cobra; drunk, he had forgotten portion of the spell that protected him
SOAMES, Mrs. (Treasure). She calls Richard Harenger to arrange a luncheon date
SODERINI, Piero (Then and Now). Sent by the Signory of Florence to Milan to hasten the expedition of four hundred lancers promised by Louis XII for the relief of the citadel at Arezzo; is an influential citizen, Gonfalonier for life, and president of the Florentine republic; brother of the Bishop of Volterra; a good friend of Niccolo Machiavelli; weak, shallow, amiable

SOLDIER #1 (Making of a Saint). He is at the gate at Forli; fetches the captain of the guard
SOLDIER #2 (Making of a Saint). Kills the last of the attackers of Checco and Matteo d'Orsi and Filippo Brandolini on a Forli street
SOLDIER (Smith). Once engaged to Emily Chapman for two or three years; killed
SOLDIER #1 (Then and Now). In Caesar Borgia's army; is sent by the officer to inform Agapito da Amalia that Niccolo Machiavelli had arrived at the Sforza Palace
SOLDIER #2 (Then and Now). Is part of the crowd surging into Caesar Borgia's apartment; he carries a pair of silver candlesticks
SOLDIER #3 (Then and Now). Is part of the crowd surging into Caesar Borgia's apartment; carries an ornamental goblet of silver gilt, as well as two silver platters
SOLDIERS (Ashenden/Mr. Harrington's Washing). Two of them; attack an old woman on a Petrograd sidewalk and take her basket of provisions
SOLDIERS (Hour Before the Dawn). Two of them; strolling in St. James's Park, London
SOLDIERS (Irish Gentleman). At the frontier; they seize Robert O'Donnel
SOLDIERS (Irish Gentlemen). Two of them; at the dungeon of Wartburg Castle; bring candles to Robert O'Donnel
SOLDIERS (Making of a Saint). A troop of them; protected head of customs as he returned from Forli palace
SOLDIERS (Making of a Saint). Two or three of them who guard Caterina Sforza as she enters the Forli piazza
SOLDIERS (Making of a Saint). Two of them; with Jacopo Ronchi, posted by the Church of San Stefano to await Girolamo Riario
SOLDIERS (Making of a Saint). Two of them; after the assassination of Girolamo Riario, they are posted to guard Caterina Sforza and her children
SOLDIERS (Making of a Saint). Of Lodovico Sforza; they escort Marco Scorsacana and Pietro Albanese to their executions in the piazza at Forli
SOLDIERS (Marriage of Convenience, 1906). Are at the village on the island off the coast of Tunis; two of them; accompany the sergeant to arrest the Narrator
SOLDIERS (Moon and Sixpence). Three of them; sitting at a table at the bar off the Rue Bouterie, Marseilles;

Characters

Tough Bill knocks over beer belonging to one of them
SOLDIERS (Mrs. Craddock). At Rome; are in gay uniforms
SOLDIERS (Narrow Corner). Two of them; at Singapore; dark skinned; they strutted past the Van Dyke Hotel
SOLDIERS (Painted Veil). At the French convent at Mei-tan-fu; perform the duties in the convent infirmary
SOLDIERS (Painted Veil). At Mei-tan-fu; they are seen wrapped in their blankets and huddled in small groups
SOLDIERS (Painted Veil). Escorting Kitty Fane from Mei-tan-fu to Hong Kong; shuffle along with a clumsy walk
SOLDIERS (Then and Now). Drag the two Gascon soldiers into Caesar Borgia's apartment
SOLDIERS (Then and Now). Two or more of them; ordered by Caesar Borgia to stand guard over the bodies of the Gascon soldiers until noon
SOLDIERS (Unknown). In John Wharton's company; when they did things that Wharton thought were wrong, he would humor them
SOLICITOR (Bad Example). Is in the habit of taking with him, on muddy days, an articled clerk to walk on the outside of the street to protect him from flying mud
SOLICITOR (Bread-Winner). Of Charles Battle; he agrees that Charles should hand over his twenty thousand pounds worth of bonds to his creditors
SOLICITOR (Explorer [novel]). Gave Julia Crowley away at her wedding to Dick Lomas
SOLICITOR (Jack Straw). He writes to Lord Serlo to remind him of his engagement to "a woman who can kick a man's topper off"
SOLICITOR (Lady Frederick). Writes to Captain Montgomerie, informing him he has purchased Crowley Castle on his behalf
SOLICITOR (Magician). Of Arthur Burdon; Arthur will communicate with Oliver Haddo only through him; he assures Arthur that Haddo will not contest Margaret Haddo's divorce case
SOLICITOR (Man of Honour). Basil Kent cannot force him to give him briefs
SOLICITOR #1 (Merry-Go-Round). To the Dwarris family; he read Elizabeth Ann Dwarris's will
SOLICITOR #2 (Merry-Go-Round). Of Basil Kent; Basil announces to him his approaching marriage to Jenny
SOLICITOR #3 (Merry-Go-Round). Of Polly Ley; he is at

Lancaster Gate, London; is elderly and rubicund; with mutton-chop whiskers; tells Polly that she can never force anyone to take her money; he draws Polly's will

SOLICITOR #1 (Of Human Bondage). For the Carey family; informs William Carey of the financial circumstances after the deaths of Philip Carey's father and mother

SOLICITOR #2 (Of Human Bondage). Informs Mildred Rogers she has no claim on Emil Miller and warns her not to molest him

SOLICITOR (Tenth Man). Catherine Winter plans to see him for the purpose of filing her divorce petition

SOLICITOR (Unattainable). Of Stephen Ashley; tells Sir Henry Lester of Stephen's death

SOLICITORS (Bishop's Apron). In Josiah Spratte's law firm; they gave Josiah briefs, but hated him; Josiah, in turn, treated them as though they were only vermin

SOLICITORS (Mrs. Craddock). Of Polly Ley; informed her by telephone of her brother's death

SOLICITORS (Painted Veil). Sent Bernard Garstin briefs; Mrs. Garstin flattered them

SOLICITORS (Unattainable). Of Caroline Ashley; of the firm of Lester and Lester; cable Nairobi to determine if Stephen Ashley has actually died

SOLICITOR'S CLERK (Loaves and Fishes). Once engaged to Louise Railing; a rather ordinary young fellow; had not the remotest ideas about art, and he would not attend a stage play unless it would make him laugh

SOMERSET, Duchess of (Alien Corn). Ferdy Rabenstein introduces Mrs. Langtry to her; a little ugly old hag with beady eyes

SOMERVILLE (Ashenden/Hairless Mexican/Traitor). Alias given Ashenden by Colonel R for his visas to France, Italy, and Switzerland; claims (in "The Traitor") to work for the censorship office

SON (Caesar's Wife). Of Abdul Said; fell ill and died

SON (Explorer [novel]). Of Mohammed the Lame; he took advantage of his father's illness, revolted, and then fortified himself in a stockade

SON #1 (Magician). Of the patron of the Chien Noir, at Paris; his father had taken to victualizing to build a business for him

SON #2 (Magician). Of Dr. Porheot's friend in Alexandria; the sheik draws a square and certain mystical

marks on the palm of his right hand; sees, in the ink on his hand, a man sweeping the ground; he also sees the form of Jeanne-Marie Porhoet lying in bed, dead
SON #3 (Magician). Of the Great Khan; he accompanied Paracelsus to Constantinople
SON (Merry-Go-Round). Of a millionaire; works ten hours a day in a bank
SON #1 (Narrow Corner). Of Catherine [Frith] and her first husband; he died of diptheria when still a baby
SON #2 (Narrow Corner). Of Catherine and George Frith; he died when Louise Frith was only a child
SON #3 (Narrow Corner). Of Kim Ching; lives at Takana; he comes to the beach to see Dr. Saunders leave
SONS (Cakes and Ale). Of George Kemp; they attended the grammar school at Haversham, which meant that young William Ashenden could have nothing to do with them
SONS (Narrow Corner). Of Kim Ching; three of them; two (see above for the third) of middle age and live at Fu-chou; friends and patients of Dr. Saunders; with money, persuade Saunders to come to Takana to treat their father
SOPHIE (Cakes and Ale). William Ashenden's aunt; lived at Blackstable, Kent; is the wife of the vicar there; she came from a noble but impoverished German family; simple, old, and of a meek and Christian disposition
SOPHIE (Razor's Edge). Maugham's (the Narrator's) aunt
SOUTH, Dr. (Of Human Bondage). A physician at Farnley, Dorsetshire; described as a crusty, funny old fellow; Philip Carey sent to assist him for a month when his regular assistant develops the mumps; more than forty years ago he had been a medical student at St. Luke's Hospital, London; had been in the Royal Navy; opposed to all of the medical advances of the past thirty years; medium height and thin; white hair cut short; long mouth that closed tightly; small white whiskers; he had the appearance of a respectable farmer in the middle of the nineteenth century; has been a widower for thirty years; offers Philip Carey a partnership
SOUTH, Mrs. (Of Human Bondage). Wife of Dr. South; has been dead for thirty years
SPANIARD (Man from Glasgow). Was, supposedly, a trusted employee of the Glasgow and South Spain Oil Company; dismissed for theft at Ecija

SPANIARD (Point of Honour). Beautiful hands, thin long fingers; he meets the Narrator at the bullfight in Seville and takes him to his house; there, he relates the story of Don Pedro Aguira

SPANIARD (Spanish Priest). In the taverns of Gibraltar; smokes the incessant cigarette, he and sips the light white wine of the Manzanilla

SPANIARD'S WIFE (Point of Honour). Is very beautiful; magnificent eyes; has a straight nose with delicate nostrils; pale smooth skin; abundant black hair, with a broad, white streak; tall; unlined face; she is no more than thirty years of age

SPANISH CONVICT (Official Position). Awaits execution

SPANISH LADY (Choice of Amyntas). At Cadiz; comes upon Amyntas in the orange grove, after he has awakened; olive skin; dark and lustrous eyes; luxuriant hair; she entertains Amyntas at her house and, in exchange, she relieves him of all ten of his golden guineas

SPANISH NOBLE #1 (Catalina). He is related to the Duke of Alva; provides Manuel de Valero with a letter of introduction to the Duke

SPANISH NOBEL #2 (Catalina). Attached to the Spanish embassy in Rome; embraced the cult of Plato; he and Demitrios Christopolous read Plato together; recalled to Spain, and takes Christopoulos with him; appointed Viceroy for the Kingdom of Valencia; dies in Valencia

SPANISH WOMAN (Happy Man). Lives with Dr. Stephens in Seville; she is no longer young, but is still "boldly and voluptuously beautiful"

SPANISH WOMAN (Point of Honour). Is at the bullfight at Seville; particularly beautiful; she smiles and bows without embarrassment

SPECIAL CORRESPONDENTS (Hero). James Parsons believes they will decide, in the future, which army has won a battle

SPECIALIST (Bad Example). Is summoned by the Scottish doctor for a consultation with James Clinton; tall; untidily dressed; wild and straggling hair; believes everyone to be stupid; declares Clinton to be insane

SPECIALIST (Hour Before the Dawn). Told May Henderson there was nothing preventing her from having a child; examined Roger Henderson and told him that there was nothing in him that would account for May's sterility

Characters 385

SPECIALIST (Sanatorium). Seen by Ashenden in London; sent him to the sanatorium in the north of Scotland

SPECIALISTS (Sacred Flame). Several; saw Maurice Tabret

SPENCER, Dr. (Mrs. Craddock). Physician at Tercanbury, Kent; a specialist brought to Court Leys to consult with Dr. Ramsay during the birth of Bertha Craddock's baby; undersized; squeaky voice; gesticulative manner

SPIES (Making of a Saint). Of Checco d'Orsi at Forli; relay events at Forli to Checco in Citta di Castello

SPINA, Luciano (Mask and the Face). A bachelor lawyer; engaged to Marta Setta, but attentive to Savina Grazia; defends Paolo Grazia at his trial; marries Marta

SPINSTER (Explorer [novel]). Serious; is routed with religious leanings by Dick Lomas's exact knowledge of the result of missionary endeavor in Central America

SPINSTERS (Moon and Sixpence). At a London tea party attended by the young Narrator; are mouse-like; soft voices and shrewd glances; kept their gloves on while they ate buttered toast

SPIRITUAL DIRECTOR (Catalina). To the Prioress Dona Beatriz at the Carmelite Convent of the Incarnation at Castel Rodriguez; a worthy and simple man; he is esteemed for his piety, but is lacking intelligence

SPORTING GENTLEMAN (Liza of Lambeth). He offers odds during the fight between Liza Kemp and Mrs. Blakeston

SPORTSMAN (Ashenden/Mr. Harrington's Washing). Willing to assassinate King B for a five-thousand pound fee

SPRATTE, Canon (Explorer [novel]). Vicar of the London church that Lady Alice Kelsey attends; has an air of breezy courtliness; handsome, urbane, attentive; he awaits the offering of a vacant bishopric; does not like Dick Lomas, whom he believes talks too much; no gathering could ever be tedious when he was present

SPRATTE, Dorothy (Bishop's Apron). The wife of Theodore Spratte and mother of Lionel and Winnie; she has been dead for ten years; was the youngest daughter of Lord Frampstone; remained dazzled her husband; in turn was treated by Theodore as though she were a congregation; was happy only within the bosom of her family

SPRATTE, First Earl of (Loaves and Fishes). Former Lord Chancellor of England; father of Sophia, Theodore, and Thomas Spratte; his full portrait hangs prominently on a drawing room wall of St. Gregory's vicarage

SPRATTE, Josiah the elder (Bishop's Apron). Father of Josiah Spratte the younger; a direct descendant of the Montmorencys; Theodore Spratte (although only age seven when his grandfather died) refers to him as having been a distinguished banker and a polished and accomplished gentleman; but, according to Thomas and Sophia Spratte, their grandfather was merely a seedy bill broker who dabbled in usury; shabby and old; invited to dinner a day after a party to eat the scraps

SPRATTE, Josiah the younger, first Earl (Bishop's Apron). Father of the first Lord Rallington, Sophia, Thomas, and Theodore Spratte; the husband of Maria; the Lord Chancellor of England; strong, large hands, from which tendons stood out; shaggy brows; strong features; hard, cruel mouth; an indomitable will and a truculent savagery; fluent speech; an imperturbable self-confidence; physique of extraordinary vigor; was insolent, overbearing, and impatient; he rose from Attorney General to Lord Chancellor; raised to the peerage; with a second term of office, he became Earl Spratte of Beachcombe and Viscount Rallington; objected to potatoes baked in their skins; favorite relaxation playing whist at his club; the most disagreeable man the Prime Minister Lord Stonehenge ever knew

SPRATTE, Lionel (Bishop's Apron). Son of Canon Theodore and Dorothy Spratte; brother of Winnie; his father's curate; tall and fair; lacks his father's energy and force of character; dresses as little like a clergyman as possible; educated at Eton and Oxford; he had inherited his mother's lack of ambition rather than his father's spirit; deciding whether to marry Gwendolyn Durant, but will not be rushed into the affair

SPRATTE, Lionel (Loaves and Fishes). Son of Canon Theodore Spratte and nephew of Lady Sophia; curate of St. Gregory's, South Kensington, London; young, tall, and languid; fair-haired; uncertain if he wishes to marry Gwendolyn Durant

SPRATTE, Lord (Bishop's Apron). Eldest son of Josiah the younger and Maria Spratte; as a child, he spoke in whispers in his father's presence; he assumed the title of Viscount Rallington; he refused to marry the heiress whom his father singled out for that purpose; written out of his father's will and dismissed from the Spratte household; went abroad and died a month before his father's death

SPRATTE, Maria (Bishop's Apron). Wife of Josiah Spratte the younger; mother of Viscount Rallington, Sophia, Thomas, and Theodore; she trembled before his husband

SPRATTE, Mr. (Loaves and Fishes). Deceased grandfather of Thomas, Sophia, and Theodore Spratte; Theodore labels him a distinguished banker; Thomas terms him a seedy bill broker and usurer; Sophia recalls that he came to dinner a day after a party to eat the scraps

SPRATTE, Mrs. (Jack Straw). Is a guest at the Parker-Jennings' garden party in Cheshire

SPRATTE, Mrs. (Loaves and Fishes). The deceased wife of Canon Theodore Spratte and the mother of Lionel and Winnie; Theodore looked upon her as an angel--she was always loving, obedient, respectful, self-effacing

SPRATTE SON (Bishop's Apron). Born to Bishop Theodore and Gwendolyn (Durant) Spratte ten months after their marriage

SPRATTE, Lady Sophia (Bishop's Apron). Sister of Thomas and Theodore Spratte; daughter of Josiah the younger and Maria Spratte; as a child, she spoke in whispers in her father's presence; at age fifty-five, the oldest of the family; handsome, self-assured; unmarried; she came to live with Theodore after his wife died

SPRATTE, Lady Sophia (Loaves and Fishes). At age fifty; handsome, well-groomed, and of determined appearance

SPRATTE, Theodore (Bishop's Apron). Is the vicar of St. Gregory's, South Kensington, London and the Canon of Tercanbury, Kent; a widower, youngest son of Josiah the younger and Maria Spratte; brother of Sophia and Theodore; father of Lionel and Winnie; as a child, spoke in whispers at his father's presence; handsome, tall, slender, and erect; profuse and curling hair, turning slightly to gray; fine, blue eyes; a mobile, shapely mouth; commanding presence; married Dorothy, daughter of Lord Frampstone; his age slightly under fifty; a resonant and well modulated voice; proposes marriage to Mrs. Fitzherbert, but he hedges when he discovers that she will lose all of her income if she remarries; seeks the vacant bishopric of Barchester, but the Prime Minister offers him only the deanery of St. Olphert's, Wales, which he refuses; then proposes marriage to Gwendolyn Durant; after Dr. Gray's death, he receives the offer of the bishopric of Barchester, which he refuses; he then accepts the offer of the of the bishopric of Sheffield; he marries Gwendolyn, and they have a child

SPRATTE, Theodore (Loaves and Fishes). The vicar of St. Gregory's, South Kensington, London, and the Canon of Tercanbury Cathedral, Kent; brother of Lady Sophia and Thomas Spratte and father of Lionel and Winifred; tall and handsome; fine head of curly, white hair; is clean shaven; dignified and bland; he aspires to a bishopric; proposes marriage to Mary Fitzgerald, but before he learns (wrongly) that she will lose her income if she remarries; proposes marriage to Gwendolyn Durant; is offered the bishopric of Colchester

SPRATTE, Lord Thomas (Bishop's Apron). Age fifty; the brother of Theodore and Sophia Spratte; son of Josiah the younger and Maria Spratte; as a child, he spoke in whispers in his father's presence; he had attended Oxford only briefly before being sent down for some escapade; fresh complexion; gray hair; has quick and breezy manner; he has been known all of his life as "Tommy Tiddler"; he succeeded Josiah the younger as second Earl Spratte of Beachcombe; is a member of the House of Lords, which he detests and never attends

SPRATTE, Lord Thomas (Loaves and Fishes). Second Earl Spratte of Beachcombe, Viscount Rallington, and Baron Spratte in the United Kingdom of Great Britain and Ireland; brother of Theodore and Lady Sophia Spratte; tall and stout; age fifty+; enjoyed a brief stay at Oxford University

SPRATTE, Winnie (Bishop's Apron). The daughter of Canon Theodore Spratte, sister of Lionel; age twenty-one; fragile and delicate; she is pretty as a shepherdess; pleasant blue eyes; she has an income from her late mother of three hundred pounds per year; in love with and engaged to Bertram Railing, as well as with his work as a reformer; she refuses Lord Harry Wroxham's first offer of marriage, but accepts a second one; in love, she thinks, with two men, although her father does convince her to disengage herself from Bertram

SPRATTE, Winnie (Loaves and Fishes). Daughter of Canon Theodore Spratte; pretty and fair; age twenty-one; is pink, white, virginal; is engaged to Bertram Railing; refuses Harry Wroxham's first marriage proposal, but accepts the second one; loves both Harry and Bertram

SQUARETOES, Flossie (Jack Straw). She engages Lord Ned Serlo in a conversation at the Grand Babylon Hotel

SQUIRE (Catalina). Is fat and little; accompanies the Knight; indicates to strangers that the Knight is mad

SQUIRES (Mrs. Craddock). Neighbors of the Craddocks; they congratulated Bertha Craddock on the way her husband, Edward, managed his properties

SRI GANESHA (Razor's Edge). Is a Yogi at Ashrama; Larry Darrell goes to live with, and to learn, from him

ST. ANSELME, Sister (Painted Veil). Painted the altarpiece and the Stations of the Cross at the chapel of the French convent at Mei-tan-fu; she was a genuine artist who fell a victim of the cholera epidemic

ST. CLAIR, Edwin (Round Dozen). Small, full bodied, but not stout; curly gray hair; wrinkled face; a humorous expression; tight lips; square chin; is a London tea merchant who resides in Bayswater; an amateur actor in his younger days; husband of Gertrude St. Clair

ST. CLAIR, Gertrude (Round Dozen). Wife of Edwin St. Clair; wears heavy, antiquated jewelry; taller than her husband

ST. ERMYNS, Duchess of (Loaves and Fishes). She told Theodore Spratte that she had found Bertram Railing's book, The Future of Socialism, as exciting as a novel

ST. ERTH, Duchess of (Jack Straw). Guest at the Parker-Jennings' garden party in Cheshire

ST. ERTH, Duchess of (Penelope). According to the note in the Morning Post, she has just returned to Wales

ST. ERTH, Duchess of (Razor's Edge). The owner of St. Clement Talbot; the place was decorated by Gregory Brabazon, much to the Duchess's delight; Elliott Templeton disappointed to discover that she and her husband have employed women to wait at their table

ST. ERTH, Duke of (Human Element). The father of Betty Welldon-Burns; old, none too rich; lived in Cornwall

ST. FRANCIS XAVIER, Sister (Painted Veil). She came to Mei-tan-fu from France ten years ago; told the Mother Superior not to grieve, for wherever they were, there were France and God; her mother's only daughter; died of the cholera

ST. JOSEPH, Sister (Painted Veil). One of the nuns at the French convent at Mei-tan-fu; a farmer's daughter and a peasant at heart; short and plump; homely face; red cheeks and merry eyes; she spoke no English; was good-humored; cheerful and easy laughter; talkative, merry creature; thought that Kitty Fane was going to have a baby; in charge of the economy of the convent

ST. MARTIN, Sister (Painted Veil). A nun at the French convent at Mei-tan-fu; declared it a pity that Kitty Fane was not a Catholic

ST. OLPHERDS (Razor's Edge). According to Maugham, they want to dispose of their (John) Constable painting of Salisbury Cathedral

ST. OLPHERTS, Duke of (Merry-Go-Round). Is to sponsor Marguerite Vizard's entrance into the Catholic Church

ST. OLPHERTS, William, Duke of (Hero). Is a friend of Reggie Clibborn; gave Reggie some special port from the cellar of an Austrian nobleman

STAGE MANAGER (Theatre). Was scolded by Julia Gosselyn concerning both the electrician and the stage lights

STANLEY, Kitie (Liza of Lambeth). She and her second husband live in the same house, Vere Street, Lambeth, as Liza Kemp; cut her forehead in a fight with her husband

STANLEY, Mr. (Liza of Lambeth). He and Kitie, his wife of eighteen months, live in the same house on Vere Street, Lambeth, as Liza Kemp; responsible for a cut on his wife's head; as gentle as a lamb when sober

STARLING, Miss (Happy Couple). Lived with Miss Wingford and the sole beneficiary of Miss Wingford's will; was accused of poisoning her companion; then marries Dr. Brandon and, after their trial, assumes (as does her husband), the name of Craig

STATION BOY (Explorer [novel/play]). A big Swahili with one ear; has been running after the women and playing the fool with the Turkana woman; George Allerton declares that it was he who shot the Turkana woman

STATION MASTER (Ashenden/Mr. Harrington's Washing). At Vladivostok; delivers impassioned speech, in Russian, to J.Q. Harrington, who cannot understand one word

STATION MASTER (Mrs. Craddock). At Blackstable, Kent; an air of self-satisfaction; he told Bertha Craddock that a carriage awaited her

Characters 391

STATION MASTER'S ASSISTANT (Ashenden/Hairless Mexican). Arranges seating on the Rome express for Ashenden and Manuel Carmona

STEARMAN, Mr. (Liza of Lambeth). A Lambeth undertaker

STEPHENS, Dr. (Happy Man). Raised by two aunts; small, thick set, and stout; age thirty; a round, red face; small, dark, bright eyes; close cropped black hair atop a bullet shaped head; married for six years, but without children; a medical officer in the Camberwell Infirmary; he gains weight and loses his hair after fifteen years in Seville

STEPHENS, Mrs. (Happy Man). The wife of Dr. Stephens; at first, she is willing to risk accompanying her husband to Spain, but then she returns to Camberwell

STEWARD #1 (Catalina). Of the Duke of Castel Rodriguez; he offers Manuel de Valero an apartment in the palace

STEWARD #2 (Catalina). Of the Spanish grandee; brought his master's gift of a kid and a hunk of pork to the inn for the actors

STEWARD (Explorer [novel]). He packed Alec MacKenzie's belongings for the journey from Gibraltar to England

STEWARD (Punctiliousness of Don Sebastian). Serves wine from Cordova to Archbishop Pablo and Don Sebastian

STEWARD (Straight Flush). He tends the bar on the ship from Hong Kong

STEWARD (Theatre). To Julia Lambert; trembling and old

STEWARD (Virtue). At Narrator's London club; is portly; jostles the Narrator while showing two men to a table

STEWARD (Winter Cruise). He serves supper on board the Friedrich Weber

STEWARDS (Winter Cruise). Decorate the dining salon of the Friedrich Weber for Christmas and New Year's Eve

STEWART, Mrs. (De Amicitia). Mother of Valentia; lives in Cincinnati, Ohio

STEWART, Valentia (De Amicitia). She is an art student at Paris; from Cincinnati, Ohio; is pretty, in her American way; a long face; hair parted in the middle and hanging over the nape of the neck; classic mouth; admirable figure; travels to Holland with Ferdinand White; she finally declares her love for Ferdinand

STOCKBROKER (Landed Gentry). Jewish; with his pockets full of money; the only person the people welcome in the country

STOCKBROKER (Moon and Sixpence). Charles Strickland's partner; he knew where to find Strickland in Paris

STOKER (Merry-Go-Round). Herbert Field envied him for his iron muscles and his ability to breathe freely

STOKER (Moon and Sixpence). Was from a ship bound for Australia; had thrown himself overboard off Gibraltar in the midst of an attack of the delirium tremons

STONEHENGE, Lord (Bishop's Apron). The Prime Minister; father of Lady Patricia Stonehenge; stupid and corpulent; bearded; Theodore Spratte expects him to offer the bishopric of Barchester to him, he only offers Theodore the deanery of St. Olphert's, Wales; after Dr. Gray's death, he offers Theodore Spratte first the bishopric of Barchester, then that of Sheffield

STONEHENGE, Lady Patricia (Bishop's Apron). Daughter of Lord Stonehenge; shared her father's predilection for undangerous mediocrity; found topics of conversation only with difficulty

STOPFORT, Mrs. (East of Suez). Wife of Reggie Stopfort; fell in love with Andre Leroux; the ladies of Peking are giving her "the frozen silverside"

STOPFORT, Reggie (East of Suez). He is the husband of Mrs. Stopfort; a drunken brute who has mistreated his wife for ten years; he is preparing to divorce her

STRANGER (Of Human Bondage). From London; married and had children; attended church and placed a florin in the collection plate

STRATTON, Captain (Door of Opportunity). The captain of constabulary; he is a small, red-faced man with a red moustache; bow-legged, but still hearty and dashing

STRATTON, Collie (For Services Rendered). Age between thirty-five and forty; bachelor, with a school-boyish manner; a pleasant and frank look; he had been the commander of a destroyer in the Royal Navy; torpedoed during the war; received the D.S.O. and the Legion of Honor; in a purely economic move, dismissed from the service after twenty years; he operates a garage; his business in difficulty and he owes Radley 187 pounds; no one will lend him money; passes several post-dated checks in payment of various accounts, knowing full well he has no money to cover them; he shoots himself

STRAW, Jack (Jack Straw). A waiter at the Grand Babylon Hotel; of somewhat striking physique; Ambrose Holland first met him in the United States; formerly a member of a traveling company; he also had been a sailor, bartender in New York, engine driver on the Canadian Pacific Railroad, miner in the Klondike, Texas ranch hand; possesses an uncontrollable love of adventure; assumes identity of Archduke Sebastian of Pomerania to help Lady Wanley fool the Parker-Jennings; falls in love with Ethel Parker-Jennings, and then proposes marriage to her; his actual identity is finally revealed to all as Archduke Sebastian of Pomerania

STRICKLAND, Amy (Moon and Sixpence). Wife of Charles Strickland and mother of Robert and a daughter (Mrs. Ronaldson); the younger sister of Dorothy MacAndrew; referred to by her husband as an excellent woman, but he also wished that she were in Hell; the daughter of an Indian civilian; she had led a quite youth in the country; had met Charles Strickland at age twenty; was married to him for seventeen years before he left her; gives parties; met the Narrator at a tea party at Rose Waterford's house; then age thirty-seven; she is tall and plump; a pleasing face; sallow skin and kind brown eyes; pleasant voice; dark hair; wore no makeup; close to sixty years of age when the Narrator sees her after his return from Tahiti; her thin face not noticeably lined, and her hair not yet very gray

STRICKLAND, Charles (Moon and Sixpence). A painter; the husband of Amy Strickland; age twenty-three when he first met his future wife; he had been married to her for seventeen years before he went off to Paris; was initially a London stockbroker on the Exchange; he is described as a nice, dull, honest, plain person; age forty when the Narrator met him; was broad and heavy; large hands and feet; good but not handsome features; clean shaven; large face; his reddish hair cut very short; small, blue-gray eyes; five years later, in Paris--grows a ragged and untrimmed beard that hides much of his face; long hair; extremely thin; his nose protrudes arrogantly; cheekbones and eyes enlarged; deep hollows in his temples; hands large and strong, merely bones and sinew; is generally cadaverous in appearance; leaves Paris for Marseilles, then moves on to his final stop, Tahiti; he eventually contracts leprosy; is blind during the final years of his life

STRICKLAND, Mr. (Moon and Sixpence). Father of Charles Strickland; forced his son to enter business because he said that there was no money to be made in art

STRICKLAND, Rev. Robert (Moon and Sixpence). The son of Charles and Amy Strickland; candid, brown, and fine reflective eyes; educated at Rugby and Cambridge; was recommended for the Military Cross; he wrote (1913) a biography of his father

STRINGER, Lady Edward (Merry-Go-Round). Small and old; false teeth; bright chestnut wig; withered neck; she wealthy; unlimited credit with the world; related to Lord Vizard, but she is not overly friendly with him

STROEVE, Blanche (Moon and Sixpence). Married to Dirk Stroeve; English; rather tall, with beautiful figure; has abundant brown hair; pale face; quiet gray eyes; formerly governess in the family of a Roman prince, where the son of the house seduced her; falls in love with Charles Strickland; poses in the nude for him; she dies from a self-administered dose of oxalic acid

STROEVE DAUGHTER (Moon and Sixpence). Is Dirk Stroeve's sister; she married the captain of a fishing smack

STROEVE, Dirk (Moon and Sixpence). Is a Dutch friend of the Narrator, living in Paris; a buffoon and a bad painter; as a young man, he won an art scholarship to study in Amsterdam; he went to Italy, then came to Paris and settled into a studio in Montmarte; married to Blanche Stroeve; slightly over thirty years old; fat and small; short legs; prematurely bald; a round face, high color, white skin, red cheeks; red lips; round, blue eyes; fair eyebrows; he wears spectacles

STROEVE, Mr. (Moon and Sixpence). He is Dirk Stroeve's father; lives in the north of Holland; a poor, fifth-generation carpenter; is a spare old man with gnarled hands; silent and upright

STROEVE, Mrs. (Moon and Sixpence). She is the mother of Dirk Stroeve; a woman of passionate orderliness; neat and small, with cheeks like apples

STRONG, Edith (Cupid and the Vicar of Swale). Age about thirty-nine; six feet tall; massive proportions; well cut features; clear, steady eyes; perfect teeth that she overly displayed; handsome; good natured and good humored; is a widow with an income of fifteen hundred pounds per year, which will end if she marries again

STROUDS (Door of Opportunity). They arranged to meet the Maudys at the Trocadero Grill Room, in London
STUBBS the elder (Honolulu). A missionary who had first come to work in Honolulu more than seventy years ago
STUDENT #1 (Mirage). At medical college, St. Thomas's Hospital, London; discovered reading a newspaper at an anatomy lecture
STUDENT #2 (Mirage). At medical college, St. Thomas's Hospital, London; hands the newspaper to the anatomy lecturer and identifies the paragraph that all of the students had been reading during the lecture
STUDENT (Woman of Fifty). Calls Wyman Holt at 11:00 p.m. to inquire into how evil had come into the world
STUDENTS (Buried Talent). At the Conservatoire, Paris; Charmian Pelter may well have slept with half of them
STUDENTS (Magician). At the Luxembourg Gardens. Paris; they stroll about, uneasy with the fear of ridicule because of their attire
STUDENTS (Mrs. Craddock). At the Villa Medici, in Rome; saw Bertha Craddock and wondered about the beautiful woman who sat for so long, unaware of their presence
STUDENTS (Mrs. Craddock). In attendance at the parson's cramming sessions; not one of them knew poker; within four days, Gerald Vaudrey "walloped 'em thirty quid"
STUDENTS (Razor's Edge). A few of them; they attend the the Sorbonne, Paris; lodge in the attics of the same hotel where Larry Darrell has a room
STUDENTS (Up at the Villa). Colleagues of Karl Richter attended an Austrian university; protested against the Anschluss; two were shot; the rest were confined to a concentration camp
STULTZ (Our Betters). He is a tailor in London; German
STURREY, Lord (Our Betters). An English politician; has always managed to escape Lady Pearl Grayston's dinner parties; scheduled to come to the Graystons' country house in Suffolk
SUBALTERNS (Hero). Of a native Indian regiment; could be observed hanging perpetually about Mrs. Pritchard-Wallace's skirts
SUBALTERNS (Spanish Priest). At Gibraltar; they attend to the needs of mature English ladies on their rides
SUBDEACON (Catalina). Of the Collegiate Church; they held chalice and paten enveloped in the humeral veil

SUBJECTS (Choice of Amyntas). Of Maiden #2; they reside on an island in the north; fat and well content; the richest in the world

SUBPRIORESS (Catalina). She receives Blasco de Valero, Bishop of Segovia; kisses his ring and ushers him in to see Beatriz

SUCCESSOR (Ashenden/Mr. Harrington's Washing). To King B; his political sympathies are not yet definite; he might be persuaded to keep his country's neutrality

SULTAN (Book-Bag). Age fifty; short and stout; large, handsome, friendly eyes; affable; has four wives and twenty-four children

SULTAN (Explorer [novel]). Of the most powerful state in British East Africa; he held Alec MacKenzie for a year in a condition that bordered on sheer captivity

SULTAN (Neil MacAdam). Keen interest in natural history

SULTAN'S SON (Book-Bag). Is a shy and smiling youngster

SULTANS (Magician). Of the East; in Margaret Dauncey's vision

SUNBURY, Beatrice (Kite). Herbert Sunbury's mother and wife of Samuel Sunbury; always insisted that her son and her husband be addressed by their full Christian names; small, strong, wiry, and active; sallow skin; sharp, regular features; small beady eyes; black hair

SUNBURY, Betty (Kite). Daughter of Mrs. Bevan #1; wife of Herbert Sunbury; small features and sharp beady eyes; short, wavy black hair; smashed Herbert's kite

SUNBURY, Herbert (Kite). A prisoner at Wormwood Scrubs; only child of Beatrice and Samuel Sunbury; five feet ten inches tall; nice looking, with regular features and dark hair; has blue eyes; smooth, pale, and clear skin; an accountant; he developed a passion for kites

SUNBURY, Samuel (Kite). Husband of Beatrice Sunbury and father of Herbert; small and thin; thin sandy hair; pale blue eyes; pasty complexion; he has been a clerk in a lawyer's office for the past twenty-four years

SUNG, Herr (Of Human Bondage). Is a Chinese lodger at Helene Erlin's Heidelberg pension; yellow face and expansive smile; almond eyes; small even white teeth; studies Western conditions at Heidelberg University; spoke quickly; elopes with Fraulein Cacilie to Italy

SUPERCARGO (Four Dutchmen). Served on the S.S. Utrecht; one of four Dutchmen; dark and fat; a large, red face

Characters 397

SUPERINTENDENT (Treasure). Of the employment registry; Richard Harenger explains at length to her his needs for a house parlor maid and a valet

SUPERIOR (Making of a Saint). At the Benedictine convent at Citta di Castello; houses Giulia dall' Aste

SURRENNES, Gaston, Duke de (Our Betters). Is the former husband of Minnie Surrennes

SURRENNES, Marquise de (Bishop's Apron). Old; is one of the most saintly women Theodore Spratte has known; wiped her knife and fork with a napkin before eating

SURRENNES, Minnie, Duchess de (Our Betters). Formerly a Miss Hodgson; from Chicago; age forty-five; large and dark; scarlet lips and painted cheeks; outrageously sensual; good looking; divorced from Gaston, Duke de Surrennes; she is holding on doggedly to Tony Paxton, her present companion

SURGEON (Cakes and Ale). He is at St. Luke's Hospital, London; Ashenden accompanies him on his daily rounds

SURGEON (Magician). At St. Luke's Hospital, in London; Arthur Burdon tells him that he must leave London on private business and then turns his work over to him

SURGEON (Moon and Sixpence). One of the senior surgeons at St. Thomas's Hospital, London; obtained Abraham a berth as surgeon on a tramp steamer for the Levant

SURGEON (Mrs. Craddock). Young; tends Edward Craddock after the latter has been thrown from his horse and broken his collarbone; he advises Edward to go home

SURGEON #1 (Narrow Corner). Dutch; at Macassar; he is perfectly competent to perform a cataract operation

SURGEON #2 (Narrow Corner). Dutch; at Amboyna; he is perfectly competent to perform a cataract operation

SURGEON (Of Human Bondage). At St. Luke's Hospital, in London; is in competition with a colleague as to who could remove an appendix in the shortest time, with the smallest incision; Philip Carey dressed for him

SURGEON (P.&O.). Boyish, cheerful face; native of Edinburgh; is attracted to Mrs. Linsell; treats Gallagher

SURGEON (Painted Veil). Operated on Mrs. Garstin; said that there had never been any hope for her recovery

SURGEONS (Magician). At London; of repute; furnished Arthur Burdon with letters to their French colleagues

SURVEYOR (Casual Affair). A guest at the Lows' dinner

SUTCLIFFE, Arrow (Three Fat Women of the Antibes). An

American; divorced two husbands; age well into the forties; not as fat as Mrs. Richman or Mrs. Hickson

SUZANNE (Our Betters). She is a dressmaker in the Place Vendome, in Paris; Lady Pearl Grayston owes her money

SWAHILI BOY (Explorer [novel]). Remains by the side of Alec MacKenzie as the explorer lies desperately ill from an almost fatal attack of the blackwater fever

SWAHILIS (Explorer [novel]). On Alec MacKenzie's latest African expedition; Alec brought them from the coast, drilled them, and gave them guns; they assumed an unaccustomed silence during Alec's serious attack of blackwater fever; went with tears down their cheeks

SWALECLIFFE, Rev. William (Tenth Man). A Nonconformist minister at Middlepool; a busybody; clean shaven; has a sallow, grave face; he is married, with children

SWAMI (Razor's Edge). Is on the ship from Alexandria to Bombay; fat and small; wore a clerical collar; brown round face; encourages Larry Darrell to visit India; meets up with Larry at Elephanta; he belonged to the Ramakrishna Swamis

SWAN, Catherine (Narrow Corner). See Catherine FRITH

SWAN, Jack (Narrow Corner). George Frith's father-in-law; Catherine Frith's father; Louise Frith's grandfather; the actual owner of the nutmeg plantation on Kanda; little and old; pale blue eyes and red-rimmed, hairless lids; darting, mischievous glance; a Sweden; formerly the captain of a schooner engaged in the slave trade, a blacksmith, a trader, and a planter; he spent seven years in New Guinea; has a hernia in his chest; had four wives and more children than he can count; he now lives with George and Louise Frith

SWAN, Mr. (Rain). A ship's quartermaster; he is small, shrivelled, and extremely dirty

SWAN, Mrs. (Narrow Corner). One of Jack Swan's wives and the mother of Catherine Frith

SWEDE (Alien Corn). A friend of George Bland at Munich

SWEDISH LADY (Ashenden/His Excellency). Is a countess; beautiful; had captured the affections of Ambassador Wilbur Schafer; she is actually a spy for the Germans

SWEDISH PAINTER (Alien Corn). Ferdy Rabenstein's dinner guest

SWELLS (Liza of Lambeth). Several of them; are from the West End, London; at the Saturday evening prize fight

SWIFT, Sir Edgar, K.C.S.I (Up at the Villa). Is in the Indian Civil Service; governor, for five years, of the northwest provinces; Mary Panton had known him all of her life; age fifty-four; a contemporary of Mary's father; tall and spare; he looked athletic and distinguished; black, curly hair, hardly touched with gray; a lean face, bronzed by the Indian sun; strong chin and aquiline nose; brown eyes under heavy brows; he had dignity, but without any trace of arrogance

SWINEHERD (Choice of Amyntas). In Spain; guarding his flock by a rock path; offers Amyntas food and shelter in exchange for his company

SWISS (Traveller in Romance). According to the commercial traveler on the post chaise, they have souls the of shop-walkers; extortionate, mean, and overbearing; insolent to their inferiors, servile to their betters

SWISS AGENT (Ashenden/Miss King). At the Intelligence Department, in Berne; is tall and very tired looking

SWISS PEASANTS (Traveller in Romance). The commercial traveler on the post chaise knew nothing about them

T

TABRET, Colin (Sacred Flame). Is the brother of Maurice Tabret; in his early thirties; tall, dark, handsome; he went to Guatemala just before Maurice crashed; has done well in the coffee plantation business; in love with Stella Tabret; father of her yet unborn child

TABRET Maurice (Sacred Flame). The invalid husband of Stella Tabret and brother of Colin; is trim and neat; close cropped hair and clean shaven face; a handsome head; hearty and cheerful manner; has very thin, pale and hollow cheeks; enormous dark eyes; formerly an aviator; he emerged from the war unscathed; however, while testing a new plane, he crashed; he broke the lower part of his spine and suffered severe burns; he has been confined for the past six years; he dies

TABRET, Millie (Sacred Flame). Is the widowed mother of Maurice and Colin Tabret; slim, small; gray haired; gentle manner; determined face; she has known Major Liconda for thirty years

TABRET, Mr. (Sacred Flame). Husband of Millie Tabret; father of Maurice and Colin; had been in the Indian

Civil Service; dead
TABRET, Stella (Sacred Flame). Wife of Maurice Tabret; age twenty-eight; is very beautiful; is in love with Colin Tabret and expecting his child
TAHITIAN GIRLS (Moon and Sixpence). Two or three; employed in the kitchen of the Hotel de Fleur, on Tahiti
TAILOR (Bread-Winner). Is sufficient enough for Charles Battle, but is not smart enough for Patrick Battle
TAILOR (Christmas Holiday). Made clothes to measure at low price; Robert Berger's suit came with extra pants
TAILOR (Loaves and Fishes). Of Thomas Spratte; Thomas never pays him
TAILOR (Of Human Bondage). In London; is demanding that Harry Griffiths pay him
TAILOR (Perfect Gentleman). Rich in original and daring ideas; outfits Monsieur Jourdain; has sent the latter some silk stockings; also tells him that persons of title wear Indian dressing gowns during the mornings
TAILOR #1 (Razor's Edge). The best one in London; made Elliott Templeton's clothes
TAILOR #2 (Razor's Edge). At London; he made Maugham's clothes; makes Larry Darrell a suit within four days
TAILOR (Theatre). Expensive; Thomas Fennell ordered new suits from him
TAILOR (Treasure). He had taught Pritchard to press gentleman's clothes
TAILOR'S ASSISTANT (Of Human Bondage). Thorpe Athelny maintained that he enlisted in the army because his daughter, Sally Athelny, would not say hello to him
TAIPAN (Taipan). English; he had come to China thirty years ago as a clerk and had worked his way up to the top position in an important English firm in China; originally from the London suburb of Barnes; educated at St. Paul's School
TAITBOUT, Jane (Theatre). An old actress (over sixty years of age) who had been societaire of the Comedie Francais; she retired to St. Malo and came in contact with Madame Falloux; boisterous, fat; she loved food more than anything else in the world; gave twelve-year-old Julia Lambert her very first acting lessons
TAMERLEY, Lord Charles (Theatre). The oldest and most constant of Julia Lambert Gosselyn's admirers; he had inherited a considerable fortune; separated from Lady

Characters

Clara Tamerley; a small head on an elegant body; not very good looking, but is distinguished in appearance

TAMERLEY, Lady Clara (Theatre). Is separated from her husband, Lord Charles; she initiated the false notion that Julia Lambert Gosselyn was the mistress of Lord Charles Tamerley; once had the reputation of a beauty

TAMIL OVERSEER (Back of Beyond). In the employ of Tom Saffary; long, black hair done in a chignon (or bun)

TAMILS (Narrow Corner). At Singapore; tall and emaciated; they saunter in silence past the Van Dyck Hotel

TANE (Moon and Sixpence). A Tahitian boy; no one knew from where he came or to whom he belonged; settled in with Ata, Charles Strickland, their baby, and the old woman's granddaughter; escorts Dr. Coutras from Strickland's plantation to the village of Taravao

TANGATU (Mackintosh). Chief of the village of Matautu, Samoa; father of Manuma

TANNER, Dr. (Bishop's Apron). Dean of St. Olphert's, in Wales; he is extremely ill and is planning to retire

TARTARS (Magician). They took Paracelsus prisoner and brought him to the Great Khan

TAXI DRIVER (Cakes and Ale). At Blackstable, Kent; he takes Ashenden from the station to the Bear and Key; he also deposits his bag

TAXI DRIVER (Christmas Holiday). At Paris; he conveys Charley Mason from the railway station to his hotel

TAXI DRIVER (Razor's Edge). Takes Isabel Macdonald from Isabel Maturin's apartment in Paris to Hakim's house

TAXI DRIVER (Treasure). Conveys Pritchard and Richard Harenger to the restaurant in Oxford Street, London

TAYLOR (Home and Beauty). She is Victoria's parlor maid

TAYLOR, Dr. (Magician). The superintendent of an asylum somewhere in Britain, where Oliver Haddo's mother has been committed; tall; with gold spectacles; wearing a frock coat; tells Arthur Burdon he has doubts about Haddo's sanity

TAYLOR, Frank (Land of Promise). One of Edward Marsh's hired men; tall and strong; clean-cut features; frank humorous eyes; clean shaven; sure of himself; he has worked as a trapper, railroad man, and freighter; he owns his own farm in Prentice, Manitoba; a hail storm has destroyed his crops and forced him to hire out as a farm laborer; marries Norah Marsh and returns with her to the farm at Prentice

TAYLOR, Norah (Land of Promise). See above, Norah MARSH

TAYLOR, Van Bueche (Moon and Sixpence). Is an American critic; asks Amy Strickland's help in writing a work on her husband, Charles; thin; large bald head, bony, shining; yellow, deep-lined face; New England accent

TEACHER (Catalina). Of theology at Salamanca; advised Blasco de Valero to have little or nothing to do with women--be polite to them and keep them at a distance

TEACHER (Razor's Edge). At Paris; he provides Larry Darrell with lessons in Greek; he has a sister

TEACHERS (Hero). At Little Primpton school, Kent; they stood by the girls during the welcome home ceremony for James Parsons

TED (For Services Rendered). He had been engaged to Ava Ardsley; killed in the war

TELEGRAPH BOY (Hero). Delivers James Parsons' telegram to the Parsons' servant

TELEGRAPH BOYS (Magician). At the Luxembourg Gardens, Paris; a group of them; they stand around a painter

TEMPLE, Richard (Outstation). Sultan's representative; advises Warburton to exercise tolerance toward Cooper

TEMPLETON, Elliott (Razor's Edge). In 1919, in his late fifties; tall, elegant, good features; thick waving dark hair, graying only slightly; age sixty-five in 1926, at which point he had gray hair, a lined face, pouches under his eyes; from an old Virginia family; had an apartment in Paris, on the Rive Gauche in the fashionable Rue St. Guillaume; he lived at Claridge's when in London; "adviser" to wealthy art collectors, which meant he had made a fortune dealing in works of art; social relationships the ruling passion of his life; a colossal snob; an Episcopalian who became a zealous Catholic; made papal chamberlain and received Order of the Holy Sepulchre; he spoke French fluently and correctly; had joined an ambulance corps in 1914, serving in Flanders and the Argonne; in 1915, secured a position with the Red Cross in Paris; for favors, Pope Pius XII restored him to the old family title of Count de Lauria; dies from a liver ailment at Antibes

TEMPLETON, George (Sanatorium). He is a patient at the sanatorium for three or four months; tall, good looking; dusky, sallow face; dark eyes; has a neat black moustache; slightly over forty years of age; resigned his major's commission in the Grenadier Guards after the war; ill and dying; in love with Ivy Bishop

TEMPLETON, Mr. the elder (Razor's Edge). Grandfather of Elliott Templeton; he was an eminent Episcopal divine

TEMPLETON, Mr. the younger (Razor's Edge). The father of Elliott Templeton; he had been the president of a Southern university

TEMPLETON, Mrs. (Razor's Edge). The mother of Elliott she traced her son's descent to one of the signers of the Declaration of Independence

TENANT (Hour Before the Dawn). At Graveney; informs May Henderson that Dick Murray has been wounded in Egypt

TENNIS PLAYER (Three Fat Women of Antibes). A professional at Carlsbad; he exercises Miss Hickson, Mrs. Richman, and Mrs. Sutcliffe

TENOR (Merry-Go-Round). Is in the choir of Tercanbury Cathedral, Kent; his voice rang out alone the melody of an old fashioned anthem

TERESA (Mask and the Face). Is not described in summary

TERRIS, Bill (Cakes and Ale). Lends Harry Retford two pounds to take Rosie Driffield to dinner at Romano's, in London, following the death of Rosie's child

TERRY, Dame Ellen Alice (Circle). The English actress (1848-1928); her picture appears in Clive Champion-Cheney's old photograph album; Clive in love with her

TERRY-MASON, Lady (Christmas Holiday). The wife of Sir Wilfred Terry-Mason; to present Patsy Mason at Court

TERRY-MASON, Sir Wilfred (Christmas Holiday). The only surviving child of Sibert Mason's eldest son; married a woman named Terry; a member of Parliament; created a baronet during the reign of George V (1910-1936); owned three-eights of Mason Estate; clever, energetic

TERRY-MASONS (Christmas Holiday). Cousins of Charley and Patsy Mason; resided at Godalming; always spent Christmas with the Masons

THACKERAY, William Makepeace (Round Dozen). The English novelist (1811-1863) who used to dine with Gertrude St. Clair's father, Mr. Sargeant Saunders

THEODORE, Grand Duke (Ashenden/Giulia Lazzari). Lover of Madame De Brides

THIN MAN (Ashenden/His Excellency). An acrobat; a large black moustache; dressed in ill-fitting, pink tights with green satin trunks; performs at the Metropolitan on Edgware Road, London

THIRD MATE (Moon and Sixpence). On the Tropic Bird; had an affair with Tiare Johnson before she was fifteen years old; a good looking boy

THOMAS, Sir Arthur (Penelope). London physician; three months ago, he gave Mrs. Watson the same medicine as Dr. Dickie O'Farrell currently prescribes for her

THOMPSON (Explorer [novel]). He is a member of Alec MacKenzie's expedition against the East African slave traders; now lying, unconscious, with a bullet in his skull; Dr. Adamson does not believe that he will last until the morning; he had once been a gold prospector

THOMPSON (Lady Frederick). A valet to Paradine Fouldes for the past twenty-five years

THOMPSON (Lion's Skin). Owner of the garage off Bruton Street; he employed young Robert Forestier as a car washer; knew Robert's father

THOMPSON (Mrs. Dot). A servant at Dot Worthley's house; serves coffee

THOMPSON (Of Human Bondage). A clerk at Messrs. Herbert Carter and Company; Philip Carey went to various places with him to pursue company business; sallow; age forty; long and lean; black hair and ragged moustache; hollow cheeks; deep lines on each side of his nose; oppressed by large family and a hopeless future

THOMPSON (Tenth Man). He is the Etchinghams' butler; announces visitors and guests

THOMPSON, Mr. (Land of Promise). At Pratt; formerly a Yorkshire bricklayer; he came to Canada, and now he has seven thousand dollars saved away in the bank

THOMPSON, Mr. (Smith). The butler at Mary Smith's first place of service; he trained her

THOMPSON, Mr. the elder (Mrs. Craddock). Father of Mr. Thompson the younger; a bricklayer

THOMPSON, Mr. the younger (Mrs. Craddock). He is the veterinarian at Blackstable and Leanham, in Kent; he holds out no hope for Edward Craddock's sick cow

THOMPSON, Sadie (Rain). Age twenty-seven; she is plump, but coarsely pretty; fat calves; supposedly had been bound for Apia and a position as a cashier

THORMAN, Captain (Choice of Amyntas). Of the Calderon, the ship that will carry Amyntas to Cadiz; Amyntas

finds him drinking rum punch inside a Plymouth tavern
THORNTON (Land of Promise). Keeper of a London gambling hall; sued Reginald Hornby for giving him a bad check
THOROLD, Bishop (Mrs.Craddock). Bishop of Rochester and Winchester; at Mrs. Branderton's dinner party, Mrs. Mayston Ryle relates the story about his white hands
TICKET COLLECTOR (Mrs. Craddock). Seen at the railway station at Blackstable, Kent; he stood at the wicket
TIDDLER, TOMMY (Bishop's Apron). See Thomas SPRATTE
TIKE, Mrs. (Liza of Lambeth). Lives in the house next to Liza Kemp and her mother; can provide the blacking to polish boots
TILLY, Mrs. (Bad Example). A neighbor of the Clintons, on the Adonis Road, Camberwell; she has finally taken down her summer curtains
TIMOTEO, Fra (Then and Now). He is confessor for Monna Caterina Cappelo, Bartolomeo Martelli, and Aurelia Martelli; a Franciscan; he receives money from Monna Caterina to pray that Aurelia will conceive a child; medium stature and pleasingly corpulent; fine beard; full red lips; a bold, hooked nose; fine black eyes
TOADS (Magician). Are in Margaret Dauncey's vision; enormous; their paws are pressed to their flanks
TOM (Liza of Lambeth). He is a resident of Vere Street, Lambeth; young; yellow hair; a small fair moustache; light complexion; blue eyes; a factory worker; he is in love with Liza Kemp and really wants to marry her
TOM (Merry-Go-Round). A clerk; engaged to Jenny Bush; young and undersized; false teeth; a jaunty air; he makes sheep's eyes across the bar while he drinks innumerable whiskies-and sodas
TOMLINSON, Violet (Razor's Edge). Is a friend of Isabel Bradley; the birth of her baby cost $1250
TOMMIES (Hero). The British soldiers in James Parsons' regiment; they curse continually as they kill Boers
TOMPKINSON (Explorer [novel]). Alec MacKenzie kicked him once at Eton; he has now written an article in Blackwood concerning the beauty of Alec's character
TONGA ISLANDERS (Narrow Corner). The Sydney Bulletin reports two of them involved in a stabbing incident
TOREL, Alban (Door of Opportunity). Just under six feet tall; slim; thick, fair hair; blue eyes; faint yellow skin; a long neck; straight nose; pale eyebrows and

pale eyelashes; thin lips; has served as the district officer in Sondurah; is known as an excellent pianist

TOREL, Anne (Door of Opportunity). Wife of Alban Torel; a neat figure; large, deep brown eyes; dark; frizzy black hair; swarthy skin; she has a small fleshy nose with large nostrils; large mouth

TOREL, Brigadier-General (Door of Opportunity). Father of Alban Torel; he was killed during World War I

TORIES (Tenth Man). At Middlepool; printing the article on posters from The Financial Standard about the mine at Campo del Oro

TORNIELLI, Niccolo (Making of a Saint). The President of the Council at Forli

TORRE, Diego (Poet). Friend of the Narrator; proposes to introduce him to Calisto de Santa Ana

TORRENS, Lord Ernest (Merry-Go-Round). A co-respondent in the divorce petition filed by Lord Vizard against Lady Vizard; he owns "a nice little shanty" on Curzon Street, London, that, after the divorce trial, he offers to lend to Lady Vizard

TOUGH BILL (Moon and Sixpence). Master of the sailors' boarding house near the Quai de la Joliette, Marseilles; a huge mulatto with a heavy fist; married to an American woman; Charles Strickland did his portrait

TOWER, Marion (Jane). She is seized with the prevailing passion for decoration; past fifty years of age; dyed red hair; handsome; is Jane Fowler's sister-in-law

TOWN CRIER (Then and Now). Ordered by Caesar Borgia to inform the population of Imola, at proper intervals, that they can certainly rely on justice from the Duke

TOWNSEND, Charlie (Painted Veil). Husband of Dorothy Townsend; assistant colonial secretary at Hong-Kong; having an affair with Kitty Fane; age forty-one; blue eyes; charming smile; shapely mouth; small white even teeth; deeply sun burned; healthy colored his cheeks; black hair, short and brushed sleek; thick and bushy eyebrows; little trim, curly moustache; lithe figure; the springing steps of a boy; he wears spectacles for reading; never spoke of his wife, who bored him; despite his "love" for Kitty Fane, he does not want to divorce Dorothy, since he is "keen" on his desire to be colonial governor; is vain, cowardly, self-seeking

TOWNSEND CHILDREN (Painted Veil). Three boys of Charlie

and Dorothy Townsend; the oldest is age fifteen; two are at school in England and the third, age six, whom Dorothy would take home next year

TOWNSEND, Dorothy (Painted Veil). The wife of Charlie Townsend; daughter of a retired colonial governor; at least thirty-eight years of age; tallish; is neither stout nor thin; a good deal of pale brown hair; not especially pretty; has good features; cold blue eyes; colorless cheeks; a pleasant voice; maintains that it is really not very flattering to her that women who fall in love with Charlie seem uncommonly second-rate

TRADER (Moon and Sixpence). At the village of Taravao, Tahiti; sold various items to Ata

TRADESMEN (Making of a Saint). At Forli; gathered at their doors and talking with one another

TRADESMEN (Man of Honour). Jenny and Basil Kent have bills with them

TRADESMEN (Merry-Go-Round). Subpoenaed by Lord Vizard to the divorce proceedings; swore by whom accounts for Lady Vizard's jewelry and clothes had been paid

TRADESMEN (Mrs. Craddock). At Leanham; practically all of them attend the Dissenters' chapel

TRAFFORD, Barton (Cakes and Ale). The husband of Isabel Trafford; is a clerk in the Home Office; a well-known authority on prehistoric man; wrote the biography of a great novelist who had been friendly with his wife; he wrote letters and luncheon invitations to those writers his wife admired, and he reviewed their books

TRAFFORD, Isabel (Cakes and Ale). Is the wife of Barton Trafford; Ashenden met her at one of the Driffields' Saturday afternoon teas in London; then age fifty; of a Scottish family; small and slight, but rather large features; crisp white hair; small pale eyes; conveyed an impression of having no bones in her body; shaking her hand "like taking a fillet of sole"; unhappily married in early life; known for her friendship with and inspiration for a great novelist who had died a few years earlier; a great reader; her own claim to fame rested upon her genius for friendship; occupied a block of flats situated on the Thames Embankment

TRAIL, Colonel (Up at the Villa). English; husband of Lady Grace Trail; traveling; a guest at Princess San Ferdinando's dinner party; is tall and thin; weather-beaten, red, lean face; a gray toothbrush moustache; an air of imbecility

TRAIL, Lady Grace (Up at the Villa). English; traveling; wife of Colonel Trail; guest at the Princess San Ferdinando's dinner party; a cousin of Rowley Flint

TRAIN PASSENGERS (Door of Opportunity). Man and wife; had been fellow passengers of the Torels on the ship from Singapore to England

TRAM CONDUCTOR (Mother). Is a resident of the tenement house in La Macarena, Seville; he played the guitar while Rosalia danced

TRAVELER (Explorer [novel]). Is on board the train from Lancashire to London; offered Alec MacKenzie (whom he does not know or recognize) a copy of the Daily Mail containing Fergus Macinnery's accusations; he claims that all MacKenzie can do now is to shoot himself

TRAVELING SERVANT (Casual Affair). Employed by Narrator

TRENCH (Isabella (Unattainable). Is age thirty-five; plump; pretty; debonair; an attractive softness and a great gift of sympathy; her husband is safely tucked away in India

TREVELYAN (Neil MacAdam). Resident at Kuala Solor; tall and fat; close cropped white hair; large, comic face; a bachelor

TREVOR, Miss (Smith). Daughter of Mr. and Mrs. Trevor; young and lovely; Algernon Peppercorn engaged to her

TREVOR, Mr. and Mrs. (Smith). Parents of Miss Trevor; rich Americans; will lunch with Algernon Peppercorn

TREVOR-JONES, Mr. and Mrs. (Mrs. Craddock). Will never forgive Polly Ley and Bertha Craddock of the latter do not attend their dinner party

TREVULZIO, Marshal (Then and Now). He captured Milan; his soldiers destroyed Leonardo's equestrian staute of Francesco Sforza

TRISMEGISTUS, Hermes (Magician). Knew about the Tinctura Physicorum being one of the alchemical mysteries

TROLLOPE, Anthony (Round Dozen). The English novelist (1815-1882) who used to dine with the St. Clairs at Leicester Square

TROLLOPS (Of Human Bondage). A few of them; customers at the Au Bon Plaisir restaurant, Dean Street, London

TROOPS (Magician). In Margaret Dauncey's vision; they drove the oppressed throngs through narrow streets

Characters

TROTTER, Benjamin (Land of Promise). Is one of Edward Marsh's hired men; English; formerly a bricklayer; his teeth are broken and discolored; hair cut short

TRUFFALDIN (Perfect Gentleman). Is in the intermezzo; he performs with the troupe of Italian dancers

TURKANA WOMAN (Explorer [novel/play]). Had been shot; still alive when found; died an hour later; said that George Allerton had shot her

TURKISH PASHA (Human Element). He had sold his estate on Rhodes to Betty Welldon-Burns

TURNER (Friend in Need). Known by both the Narrator and Lenny Burton; a remittance man in Yokohama; he is an excellent bridge player

TURNER, Algy (Hero). Clara Clibborn maintains that he either poisoned himself or died from a broken heart because he loved her; Reggie Clibborn counters that Algy died of cholera

TURNER, Bertie (Bread-Winner). Stockbroker; telephones the Battles' home to say Charles Battle is ruined

TURNER, Ernest (Sheppey). Is age twenty-two or twenty-three; extremely good looking; has long wavy hair and fine eyes; alert, vibrant, and charming; a master in one of the County Council schools; is a favorite with his pupils; he has been engaged to Florrie Miller for two years; envisions himself standing for Parliament

TURNER, Mr. (Of Human Bondage). He is known as "Tar"; a master at King's School, Tercanbury; short, with an immense belly; his black beard turning gray; swarthy skin; in his clerical garb he resembled a tar barrel; age fifty-five; he is possessed of a bitter tongue

TURNER, Mr. (Sheppey). Father of Ernest Turner; a clerk in the city, and a gentleman; on the Stock Exchange

TURNER, Mrs. Violet (Taipan). Small and pretty; had an affair with the Taipan; lies in the English cemetery

TURNKEY (Official Position). Assigned to assist Louis Remire; killed a farmer and his wife; looked brutish

TURNPIKE KEEPER (Of Human Bondage). Emma's father; kept a turnpike (toll gate) on the high road to Exeter

TUTOR (Explorer [novel]). In mathematics at Oxford; had a precious gift for making all people feel thoroughly uncomfortable; said he would rather teach mathematics to a brick wall than attempt to teach Alec Mackenzie

TUTOR (Facts of Life). At Cambridge University; tennis

player; had no objections to Nicholas Garnet leaving Cambridge for Monte Carlo
TUTOR (Merry-Go-Round). To Reggie Barlow-Bassett; was supposedly to read with his pupil in Brighton; wires to Emily Barlow-Bassett that he has not seen Reggie since July; has been in London throughout the summer
TUTOR (Mrs. Craddock). To Gerald Vaudrey; told General Vaudrey that if he did not remove Gerald, "he'd give me the shoot" (dismiss him)
TWICKENHAM, Lord John (Sheppey). Is the younger brother (by fifteen years) of the Marquess of Twickenham, and a customer at Bradley's Hairdressing and Barber's Saloon, Jermyn Street, London
TWICKENHAM, Marchioness of (Home and Beauty). Following her divorce, she had her ravaged face restored with a course of twelve treatments by Esmeralda Mountmorency
TWICKENHAM, Marquess (Sheppey). Older brother of Lord John Twickenham; a customer at Bradley's Hairdressing and Barber's Saloon, in Jermyn Street, London; he insisted on trying a bit of German hair preparation
TWICKENHAM, Sadie (Our Betters). An American woman who is married to an Englishman, and unfaithful to him
TWINING, Richard (Moon and Sixpence). A writer; a guest at Amy Strickland's luncheon
TWINING, Richard (Our Betters). A writer; he has been invited to a dinner at Lady Pearl Grayston's house
TYPIST (Of Human Bondage). At the linen drapery firm of Lynn and Sedley, London; types the manager's letters
TYRANTS (Magician). Grim; in Margaret Dauncey's vision
TYRELL, Dr. (Of Human Bondage). Age thirty-five; tall and thin; a small head; red hair cut short; prominent blue eyes; a bright scarlet face; a large, successful practice, with prospect for knighthood; Philip Carey becomes his out-patients' clerk; he examines Cronshaw

U

UNCLE (Explorer [novel]). Of Alec Mackenzie; he owned a ranch in Texas that he willed to Alec
UNCLE (Jack Straw). To one of the Parker-Jennings; from the North; a hardware manufacturer; died suddenly and left the Parker-Jennings nearly two million pounds
UNCLE (Liza of Lambeth). Of Sally; he is a man of some

means; marches arm-in-arm with Sally's mother to his niece's wedding; then buys beer for the wedding party prior to the ceremony

UNCLE (Of Human Bondage). Of Emily Wilkinson, on her mother's side; was wealthy; he had married his cook

UNCLE (Sheppey). Of Jim Cooper's mother; used to live with the Coopers; thought he was a loaf of sugar, and thus would not bathe

UNDERHILL, Jean-Paul (Cakes and Ale). A resident of New York; wishes to look at the Driffield house and garden; tall, young, broad shouldered; heavy; a swarthy face; clean shaven; handsome eyes; thick black hair; horn-rimmed spectacles; on a literary tour of England

UNDERSECRETARY (Explorer [novel]). For Foreign Affairs; in debate, spoke of Alec Mackenzie with honeyed words

UNDERTAKER (Daisy). Opens a shop in Blackstable, Kent; causes Robert Griffith to lose the most remunerative part of his business

UNDERTAKER #1 (Of Human Bondage). At London; a little fat Jew; curly, long, and greasy black hair; he wore a large diamond ring on a podgy finger

UNDERTAKER #2 (Of Human Bondage). At Blackstable; also the carpenter

UNDERTAKER (Razor's Edge). At Toulon; is recommended by the chief inspector of police to Maugham concerning Sophie Macdonald's burial; is brisk and businesslike

UNDERTAKER'S MEN (Razor's Edge). At Antibes; they place Elliott Templeton's embalmed body inside the coffin

UNTEL, Monsieur (Man with a Conscience). Owner of a La Havre shipping firm who proposed to hire Henri Renard

UPJOHN, Leonard (Of Human Bondage). A literary critic; Philip Carey met him at Paris with Cronshaw in a cafe of the Quarter; found London publisher for Cronshaw's poems; age thirty-five; looked weedy; long pale hair, white face; patronizing; liked to hear himself talk

URCHIN (Hour Before the Dawn). One of several children evacuated to the Hendersons' estate at Graveney Holt; asks Jane Foster why she has no children of her own

URCHIN (Then and Now). Conducts Niccolo Machiavelli and Piero Giacomini to the house of Bartolomeo Martelli

URCHINS (Making of a Saint). Are at the market place in Forli; they glide in and out and chase one another

URCHINS (Merry-Go-Round). At the port at Brindisi; they

played merrily on the quay
URCHINS (Mrs. Craddock). Seen at Rome; ragged; they are quaintly costumed and importunate
UTAN (Narrow Corner). Is a Black crew member on Captain Nichols' lugger; a Torres Straits islander; strong, fine figure; spoke English well

V

VALET (Jack Straw). Employed by the Pomeranian attache; the attache introduced him to an American woman as a count; she asked him to dinner
VANCOUVERS (Constant Wife). To dine with Mortimer and Marie-Louise Durham at 8:15
VAN HASSELDT (Door of Opportunity). The Dutch manager of the timber camp; very fat
VANHATTON (Bishop's Apron). He is the secretary to Lord Stonehenge; informed the Prime Minister that he had promised to do something for Theodore Spratte before the last election
VAN HOOG, Miss (Our Betters). See Flora DELLA CERCOLA
VAN RYK (Narrow Corner). Half-caste; assistant manager at the hotel on Kanda; spoke Dutch
VAN TIEFEL (Choice of Amyntas). Is a Dutch merchant who lives at Cadiz; a friend of the Parson; he asks the Parson for an English clerk; then forced to leave the country and all his properties seized by the Spanish authorities--all occurring prior to Amyntas's arrival
VAN VECHTEN, Carl (Creative Impulse). American critic (1880-1964) who chastised the public for its failure to recognize the true merits of Mrs. Albert Forrester
VANUZZI, Mr. (Cakes and Ale). He phones Rosie Driffield during her conversation with Ashenden in Yonkers, New York; one of Rosie's beaux; retired; formerly owned a grocery store in New York City
VARSITY BOY (Sheppey). Horse upon which Sheppey placed a bet, a shilling each way
VASQUEZ, Rosalia (Catalina). Is an actress engaged by Alonso Fuentes to console himself over the loss of his wife and to play minor roles and stand-in parts
VAUDREY, Betty (Mrs. Craddock). Wife of General Vaudrey and mother of Gerald; she writes to her sister, Polly Ley, concerning her son's philandering with her maid

Characters   413

VAUDREY COUSINS (Mrs. Craddock). Gerald Vaudrey labels them as "frumps"

VAUDREY DAUGHTERS (Mrs. Craddock). Of General and Betty Vaudrey; in tears over Gerald's philandering with his mother's maid

VAUDREY, General (Mrs. Craddock). The husband of Betty Vaudrey; father of Gerald; brother-in-law of Polly Ley and Bertha Ley's father; irascible; bald; is in a passion over his son's philandering with his wife's maid; has given Gerald five hundred pounds and told him to go to the devil

VAUDREY, Gerald (Merry-Go-Round). Nephew of Polly Ley; mentioned in Polly's will to receive one-third of her estate; a scamp; Polly certain that he will squander the money in riotous living

VAUDREY, Gerald (Mrs. Craddock). The son of General and Betty Vaudrey; age nineteen; slight; small, girlish face; tiny, straight nose; freckled complexion; dark and curly hair, worn long; handsome green eyes; has a charming expression; a sensual mouth always smiling; expelled from Rugby, and then dismissed by a series of crammers; Bertha Craddock's cousin (Polly Ley his aunt); he has been philandering violently with his mother's maid; goes to Florida and then to London; he falls in love with Bertha Craddock

VAUGHAN, George (Narrow Corner). On one of the Jardine boats going to Amoy; suffered so badly from dyspepsia that he hanged himself

VENNING (Of Human Bondage). A student at King's School, Tercanbury; small

VERGARA, Father (Catalina). A Dominican; he hears the confessions of Maria Perez Orta and of Catalina; he is a simple man of no significant amount of learning

VERGER (Explorer [novel]). Of a deserted London church; he signed the book at the wedding of Dick Lomas and Julia Crowley

VERGER #1 (Merry-Go-Round). Is at Tercanbury Cathedral, Kent; he told Herbert Field the cathedral would close

VERGER #2 (Merry-Go-Round). In attendance at All Soul's Church, London, at the marriage between Hilda Murray and Basil Kent

VERGER (Mrs. Craddock). At Westminster Abbey, London; black-robed; guided a party of Americans and English country folk

VERMONT, Elizabeth (Promise). Lunches with the Narrator at Claridge's; an agreeable smile; age fifty; black hair, sleek and shining; very slim; white hands; the daughter of the seventh Duke of St. Erth; married at age eighteen, followed by divorce and a succession of husbands and lovers; current husband is Peter Vermont

VERMONT, Peter (Promise). Current husband of Elizabeth Vermont; he married her at age twenty-one, she being forty; eventually falls in love with Barbara Canton

VERNON, Helen (Landed Gentry). Age thirty-five; slight, faded, and gaunt; independent and affluent; resides at Foley, Somersetshire; the heiress to five thousand acres and a house that has recently been remodeled; the Insoleys had wanted her to marry Claude, and now want her to wed Archibald; still in love with Claude

VERNON, Mary (Landed Gentry). Is Helen Vernon's great-grandmother; an abandoned hussy who supposedly had an affair with the Regent

VERNON, Monte (Theatre). The actor who plays the lead role in the very first play produced by the Gosselyns

VERSINDER, Lady (Treasure). She will have lunch with Richard Harenger on Thursday, the eighth of the month

VETERINARIAN (Marriages Are Made in Heaven). The father of Lottie Vivian; lives in the country

VETERINARIAN (Theatre). In Colonel Gosselyn's regiment; an officer, and one of the best

VICAR #1 (Cakes and Ale). William Ashenden's uncle and vicar of Blackstable, Kent; had been to Oxford; he sold subscriptions to the Additional Curates' Society

VICAR #2 (Cakes and Ale). Of Blackstable, Kent; William Ashenden's uncle's successor, twice removed; wrote to the Daily Mail asking to have Edward Driffield buried beneath the Kentish elms of Blackstable; attended a a Driffields' luncheon at Ferne Court, Blackstable, with his wife, William Ashenden, Lady Hodmarsh, the fat duchess, and Lord Scallion

VICAR (Cupid and the Vicar of Swale). Of Swale; over eighty years old at his death; Robert Branscombe's immediate predecessor

VICAR (Jack Straw). Was Lewis Abbott's predecessor at Taverner; died from influenza

VICAR #1 (Of Human Bondage). Of Whitestone church, East

Anglia; a bachelor; had taken up farming; filed cases in the county court against laborers and tradesmen
VICAR #2 (Of Human Bondage). Of Ferne, in East Anglia; bearded; fine figure; was terribly cruel to his wife
VICAR #3 (Of Human Bondage). Of Surle, in East Anglia; he spent every evening lounging in the public house
VICAR #1 (Verger). The predecessor of Vicar #2 at St. Peter's, Neville Square; clergyman of the old school; silvery voiced
VICAR #2 (Verger). The recently appointed vicar of St. Peter's, Neville Square; age in the early forties; red faced and energetic; had come from the East End
VICEROY (Our Betters). Formerly in India; sat opposite of Bessie Saunders at Pearl Graystone's dinner party
VICTOR (Sheppey). Number three barber, Bradley's Hairdressing and Barber's Saloon, Jermyn Street, London
VILLAGERS (Faith). Of San Lucido, Spain; crowd around the frozen body of Brother Jasper
VINCENT (Razor's Edge). Waiter at a Rue de Lappe cafe, Paris; he refuses to get a chair for Sophie Macdonald
VINCENT, Mrs. Alfred (Land of Promise). Sends a wreath to Miss Wickham's house
VINEYARD OWNER (Lotus Eater). Thomas Wilson rents his house; he lives with his wife, Assunta, in a nearby cottage
VIRGILIO, Marcello (Then and Now). Secretary of state of the Republic of Florence and Niccolo Machiavelli's immediate superior; he is a gifted orator; handsome
VIRGO, Victoria (Of Human Bondage). Is a London music hall artiste who had all her clothes made at Lynn and Sedley's, London; she once invited Mr. Sampson to dinner on a Sunday at her house, in Tulse Hill
VITELLI the elder (Making of a Saint). The tyrant of Castello; signed a warrant for the arrest of Filippo Brandolini; died recently
VITELLI the younger (Making of a Saint). The son of the tyrant Vitelli; undid all of his father's evil deeds; he was attracted to the abilities of Checco d'Orsi
VITELLI, Paolo (Then and Now). A brother of Vitellozzo Vitelli; taught the profession of arms to Oliverotto da Fermo; tortured and executed by the Florentines
VITELLI, Vitellozzo (Then and Now). A mercenary captain in the service of Caesar Borgia and the ablest of his

commanders; lord of Citta di Castello; a bitter enemy of the Florentines, whom he defeated at Arezzo; he is sullen, suspicious, moody; is subjected to attacks of depression resulting from mercury to counteract his syphilis; the best artilleryman in Europe; initially, a powerful physique, big and strong; later, he became gaunt, sallow, and clean shaven; he has an aggressive nose and a small, receding chin; drooping eyelids

VIVYAN, Lottie (Marriages Are Made in Heaven). Is age twenty-eight; handsome; self-possessed; with an easy manner suggesting that she has consorted with men, rather than with women; is preparing to marry Jack Rayner; had grown up in the country, the daughter of a veterinarian; came to London after an affair with a man at Oxford; has an income of twelve hundred pounds a year that has been settled on her by Lord Feaverham

VIZARD, Grace (Explorer [novel]). Niece of Lady Vizard; the prettiest girl seen at Lady Alice Kelsey's dance

VIZARD, Lady (Bishop's Apron). Canon Theodore Spratte to have lunch with her in order that she can meet the Princess of Wartburg-Hochstein

VIZARD, Lady (Explorer [novel]). Grace Vizard's aunt; a pattern of all the proprieties; is a devout member of the Church of Rome

VIZARD, Lord (Merry-Go-Round). Married Marguerite Kent (Basil Kent's mother) following the death of her husband; is younger than his wife; neither rich nor generous; ill-tempered and not always sober; related to Lady Edward Stringer; filed a petition for divorce

VIZARD, Marguerite Elizabeth Claire (Merry-Go-Round). Mother of Basil Kent and the widow of Mr. Kent #1; married Lord Vizard shortly after her husband died; is a beautiful woman; dark, flashing eyes; beautiful teeth; magnificent hair dyed in harmony with her eyes and complexion; tall, with a splendid figure; walked with the majesty of an Eastern queen; hated old Mrs. Kent; notoriously extravagant; detested both of her husbands; filed a counter-petition for divorce from Lord Vizard; to be received into the Catholic Church

VOLTERRA, Cardinal of (Then and Now). Brother of Piero Soderini; when he was a bishop, accompanied Niccolo Machiavelli to Urbino to confer with Caesar Borgia, following the capitulation of the citadel at Arezzo

Characters

VON BREMER, Count Adrien (Jack Straw). The Pomeranian ambassador; lives next door to the Parker-Jennings in the country; old and distinguished; wears an eyeglass

VON CRAMM (Facts of Life). Tennis player at Monte Carlo

VON GRABAN, Peter (Irish Gentleman). Court chamberlain of Wartburg-Hochstein; he is wizened, with a skin of parchment; brings Robert O'Donnel fifty pounds from John-Adolphus for having rescued the Princess Mary

VON KUFFSTEIN, Count Johann-Ferdinand (Magician). He generated spirits (or homunculi) in the Tyrol in 1775

VON P., Major (Ashenden/Traitor). Head, German Intelligence Department at Berne; Grantley Caypor's superior

VON SCHEILDLEINS (Caesar's Wife). Invited to Sir Arthur and Lady Violet Little's party

VON THUN, Count Franz-Joseph (Magician). Saw homunculi

W

WADDINGTON (Painted Veil). Deputy Commissioner at Mei-tan-fu; well under forty years old; small and thin; bald head; a small and bare face, unlined and flesh colored; a small nose and mouth; small, bright blue eyes; fair, scanty eyebrows; bore an ugliness that was not without charm; shrewd; drinks; had developed an eccentric freedom, full of fads and oddities; has been in China for twenty years; had been at Hankow before coming to Mei-tan-fu; speaks Chinese easily; knows and dislikes Charlie Townsend; describes himself as an old-fashioned little man who likes a well-bred woman; lives with a Manchu woman from Hankow; he reads the funeral service at Walter Fane's burial

WAGGETT, Lady (Mrs. Craddock). She is a guest at Mrs. Branderton's dinner party; the widow of a city knight

WAITER (Cakes and Ale). At Alroy Kear's club, St. James Street, London; waits on Kear and Narrator at lunch

WAITER #1 (Christmas Holiday). At the Serail, Paris; he brings Simon Fenimore an orangeade

WAITER #2 (Christmas Holiday). At Charley Mason's Paris hotel; takes Charley's order for lunch

WAITER #3 (Christmas Holiday). At the large cellar bar, Paris; slatternly and in shirt sleeves; finds Charley Mason and Lydia Berger seats and takes their orders

WAITER #1 (Cousin Amy). At the Ritz, London; hands the

Narrator the menu
WAITER #2 (Cousin Amy). At the Ritz, London; brings the Narrator the wine list
WAITER (Dream). Is at the train station restaurant at Valdivostok
WAITER #1 (Explorer [novel]). Is in Walker's vision; at his club; an obsequious menial who brings rumpsteak and fried potatoes
WAITER #2 (Explorer [novel]). Is in Walker's vision; at his club; a liveried flunky; brings a pewter tankard of foaming ale
WAITER (Gigolo and Gigolette). At the Casino; he serves the Barrett party
WAITER #1 (Human Element). The bar waiter at Claridge's
WAITER #2 (Human Element). Dining room, the Plaza, Rome
WAITER #3 (Human Element). Lounge, Hotel Plaza, in Rome
WAITER #1 (Jack Straw). The Grand Babylon Hotel; tells Ambrose Holland his waiter will arrive in one minute
WAITER #2 (Jack Straw). Is at the Grand Babylon Hotel; Marie Parker-Jennings complains to him that others have occupied the one table reserved for their party
WAITER #3 (Jack Straw). At the Grand Babylon Hotel; he offers and serves cigars at the Parker-Jennings table
WAITER (Lion's Skin). The bar on the Croisette; serves the table of Robert Forestier and Frederick Hardy
WAITER (Love in a Cottage). Hotel Splendide; an Italian
WAITER (Luncheon). At Foyot's restaurant, Paris; serves luncheon to the woman and the Narrator
WAITER #1 (Magician). At Lavenue's, in Paris; Marie's lover; he beats her
WAITER #2 (Magician). At a Monte Carlo restaurant; he engages in a most disgraceful altercation with Oliver Haddo after the latter gave him a counterfeit coin
WAITER (Man with a Conscience). An ex-convict who lives with the woman who operates the hotel at St. Laurent de Maroni; he waits tables there
WAITER #1 (Merry-Go-Round). At the Carlton, in London; he serves Reggie Barlow-Bassett and Grace Castillyon
WAITER #2 (Merry-Go-Round). At the hotel dining room in Rochester; he places Polly Ley at a little table
WAITER #1 (Moon and Sixpence). At the Hotel des Belges, Rue des Moines, Paris; he is young; furtive eyes and a sullen look

Characters 419

WAITER #2 (Moon and Sixpence). Is at the cafe on the Avenue de Clichy, Paris, where Charles Strickland and the Narrator play chess

WAITER #3 (Moon and Sixpence). At the inn off the Rue Bouterie, Marseilles; is an undersized youth; a flat, spotty face; he scurries back and forth serving beer

WAITER (Mrs. Craddock). In the old coffee room of the Ship, Greenwich; black; absurdly extolled the dishes

WAITER #1 (Of Human Bondage). At Hotel des Doux Ecoles, Paris; he carries Philip Carey's luggage to his room

WAITER #2 (Of Human Bondage). At La Closerie de Lilas, Paris; serves Cronshaw and his guests; he is a jovial fellow who knew Cronshaw intimately

WAITER #3 (Of Human Bondage). At the cheap, respectable restaurant in Soho; French; seedy; is attempting to learn English

WAITER #1 (Razor's Edge). At the Dome, Paris; he serves drinks to Maugham and Larry Darrell

WAITER #2 (Razor's Edge). At the cafe in Toulon; serves drinks to Maugham and Sophie Macdonald

WAITER #3 (Razor's Edge). At the Brasserie Graf, Avenue de Clichy, Paris; he serves Larry Darrell and Maugham

WAITER (Round Dozen). He serves port to Mr. St. Clair

WAITER (Tenth Man). At the Palace Hotel, Middlepool; is told by Frederick Bennett to bring the London newspapers as soon as they arrive

WAITER (Theatre). In the dining car on the train from Paris to Cannes; he collects the payments for bills

WAITER (Three Fat Women of Antibes). Is at the "Monkey House" at Antibes, overlooking the sea

WAITER (Treasure). At the restaurant in Oxford Street; he serves Pritchard and Richard Harenger

WAITER (Virtue). At Charlie Bishop's London club; he has been employed there for thirty years

WAITERS (Bread-Winner). Two of them; are at the Stock Exchange, London; they appear at the stands, take off their hats, and beat with a wooden mallet three times

WAITERS (Christmas Holiday). At the Serail, Paris; in Turkish dress

WAITERS (Christmas Holiday). At the Select, Boulevard Montparnasse, Paris; getting restive

WAITERS (Explorer [novel]). Lady Alice Kelsey's dance; at the end, they stand with heavy eyes behind tables

WAITERS (Jack Straw). Some two or three of them; at the lounge and winter garden of the Grand Babylon Hotel; they are seen standing about or serving customers

WAITERS (Mrs. Craddock). At the London restaurant where Gerald Vaudrey and Bertha Craddock dine; busy; glide to and fro

WAITERS (Of Human Bondage). One or two of them; out of work; are customers at the Au Bon Plaisir restaurant, Dean Street, London

WAITERS (Tenth Man). Two of them; at the Palace Hotel, Middlepool; bring champagne to George Winter's rooms after the votes have been counted

WAITRESS (Ashenden/Traitor). Ashenden's hotel, Lucerne

WAITRESS (Of Human Bondage). At the tea shop in Parliament Street, London; is impressed by Philip Carey's drawing of Mildred Rogers

WAITRESS (Theatre). At a Lyons tea shop, Edgware Road, London; serves tea to Julia Lambert Gosselyn and the young man, as well as scone and butter to the latter

WAITRESSES (Christmas Holiday). At the restaurant in the Avenue du Maine, Paris; anxious for Charley Mason and Lydia Berger to leave

WALKER (Explorer [novel]). Young; he had recently been sent to take charge of the most northerly station of the North East Africa Company; had been with Alec Mac Kenzie's expedition for a year; funny and fat; round face and comic manner; was eminently unsuited for the life he led; had squandered his small inheritance; is honest, loyal, unbending; had received a wound in the arm; killed in last attack against Arabs and slavers

WALKER (Mackintosh). The administrator of Talua, one of the larger Samoan islands; sixty years old; a little man, of less than middle height; is enormously stout; has a large, fleshy face, with hanging cheeks; has three vast chins; almost completely bald; blue eyes; he wears spectacles; he speaks in a loud, gruff voice

WALKER (Mrs. Craddock). A baker at Leanham; has ceased coming to church

WALTERS #1 (Of Human Bondage). He is a pupil at King's School, Tercanbury; had his ears boxed with a book by Rev. B.B. Gordon; his hearing affected to the point where he had to leave school; Walters #2's brother

WALTERS #2 (Of Human Bondage). Is the younger brother of

Walters #1, and a pupil at King's School, Tercanbury

WALTERS, Mr. (Of Human Bondage). Father of Walters #1 and #2; is a brewer and resident of Tercanbury, Kent

WALTON (Casual Affair). Is a member of the club in the north of Borneo; had known Jack Almond at Singapore

WANLEY, Lady (Jack Straw). Handsome widow of uncertain age; poor; two sons; falls in love with Jack Straw

WARBURTON, George (Outstation). Resident of Sembulu, in Borneo; hot temper; red face; his red hair whitening; blue eyes; is age fifty-four; Oxford educated; a snob

WARD, Mrs. Humphry [Mary Augusta Arnold] (Cakes and Ale). British novelist (1851-1920); niece of Matthew Arnold; Mrs. Encombe knew her as a woman of the highest character

WARDER (Episode). Looks on whenever Grace visits Fred at Wormswood Scrubbs

WARDER #1 (Official Position). A big, powerful man; had fainted at an execution

WARDER #2 (Official Position). In charge of the working party out in the jungle; he notices a great flock of vultures clustered around a tree

WARDER (Vessel of Wrath). He is in charge of the ten prisoners sent to Maputiti, one of the outer Islands

WARDERS (Christmas Holiday). Two of them; escort Robert Berger into the courtroom

WARE, Lady Mary (Jack Straw). A cousin of Lady Wanley; brother of Tregary Ware; Vincent Parker-Jennings saw her driving with Lady Wanley

WARE, Tregary (Jack Straw). Brother of Lady Mary Ware; cousin of Lady Wanley; Vincent Parker-Jennings claims to have been "a great pal" of his while at Oxford

WARING (Neil MacAdam). Employed in the customs at Kuala Solor; shared a house with Johnson

WARMINGTON, Maria Penn (Ashenden/Mr. Harrington's Washing). J.Q. Harrington's great aunt

WARRNE (Magician). Small and bald; his pate shiny as a billiard ball; pointed beard; rubicund; protruding, brilliant eyes; is always drunk; very nearly a great painter and a delightful interpreter of Paris; his memory for names was defective

WARREN, Miss (Creative Impulse). Pours at Mrs. Forrester's Tuesday afternoon teas; types her manuscripts

WARRIORS (Magician). In Margaret Dauncey's vision; in

their steel

WARTBURG-HOCHSTEIN, Princess of (Bishop's Apron). Is to lunch with Lady Vizard and Canon Theodore Spratte

WARTBURG-HOCHSTEIN, Princess of (Loaves and Fishes). Had lunch with Theodore Spratte and Lady de Capit; she found Bertram Railing's book to be most readable

WARTON, Mary (Social Sense). Wife of Thomas Warton; she sits next to the Narrator at the Macdonalds' dinner party; once a well-known concert singer; age fifty-three; haggard, with mannish features; weather-beaten skin; short, thick, and curly gray hair; fine eyes bright with intelligence; she is fond of reading and painting, as well as music

WARTON, Thomas (Social Sense). Husband of Mary Warton; he is a not too successful portrait painter; a decent craftsman without originality or imagination; on the surface is amiable and kind, but actually is narrow, argumentative, and conceited

WATCHMAKER (Christmas Holiday). At Neuilly, a quarter of a mile from the Bergers' house; he repaired Lydia Berger's watches

WATCHMAN (East of Suez). He found Se Shi Ming with a dagger in his heart

WATCHMAN (Punctiliousness of Don Sebastian). He is at Xiormonez, Spain; after the cathedral bells strike the hour, he cries, "Protect us, Mary, Queen of Heaven; protect us, Mary!"

WATER CARRIER (East of Suez). Seen in a crowded Peking street; with a creaking barrow; he slops the water

WATERFORD, Rose (Creative Impulse). Well known novelist who repeated to Mrs. Forrester Clifford Boyleston's remark about Albert Forrester

WATERFORD, Rose (Moon and Sixpence). Novelist; extended kindness to the young Narrator; combined masculine intelligence with feminine perversity; was a cynic

WATKIN, Henrietta (Of Human Bondage). Is Philip Carey's godmother; lives in Onslow Gardens, London, with her elder sister; stout; she has a red face and dyed hair

WATKIN, Miss (Of Human Bondage). Is Henrietta Watkin's elder sister; resigned herself contentedly to old age

WATSON (Of Human Bondage). A clerk at Messrs. Herbert Carter and Company, London; son of a brewer (Watson, Craig, and Thompson); young; large, stout; educated at Winchester School and Oxford; is spending a year to learn the business

WATSON, Dr. (Painted Veil). A missionary to Mei-tan-fu; he sent his wife and children to Hong Kong because of the cholera epidemic that eventually took his life; buried at Mei-tan-fu; the Fanes occupy his bungalow

WATSON, Dr. (Penelope). Dead husband of Mrs. Watson; subscribed to the Lancet and British Medical Journal

WATSON, Helen (Of Human Bondage). The wife of the headmaster of the preparatory school of King's School, at Tercanbury, Kent; dark, with black hair parted in the middle; she has thick lips and a small round nose

WATSON, Mrs. (Penelope). Widow of Dr. Watson; small and old; a patient of Dr. Richard O'Farrell; leaving with her daughter for the Riviera; likes to be examined by doctors

WATSON, Rev. (Of Human Bondage). The Headmaster of the preparatory school of King's School, Tercanbury; the archdeacon of Tercanbury Cathedral; is over six feet tall; broad; enormous hands; great red beard; jovial and aggressively cheerful; is married to Helen Watson

WAYLAND, Beatrice (Sacred Flame). A nurse; age twenty-seven; handsome; fine eyes; a fine figure; has tended to Maurice Tabret for almost five years, and is in love with him; she believes that Maurice was murdered

WAYLAND, Miss (Sacred Flame). She is Beatrice Wayland's sister; lives in Japan

WEBER BROTHERS (Winter Cruise). Owners of the Friedrich Weber; residents of Hamburg; always ready to send the ship on any route, as long as it proved profitable

WEEKS (Of Human Bondage). One of the American lodgers at Frau Helen Erlin's pension at Heidelberg; theological student and a graduate of Harvard, where he had taught Greek literature; he wore a black coat; thin; skin yellow and dry; a scholarly stoop; long and ugly head; pal,e scanty hair; thin mouth; long thin nose; a great protuberance of his frontal bones; had a New England accent; spoke bad German; was slightly over thirty years of age; bore a cold and precise manner

WEITBRECHT-ROTHOLZ, Hugo (Moon and Sixpence). A psychopathologist and a student of art; he published (1914) an enthusiastic monograph on the painting of Charles Strickland; he belonged to that school of historians that believes human nature to be not only as bad as it can be, but considerably worse than it actually is

WELLDON-BURNS Elizabeth (Human Element). Betty; is age thirty-four; lives in Rhodes; former London resident; the daughter of the Duke of St. Erth; wife of James Welldon-Burns; hospital nurse during World War I; she lived a life of hectic gaiety brown hair; deep blue eyes; "milk and roses" skin; a great beauty; a poet

WELLDON-BURNS, James (Human Element). Jimmie; husband of Betty Welldon-Burns; son of a manufacturer; Eton schoolmate of Humphrey Carruthers; contracts tuberculosis and dies

WELLINGTON, Arthur Wellesley, Duke of (Mrs. Craddock). British soldier and statesman (1769-1852); at Mrs. Branderton's dinner party, General Hancock told celebrated stories about him

WESTCOTT, Sandy (Gigolo and Gigolette). Waits for Eva Barrett at the Casino bar; at the Casino every night

WESTREYS, Duke of (Theatre). Is young; he looked like a stable boy; he sat next to Julia Lambert Gosselyn at Charles Tamerley's luncheon; he claimed that he knew and spoke French slang far better than any Frenchman

WHARTON (Of Human Bondage). English; is studying for a philological degree at Heidelberg University; Philip Carey goes to his lodgings for mathematics lessons; is short and stout; heavy moustache and long, unkempt hair; an excessive beer drinker; had been in Germany for five years after taking his degree at Cambridge

WHARTON, Evelyn (Unknown). The wife of Colonel George Wharton; married for thirty-five years; the mother of John; age fifty-five; slight, tall; deliberate features; kind eyes; gentle look; dark hair turning gray

WHARTON, Colonel George (Unknown). Husband of Evelyn, father of John; married for thirty-five years; considerably older than his wife; thin; frail; white hair; bronzed face; erect; he is fatally ill and will not live much longer; he had served in India, Egypt, and South Africa; fears death; he dies quite peacefully

WHARTON, Major John (Unknown). Son of Evelyn and George Wharton; age thirty; engaged to Sylvia Bullough for seven years; recently returned from the war on three weeks' leave; had been wounded; earned the Military Cross and the D.S.O.; served in India and Gallipoli;

Characters   425

   he has lost his faith in God
WHEELER, Bananas (Honolulu). Is Captain Butler's mate;
   tall, dark-skinned Hawaiian native; inclined toward
   stoutness; crisply curling thick gray hair; his upper
   front teeth are cased in gold; he has a marked squint
WHIST PLAYERS (Of Human Bondage). Two of them; come to
   see Harry Griffiths while he is nursing Philip Carey
WHITE, Ferdinand (De Amicitia). A poet and playwright
   at Paris; from Oxford; had spent his childhood in a
   country parsonage; travels to Holland with Valentia
   Stewart and falls in love with her
WHITE MEN (Explorer [novel]). Sixteen of them, on Alec
   MacKenzie's latest expedition to Africa; except for
   occasional fever, they endured the climate quite well
WHITSABLE, Lady (Smith). She is identified as a former
   "employer" of Algernon Peppercorn; she wanted the
   earth, but she wanted it at a considerable reduction
WICKHAM, Dorothy (Land of Promise). The wife of James
   Wickham; young and pretty
WICKHAM, James (Land of Promise). Husband of Dorothy
   Wickham; nephew of Louisa Wickham; clean shaven; thin
   face; baldish; eventually sends Norah Marsh (now in
   Canada) five hundred pounds from what Louisa left him
WICKHAM, Louisa (Land of Promise). Resided at Tunbridge
   Wells; exacting, domineering, disagreeable; thought
   to have been a detestable old woman; wealthy; she has
   just died; left all of her fortune to James Wickham
WIDOW (Catalina). Takes Demetrios Christopoulos into
   her home after the death of the Viceroy
WIDOW (Explorer [novel]). Is skittish and of uncertain
   age; she retired in disorder before Richard Lomas's
   complete acquaintance with the Restoration dramatists
WIDOW (Hero). Of the late incumbent of Stone Fairley,
   Kent; to move from the vicarage in six weeks, giving
   Thomas and Mary (Clibborn) Dryland time to honeymoon
WIDOW (Lady Frederick). Of a city knight; Lady Frede-
   rick Berolles sees her and Capt. Montgomerie lunching
WIDOW (Razor's Edge). With money; she marries Artist #2
WIDOWER (Lion's Skin). Was the first husband of Mrs.
   Forestier; a prominent citizen with growing children
WIFE (Bad Example). Of the seventy-year-old Man #1; she
   died before her husband did
WIFE (Cakes and Ale). Of the vicar, Blackstable, Kent;

she lunches at the Driffields' with her husband, Lord Scallion, fat duchess, Lady Hodmarsh, and Narrator

WIFE #1 (East of Suez). Of Sen Shi Ming; sitting with her husband, looking at a Tang bronze, when a cry for help came from outside

WIFE #2 (East of Suez). Of the Consul at Chung-King; is charming

WIFE #1 (Explorer [novel]). Of Mohammed the Lame; one of several; according to the natives, Mohammed's illness the result of a magic spell she had cast on him

WIFE #2 (Explorer [novel]). Of the medical missionary; her loving-kindness, when combined with her husband's medical skills, brings Alec MacKenzie out of danger

WIFE #3 (Explorer [novel]). Of Miner #3; waited for her husband at the mouth of the pit in Lancashire, with her children by her side

WIFE (Good Manners). Of the rector; with her husband, a guest at one of August Breton's little dinners; once ventured to eat an orange while she drank her port

WIFE #1 (Hour Before the Dawn). Of foreign ambassador; she and her husband at a dinner with Roger and May Henderson; Roger sits next to her, and and pays her unusually close attention; she is a massive beauty

WIFE #2 (Hour Before the Dawn). Of French ambassador; Roger Henderson able to obtain the large gold chain before she could buy it

WIFE #3 (Hour Before the Dawn). Of Michel; plump, tall, middle aged

WIFE (Letter [play]). Of the Attorney-General at Singapore; Dorothy Joyce knows her; believed that Leslie Crosbie should never have been brought to trial

WIFE (Liza of Lambeth). Of John; urges her husband to disrupt the fight between Jim Blakeston and his wife

WIFE (Magician). Of Eliphas Levi; a fair damsel; she ran away with her lover

WIFE (Making of a Saint). Formed a discreditable union with the mythical Consul of a Roman Republic to found the family of Brandolini

WIFE (Marriage of Convenience). Of a retired French official; accompanies her husband on board the ship out of Bangkok; tall and generally large; statuesque; is a native of Geneva, Switzerland; had spent fifteen years nursing her invalid mother; is age fifty-five

Characters

WIFE #1 (Merry-Go-Round). Of the Bishop of Rochester; had been a governess
WIFE #2 (Merry-Go-Round). Second wife of the Archdeacon of Tercanbury, in Kent; she was the author of a novel
WIFE #3 (Merry-Go-Round). Of Algernon Langton's Portsmouth parishioner; her husband had cut her throat six months after their marriage
WIFE #4 (Merry-Go-Round). Of Friend #2; wrote to Bella Field after Bella and Herbert Field had gone to Italy
WIFE #1 (Moon and Sixpence). Of a government official; a guest at the Stricklands' dinner party
WIFE #2 (Moon and Sixpence). Of a King's Council; she was a guest at the Stricklands' dinner party
WIFE #3 (Moon and Sixpence). Of a member of Parliament; a guest at the Stricklands' dinner party
WIFE #1 (Mrs. Craddock). Of the pasty-faced clerk; at the station, Blackstable, Kent; followed her husband, carrying their second child and innumerable parcels
WIFE #2 (Mrs. Craddock). Married to Gerald Vaudrey's last tutor; "the most awful old geyser you ever saw"
WIFE (Narrow Corner). Of Dutchman #1; is in the hotel dining room, on Kanda; half-caste; stout and listless
WIFE #1 (Of Human Bondage). Of the curate at Blackstable vicarage; plays tennis against Emily Wilkinson
WIFE #2 (Of Human Bondage). Of the manager of the Hotel St. Georges, Paris; she has dinner with her husband, Mr. Goodworthy, and Philip Carey
WIFE #3 (Of Human Bondage). Of the proprietor of the cheap but respectable restaurant in Soho
WIFE #4 (Of Human Bondage). Of Vicar #2; she left her husband because of his cruelty toward her; filled the neighborhood with stories of his extreme immorality
WIFE #1 (Official Position). Of a liberated prisoner; a young, pretty, Black woman; has a neat little figure; mischievous eyes; partly responsible for the death of Louis Remire's predecessor
WIFE #2 (Official Position). Of the governor of the prison island; she hard bargained with Louis Remire over the price he asked for a fish that he had caught
WIFE #3 (Official Position). Of a prison official; she spent long hours of a day gossiping with Louis Remire
WIFE (P.&O.). Of a missionary to China; had traveled on the P.&O. for thirty-five years; had never heard of

second-class passengers being invited to a dance in
the first-class saloon
WIFE #1 (Painted Veil). Of A.P.C. man; Kitty Fane met
her at a tea party; she said that she and her husband
had left Mei-tan-fu because of the cholera epidemic
WIFE #2 (Painted Veil). Of the Governor of Hong Kong;
came to drink a quiet cup of tea with Kitty Fane
WIFE #3 (Painted Veil). Of the Admiral at Hong Kong;
came to drink a quiet cup of tea with Kitty Fane; she
invited Kitty to her luncheon at Government House
WIFE #4 (Painted Veil). Of the Chief Justice of Hong
Kong; came to have a quiet cup of tea with Kitty Fane
WIFE (Razor's Edge). Of Joseph; insists that Elliott
Templeton receive the last sacraments of the Church
WIFE #1 (Theatre). Of the Spanish attache in Paris; she
is on holiday with her husband and daughter at Cannes
WIFE #2 (Theatre). Of Chauffeur #2; she cleaned Thomas
Fennell's new flat and cooked his breakfast
WIGRAM, Dr. (Of Human Bondage). Had a house on the high
street of Blackstable; served as chairman of the Conservative political rally at Blackstable; two daughters had married successive assistants; friends who
came to stay with him brought the news of the outside
world; tends to the elderly William Carey during his
bout with bronchitis; he had practiced in Blackstable
for thirty-five years; he is extremely conservative
WIGRAM, Mrs. (Of Human Bondage). Wife of Dr. Wigram and
mother of two daughters; she sat sewing at her window
WILBERFORCE, Samuel (Mrs. Craddock). Bishop of Oxford
and Winchester (1805-1873); at one of Mrs. Branderton's dinner parties, Mrs. Mayston Ryle relates the
story about him and the bloody shovel
WILKINS, Mr. (Marriage of Convenience). American circus
proprietor on board the ship out of Bangkok; is short
and fat; a red, clean shaven face; merry blue eyes;
untidy sandy hair; he was born at Portland, Oregon
WILKINS, Mrs. (Marriage of Convenience). Wife of Mr.
Wilkins; with her husband aboard the ship from Bangkok; small and fat; round red face; sandy untidy hair
WILKINSON (Landed Gentry). He is Mrs. Insoley's milkman
WILKINSON, Emily (Of Human Bondage). A daughter of Rev.
Wilkinson; friend of William Carey; lived in Berlin;
had served as a governess in France and Germany; her

age was calculated somewhere between twenty-seven and thirty-nine; black, shiny, and hard hair; large black eyes; aquiline nose; prepossessing full face; a large mouth; big and yellow teeth; has thick and ungainly ankles; she spoke with a slight French accent; very affable; she gives Philip Carey voice lessons; Philip generally accepts the truth of her stories; she and Philip have an affair; eventually marries a widower

WILKINSON, Mr. and Mrs. (Unknown). Mrs. Littlewood plans to ask them to play bridge

WILKINSON, Rev. (Of Human Bondage). The father of Emily Wilkinson and rector of a village church in Lincolnshire; William Carey had been his curate; is now dead

WILLI (Unconquered). German soldier; small, dark, thin faced; he had been a dress designer in civilian life

WILLIS (Yellow Streak). Resident of Kuala Solor; places Campion in the care of Izzart; small, elderly; thin gray hair and yellow face

WILLOUGHBY, Charles Stuart (Road Uphill). An interior decorator; he wants to re-design Cornelia Sheridan's drawing room; engaged by Howard and Ruth Green to decorate their new home; plans to revolutionize Cornelia's garden; Joseph Sheridan frightens him out of his mother's house

WILSON (Loaves and Fishes). Is a newspaper man who does the clerical intelligence for two or three important London papers; Theodore Spratte writes to him, denying the "rumors" that he has been offered the vacant bishopric of Colchester

WILSON #1 (Lotus Eaters). Daughter of Thomas Wilson and his wife; lived with her maternal grandmother following the death of her mother; dies of blood poisoning

WILSON #2 (Lotus Eaters). Thomas Wilson's uncle; went to Australia before his nephew was born

WILSON, Edward (Vessel of Wrath). Full and legitimate name of "Ginger Ted" (see above)

WILSON, Mr. (Bishop's Apron). An acquaintance of Canon Theodore Spratte, and a clerical correspondent for an important paper; Theodore writes to him, disclaiming the "rumor" that he has been offered the vacant bishopric of Colchester

WILSON, Mr. (Of Human Bondage). Is the richest man in Blackstable; has an income of five hundred pounds per year; married his cook; the only man in Blackstable with a bathroom in his house

WILSON, Mrs. (Lotus Eaters). The wife of Thomas Wilson; was always concerned about what other people thought; died of bronchial pneumonia

WILSON, Mrs. (Of Human Bondage). The wife of Mr. Wilson of Blackstable; before her marriage, Wilson's cook

WILSON, Thomas (Lotus Eaters). His teeth not very good; deeply sunburned; lined, long face; thin lips; small gray eyes close together; gray hair; age forty-nine; formerly manager of the Crawford Street branch of the York and City Bank

WILSON, Sir William (Penelope). A physician; told Mrs. Watson not to follow the advice of Dr. Broadstairs

WINE WAITER (Virtue). At the Narrator's club; carries a bottle of hock and two long-stemmed glasses to the cashier's desk

WINGFIELD, Miss (Happy Couple, 1908). A rich spinster of mature age; lived in the country with a companion, the future Mrs. Craig; died and buried; left everything to her companion

WINGFORD, Miss (Happy Couple, 1952). A rich spinster of mature age; a healthy woman woman for her age, but she died rather suddenly

WINKS (Of Human Bondage). The master of the upper-third form at King's School, Tercanbury, Kent; kind; gentle and foolish; weak-kneed; drooping eyelids; too tall for his strength; slow and languid in his movements

WINTER (Honolulu). An American; born in Honolulu; age forty to fifty; his scanty black hair, graying at the temples; sharply featured thin face; wears large horn spectacles; tall, thin; once an actor, but then went into his father's department store; amateur painter

WINTER, Catherine (Tenth Man). Wife of George Winter, M.P., to whom she has been married for four years; a daughter of Lady Angela and Lord Francis Etchingham; sister of Anne Etchingham; she has left her husband; a graceful, strong, passionate face; she is in love with Robert Colby; seeks a divorce; openly questions George's honesty; following the election, she tells her husband that she plans to leave him permanently

WINTER, George. M.P. (Tenth Man). Husband of Catherine Winter; six feet tall; powerful build; fine hair and fine eyes; a short red beard; inclined to corpulence; jovial and bland; is always in control of his temper; had been to sea at age fourteen; began as a clerk in a bucket shop (a disreputable stock brokerage) at twenty-five shillings per week; he is now a prominent financier; a Radical who represents Middlepool in the Parliament; unfaithful to his wife; he has discovered blackmail as the simplest means to success; tries to blackmail Catherine into returning to him; promises Edward O'Donnell a job; wins re-election to Parliament; he throws himself in front of a train near the Palace Hotel, Middlepool

WINTER, Mr. (Tenth Man). The deceased father of George Winter; a hatter at Middlepool; he was "an aitchless" Nonconformist

WISE MEN (Magician). Relied on the Electricum Magicum to make mirrors in which they could see past and present events, and the day and night activities of men

WITHERS (Letter [story]). Assistant District Officer; first person on the scene following the shooting of Geoffrey Hammond; age fifty; tall, drawn, and faded

WITHERS, Fanny (Jack Straw). Wife of Horton Withers; honest and simple; not distinguished; is good natured and kindly; attended Brixton High School with Maria Parker-Jennings, and served as one of the bridesmaids at her wedding; Maria always refers to her as Florrie

WITHERS, Horton (Jack Straw). Husband of Fanny Withers; honest, simple; undistinguished; good natured, kindly

WITHERS, John (Letter [play]). The Assistant District Officer at Singapore; young

WITHERSPOON, Lady Anne (Ashenden/His Excellency). Wife of Sir Herbert Witherspoon

WITHERSPOON, Sir Herbert (Ashenden/His Excellency). The British ambassador to X; appointed, age fifty-three; career diplomat; is tall and thin; an uninterestingly handsome; neat gray hair; pale and clean shaven face; delicate straight nose; gray eyes under gray eyebrows

WIVES (Caesar's Wife). Of cabinet ministers; are at the duchess's weekend party; protruding teeth; stared at Violet (Little) up their noses; looked like camels

WIVES (Cakes and Ale). Of Kentish farmers; they are all highly colored and robust; have grown portly on good butter and on home-made bread, cream, and fresh eggs

WIVES (Making of a Saint). Of those men who ransack the Palazzo Orsi at Forli; receive the plunder from their husbands and take it home
WIVES (Painted Veil). Of the solicitors who sent briefs to Bernard Garstin; Mrs. Garstin familiar with them
WIVES (Painted Veil). Of several judges; Mrs. Garstin obsequious to them
WOLFE, Miss (Cakes and Ale). Of Ferne Court, in Blackstable, Kent; Edward Driffield's father her bailiff
WOMAN (Ant and the Grasshopper). Engaged to Tom Ramsay; is old enough to be his mother; dies and leaves Tom a half-million pounds
WOMAN (Ashenden/Hairless Mexican). Flashing eyes, white teeth; dances with Manuel Carmona in a Naples tavern
WOMAN #1 (Bad Example). Holds James Clinton's hat while policeman questions him; asks Clinton if he is better
WOMAN #2 (Bad Example). In a London slum; big-boned and very coarse-featured; James Clinton enters her house
WOMAN (Caesar's Wife). Invited Violet and Arthur Little to a weekend party
WOMAN (Cakes and Ale). Poor; at the fried fish shop in Horseferry Row; she bought "two penn'orth of mixed"
WOMAN #1 (Catalina). Pregnant; her torture postponed by Blasco de Valero until the end of her confinement
WOMAN #2 (Catalina). Is involved in a relationship with the archpriest of the Collegiate Church
WOMAN #3 (Catalina). A middle-aged actress; she played duennas, wicked stepmothers, and widowed queens; she also served as the wardrobe mistress for the troupe
WOMAN #1 (Christmas Holiday). At Paris; in a limousine; in a sable coat; painted cheeks and lips; a profile of incredible distinction; Charley Mason sees her from his taxi
WOMAN #2 (Christmas Holiday). At the Serail, in Paris; is beautifully dressed in black; a string of emeralds around her neck; she dances with the two other girls
WOMAN #3 (Christmas Holiday). A cloak room attendant at the Select, Boulevard Montparnasse, in Paris; brought Charley Mason's coat
WOMAN #4 (Christmas Holiday). Elderly; from the window of his Paris hotel room, Charley Mason observes her watering a flower pot
WOMAN #5 (Christmas Holiday). At Simon Fenimore's

lodgings, in Rue Campagne Premiere, Paris; little and old; she directs Charley Mason to where Simon lives

WOMAN #6 (Christmas Holiday). Her vanity case stolen by Robert Berger, who, in turn, gave it to Lydia Berger; identified Berger as the man who had given her a lift in his stolen car

WOMAN #7 (Christmas Holiday). Her gold watch stolen by Robert Berger, who, in turn, gave it to Lydia Berger; she thought that she recognized Robert Berger's voice

WOMAN #8 (Christmas Holiday). She works at the gloves department at Trois Quartiers, Paris; said that she remembered having sold Robert Berger a pair of gloves on the very day of Teddie Jordan's murder; age forty

WOMAN #9 (Christmas Holiday). Is at the cellar bar in Paris; she claims that La Marishka had diamonds worth millions, but the Bolsheviks took everything from her

WOMAN (Circle). Hughie Porteus fell in love with her after he had run away with Catherine Champion-Cheney

WOMAN (Closed Shop). Young; from Michigan; possessed a feminine weakness for marriage

WOMAN (Colonel's Lady). Gushes at George Peregrine at the publisher's cocktail party and raves to him about Evie Peregrine's book

WOMAN (East of Suez). In a crowded Peking street; old and blind; a masseuse; she strikes wooden clippers to proclaim her calling

WOMAN #1 (Explorer [novel]). In a kraal in British East Africa; her face was blown away by some clumsy gun

WOMAN #2 (Explorer [novel]). On the Isle of Wight; had formerly served Lucy Allerton at Hamlyn's Purlieu; Lucy engages rooms in her house following the release of her father from prison

WOMAN #3 (Explorer [novel]). In Walker's dream; pretty; she was seen crossing Piccadilly at Swan and Edgar's

WOMAN #4 (Explorer [novel]). English; is slab-sided and round-shouldered; she asked Julia Crowley to visit her sister in Jonesville, Ohio

WOMAN (Explorer [play]). In Dick Lomas's dream; pretty; she was seen crossing Piccadilly at Swan and Edgar's

WOMAN (Facts of Life). At the roulette table at Monte Carlo; speaks English with a foreign accent; Nicholas Garnet lends her a thousand francs; has neat, slight figure; pretty little face and a trim head; claims to

be the wife of an administrator in Morocco, and the
mother of a small child
WOMAN (Faith). At San Lucido, Spain; paralyzed arm; she
comes near the frozen body of Brother Jasper, touches
his cowl, then claims that her arm has been restored
WOMAN (Force of Circumstances). Is from the Kampong;
slight, small; dark, starry eyes; raven black hair;
heavy features; dark skin; pretty; has three children
fathered by Guy; at age fifteen when she came to Guy
WOMAN #1 (Hero). On the same train from London as Major
William Forsyth; according to his account, she was
the prettiest woman he has seen for a long time; For-
syth made eyes at her, but she would not look at him
WOMAN #2 (Hero). In a London park; gallops toward James
Parsons; she closely resembles Mrs. Pritchard-Wallace
WOMAN #3 (Hero). Friend of Mary Clibborn; she cured her
husband (see Man #4) of swearing by countering his
vulgarities with her own
WOMAN #1 (Hour Before the Dawn). At St. James's Park,
London; is tired looking; on a chair, reading a book
WOMAN #2 (Hour Before the Dawn). She talks with Dora
Friedberg at St. James's Park, London; is tall; dark
and marked features; Dora identifies her as a German
refugee; Jim Henderson believes her to be a member of
the staff of the German embassy
WOMAN #3 (Hour Before the Dawn). Mother of six children
evacuated to the Hendersons' estate at Graveney Holt;
fierce and hard-featured; calls Mrs. Henderson a lady
WOMAN #4 (Hour Before the Dawn). At the inn in a small
French village; she is sweeping the floor; friendly
but frightened; she gave Roger Henderson and Nobby
Clark food and drink; her husband is away in the army
WOMAN #5 (Hour Before the Dawn). In the London air raid
shelter; she leads in singing "Role out the barrel"
WOMAN #6 (Hour Before the Dawn). She lives in the same
house as the Clark family, in London; she is about to
deliver a baby, and asks the lad to fetch Mrs. Clark
WOMAN #7 (Hour Before the Dawn). Is at the Dorchester
Hotel; a friend of Jane Foster; lends Jane a dress
WOMAN #8 (Hour Before the Dawn). Old; maintained the
general store at Graveney, Kent; tells Jim Henderson
that she has not sold or carried "fusees" for years
WOMAN (Human Element). Fine eyes; is drinking lemonade

Characters 435

    with young officer in the lounge, Hotel Plaza, Rome
WOMAN (Land of Promise). After Louisa Wickham's death, she offered to employ Norah Marsh for ten shillings a week and lunch; she expected Norah to pay for her own room, breakfast, supper, and clothes
WOMAN (Landed Gentry). Old, curtsied to Mrs. Insoley as she passed
WOMAN #1 (Liza of Lambeth). A resident of Vere Street, Lambeth; asks Polly when her child is due
WOMAN #2 (Liza of Lambeth). A resident of Vere Street, Lambeth; speculates on the arrival of Polly's child
WOMAN #3 (Liza of Lambeth). A resident of Vere Street, Lambeth; stout; is a woman of great importance; hopes Polly will have an easier time than the last in the delivery of her child
WOMAN (Loaves and Fishes). She is a widow who told Mary Fitzgerald that when she read of Mary's engagement in the newspaper, she exclaimed aloud, "Talk of tarpon"
WOMAN (Luncheon). She meets the Narrator at a play; is extremely heavy; has not seen him in twenty years, at which time she was forty years of age; more imposing than attractive; displays white, large, even teeth
WOMAN #1 (Magician). Pregnant; Sheik saw her in mirror
WOMAN #2 (Magician). Seen at the gaming table at Monte Carlo; is painted; notoriously disreputable; Margaret Haddo smiles and nods to her
WOMAN #1 (Making of a Saint). Employed at the house of Ercole Piacentini; opened a small door and conducted Filippo Brandolini into the room of Claudia Piacentini; evidently well used to the nature of her business
WOMAN #2 (Making of a Saint). A seller of cheap jewelry at the market place in Forli; is huge; a treble chin; red face dripping with perspiration; bulged out her cheeks and blew a blast that nearly carried Filippo Brandolini away; she violently attacked Matteo d'Orsi
WOMAN #3 (Making of a Saint). Serves Caterina Sforza; she warns Giulia dall' Aste that she will be arrested
WOMAN (Man of Honour). She is with Robert Brackley at a play; a fair charmer; green eyes; dyed yellow hair
WOMAN (Man with a Conscience). Black; she maintains the hotel at St. Laurent de Maroni
WOMAN (Marriage of Convenience, 1906). At a village on an island off of Tunis; she rents the Narrator a room

WOMAN #1 (Merry-Go-Round). Manages a tea shop in Bond Street, London; Mrs. Castillyon thinks her impudent

WOMAN #2 (Merry-Go-Round). At Florence; good looking; Bella Field calls Herbert Field's attention to her

WOMAN #3 (Merry-Go-Round). Is a peasant at Pisa, Italy; Herbert Field wrote a single sonnet about her ankles

WOMAN #4 (Merry-Go-Round). Had thrown herself into the Thames, London, at a spot where the water was deep and the bank shelved suddenly

WOMAN #1 (Moon and Sixpence). Guest at the Stricklands' dinner; chats with Narrator, who escorts her to table

WOMAN #2 (Moon and Sixpence). At the Hotel des Belges, Paris; seen in a dressing gown and with tousled hair

WOMAN #3 (Moon and Sixpence). Sells bread to Charles Strickland; recommends him to the retired plumber, who wants someone to paint his portrait

WOMAN #4 (Moon and Sixpence). Behind the bar of a cafe, the Rue Bouterie, Marseilles; sits nursing her baby

WOMAN #5 (Moon and Sixpence). Old; Tahitian; helped Ata through her pregnancy

WOMAN #1 (Mother). Resident of the tenement house in a back street of La Macarena, Seville; reports that La Cachirra is arguing with the porter; nudges Woman #2

WOMAN #2 (Mother). She listens to the argument between La Cachirra and her porter; she then nudges Woman #1

WOMAN (Mrs. Dot). On the crowded train from the city; old and tired; had to stand

WOMAN #1 (Of Human Bondage). A companion of Hayward; is charming; is possessed of a real feeling for art and literature

WOMAN #2 (Of Human Bondage). At a Paris revue; appeared with practically nothing on

WOMAN #3 (Of Human Bondage). Enters the Closerie des Lilas, in Paris; has scarlet lips and vividly colored cheeks; had blackened her eyebrows and eyelashes; eye lids painted bold blue; dark hair done over her ears

WOMAN #4 (Of Human Bondage). Lives with Cronshaw and their scrubby, unwashed baby in a small sixth-floor apartment of a dilapidated house on the Quai des Grands Augustins, Paris; supposedly the daughter of the concierge of the building; dark, small, fat, and young; black hair; red cheeks; large, sensual mouth; shining lewd eyes; displayed a flaunting vulgarity

WOMAN #5 (Of Human Bondage). Young; another woman with whom Dunsford found occasion to flirt

WOMAN #6 (Of Human Bondage). In Philip Carey's imagination; tall, dark, beautiful; eyes like the night; has black hair

WOMAN #7 (Of Human Bondage). Is leaving the restaurant; she bought her furs at the Bon Marche in Brixton

WOMAN #8 (Of Human Bondage). At the cheap, respectable restaurant in Soho; she wore a red feather in her hat

WOMAN #9 (Of Human Bondage). She keeps the house in Highbury where Emil Miller and Mildred Rogers rent furnished rooms; she speaks terribly ill of Mildred

WOMAN #10 (Of Human Bondage). Out-patient at St. Luke's Hospital, London; age eighteen; delicate features and large blue eyes; fair, golden hair; beautiful skin; she had been coughing and generally losing weight

WOMAN #11 (Of Human Bondage). The sister of Woman #10; she brought the latter to the out-patient room of St. Luke's Hospital, London

WOMAN #12 (Of Human Bondage). Mother of Woman #10 and Woman #11; she died of pthisis (tuberculosis of the lungs), as had her husband and two other children

WOMAN #13 (Of Human Bondage). Out-patient at St. Luke's Hospital, London; a member of the ballet at a famous music hall; looked fifty years old, but gave her age as twenty-eight; large black eyes; yellow teeth; had chronic bronchitis

WOMAN #14 (Of Human Bondage). Lives on the first floor of the house in Hyde Street, London, where Chronshaw lives; she looks very suspiciously at Philip Carey

WOMAN #15 (Of Human Bondage). Is employed by the London undertaker to lay out Cronshaw's corpse

WOMAN #16 (Of Human Bondage). Opens the door for Philip Carey and Mildred Rogers to the rooming house in the Gray's Inn Road neighborhood; elderly; tall; stares at Philip and speaks to Mildred in an undertone

WOMAN #17 (Of Human Bondage). Opens the door for Philip Carey at a shabby lodging house in a sordid London street, and she directs him to Mildred Rogers' room

WOMAN #18 (Of Human Bondage). Is at London; wife of Man #18; blousy and middle aged; had a long succession of still-born children; is attended to by Philip Carey

WOMAN #19 (Of Human Bondage). Is the wife of Harry; age

sixteen; is pretty; delicate features and large blue eyes; with a mass of dark hair; Philip Carey called to deliver her baby; she dies

WOMAN #20 (Of Human Bondage). Near Trafalgar Square, in London; Philip Carey mistakes her for Mildred Rogers; she is much older than Mildred; has lined yellow skin

WOMAN #1 (Our Betters). Recommended by Compton Edwardes and comes every morning to do Minnie Surennes' face

WOMAN #2 (Our Betters). She teaches all of the American peeresses how to speak proper British English

WOMAN #1 (Painted Veil). At Mei-tan-fu; is with a child tied on her hip; she rows the sampan across the river

WOMAN #2 (Painted Veil). At Mei-tan-fu; she is washing her hands and face by the light of a taper

WOMAN #3 (Painted Veil). Seen between Mei-tan-fu and Hong Kong; she is tottering along on her bound feet

WOMAN #4 (Painted Veil). Old; passing along a causeway; face with a thousand little wrinkles; walked on tiny feet and leaned on a long black staff

WOMAN #1 (Poet). Of Ecija, in Andalusia, Spain; attired in black; she is observed on her way from church

WOMAN #2 (Poet). She attends the front gate of the old man's house; old; a heavy moustache; fine black eyes

WOMAN #1 (Punctiliousness of Don Sebastian). Is at the hotel in Xiormonez, Spain; she opens the door for the porter and the Narrator

WOMAN #2 (Punctiliousness of Don Sebastian). Had nursed Don Sebastian in his childhood; after the death of Dona Sidona, she disobeys Don Sebastian's order and brings him food

WOMAN (Raw Material). Lunches at the Ritz, in New York, with the Narrator; later, she hosts a small party attended by the Narrator, Peterson, and Campbell

WOMAN #1 (Razor's Edge). Old; at Chicago; she wanted to invest one thousand dollars in some wildcat scheme that had been recommended to her by her minister

WOMAN #2 (Razor's Edge). Kept by a gentleman; lodges at the cheap hotel in Paris; she and Larry Darrell have the only rooms with a bath

WOMAN #3 (Razor's Edge). At the Brasserie Graf, Avenue de Clichy, Paris; young, shabby, heavily painted; she joins the bearded man; slaps him in the face; curses the manager

WOMAN (Sanatorium). She is a patient at the sanatorium; "pretty hot stuff"; carrying on with another patient

WOMAN #1 (Sheppey). Seen at the Lambeth Police Court, London; respectable looking; had been caught stealing a bit of steak off of a barrier; the mother of three children; had to keep them and herself on eighteen shillings per week

WOMAN #2 (Sheppey). She appears to Sheppey Miller in a death vision, first as Bessie Legros, then as Death

WOMAN (Smith). A maid; Emily Chapman's Jewish fiancee felt that he should marry her; the fiancee told Emily he had ruined the woman and she had lost her position

WOMAN (Spanish Priest). Is in the Calle Alfonso Trece, Granada; she tells the English man that Vicente Oria y Mazallon had gone away a fortnight ago

WOMAN (String of Beads). She turns down, at the last moment, her invitation to dine with the Livingstones

WOMAN #1 (Then and Now). Old; is part of the crowd that surges into Caesar Borgia's apartment

WOMAN #2 (Then and Now). An old crone at Imola; popped her head out of the window; shouted at the man with the assess' milk; appeared at the door with a beaker

WOMAN #3 (Then and Now). At Imola; trying on a pair of shoes at the shoemaker's shop

WOMAN #4 (Then and Now). At Imola; tells Piero Giacomini about the two Gascon soldiers who have been hanged

WOMAN #5 (Then and Now). Of a house, Citta della Piave, where Niccolo Machiavelli and Piero Giacomini lodged

WOMAN (Traveller in Romance). A passenger on the post chaise from St. Moritz into Italy; is close to fifty years old; got out; ill-favored; got off at Kampfer

WOMAN (Unconquered). Sad-faced; cries when the Periers ask to see Doctor #3; informs them of his arrest, but gives them the name of a midwife

WOMAN #1 (Unknown). At the London hotel; both she and Charlotte Littlewood go to the Gaiety and the Empire

WOMAN #2 (Unknown). She comes to the Whartons' house to prepare the body of George Wharton for burial

WOMAN (Up at the Villa). Rowley Flint is named a co-respondent in her divorce case

WOMEN (Bad Example). Two of them; seated on a doorstep in a London street

WOMEN (Christmas Holiday).The two of them; middle aged;

dining at a restaurant in the Avenue du Maine, Paris
WOMEN (Circle). At London parties; they are middle aged and painted; in beautiful clothes; lolloping around ballrooms with rather old young men
WOMEN (Colonel's Lady). Two of them; sitting together on a sofa at the publisher's cocktail party; George Peregrine believes that they are talking about him
WOMEN (De Amicitia). At Volendam, Holland; sitting at their doors mending nets
WOMEN (East of Suez). Of various sorts; in a crowded street in Peking; stroll the streets or enter shops
WOMEN (Episode). Two of them; guests at dinner attended by Ned Preston and the Narrator; clever and nice
WOMEN (Explorer [novel]). At the tiny kraal in British East Africa; in groups, grinding their corn; chatter
WOMEN (Explorer [novel]). In Piccadilly Circus, London; they sat around the fountain and sold their flowers
WOMEN (Explorer [novel]). A throng of them outside the house opposite that of Lady Alice Kelsey in London
WOMEN (Liza of Lambeth). Two of them; on Vere Street, Lambeth; squatting on the doorstep
WOMEN (Liza of Lambeth). Two or three; on Vere Street, Lambeth; seated on chairs, nursing babies; pregnant
WOMEN (Liza of Lambeth). Gathered near the public house in Vere Street; see altercation between Liza Kemp and Mrs. Blakeston; unsympathetic; virtuously indignant
WOMEN (Lord Mountdrago). Two of them, seen in a dream; performing a grotesque exercise in front of a fireplace in a Limehouse pub; one of them is a prostitute
WOMEN (Magician). The wives, or near-wives, of a few Frenchmen for whom a small room with three tables was reserved at the Chien Noir, Paris; young; their manner had a definite air of matrimonial respectability
WOMEN (Magician). In the vision of Son #2; in the room of Jean-Marie Porhoet, crying; kneel before the bed; they are wearing little white caps and black dresses
WOMEN (Magician). Fierce and evil; of olden time; in Margaret Dauncey's vision; they pass by her side
WOMEN (Magician). At the tavern on the Boulevard des Italiens, in Paris; reflected in innumerable mirrors; they are admirably gowned and laughing boisterously
WOMEN (Magician). South Americans; seen with prodigious diamonds; often in the Haddos' company at Monte Carlo

WOMEN (Magician). At the London opera house; Susie Boyd examines them as they enter boxes of the grand tier

WOMEN (Magician). Six of them; at the Savoy, London; according to Susie Boyd, they turned green with envy at the sight of her frock; Susie believes them to be French and to think that she is not respectable

WOMEN (Magician). Are of the Liverpool and Manchester docks; vile; after periods of debauch, Oliver Haddo returned to Skene, his mouth hot with their kisses

WOMEN (Making of a Saint). Are in waiting to Caterina Sforza; weep and wail when they hear of the death of Girolamo Riario and of the announcement that Filippo Brandolini prepares to take their mistress prisoner

WOMEN (Making of a Saint). In the square at Forli; of the lower classes; after the assassination of Girolamo Riario, they join their shrill cries to the shouts of the men

WOMEN (Making of a Saint). At Forli; madly flourished their handkerchiefs after learning that Checco d'Orsi would place the town under the protection of the Pope

WOMEN (Making of a Saint). At Forli; are praying and weeping in the churches after the arrival of Lodovico Sforza and his army

WOMEN (Marriage of Convenience, 1906). At the island village off of the coast of Tunis; magnificent eyes

WOMEN (Merry-Go-Round). In Bond Street, London; painted cheeks and dyed hair; dressed in a manner which even a courtesan would think startling; in them, Polly Ley recognizes the leaders of London fashion

WOMEN (Merry-Go-Round). At Chatham; Grace Castillyon believes that Reggie Barlow-Bassett would go after some of them if she left him alone in Rochester

WOMEN (Merry-Go-Round). Polly Ley met them at Venice and Capri; they confessed to her how, for love, they had been willing to break down the pillars of heaven

WOMEN (Merry-Go-Round). Of various rank; had written letters to Reggie Barlow-Bassett

WOMEN (Merry-Go-Round). In London slums; dirty aprons; blowzy and disheveled; lounging about their doorsteps

WOMEN (Moon and Sixpence). Were at a London tea party attended by the young Narrator; large and unbending; great noses and rapacious eyes; wore their clothes as though they were armor

WOMEN (Moon and Sixpence). Two or three of them; from the Tahitian village; accompanied Ata to gather fruit

WOMEN (Mrs. Craddock). At the London restaurant where Bertha Craddock and Gerald Vaudrey dine; they glitter in their diamonds

WOMEN (Mrs. Dot). Two of them; standing on the stairs of the Army and Navy Store, discussing their servants and blocking the entrance

WOMEN (Narrow Corner). Dr. Saunders remembers them in the old days, in the boxes at Covent Garden Theatre, London; in tiaras and with pearls round their necks

WOMEN (Of Human Bondage). They are in the stalls at the Shaftesbury Theatre, in London; their dyed and false hair sets attract the interest of Mildred Rogers

WOMEN (Painted Veil). At a dinner party; Walter Fane talked with them, looking at them with steady and unblinking eyes; tried to indulge Walter in small talk

WOMEN (Razor's Edge). Two of them; with the American banker at the Brasserie Graf, Avenue de Clichy, in Paris; painted; middle aged

WOMEN (Razor's Edge). Two of them; are at the Brasserie Graf, Avenue de Clichy, Paris; fat and somber; are tightly fitted into mannish clothes

WOMEN (Round Dozen). Two of them; elderly; are wearing short skirts and stout shoes

WOMEN (Sanatorium). Several of them; elderly patients at the sanatorium; resentful because they could not lunch at the table with McLeod, Campbell, Miss Atkin

WOMEN (Then and Now). Young and of humble station; kept as mistresses by Bartolomeo Martelli during the lifetime of his two wives

WOMEN (Then and Now). Two; pray in Fra Timoteo's church

WOMEN (Then and Now). Old; pretended to have herbs to make women conceive; had no effect upon the wife of Giuliano degli Albertelli

WOMEN (Voice of the Turtle). Two of them; they host the sherry party in Bloomsbury; large, middle aged; they are independent and affluent

WOMEN (Wash-Tub). Two of them; sturdy; carry the Narrator's bags on their heads to the hotel at Positano

WOODSMEN (Then and Now). At Niccolo Machiavelli's farm, San Casciano, situated some three miles from the city of Florence; Machiavelli stops to talk with them

Characters 443

WORKING MEN (Tenth Man). At Middlepool; a large number among them voted when the polling stations opened

WORKMAN (Liza of Lambeth). One of the two who had seen Liza Kemp and Jim Blakeston together; Jim meets him in a pub, but he says nothing about having seen them

WORKMAN (Moon and Sixpence). Is a resident of the same Paris house, and on the same floor, where Charles Strickland lives

WORKMEN (Liza of Lambeth). Two of them; returning home to Vere Street, Lambeth, from a job at Vauxhall; walk past Jim Blakeston and Liza Kemp

WORKMEN (Loaves and Fishes). According to Rev. Theodore Sprattte, their slowness will force Mary Fitzgerald to stay with the Sprattes for a week

WORTHIES (Making of a Saint). Members of the Council of Forli; one by one they extend their thanks to Checco d'Orsi for the freedom that he has bestowed upon them

WORTHLEY, Frances Annandale (Mrs. Dot). Known as Mrs. Dot; she is Freddie Perkins' widowed aunt; pretty and small; the owner of a brewery, Worthley's Entire and Worthley's Half-crown Family Ale; receives pleasure from giving away money; in love with Gerald Halstane

WRIGHT, Mr. the elder (Mrs. Dot). Father of Mr. Wright the younger; Rixon saw him on a matter of business

WRIGHT, Mr. the younger (Mrs. Dot). A tailor; son of Mr. Wright the elder; is young, dapper, and smartly dressed; is the junior partner of Andrews and Wright

WRITER (Ashenden/Mr. Harrington's Washing). Writes on political economy; is pregnant with child by Vladimir Semenovich Leonidov

WRITER (Consul). Employed by Mr. Pete, who assails him for no apparent reason

WRITER (Of Human Bondage). At Paris; an acquaintance of Clutton; his wife died in childbirth

WROXHAM, Lord Harry (Bishop's Apron). Age twenty-five; son of Lady Wroxham; slender and of moderate height; short, crisp hair and small moustache; blue eyes are prominent and short-sighted; wore gold-rimmed pinznez; an insignificant appearance; pleasant, earnest face, kindly, but not handsome; is in love with and wishes to marry Winnie Spratte; left fatherless in early boyhood; head of an ancient and distinguished family (is the twenty-first Lord Wroxham); educated at Eton and Oxford; a member of the House of Lords; has three houses, a number of acres, and an income of twenty thousand pounds per year; Winnie rejects his first marriage proposal, but accepts the second one

WROXHAM, Lord Harry (Loaves and Fishes). He wishes to marry Winnie Spratte; had gone to Eton with Lionel Spratte; has an income of thirty thousand pounds per year and an assured position in the House of Lords; proposes to Winnie, but she refuses him; dark; small moustache; wears a pinz-nez; not good looking, but of a gentlemanly appearance; proposes to Winnie a second time, and she accepts; he chaired a meeting at which Bertram Railing spoke, and he has read Bertram's book

WROXHAM, Lady (Bishop's Apron). Mother of Lord Harry Wroxham; charming, with a deeply religious spirit

WROXHAM, Lady (Loaves and Fishes). Mother of Lord Harry Wroxham; she invites Winnie Spratte to the opera

WU (East of Suez). Is a Chinese servant of the British American Tobacco Company, Peking; a model servant who has intelligent anticipation; he is employed by the Andersons after they marry

WYNNE, Clement (Land of Promise). Is Louise Wickham's solicitor and Dr. Evans' brother-in-law; tallish and bald; has prominent red cheeks and hearty countenance

WYNNE, Norman (Merry-Go-Round). A co-respondent in Lord Vizard's divorce petition filed against Lady Vizard

Y

YELLOW-HAIRED WOMAN (Ashenden/Miss King). Drugs French minister at Nice and steals his dispatch case with important documents

YOGI #1 (Razor's Edge). In India; he told Larry Darrell about Yogi #2, who walked on the surface of the water

YOGI #2 (Razor's Edge). In India; came to a river, did not have money to pay for the ferry to cross it, and walked on the surface of the water to the other side

YOGI #3 (Razor's Edge). In Travancore; Larry Darrell spent two years in his company; peace and blessedness irradiated from his presence; medium height, neither fat nor thin; palish brown in color; clean-shaven; close-cropped white hair; he wore only a loincloth

YOGI #4 (Razor's Edge). In India; old; he cured Larry

Darrell's insomnia

YOKELS (Hero). Of Little Primpton, in Kent; stood about with open mouths and in admiration during the welcome home ceremony for James Parsons

YOUNG CHILDREN (Liza of Lambeth). Seen on Vere Street, Lambeth; sat about the road, as disconsolate as poets

YOUNG LADIES (Cupid and the Vicar of Swale). Literary; Edith Strong reminded them of warrior-queen Boadicea

YOUNG LADY (Cakes and Ale). At the vicarage tea party; she claimed that she had given up playing and had not brought her music with her

YOUNG LADY (Sheppey). A friend of Albert; he is taking her to the pictures

YOUNG MAN (Appearance and Reality). Lisette's lover; a traveling salesman for a Lyons silk firm; discovered by Raymond Le Sueur upon his unexpected return to Lisette's flat; big eyes and wavy hair; a divine dancer

YOUNG MAN (Ashenden/Miss King). He wears spectacles; sitting in the cafe in Geneva, writing a long letter

YOUNG MAN (Bad Example). Riding in a cab near Westminster abbey; gilded in an opera hat and wearing evening clothes; James Clinton believes that he has too much money and nothing to do

YOUNG MAN (Christmas Holiday). At Paris; bearded; in a broad-brimmed hat; walks arm-in-arm under an umbrella with a girl; Charley Mason observes him from his taxi

YOUNG MAN (Colonel's Lady). Clerk at the bookseller's in Piccadilly; waits on George Peregrine; short and stout; a shock of untidy red hair; he is bespectacled

YOUNG MAN (Constant Wife). A.D.C. to one of the governors in India; came back to England on the same boat as Marie-Louise and Mortimer Durham; Marie-Louise is madly in love with him

YOUNG MAN (Explorer [novel]). At Alice Kelsey's dance; spruce; he dances with Lucy Allerton and Grace Vizard

YOUNG MAN (Flirtation). At Lady Mereston's party; wants to talk with Mrs. Parnaby

YOUNG MAN (Kite). Helps Samuel and Beatrice fly their kite on the common

YOUNG MAN (Louise). Friend of the Narrator; eventually marries Iris Maitland

YOUNG MAN (Making of a Saint). Is in attendance at the gathering at Palazza Orsi; tells Nicolo to be quiet

YOUNG MAN (Razor's Edge). At entrance to Sri Ganesha's compound at Ashrama; leads Larry Darrell to the yogi

YOUNG MAN (Sanatorium). A patient at the sanatorium; age twenty; sub-lieutenant in the submarine service; tall and good looking; curly brown hair; blue eyes; a sweet smile; he died within two months of his arrival

YOUNG MAN (Theatre). Follows Julia Lambert Gosselyn for ten minutes along the Edgware Road, London; short and stocky; black hair; fine eyes; poor teeth; pale skin; looked like a clerk or a shop walker; wants Julia's autograph for his fiancee, Gwen, whom he plans to wed in August

YOUNG MAN (Unattainable). Will marry Cooper at Christmas; she would not marry him had she better prospects

YOUNG MEN (Caesar's Wife). A half dozen Egyptians; are under lock and key for their parts in a plot to kill Sir Arthur Little

YOUNG MEN (Christmas Holiday). At the Dome, Paris; they are in turtle neck sweaters and with short beards

YOUNG MEN (Circle). Rather old; at London parties; lollop around ballrooms with middle aged, painted women

YOUNG MEN (Explorer [novel]). Are of the Turkana tribe; after George Allerton shot the Turkana woman, they agitate among the neighboring tribes against Alec Mac Kenzie's men and enter into communication with Arabs

YOUNG MEN (Flirtation). A dozen of them; at Lady Mereston's party; see Mrs. Parnaby more charming than ever

YOUNG MEN (Liza of Lambeth). On Vere Street, Lambeth; tease Liza Kemp about her affair with Jim Blakeston

YOUNG MEN (Liza of Lambeth). Two or three of them; they noticed Liza Kemp's black and blue eye

YOUNG MEN (Making of a Saint). At the piazza at Forli; talk excitedly after the slaying of Girolamo Riario

YOUNG MEN (Merry-Go-Round). Purchased the portraits of celebrated beauties whom they did not even know

YOUNG MEN (Of Human Bondage). Two of them; ages eighteen; at a London restaurant; dining at a table near Philip Carey and Mildred Rogers

YOUNG MEN (Penelope). Take night trips to Paris with the objects of their affection

YOUNG ROUGH (Razor's Edge). Seen at the Brasserie Graf, Avenue de Clichy, Paris; he came with the Englishman; sat at a table and greedily ate a plate of sandwiches

Characters

YOUNG WOMEN (Christmas Holiday). At the Serail, Paris; ten or twelve of them; lower parts of their bodies are clad in Turkish costume; their upper parts naked

YOUNG WOMEN (Mrs. Craddock). Four of them; dancers at a Gaiety burlesque in London; appeared on stage in thin tights and nothing else worth mentioning; danced a singularly ungraceful jig

YOUTH (Choice of Amyntas). With a withered hand; lives in a palace with Maiden #1 and rules a mighty empire

YOUTH (Faith). At San Lucido, Spain; is lying on a bed, wasted by illness; so thin that the protruding bones and formed sores on his skin; brought to the frozen body of Brother Jasper; he rouses himself after being touched with Jasper's garment

YOUTH, (Man from Glasgow). At Naples; he is pursued and killed by a man with a knife

YOUTH (Merry-Go-Round). Strapping, and with a military air; he accompanies Lady Paperleigh to the theatre

YOUTH (Narrow Corner). Rides to the Kanda hotel on his bicycle to deliver Dr. Saunders' cable to the manager

YOUTHS (Christmas Holiday). At the Dome, Paris; Scandinavian; tall and fair haired

YOUTHS (Painted Veil). Amorous; they filled the Garstin drawing room in South Kensington, London, on Sunday afternoons; flirted with Kitty and proposed to her

YU, Colonel (Painted Veil). Commander of the troops at Mei-tan-fu; is tall and stockily built; yellow, flat face; is having a difficult time keeping his men from looting; is with Walter Fane throughout his illness

YU, Mr. (Consul). Married Miss Lambert two years ago; he had been in England studying at the University of London; he has to keep the peace among three warring women; his hair grown on his forehead

YU, Mrs. #1 (Consul). Yu's mother; she cannot get along with Miss Lambert

YU, Mrs. #2 (Consul). Yu's first wife; Chinese; cannot get along with Miss Lambert

YU, Mrs. #3 (Consul). An English woman, formerly Miss Lambert; she had married Yu in London and returned to China with him; discovers that she is the second of her husband's extant wives, which technically negates the marriage; young, solid, thick-set, and plain; bad teeth; muddy skin; large hands; has a cockney whine

YVONNE (Ashenden/His Excellency). O'Malley's sluttish French mistress, with whom he lived at the Rue de Cherche Midi, Paris

Z

Z, Professor (Ashenden/Mr. Harrington's Washing). Held absolute authority over all of the Czechs in Russia

ZAMPA, Celestine (Rehearsal). The first of the great dancers of her family; danced before Napoleon; she refused his Imperial crown

ZAMPA, Genevieve (Rehearsal). Is the <u>premiere danseuse</u>; passionately devoted to the conventions of her art; small; flashing eyes; lovely teeth; engaged to Lucien Smith; initially refuses to dance in Lucien's ballet attired in skirts and high heels; she breaks off her engagement, but, in the end, reconciles with Lucien

ZAMPA, Mademoiselle (Rehearsal). Deceased wife of Rene de Pornichet de la Paule, Monsieur Zampa; the mother of Genevieve; all Europe at her feet; kings desired in vain to kiss her hand

ZAMPA, Rene-Antoine-Joseph-Marie de Pornichet de la Paule, Monsieur (Rehearsal). The father of Genevieve Zampa; short and fat; iron gray hair, cut short and standing straight on end; a fierce moustache; round red face; small and enthusiastic eyes; strong French accent; believes Lucien Smith has insulted Genevieve, and therefore he challenges him to a duel

ZAMPESCHI (Making of a Saint). Seized Girolamo Riario's castle at San Marco

ZANOTTI, Cirillo (Mask and the Face). Banker; cynical, philosophical, and elderly; husband of Elisa Zanotti; he overhears the flirtation between Elisa and Giorgio Alamari; he eventually reconciles with his wife

ZANOTTI, Elisa (Mask and the Face). The wife of Cirillo Zanotti; young; flirts with Giorgio Alamari; upset by her husband's kindness; she prefers to be terrorized by a jealous husband, such as Paolo Grazia, but is sharply repulsed by him; reconciles with her husband

ZAPATA, Pepe (Voice of the Turtle). Former husband of La Falterona, whom he meets while in Buenos Aires

ZERBINETTA (Perfect Gentleman). Member of the troupe of Italian dancers hired to perform in the intermezzo

Editions and Secondary Sources Consulted

A. Editions

Ashenden; or, the British Agent. Garden City, New York: Doubleday and Company, Inc., 1941.
The Bishop's Apron. A Study in the Origins of a Great Family. London: Chapman and Hall, Ltd, 1906.
Cakes and Ale; or, The Skeleton in the Cupboard, and Twelve Stories. Garden City, New York: Doubleday and Company, Inc., 1967.
Catalina. A Romance. Garden City, New York: Doubleday and Company, Inc., 1948.
Christmas Holiday. New York: Doubleday, Doran and Company, Inc., 1939.
The Collected Plays of W. Somerset Maugham. 3 vols. London: Heinemann, 1931.
The Complete Stories of W. Somerset Maugham. I. East and West. Garden City, New York: Doubleday and Company, Inc., 1953.
The Complete Stories of W, Somerset Maugham. II. The World Over. Garden City, New York: Doubleday and Company, 1953.
The Explorer. New York: Carroll and Graf Publishers, Inc., 1991.
The Explorer. A Melodrama. In Four Acts. Chicago: The Dramatic Publishing Company, n.d.
The Hero. London: Hutchinson and Company, 1901.
The Hour Before the Dawn. A Novel. Garden City, New York: Doubleday, Doran and Company, 1942.
Landed Gentry. A Comedy in Four Acts. London: William

Heinemann, Ltd., 1924.
The Letter. A Play in Three Acts. New York: George H. Doran Company, 1925.
Liza of Lambeth. London: Penguin Books, Limited, 1967.
Loaves and Fishes. A Comedy in Four Acts. London: William Heinemann, Ltd., 1924.
The Magician. Garden City, New York: Doubleday, Doran and Company, 1957.
The Making of a Saint. A Romance of Medieval Italy. New York: Farrar, Straus and Giroux, 1966.
A Man of Honour. A Tragedy in Four Acts. Chicago: The Dramatic Publishing Company, 1912.
The Merry-Go-Round. London: William Heinemann, 1969.
The Moon and Sixpence. New York: Doubleday, Doran and Company, 1919.
Mrs. Craddock. London: William Heinemann, Ltd., 1967.
The Narrow Corner. Garden City, New York: Doubleday, Doran and Company, 1935.
Of Human Bondage, in Mr. Maugham Himself, selected by John Beecroft. Garden City, New York: Doubleday and Company, Inc., 1954, pp. 1-446.
"'The Perfect Gentleman.' Adapted from Moliere's Le Bourgois Gentilhomme" in Theatre Arts, 39 (November 1955): 49-64.
Princess September and the Nightingale. Illustrated by Richard C. Jones. London, New York, and Toronto: Oxford University Press, 1939.
The Razor's Edge. A Novel. Garden City, New York: Doubleday and Company, Inc., 1944.
Seventeen Lost Stories by W. Somerset Maugham, ed. by Craig V. Showalter. Garden City, New York: Doubleday and Company, Inc., 1969.
Six Comedies. New York: Doubleday, Doran and Company, 1937.
A Traveller in Romance. Uncollected Writings, 1901-1964 ed. John Whitehead. New York: Clarkson N. Potter, Inc, Publishers, 1984.
The Tenth Man. A Tragic Comedy in Three Acts. London: William Heinemann, 1913.
Theatre. New York: Doubleday and Company/Bantam Books, 1964.
Then and Now. A Novel. Garden City, New York: Doubleday and Company, Inc., 1946.

Editions and Secondary Sources Consulted   451

Up at the Villa. New York: Doubleday, Doran and Company, Inc., 1941.

B. Secondary Sources

Archer, Stanley. W. Somerset Maugham: A Study of the Short Fiction. New York: Twayne Publishers, 1993.
Brophy, John. Somerset Maugham. London: Longmans, Green and Company for the British Council and the National Book League, 1958.
Burt, Forrest D. W. Somerset Maugham. Boston: Twayne Publishers, 1986.
Calder, Robert Lorin. Willie: The Life of W. Somerset Maugham. New York: St. Martin's Press, 1990.
Curtis, Anthony. Somerset Maugham. Windsor, Berkshire, England: Profile Books, 1982.
Hawkinson, Kenneth Steven. Three Novels by W. Somerset Maugham: An Analysis Based on the Rhetoric of Wayne C. Booth. Unpublished Dissertation. Southern Illinois University at Carbondale, 1986.
Loss, Archie K. Of Human Bondage. Coming of Age in the Novel. Boston: Twayne Publishers, 1990.
_____. W. Somerset Maugham. New York: Ungar, 1987.
Makolkin, Anna. Semiotics of Misogyny through the Humor of Chekhov and Maugham. Lewiston, New York: Edwin Mellen Press, 1992.
Mander, Raymond, and Joe Mitchenson. Theatrical Companion to Maugham. A Pictorial Record of the First Performances of the Plays of W. Somerset Maugham. New York: The Macmillan Company, 1955.
Maugham, W. Somerset. On a Chinese Screen, intro. H.J. Lethbridge. New York: Paragon House, 1990.
Morgan, Ted. Maugham. New York: Simon and Schuster, 1980.
Nguyen, Hien Le. Doi Nghe Si. Westminster, California: Van Nghe, 1993 [in Vietnamese; biographical sketches of Walt Disney, Somerset Maugham, Goethe, Chateaubriand, and Honore de Balzac].
Raphael, Frederic. Somerset Maugham. 1976; rev. and expanded ed. London: Cardinal Books, 1989.
Sharma, Krushal Kishore. Tradition in the Modern Novel. Atlantic Highlands, New Jersey: Humanities Press, 1981 [re: Maugham and E.M. Forster].

Stott, Raymond Toole. A Bibliography of the Works of W. Somerset Maugham. Edmonton: The University of Alberta Press, 1973.

Whitehead, John. Maugham: A Reappraisal. London: Vision Publications; Totowa, New Jersey: Barnes and Noble, 1987.

Wright, Reg, ed.. Early Modern Novelists. New York: M. Cavendish, 1989 [focus on Henry James, H.G. Wells, John Galsworthy, and Somerset Maugham].

Index of Titles

Unless indicated otherwise, the date following the title refers to the year of publication. In the instance of two dates for plays and novels, the intent is to provide first, the initial year of publication (most likely in a periodical) and second, the date of the work as a single volume. For those stories that appeared under different titles, the first date refers to the initial publication in a periodical and the second to publication in a bound collection. The listing cites the most recent and most recognizable title of a work.

As an index, those numerals that follow the year of publication refer to page numbers. Bracketed figures refer to the number of references found on that page.

A. Novels

Ashenden (1928), 8 [3], 15, 16, 17, 18, 21, 26, 27, 36 [2], 38, 42, 55, 56, 57, 59, 63, 65, 71, 73, 75, 77, 88, 92, 93, 116, 117, 118, 119, 121, 123 [2], 125, 140, 145, 148, 150 [2], 152, 155 [2], 158, 163, 168, 173, 176, 183, 185 [2], 196 [2], 200, 201 [2], 203, 207, 208 [2], 222, 223, 226 [2], 231, 235, 238 [2], 241, 243, 251 [2], 256 [2], 298, 306, 307, 312 [4], 313, 315, 317, 323, 324, 330, 334, 336, 345, 346, 349, 354, 358 [3], 360, 361, 363, 380, 382, 385, 390, 391, 396, 398, 399, 403 [2], 417, 420, 421, 431 [2], 432, 443, 444, 445, 448 [2]

Bishop's Apron, The (1906), 8, 16, 39 [2], 56, 63, 65, 69, 82, 91, 96 [2], 98, 101 [2], 104, 120, 125, 138, 139, 141, 150, 155 [2], 156, 162, 166, 167, 178 [2], 180, 181, 182, 187, 190, 191 [2], 198 [2], 201, 203 [2], 210, 218 [2], 227, 228 [3], 244, 256 [2], 267, 270, 271 [2], 278, 292 [2], 307, 309, 313, 320 [3], 325, 333, 335 [2], 336, 341, 347 [5], 348 [2], 351, 368 [2], 371, 374, 379 [2], 382, 385, 386 [4], 387 [4], 388 [2], 392 [2], 397, 401, 405, 412, 416, 422, 429, 443, 444

Cakes and Ale (1930), 2, 17 [2], 20, 22, 25, 26, 29 [2], 31, 45, 54 [2], 55, 57, 63 [2], 67, 72, 79 [2], 105, 116, 117, 125, 129, 134, 135 [3], 136, 137, 142, 143, 152, 159, 169, 170 [4], 173, 177, 185, 188 [2], 196, 202 [2], 205, 208, 214, 219 [2], 220 [2], 221 [2], 225, 227, 228 [2], 231, 232 [2], 247, 251 [2], 254, 264, 270, 272, 278 [2], 286, 291, 294 [2], 305, 317, 320, 330, 333 [2], 336 [3], 340, 341, 342, 349, 351, 352 [2], 356, 360, 363, 365 [2], 374, 378, 379, 383 [2], 397, 401, 403, 407 [2], 411, 412, 414 [2], 421, 431, 432 [2], 445

Catalina. A Romance (1940), 2, 6, 7, 8 [2], 11, 12 [2], 17 [2], 19, 21, 27, 28, 29, 38, 46, 73 [2], 74, 86, 116 [4], 117, 121, 122 [6], 125, 130, 137, 138, 139, 140, 141, 144, 147, 148, 150, 158, 162, 163, 165 [3], 168 [2], 170, 192, 209 [2], 224, 226, 227, 228 [2], 229, 232, 235 [3], 238, 256, 267, 269 [2], 273, 282, 284, 292, 293, 294, 298, 307 [3], 308 [6], 315 [3], 325 [2], 326, 327 [2], 329, 330, 336 [2], 339, 341 [2], 342 [2], 343 [5], 350, 354, 364, 365, 368 [2], 371, 384 [2], 385, 389, 391 [2], 395, 396, 402, 412, 413, 417, 425 [2], 432 [3]

Christmas Holiday (1939), 7, 8 [2], 13, 14, 16, 26, 37 [4], 46 [2], 49, 73, 81 [2], 88, 94, 95 [3], 98, 110, 121 [2], 124 [2], 126 [2], 129 [2], 134, 141, 146, 147 [2], 151, 152 [2], 153, 154, 166, 178 [9], 181 [2], 208, 216 [2], 218 [2], 226, 229, 230, 237 [2], 239, 244, 245, 251 [2], 254, 256 [3], 257 [4], 266, 270 [3], 271 [5], 272, 278, 279, 288, 294, 297, 303 [2], 305, 306, 323 [2], 328, 331, 333, 336, 337 [2], 340, 341, 345, 351, 354, 357, 359, 363 [2], 368, 376, 400, 401, 403 [3], 417 [3], 419 [2], 420, 421, 422,

Index: Novels

432 [5], 433 [4], 439, 445, 446, 447 [2]

Explorer, The (1908), 3, 4, 8, 9 [2], 10, 11 [3], 13, 18 [4], 22, 27, 34, 41, 45 [3], 46]2], 57, 63 [2], 65, 69, 78, 80, 82 [2], 94, 96, 97, 102, 105 [2], 106, 109 [2], 114, 115, 124 [2], 125, 126 [2], 131, 133, 134, 137, 147, 156, 157, 158, 159, 171, 183, 184, 191, 198, 210, 211, 213, 218, 220 [3], 234, 242, 243, 248, 249, 250 [3], 251 [2], 252, 256, 257, 258 [2], 264, 270, 276, 279 [2], 283, 284, 285, 286, 288 [4], 290, 302 [2], 303 [3], 304, 322 [2], 325, 328, 337 [2], 338, 339, 345, 350 [2], 352, 353, 355 [2], 359, 362, 363, 364, 366, 376 [2], 378 [2], 381, 382, 385 [2], 390, 391, 396, 398 [2], 404, 405, 408, 409 [2], 410, 411, 413, 416 [2], 418 [2], 419, 420, 425 [2], 426 [3], 433 [4], 440 [3], 445, 446

Hero, The (1901), 19, 27, 30, 38, 43, 58, 59 [2], 80, 90 [3], 91, 94, 113, 137 [2], 161, 169 [2], 170, 179, 181, 187 [2], 188, 197, 198, 201, 205, 211, 212, 215, 227, 229, 230, 233 [2], 234 [3], 254, 258 [4], 299, 304, 311, 321 [3], 335, 337, 338, 339, 344 [2], 346, 354, 363, 367 368 [2], 384, 390, 395, 402 [2], 405, 409, 425, 434 [3], 445

Hour Before the Dawn, The (1941, 1942), 5, 6 [2], 8, 12, 33 [2], 35, 46 [3], 50, 56, 63, 67, 71, 72 [2], 76, 79 [2], 80 [2], 85, 87 [3], 94, 96, 97, 126, 137 [2], 146, 151, 158, 161 [2], 165, 166 [2], 168, 174, 176 [3], 181, 199 [6], 200, 203 [2], 205, 213 [2], 227, 252 [3], 254, 258, 267, 279 [3], 285, 286, 288, 289, 294, 297 [2], 308, 309, 333 [3], 346, 365 [2], 371, 380, 384, 403, 411, 426 [3], 434 [8]

Liza of Lambeth (1897), 25 [2], 31 [2], 38, 41, 42 [2], 43, 47 [5], 50 [2], 82, 88, 91, 93, 101 [2], 103, 107, 110, 126 [4], 146, 152, 157, 158, 166 [2], 179 [4], 181 [3], 202, 207, 215, 221 [3], 229, 258 [4], 259 [2], 269, 275, 279 [4], 280 [2], 295, 306, 314, 319, 322 [2], 330, 334, 335, 338, 340, 344, 375, 385, 390 [2], 391, 398, 405 [2], 410, 426, 435 [3], 440 [3], 443 [2], 445, 446 [2]

Magician, The (1908), 3 [2], 13, 16, 19, 28, 38, 43,

47, 49, 56, 58, 59, 60 [2], 65, 66, 67, 68, 69, 76, 81, 82, 87, 88 [3], 89, 91, 95 [3], 97 [2], 102, 104 [3], 109, 113, 114 [3], 116, 121, 131, 134, 136, 141, 150, 151, 152 [2], 157, 158, 160, 163, 164 [2], 165 [2], 166 [4], 167 [3], 169, 173, 175 [2], 185, 191 [3], 192 [4], 198, 203 [2], 206, 210, 212, 215, 219, 227 [2], 229 [2], 237, 238, 239, 240, 241, 242, 244, 251, 259 [4], 267, 273, 280 [7], 284 [2], 285 [2], 290 [2], 295, 298, 303, 309, 310, 313 [2], 317, 318 [2], 319, 320, 323, 324, 325 [4], 326 [4], 328, 329 [2], 331, 334 [2], 336 [2], 337, 341 [3], 346, 353, 356, 357, 358, 363, 366, 368, 369 [3], 371 [2], 374, 379 [2], 381, 382 [2], 383, 395, 396, 397 [2], 401 [2], 402, 405, 408 [2], 410, 417 [2], 418 [2], 421 [2], 426, 431, 435 [2], 440 [5], 441 [3]

Making of a Saint, The (1898), 6, 7, 13 [2], 16 [2], 29, 35, 44, 53 [3], 54 [2], 57, 58, 62, 66, 68 [3], 74, 82, 87 [2], 89, 96, 97, 103 [2]. 104 [3], 111 [3], 113, 118 [2], 119, 132 [5], 136, 141, 144, 148 [2], 150, 160, 162, 163, 165, 167 [2], 169, 174, 175 [2], 182 [2], 191 [4], 194, 198, 208 [2], 209, 227 [2], 228, 229, 232, 234, 244, 259 [5], 260 [2], 276, 280 [6], 281 [3], 282, 283, 284 [2], 285 [3], 289, 290, 291, 293 [3], 294, 295, 298, 306, 312 [2], 313, 316, 317 [3], 318, 322, 324, 326, 331 [3], 332, 336, 344, 345 [2], 350, 352 [2], 356, 363 [2], 364, 366, 367, 369 [7], 371 [4], 372, 373 [4], 375, 377, 380 [7], 385, 397, 406, 407, 411, 415 [2], 426, 432, 435 [3], 441 [4], 443, 445, 446, 448

Merry-Go-Round, The (1904), 28, 30 [3], 31, 39 [2], 44, 55 [4], 61 [3], 62 [2], 64 [4], 66 [3], 68, 74 [5], 78, 82, 89, 92 [2], 99 [2], 105, 107, 110, 116, 126 [3], 127 [4], 139, 140, 149 [2], 154 [3], 157, 158 [2], 165, 167 [2], 169, 175, 179, 182 [2], 185, 198, 200, 201 [3], 204, 206, 207, 210, 214, 216, 218, 220, 221, 222 [4], 223, 228, 229, 232, 233 [2], 235, 239, 240, 241 [2], 243, 250, 252 [5], 260 [6], 269, 277, 281 [3], 286, 288, 289 [2], 290, 296, 297, 303, 304, 306, 319 [2], 330, 331, 332, 333, 334, 337 [2], 338, 342, 350, 356, 360, 370 [5], 372 [4], 376, 377, 381 [3], 383, 390, 392, 394, 403, 405, 406, 407, 410, 411, 413 [3], 416 [2], 418 [2], 427 [4], 436 [4], 441 [5], 444, 446 , 447

Index: Novels 457

Moon and Sixpence, The (1919), 2, 6, 14, 16, 20 [2], 21, 23, 26, 43, 47 [4], 58 [2], 71 [2], 82 [2], 83 [2], 84, 92 [2], 93, 95 [4], 105, 127 [2], 136, 139, 144 [2], 150, 164 [3], 174, 179, 181, 185, 188, 196 [2], 200, 206, 213, 214, 216 [2], 223 [2], 232, 237, 246 [2], 252, 254, 260 [2], 266, 272, 278, 281, 290 [2], 291, 301, 305 [3], 308, 317, 318, 332, 345 [2], 348, 354, 356 [2], 359, 360, 380, 385, 392 [2], 393 [2], 394 [7], 397, 400, 401, 402, 404, 406, 407, 410, 418, 419 [2], 422, 423, 427 [3], 436 [5], 441, 442, 443

Mrs. Craddock (1902), 16, 21, 22, 26, 28, 38, 52 [2], 53, 57, 58, 66 [2], 67, 68, 82 [2], 85, 89, 90, 92, 94, 96, 99 [2], 102, 103, 104 [2], 105 [2], 106 [2], 107 [2], 109, 116 [2], 123, 124, 125, 127 [2], 134, 141, 144, 150, 163, 167 [3], 171, 181, 182 [4], 194 [2], 202, 205, 208, 210 [2], 212, 216 [2], 226 [2], 229 [2], 232, 240, 241 [3], 245 [2], 252, 260 [2], 261, 281, 286, 290 [2], 291, 304, 308, 314, 317, 319, 320, 321, 326, 332, 337 [2], 339 [2], 340, 341 [2], 348 [3], 355 [2], 357, 359, 360, 366, 370 [4], 372, 374 [2], 381, 382, 385, 389, 390, 395 [2], 397, 404 [2], 405 [2], 407, 408, 410, 412 [2], 413 [5], 417, 419, 420 [2], 424, 427 [2], 428, 442, 447

Narrow Corner, The (1932), 4, 6, 18, 25, 31, 32, 40, 41 [5], 43, 45, 48 [3], 50, 53, 57, 69, 80, 82, 83, 84 [3], 85, 86 [3], 89, 90, 97, 99 [2], 100 [2], 102, 127 [5], 133, 134, 140 [5], 167, 168 [2], 175, 204, 205, 206 [2], 212, 213, 215, 222, 223, 245, 253, 255 [2], 256, 261 [4], 264, 272, 281, 284, 293, 295, 296, 302 [2], 303, 305 [2], 310, 312, 316, 322 [2], 332 [2], 333, 353, 359, 362, 377, 378 [4], 381, 383 [4], 397 [2], 398 [3], 401, 405, 412 [2], 413, 427, 442, 447

Of Human Bondage (1915), 3 [2], 4, 6, 13 [2], 14, 17, 21 [3], 22 [2], 23 [5], 24 [9], 25, 26 [3], 27, 28, 30 [2], 35, 36, 39, 40, 44, 48 [3], 50 [2], 55, 57, 62, 63, 65, 66 [2], 67, 69, 70 [4], 72 [2], 73, 75, 76, 77, 79, 82, 86, 89 [2], 91, 92, 93, 95, 96 [2], 97 [2], 99, 101, 102, 105, 107, 110 [2], 113 [3], 115, 116, 119, 125 [2], 127, 128 [5], 131, 134 [2],

138 [3], 141 [2], 142 [3], 143 [4], 145 [4], 155 [2], 156 [3], 157 [2], 159, 161, 162 [4], 164 [3], 170 [2], 171 [2], 174 [3], 177, 179 [3], 183 [4], 186, 187, 190 [3], 192, 195, 196, 197, 202 [4], 204, 205, 207 [3], 208, 212, 214 [2], 215, 217, 221, 223, 224 [2], 226, 227, 228 [4], 230 [6], 231 [4], 235, 239 [2], 241, 242, 244, 246, 247, 253 [6], 254, 261 [9], 262 [9], 264, 265, 270 [2], 272 [3], 274, 276 [5], 277 [10], 278, 281 [2], 282 [2], 284 [2], 286 [3], 287, 288, 289 [2], 290, 295 [4], 304 [2], 306, 307 [2], 309 [4], 310 [2], 316 [2], 317 [2], 322, 328 [2], 330 [3], 331, 334, 335, 337 [3], 338 [3], 340 [4], 341, 343, 344, 349 [3], 352 [2], 355 [3], 356, 361, 365 [2], 367, 370 [2], 372, 373, 375 [2], 376, 377 [2], 382 [2], 383 [2], 392, 396, 397, 400 [2], 404, 408, 409 [2], 410 [2], 411 [4], 413, 414, 415 [3], 419 [3], 420 [4], 421, 422 [3], 423 [3], 424, 425, 427 [4], 428 [3], 429 [2], 430 [2], 436 [4], 437 [15], 438, 442, 443, 446

Painted Veil, The (1925), 1, 2, 4 [4], 11, 12 [4], 17, 19, 28 [2], 34 [5], 35, 36, 48 [7], 49 [4], 50 [4], 80, 81, 82, 83 [3], 84 [4], 85 [2], 89, 99, 100 [5], 101, 105 [3], 119, 120, 123, 148, 149, 150, 151 [3], 171, 172 [4], 173 [2], 179, 180, 181 [2], 185, 186, 197, 198, 205, 208, 218, 224, 225, 233, 251, 262 [3], 265, 276, 281 [2], 284, 291, 295 [2], 304, 308 [2], 309, 310, 311 [3], 313, 314, 319, 322 [2], 324 [4], 335, 351, 367, 376, 381 [3], 382, 389 [2], 390 [2], 397, 406 [2], 407, 417, 423, 428 [4], 432 [2], 438 [4], 442, 447 [2]

Razor's Edge, The (1943, 1944), 1 [3], 3, 5, 7, 11, 13 [2], 14 [3], 17, 21 [5], 23, 28 [2], 29 [2], 32 [2], 33, 34 [4], 35 [2], 36 [2], 39, 51 [4], 52 [5], 55, 56, 62, 64 [3], 67, 76, 78, 79 [3], 81, 92, 93, 96 [2], 102, 103, 112 [4], 114, 117 [4], 119, 120, 121, 123 [2], 128 [4], 129 [4], 131, 134, 136 [2], 137 [2], 138, 140, 142 [2], 143 [2], 144, 146, 147, 150, 154 [2], 155, 156, 158, 159, 160, 162, 163, 164, 165, 167, 172, 174, 175, 180 [2], 184, 185, 186, 196, 201, 208 [3], 210, 214, 217, 220, 223 [2], 230 [2], 232, 246 [2], 247 [3], 250, 251, 254, 263 [6], 265 [3],

Index: Novels/Stories   459

267 [3], 269, 272, 273 [2], 274 [7], 281, 282 [2],
285, 288, 289 [3], 291, 295, 301, 303, 305, 307 [3],
309 [2], 310, 312 [2], 316 [2], 323 [3], 329, 331,
332 [2], 334, 335, 341, 342, 344, 346, 352, 357 [4],
358, 360, 362, 363, 366, 370, 375, 377, 383, 389 [2],
390, 395, 398, 400 [2], 401, 402 [2], 403 [3], 405,
411 [2], 415, 418 [[3], 425, 428, 438 [3], 442 [2],
444 [4], 446 [2]

Theatre (1937), 1, 3 [4], 15, 16 [2], 17, 25, 27 [2],
36, 51, 58, 64, 66, 79 [2], 80, 86, 94 [2], 96, 99,
102, 107 [2], 114, 120 [4], 123 [4], 134, 147, 148
[2], 153 [2], 154, 176, 177, 180 [2], 183 [2], 184
[3], 192, 214, 215, 228, 230, 231 [2], 233, 235, 238,
244, 253, 263, 264, 267, 274, 275, 282, 304, 330,
340, 342, 353, 390, 391, 400 [2], 401, 414 [2], 419,
420, 424, 428 [2], 446
Then and Now (1946), 5 [4], 7 [3], 12, 13, 16, 17, 20,
28, 29, 36 [2], 37, 38, 39, 41, 44 [6], 52, 56, 59
[2], 62, 66 [2], 68 [2], 69 [2], 94 [2], 103, 104
[6], 110 [2], 111 [3], 114, 115, 117 [2], 118 [3],
121, 124, 130 [2], 131, 142, 145 [3], 148, 149, 153,
154 [3], 157 [3], 163, 165, 169, 172 [2], 176 [2],
177, 187, 190, 191, 208, 209 [2], 210, 225, 226, 232,
238, 241, 244 [2], 245, 248 [3], 253, 264 [4], 266
[3], 268 [2], 269 [3], 282 [2], 283, 284, 285, 287,
303, 306 [2], 311 [3], 314, 315 [2], 317, 324, 329
[2], 330, 332, 359 [2], 361, 365, 366 [3], 367, 370,
371 [2], 372 [2], 373 [2], 379, 380 [3], 381 [2],
405, 406, 408, 411, 415 [3], 416, 439 [5], 442 [4]

Up at the Villa (1940, 1941), 4, 23, 25 [2], 86, 97,
136, 146, 157 [3], 159, 177, 235 [2], 237, 245, 295,
306, 307, 318 [2], 326, 353 [2], 361 [2], 364, 376,
394, 399, 407, 408, 439

                            B. Stories

"Alien Corn" (1931), 3, 14, 17, 33, 35, 42 [4], 107,
166 [3], 200, 233, 255, 267, 280, 317, 330, 333, 346
[2], 351, 368, 382, 398 [2]
"Ant and the Grasshopper, The" (1924), 107, 298, 348
[2], 432

"Appearance and Reality" (1934), 94, 95 [2], 121, 234 [2], 238 [4], 251, 274, 298, 344, 360, 365, 445

"Back of Beyond, The" (1931, 1933), 38, 87 [2], 133, 197, 204, 215, 255, 256, 278, 292 [3], 314, 359 [2], 401

"Bad Example" (1899), 7, 30, 82 [2], 88, 90, 91, 102 [2], 113, 123, 125 [2], 147, 152, 157, 159, 177, 180, 219, 256 [3], 278, 294, 303, 318, 333, 349 [3], 371, 381, 384, 405, 425, 432 [2], 439, 445

"Before the Party" (1926), 17, 39, 81, 115, 125, 162, 189 [2], 196, 201 [2], 215, 288, 376, 377 [3]

"Book-Bag, The" (1932), 12, 45, 83, 98, 151, 195 [5], 197 [2], 204, 256, 298, 366 [2], 367 [2], 396 [2]

"Bum, The" (1929, 1936), 29, 35, 333

"Buried Talent, The " (1958?), 13, 35, 79, 97 [2], 178, 246 [2], 278 [2], 324 [2], 352, 395

"Casual Affair, The" (1934), 11, 46, 63, 81, 85, 125, 151, 158, 185, 219 [2], 221, 241, 244 [2], 298, 314 [2], 334, 354, 358, 375, 397, 408, 421

"Choice of Amyntas, The" (1899), 14, 21, 29, 36, 40, 44, 152, 200, 212 [2], 215, 253, 254 [3], 256, 269, 278 [2], 283, 286, 293, 321, 324, 329 [3], 338, 362, 374, 384, 396, 399, 404, 412, 447

"Closed Shop, The" (1926), 26, 71, 102, 130 [2], 226, 251, 279, 299, 312, 340, 364, 365, 433

"Colonel's Lady, The" (1946), 13, 29, 42, 63, 107, 112 [2], 144, 257, 326 [2], 327 [2], 433, 440, 445

"Consul, The" (1922), 46, 88, 230, 231 [2], 329, 417, 418, 443, 447 [4]

"Cousin Amy" (1908), 14 [2], 257, 299

"Creative Impulse" (1926), 13, 49, 59, 72, 78, 98, 160 [2], 173, 194, 299, 309, 337, 364, 376, 412, 421, 422

"Cupid and the Vicar of Swale" (1900), 29, 54 [2], 63, 227, 257, 299, 344 [3], 376 [3], 394, 414, 445

"Daisy" (1899),46,58, 71, 110, 149, 154, 167, 171, 182, 189 [6], 190, 202, 205, 213 [2], 230 [2], 257, 316 [2], 335, 350, 371, 411

"De Amicitia" (1899), 27, 46, 165, 209, 257, 279,

Index: Stories   461

286,   299, 339, 356, 359, 391, 425, 440
"Door of Opportunity, The" (1931), 43, 194 [2], 204, 274, 302, 310, 314, 316, 317, 333, 338, 345, 365, 375, 392, 394, 405, 406 [2], 408, 412
"Dream, The" (1924), 242, 299, 358 [2], 418

"End of the Flight, The" (1926), 2, 46, 84, 88, 125, 140, 299, 377 [2]
"Episode" (1947), 60 [2], 72 [2], 73, 81, 203, 204, 229, 251, 257, 266 [2], 299, 340, 421, 440
"Escape, The" (1925, 1936), 30, 78, 284, 299

"Facts of Life, The" (1939), 2, 27, 50, 115, 171 [5], 258 [4], 345, 409, 417, 433
"Faith" (1899), 213, 291, 307, 324, 337, 343 [2], 374, 415, 434, 447
"Fall of Edward Barnard, The" (1921), 6,31 [2], 54, 78, 151, 206 [2], 211 [2], 212, 243 [3]
"Flirtation " (1906), 66, 134, 283, 320, 374, 445, 446
"Flotsam and Jetsam" (1947), 41, 72, 84, 125, 140 [2], 186 [2], 198, 205, 224, 318 [2], 377
"Footprints in the Jungle" (1927), 30, 56, 57, 59, 71, 73 [2], 84, 129, 173, 197, 299, 323, 333, 366
"Force of Circumstances, The" (1924), 2, 131, 192, 205, 434
"Fortunate Painter, The" (1906), 32, 81, 90, 110, 151, 189, 225 [2], 227 [2], 237, 319, 357
"Four Dutchmen, The" (1928), 4, 68, 81 [2], 140, 204, 255, 299, 364, 396
"French Joe" (1926, 1936), 32, 102, 120, 204, 299, 308, 359
"Friend in Need, A" (1925, 1936), 46, 61 [4], 299, 409

"German Harry" (1924), 78, 176, 299, 323, 378
"Gigolo and Gigolette" (1935), 4 [2], 16, 31, 32 [2], 56, 94, 103 [2], 116, 121, 143, 146, 177, 183, 204, 210, 233, 325 [2], 340, 342, 358, 364, 418, 424
"Giulia Lazarri" (1928), 17, 21, 77, 93, 116, 117, 121, 125, 152, 201 [2], 226, 235, 251, 256, 313, 349, 403
"Good Manners" (1907), 5, 29, 55, 142, 150, 186, 241, 299, 348, 350, 368, 426

"Hairless Mexican, The" (1927), 15 16,21, 71, 123, 140,

145, 226, 243, 382, 391, 432
"Happy Couple, The" (1908, 1952), 16, 54, 88, 106 [2], 107 [4], 121, 141, 187, 206, 232, 235 [2], 240, 254, 299, 304, 306, 308, 390, 430 [2]
"Happy Man, The" (1924), 299, 337, 384, 391
"His Excellency" (1928), 8, 21, 26, 57, 63, 65, 150, 158, 200, 312, 363, 398, 403, 431 [2], 448
"Home" (1925), 242, 273, 275, 276 [6], 300
"Honolulu" (1921), 65, 119, 179 [2], 215, 300, 302, 375, 425, 430
"Human Element" (1930), 2, 7, 64, 72, 159, 176, 185, 241, 244, 300, 311, 312, 320, 341, 345, 346, 350, 389, 409, 418 [3], 424 [2], 434

"In a Strange Land" (1924), 133, 188, 300, 305 [3], 314 [2], 319
"Irish Gentleman, An" (1904), 98, 132, 143, 145, 174, 209, 214, 215, 229, 270, 310, 311, 380 [2], 417

"Jane" (1923), 11, 64, 123, 162, 168, 298 [2], 300, 351, 400, 406
"Judgment Seat, The" (1934), 16, 146, 215, 269, 330, 359

"Kite, The" (1947), 38 [3], 134, 300, 340, 396 [4], 445

"Lady Habart" (1900), 25, 80, 192 [2], 300, 349, 358, 369, 379
"Letter, The" (1924), 84, 85, 108, 109, 121, 194, 217, 218, 248, 273, 275, 313, 350, 431
"Lion's Skin, The" (1938), 47, 160 [4], 177, 195 [2], 218, 252, 300, 342, 404, 418
"Lord Mountdrago" (1939, 1940), 26, 27, 68, 96, 155, 76, 190 [3], 259 [3], 288, 290, 295, 296 [2], 320, 365, 440
"Lotus Eater, The" (1935), 17, 23, 56, 65, 107, 131, 143, 204, 300, 415, 429 [2], 430 [2]
"Louise" (1925), 164, 255 [3], 300, 445
"Luncheon, The" (1924), 300, 418, 435

"Mabel" (1953), 47, 56, 100, 131, 175, 245, 300, 365, 378
"Mackintosh" (1920), 6, 213, 214 [2], 266, 334, 401, 420
"Making of a Millionaire" (1906), 43 [2], 56, 89, 90,

Index: Stories 463

264, 286, 356 [3], 369, 371, 373
"Man from Glasgow, A" (1947), 154, 217, 232, 252, 260, 294, 300, 312, 374, 383, 447
"Man with a Conscience, A" (1939), 18, 78, 94, 97, 98 [5], 124, 185, 285 [2], 300, 302, 351 [2], 411, 418, 435
"Man with the Scar, The" (1925), 3, 173 [2], 300, 302, 311, 350, 361
"Marriage of Convenience, A" (1906, 1908), 18 [3], 35, 47, 69, 89, 93, 104, 105, 120, 121, 141, 142, 163 [2], 164, 211, 215, 288, 289, 300 [2], 327, 342, 344, 364, 365, 367, 378, 380, 426, 428 [2], 435, 441
"Masterson" (1929, 1951), 47, 61, 99, 170, 260, 272, 300, 352, 370
"Mayhew" (1924), 260, 274, 300
"Mirage" (1929), 47, 116, 164, 236, 251, 300, 312 [2], 337, 353, 354, 394 [2]
"Miss King" (1928), 8 [2], 18, 36, 38, 42, 55, 59, 73, 117, 148, 150, 163, 173, 176, 201 [2], 203, 208 [2], 222, 223, 241, 251, 298, 306, 317, 324, 334, 336, 354, 360, 399, 444, 445
"Mother, The" (1909), 36, 127, 225, 232, 266, 270, 332, 333, 337, 356, 361 [2], 362, 408, 436 [2]
"Mr. Harrington's Washing" (1928), 21, 27, 36, 56, 117, 119, 123, 196, 200, 207, 238 [2], 256, 312 [3], 315, 323, 330, 345, 358 [3], 361, 380, 385, 390, 396, 421, 443, 448
"Mr. Know-All" (1925), 127, 221, 301, 348 [2]

"Neil MacAdam" (1932), 6, 25, 39, 48 [2], 54 [2], 83, 85, 127, 140, 179, 212 [2], 216, 245 [2], 256, 296 [2], 334, 396, 408, 421
"Noblest Act" (1942?), 127, 149, 150 [2], 275

"Official Position, An" (1937), 8, 84, 94, 147 [3], 163, 185, 333, 334, 351 [2], 384, 409, 421 [2], 427 [3]
"Outstation, The" (1924), 1, 7, 32 [2], 101, 159, 169, 191, 197, 200 [2], 202, 242, 301, 314, 402, 421

"P. & O." (1923), 128, 169, 193 [2], 212, 213, 227 [2], 241 [2], 255, 289, 312, 332, 345, 397, 427
"Poet, The" (1926, 1936), 208, 263, 291 [2], 301, 361, 406, 438 [2]

"Point of Honour, The" (1947), 2 5 [2], 6, 12 [2], 130, 263, 272, 301, 331, 340, 361, 370, 384 [3]
"Point of Law, A" (1904), 4 [2], 89 [2], 112, 113 [3], 134, 137, 231, 271 [2], 301, 372
"Pool, The" (1921), 55 [2], 74 [2], 77 [2], 146, 211, 235 [2], 287, 296, 301, 303, 304, 324
"Portrait of a Gentleman" (1925, 1936), 40, 44, 301
"Princess and the Nightingale, The" (1922; see Princess September)
"Princess September" (1939), 18, 26, 39 [2], 152, 211, 212, 218 [2], 223 [2], 254, 267, 274, 345, 367
"Pro Patria" (1903), 5 67 [2], 184, 243, 251, 316, 339 [3], 377
"Promise, The" (1925, 1936), 26, 68 [2], 255, 301, 302, 414 [2]
"Punctiliousness of Don Sebastian, The" 1898), 1, 19, 49, 103, 118, 119 [2], 130 [3], 153, 176, 191, 198, 283, 301, 317, 326, 330, 338 [2], 348, 364, 365, 370, 372, 391, 422, 438 [2]

"Rain" (1921), 115 [2], 185, 203 [2], 275 [2], 312, 398, 404
"Raw Material" (1923, 1936), 67, 301, 330, 438
"Red" (1921), 107, 143, 187, 273, 303, 350, 360
"Romantic Young Lady, The" (1947), 19 72, 133 [2], 237, 266, 301, 338, 361
"Round Dozen, The" (1924), 11, 32, 57, 114, 142, 156, 175, 180, 205, 210, 213, 230, 265, 286, 301, 336, 338, 342, 363, 389 [2], 403, 408, 419, 442

"Salvatore" (1925), 23, 49, 180 [3], 263, 301, 360 [4]
"Sanatorium, The" (1938), 21, 24, 40 [2], 67, 80 [2], 128, 130, 173, 208, 228, 237, 253 [2], 263, 273, 275, 295, 309 [2], 322, 351, 385, 402, 439, 442, 446
"Social Sense" (1929, 1936), 247 [2], 266 [2], 301, 422 [2]
"Spanish Priest, The" (1958?), 15 [2], 18, 49, 89, 138, 143, 144, 181, 232, 242, 263, 265, 302, 303, 314, 328, 360, 363, 383, 395, 439
"Straight Flush" (1929), 131, 275 [2], 302, 322, 332, 357, 391
"String of Beads, A" (1927, 1936), 20, 23, 29, 45, 115, 188, 234, 242 [2], 245, 282, 302, 354, 439

Index: Stories/Plays   465

"Taipan, The" (1928), 50, 57, 69, 76 [2], 83, 89, 97,
   101, 128, 155, 263 [4], 282, 289, 296, 329, 364, 400,
   409
"Three Fat Women of the Antibes, The" (1933), 64, 80,
   129 [2], 154, 353, 354, 397, 403, 419
"Traitor, The" (1927), 21, 77, 88, 92, 155 [2], 168,
   183, 185 [2], 231, 382, 417, 420
"Traveller in Romance, A" (1958?), 136 [2], 264, 265,
   282, 302, 339, 399 [2], 439
"Treasure, The" (1934, 1940), 64, 120, 175, 191 [2], 196
   [2], 213, 235, 306, 310, 317, 338, 343, 344, 379,
   397, 400, 401, 414, 419

"Unconquered, The" (1943), 129 [3], 164 [2], 173, 176,
   194 [3], 236, 286, 327 [5], 328, 429, 439

"Verger, The" (1929, 1936), 29, 73, 86, 100, 159 [2],
   314, 415 [2]
"Vessel of Wrath, The" (1931), 16, 83, 84, 85, 86, 177,
   180, 190, 197, 198 [2], 205, 214, 216 [2], 266, 275,
   276, 285, 302, 333, 334, 364, 367, 421, 429
"Virtue" (1931), 40 [2], 79, 83, 129, 217, 253, 265,
   268, 294, 301, 318, 334, 391, 419, 430
"Visit" (1928), 21
"Voice of the Turtle, The" (1935), 33, 44, 109, 182,
   210, 226, 278, 291 [2], 302, 303, 354, 358, 442, 448

"Wash-Tub, The" (1919, 1936), 31 [3], 105, 181, 253,
   302, 366, 442
"Winter Cruise" (1943, 1947), 5 [2], 43, 81, 129, 145,
   224, 225, 342 [2], 346, 351 [2], 391, 423
"Woman of Fifty, A" (1946), 88, 124 [2], 188 [3], 189,
   194, 195, 203, 211, 302, 395

"Yellow Streak, The" (1925), 54, 67, 140, 183, 197, 207,
   211 [2], 255, 275 [2], 319, 338, 429

C. Plays

Bread-Winner, The (1930), 27, 33 [4], 44, 79, 145, 186
   [4], 216, 238, 381, 400, 409, 419

Camel's Back, The (produced 1923; not published), 16,

123, 125, 236 [4], 331, 362
Caesar's Wife (1922), 2, 17, 18, 20, 57, 63, 102, 123, 137, 146, 170, 222, 242 [2], 294 [2], 315, 320, 325, 328, 341, 343 [2], 360 [3], 365, 368, 371, 376 [2], 382, 417, 431, 432, 446
Circle, The (1921), 4, 7, 15, 63 [2], 65, 73, 76 [2], 77 [2], 97, 104, 120, 133, 138, 175, 197, 211, 233, 244, 245, 265, 277, 291 [2], 294, 307, 308, 315, 323, 339 [2], 349, 371, 374 [2], 403, 433, 440, 446
Constant Wife, The (1927), 37, 98, 109 [2], 132 [2], 151, 166, 222, 241, 285, 286 [2], 293, 412, 445

East of Suez (1922), 1, 2, 12, 15 [2], 22, 29 [3], 35, 46 [2], 49, 50, 57 [2], 71, 83 [3], 84 [2], 85, 86, 87, 90, 98 [2], 100 [4], 126, 147, 151 [2], 154, 179, 189, 197, 224 [3], 225, 236, 238, 279 [2], 283, 288, 289, 290, 291, 297, 349 [2], 354, 367, 368, 375, 392 [2], 422 [2], 426 [2], 433, 440, 444
Explorer, The (1912), 3, 9, 10 [2], 11, 18, 27, 31, 45, 69, 78, 80, 94, 103, 109, 134, 167, 210, 218 [2], 220, 223, 243, 249, 250, 252, 256, 258, 265, 282, 286, 288, 302, 303 [2], 306, 328, 353, 364, 366, 368 [2], 390, 409, 433

For Services Rendered (1932), 19 [4], 20 [2], 22, 29, 32 [5], 75 [3], 88, 142, 176, 182, 218, 219, 297, 340, 346, 392, 402

Home and Beauty (1923), 69 [3], 87, 92, 93, 98, 110, 119, 121, 126, 163, 173, 174 [5], 176, 207, 215, 216, 244 [3], 267, 273, 292, 308, 323, 332, 346, 375, 401, 410

Jack Straw (1912), 1, 2, 14, 15, 27, 56, 137, 143, 158 [2], 198, 202, 203, 212, 223, 229, 231, 243, 284, 304, 319 [2], 320 [3], 332, 335, 364, 367 [2], 368, 369, 374, 375, 381, 387, 389 [2], 392, 410, 412, 414, 417, 418 [3], 420, 421 [3], 431 [2]

Lady Frederick (1912), 16, 36, 38 [4], 39, 71 [2], 88, 92, 123, 131, 142, 162, 225, 239, 283 [3], 291, 313 [2], 320, 328, 369 [3], 381, 404, 425
Land of Promise (1913, 1922), 22, 126, 144, 147, 204

Index: Plays 467

[3], 204, 208, 210, 218, 219, 268 [4], 342 [3], 374 [2], 301, 402, 404, 405, 409, 415, 425 [2], 435, 444

Landed Gentry (1913), 28 [3], 92 [2], 98, 115, 130, 157, 169, 170 [2], 193, 205, 209 [5], 210, 218, 224, 239, 252 [3], 279, 293, 325, 352, 354, 356, 391, 414 [2], 428, 435

Letter, The (1925), 6, 26, 46 [2], 67, 83, 85 [2], 86, 107 [2], 166, 193, 197 [3], 217 [2], 218, 255 [3], 264, 275 [2], 313, 319, 333, 350, 426, 431

Loaves and Fishes (1924), 39, 50, 71, 93, 96 [2], 98, 101, 107, 155 [3], 187, 270, 278 [2], 292 [3], 308, 323, 325, 334, 335, 342, 347 [4], 348, 363, 379, 382, 385, 386, 387 [3], 388 [3], 389, 400, 422, 429, 435, 443, 444 [2]

Love in a Cottage (written 1917, produced 1919; never published), 20, 30 [2], 35, 58, 65 [2], 80, 115 [2], 121, 133, 139 [2], 142, 157, 204, 210, 211, 259 [2], 308, 318 [2], 335, 349, 355, 418

Mademoiselle Zampa (produced 1904; not published); see Rehearsal

Man of Honour, A (1903), 4, 27, 51, 61 [2], 62 [2], 64, 78, 92, 97, 102, 126 [2], 149, 185, 190, 193 [3], 221, 222, 260, 269, 296, 296, 303, 381, 407, 435

Marriages Are Made in Heaven (1903), 39, 113, 151, 260, 322, 349, 369, 414, 416

Mask and the Face, The (translated from a play by Luigi Chiarelli; produced 1933; never published), 6, 13, 16, 152, 155, 177, 187, 188, 207, 275, 286, 345, 367, 372, 385, 403, 448 [2]

Mrs. Dot (1912), 43, 64, 78, 89, 133, 158, 174, 175, 179, 185, 193, 202, 203 [2], 248, 261, 296 [2], 304, 328 [2], 354, 366 [3], 404, 436, 442, 443 [3]

Noble Spaniard, The (1953), 76, 119 [2], 151, 200, 223, 232, 245, 270, 291, 298 [2], 304, 343, 344, 345, 362

Our Betters (1923), 8, 12 [2], 16, 20, 41 [2], 42, 48, 64, 66, 79, 88 [2], 99, 118 [2], 132, 141, 145, 153, 159, 182, 187 [3], 194, 197, 202 [2], 225, 234, 272, 293 [2], 295, 323, 333, 362 [3], 395, 397 [2], 398, 410 [2], 412, 415, 438 [2]

Penelope (1912), 2, 15, 22, 30, 33 [2], 56, 88, 114, 128, 153, 154, 176, 181, 182, 183, 199, 203, 223, 249 [2], 253, 268, 284, 311 [2], 322, 330, 354, 355, 367, 389, 404, 423 [2], 430, 446

Perfect Gentleman, The (1955), 20, 23, 28, 56, 88, 94, 100, 112, 131 [2], 136, 141, 152, 159, 196, 217 [3], 272, 281, 297, 298, 305, 363, 376, 377, 400, 409, 448

Rehearsal, A (1904), 79, 92, 141, 189, 205, 213, 221, 223, 226, 298, 378, 448 [4]

Road Uphill, The (written 1924; never produced or published), 7, 115, 136, 163, 188 [2], 219, 234 [2], 250, 375 [3], 429

Sacred Flame, The (1928), 8, 27, 41, 102, 167, 171, 241, 309, 385, 399 [4], 400, 423

Sheppey (1933), 6, 43, 51, 52, 101, 110 [3], 114, 128, 134, 144, 161, 169, 170, 175 [3], 177, 212, 213, 214, 219, 237, 250, 251, 265, 282, 283 [3], 284, 287 [4], 326, 351, 354 [2], 360, 370, 375, 377, 409 [2], 410 [2], 411, 412, 415, 439 [2], 445

Smith (1913), 40, 66, 77, 85, 92, 99 [2], 111 [2], 134, 156, 158, 163 [2], 180, 186 [2], 214, 222, 256, 273, 284, 309, 326 [2], 334, 338, 339, 357 [6], 358, 372, 377, 378, 379 [2], 380, 404, 408 [2], 425, 439

Tenth Man, The (1913), 36, 49, 56, 79, 81 [2], 93, 121, 146 [3], 152, 159, 200, 201, 230, 234, 239. 246, 250, 253, 265, 272, 282 [2], 285, 294, 311 [2], 328, 335, 342, 355, 377, 382, 398, 404, 406, 419, 420, 430 [2], 431, 443

Unattainable (1923), 22 [3], 43, 58, 78, 89, 99, 100, 101, 102, 109, 169, 172, 177, 180, 227, 238, 248, 254, 264 [2], 312, 329 [2], 334, 382 [2], 446

Unknown, The (1920), 40, 59 [2], 62, 71, 93, 100, 170, 171, 194, 197, 219, 220, 242 [3], 248 [2], 295, 317, 335 [2], 354, 381, 424 [3], 429, 439 [2]

About the Author

SAMUEL J. ROGAL is chair of the Division of Humanities and Fine Arts at Illinois Valley Community College. His most recent publications include *Medicine in Great Britain from the Restoration to the Nineteenth Century, 1660–1800* (1992), *Agriculture in Britain and America, 1660–1820: An Annotated Bibliography of the Eighteenth-Century Literature* (1994), and SING GLORY AND HALLELUJAH! Historical and Biographical Guide to *Gospel Hymns Nos. 1 to 6 Complete* (1996), all published by Greenwood Press.

ISBN 0-313-29917-X

OHIO UNIVERSITY LIBRARY